Social Inequality in Canada

Patterns, Problems, and Policies

Fourth Edition

Edited by

James Curtis
University of Waterloo

Edward Grabb
University of Western Ontario

Neil Guppy
University of British Columbia

PEARSON

Prentice
Hall

Toronto

National Library of Canada Cataloguing in Publication

Social inequality in Canada : patterns, problems, and policies / edited by James Curtis, Edward Grabb, Neil Guppy. — 4th ed.

Includes bibliographical references and index.
ISBN 0-13-035150-4

1. Equality—Canada. 2. Social classes—Canada. 3. Canada—Social conditions—1991– I. Curtis, James E., 1943– II. Grabb, Edward G. III. Guppy, L. Neil, 1949–

HN110.Z9S6 2004   305'.0971   C2003-900217-9

ISBN 0-13-035150-4

Vice President, Editorial Director: Michael J. Young
Executive Acquisitions Editor: Jessica Mosher
Senior Marketing Manager: Judith Allen
Associate Editor: Patti Altridge
Editorial Coordinator: Söğüt Y. Güleç
Copy Editor: Lu Cormier
Proofreader: Karen Bennett
Production Coordinator: Patricia Ciardullo
Page Layout: B.J. Weckerle
Art Director: Mary Opper
Cover and Interior Design: Anthony Leung
Cover Image: PhotoDisc/The Signature Series/Colourful Contrasts

Statistics Canada information is used with the permission of the Minister of Industry, as Minister responsible for Statistics Canada. Information on the availability of the wide range of data from Statistics Canada can be obtained from Statistics Canada's Regional Offices, its World Wide Web site at http://www.statcan.ca, and its toll-free access number 1-800-263-1136.

2 3 4 5   08 07 06 05 04

Printed and bound in Canada.

Contents

iii

Preface

Our purpose in this book is to introduce students to issues of social inequality in Canada. We do this by presenting a collection of thirty-one articles that address virtually all of the major aspects or dimensions of social inequality. The result is a book dealing with topics that are central to a range of courses, including Social Inequality, Social Class, Social Stratification, Social Issues, and Canadian Society.

This new fourth edition begins from the same premise that guided the earlier versions of the book. The premise is that social inequality entails two broad components: *objective or structural conditions* of social inequality (power, poverty and wealth, occupations, and educational attainment, in particular) and *ideologies* that help support these differences. The ideologies—expressed in formal laws, public policies, dominant values, and so forth—provide justification for the objective patterns of inequality such as income differences by sex, region, or education level.

Of course, there are other, less influential, ideologies in society too—"counter-ideologies"—that often reflect the interests of the disadvantaged. These counter-ideologies, which are expressed, for example, by social movements promoting the interests of women, visible minorities, or native people, frequently call for changes to existing conditions of inequality in order to better the lot of the disadvantaged. The proper study of social inequality involves the scrutiny of both of these structural and ideological components.

In this revised collection we have also sought to retain the core strengths of the earlier editions. As before, we have chosen articles with an eye to reflecting the range of theoretical perspectives and research approaches used to address issues of inequality. In addition, we have retained our emphasis on papers that are imaginative and clear expositions of results and theories. Also, we have preserved our commitment in the earlier editions to the historical context of patterns of inequality. Furthermore, we have worked very hard to ensure that various dimensions of inequality—for example, gender and ethnicity—have not been confined exclusively to isolated sections. While separate sections for gender and race and ethnicity are maintained, we include several articles in other sections that deal with these dimensions as well (e.g., in the sections on education, income, and occupation). Finally, in keeping with the earlier editions, all sections of the book stress politics and ideologies related to inequality.

In this new edition, ten of the thirty-one pieces from the third edition are retained in unaltered form, while fourteen others have been revised and updated, and seven are new. Of the thirty-one papers, only twelve have been taken from previously published sources, while nineteen were written expressly for this book. As with the earlier editions, the substantial changes that we have made this time illustrate the extensive additions to research on social inequality that have been made in recent years.

Readers familiar with previous editions will note another substantial change. Although we were reluctant to do so, we have decreased somewhat the average length of the articles. While this made our selection of material even more difficult than before, there was little choice if we were to keep the book's price within reason and still maintain a large number of selections and breadth of coverage of topics.

Space constraints have meant, again, that we have had to include some choices, to the exclusion of many other fine works on the same topic. Our "Further References" sections, and the references in the selections themselves, only begin to suggest the amount of important research now available and the difficulty we have had in making choices.

The study of social inequality in Canada has moved forward rapidly toward a much better understanding of the phenomenon. Those of us who would prefer to see our society changed to provide greater equality of opportunity and condition can take heart at this improved understanding. It is another matter, though, to turn our understanding into action and achieve social change. The following pages will show that many patterns of inequality are terribly resistant to change because they are maintained by formidable forces, especially by the *economic, political, and ideological control* of highly privileged groups. Some of this control operates through the apparatuses of the state, as certain chapters of the book will emphasize.

This volume will show that there are types of inequality that are becoming more marked over time—as is the case with the increased concentration of wealth and corporate control, for example. There are also other forms of inequality that have considerably diminished—as with differences in the attainment of university degrees by women relative to men, and differences in the earnings and occupations of some ethnic groups, especially those who are not visible minorities. And finally, there are other patterns, such as the distribution of income, that show little change in recent decades. Thus, those readers who would prefer a more egalitarian society than currently exists in Canada will find reasons for both optimism and pessimism in the research presented here.

We would like to thank many people for their help with this project. First, of course, are the contributors to the volume. The strengths of the book are largely their doing. Second, we are indebted to many people for helpful suggestions in improving our editions. In particular, we thank the many students, over several cohorts, who have given us valuable feedback on the volume in their courses. Also, those who have provided helpful suggestions include Bruce Arai, Gillian Creese, Dawn Currie, Brian Elliott, Dawn Farrough, Martha Foschi, and Robin Hawkshaw from the University of British Columbia; Anton Allahar, Doug Baer, Catherine Corrigall-Brown, Paul Maxim, Kevin McQuillan, and Jim Rinehart at the University of Western Ontario; Bill Johnston from the University of Alberta; Monica Boyd, John Myles, and Lorne Tepperman at the University of Toronto; John Goyder, John Hirdes, and Ron Lambert at the University of Waterloo; and Tony Williams from Okanagan University College in B.C. Third, we appreciate the continuing support of personnel from Prentice Hall Canada/Pearson Education Canada, both past and present, including Laura Pearson, David Stover, David Jolliffe, Lisa Phillips, Matthew Christian, Jim Zimmerman, Jessica Mosher, and Patti Altridge. Fourth, the support staffs at our respective universities have been extremely helpful with each edition. For their fine work on the present edition, we are particularly grateful to Terry Stewart for computing work, and to Julie Dembski and Robin Hawkshaw for their help with preparation of materials. We also thank Denise Baker, Joyce D'Souza, Veronica D'Souza, Denise Statham, Lois Wilbee, and Carol Wong.

J.C.

E.G.

N.G.

General Introduction

CONCEPTUAL ISSUES IN THE STUDY OF SOCIAL INEQUALITY

Edward Grabb

That human beings are often very different from each other is one of those basic truths about life that we can all recognize. We need only observe the various sizes, shapes, and colours of other people, the different group affiliations they adopt, and the distinct goals or interests they pursue, to be reminded of the numerous differences that can be drawn among us. It is also true that many of these differences probably have little or no lasting influence on our existence. And yet, it is clear that certain human differences regularly have significant consequences for the lives that we are able to lead in society.

The study of social inequality is really the study of these consequential human differences. In particular, inequality refers to differences that become socially structured, in the sense that they become a regular and recurring part of how people interact with one another on a daily basis. Structured inequality involves a process in which groups or individuals with particular attributes are better able than those who lack or are denied these attributes to control or shape rights and opportunities for their own ends. One major factor in this process is that the advantaged groups or individuals tend to obtain greater access to the various rewards and privileges that are available in society. These benefits, in turn, serve to reinforce the control over rights and opportunities enjoyed by the advantaged factions, in a cyclical process that structures and reproduces the pattern of inequality across time and place.

In general terms, at least, this view of social inequality is held by most theorists and researchers in the social sciences, including many of those who study Canadian society. In this book we have brought together recent exemplary works by some noted Canadian writers, all of whom share an interest in understanding the consequential differences among people and the inequalities that they engender.

The main goal of this opening chapter is to provide an integrative background for the papers that have been selected, and a context within which the substance of our selections can be more easily located and comprehended. This is not an entirely straightforward task, since in the study of inequality, as in most vibrant and continuing areas of inquiry, there are clear divergences in theoretical orientations and research traditions.

Given these divergences, there is little possibility at present of establishing a single, universally accepted approach to analyzing the problem. In other words, a complete synthesis of existing thought and knowledge is currently not feasible. Nonetheless, we can arrive at a general understanding of the major theoretical issues and empirical questions that have held the attention of contemporary students of social inequality. This under-standing should also help us to appreciate important areas of agreement and dispute among scholars in the field.

The central questions we shall address in this opening chapter are theoretical in nature. Our discussion here will provide the conceptual background for the selection and classification of papers in this volume. In particular, we will assess the two most important ideas in most theories of social inequality: the concept of class and the concept of power, or domination. In doing so, we will demonstrate that class and power are closely tied to questions of economic control and also to questions of ideological and political control. The combined effects of these factors are what give rise to the key bases for social inequality that operate in Canada and most modern societies.

SOCIAL INEQUALITY AND THE CONCEPT OF CLASS

If we were to ask most people what inequality is about, we would probably find that their responses put considerable stress on economic or material distinctions, on differences in economic rights, opportunities, rewards, and privileges between themselves and others. Although such differences might not be their sole focus, people do show a notable interest, for example, in whether or not they earn as much money as others in different occupations; they might wonder if their own share of society's wealth is growing or shrinking over time; they might even raise such questions as whether or not it is true that a small number of businesses increasingly control more and more of their country's economic resources.

In fact, until relatively recently these same kinds of questions—about economic control and material privilege—have also been the predominant concern among most of the social scientists interested in the topic of inequality. Such a focus is understandable, of course, since economic differences involve the most immediate or fundamental inequality in social settings: people's relative access to the material necessities of life itself. Undoubtedly, this emphasis is at least partly responsible for the central role that the concept of economic class has always played in social analysis, particularly since the early writings of Karl Marx and Max Weber (see Marx 1867; Weber 1922).

Unfortunately, the concept of class has provoked long-standing and still unresolved questions about its precise meaning and significance. Of these questions, five in particular should be raised in this opening section. First, there is the question of whether classes are just categories of individuals who share similar economic circumstances, or whether the term *class* should refer only to an economic category that is also a real social group, a set of people with a shared sense of common membership or purpose. Second, analysts have debated whether classes are best thought of as simply the same as *strata*—ranked layers of people separated according to income or occupation level, for instance—or whether the dividing lines between classes are less arbitrary, less variable, and more fundamental than these stratum distinctions suggest. Third, some writers contend that classes are best understood as sets of *people*, while others say they are really sets of *places* or positions, like boxes or containers in which the people are located. Fourth, there is the question of whether classes should be defined principally by differences in the amount of material rewards *distributed* to them for consumption purposes, or whether such differences are secondary to, and largely derivative from, structured economic *relationships*, especially relationships that give sustained control over material life to some and not others. For some theorists, such control provides the real means by which classes are defined and delineated. Finally, many writers disagree on how many classes there are in modern societies. Are there just two, a small dominant one and a large subordinate one? Are there instead some intermediate classes between top and bottom and, if so, how many? Or is it the case that there are no easily identifiable classes, but instead a continuous hierarchy without clear class distinctions?

The difficulties inherent in any attempt to answer all of these questions are obvious from the volume of work that has been generated on the concept of class (for a review, see Grabb 2002). These differing perspectives cannot be fully incorporated within a single conception or definition of class. Nevertheless, there is sufficient common ground for class to be viewed in a manner that, at least in general terms, is consistent with most major works in the field, including those of the key classical writers, Marx and Weber, and of subsequent writers broadly sympathetic to either or both of these theorists (for example, Poulantzas 1975; Carchedi 1977, 1987; Wright 1979, 1985, 1989, 1994, 1997; Wright et al. 1992; Parkin 1979; Giddens 1973, 1981a, 1981b, 1984, 1989, 1994, 1998, 2000).

Our approach to defining the concept of class involves the following answers to the five questions listed above:

1. Classes exist primarily as *categories* of people, and need not be defined as real groups. In other words, classes typically will not be sets of people having a common sense of group membership and capability to act in unison toward some collective goal. This is not to say that such united action is never possible; classes sometimes become groups, but only sometimes. As Giddens notes, for example, class systems exist on a national or even international scale in modern times, making such co-ordination and common purpose exceedingly difficult to generate, at least in the mass of the population (Giddens 1973:84). In those rare instances where simple economic classes also develop these group-like characteristics, some writers find it useful, following Weber, to refer to such groups as social classes (Weber 1922:302–305; see also Giddens 1973:78–79; Grabb 2002:52).

2. While classes normally are not real groups, neither are they merely equivalent to strata, as certain writers seem to suggest (e.g., Johnson 1960:469; Barber 1957:73; Parsons 1951:172). That is, strata are usually ranked statistical aggregates, for which the criteria used in ranking are quite variable (including such characteristics as income education, occupation, and general prestige level) and where the choice of boundaries is an arbitrary decision made by the researcher. In contrast, class divisions are traceable to more fundamental, deep-seated, and uniform cleavages than the ones implied by these stratum distinctions.

3. Classes are most completely comprehended if we recognize that they are neither just sets of people nor just structural categories, the containers that separate or encapsulate sets of people; they really are both of these things in combination. This double meaning of class is one aspect of a more general process that Giddens has called the "duality" of social structures (Giddens 1979, 1981b, 1984, 1989). Hence, classes exist as structural entities because certain enforceable rights or opportunities—such as the right to own and to exclude others from owning productive property—define them and distinguish them from each other. However, classes have almost no meaning if they are not also seen as real people, for it is people who create the rights or opportunities that define classes in the first place; it is people who enjoy or suffer the consequences of class inequalities, and it is people alone who are capable of changing or consolidating class structures through social action.

4. Classes are most readily defined as *economically based* entities. However, as will be discussed later, they also have an important part to play in the political and ideological spheres of society and can be said to exist, in a sense, within and across all social structures, not just the economic (see Wright 1978, 1980, 1989:343–345; 1997:303–304, 544–545). In delineating classes, we can conform with Marx, Weber, and most leading contemporary theorists by treating one distinction—between those who own or control society's productive property or resources and those who lack this attribute—as the initial and most fundamental division in modern class systems (e.g., Marx and Engels 1848a:58, 92; Weber 1922:927; Giddens 1973:100; Poulantzas 1975:14; Wright 1978:73; Parkin 1979:53).

While this basic division is the crux of most class structures, there are other forms of social inequality that can occur. The relations of domination and exploitation established by this division are the primary factors in class formation, but the distribution of material benefits such as income can also be significant for delineating classes, if only in an indirect way. Such benefits can enhance or blur the division between the dominant and the subordinate classes, depending on whether or not these benefits are distributed so that the two classes have markedly distinct consumption habits and qualities of life.

In addition, despite what some writers seem to suggest, the distribution of material benefits need not be an insignificant factor in the formation of classes. For example, some Marxist theorists tend to consider all wage and salary employees as simply members of the working class, or *proletariat*, because they depend for their livelihood on the sale of labour power to the propertied owning class, or *bourgeoisie*. However, wage and salary employees sometimes are paid sufficiently high incomes for them to be able to accumulate some surplus funds, over and above what they need for basic survival. These funds can be, and occasionally are, used to gain some control over productive resources in the acquisition of such holdings as stocks, rental properties, interest-bearing bonds, annuities, pension plans, and so forth. To be sure, these are relatively minor forms of economic control or ownership, and in most cases are somewhat like that of the *petty bourgeoisie*, who own small-scale businesses or farms but employ no workers themselves. Nonetheless, such resources provide a means by which distributive inequalities can give rise to economic categories that are distinct to some degree from both the bourgeoisie and the proletariat (see Wright 1989:325, 333; 1994:45–48).

A related point of note is that those with a distributive surplus have the opportunity to expend these funds in another manner: to help finance special educational qualifications or technical training for themselves or their children. Here again, distributive inequalities need not merely signify consumption differences. Some writers suggest that educational credentials themselves are another form of productive "property." This may be true to the extent that educational certificates are tangible possessions that can generate material dividends all their own and that, as a result, can provide a basis for economic control otherwise unattainable by those who lack similar credentials (Giddens 1973; Collins 1979; Parkin 1979). Hence, educational advantage or opportunity may be yet another basis on which divisions can arise in the class structure and be passed on or reproduced over generations. The important role of educational certification or "credential assets" in class formation has increasingly been acknowledged by recent Marxist scholars (e.g. Wright 1985, 1989, 1994, 1997), in contrast to some earlier Marxists who ignored or downplayed the importance of this factor.

5. The final, and probably most controversial, question to address about class is how many classes actually exist in current capitalist societies. Again, complete agreement on this question is at present unattainable. Nevertheless, most writers now concur that modern class systems are more complex or pluralist in nature than the traditional Marxist division between bourgeoisie and proletariat is alone capable of representing. On the surface, this may seem to contradict standard Marxist accounts on the subject of class, especially those offered by Marx's early disciples. However, we should note that, on closer inspection, some allowance for a more complex portrayal of modern class systems is really quite consistent with Marx's own analysis and with more recent treatments by Marxist scholars.

At several points in his original writings, it is clear that Marx himself speaks of additional economic groupings that exist in real societies and that complicate the pure two-class model he believes will ultimately emerge in advanced capitalism. Marx refers to these complicating elements in various ways, calling them *Mittelstande* ("middle estates or strata"), *Mittelstufen* ("middle stages or ranks"), and *Mittelklassen* ("middle classes") (Marx and Engels 1848b:472; Marx 1862:368; 1867:673, 688, 784, 791; 1894:892). Most current Marxists describe similar complications in contemporary class structures, although they usually avoid referring to these additional elements as genuine classes (but see Carchedi 1977; Wright and Martin 1987; Wright 1989, 1994, 1997). Such elements may include the traditional petty bourgeoisie of small-scale owners but also involve a diverse range of salaried personnel that, because of attributes such as educational training, technical knowledge, administrative authority, and so on, persist as "fractions," "contradictory class locations," or similar elements complicating the basic two-class structure of capitalism (Poulantzas 1975:23, 196–199, 297; Wright 1978:90–91; 1979:46–47; 1985:88–89; 1989:301–348; 1994:45–48, 252).

Among most non-Marxists, the existence of intermediate categories in the class structure is readily acknowledged. In fact, some non-Marxists argue that there are so many complexities and fine distinctions in today's economic structure that what we really have is a *continuous hierarchy* with no distinct classes at all (Nisbet 1959; Faris 1972). Other non-Marxists have tried to adhere to this notion of a continuum while simultaneously retaining the concept of class in their analyses. One approach is to conceive of a general social hierarchy that is continuous and yet can also be divided into identifiable class clusters. In contrast to Marxist writers, some non-Marxist analysts, especially the so-called "structural functionalist school," see classes as sets of *occupations* that share a similar level of *prestige* because they are similar in their supposed value to society as a whole (Parsons 1940, 1953; Barber 1957).

Among many recent non-Marxist scholars, however, it is common to reject this conception, primarily because it tends only to confuse classes with statistical categories or strata. Instead, leading contemporary writers outside the Marxist circle now conclude that it is essential to retain key aspects of Marx's original conception of class, provided these are revamped or supplemented to take account of subsequent developments in advanced class systems.

The latter approach is reminiscent of that adopted by Max Weber, the best-known non-Marxist among major classical theorists in the field of inequality. Weber's work entails a constructive critique of Marx's writings. Weber envisions a class structure broadly similar to Marx's, involving a dominant bourgeoisie, or owning class at the top, a propertyless working class at the bottom, and a mix of "various middle classes" (*Mittelstandklassen*) in between (Weber 1922:303–305). There are several differences between the views of Marx and Weber, of course. Perhaps the most crucial difference concerns their expectations for the eventual fate of the middle categories in the class system. In contrast to Marx, Weber believes that the growing need for intermediate bureaucratic and technical personnel in modern societies means that the middle class will not fall into the proletariat with time, but will continue to endure as a significant force in the future; hence, Weber is far less convinced than Marx that a growing split will emerge between the top and the bottom classes or that an ultimate revolt by the working class against capitalism is likely to occur.

Weber's approach to the study of class has had a notable influence on virtually all current non-Marxist theorists. For example, some recent writers see classes arising because some people are able to gain greater access to certain important "capacities" and "mobility chances" (Giddens 1973:101–103) or to special "resources and opportunities" (Parkin 1979:44–46) that serve to exclude other people from advantaged positions (see also Scott 1996; Tilly 1998). Certainly, these more recent approaches are not identical to one another, nor do they correspond precisely to the views of either Marx or Weber in their subtler details. Still, the class structures they portray are generally akin to one another and to the classical conceptions, for they also arrive at three key groupings: a *dominant class* composed mainly of those who own or control large-scale production; a *working class* made up of people who lack resources or capacities apart from their own labour power; and, in between, a *mixed intermediate range* that mainly includes professional, technical, or white-collar personnel who have some degree of special training or education (Giddens 1973:101–110; Parkin 1979:47–58, 102–110).

Thus, even a brief review of classical and contemporary conceptions of class indicates that what is really at issue among most theorists is not whether complications exist in the class system, but whether the complexities that do occur, especially those found in the centre of the structure, in fact constitute classes in their own right. Marxists usually say no, perhaps because they consider any middle segments as both transitional and heterogeneous, destined to fall eventually into the proletariat and to blur only temporarily the real two-class system that underlies capitalism. In contrast, non-Marxists routinely treat such central segments as a middle class (or set of middle classes), either because such writers use the term *class* differently or because they genuinely believe these intermediate categories are fundamental and persistent realities within modern class systems.

While no complete resolution of this debate is possible, the view put forth here is that, at least for the current stage of capitalist development, it is reasonable to use the term *middle class* to label these central categories. There are three reasons for taking this position.

First, there is nothing inherent to the word *class* that suggests that it must be reserved solely to refer to permanent and lasting social categories. Thus, while all Marxists treat the bourgeoisie as a real class within capitalism, Marxists also contend that this class is destined for eventual dissolution in future socialist societies. Similarly, then, whether or not the middle categories in the class system are destined to be transitional entities should not be a crucial concern for deciding whether or not they form a class at present. Marx clearly saw this himself since, as noted already, he sometimes spoke of the existence of a middle class even though he had no doubt that its days were numbered.

Second, it can be argued similarly that although the middle segments of the class structure are indeed heterogeneous, their diversity is insufficient grounds for denying that they form a distinct class. For, as leading Marxists and others acknowledge, the contemporary bourgeoisie and proletariat are also marked by considerable heterogeneity but are deemed to be classes all the same (Poulantzas 1975:23, 139, 198).

Finally, between the proletarian or bourgeois classes, on the one hand, and the set of intermediate categories, on the other hand, there is some conceptual parity that suggests the latter also may be seen as a class. By conceptual parity we mean that the middle class is definable by means of the very same criteria used to delineate the bourgeoisie and proletariat. These criteria are the measure of people's relative control over society's productive resources and the extent to which such control separates sets of individuals (and the positions they occupy) from one another. What is most distinct about the members of the middle class is their mixed, or hybrid, situation in the productive system relative to people from other classes. As suggested previously in point 4, middle-class incumbents are unlike those in the proletariat, and similar to people in the bourgeoisie, because they retain some control over productive resources or assets—the acquisition of property and investments or of educational credentials and skills, in particular. However, at the same time, middle-class members are unlike those in the bourgeoisie, and closer to people in the proletariat, because the resources they control are typically minor in scale and are often derived from a relatively small surplus fund accumulated from salaried or wage-based earnings. That these middle locations tend to commingle characteristics of the other two classes, and yet still remain marginal to both of them, is what most clearly identifies the middle class as a separate entity (see Wright 1989:333; Wright et al. 1992:41).

Given these considerations, we can deal with point 5 by provisionally suggesting that Canada, as well as most advanced capitalist countries, retains a class structure that, although highly complex and internally diverse, tends at its core to comprise three basic elements. The first is a predominant class of large-scale owners of productive property, the so-called *capitalist class* or *bourgeoisie* in classical Marxian terminology. The second element is a subordinate class of workers who live primarily through the sale of their labour power to the owning class and who are usually termed the *working class* or *proletariat*. The third major element is a mixed and more heterogeneous middle category of small-scale business people, educated professional-technical or administrative personnel, and various salaried employees or wage earners possessing some certifiable credentials, training, or skills. The latter grouping, while it is for some writers just a set of complicating fractions or fragments within a basic two-class model, can be considered a third or *middle class* for the reasons already outlined (see Grabb 2002:227–228).

Still, as has been pointed out from the beginning of this chapter, this provisional characterization cannot be presented as a universally acceptable conception of modern class structures. Rather, it can best be seen as an approximation, a compromise view with which the differing perspectives that are considered in this book can be compared and contrasted. Such an approximation allows us to recognize some level of agreement on how to think about the concept of class. Even so, other theoretical issues still remain to be addressed. In particular, we should be aware that many analysts believe a focus on class is too narrow to provide by itself a complete conceptualization of social inequality in all its forms. Such contentions move us beyond the problems of economic class and control over material or productive resources. They lead to a broader range of concerns that require us to consider the second key idea in most theories of social inequality—the concept of power or domination.

SOCIAL INEQUALITY AS POLITICAL AND IDEOLOGICAL CONTROL

In our opening remarks it was suggested that social inequality is primarily a question of consequential human differences, especially those that become structured and recurring features of our everyday lives. To this point, we have considered what many feel are the most familiar and fundamental illustrations of such differences: the inequalities that derive from differential *economic* control, or people's command over material and productive resources in society. In addition, however, many writers suggest at least two other major mechanisms that are crucial to the creation and continuation of social inequality. The first of these involves control over people and their conduct, over what some might call "human resources." This command over human resources is the essence of *political* control, as broadly defined by various analysts. The third major mechanism can be referred to as *ideological* control. It entails the control of ideas, knowledge, information, and similar resources in the establishment of structured inequality between groups or individuals (Mann 1986, 1993; Runciman 1989; Grabb 2002).

A basic premise of the current discussion is that these two additional forms of control, though they typically occur in conjunction with economic control (and with each other), are not simply reducible to or a consequence of economic control, since both political and ideological control actually have their own distinct origins. In other words, it is possible to gain positions of dominance in society and to establish inequalities between factions without relying purely on control over material resources.

For example, inequality can result from political control when enforceable policies, statutes, or laws are invoked to ensure the compliance of subordinates with the will of others. The government or *state* is most commonly identified with the idea of political control, since it takes primary responsibility for creating the laws that govern the behaviour of people and can ensure compliance, if necessary, through the use of police or military force. However, political control in the broadest sense occurs whenever individuals' actions are constrained by rules of conduct established by others in authority over them in various organizations—when employees obey the work regulations of their jobs or when students comply with the academic regulations of their university, for example. The most extreme or blatant form that political control can take is one that is usually exercised by the state. This is the use of physical force by one faction on another, what Poulantzas quite literally calls the "coercion of bodies and the threat of violence or death" (Poulantzas 1978:28–29).

In addition to economic and political control, inequalities can also be created through or reinforced by ideological forces. *Ideology* refers to the set of ideas, values, and beliefs that describe, explain, or justify various aspects of the social world, including the existence of inequality (Porter 1965, chs. 15, 16; Marchak 1988). Thus, for example, a belief in racial superiority or inferiority is central to the ideological system that helped create and justify the unequal treatment of blacks by whites in the nineteenth-century southern United States and in the old apartheid system in South Africa. Similarly, the belief in the divine right of kings was important in establishing and maintaining the rule of monarchs and nobles over other people in much of medieval Europe. Of course, it is also possible for ideologies to support *reductions* in inequalities among groups. For example, the Canadian Charter of Rights and Freedoms is one relatively recent attempt in Canada to implement the belief in equal rights and opportunities for all people, regardless of "race, national or ethnic origin, colour, religion, sex, age, or mental or physical disability." In each of these examples, ideas and beliefs about inequality were also converted by governments into official policy or formal laws. This illustrates the often close connection between politics and ideology in society.

We should also recognize, though, that ideology can be fundamental to the third major type of control we have been discussing: economic control. For example, the belief that it is acceptable for people to own private property is clearly an essential ideological prerequisite for the existence of economic inequalities based on such ownership. Similarly, the belief that people with unequal talents or motivation should also be unequal in the material rewards they receive can be used as both an explanation and justification for the economic differences that arise among individuals. In both of these examples, the extent to which people believe or reject ideas about themselves and their society will have an important bearing on how much inequality exists, and how likely it is to change with time.

POLITICAL AND IDEOLOGICAL FACTORS IN CLASS DIFFERENCES

The recognition of multiple mechanisms of control and the distinct resources they entail suggests that there is some degree of pluralism in the processes that generate social inequality. This, in turn, implies that any investigation based solely on economic class, especially if classes are conceived only in conventional terms as groupings within the structure of material production, is not sufficient by itself to capture and express this pluralism.

Perhaps for this reason, some Marxists have sought to include in their conceptions of class the sense that not only economic control but also political and ideological control are crucial to the formation of class structures (Poulantzas 1975; Wright 1979, 1985, 1989, 1994, 1997). The incorporation of these additional elements into conventional conceptions of the class system is a significant innovation. Their inclusion permits us to recognize that classes, although they are primarily economic groupings, can also be important for other reasons and, in a way, may be fundamentally embedded within and across all social structures, both economic and noneconomic.

Here we should also note that, in addition to a revised notion of the class system, other complicating elements have come to be recognized in the multifaceted structure of inequality that characterizes most societies. As both Marxists and non-Marxists now generally acknowledge, various patterns of inequality exist that are at least partially independent of, and not reducible to, class inequality alone. The more prominent examples of these other bases for inequality include gender and race or ethnicity. Other important bases include age, region, and, in some cases, language and religion. Non-Marxists sometimes refer to these factors as different bases for "social closure" (Parkin 1979), while Marxists sometimes call them "multiple oppressions" (Wright 1985:57). Whatever label they are given, however, they represent important additional areas of inquiry for students of inequality and require a conceptual approach that is broader than what the class concept by itself can provide.

SOCIAL INEQUALITY AS THREE FORMS OF POWER

It is primarily for this reason that some writers have recommended that the concept of power be used in conjunction with class theory, in an effort to move us toward a more general framework for analyzing and thinking about inequality in all its forms. Some Marxist scholars have been reluctant to take this approach, especially if it relegates class analysis to a secondary concern (Wright 1985:57; Clement 1982:481). And, indeed, it is essential when analyzing other crucial problems in social inequality that we not ignore or downgrade the continuing importance of class in contemporary societies. Thus, although some now suggest that class may be "dying" as a significant issue or concept in sociology (e.g., Clark and Lipset 1991; Clark et al. 1993), existing research, including many of the studies presented in this book, make it clear that this suggestion is mistaken.

As noted already, however, it can be argued that class analyses are improved significantly by a fuller appreciation of the other forms of inequality and power relations in society. In other words, power can be used as a more generalizable, if not a more fundamental, concept than class, because it can be used to describe and analyze both class and nonclass forms of social inequality (Giddens 1981a; Grabb 2002:226–230). Those who adopt the latter perspective contend that class is pivotal in any complete understanding of social inequality, but that class differences represent one manifestation of the more general structure of power that is responsible for generating the overall system of inequality in most societies. Other crucial manifestations of inequality, such as those based on gender and race, can therefore be understood as the results of differential access to the different forms of power or domination in society (see, for example, Blalock 1989, 1991; Wilson 1973; Huber and Spitze 1983; Blumberg 1984; Milkman 1987; Connell 1987; Collins 1988; Li 1988; Mackie 1991; Chafetz 1990, 1997; Walby 1990, 1997; Agger 1993; Andersen and Collins 1995).

However, even if power can serve this more general conceptual purpose, the question still remains: What precisely does the concept of power signify? This is not a simple question to answer since power, like class, is an idea that has stimulated numerous debates over its definition and meaning (see, for example, Lukes 1974; Wrong 1979; Mann 1986, 1993; Runciman 1989; Scott 1996). For our purposes, however, *power* can be defined briefly as the differential capacity to command resources and thereby to control social situations. We have already suggested that there are three major types of resources operating in social settings (material, human, and ideological) and three mechanisms of control corresponding to them (economic, political, and ideological). These three mechanisms can be seen as the key forms of power in society.

Whenever differences in economic, political, or ideological power are sufficiently stable and enduring that they promote regular, routinized relations of ascendance and subordination among people, the resulting pattern of interaction is a case of *structured power*, or what might be termed a *structure of domination* (Grabb 2002). Using abstract imagery, we can think of the overall system of inequality in a society as a kind of framework, involving all three forms of power and the three corresponding structures of domination. In more concrete terms, the structures of domination exist mainly as bureaucratic or corporate organizations: business enterprises in the economic sphere, departments of government in the political sphere, church hierarchies and institutions of higher learning in the ideological sphere, and so forth. It is within all of these concrete settings that power differences among people (and among the positions they occupy) become manifested, thereby producing organized patterns of inequality.

Another point to note in this abstract imagery is that there is no perfect one-to-one linkage between each of the three forms of power and each set of concrete structures. These are just the *primary linkages*, since each of the means or forms of power can operate in at least a secondary fashion in any of the three structures. Thus, as noted earlier, political power (control over people or human resources) may indeed be the principal jurisdiction of the set of political or state organizations, but it is also exercised in the control imposed by owners on their workers in the economic structure. At the same time, the various political organizations composing the modern state do not derive all their power from the capacity to legislate or coerce human behaviour, for they also control material resources through their command over tax revenues, government ownership of some business enterprises, and so on. As for control of ideas or knowledge, this is most obviously identified with ideologically oriented structures such as the mass media, the education system, and the church. However, as mentioned in a previous section, such ideological control is clearly a means for wielding power elsewhere too. This is illustrated by the policy-making, information-gathering, and surveillance capacities within the state and by the control over technical ideas and knowledge that occurs in the economic sphere (Giddens 1981b, 1985, 1989).

The combined operation of all the structures of domination, or rather the concrete organizations to which they correspond, establishes the major contours of the overall structure of inequality. The organizations themselves are patterned according to formal rules, laws, and rights of office, and their personnel exercise power in accordance with these formal guidelines. In addition, however, the inequalities that may develop within organizations, as well as the inequalities that organizations may engender for people outside them, are at least partly determined by informal practices or traditions, customs or habits, beliefs or prejudices. Not only formal rights or powers, but also informal privileges or advantages, tend to determine the nature and extent of inequality in society. Both act together to designate what the key bases of social inequality will be and how much each of them will matter.

THE BASES OF SOCIAL INEQUALITY IN CANADA

There is a final conceptual issue to consider. This involves the identification of the central bases of social inequality that arise from the exercise of power in Canada. As we have already suggested, the notion that there are several distinct bases for inequality in society is one that has achieved increasing acceptance by theorists and researchers in the field, among both non-Marxist and Marxist scholars. What has increasingly been argued is that there exists a multiple set of human characteristics or socially defined attributes that are consequential for determining the quality of life of most people. It will be recalled that this is the idea with which we began our introduction to the topic of social inequality in this chapter.

But what are these major bases for inequality, and why do these particular characteristics matter more than others? While it is difficult to provide answers to these questions that will satisfy all theoretical camps, we can see at least some common ground in the responses that most observers would give to both queries.

Perhaps the more difficult question to deal with is the second: Why are some attributes of people more likely than others to lead to important inequalities? Why, for example, has colour of skin had such a sustained impact on the rights and rewards of people historically, but not colour of eyes or hair? In general terms, it is possible to conceive of this problem by looking once again at the idea of power, or domination, and by considering which factions within the population have historically been the most or the least successful in turning to their advantage the various economic, political, and ideological mechanisms of power that operate within social structures. That is, to the extent that those in positions of ascendancy are able to use the three forms of power to establish and routinize structures of domination, they will be relatively more successful in reproducing across time and place important advantages for themselves and others with similar backgrounds or characteristics. For example, within any capitalist society, those individuals who retain private ownership or control over productive property will clearly enjoy special advantages and may well attempt to use their strategic position to encourage the further institutionalization of property rights in law, to foster belief systems favourable to such rights, and to employ other comparable means to help ensure that the privileges of property are maintained for themselves and succeeding generations of capitalists. In a similar fashion, those who have recognized training and skills, notably those who possess formal credentials or degrees in such areas as medicine and law, will themselves benefit from the advantages such exclusive accreditation brings and will also tend to favour the continuation of the system of special certification (and attendant privileges) for themselves and the cohorts who follow.

In both of these illustrations, we have noted important bases for inequality—property and educational credentials—which also happen to correspond to two of the key types of economic or productive resources that are in demand in most societies. In the present context, however, these are not just resources but socially defined human attributes, or capacities of real people. In this form, they become recognized by others as crucial characteristics for differentiating some individuals or factions from others and for determining the rights, opportunities, rewards, and privileges of those who do or do not have them. We should note that this distinction, between resources, on the one hand, and human attributes, on the other hand, illustrates once again what has elsewhere been referred to as the duality of social structures. In addition to these attributes, though, there is a whole range of other consequential human differences that should be identified. Gender and race or ethnicity probably are the best contemporary examples. Inequalities based on gender and race or ethnicity are neither identical to nor reducible to class inequality. Nevertheless, like class inequality, these two bases of inequality can be conceived of as the product of long-standing factional antagonisms, struggles, or contests in which economic, political, and ideological mechanisms of power have played significant roles in establishing and structuring advantages for one grouping of people relative to others.

In fact, a full range of attributes or capacities can be delineated, comprising all the major bases of inequality. In the contemporary Canadian context, these include the set of class-related bases—property ownership, education, occupation, and possession of wealth or income—as well as the key nonclass bases—gender, race, ethnicity, language, region, and age (see Grabb 2002). As the papers in this volume will show, there is evidence to indicate that social groupings that are distinguishable from others on these dimensions have often been able to maintain significant advantages within the system of social inequality in Canada, and have done so largely because of superior access to economic, political, and ideological power.

In considering such a list, of course, we should also be aware that not all of these factors will be equally influential in shaping the general patterns of inequality in Canadian society. It is also important to acknowledge that other factors may matter, in different historical periods or different places, and that there may be considerable variability over time in the importance or prevalence of some bases of inequality relative to others. One example is religious affiliation. This is one social characteristic that we have not listed here, but which in the past was probably a significant basis for inequality in Canada. Nevertheless, most analysts would agree that now religion is of relatively little consequence in influencing the power or rank of Canadians, especially compared with a century ago. At the same time, though, it is true that religious differences still play a major part in shaping the structure of inequality in other countries, in contemporary Northern Ireland or Iran, for example.

PLAN OF THE BOOK

The selections incorporated into this book reflect rather clearly the central role that the study of class and power has played in theory and research on inequality in Canada (see, in particular, Sections 1 and 2). Various chapters also discuss the array of social characteristics that have arisen as important bases for inequality in this country (in particular, Sections 2 and 3). As the title of the book suggests, we have attempted within each section to attend not only to the patterns of social inequality and some of the problems these patterns pose for our society but also to the policies and ideologies involved in inequality. Section 4 traces out some of the varied consequences of inequality for individuals.

Our choice of "Power and Class" as the topic for our first section is meant to underscore that control over productive property provides a fundamental context within which the other bases for inequality operate in Canada and other capitalist societies. This section, therefore, provides necessary groundwork for understanding the patterns of inequality that are dealt with in the other sections.

We have said that certain key inherited or attained socio-economic characteristics are very important in defining the contours of inequality in our society. This issue is the principal focus of the second section of the book, which deals with the distribution of personal wealth or income, occupational status, and educational attainment. These are three bases for inequality that are distinct from each other and from the ownership factor itself, but which are also involved in shaping the system of economic classes. Ownership of productive property is the essential basis for class inequality, particularly that which exists between the owning class and the working class. At the same time, however, educational credentials and surplus wealth or income are, as we have seen, potentially important for distinguishing the "middle class," or comparable intermediate categories, from the two major classes. The reason for including occupation in the same section is perhaps less obvious, but follows from two considerations. First, occupation has long been used in social research as an approximate indicator of class location, although methodological problems associated with this have been of some concern to many writers, especially Marxists. Second, the analysis of occupational inequality is useful in a supplementary or residual sense, because occupation subsumes such phenomena as skill level, manual versus nonmanual labour power, and so on, which are not fully captured in research that is restricted to the study of ownership, wealth or income, and education.

In Section 3 the central concern is with factors of social ascription. In Canada, these include gender, race, ethnicity, language, age, and region of residence. This third set of attributes is discussed separately from class and the socio-economic status characteristics for two reasons. First, these bases for inequality are conceptually independent of class distinctions, although, as we shall see, they may be correlated with class location and may give rise to important divisions within classes. Second, these attributes are ascriptive in nature, involving statuses that are not achieved or attained by people, but rather given to them. The ascriptive process is most clear in such characteristics as gender, race, and ethnicity, which are all essentially assigned to people at birth. Age is another social characteristic that, though constantly changing, is assigned and beyond the control of people. Language and region of residence are also assigned characteristics. For adults, there is some reason to dispute the ascriptive label for these last two attributes, because adults can elect to alter the language they speak or move to another place to live. However, even in adulthood, these attributes are more ascriptive than they appear, because of the pressures upon many Canadians to retain the language and place of residence they are born into. Language barriers and regional divisions tend to reproduce themselves over time, in spite of any policy efforts to change or reduce them.

The first three sections of the volume concentrate on structural questions: the character of class divisions and the other key bases of social inequality, and the ways in which such inequalities have been developed and maintained. The final section serves a different purpose, by providing a broad sampling of evidence to show that all of the various bases of inequality can influence the quality of life enjoyed or endured by Canadians. Of course, the earlier parts of the book also deal with the consequences of inequality, to the extent that these sections examine the effects of class, gender, or ethnicity on education, occupation, or income, for example. Section 4, however, goes beyond the early sections to show the wide-ranging impact that social inequality can have on aspects of life as diverse as health and mortality, the incidence of racial prejudice, and people's beliefs about the causes of inequality. Taken together, the collection of papers in this volume should give the reader a good sense of the array of important issues that Canadian researchers have addressed in the study of social inequality.

REFERENCES

Agger, Ben 1993. *Gender, Culture, and Power.* Westport, Connecticut: Praeger.

Andersen, Margaret, and Patricia Collins (eds.) 1995. *Race, Class, and Gender.* Belmont, California: Wadsworth.

Barber, Bernard 1957. *Social Stratification.* New York: Harcourt Brace and World.

Blalock, H.M., Jr. 1989. *Power and Conflict: Toward a General Theory.* Newbury Park: Sage.

Blalock, H.M., Jr. 1991. *Understanding Social Inequality.* Newbury Park: Sage.

Blumberg, Rae Lesser 1984. "A general theory of gender stratification." In R. Collins (ed.), *Sociological Theory 1984,* pp. 23–101. San Francisco: Jossey-Bass.

Carchedi, Guglielmo 1977. *On the Economic Identification of Social Classes.* London: Routledge.

Carchedi, Guglielmo 1987. *Class Analysis and Social Research.* Oxford and New York: Basil Blackwell.

Chafetz, Janet Saltzman 1990. *Gender Equity: An Integrated Theory of Stability and Change.* Newbury Park: Sage.

Chafetz, Janet Saltzman 1997. "Feminist theory and sociology: underutilized contributions for main-stream theory." *Annual Review of Sociology* 23:97–191.

Clark, Terry Nichols, and Seymour Martin Lipset 1991. "Are social classes dying?" *International Sociology* 6:397–410.

Clark, Terry Nichols, Seymour Martin Lipset, and Michael Rempel 1993. "The declining political significance of class." *International Sociology* 8:293–316.

Clement, Wallace 1982. "Corporations, power, and class." In D. Forcese and S. Richer (eds.), *Social Issues: Sociological Views of Canada,* pp. 469–485. Scarborough, Ontario: Prentice-Hall Canada.

Collins, Randall 1979. *The Credential Society.* New York: Academic Press.

Collins, Randall 1988. *Theoretical Sociology.* San Diego: Harcourt Brace Jovanovich.

Connell, R.W. 1987. *Gender and Power: Society, the Person and Sexual Politics.* Cambridge: Polity Press.

Faris, Robert E. L. 1972. "The middle class from a sociological viewpoint." In G. Thielbar and S. Feldman (eds.), *Issues in Social Inequality,* pp. 26–32. Boston: Little Brown and Company.

Giddens, Anthony 1973. *The Class Structure of the Advanced Societies.* London: Hutchinson.

Giddens, Anthony 1979. *Central Problems in Social Theory.* Berkeley: University of California Press.

Giddens, Anthony 1981a. "Postscript (1979)." *In The Class Structure of the Advanced Societies* (2nd ed.), pp. 295–320. London: Hutchinson.

Giddens, Anthony 1981b. *A Contemporary Critique of Historical Materialism.* Vol. 1, Power, Property, and the State. London: Macmillan.

Giddens, Anthony 1984. *The Constitution of Society.* Berkeley and Los Angeles: University of California Press.

Giddens, Anthony 1985. *A Contemporary Critique of Historical Materialism. Vol. 2, The Nation-State and Violence.* Berkeley and Los Angeles: University of California Press.

Giddens, Anthony 1989. "A reply to my critics." In D. Held and J. Thompson (eds.), *Social Theory of Modern Societies,* pp. 249–301. Cambridge: Cambridge University Press.

Giddens, Anthony 1991. *Gender Relations in Canada.* Toronto: Butterworths.

Giddens, Anthony 1994. *Beyond Left and Right: The Future of Radical Politics.* Stanford: Stanford University Press.

Giddens, Anthony 1998. *The Third Way: The Renewal of Social Democracy.* Cambridge: Polity Press.

Giddens, Anthony 2000. *The Third Way and Its Critics.* Cambridge: Polity Press.

Grabb, Edward G. 2002. *Theories of Social Inequality: Classical and Contemporary Perspectives* (4th ed.). Toronto: Harcourt Canada.

Huber, Joan, and Glenna Spitze 1983. *Sex Stratification: Children, Housework, and Jobs.* New York: Academic Press.

Johnson, Harry M. 1960. *Sociology: A Systematic Introduction.* New York: Harcourt, Brace and World.

Li, Peter S. 1988. *Ethnic Inequality in a Class Society.* Toronto: Wall and Thompson.

Lukes, Steven 1974. *Power: A Radical View.* London: Macmillan.

Mackie, Marlene 1991. *Gender Relations in Canada.* Toronto: Butterworths.

Mann, Michael 1986. *The Sources of Social Power, Vol.1.* Cambridge: Cambridge University Press.

Mann, Michael 1993. *The Sources of Social Power, Vol. 2.* Cambridge: Cambridge University Press.

Marchak, M. Patricia 1988. *Ideological Perspectives on Canada.* Toronto: McGraw-Hill Ryerson.

Marx, Karl 1862. *Theories of Surplus Value, Vol. 2.* Moscow: Progress Publishers.

Marx, Karl. 1867. *Capital, Vol. 1.* New York: International Publishers.

Marx, Karl. 1894. *Capital, Vol. 3.* New York: International Publishers.

Marx, Karl, and Friedrich Engels 1848a. *The Communist Manifesto.* New York: Washington Square Press.

Marx, Karl, and Friedrich Engels 1848b. *The Communist Manifesto* (German version). In *Marx Engels Werke, Vol. 4.* Institut fur Marxismus-Leninismus Beim Zk Der Sed. Berlin: Dietz Verlag.

Milkman, Ruth 1987. *Gender at Work.* Urbana and Chicago: University of Illinois Press.

Nisbet, Robert A. 1959. "The decline and fall of social class." *Pacific Sociological Review* 2:11–17.

Parkin, Frank 1979. *Marxism and Class Theory: A Bourgeois Critique.* London: Tavistock.

Parsons, Talcott 1940. "An analytical approach to the theory of social stratification." In T. Parsons, *Essays in Sociological Theory,* pp. 69–88. New York: The Free Press.

Parsons, Talcott 1951. *The Social System.* New York: The Free Press.

Parsons, Talcott 1953. "A revised analytical approach to the theory of social stratification." In T. Parsons, *Essays in Sociological Theory,* pp. 386–439. New York: The Free Press.

Porter, John 1965. *The Vertical Mosaic: An Analysis of Social Class and Power in Canada.* Toronto: University of Toronto Press.

Poulantzas, Nicos 1975. *Classes in Contemporary Capitalism.* London: New Left Books.

Poulantzas, Nicos 1978. *State, Power, Socialism.* London: New Left Books.

Runciman, W.G. 1989. *A Treatise on Social Theory. Vol. 2, Substantive Social Theory.* Cambridge: Cambridge University Press.

Scott, John 1996. *Stratification and Power.* Cambridge: Polity Press.

Tilly, Charles 1998. *Durable Inequality.* Berkeley: University of California Press

Walby, Sylvia 1990. *Theorizing Patriarchy.* Oxford: Basil Blackwell.

Walby, Sylvia 1997. *Gender Transformations.* London: Routledge.

Weber, Max 1922. *Economy and Society, Vols. 1–3.* New York: Bedminster Press.

Wilson, William Julius 1973. *Power, Racism, and Privilege.* New York: Macmillan.

Wright, Erik Olin 1978. *Class, Crisis, and the State.* London: New Left Books.

Wright, Erik Olin 1979. *Class Structure and Income Determination.* New York: Academic Press.

Wright, Erik Olin 1980. "Class and occupation." *Theory and Society* 9:177–214.

Wright, Erik Olin 1985. *Classes.* London: Verso.

Wright, Erik Olin 1989. *The Debate on Classes.* London: Verso.

Wright, Erik Olin 1994. *Interrogating Inequality: Essays on Class Analysis, Socialism, and Marxism.* London: Verso.

Wright, Erik Olin 1997. *Class Counts: Comparative Studies in Class Analysis.* Cambridge: Cambridge University Press.

Wright, Erik Olin, Andrew Levine, and Elliott Sober 1992. *Reconstructing Marxism.* London: Verso.

Wright, Erik Olin, and Bill Martin 1987. "The transformation of the American class structure, 1960–1980." *American Journal of Sociology* 93:1–29.

Wrong, Dennis 1979. *Power: Its Forms, Bases and Uses.* New York: Harper and Row.

POWER AND CLASS

We begin our look at social inequality in Canada with a series of papers dealing with the interplay of power and class structure in our society. This is a logical starting point because, as was discussed in the general introduction, the concepts of class and power are pivotal to any general understanding of social inequality. In this section, we are especially interested in the power that derives from ownership and control of productive property and resources, and the nature of the class structure that is defined by such power. Some of the selections also explore the connections between economic classes and the state, most notably the roles that government activities and policies play in shaping the pattern of both ownership and class inequality in Canada.

In capitalist countries like Canada, and perhaps in all societies, ownership of property is arguably the key defining criterion for those who wish to understand the nature of material inequality and the emergence of economic classes. But what is really meant by the notion of property ownership in this context? Most theorists agree that property does not refer to the simple possession of material resources that are used only for personal consumption, such as food, clothing, shelter, and the like. This is not to say that the distribution of these and other consumer items is unimportant to the study of inequality, nor is it to deny the tremendous significance of such items for those who experience a shortage or abundance of them in their daily lives. Rather, it is to recognize that the possession of material benefits or products is not only, or even primarily, what constitutes property ownership. Ownership of property, in its most crucial sense, entails the *right of disposition over the economic process in general.*

The essence of property ownership is having the capacity to command the various activities and organizational processes that are involved in producing, accumulating, investing, or expending society's material or economic resources. Ultimately, it is from this capacity that decisions are made about the distribution of economic benefits to people, and it is through this capacity that some groups and individuals can exclude others from economic control or influence. Perhaps the most important outcome of this process is that the class of people who own society's productive property is in a position to establish relations of domination and exploitation over the class of non-owners, who in turn must sell their labour in order to survive. The non-owners, or working class, may resist this pattern of relationships through political organization, unionization, and other forms of collective action. However, as both classical and contemporary social theorists have often pointed out, the owning class is typically able to override or limit the success of such opposition, given the rights of this class to private productive property and the protection of these rights by the state or government.

The first chapter in this section, by Edward Grabb, assesses evidence on the concentration of economic power in Canada, in order to answer three related questions: Has the share of Canada's economy that is controlled by private-sector corporations increased in recent decades; what part do foreign-controlled companies play in Canada's ownership structure; and how does the state's power and influence compare with that of private business interests when it comes to owning and directing the contemporary Canadian economy?

The second paper in this section, by Gordon Laxer, broadens the analysis of social inequality to include the important question of international class and power relations. His discussion of globalization and the global capitalist system underlines the importance of large-scale private-sector companies. Many of these large companies operate throughout the world as multinational or transnational enterprises, with business holdings in numerous countries. In some cases these individual enterprises actually rival or surpass the economic power of entire nations. A major issue that Laxer's analysis addresses is the prospect of democratic collective action and solidarity within the wider population of contemporary societies, given the increasing prominence of these globally oriented businesses.

In the third article, James Conley considers the processes and forces that have been involved in the formation of the Canadian working class in the twentieth century. Beginning with Marx's and Weber's classical approaches to understanding capitalist class structures, the author then focuses on a review of Canadian evidence relating to four key topics. These include the alleged tendency for increased class polarization in modern capitalism; the changing organization of the workplace and its possible effects on working-class solidarity; the likelihood of increasing class awareness or class consciousness within the working class; and the prospects for mobilization, formal organization, and collective action among workers in Canada today.

For many observers, the high concentration of economic control in relatively few hands is a potentially serious problem. The main concern is that far too much power has been wielded historically by the owners of productive property. Any further centralization of ownership only enhances the likelihood that such power could be abused, with the rest of the population facing increased exploitation and domination by the owning class.

The final chapter in the section, by Robert Brym, looks at power and class from the point of view of the working class, especially the struggles over power that give rise to workers' strikes. The author finds that, in contrast to the pattern in earlier times, the strike has not been a particularly effective mechanism for improving the situation of workers relative to the capitalist owning class. He suggests that this change, which has been in place since the mid-1970s, is reflective of a major redistribution of power away from workers and in favour of employers.

The overall message conveyed by this section of the book is that ownership of productive property or resources, especially through the mechanism of giant private-sector business enterprises, is perhaps the most fundamental force generating the overall pattern of social inequality, both in Canada and in the larger international context. Moreover, the available evidence suggests that this will continue to be true for some time in the future.

ECONOMIC POWER IN CANADA: CORPORATE CONCENTRATION, FOREIGN OWNERSHIP, AND STATE INVOLVEMENT

Edward Grabb

(Revised from the previous edition of this volume.)

INTRODUCTION

Social scientists have long been concerned with understanding the structure of economic power in Canada. In particular, a number of investigators have been interested in determining the extent to which the economy is controlled by a few powerful groups and organizations. Research on this question began in the early part of the twentieth century (e.g., Myers 1914; Creighton 1937), but it was John Porter's extensive analyses in the 1950s and 1960s that first provided detailed evidence on the high concentration of economic ownership and control in this country (Porter 1956, 1957, 1965). One of Porter's main conclusions from his research was that less than 200 large corporations and their directors appeared to dominate much of Canada's economic power structure at that time.

Porter's findings set the stage for most of the later attempts to understand Canadian patterns of ownership and control. The next influential series of studies arose from Wallace Clement's research on Canada's "corporate elite" (Clement 1975, 1977a, 1977b). Clement's findings suggested that, by the 1970s, economic control in Canada was probably even more concentrated than in the period Porter considered, with 113 powerful companies accounting for the majority of business activity.

Since Porter and Clement published their findings, numerous academics, commentators, and journalists have added to what is now a sizeable body of literature on the workings of the Canadian economy (e.g., Newman 1979, 1981; Marchak 1979; Niosi 1978, 1981, 1985; Ornstein 1976; Carroll, Fox, and Ornstein 1982;

Carroll 1982, 1984, 1986; Richardson 1982; Brym 1985, 1989; Antoniou and Rowley 1986; Francis 1986; Veltmeyer 1987; Laxer 1989; Fox and Ornstein 1986; Grabb 1990; O'Connor 1999; Carroll and Alexander 1999). Most of this research suggests that, by the 1990s, the concentration of economic power was still on the rise, with a shrinking group of large, often interconnected, and mainly private-sector corporations at the centre of Canada's ownership structure.

In the past, many of these powerful companies were owned or effectively controlled by a relatively small number of people. For much of our history, in fact, a few prominent and long-established families formed a major component of Canada's economic elite (see Newman 1979; Antoniou and Rowley 1986; Francis 1986). These included such well-known names as the Eatons, the Molsons, the Westons, and the McCains, to name just four examples. In more recent years, another component of our economic elite has involved less established individual entrepreneurs who, through what are commonly called "conglomerates" or "holding companies," control interrelated sets of large and often quite diverse businesses. A prime illustration is Paul Desmarais who, through Power Corporation, has interests in major enterprises in such areas as forestry, oil and gas, newspaper publishing, and life insurance. As the principal investors and shareholders in many of Canada's biggest businesses, these families and individual business leaders have tended to enjoy an inordinate amount of influence in determining the general nature and overall direction of our economy.

Apart from private-sector companies and their owners, most writers have identified two other principal components that are believed to be integral to Canada's economic power structure. The first of these is foreign-owned private businesses, which have played a significant part in our economy for some time, but became especially prominent during the latter half of the twentieth century. The degree to which our economy has been controlled by such outside interests has occupied the attention of numerous researchers and observers over the years (e.g., Levitt 1970; Clement 1977a; Laxer 1989).

The final key factor to consider when assessing who controls or directs the Canadian economy is the role of the government or state. Especially since the 1970s, contemporary social scientists in various countries have shown a sustained interest in the amount of state involvement in economic activity (e.g., Miliband 1973; Poulantzas 1978; Wright 1978; Friedman and Friedman 1980; Offe 1984). In Canada, as well, observers have debated the extent of state intervention into business activity and its implications for shaping our system of economic power (e.g., Panitch 1977; Calvert 1984; Banting 1986; Fox and Ornstein 1986).

The goal of the present chapter is to build on previous research and analysis on these topics by assessing the pattern of ownership and economic control in Canada, with a particular focus on the 1990s and early 2000s. We are primarily concerned with three related questions. First, what does the available evidence tell us about the trends in ownership concentration in recent decades, especially in regard to the role of Canada's large-scale private-sector businesses and corporations? Second, what part do foreign or non-Canadian companies play in our economy, and has the level of involvement by foreign-controlled corporations changed from what it was in earlier years? Finally, how does the level of ownership by major private-sector companies compare with that of state-controlled agencies or enterprises? The answers to these questions will provide a clearer picture of the nature of economic power and ownership concentration in Canada in the contemporary period.

ANALYSIS

Trends in the Concentration of Corporate Assets

Our first concern is to assess the current degree of economic concentration among privately owned corporate enterprises, and to determine if any major changes have occurred in this concentration in recent years. Research has shown that there was a high level of economic centralization in Canada in the recent past. For example, one study reported that, although 400 000 companies were operating in Canada in 1987, the largest twenty-five enterprises by themselves accounted for over 41% of all corporate assets in that year (O'Connor 1999:36). Previous research has also indicated that this level of ownership concentration was significantly greater in the mid-1980s than it had been just ten years before (e.g., Francis 1986:3; Grabb 1990:77).

More recent evidence suggests certain changes in the structure of corporate ownership. First of all, a number of the established family "dynasties," including the Eatons, the Reichmanns, and the Bronfmans, have experienced the loss or sale of some of their corporate holdings and some reduction in their overall influence (see Francis 1997:38; Associated Press 2000, 2002). Nevertheless, other family-based enterprises continue to be very important. For example, the Westons, who are best known for their vast food empire, the Bombardier family, who have long been leaders in the manufacture of trains, recreational vehicles, and other transportation equipment, and the Stronach family,

whose Magna International is a major force in vehicle parts manufacturing, continued to control three of the top twenty corporations operating in Canada as of 2000, and were still among the major decision-makers on the Canadian economic scene (*National Post* 2001:112–113). Similarly, although some prominent individual entrepreneurs, such as Conrad Black, have reduced their holdings, others have continued to thrive and expand. A prime example is Paul Desmarais, who is the majority owner of Power Corporation. This company, as mentioned earlier, is a large conglomerate with investments in a number of business endeavours. It has consistently ranked among the top fifteen or twenty companies in Canada over the years (see, e.g., *Financial Post* 1985, 1995; *National Post* 2001).

It may not be surprising, then, that government statistics and other evidence suggest a continued trend toward higher levels of economic concentration. From 1987 to 1993, for example, the share of Canada's corporate assets controlled by the largest twenty-five enterprises rose once again, from 41% to 46% of the national total (Statistics Canada 1995a: 50). Thus, by the mid-1990s, almost half of Canada's corporate assets were held by the top twenty-five businesses, a trend that is also consistent with the increase in mergers and acquisitions involving major companies (*Maclean's* 1993:34; Canadian Press 1996, 1997). Corporate takeovers in Canada have occurred at an unprecedented rate in recent times. In 1997, there were a record 1274 mergers and acquisitions involving more than $100 billion of assets (Greenwood 1998). In 2000, the asset value of corporate takeovers was more than double the 1997 figure (Arab 2000). Although this merger "fever" had declined somewhat by 2001 (Canadian Press 2001), the general trend in mergers and acquisitions has clearly been upward over the last decade or more, leading to an overall increase in ownership concentration.

The high degree of concentration is apparent throughout most of the economy, but is especially pronounced in the financial sector, where only a handful of banks, trust companies, and insurance firms have consistently predominated (e.g., Francis 1986:242). Recent mergers and acquisitions in the financial sector have only added to this centralization. Some of the most prominent examples include the 1997 purchase of National Trust Company by the Bank of Nova Scotia, the 1997 takeover of London Life Insurance by Great West Life Assurance (which in turn is controlled by the major conglomerate Power Corporation), the 2000 takeover of Canada Trust by the Toronto-Dominion Bank, and the 2002 acquisition of Clarica Life Insurance by Sun Life Insurance (Statistics Canada 2000a:25; Newman 1997:54; Ferguson 2000; Arab 2002). The most recent government statistics available are for 1998, and so do not reflect the latter two mergers; however, even without including these major transactions, the evidence of ownership concentration in the financial sector is striking. Data from Statistics Canada indicate that financial industries in Canada owned assets worth $1.655 trillion in 1998 (Statistics Canada 2000b:64–65). The *Financial Post* (1999: 174) reported that $1.194 trillion of these financial assets, or more than 70% of the total for 1998, were held by the five largest Canadian banks alone: the Canadian Imperial Bank of Commerce, the Royal Bank, the Bank of Nova Scotia, the Bank of Montréal, and the Toronto-Dominion Bank.

The mass media represent another area of the economy that has recently seen high levels of ownership concentration. Perhaps the best illustration concerns the holdings of the Asper family, who own CanWest Global and other media enterprises. As of March 2002, the Aspers by themselves controlled 60% of Canada's newspapers and television outlets (Worthington 2002; Canadian Press 2002). Concentration has also been high in some resource industries. For example, Silverberg found that the top five mining companies in Canada, which in 1972 controlled 49% of that industry, by 2000 had raised their ownership share to 72%. He also found that the top five forestry companies increased their assets substantially, from 26% to 43% of the total, during this same period (Silverberg 2001:152, 191). There is good reason to conclude, then, that the concentration of economic ownership in Canada is probably more pronounced now than it has ever been.

Changes in Foreign Economic Influence

From Canada's beginnings as a colony, first of France and then of England, our economy has been marked by a considerable amount of foreign control and influence. While Canada in the modern era has evolved into one of the most prosperous and industrialized nations in the world, we have continued to experience a relatively high level of foreign involvement in the economy, at least in comparison with other developed countries.

Much of the research on foreign ownership in Canada has focused on the influx of American-based transnational corporations during the twentieth century (e.g., Levitt 1970; Clement 1975, 1977a; Laxer 1989). Evidence indicates that this American involvement developed in a series of stages, but became especially important during a period of about twenty-five years after World War II. Between 1970 and the mid-1980s, however, Canada witnessed a decline in the general level of American and other foreign ownership (Niosi 1981:31–33; Grabb 1990:78).

The most recent available data indicate that foreign involvement is still a prominent feature of the Canadian economy, although the level of influence has fluctuated over time. For example, foreign companies accounted for 36% of the assets of nonfinancial companies operating in Canada in 1970. This proportion had declined to 23% by 1983, before rising again to about 27% by 1998 (Statistics Canada 1995a:33; 2001:15). In the financial sector, where Canadian companies have always enjoyed government protection from external competition, the foreign presence is less evident. However, the share of assets held by non-Canadian financial companies is more substantial than it was in years past, rising from under 12% in 1983 to more than 18% by 1998 (Statistics Canada 1993:17, 41; 2001:25).

Over the years, some of the strongest evidence of foreign control in our economy could be found at the very top of the nonfinancial sector, where a few major non-Canadian corporations tended to predominate. In the mid-1980s, for example, six of the top ten companies operating in Canada were foreign-owned. These included the Canadian subsidiaries of the three American automotive giants (General Motors of Canada, Ford of Canada, and Chrysler Canada), as well as two American-owned oil subsidiaries (Imperial Oil and Texaco Canada) and one Dutch-controlled oil company (Shell Canada) (*Financial Post* 1985). By 2000, there was some evidence of a reduced foreign presence among the very largest businesses, with four non-Canadian companies among the top ten. These again included the three major automobile firms—General Motors of Canada, Ford of Canada, and DaimlerChrysler Canada

(now renamed after Mercedes Benz's takeover of Chrysler in the United States)—and Seagram, a firm that was once Canadian-owned but was sold by the Bronfman family to the French company Vivendi in 2000 (*National Post* 2001: 112–113; Associated Press 2000).

Despite this decline in foreign enterprises in the top ten in recent years, the influence of foreign companies continues to be substantial. For example, as of 2000, twenty-three of the leading 100 companies in Canada were wholly owned or majority owned by non-Canadians. Moreover, if only nonfinancial companies are considered, this number rises to twenty-eight out of the top 100 (*National Post* 2001: 112–117). Of the top fifty foreign-controlled companies doing business in Canada in 2000, thirty-two were American, with fourteen based in Europe, three in Japan, and one in Barbados (*National Post* 2001:148). The predominant American role in the foreign sector of the economy is also confirmed by recent government statistics, which show that companies based in the United States accounted for 69% of the total operating revenues earned by foreign companies in Canada in 1998 (Statistics Canada 2001:14). This proportion is down slightly from the 73% that American firms received in 1975, but is similar to the share that they have held since the mid-1980s. Companies from European nations accounted for another 18% of the foreign-controlled revenues in 1998, with the remaining 9% held in the rest of the world (see Statistics Canada 1996:25–26; 2001:14).

The State and Economic Power

The next question to address is the role of Canada's various levels of government in the contemporary Canadian economy.

Historically, business activities have often been influenced by state involvement, although sometimes in contradictory ways. At certain times, for example, governments have lent money to Canadian capitalists and imposed tariffs or other trade restrictions on foreign competitors, in order to promote and protect Canadian companies. At other times, however, governments have offered tax reductions and other incentives to encourage foreign business ventures in Canada, and have also established state-run enterprises that compete directly with Canada's private-sector firms (Clement 1975, 1977b; Traves 1979; Marchak 1979; Laxer 1989).

In recent decades, a good deal of the discussion on the role of the Canadian state has centred on whether or not government economic intervention has gone too far. Some researchers suggest that the state's role in the Canadian economy is actually rather small. Such analysts usually acknowledge that the state spends a considerable portion of the national wealth, with governments covering the costs of providing and maintaining public education, health care, a wide range of social services, transportation facilities, and the like. However, most of these writers also contend that, otherwise, the state has normally been a limited player in the Canadian economy, with private business interests still acting as the pre-eminent force (e.g., Calvert 1984; Fox and Ornstein 1986; Brym 1989; O'Connor 1999).

There are other observers, however, who allege that the various branches of the state have become exceedingly influential within our economic system. These writers argue that governments at all levels have too often used their considerable taxation and spending powers to fund a number of poorly conceived endeavours, including expensive, loosely administered

social programs and unprofitable, inefficient government enterprises (see, e.g., Horry et al. 1992; Francis 1995:13; Walker 1997). Similar views appear to be found among many private-sector capitalists, who see the government as an intruding competitor in the business arena (Ornstein 1985, 1999). Added to these perceptions is the belief that state-owned companies usually have an unfair advantage over private businesses, which need to turn a profit to survive and cannot rely on government financial assistance to bail them out of difficulty.

One direct means for measuring state economic power is to determine the proportion of major enterprises that are government-controlled. Previous research found that, in both 1975 and 1985, only four of the top twenty-five nonfinancial corporations operating in Canada were state-owned, and less than ten of the top 100 (Grabb 1990:79). More recent business rankings suggest an even smaller government presence at the highest level. For example, in 2000, Québec's electric utility, Hydro Québec, was the only government-directed enterprise among the leading twenty-five companies. A total of eleven government-controlled companies ranked within the top 100 enterprises; these included other utilities such as Ontario Power Corporation, Hydro One (Ontario), and B.C. Hydro, as well as Canada Post, the Canadian Wheat Board, and two major provincial lottery agencies, Loto-Québec and the Ontario Lottery Corporation (*National Post* 2001: 112–115). On this basis, however, it is difficult to argue that government enterprises dominate the Canadian economy.

Perhaps a more comprehensive gauge of government economic influence is the share of the nation's total assets held by the various branches of the state. One earlier study, using government data on the "national balance sheet," estimated that, by the mid-1980s, less than one-fifth of Canada's total assets were owned by government entities of different kinds. These included state-run agencies, business enterprises, pension funds, and related organizations (Grabb 1990:86–87). Such findings indicate that government economic control in Canada, though notable, was not nearly as great as some observers have argued, and was far lower than that enjoyed by the private business sector, in particular.

Table 1-1 presents broadly similar data on the national balance sheet, for ten-year intervals between 1961 and 2001. These figures show clearly that the government or public sector accounts for a relatively minor segment of Canada's ownership structure. These data also reveal that the level of government control over assets has declined significantly over this forty-year time span, especially in the last two decades. As of 2001, the government controlled less than 11% of all assets held

within Canada, compared with about 16% in 1981 and 18% in 1961.

Although numerous factors probably account for this trend, one major cause has been the changing policies of the federal government and many provincial administrations in recent years. In particular, state leaders have been increasingly motivated to encourage private-sector economic expansion and also to sell off various government-run enterprises to private interests. This pattern began in the mid-1980s, around the time of the election of the federal Progressive Conservatives, under Brian Mulroney. However, despite suggestions to the contrary prior to their election in 1993, the federal Liberals, led by Jean Chrétien, adopted much the same set of policies and have followed them right up to the early 2000s. Similar initiatives to reduce state involvement in the economy have recently been put forward at the provincial level as well, especially by the Conservative-led governments of Alberta and Ontario (see, e.g., Denis 1995).

TABLE 1-1	Estimated Disribution of Total Assets Held within Canada, 1961 to 2001				
Year	**1961**	**1971**	**1981**	**1991**	**2001**
Sector					
I. Persons and Unincorporated Businesses	39.8%	37.4%	36.4%	37.2%	34.4%
II. Private Sector	33.8%	36.3%	39.3%	41.0%	45.7%
1. Nonfinancial enterprises	20.5	20.3	20.5	18.6	17.9
2. Financial institutions	13.3	16.0	18.8	22.4	27.8
III. Public Sector	18.0%	18.3%	15.8%	13.3%	10.6%
1. Nonfinancial enterprises	4.1	4.0	4.2	3.5	2.4
2. Financial institutions	2.4	2.8	1.9	1.6	1.7
3. Other (pensions, social security funds, other levels of government, etc.)	11.5	11.5	9.7	8.2	6.5
IV. Nonresidents	8.4%	8.0%	8.5%	8.5%	9.3%

Source: Calculated from CANSIM II, 2002, National Balance Sheet Accounts, Total Assets in Dollars, by Sectors, Table 3780004. These data originate from the Statistics Canada CANSIM Data Base. CANSIM is an official Mark of Statistics Canada.

As we would expect given the evidence reported earlier in this chapter, Table 1-1 shows that private-sector corporations continue to hold the largest single portion of our national assets, with a share of about 46%, or almost half of the total, as of 2001. This share represents a substantial increase over time, since private corporations controlled only about 34% of the nation's assets in 1961, and about 39% in 1981. The biggest change in the private sector has been the steady rise in the proportion of assets held by private financial companies, from about 13% in 1961 to almost 28% by 2001. This pattern was counterbalanced somewhat by a small decline in the assets of private nonfinancial companies, from just over 20% to just under 18% of the total during the same period.

One sector that traditionally has rivalled private corporations in terms of assets share is the "persons and unincorporated businesses" category. This is a heterogeneous grouping that subsumes the personal possessions, savings, real estate, and private pension funds of individual citizens, as well as the assets of small businesses, farms, and nonprofit organizations that are not officially constituted as corporate entities. It is notable that, although this category accounted for the largest single share of assets in 1961, with almost 40% of the total, by 2001 its proportion had declined to about 34% and is now less than the amount owned by private-sector businesses. The remaining assets in the Canadian economy are owned by nonresidents, most notably in the financial holdings of foreign investors and business interests. These have hovered between 8% and 9% of the total throughout the last forty years.

SUMMARY AND CONCLUSION

Our review of recent evidence on economic control and ownership in Canada has revealed that, by the early 2000s, many of the same patterns of ownership that existed in previous decades are still in place. That is, we have found a relatively high concentration of economic power in a small group of giant private-sector corporations operating at the top of the ownership structure. Moreover, this level of concentration has continued to rise compared with the situations that obtained in the past. It seems clear, then, that large-scale financial and nonfinancial business enterprises, along with the major shareholders and directors that control them, are as powerful as they have ever been in the Canadian economy.

We have also considered the level of foreign involvement in Canada's ownership structure. In this case we determined that non-Canadian businesses play a substantial role in the economy, though probably somewhat less so than they did in the peak years of foreign activity around 1970. Even so, the most powerful and profitable enterprises currently operating on the Canadian scene still show a notable foreign presence, with about a quarter of the top 100 companies owned by non-Canadian, mostly American, transnational corporations.

The final major issue we addressed was the degree of state control over Canada's economic affairs. In keeping with earlier research from previous decades, we have seen that the government role, though notable in some respects, is really quite minor in comparison with that played by private corporations. Moreover, the government's presence on the economic scene has declined in the past several decades, both in regard to its role as a director of large-scale business enterprises and in its control over national assets. Now very few of Canada's largest enterprises are government-owned, and the proportion of Canadian assets owned by all branches of government is down to about one-tenth of the total. In addition, during the 1990s and the early 2000s, we have seen concerted drives by the federal and provincial governments to cut back on services in the interest of eliminating government deficits and reducing the nation's debt. These policies make it evident that there has been some curtailment of state economic activity in the spending area as well. The government strategy for the future clearly appears to be one in which political leaders look primarily to the private sector, and not to state-sponsored programs, to promote economic activity. Overall, the current climate is one in which private-sector businesses continue to determine the major contours and direction of Canada's economic power structure.

REFERENCES

Antoniou, Andreas, and Robin Rowley 1986. "The ownership structure of the largest Canadian corporations, 1979." *Canadian Journal of Sociology* 11:253–268.

Arab, Paula 2000. "Corporate takeovers reach fever pitch." In the *London Free Press*, October 7:D8.

Arab, Paula 2002. "Sun Life swallows Clarica to become No. 1." In the *London Free Press*, October 7:C3.

Associated Press 2000. "Seagram dead at 76." Reported in the *London Free Press*, June 21:A1, A3.

Associated Press 2002. "Deal allows Vivendi to avoid bankruptcy." Reported in the *London Free Press*, August 20:C6.

Banting, Keith 1986. *The State and Economic Interests*. Toronto: University of Toronto Press.

Brym, Robert 1985 (ed.). *The Structure of the Canadian Capitalist Class*. Toronto: Garamond.

Brym, Robert 1989. "Canada." In T. Bottomore and R. Brym (eds.), *The Capitalist Class. An International Study,* pp. 177–206. New York: New York University Press.

Calvert, John 1984. *Government, Limited.* Ottawa: Canadian Centre for Policy Alternatives.

Canadian Business 1995. The Canadian Business 500, Volume 68 (June).

Canadian Press 1996. "Mergers, acquisitions hit record in 1995." Reported in the *London Free Press*, January 6:B9.

Canadian Press 1997. "Can the merger mania last?" Reported in the *London Free Press*, December 30:D3.

Canadian Press 2001. "Corporate takeovers down 39% this year." Reported in the *London Free Press*, April 25:D3.

Canadian Press 2002. "CanWest reduces media assets." Reported in the *London Free Press,* July 11:C6.

Carroll, William 1982. "The Canadian corporate elite: financiers or finance capitalists?" *Studies in Political Economy* 8:89–114.

Carroll, William 1984. "The individual, class, and corporate power in Canada." *Canadian Journal of Sociology* 9:245–268.

Carroll, William 1986. *Corporate Power and Canadian Capitalism.* Vancouver: University of British Columbia Press.

Carroll, William, and Malcolm Alexander 1999. "Finance capital and capitalist class integration in the 1990s: networks of interlocking directorships in Canada and Australia." *Canadian Review of Sociology and Anthropology* 36:331–354.

Carroll, William, John Fox, and Michael Ornstein 1982. "The network of directorship links among the largest Canadian firms." *Canadian Review of Sociology and Anthropology* 19:44–69.

Clement, Wallace 1975. *The Canadian Corporate Elite.* Toronto: McClelland and Stewart.

Clement, Wallace 1977a. *Continental Corporate Power.* Toronto: McClelland and Stewart.

Clement, Wallace 1977b. "The corporate elite, the capitalist class, and the Canadian state."

In L. Panitch (ed.), *The Canadian State,* pp. 225–248. Toronto: University of Toronto Press.

Creighton, Donald 1937. *The Commercial Empire of the St. Lawrence.* Toronto: Macmillan.

Denis, Claude 1995. "'Government can do whatever it wants': moral regulation in Ralph Klein's Alberta." *Canadian Review of Sociology and Anthropology* 32:365–383.

Ferguson, Rob 2000. "Ottawa expected to go slow on bank mergers." In the *Toronto Star,* June 4:B4, B5.

Financial Post 1985. *The Financial Post 500,* Summer 1985.

Financial Post 1995. *The Financial Post 500,* Summer 1995.

Financial Post 1999. *The Financial Post 500,* June 1999.

Fox, John, and Michael Ornstein 1986. "The Canadian state and corporate elites in the post-war period." *Canadian Review of Sociology and Anthropology* 23, 4 (November):481–506.

Francis, Diane 1986. *Controlling Interest.* Toronto: Macmillan.

Francis, Diane 1989. *Open for Business.* Toronto: Oxford University Press.

Francis, Diane 1995. "The need for laws to limit spending." *Maclean's,* February 13.

Francis, Diane 1997. "When famous families lose touch." *Maclean's,* March 17.

Friedman, Milton, and Rose Friedman 1980. *Free to Choose.* New York: Harcourt Brace Jovanovich.

Grabb, Edward 1990. "Who owns Canada? Concentration of ownership and the distribution of economic assets, 1975–1985." *Journal of Canadian Studies* 25:72–93.

Greenwood, John 1998. "Corporate takeovers soar to record." In the *London Free Press,* January 10:D8.

Horry, Isabella, Filip Palda, and Michael Walker 1992. *Tax Facts 8.* Vancouver: The Fraser Institute.

Laxer, Gord 1989. *Open for Business.* Toronto: Oxford University Press.

Levitt, Kari 1970. *Open for Business.* Toronto: Oxford University Press.

Maclean's 1993. "The return of the big deal in mergers." October 25.

Marchak, Patricia 1979. *In Whose Interests? An Essay on Multinational Corporations in a Canadian Context.* Toronto: McClelland and Stewart.

Miliband, Ralph 1973. *The State in Capitalist Society.* London: Quartet Books.

Myers, Gustavus 1914. *A History of Canadian Wealth.* Toronto: James Lewis and Samuel.

National Post 2001. *The National Post Business FP500.* Canada's Largest Corporations, June.

Newman, Peter 1979. *The Canadian Establishment.* Toronto: McClelland and Stewart-Bantam.

Newman, Peter 1981. *The Acquisitors.* Toronto: McClelland and Stewart-Bantam.

Newman, Peter 1997. "How Power trumped the Royal Bank." *Maclean's,* September 1.

Niosi, Jorge 1978. *The Economy of Canada.* Montréal: Black Rose Books.

Niosi, Jorge 1981. *Canadian Capitalism: A Study of Power in the Canadian Business Establishment.* Toronto: Lorimer.

Niosi, Jorge 1985. *Canadian Multinationals.* Toronto: Garamond.

O'Connor, Julia 1999. "Ownership, class, and public policy." In J. Curtis, N. Guppy, and E. Grabb (eds.), *Social Inequality in Canada: Patterns, Problems, Policies* (3rd ed.), pp. 35–47. Scarborough: Prentice-Hall Allyn Bacon Canada.

Offe, Claus 1984. *Contradictions in the Welfare State.* Cambridge, Mass.: MIT Press.

Ornstein, Michael 1976. "The boards and executives of the largest Canadian corporations: size, composition, and interlocks." *Canadian Journal of Sociology* 1:411–437.

Ornstein, Michael 1985. "Canadian capital and the Canadian state: ideology in an era of crisis." In R. Brym (ed.), *The Structure of the Canadian Capitalist Class,* pp. 129–166. Toronto: Garamond.

Ornstein, Michael 1999. *Politics and Ideology in Canada.* Montréal and Kingston: McGill-Queen's University Press.

Panitch, Leo (ed.) 1977. *The Canadian State.* Toronto: University of Toronto Press.

Porter, John 1956. "Concentration of economic power and the economic elite in Canada." *Canadian Journal of Economics and Political Science* 22:199–220.

Porter, John 1957. "The economic elite and the social structure of Canada." *Canadian Journal of Economics and Political Science* 23:377–394.

Porter, John 1965. *The Vertical Mosaic.* Toronto: University of Toronto Press.

Poulantzas, Nicos 1978. *State, Power, Socialism.* London: New Left Books.

Richardson, R.J. 1982. "'Merchants against industry': An empirical study of the Canadian elite." *Canadian Journal of Sociology* 7:279–295.

Silverberg, Shane 2001. "Concentration of ownership in Canada's resource industries: historical and recent trends in mining, petroleum, and forestry." Unpublished Master's thesis, University of Western Ontario.

Statistics Canada 1986. *National Balance Sheet Accounts, 1961–1985.* Catalogue 13-214.

Statistics Canada 1993. *Corporations and Labour Unions Returns Act. Preliminary 1992.* Catalogue 61-220.

Statistics Canada 1995a. *Corporations and Labour Unions Returns Act. Preliminary 1993.* Catalogue 61-220.

Statistics Canada 1995b. *National Balance Sheet Accounts, 1984–93.* Catalogue 13-214.

Statistics Canada 1996. *Corporations and Labour Unions Returns Act. Preliminary 1994.* Catalogue 61-220.

Statistics Canada 2000a. *Inter-Corporate Ownership 2000.* Catalogue 61-517.

Statistics Canada 2000b. *Financial and Taxation Statistics for Enterprises 1998.* Catalogue 61-219.

Statistics Canada 2001. *Corporations Returns Act. 1998.* Foreign Control in the Canadian Economy. Catalogue 61-220.

Traves, Tom 1979. *The State and Enterprise: Canadian Manufacturers and the Federal Government, 1917–1931.* Toronto: University of Toronto Press.

Veltmeyer, Henry 1987. *Canadian Corporate Power.* Toronto: Garamond.

Walker, Michael 1997. "The law of diminishing returns applies to government." In the *London Free Press,* January 2:B7.

Worthington, Peter 2002. "Asper chain redefines 'loopy.'" In the *London Free Press,* March 16:F5.

Wright, Erik Olin 1978. *Class, Crisis, and the State.* London: New Left Books.

DEMOCRACY AND GLOBAL CAPITALISM

Gordon Laxer

(Adapted from Gordon Laxer, "Social Solidarity, Democracy, and Global Capitalism." *Canadian Review of Sociology and Anthropology* 32, August 1995, pp. 287–313. Reprinted with permission.)

INTRODUCTION

If someone were to tabulate the top forty words used today on the political newspeak charts, "globalization" would be at or near the top. "Globalization" is a short form for a cluster of related changes. Economic changes include the internationalization of production and the greatly increased mobility of capital and of transnational corporations (henceforth "transnationals"). Cultural changes involve trends toward a universal world culture and the erosion of the nation-state.

This paper challenges the globalization assumptions on three points. First, regarding the claim of greater global economic integration, is the relative level of transnational ownership and control higher now than in the past? Second, has globalization resulted from technological change or from the political project of the new right? Third, is democracy strengthened by global "market reforms"? The remainder of the paper examines the prospects for social solidarity in the future.

TRANSNATIONALS THEN AND NOW

In 1991 Robert Reich forecast a new age in which there would soon be no "national corporations" and no "national economies." In 1989 "over 7% of the aggregate value of the world stock market was held by foreign investors" (138). Do Reich's claims of a higher level of global corporate integration withstand scrutiny?

Reich's figures do not impress. According to John Dunning (1988), the relative level of foreign direct investment (FDI) "was more significant" from 1900 to 1914 "than at any time before or since" (72). In contrast to Reich's 7% figure for 1989, Dunning estimates that FDI represented 35% of long-term international debt then. Although there were new waves of transnational investment after 1914, the World Wars, revolutions, decolonization, and repatriations weakened transnational control relatively from 1914 through the 1970s (Wilkins 1974:221; Dunning 1993: 119, 126).

When foreign ownership was at its height before 1914, about three-fifths was located in what is now called the Third World. Its territorial compass was wider, much of it concentrated in Russia and China, areas to which it has only recently started returning.

Transnationals and foreign ownership are not new. Once entrenched they can be removed. It is their nature that is different. Before 1914 foreign ownership often involved freestanding companies and fairly autonomous subsidiaries (Dunning 1993:120). Global communications were difficult. Recent technological changes greatly enhance the ability of transnationals to move capital globally and to run subsidiaries and affiliates from afar. Computers, telephones, fax machines, high-resolution monitors, satellites, and modems allow corporations to link a global network of suppliers, designers, engineers, and dealers, and to develop flexible manufacturing processes. They can form alliances with companies anywhere to work on such things as research and development.

The recent upsurge in Japanese and European transnationals has restored the relative importance of transnationals globally to roughly that before 1914. According to Dunning (1993), transnationals "accounted for between 25% and 30% of the gross domestic product of the world's market economies in the mid-1980s. They were also responsible for around three-quarters of the world's commodity trade" (14). Stopford et al. (1991) add that transnationals control "80 per cent of the world's land cultivated for export crops, and the lion's share of the world's technological innovations" (15). Although there were up to 20 000 transnationals in 1988, the largest 300 "are thought to account for 70 percent of the total foreign direct investment stake" (15).

The technology is now at hand for global production that takes little account of borders, cultures, or democracy. The main barriers to transnationals' strategies have been myriad social and political arrangements among governments, businesses, unions, and citizens in each polity. Current assumptions about the irreversibility of "globalization" and the decline of national sovereignty help to eliminate these barriers.

Technological Determinism or Political Agency

The inevitable direction of history has shifted recently. As late as the 1970s it was widely thought that history was inevitably moving toward international socialism. Now history has swung toward the globalization of the new right.

New technologies put much of the world in touch with common cultural products such as American films and English-language rock music and television programs. The Internet allows people in different countries to converse with one another. We have seen as great a revolution in transportation as in information. Everywhere on earth is quickly accessible for a price. Has the migration of labour across borders accelerated as has the international migration of corporations?

International labour migration has likely declined relatively since the great migration from Europe to the "New World" between the 1880s and 1914 (Hobsbawm 1990:91). No political revolution comparable to new-right globalization has taken place to free labour mobility. Elites have been content to leave labour where it is. Exceptions have been made to allow managers, diplomats, businesspeople, investors, and certain professionals to migrate with the transnationals. But most wage-earners in the privileged countries have stayed put. Corporations can move from one labour market to another, playing off one set of wage-earners and one set of social citizenship rights against another. The smaller and weaker the polity, the easier it is to deploy economic blackmail strategies.

We can now see how peculiar the period between the 1940s and 1970s was for business and for the political right. The stark contrast between the 1930s depression under free-market conditions and the prosperity of the war years under government stimulus taught a lesson to many people outside war-torn areas. A positive state role was now widely thought to be necessary for economic growth. The prosperity of the thirty years after 1945 saw the expansion of the welfare state and the growing influence of unions and social democratic parties (Hobsbawm 1994: 272). The right had been defeated, morally as well as militarily, in the war against fascism. Ideas with similarities to fascism were discredited (176–177).

In this unique context the power of organized workers and citizens grew. The ideas of renegade members of the establishment before World War II—Henry Ford and John Maynard Keynes among them—had highlighted underconsumption as the cause of economic crises. They challenged free-market capitalism, and their views became the ruling orthodoxy. Under "Fordism," corporations granted workers a share in productivity gains. Under "bastard" Keynesianism, governments stimulated demand through full-employment policies and public social services, and regulated economic cycles through fiscal and monetary policies (Lipietz 1992:5–7). A "great compromise" among capital, labour, and the state emerged in the advanced countries. It was sometimes forgotten that the consensus came only after major struggles by organized workers and in anti-Nazi resistance movements (7–8).

In the compromise, corporations acknowledged the legitimacy of unions and implicitly recognized some obligation to workers and citizens. Labour accepted corporate control over production and investment and gave up its historic goal of overturning capitalism. There were different versions and levels of commitment to this compromise in each country (Esping-Andersen 1990).

Seduced by these changes arising from a unique historical conjuncture, most Western socialists proclaimed old-style capitalism dead. It is curious to read their assertions now. All the state had to do, so they said, was regulate, not socialize, capital.

It went unnoticed that the great compromise was built on twin foundations: the politics of support for regulation and the embeddedness of corporations in communities. By the 1980s neither condition held.

Patricia Marchak (1991) has outlined the rise of the new right. Corporate

leaders and their allies, organized institutes and business associations, aimed at
undermining the ideological underpin-
nings of the Keynesian welfare state. The
Trilateral Commission, founded in 1973
by David Rockefeller and other powerful
leaders in North America, Europe, and
Japan, was one of the most prominent of
these (103). The "Trilateralists" identified
an "excess of democracy" as a major problem in the advanced countries. Their solutions were to strengthen governments relative to citizens and to give transnationals
greater freedom to make investments
(Crozier et al. 1975:162, 173).

The corporate agenda joined with two
others to form the new right. One was a
revived neo-liberal economics that projected the image of championing the "little
guy" against entrenched interests, especially in government. A third agenda,
"neoconservatism," brought a popular
base for the new right. Reaction to feminism was at the heart of the backlash
(Eisenstein 1982; Gilder 1989). So too
were reactions against rights for racial
minorities, gays and lesbians, and immigrants. As unemployment and social benefits rose, the welfare state created a tax
backlash (Esping-Andersen 1990). Finally,
there was a religious backlash, especially
in the U.S., against secularism and the per-
missive values of the 1960s.

Intellectually the new right was a
strange brew. The corporate agenda called
for greater state authority, while libertarian economics wanted limited government.
The latter allied with neoconservatives
urging the state to legislate morality and
enforce law and order (Nisbet 1986:
102–103; Lipset 1988). When it was all
put together, freedom was for the corporations, and discipline for wage-earners and
citizens.

The new right agenda had national and
global components. The global component

involved freeing corporations from obligations to wage-earners and citizens, and
reducing the autonomy of countries. This
was done through "trade" agreements.
Although they invoked the image of "free
trade," these agreements were concerned
with granting citizen-like rights to
transnationals and with using the state to
entrench their monopoly positions.

The information revolution enhanced
corporate mobility. New-right liberalism
and its bedfellow "neoconservatism" provided the rationale and the popularity
to allow corporations to cut their moor-
ings. Have these changes strengthened
democracy?

DEMOCRACY WITHOUT SOVEREIGNTY

Fukuyama (1992) embraces Lord Bryce's
definition of political liberalism as exemptions from societal control over property
rights, religion, and political matters
unnecessary to the welfare of the whole
community. Democracy, on the other
hand, calls for citizens to share in political
power (42–43). Transnationals make up
forty-seven of the 100 largest economic
entities in the world, while states make up
the other fifty-three (Goldstein and Weiss
1991). Shifting power from governments
to "market forces" under these conditions
means transferring power from democratic bodies to giant corporations. If neo-lib-
eralism exempts most societal spheres
from democratic control and reduces the
sovereignty of political communities, is
real democracy still possible?

Global citizenship rights for corporations enables them to escape obligations to
country. The implicit threat is: Bring in
strict anti-pollution regulations, promise
public auto insurance or higher minimum
wages, and we the corporation will move
out. You the wage-earners and citizens

who voted for such policies will be left hurting. Not us: We are mobile and responsible to shareholders, not communities. Global corporate-citizenship rights enhance the transnationals' ability to use blackmail to discipline democracies.

The global marketplace is the arena for transnationals, the rich, and some business professionals, where rights and power are based on unequal command of property. The arena for most wage-earners and most citizens is countries and regions where the principles of democracy and equality are widely recognized. Capital is mobile. Labour, by and large, is not. Most people do not want to roam the globe in search of a job. If most people are relatively immobile, then the sovereignty of their political communities to determine their destinies is fundamental to democracy.

PROSPECTS FOR SOCIAL SOLIDARITY IN THE GLOBAL ECONOMY

Are there alternatives to new-right globalization?

What is new about the 1990s is that socialist alternatives to capitalism are, for the first time in over a century, not credible. This is not to say that new versions of democratic socialism cannot become credible as the bases for powerful movements. In place of the old socialisms, new language and concepts are needed that are more inclusive than that of class, and that place less emphasis on unity as uniformity.

Class is still with us. If anything, recent globalization has accentuated class inequalities. But, as feminist, racial, and national liberation movements have shown us, class is not the only form of domination and exploitation.

For democratic-egalitarian projects to succeed in challenging the power and unitary vision of the transnationals, they must be able to incorporate social movements that are class-based with those that are not. They must also be able to demonstrate that they, and not the elites, better represent the whole of the political community.

We know from historical experience that the mere socialization of work did not necessarily lead to the formation of communities of workers who rejected the logic and power of capitalism and campaigned for its replacement. The socialization of work created unfavourable as well as favourable conditions for the rise of such oppositional communities. Generally, circumstances favourable to union organizing were the ones with emancipatory potential.[1] Organized working-class power has been crucial to the development of social services, citizens' rights, and democracy.

What if we are now experiencing a historical reversal: the desocialization of work? The signs are not entirely clear. There is high real unemployment in all advanced countries, more part-time work, home-based work, self-employment, and contracting out from corporations and the state to small businesses in which employment is often temporary (Krahn and Lowe 1993). These conditions are not conducive to building communities of wage-earners. The trends vary by country and are influenced by politics. Nevertheless, they seem to point to a reduction in the demand for labour and to the transference of work from the developed to the Third World.

Capitalism has been in crisis since 1973, recording lower productivity gains and lower profits. This crisis is at the heart of trends to end permanent jobs and to reduce wages and employment.

The 1990s have witnessed similar changes in the public sector. The 1990s recession and high-interest-rate policies led to a fiscal crisis of the state in most advanced countries.[2] The new right took advantage of this situation to demand major cutbacks in government services and the privatization of much that remained to be delivered (Osborne and Gaebler, 1992). The combined effect was massive cuts in public sector workforces and the weakening of public sector unions.

What are the emancipatory prospects for movements based outside communities of wage-earners? I am referring to feminist, civil-rights, transformative-nationalist, environmental, religious-reformist, and other bases for social movements.

Non-work-based movements are fragmented in their identities, in their issues of concern, and in the sites of their political actions. They lack an overarching vision.

Many things keep these movements apart, but several may bring them together. Shared democratic and egalitarian values are spreading into more and more spheres of life. National sovereignty and democracy are powerful rallying cries for citizens and wage-earners who are rooted in place and attached to their communities (Laxer 1995). The most powerful impetus for cooperation may be the new right's globalization project, which is totalizing in its ambitions and focuses on culture as much as on production.

The transnationals will not necessarily succeed in homogenizing world culture or in maintaining capital mobility. The scope of and opportunities for social movements are expanding. Many new social movements recruit mainly from the growing and diverse groups outside the traditional working class. Greater formal education, more leisure time, and better communications encourage a rich life of networking locally, nationally, and internationally.

Because environmentalists, feminists, economic nationalists, and others are all threatened by new-right globalization, they can develop coalitions for common purposes. I use the word "can" rather than "must" because there is nothing inevitable about this. Non-work-based movements must develop means of dealing with the state, with elections, and with political parties.

Can such coalitions agree upon enough of a common vision, while respecting differences, to transform political communities into more egalitarian, democratic, communitarian societies? The answers will come from further research and thinking and from concrete attempts at coalition-building.

To pose alternatives to the transnationals, coalitions of labour and other social movements would have to be powerful and would have to occur in many countries. I am not optimistic that it is possible to build an effective, democratic internationalism from below to counter globalization from above, but it is worth trying. If popular democratic control is to be enhanced, there remains a major role for democratic states with sufficient sovereignty to represent immobile labour and territorially based communities.

CONCLUSION

One element of relative continuity is that the values and aspirations of democratic-egalitarian social movements have remained similar. People want a sense of belonging, security, equality, respect, personal development, and freedom. These can best be fulfilled in socially supportive, democratic, and egalitarian communities. Globalization by the transnationals is not indifferent to these needs and aspirations; it is hostile to them.

NOTES

1. See Krahn and Lowe (1993:247).
2. Of the twelve countries in the European Union in September 1994, only Ireland and

Luxembourg had debt ratios of less than 60% of GDP and current deficits of 3% or less. Those were the convergence criteria for joining the European Monetary Union (*The European*, September 23–29, 1994:1).

REFERENCES

Crozier, M., S.P. Huntington, and J. Watanuki 1975. *The Crisis of Democracy: Report on the Governability of Democracies to the Trilateral Commission.* New York: New York University Press.

Dunning, J.H. 1988. *Explaining International Production.* London: Unwin and Hyman.

Dunning, J.H. 1993. *Multinational Enterprises and the Global Economy.* Wokingham, England: Addison-Wesley.

Eisenstein, Z. 1982. "The sexual politics of the new right: understanding the 'crisis of liberalism' for the 1980s." *Signs*, Vol. 7, No. 3 (Spring):567–588.

Esping-Andersen, G. 1985. *Politics against Markets: The Social Democratic Road to Power.* Princeton: Princeton University Press.

Esping-Anderson, G. 1990. *The Three Worlds of Welfare Capitalism.* Princeton: Princeton University Press.

Fukuyama, F. 1992. *The End of History and the Last Man.* Toronto: Maxwell Macmillan Canada.

Gilder, G. 1989. *Men and Marriage.* Gretna: Pelican.

Goldstein, K. and M. Weiss 1991. "The Top 100." *Across the Board:*16–19.

Gonick, C. and J. Silver 1989. "Fighting free trade." *Canadian Dimension*, Vol. 23, No. 3 (April):6–14.

Hobsbawm, E. 1990. *Nations and Nationalism since 1780: Programme, Myth, Reality.* Cambridge: Cambridge University Press.

Hobsbawm, E. 1994. *Age of Extremes: The Short Twentieth Century 1914–1991.* London: Michael Joseph.

Krahn, H. and G. Lowe 1993. *Work, Industry and Canadian Society* (2nd ed.). Scarborough, Ontario: Nelson Canada.

Laxer, G. 1995. "Opposition to continental integration: Sweden and Canada." *Review of Constitutional Studies,* Vol. 2, No. 2:342–395.

Lipietz, A. 1992. *Towards a New Economic Order: Postfordism, Ecology and Democracy.* New York: Oxford University Press.

Lipset, S.M. 1988. "Neoconservatism: Myth and reality." *Society*, Vol. 25, No. 5:30–37.

Marchak, P. 1991. *The Integrated Circus: The New Right and the Restructuring of Global Markets.* Montréal and Kingston: McGill-Queen's University Press.

Nisbet, R. 1986. *Conservatism: Dream and Reality.* Minneapolis: University of Minnesota Press.

Osborne, D. and T. Gaebler 1992. *Reinventing Government: How the Entrepreneurial Spirit Is Transforming the Public Sector.* New York: Plume.

Reich, R. 1991. *The Work of Nations: Preparing Ourselves for Twenty-First Century Capitalism.* New York: Alfred A. Knopf.

Stopford, J.M., S. Strange, and J.S. Henley 1991. *Rival States, Rival Firms: Competition for World Market Shares.* Cambridge: Cambridge University Press.

Wilkins, M. 1974. "Multinational enterprises." In *The Rise of Managerial Capitalism*, H. Daems and H. van der Wee (eds.), pp. 213–235. The Hague: Martinus Nijhoff.

3

WORKING-CLASS FORMATION IN CANADA

James Conley

(Revised from the previous edition of this volume.)

INTRODUCTION

In the first six months of 2002, teachers, health care workers, social workers, and other members of public-sector unions in British Columbia protested against large-scale cutbacks to government services and jobs by the Liberal government that was elected in the previous year. They engaged in illegal strikes and, along with thousands of other people (including students, seniors, and community activists), took part in protest rallies and demonstrations in various locations across the province. Meanwhile, as leaders of the G8 group of advanced industrial nations prepared for a summit in Kananaskis, Alberta, a variety of anti-globalization activist organizations, including a number of both private-sector and public-sector unions, made their own preparations for protests against what they argue is a corporate agenda

being promoted by this and other recent summits, including the summit in Québec City a year earlier.

What is the relationship between a series of protests by unionized workers and others, and the sociological study of social inequality? Social conflicts such as these, and the social changes that sometimes result from them, are related to inequalities of power. Inequalities of power have always been central components of sociological inquiry into social inequality. "Who has power?" "What are the institutional bases of power?" "How is power used?" These are among the many questions that are asked by sociologists, and that are addressed in other chapters of this volume. The classical theories of class, which still define most theoretical debates and empirical research in this area, concentrate on identifying sources of power and conflicts of interest in the ownership of productive property (Marx) or in positions in markets and organizations (Weber).

The identification of inequalities of power and antagonistic interests in structured social relationships is only the first step to understanding social conflicts and social change, however. Intervening between structural inequalities of class power and class conflict are processes of class formation and mobilization. These processes involve consideration of the sources of conflict and the resources available to classes; the existence of solidarity within classes; the awareness of class interests and dispositions to act on them by class members; the mobilization of classes by organizations; and the forms of collective action that class members undertake.

The resources, social organization, dispositions, and mobilization of dominant classes are often taken for granted, for their power is firmly institutionalized. Attention here will focus on the working class. Like most studies of working-class formation and collective action, this chapter starts from the ideas of Marx and Weber before turning to the dynamics of working-class formation in Canada.

CLASS FORMATION AND CLASS CONFLICT IN THEORY

The power of the capitalist class rests on its control over society's productive resources. Ownership of property gives businesses the right to exclude others from the use of those resources, to allocate them to different uses, to move them, to choose production technologies, and so on. These powers also give the capitalist class leverage on the state. But what are the bases for opposition to capitalist class power?

Marx

For Marx, the reasons for working-class opposition to the power of the capitalist class lie in workers' experiences of exploitative and alienating work, and in the consequences of capitalist profit-making strategies for working-class standards of life. The "general law of capitalist accumulation," Marx argues, is "that in proportion as capital accumulates, the lot of the labourer, be his pay high or low, must grow worse... accumulation of wealth at one pole is, therefore, at the same time accumulation of misery, agony of toil, slavery, ignorance, brutality, mental degradation, at the opposite pole" (Marx 1887:604). Either in absolute terms, or relative to that of the capitalist class, the standard of living of workers falls as capitalism develops, and the conditions of work become more toilsome (Grabb 2002; Braverman 1974).

For Marx, capitalism created not only grievances among workers, but also the conditions of class formation and class power for workers to act to eliminate the sources of their distress. Specifically, Marx expected capitalism to create three conditions giving workers the organization and resources to resist capitalist power. First, changes in the production process would bring workers together in larger workplaces, and a more cooperative production process would lead to solidarity between workers. Unlike Durkheim (1893), who expected the increasing division of labour to lead, at least under certain circumstances, to organic solidarity between classes in modern societies, Marx expected that changes in production would obliterate skill differences, levelling workers to what are today called semi-skilled workers. Mechanized production would also reduce the importance of physical strength, and gender differences between workers would cease to be significant. This process of homogenization would create mechanical solidarity within the working class (Sørensen 1994) and increase the possibility of and necessity for workers to organize on a broad, inclusive basis. The changing character of production also gave workers power: Even as the demise of craft production and the introduction of machine pacing deprived workers of control over the process of production as individuals, they gained power as a collectivity.

Second, Marx emphasized the power that derives from class size. The class structure in capitalism would polarize as the petty bourgeoisie of small proprietors disappeared, and the capitalist class would grow smaller and more concentrated as large capitalists swallowed up smaller capitalists. As a consequence, the working class would become the largest class in capitalist societies, confronting a small capitalist class in a conflict without any intermediaries.

However, structural tendencies in capitalism toward homogenization of the working class and polarization of the class structure only furnish preconditions for working-class power. The problem of collective action remains: Individual workers do not have the resources to counter the power of capitalists,[1] and size is not enough for power unless it is organized. Therefore, as a third condition, Marx expected that, in the course of conflict with capitalists, workers would develop increasingly broad levels of organization: Unions would form on local, then on industrial, and finally on national levels, at the same time as political parties advancing the interests of workers would grow (Marx and Engels 1848). In other words, out of the experience of conflict, increasingly inclusive and politicized forms of organization of workers would result, and increasingly broad struggles would follow between workers, on the one hand, and capitalists and the state, on the other hand.

Weber

Weber is often described as involved in a debate with Marx's ghost. This certainly applies to Weber's thoughts on social inequality, which assume much of what Marx had to say, but go on to add to and amend Marx's views (see Grabb 2002). Unlike Marx, who almost exclusively emphasized class, Weber considered classes, status groups, and parties as "phenomena of the distribution of power" within societies (Weber 1922:927). Weber expected that, in addition to or instead of conflict occurring on class lines, there would be organized conflict based on status groups and factions competing for power in organizations, especially the state.

Like Marx, Weber thought that property was central to the concept of class. However, unlike Marx, Weber conceived of classes as based on positions in markets, not in production. From this perspective, classes are distinguished by differences in the possession of marketable, income-producing goods and services. Thus, Weber's analysis points to possible lines of differentiation among workers based on possession of skills and other advantages in labour markets. Such differentiation in labour markets need not promote the general impoverishment of the working class that Marxian theory seems to suggest, because there would be distinct segments or strata within the working class, with different experiences, different interests, and different capacities for organization and collective action.

Weber's concept of *social classes*, "within which individual and generational mobility is easy and typical" (Weber

1922:302), adds another layer of complexity to working-class formation. Weber believed that the development of a new middle class of white-collar employees, technical specialists, and professionals, due to the expansion of bureaucratic forms of administration in modern times, provides an avenue for mobility out of the working class (Weber 1922:304). Because stability in class membership, both within and between generations, is positively associated with class formation, a high degree of mobility or fluidity between classes tends to hinder the formation of networks of solidarity or a strong sense of class identification. In addition, the existence of a middle class between the working class and the capitalist class works against the Marxian expectation that the capitalist class structure would become polarized over time.

Weber's concept of status is the second aspect of power that affects class formation. The existence of status groups that cut across different classes may also complicate or retard the increasing homogeneity of the working class that Marx envisioned. Moreover, rather than groups forming purely on the basis of class location, groups may form around status-related issues, including shared consumption patterns and styles of life. Thus, status groups based on gender, ethnicity, region, or education can divide members of one class and create solidarity between members of different classes. Finally, relations of domination between such status groups may be more "transparent" than class relations, and therefore may be a more readily available source of group identity than class.

Party is the third key aspect of power that Weber distinguishes. With respect to problems of class formation, Weber's insight here is that when groups organize to pursue power and its rewards in organi-zations, and above all in states, they may do so on bases other than class or status. The best example may be forms of political party organization. The history of party systems and of political cleavages in societies can thus be expected to have effects on working-class formation and the organization of class conflict.

Even today, the ideas of Marx and Weber continue to provide a basis for the way sociologists think about class formation and class conflict. Marx tended to see working-class formation and collective action as a series of steps toward an endpoint, a terminus on the road to a revolution that would overthrow capitalism. Weber, in contrast, presents a more complex and contingent view of class formation, as one of several possible lines along which groups in conflict might form.

CLASS FORMATION AND CLASS CONFLICT IN CANADA

What do we know about class formation and class conflict in Canada at the beginning of the twenty-first century? Evidence on working-class formation and conflict will be presented with respect to the following issues: (1) the structural tendencies of class formation, with particular attention to the process of polarization expected by Marx; (2) the changes in social organization in workplaces and labour markets that have affected working-class solidarity; (3) the dispositions of members of different classes; and (4) levels of mobilization in unions and political parties, along with conflict in social movements and strikes.

Class Structure: Polarization?

As we have seen, Marxists have expected that working-class formation would be facilitated by a polarization of the class structure. This polarization has three aspects: decline of the petty bourgeoisie, polarization of incomes, and polarization of skills. While generally agreeing on the demise of the petty bourgeoisie, Weber and his followers are less sure about the other two predictions. What does the Canadian evidence show?

Marx expected that the petty bourgeoisie, comprising self-employed artisans, farmers, shopkeepers, and the like, would disappear under the pressure of competition from larger, more efficient capitalist enterprises. The result would be a class structure polarized between workers on the one hand and capitalists on the other hand. Weber, in contrast, did not expect a polarization, because a new middle class of salaried employees with educational credentials would develop in tandem with bureaucratic organizations and interpose itself between the capitalists and the workers.

In Canada, evidence on levels of self-employment over the course of the twentieth century largely bears out Marxist expectations about the decline of the petty bourgeoisie.[2] The self-employed did decline from about 25% of the total labour force in 1931 to about 10% or 12% of all workers in the 1970s. Since then, however, the trend has reversed, both in Canada and in other countries. By the end of the twentieth century, more than 15% of Canada's work force was in the self-employed category.

Most of the historical decline of the petty bourgeoisie in Canada was due to falling employment in the agricultural sector, where levels of self-employment have always been, and continue to be, very high.[3] Recent increases have occurred across all industries. In addition to farming, levels of self-employment have remained higher than average in the construction, business-services and amusement, and personal and household-services industries. As Marx would have expected, the lowest level of self-employment is in manufacturing (Gardner 1995; Crompton 1993; Statistics Canada 1997a; Arai 1997).

Despite its recent growth, the petty bourgeoisie has nonetheless declined in prominence over the longer term, much as Marx expected. Has this polarized the class structure, making class conflict and working-class formation more likely? As noted earlier, Weberian understandings of the class structure point to the growth of a new middle class of employees characterized by authority within bureaucratic organizations and by the possession of educational credentials. Although the causes, characteristics, conceptualization, and future prospects of the new middle class have been the subject of considerable theoretical debate by neo-Marxist and neo-Weberian theorists (see Grabb 2002), there is agreement that the numbers of middle-level administrators and managers, professionals, and skilled technical employees constitute a significant and generally growing part of the post-industrial class structure, one which is relatively distinct from the bourgeoisie, the petty bourgeoisie, and the working class (Myles and Turegin 1994). In the only large-scale Canadian study to use neo-Marxist class categories, the new middle class, defined as lower-level managers and supervisors with authority to impose sanctions on other employees, was found to represent about 25% of the labour force in the early 1980s, compared with nearly 60% for the working class, over 10% for the petty bourgeoisie, and 6% for employers (Clement and Myles 1994). Since the early 1980s, however, it has been suggested that the middle class has been in decline. This position was given credibility by the wave of "downsizing" that began in the 1980s, involving well-publicized layoffs of middle managers in large corporations, and reductions in employment in the public sector.

Nevertheless, based on census data on occupations, those occupations that have the closest fit to what Marxists and Weberians consider the new middle class composed slightly over a quarter of the labour force in both 1986 and 1991 (Table 3-1). This proportion, moreover, has changed little from the 1971 and 1981 censuses (Pineo 1985). Unfortunately, changes in the occupational categories used in the 1996 census make it impossible to generate comparable data after 1991. However, if we use the category of "upper-tier" service jobs as a rough indicator of membership in the new middle class, then the findings reported by Graham Lowe in Chapter 11 of this volume suggest that growth in these jobs during the period from 1990 to 2000 has generally been greater than the average for all jobs. This is especially true of "professional, scientific, and technical services" occupations and of "managerial, adminis-trative, and other support services" positions. Although the evidence cannot be considered definitive because of the classification used, it provides no support for the proposition that the new middle class has been in decline. On the contrary, this class has been growing faster than the labour force as a whole, with the only declining category being lower-level blue-collar supervisors (forewomen and foremen). In addition, generally rising levels of post-secondary education point to growth in the new middle class, despite the existence of a gap between the employees' educational credentials and the tasks they actually perform on the job (Guppy and Davies 1998; Livingstone 1999).

The economic restructuring that has occurred in both Canada and other advanced capitalist societies since the 1970s has spawned another debate about the new middle class. This debate concerns whether this class has declined, not in numbers, but in income and quality of working conditions. First of all, some writers suggest that the long-term processes of routinization, de-skilling, and loss of autonomy that occurred with manual and

TABLE 3-1	Occupational Change 1986–1991		
Occupational Group	**1986**	**1991**	**% Change**
Middle Management	803 935	1 095 170	36.2
Employed Professionals	922 606	1 074 025	16.4
Semi-Professionals	819 170	1 008 825	23.2
Technicians	225 225	273 580	21.5
Supervisors	354 110	375 460	6.0
Foremen and Forewomen	325 235	289 545	−11.0
"New Middle Class"	3 450 281	4 116 605	19.3
Percentage	27.1	28.9	
All Occupations	12 740 225	14 220 230	11.6

Source: Statistics Canada 1993, Table 1. Occupational Classification: Revised Pineo-Porter-McRoberts Socioeconomic Classification of Occupations (Pineo 1985).

clerical workers in previous stages of industrialization are now extending to professional employees and middle-level administrators in the post-industrial period. However, evidence from the early 1980s has not shown any decline in skill requirements in new-middle-class occupations; instead, the shift to a post-industrial service economy has created both skilled and unskilled jobs, but on balance the former have grown more than the latter (Clement and Myles 1994).

The possible effects of further changes since the 1980s have yet to be determined. It may be that at least part of the recent increase in self-employment stems from members of the new middle class going into business for themselves because of the reduced job security produced by large companies either downsizing or contracting out work. Technological changes, especially computer technologies, make such arrangements possible, and also provide opportunities for self-employment in consulting work (Arai 1997; Statistics Canada 1997b).

The third possible pattern of class polarization to receive attention in recent decades concerns the polarization of earnings. In this case, the middle class is conceptualized in a gradational, distributive way, and is represented by those individuals in the middle categories of the income structure. Any shrinkage among middle-income earners could have important implications for class formation, because this group would include not only many members of the new middle class, as defined in Marxist or Weberian terms, but also the more affluent part of the working class. In Canada, increases in real incomes for men, which began after World War II, actually stopped in the early 1980s, and have been largely stagnant until recently. Among women, both labour-force participation and earnings have slowly risen, with

the increasing prevalence of dual-income households helping to prevent declines in economic circumstances for many working-class families. Income polarization has occurred, but it is mainly on the basis of age and marital status, with declines in the earnings of younger workers relative to older workers, and of lone-parent families (which are primarily female-headed) relative to two-parent families (Picot and Myles 1995; Morissette 1997).

What, then, can we conclude from the evidence on polarization in the class structure? First, Marx and Weber were broadly correct about the decline of the petty bourgeoisie, but its decline has not been uniform across all sectors of the economy, and the long-term trend has been reversed somewhat in the last two decades. Second, there has been growth in new-middle-class positions in the class structure, as Weber expected, and they have not been subject to the de-skilling expected by many neo-Marxists. Moreover, although there has been a decline in job security for some middle-class workers in both the private and the public sectors since the 1980s, neither the absolute numbers nor the proportions of such jobs have decreased. Third, polarization of earned incomes has occurred, but it has not been clearly along class lines. Instead, polarization has involved falling incomes for workers in the most vulnerable labour market positions, with others in more secure positions being somewhat better protected. The result has been a more complex class structure than classical Marxism tends to suggest.

Social Organization: Homogenization of the Working Class?

Marx expected capitalism to facilitate working-class solidarity through the concentration of workers in larger workplaces, with a more cooperative labour process and fewer skill differences between workers. He also expected the significance of gender differences within the working class to decline. What has happened in Canada?

Workplace Size

On average, workplace size grew for much of the twentieth century, especially in manufacturing, but in the last twenty-five years this trend has reversed. Table 3-2 shows that between 1925 and 1970 the proportion of manufacturing employees working in establishments with fewer than 100 workers dropped from 40% to 30%. At the same time, the proportion of employees in large establishments (500 and over) rose from less than 24% to more than 32%. From 1975 to 1995, however, the share of employment in small plants rose, while employment in large plants fell back to less than 25% of manufacturing employment. Not all of this shifting has involved blue-collar production workers. Consistent with Weber's expectations, evidence from the 1986 Labour Market Activity Survey suggests that the proportion of professional and managerial employees has generally risen with increases in workplace size (Morissette 1991:37).

Outside of manufacturing, average workplace size in the private sector of the economy tends to be smaller. Between 1978 and 1988, in the Canadian commercial economy (excluding the agriculture,

TABLE 3-2	A. Employees by Size of Establishment (Manufacturing) 1925–1970		
Year	**Employees (%)**		
	<100	**100–499**	**500+**
1925	40.8	35.4	23.8
1930	39.3	35.0	25.7
1940	35.3	34.5	30.2
1950	34.5	31.8	33.7
1960	35.7	32.4	31.9
1970	30.5	37.1	32.5

B. Manufacturing Employment by Plant Size, 1975–1995			
Year	**Employees (%)**		
	0–100	**101–500**	**500+**
1975	30.7	38.6	30.7
1980	32.0	37.8	30.2
1985	34.9	37.9	27.2
1990	39.4	36.2	24.4
1995	36.8	39.5	23.7

Sources:
(A) Adapted from the Statistics Canada publication *Historical Statistics of Canada*, Catalogue 11-516, 1983, Series R795-811, 812-825.
(B) Adapted from the Statistics Canada publication *The Trend to Smaller Producers in Manufacturing: A Canada/U.S. Comparison*, Catalogue 11F0027, No. 003, May 2002.

health, education, and government sectors), about 35% of employees worked for *companies* (not workplaces) with fewer than fifty employees, while 40% worked for companies with 500 or more employees. However, since large companies in particular may have more than one establishment or workplace, these figures overestimate the size of workplaces in Canada (Picot and Dupuy 1996).

As noted earlier, since the 1980s, the share of private-sector employment accounted for by small companies and small establishments has risen. This increase has potentially significant implications for working-class formation, since workers in small firms receive less pay and fewer benefits than workers in larger firms, and are more likely to be laid off (Clement and Myles 1994:57–59). Given these considerations, we might expect workers to be more class-conscious in small firms. However, as Stinchcombe (1990) points out, the social relations and employment relationship in small firms tend to reduce class solidarities. This is partly because the social distance between employer and employee is likely to be smaller than in larger firms, the employer is more likely to work alongside the employee, and employees can perceive opportunities for themselves to move up into the role of small employer. In smaller firms, there are also likely to be more individualized labour contracts and less routinized production. By comparison, larger companies tend to have more bureaucratized labour relations, with internal labour markets, standardized employment conditions, and extensive quasi-judicial procedures for grievances. In recent years, some large employers have adopted new forms of workplace organization such as Japanese-style approaches to production management and flexible specialization. These forms of organization recreate, to some extent, the social relations of small firms, and are also supposed to empower workers through multi-tasking, job rotation, and reduction in status distinctions between workers and management. According to some analyses, however, these new forms of control are simply "old wine in new bottles," and have not reduced either workplace conflict or worker solidarity (Rinehart et al. 1997).

Class and Social Mobility

Social mobility refers to the movement of people into or out of different social groupings, including classes. The lower the amount of mobility between classes, the more stable will be the composition of any one class over time. In turn, the more stable the composition of a class, the more likely it is that its members will develop a sense of class solidarity and identity. Table 3-3 provides evidence on patterns of class mobility or stability among Canadian males from the early 1980s, by comparing the class position of fathers with the class position of their adult sons. The data show that the employer, petty bourgeois, and working classes were the most stable, with 38.1%, 47.4%, and 39.7% of respondents in these three classes having fathers with the same class locations. Class stability is particularly evident among the propertied classes, with nearly three-quarters of employers and petty-bourgeois respondents coming from either employer or petty-bourgeois backgrounds. As might be expected, the growing new-middle-class positions are much less stable than the propertied or working classes, as a third or more of expert managers, managers, and semi-professionals have worker backgrounds. In addition, a third of professionals have employer backgrounds. For males, at least, the tendency toward stability in the formation of social classes,

TABLE 3-3	Intergenerational Class Mobility of Canadian Males, 1982 (Inflow Percentages)							

Class of Origin

Class of Destination	Employer	Petty-Bourg.	Expert Mgr.	Manager	Prof.	Semi-Prof.	Worker	N
Employer	38.1	34.4	6.0	3.1	0.0	3.0	15.2	860
Petty-Bourgeoisie	24.5	47.4	8.7	3.5	0.6	1.3	14.0	1354
Expert Manager	17.6	11.5	12.2	13.6	2.3	9.6	33.3	1401
Manager	14.8	15.6	8.3	20.8	0.5	2.6	37.5	1246
Professional	34.3	14.2	11.6	2.3	9.3	8.5	19.8	353
Semi-Professional	11.2	13.1	21.1	19.4	2.4	0.4	32.4	892
Worker	13.8	22.5	7.7	13.8	1.1	1.3	39.7	4204
All	18.4	23.3	9.7	12.5	1.4	2.9	31.8	
N	1892	2405	996	1287	148	300	3282	10 310

Source: Western and Wright, 1994:627, using data from the comparative class structure project (see Clement and Myles 1994).

therefore, appears to be strongest in the three "oldest" classes: employers, the petty bourgeoisie, and workers. Data from the mid-1980s using a different classification show that levels of class stability are not markedly different for males and females (calculated from Nakhaie 1996).

Gender and Ethnicity

Two of the most important changes in the Canadian labour force in the last fifty years have been the increased participation of women in paid work, and the rise in immigration from non-European nations. Both of these processes are well documented in other chapters in this volume. Here, our main concern is to consider their implications for working-class formation.

Although the importance of physical strength has declined in modern production, as Marx expected, the social significance of gender has not disappeared. Women are more likely than men to occupy working-class positions in the paid

labour force, and they are more likely to be employed in the service sector of the economy than in the goods-producing sector (Clement and Myles 1994:35). Not only is there gender segregation by industry, there is also segregation between women and men in occupations, so that women and men tend not to work in the same workplaces at the same jobs. Women's experiences at work are consequently different from men's. In addition, the continuing greater responsibility of women for household labour and child care further distinguishes their experience of the labour market and paid work from that of men. Women's average earnings are also less than those of men. Consequently, despite the shared interests that men and women may have as employees, women's interests may diverge from those of their male coworkers over issues such as maternity leaves, child care, pay equity, employment equity, and sexual harassment.

The changing gender composition of the Canadian working class has been accompanied by changes in its ethnic and racial composition, as immigration levels have increased from outside the traditional European sources. In the past, ethnic affiliations rooted in segregated residential communities and their institutions, and in exclusion from and competition for jobs, may have been a source of both ethnic and class solidarity (see, for example, Frager 1992). The assimilation of previous generations of European immigrants and their children has reduced the salience of ethnic differences within the working class, but the linguistic-regional differences between anglophone and francophone workers have a long history in Canadian society. As well, differences in occupation and income between those of European ethnic origin, on the one hand, and visible minority immigrants and Aboriginals, on the other hand, have continued to be significant.

As Weber long ago suggested, status differences involving gender, race, ethnicity, language, and region have often been features of working-class social organization, and have not disappeared with capitalist development. All of these differences tend to cut across class allegiances, reducing the sense of shared or common experience, especially among the working class. Located within different relations of power, status differences can be double-edged swords, contributing to working-class solidarities when class and status interests are congruent, but acting as sources of division at other times, as when males and females or blacks and whites must compete with each other for the same scarce employment opportunities.

Class Consciousness

Both class polarization and the changing social organization of workplaces and labour markets entail structural conditions

that affect the broad patterns of social cleavage in capitalist societies, as well as the solidarities of workers within them. The third feature of class formation to consider is people's interpretations of these structural conditions, and the class-based outlooks that follow from them. Despite some acknowledged methodological limitations, sample surveys of attitudes have provided a good deal of the evidence for assessing and measuring class consciousness in previous sociological research. These survey measures range from people's estimates of their own class locations, to their attitudes toward the role of corporations in the economy, to their feelings about unions and strikes, and so on. With this wide variety of attitude items, investigators seek to understand and to study different dimensions of the class consciousness of members of the various classes. Conceptually, researchers influenced by Marx have generally used a typology involving three types or degrees of class consciousness: class awareness or identity, oppositional class consciousness, and revolutionary or counter-hegemonic class consciousness (Giddens 1973; Livingstone and Mangan 1996). Class identity has been defined as awareness of membership in a distinct class, class opposition as the belief that the interests of the workers and capitalists are opposed, and counter-hegemonic consciousness as a belief in the possibility and desirability of a society organized along non-capitalist lines.

Although assessment of the results of attitude surveys is complicated by the variety of measures that have been used for both class position and class consciousness, most studies suggest that the class identity adopted by the majority of respondents in all classes is "middle class." However, members of the working class and petty bourgeoisie are more likely than members of other classes to choose a working-class identity (Livingstone and Mangan 1996; Johnston and Baer 1993). The effects of the complex position of women in labour markets and households is shown in findings that married women's class identity is affected more by their husband's class position than their own (Livingstone and Mangan 1996). This is perhaps a reflection of the persistence of the male "breadwinner" norm, and the traditional primacy accorded male jobs and male earnings in most households.

As for oppositional class consciousness, surveys have found that, on such issues as the rights of labour unions and the redistribution of income from rich to poor, the attitudes of workers and capitalists are indeed opposed: Members of the capitalist class and the petty bourgeoisie express more pro-business and less pro-labour attitudes than do industrial and service workers. The findings for the new middle class are inconsistent, with some studies showing them to be little different from workers, and other studies showing them to have more pro-business attitudes. Gender further complicates this picture, for studies also show that women are less likely than men to have attitudes that are supportive of labour. The organization of workers also has an effect on oppositional consciousness: Most studies find that membership in a union is positively associated with pro-labour attitudes (Clement and Myles 1994; Livingstone and Mangan 1996).

Finally, little research has been conducted on hegemonic class consciousness, and what research there is shows that most people in all class positions rarely see an alternative to a capitalistic economy. Members of the working class are somewhat more likely to do so, but even in this class the proportion represents a tiny minority (Livingstone and Mangan 1996; Johnston and Baer 1993).[4]

Some ethnographic studies furnish additional insights into working-class consciousness. For example, a study of young white working-class men in Thunder Bay illustrates how people's consciousness or perceptions regarding class, gender, regional, and racial identities can be intertwined in complex and often inconsistent ways (Dunk 1991). The working-class "boys" in this study expressed disdain for university-educated experts. They also promoted a cult of masculinity from which women were excluded, both at work and in leisure. Many were hostile toward and asserted moral superiority over Aboriginals, but also resented the dominant influence of corporations, governments, and outside experts in their region. Such attitudes suggest a mix of opposition to the interests of both the powerful and the powerless in Canadian society. These views may indicate a form of populist political culture, with possible roots in the traditional agrarian petty-bourgeois opposition to regional and capitalist dominance. Such cross-cutting outlooks also underscore the historical weakness of working-class mobilization and collective action in Canada, at least compared with Scandinavia and other places where class dispositions are stronger (Clement and Myles 1994; Johnston and Baer 1993).

Mobilization and Collective Action

For Marx and subsequent Marxists, class polarization, growing working-class solidarity based on changing workplaces, and oppositional and counter-hegemonic consciousness should all go hand in hand with increasing levels of working-class organization and, ultimately, power. In Canada, workers have become more organized, but power has not necessarily followed. This has had long-term effects on the other components of class formation.

Labour unions exist, partly, to defend the economic interests of their members. These interests include wages and benefits, working conditions, decent treatment by employers, and job security. Unions have largely succeeded in protecting these interests, for union jobs typically have higher wages and better benefits than do non-union jobs. This is not all that unions do, however. Many unions are also involved in movements and campaigns for broader objectives affecting working people more generally. Examples include support for social programs of the welfare state, the organization of non-unionized workers, and support for social-democratic political parties, such as the New Democratic Party.

As Marx expected, unions have grown from small local organizations, based mainly on skilled craft workers, to large national and international bodies, often encompassing workers from a wide variety of different occupations. These include many members of the new middle class, such as some of the more than one-in-five union members who have a university degree. The growth of unions in Canada occurred in three major waves: the organization of craft unions in the late nineteenth and early twentieth centuries, the spread of industrial unions in manufacturing in the 1940s, and the rapid growth of public-sector unionism in the 1960s. Union membership has expanded from 133 000 in 1911 to over 3.8 million in 2001. In Canada, union density, or the percentage of paid workers who belong to unions, has ranged from 30% to 33% since the late 1960s. In the majority of other advanced capitalist societies, however, union density has fallen, sometimes to very low levels. In the United States, for example, union density has declined from 23% to 16% in recent

years (Galarneau 1996; Akyeampong 2001a; Western 1995).

Canadian unionization rates have not suffered such declines, largely because of the strength of unionism in the public sector. The union density in the public sector is about 70%, compared with only 18% in the private sector, with members of the public sector making up more than half of all union members in Canada. However, even in Canada, union growth has not kept up with the general growth in employment in recent years, for several reasons. First, there is the shift of private-sector employment from goods-producing industries, in which union density is higher (but declining), to service industries, in which union density is lower. Second, there is the trend toward decreases in firm size, and unionization rates are generally lower in small firms. Third, there is the growth in part-time and temporary jobs, which are much less likely to be unionized (Galarneau 1995; Akyeampong 2001a). Partly as a consequence of declining levels of unionization in goods-producing industries, union density has fallen among men in particular. Among women, despite the slowness of unions to take up women's concerns in the past, unionization has risen to nearly the same level as that for men. By 2000, women made up 47% of union members, up from approximately 33% in 1982 and only 16% in 1962 (Akyeampong 2001a; White 1993).

Unions in Canada have often supported left-leaning political parties, in particular the New Democratic Party. Even so, such parties have never achieved more than third-party status in national politics, although they have formed several provincial governments. Also, the fortunes of the NDP have declined in the past decade. This has meant a relative lack of formal political power for workers, making class a less important element in political discourse than might otherwise be the case. Instead, workers have been politically mobilized according to a variety of other issues or identities. Most of the opposition of workers to the power of capitalism or big business has been manifested in strike activity and political protest campaigns.

Surges of union organization have corresponded historically with periods of heightened industrial conflict, with the two feeding off each other. The expansion of industrial unions in the 1940s and the rise of public-sector unionism in the 1960s both occurred amid waves of strikes that, at times, gave Canada among the highest rates of industrial conflict in the world (Cruikshank and Kealey 1987). In recent times, the number of strikes and the time lost to strikes have fallen to historically low levels, although the number of workers involved has remained high (Akyeampong 2001b).

In addition to their role in collective bargaining, unions have also played prominent roles in protest campaigns against government cutbacks and attempts to restrict union power. Some examples are the opposition to the federal government's imposition of wage controls in the 1970s, the Solidarity movement in British Columbia in the 1980s, opposition to the Harris government's "Common Sense Revolution" in Ontario in the 1990s, and conflict with the new Campbell government in British Columbia since 2001. At present, an important concern for unions, and working-class organizations more generally, is the threat of increasing capital mobility in today's global economy. An example of this threat is the movement of companies and investment out of one nation or region and into another nation or region that is more friendly to big-business interests. Such possibilities have meant that unions, often in alliance with other groups, have fought against free trade agreements and international institutions promoting corporate globalization. Labour strife and protests are likely to continue in the future.

CONCLUSION

In this review, we have found that, although Marxist theory furnishes many of the key ideas for an understanding of class formation and class conflict, the history of these two processes, both in Canada and in many other countries, is more variable, contingent, and dependent on other issues than Marx may have fully anticipated (see Tilly 1992; Katznelson 1986). Certain modifications of the Marxian view, including some of those provided by Weber, are also required. These include the recognition that there is no inevitable progression toward class polarization, labour homogenization, working-class consciousness and organization, and proletarian revolution. Instead, the processes of class formation and class conflict appear to involve a complex pattern of rises and declines, with varying rates of class mobility, interactions between class and status-group identities and networks, and the persistent role of unions and other traditional organizational forms in the process of mobilization.

NOTES

1. The power of individual and small-group "resistance," such as restriction of output, should not be ignored. This resistance has sometimes led to changing managerial strategies to deal with problems such as high rates of turnover.

2. The concept of self-employment does not correspond strictly to Marx's concept of petty bourgeoisie, as it includes both self-employed who do not employ paid help, and those who do, i.e., employers or capitalists. There is some debate in the

literature about how many paid employees are required before a self-employed person becomes a member of the capitalist class (e.g., Clement and Myles 1994 use three as a threshold). Over 60% of the self-employed in Canada in 1996 did not have any paid employees. Of those who were employers, more than a quarter had only one employee, and about two-thirds had fewer than five employees (Statistics Canada 1997b:39).

3. This pattern may be due less to capitalist competition than to technological changes, which have made possible larger scales of production, even for family farms. However, large-scale corporate farming has not been a major factor in Canadian agriculture. In fact, the rate of self-employment in agriculture has declined only marginally since 1931 (Gardner 1995). However, the forces that Marx expected to lead to the demise of the petty bourgeoisie have been at work: declining numbers of small producers; narrow margins between expenses and revenues, which require many farm households to combine farm and off-farm employment; increased average farm size; and larger capital investments in farm machinery and equipment (Bowlby 2002).

4. This pattern might be expected to vary according to the level of class conflict, but even in an industrial city such as Hamilton, in a period of high strike activity, Livingstone and Mangan (1996) found that there was not much spontaneous recognition of class conflict. In his study of a postal workers' strike in the same city in the same time period, Langford (1994) found little enduring change in class consciousness as a result of participation in the strike.

REFERENCES

Akyeampong, Ernest B. 1997. "A statistical portrait of the trade union movement." *Perspectives on Labour and Income* (Winter):45–54.

Akyeampong, Ernest B. 2001a. "Fact sheet on unionization." *Perspectives on Labour and Income* 13, 3:46–54.

Akyeampong, Ernest 2001b. "Time lost to industrial disputes." *Perspectives on Labour and Income* 13, 3:14–16.

Arai, Bruce 1997. "The road not taken: The transition from unemployment to self-employment in Canada." *Canadian Journal of Sociology* 22:365–382.

Baldwin, John R., Ron S. Jarmin, and Jianmin Tang 2002. "The trend to smaller producers in manufacturing: A Canada/U.S. comparison." Statistics Canada Economic Analysis Research Paper Series No. 003.

Bowlby, Geoff 2002. "Farmers leaving the field." *Perspectives on Labour and Income* 14, 1:23–28.

Braverman, Harry 1974. *Labor and Monopoly Capital.* New York: Monthly Review Press.

Clement, Wallace, and John Myles 1994. *Relations of Ruling: Class and Gender in Postindustrial Societies.* Montréal and Kingston: McGill-Queen's University Press.

Crompton, Susan 1993. "The renaissance of self-employment." *Perspectives on Labour and Income* 5, 2:22–32.

Cruikshank, Douglas, and Gregory S. Kealey 1987. "Canadian strike statistics, 1891–1950." *Labour/Le Travail* 20:85–145.

Dunk, Thomas W. 1991. *It's a Working Man's Town: Male Working-Class Culture in Northwestern Ontario.* Montréal and Kingston: McGill-Queen's University Press.

Durkheim, Emile 1893. *The Division of Labor in Society.* Translated by George Simpson. New York: The Free Press, 1933.

Frager, Ruth 1992. *Sweatshop Strife: Class, Ethnicity, and Gender in the Jewish Labour Movement of Toronto, 1900–1939.* Toronto: University of Toronto Press.

Galarneau, Diane 1995. "Unionized Workers." *Perspectives on Labour and Income* 8, 1:43–52.

Gardner, Arthur 1995. "Their own boss: The self-employed in Canada." *Canadian Social Trends* 37:26–29.

Giddens, Anthony 1973. *The Class Structure of the Advanced Societies*. London: Hutchinson.

Grabb, Edward G. 2002. *Theories of Social Inequality: Classical and Contemporary Perspectives* (4th ed.). Scarborough: Nelson Thomson.

Guppy, Neil, and Scott Davies 1998. *Education in Canada: Recent Trends and Future Challenges*. Ottawa: Statistics Canada.

Johnston, William, and Douglas Baer 1993. "Class consciousness and national contexts: Canada, Sweden and the United States in historical perspective." *Canadian Review of Sociology and Anthropology* 30, 2:271–295.

Katznelson, Ira 1986. "Working-class formation: Constructing cases and comparisons." In Ira Katznelson and Aristide Zolberg, eds. *Working-Class Formation*. Princeton: Princeton University Press.

Langford, Tom 1994. "Strikes and class consciousness." *Labour / Le Travail* 34:107–137.

Livingstone, D.W. 1999. *The Education-Jobs Gap: Underemployment or Economic Democracy*. Toronto: Garamond Press.

Livingstone, David, and J. Marshall Mangan (eds.) 1996. *Recast Dreams: Class and Gender Consciousness in Steeltown*. Toronto: Garamond.

Marx, Karl 1887. *Capital: A Critical Analysis of Capitalist Production*. Vol. 1. Moscow: Progress Publishers, 1953.

Marx, Karl, and Frederick Engels 1848. "Manifesto of the Communist Party." In Marx and Engels, *Selected Works in Three Volumes*, Vol. 1. Moscow: Progress Publishers, 1969.

Morissette, René 1991. *Canadian Jobs and Firm Size: Do Smaller Firms Pay Less?* Research Paper No. 35, Analytical Studies Branch, Statistics Canada.

Morissette, René 1997. "Declining earnings of young men." *Canadian Social Trends* 46:8–12.

Myles, John, and Adnan Turegin 1994. "Comparative studies in class structure." *Annual Review of Sociology* 20:103–124.

Nakhaie, M. Reza 1996. "The reproduction of class relations by gender in Canada." *Canadian Journal of Sociology* 21:523–558.

Picot, Garnett and Richard Dupuy 1996. *Job Creation by Company Size Class: Concentration and Persistence of Job Gains and Losses in Canadian Companies*. Research Paper No. 93, Business and Labour Market Analysis Division, Statistics Canada.

Picot, Garnett, and John Myles 1995. "Social transfers, changing family structure, and low income among children." Research Paper No. 82, Analytical Studies Branch, Statistics Canada.

Pineo, Peter C. 1985. "Revisions of the Pineo-Porter-McRoberts socioeconomic classification of occupations for the 1981 census." Research Report No. 125, Program for Quantitative Studies in Economics and Population, McMaster University.

Rinehart, James, Christopher Huxley, and David Robertson 1997. *Just Another Car Factory? Lean Production and Its Discontents*. Ithaca, NY: ILR Press.

Sørensen, Aage B. 1994. "The basic concepts of stratification research: Class, status, and power." In David B. Grusky, ed., *Social Stratification in Sociological Perspective: Class, Race and Gender*. Boulder: Westview.

Statistics Canada 1993. *Occupation: The Nation*. Ottawa: Industry, Science, and Technology.

Statistics Canada 1997a. *The Daily*. October 24.

Statistics Canada 1997b. *Labour Force Update 1, 3: The Self-Employed*. Ottawa: Minister of Industry.

Stinchcombe, Arthur L. 1990. *Information and Organizations*. Berkeley: University of California Press.

Tilly, Louise 1992. *Politics and Class in Milan, 1881–1901*. New York: Oxford University Press.

Wannell, Ted 1991. "Trends in the distribution of employment by employer size: Recent Canadian evidence." Research Paper No. 39, Analytical Studies Branch, Statistics Canada.

Weber, Max 1922. *Economy and Society*. Guenther Roth and Claus Wittich (eds.). Berkeley: University of California Press, 1978.

Western, Bruce 1995. "A comparative study of working-class disorganization: Union decline in eighteen advanced capitalist countries." *American Sociological Review* 60:179–201.

Western, Mark, and Erik Olin Wright 1994. "The permeability of class boundaries to intergenerational mobility among men in the United States, Canada, Norway, and Sweden." *American Sociological Review* 59:606–629.

White, Julie 1993. *Sisters and Solidarity: Women and Unions in Canada.* Toronto: Thompson Educational Publishing.

AFFLUENCE, POWER, AND STRIKES IN CANADA, 1973-2000

Robert J. Brym

(An original chapter written for this volume. I thank Jonah Butovsky, John Fox, Morley Gunderson, Alan Harrison, Reza Nakhaie, Gregg Olsen, and Michael Shalev for helpful comments on a draft of this chapter.)

AFFLUENCE, UNEMPLOYMENT, AND STRIKES

Common sense suggests affluence breeds contentment. On this assumption, people with secure jobs, good working conditions, and high wages are happier than people who face the prospect of unemployment, poor working conditions, and low wages. Moreover, according to the common-sense view, happier workers are less likely to strike. After all, compared with unhappy workers, their needs and demands seem closer to having been met. They appear to lack the deprivations that would motivate them to strike.

It follows from the common-sense view that there ought to be an observable association between measures of strike activity and measures of economic well-being. Figure 4-1, covering the 1973–2000 period, seems to suggest there is such an association.[1] The graph's horizontal axis shows GDP per capita (GDPpc), or the total value of goods and services produced in Canada in a year divided by the number of people living in the country at year end. GDPpc is an indicator of the economic well-being of the average Canadian. It is measured in constant (1992) dollars to eliminate the influence of inflation. In effect, this indicator of economic well-being shows the purchasing power of the average Canadian in a given year. Meanwhile, the graph's vertical axis shows weighted strike frequency, or the number of strikes that took place in Canada each year divided by the number of non-agricultural workers in the country. The curve formed by annual scores on these two variables slopes downward. This suggests that when well-being is low, propensity to strike is high; and when well-being is high, propensity to strike is low. Affluence, it seems at first glance, does breed contentment.

Case closed? Hardly. GDPpc is an average, and averages can mask more than they reveal. For instance, GDPpc could conceivably rise when the purchasing power of high-income earners (a minority of the population) rises a lot and the purchasing power of middle- and low-income earners (a majority of the population) falls a little. In that case, rising GDPpc would mask the fact that most people are worse off.

Because workers who strike are unlikely to be rich, we need a better measure of workers' well-being than GDPpc. One candidate is the *unemployment rate*. Unemployment is more likely to affect ordinary workers than the well-to-do. Doctors rarely lose their jobs, and business executives, even if they are fired, can live relatively comfortably off savings in the typically short period before they find work again. On the other hand, unemployment is likely to result in a sharp decline in living standards for ordinary workers, and sometimes the period before they find a new job is protracted.

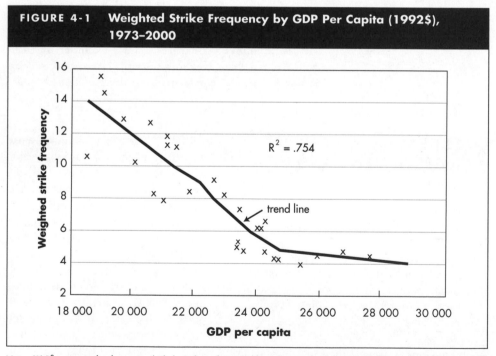

FIGURE 4-1   Weighted Strike Frequency by GDP Per Capita (1992$), 1973–2000

$R^2 = .754$

trend line

Weighted strike frequency (vertical axis)

GDP per capita (horizontal axis)

Notes: (1) R^2 measures the degree to which the independent variable is associated with (or "explains") variation in the dependent variable. If the independent variable accounts for none of the variation in the dependent variable, the value of R^2 is 0. If it accounts for all of the variation, its value is 1. The R^2 given here is adjusted for the number of cases. (2) The "trend line" is a LOWESS curve. LOWESS stands for "locally weighted scatterplot smoothing." After dividing the values of the independent variable into a number of equal parts, the LOWESS curve computes least squares regression lines for each part and then smoothes the lines. This reveals patterns in the data that may be obscured by a single linear regression line computed over all values of the independent variable.

How then does strike activity vary with the unemployment rate? Figures 4-2 and 4-3 provide the surprising answer. During the first half of the 1973–2000 period, weighted strike frequency fell when the unemployment rate rose, and rose when the unemployment rate fell (see Figure 4-2). In other words, when workers were most economically deprived, they were *least* inclined to strike, and when they were most secure in their jobs, they were *most* inclined to strike. This is just the opposite of the common-sense view outlined above. Equally unexpected are

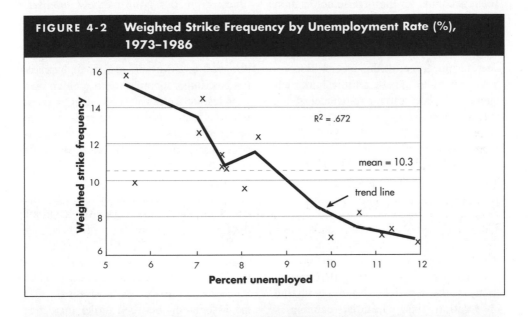

FIGURE 4-2 **Weighted Strike Frequency by Unemployment Rate (%), 1973–1986**

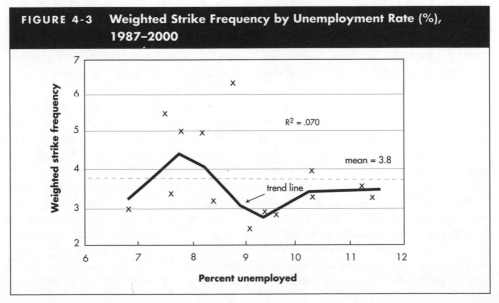

FIGURE 4-3 **Weighted Strike Frequency by Unemployment Rate (%), 1987–2000**

the results for the second half of the 1973–2000 period (see Figure 4-3). After 1986, the relationship between the unemployment rate and weighted strike frequency virtually disappeared. Thus, the trend line summarizing the association between weighted strike frequency and the unemployment rate shows little trend. What accounts for the inverse association between the unemployment rate and weighted strike frequency in the 1973–1986 period? What accounts for the near disappearance of this inverse association after 1986? These are the intriguing questions I address in the remainder of this chapter.

STRIKE RESEARCH ON THE EFFECT OF THE BUSINESS CYCLE

The existing body of strike research goes a long way toward explaining the trend for the 1973–1986 period, although not, as you will see, for the 1987–2000 period. Many strike researchers begin with the observation that capitalist economies undergo recurrent "boom and bust" cycles. During bad times, unemployment is high and business profitability low. During good times, unemployment is low and business profitability high. They then note the existence of an association between the business cycle and strike frequency (Rees 1952). They argue that, as unemployment falls, strike incidence rises. That is because workers are in a better bargaining position during good economic times. Accordingly, at the peaks of business cycles workers are more likely to enjoy higher savings and alternative job opportunities. At the same time, workers know employers are eager to settle strikes quickly since business is so profitable. Strikes are therefore relatively low-risk. In

contrast, during economic downturns, workers are less well off and have fewer job alternatives. They understand employers have little incentive to meet their demands because profitability is low and inventories high. Workers avoid strikes during troughs in the business cycle since they are riskier than in economic good times. From this point of view, workers' contentment, levels of felt deprivation, and other states of mind are unimportant as causes of strike activity. What matters is how *powerful* workers are. Their bargaining position or their ability to get their own way despite the resistance of employers is what counts. Said differently, strike research suggests we can arrive at superior explanations for variations in strike activity by thinking like sociologists, not psychologists.

The association between strike incidence and the business cycle (or its proxy, the unemployment rate) was first demonstrated empirically for the United States (Ashenfelter and Johnson 1969) and shortly thereafter for Canada (Smith 1972). Since then, researchers have shown that the association between strike incidence and the business cycle was a feature of most advanced capitalist countries in the twentieth century (Hibbs 1976). However, later research also introduced three important qualifications to the argument.

First, before World War II, the North American *system of collective bargaining* between workers and employers was not well institutionalized. In Canada, for example, the legal right to organize unions, bargain collectively, and strike with relatively little constraint dates only from 1944. Before then, strikes were often fights for union recognition. They were therefore less responsive to economic conditions (Cruikshank and Kealey 1987; Jamieson 1973 [1957]:102; Palmer 1987; Snyder 1977). As a result, in Canada and the United States, the effect of the business cycle on strike incidence is stronger for the post–World War II period than for the pre–World War II period.

The second important qualification concerns the fact that, in much of Western Europe, *the institutional environment* mitigates the effect of economic conditions on strike frequency. One important aspect of the institutional environment is the degree of centralization of bargaining units. Strikes are negotiating tools. They are therefore more frequent during periodic contract renewals than between contracts. In much of Western Europe, however, centralized, nation-wide bargaining among workers, employers, and governments means that entire sectors of the work force come up for contract renewal and negotiation at the same time. Thus, aggregate measures of strike frequency are affected not just by the phase of the business cycle but by the periodicity of contract renewal schedules. In contrast, the absence of a centralized bargaining structure in Canada and the United States makes aggregate measures of strike frequency more sensitive to the business cycle in North America (Harrison and Stewart 1994; Snyder 1977; Franzosi 1989a).

Union density, or the proportion of the non-agricultural labour force that is unionized, is another aspect of the institutional environment that influences strike activity. Unions educate workers and enable them to speak with one voice. Their organizational assets allow unions to mobilize workers. It follows that union density will influence strike action, although strike frequency is often less affected than are strike duration and the average size of strikes (Shorter and Tilly 1971).

Finally, the third condition limiting the impact of the business cycle on strike frequency is political. In many Western European countries, left-wing or social democratic parties have formed governments or at least achieved representation in cabinets. This has the effect of moving negotiations over the division of rewards in society from the labour market, where strikes are important bargaining tools, to the political sphere. Where labour is powerful enough to negotiate favourable income redistribution and welfare policies at the political level, industrial conflict tends to recede.[2] Agreeing to limit strike action has even been used as a bargaining chip in exchange for income redistribution and welfare concessions in Sweden, Germany, and other West European countries. Thus, in the 1970s and 1980s, strike frequency in Sweden, for example, was relatively insensitive to the business cycle (Franzosi 1989a; Hibbs 1978; Korpi and Shalev 1980).

In sum, a substantial body of research demonstrates an association between the business cycle and strike frequency. Moreover, it shows that the association is strongest in North America in the post–World War II era because that is the setting least influenced by mitigating institutional and political variables (Paldam and Pedersen 1982).

In the context of this research, Figure 4-2 is as ordinary as Figure 4-3 is puzzling. The strong inverse relationship between the unemployment rate and strike frequency for the 1973–1986 period is wholly in line with expectations derived from the research literature. However, contrary to what we are led to expect by the research literature, there is little discernible trend for the 1987–2000 period. The unemployment rate is very *weakly* associated with strike frequency in the latter period. Said differently, cyclicality appears to have been largely wrung out of Canada's labour relations system in the last fourteen years of the twentieth century, at least in terms of its influence on the incidence of industrial disputes. With respect to its impact on strike incidence, the business cycle was somehow repressed— and this occurred in precisely the setting (post–World War II North America) where its impact was previously the greatest.

Why? What accounts for the repression of the business cycle as a determinant of the incidence of Canadian industrial disputes? That is the question on which the remainder of this chapter turns. An intimation of my answer lies embedded in my decision to divide the recent history of Canadian industrial disputes into two 14-year periods, as in Figures 4-2 and 4-3. Inspection of scatterplots suggested that a shift in the direction of the relationship between the unemployment rate and weighted strike frequency took place after 1986. Since data were available for fourteen years following 1986, I chose to examine the relationship for a period of equal duration before 1987. That period starts in 1973.

Using 1973 as the cut-off is also justifiable on historical grounds, for 1973 was the year of the first oil shock. In that year, due to war in the Middle East, the price of oil on world markets tripled, intensifying already high inflation and galloping wage demands. As a result, a strike wave that had been growing since the mid-1950s gained force and crested in 1974–1975. In the entire history of Canadian labour, the only strike action that matched that crest was the Winnipeg General strike of 1919 and the ensuing sympathy strikes that stretched all the way from Amherst, Nova Scotia, to Victoria, British Columbia (see Figure 4.4). Understandably, therefore, the strikes of 1974–1975 caused a strong reaction among government and corporate

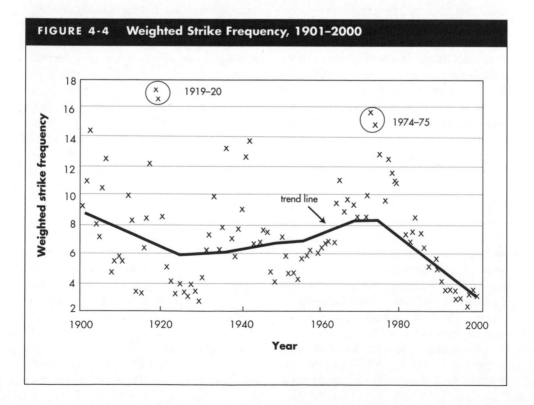

FIGURE 4-4   Weighted Strike Frequency, 1901–2000

leaders. They soon took measures to make it substantially more costly for workers to strike. Thus, 1973 marks the beginning of an historical era, one aspect of which is the substantive focus of this chapter.

In the balance of this chapter, I outline how, from the mid-1970s to the 1990s, government and corporate leaders weakened unions and made it more difficult for workers to achieve their goals. These actions had the effect of making strikes less frequent and repressing the effect of the business cycle on the propensity to strike. As you will see, they explain the near-trendless trend line in Figure 4-3.

A NEW ECONOMIC AND POLITICAL CONTEXT

Government and business leaders reacted to the 1919–1920 strike wave by sending in troops to restore order, throwing union leaders in jail, legislating strikers back to work, and changing laws to allow the deportation of British-born immigrants, who were thought to dominate the strike leadership (Bercuson 1990 [1974]). Faced with a strike wave of similar proportions in 1974–1975, government and business leaders again felt that drastic action was necessary. However, the political, institutional, and cultural environment had changed between these two extraordinary episodes of labour unrest. As a result, strategies for controlling labour were different. In 1944, Canadian workers had won the right to organize, bargain collectively, and strike with relatively little constraint. In the context of three decades of post-war prosperity, their new rights allowed them to win substantial gains in real earnings and a massive expansion of state supports and services. In the mid-1970s, business leaders and governments sympathetic to business felt they had to control labour unrest while fighting wage

gains and the growth of the welfare state. To accomplish these tasks, they organized a neo-conservative "counter-revolution" that continues to this day.

The neo-conservative counter-revolution was, however, motivated by more than just the strike wave that crested in the mid-1970s. Rising government debt and global competition also contributed to the decision to go on the political offensive (Johnston 2001).

Government borrowing rose quickly in the 1970s and 1980s. By the end of that period, interest payments were consuming a quarter of the federal government's annual budget. With indebtedness threatening to cripple government programs, the neo-conservative claim that debt reduction is sound public policy made sense to more and more people.

At the same time, global competition was becoming fiercer. By the early 1970s, Japanese and West German industry had fully recovered from the destruction of World War II. Manufacturers in these countries were exporting massive quantities of finished goods to North America and other markets. In the 1980s, South Korea, China, and other countries followed suit. With growing global competition threatening the welfare of Canadian industry, big business had to develop new strategies to survive and prosper. One such strategy involved restructuring: introducing computers and robots, eliminating middle-management positions, outsourcing parts manufacturing, and so forth. Another strategy was to increase business opportunities and to bring about job growth by creating a free trade zone encompassing Canada and the United States (MacDonald 2000).

Controlling labour while cutting debt, restructuring, and promoting free trade required deep ideological change. Business leaders therefore set about the task of redefining in the public mind the desirable features of the market, the state, and the relationship between the two. From roughly the end of World War II until the mid-1970s, labour demands focused on improving wages and state benefits. Now, an imposing ideological machine sought to convince the public that high wages and generous state benefits decrease the ability of Canadians to compete against workers in other countries. Massive job losses will result (the neo-conservative argument continued) unless wages are held in check and state benefits slashed. That was the main message of Canada's two neo-conservative, corporate-funded think tanks and pressure groups, the Fraser Institute, founded in 1974, and the Business Council on National Issues (BCNI), founded in 1976. The creation of these bodies in the mid-1970s signalled that, like its counterpart in the United States, the Canadian business elite was becoming more ideologically and politically organized and unified (Akard 1992; Langille 1987).

One important sign of neo-conservative success was the outcome of the 1988 "free trade" federal election (Richardson 1996). Just four days before the election, a Gallup poll showed the pro–free trade Progressive Conservatives with the support of only 31% of Canadians intending to vote. The anti–free trade Liberals enjoyed a commanding 43% of the popular vote while the anti–free trade New Democratic Party stood at 22%. At about the same time, an Angus Reid poll disclosed that most Canadians opposed free trade by a margin of 54% to 35%. A majority of Canadians apparently sensed that free trade might open the country to harmful competition with giant American companies, thus leading to job losses and deteriorating living standards.

Then, a mere 100 hours before the first votes were cast, a little-known organiza-

tion, the Canadian Alliance for Trade and Job Opportunities (CATJO), swung into high gear. CATJO was funded exclusively by the BCNI. With a campaign budget larger than that of the two opposition parties combined, CATJO bankrolled a media blitz promoting the PCs and their free trade policies. A barrage of brochures, newspaper ads, and radio and television commercials supported the idea that Canadian prosperity depends on the removal of all taxes and impediments to trade between Canada and the United States. CATJO argued that if goods and services could be bought and sold across the border without hindrance, and capital invested without restraint, good jobs would proliferate and Canada's economic future would be assured. The CATJO onslaught succeeded in overcoming some of the public's fears and drawing attention away from the opposition. On election day, the PCs won with 43% of the popular vote. The free trade agreement with the United States was signed just six weeks later.

The free trade agreement, later broadened to include Mexico, sharply increased competition for investment between jurisdictions, leading to a "downward harmonization" of labour policies (Gunderson 1998). Just as water seeks its lowest level, capital that is allowed to flow freely between jurisdictions will seek the jurisdiction with the lowest costs and therefore the highest profit potential, all else being the same. Increasingly, jurisdictions will compete for investment by offering outright tax concessions to investors and ensuring competitive labour costs in the form of lower state benefits, wages, and rates of labour disruption due to strikes. As Canadian workers learned, persistent demands for higher wages—indeed, failure to make wage and other concessions—increase the prospect of plant closings. Where capital mobility is unrestricted, it is only a short hop from southern Ontario to "right to work" states like Georgia or the Maquiladora free trade zone of northern Mexico. In this context, unions lose bargaining power and strikes become riskier actions with a lower probability of achieving their aims.[3]

The slew of government budget cutbacks that took place in the 1990s also had a negative influence on strike incidence. Since workers who go out on strike sometimes quit or lose their jobs, declining income-replacing state benefits make strikes riskier for them. In other words, many of the cutbacks of the 1990s increased the potential cost of job loss to workers and therefore ensured that strike incidence would drop. Restricting eligibility for employment insurance and welfare were two of the most important policy measures affecting the readiness of workers to strike.

High government debt, intense global competition, and neo-conservative publicity and lobbying continued to push the Canadian electorate to the right in the 1990s. The Reform Party became the official opposition, its popularity aided by the defection of members of the working class, most of them non-unionized, from the Liberals and the NDP (Butovsky 2001). The ruling Liberals, meanwhile, adopted much of the neo-conservative agenda. To varying degrees, all major parties supported the new industrial relations regime that had begun to crystallize in the mid-1970s.

A NEW INDUSTRIAL RELATIONS REGIME

Beginning in the mid-1970s, governments adopted a series of measures aimed at better controlling labour (Panitch and Swartz 1993 [1985]). Among them was the establishment of "wage and price controls" that, in practice, limited only wages but claimed to require equal sacrifices from labour and business. That strategy was followed by the Trudeau government in 1975 when it established the Anti-Inflation Board for a three-year period. Blessed by business and condemned by the labour movement, the anti-inflation program suspended collective bargaining for all workers in Canada. By undermining the ability of strikes to achieve wage gains, it also dampened labour militancy. A similar approach was taken in 1982, when the federal government passed the *Public Sector Compensation Restraint Act*. The Act imposed a two-year wage limit on federal employees, eliminating their right to bargain and strike. The provinces soon passed similar laws. In some cases, provincial cutbacks were even more draconian than those implemented at the federal level. Public employees in Québec, for example, took a 20% pay cut. In 1991, the federal government announced a one-year wage freeze for federal employees followed by a 3% limit on wage increases for the next two years. By 1993, even the Ontario NDP was backing wage restraint. In that year, the government of Bob Rae introduced a "Social Contract" that overruled the provisions of existing collective agreements and effectively reduced the wages of all 900 000 provincial employees for a three-year period.

A second method of labour control involved amending a variety of laws and regulations. For example, governments persistently broadened the definition of "management" and "essential service," thereby denying many public-sector workers the right to strike. Thus, in 1984 nearly 76% of public-service workers negotiating contracts were designated as providing managerial or essential services. In the preceding set of negotiations, fewer than 47% of those workers were so designated. In addition, and to varying degrees,

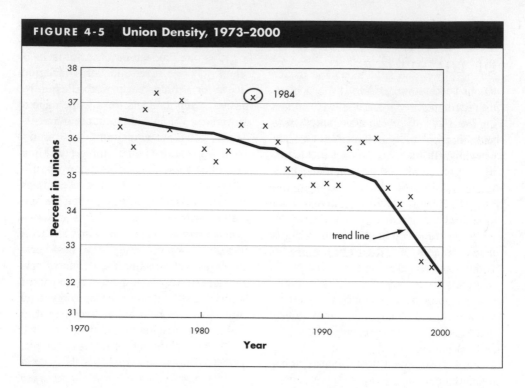

FIGURE 4-5 **Union Density, 1973–2000**

governments imposed restrictions on political strikes and secondary picketing (picketing beyond the plant or department affected by a strike). They increased employers' rights to fight organizing drives and employees' rights to attempt decertification. They banned strikes in designated work sites, weakened the ability of unions to discipline members who carried out anti-union activities, permitted unions to be sued, and, in most jurisdictions, allowed the use of replacement workers. One result of these actions was that, beginning in 1984, union density began to decline (see Figure 4-5).

Finally, throughout the 1980s, and particularly after Brian Mulroney's Progressive Conservative government was elected in 1984, federal and provincial governments increasingly adopted ad hoc back-to-work legislation to weaken workers' bargaining position and thereby limit strike action. Used on average only 0.2 times per year in the period 1950–1954, back-to-work laws were passed on average 5.0 times per year in the period 1975–1979 and 5.4 times per year in the period 1985–1989.

At first, limiting the right to strike was widely viewed as a temporary measure necessitated by fear of a resurgence of the strike wave of 1974–1975, the highest inflation rates Canada had ever seen, and the deep recessions of 1981–1982 and 1991–1992. However, limiting the right to strike became a matter of an enduring, if unstated, public policy, largely because economic and political conditions required a less expensive and less militant work force. By the mid-1980s, a new labour relations regime had crystallized. One of its main purposes was to render labour's ultimate bargaining tool—the strike—increasingly superfluous as a means of bargaining for improved terms of employment.

CONCLUSION: THE WITHERING AWAY OF THE STRIKE?

About 1960, some influential social scientists predicted that the strike was "withering away." The working class, they wrote, had become "embourgeoisified" due to growing affluence. Class conflict was supposedly becoming "institutionalized" in stable systems of collective bargaining. These developments were viewed as a sort of natural evolutionary process, part of the peaceful unfolding of the "inner logic of industrialization" (Ross and Hartman 1960; Dahrendorf 1959).

In the 1960s and 1970s, an international strike wave caught these social scientists by surprise. It cast doubt on the validity of their generalizations. Now, however, amid an international "resurgence of labour quiescence" (Shalev 1992) that has lasted more than two decades, some observers may be tempted to argue that affluence has at last caused the strike to wither away. For them, the generalizations of 1960 may appear valid after all.

My analysis suggests we should avoid this conclusion. I have shown that a measure of average affluence (GDPpc) is inversely associated with weighted strike frequency but is a poor measure of the economic conditions that shape the lives of Canadian workers. The unemployment rate is a much better indicator of workers' economic conditions; and for the 1973–1986 period, the unemployment rate varied inversely with weighted strike frequency. This suggests that the relative power or bargaining position of workers—not their level of affluence—determined their propensity to strike. Complicating the story, however, is a fact most researchers have overlooked. In the 1987–2000 period, the inverse relationship between the unemployment rate and weighted strike frequency nearly disappeared.[4] The business cycle had little effect on workers' propensity to strike. The reason? Actions taken by employers and governments from the mid-1970s to the late 1990s—introducing free trade, cutting budgets for a wide range of government assistance programs, passing laws and regulations that undermined unions—disempowered workers and rendered the strike a less effective weapon.

In sum, the history of Canadian industrial relations since the mid-1970s suggests that the "inner logic" of industrial capitalism is driven by power, not alleged evolutionary imperatives such as the rising average level of affluence. Industrial relations systems are institutionalized forms of class conflict—that is, enduring legal resolutions of historically specific struggles between workers and employers. But "enduring" does not mean "permanent." Trends lasting a few decades should not be confused with the end of history. Industrial relations systems change when power is massively redistributed between classes. In Canada, for example, a massive redistribution of power in favour of workers took place from the mid-1940s on, when workers won the legal right to unionize and strike and were in a position to extract increased disposable income and benefits from employers and governments. Another massive redistribution of power, this time in favour of employers, took place after the mid-1970s. The Canadian industrial relations regime was transformed on both occasions. The transition from the first regime to the second was marked by a change in the relationship between strike frequency and the business cycle. It follows that, however difficult it might be to imagine in the current industrial relations climate, another massive shift in the distribution of power in society could once again help the strike regain its former popularity.

NOTES

1. Data sources for this chapter are as follows:

    Population: CANSIM (2002b).

    Gross Domestic Product per Capita: CANSIM (2002a).

    Strikes: "Series E190-197..." (2001); "Chronological Perspective..." (2001).

    Union membership: "Series E175-177..." (2001); Human Resources Development Canada (2001); Union Membership (2000).

    Non-agricultural workers (1902–10 and 1912–20 interpolated): *Fifth Census...* (1915), Table 1, p. 13; *Labour Organizations...* (1973) pp. xxii–xxiii; *1994–1995 Directory...* (1995) p. xiii; Union Membership (2000).

    Unemployment: CANSIM (2001).

2. That is why the influence of union density on strike action peaks at intermediate levels of union density and then tapers off. In countries with the highest proportion of unionized workers, unions tend to exert considerable political influence.

3. As Morley Gunderson commented on a draft of this chapter, the argument developed here is also an argument about wage concessions. Moreover, for strike incidence to fall, the *joint* cost of strikes to both workers and employers must increase. In the present case, the cost of strikes to employers has increased, partly because strikes threaten the loss of global market share.

4. See, however, Cramton and Tracy (1994), who reach similar conclusions about the United States in the 1980s.

REFERENCES

Akard, Patrick J. 1992. "Corporate mobilization and political power: The transformation of U.S. economic policy in the 1970s." *American Sociological Review* 57:587–615.

Ashenfelter, Orley, and George Johnson 1969. "Bargaining theory, trade unions, and industrial strike activity." *American Economic Review* 59:35–49.

Bercuson, David Jay 1990 [1974]. *Confrontation at Winnipeg: Labour, Industrial Relations, and the General Strike* (rev. ed.). Montréal: McGill-Queen's University Press.

Butovsky, Jonah 2001. *The Decline of the New Democrats: The Politics of Postmaterialism or Neoliberalism?* Ph.D. dissertation, Department of Sociology, University of Toronto.

CANSIM 2001, "Unemployment rate age 15+ SA CDA." Retrieved April 4, 2001 (http://dc2.chass.utoronto.ca/cansim2/English/index.html).

CANSIM 2002a. "G.D.P., expenditure-based, 1992\$/gross domestic pr at market prices." Retrieved January 7, 2002 (http://dc2.chass.utoronto.ca/cansim2/English/index.html).

CANSIM 2002b. "Population of Canada, by province/Canada." Retrieved January 7, 2002 (http://dc2.chass.utoronto.ca/cansim2/English/index.html).

Cramton, Peter C., and Joseph S. Tracy 1994. "The determinants of U.S. labour disputes." *Journal of Labor Economics* 12:180–209.

Cruikshank, Douglas, and Gregory S. Kealey 1987. "Strikes in Canada, 1891–1950." *Labour/Le Travail* 20:85–145.

Dahrendorf, Ralf 1959. *Class and Class Conflict in Industrial Society*. London: Routledge & Kegan Paul.

Fifth Census of Canada, 1911 Vol. VI. 1915. Ottawa: Census and Statistics Office, Department of Trade and Commerce.

Franzosi, Roberto 1989a. "One hundred years of strike statistics: Methodological and theoretical issues in quantitative strike research." *Industrial and Labor Relations Review* 42:348–362.

Franzosi, Roberto 1989b. "Strike data in search of a theory: The Italian case in the postwar period." *Politics and Society* 17:453–487.

Gunderson, Morley 1998. "Harmonization of labour policies under trade liberalization." *Industrial Relations* 53. Retrieved April 9, 2001 (http://www.erudit.org/erudit/ri/v53no1/gunder/gunder.html).

Harrison, Alan, and Mark Stewart 1994. "Is strike behavior cyclical?" *Journal of Labor Economics* 12:524–553.

Hibbs, Douglas 1976. "Industrial conflict in advanced industrial societies." *American Political Science Review* 70:1033–1058.

Hibbs, Douglas 1978. "On the political economy of long-run trends in strike activity." *British Journal of Political Science* 8:153–175.

Human Resources Development Canada 2001. "Special tabulation on union membership, 1960–2000."

Human Resources Development Canada 2002. "Chronological perspective on work stoppages in Canada (work stoppages involving one or more workers), 1976–2000." Retrieved March 27, 2002 (http://labour-travail. hrdc-drhc.gc.ca/doc/wid-dimt/eng/ws-at/table.cfm).

Jamieson, Stuart 1973 [1957]. *Industrial Relations in Canada* (2nd ed.). Toronto: Macmillan.

Johnston, William A. 2001. "Class and politics in the era of the global economy." In Doug Baer (ed.), *Political Sociology: Canadian Perspectives*, pp. 288–306. Don Mills, Ontario: Oxford University Press.

Korpi, Walter, and Michael Shalev 1980. "Strikes, power and politics in the Western nations, 1900–1976." *Political Power and Social Theory* 1:301–334.

Labour Organizations in Canada 1972 1973. Ottawa: Economics and Research Branch, Canada Department of Labour.

Langille, David 1987. "The business council on national issues and the Canadian state." *Studies in Political Economy* 24:41–85.

Leacy, F.H. (ed.) 1983 [1965]. *Historical Statistics of Canada* (2nd ed.) Ottawa: Statistics Canada.

MacDonald, L. Ian (ed.) 2000. *Free Trade: Risks and Rewards.* Montréal and Kingston: McGill-Queen's University Press.

1998 Directory of Labour Organizations in Canada 1998. Ottawa: Workplace Information Directorate.

1994–1995 Directory of Labour Organizations in Canada 1995. Ottawa: Minister of Supply and Services Canada.

Paldam, Martin, and Peder Pedersen 1982. "The macroeconomic strike model: A study of seventeen countries, 1948–1975." *Industrial and Labor Relations Review* 35:504–521.

Palmer, Bryan D. 1987. "Labour protest and organization in nineteenth century Canada, 1820–1890." *Labour/Le Travail* 20:61–83.

Panitch, Leo, and Donald Swartz 1993 [1985]. *The Assault on Trade Union Freedoms: From Wage Controls to Social Contract* (2nd ed.). Toronto: Garamond Press.

Rees, Albert 1952. "Industrial conflict and business fluctuations." *Journal of Political Economy* 60:371–382.

Richardson, R. Jack 1996. "Canada and free trade: Why did it happen?" In Robert J. Brym (ed.), *Society in Question*, pp. 200–209. Toronto: Harcourt Brace Canada.

Ross, Arthur M., and Paul T. Hartman 1960. *Changing Patterns of Industrial Conflict.* New York: Wiley.

Schor, Juliet B., and Samuel Bowles 1987. "Employment rents and the incidence of strikes." *Review of Economics and Statistics* 69:584–592.

Shalev, Michael 1992. "The resurgence of labour quiescence." In Marino Regini (ed.), *The Future of Labour Movements*, pp. 102–132. London: Sage.

Shorter, Edward, and Charles Tilly 1971. "The shape of strikes in France, 1830–1960." *Comparative Studies in Society and History* 13:60–86.

Smith, Douglas A. 1972. "The determinants of strike activity in Canada." *Industrial Relations* 27:663–677.

Snyder, David 1975. "Institutional setting and industrial conflict: Comparative analyses of France, Italy and the United States." *American Sociological Review* 40:259–278.

Snyder, David 1977. "Early North American strikes: A reinterpretation." *Industrial and Labor Relations Review* 30:325–341.

Statistics Canada 2001. "Series E175-177: Union membership in Canada, in total, as a percentage of non-agricultural paid workers, and union members with international affiliation, 1911 to 1975 (thousands)." Retrieved March 29, 2001 (http://www.statcan.ca/english/freepub/11-516-XIE/sectione/sectione. htm#Unions).

Statistics Canada 2001. "Series E190-197: Number of strikes and lockouts, employers and workers involved and time loss, Canada, 1901 to 1975." Retrieved March 29, 2001 (http://www.statcan.ca/english/freepub/11-516-XIE/sectione/sectione.htm#Unions).

Union Membership in Canada—2000 2000. *Workplace Gazette: An Industrial Relations Quarterly* 3, 3:68–75.

FURTHER REFERENCES—
SECTION 1:
POWER AND CLASS

Allahar, Anton, and James Cote 1998. *Richer and Poorer: The Structure of Inequality in Canada.* Toronto: Copp Clark. The authors use a framework that centres on the role of dominant ideology to examine social inequality in Canada, with a special focus on issues of class, gender, age, and race/ethnicity. A key claim in this analysis is that Canadians are in a state of denial about the existence of major inequalities in their society.

Baer, Douglas (ed.) 2002. *Political Sociology: Canadian Perspectives.* Toronto: Oxford University Press. This collection includes a number of papers that deal with issues of political power and inequality, the role of the state in contemporary Canadian society, and related questions.

Carroll, William 1997. *Organizing Dissent: Contemporary Social Movements* (2nd ed.). Toronto: Garamond. This book considers the significance of contemporary social movements in Canada, including the women's movement, the Native Indian movement, and others that focus on important problems of social inequality.

Clement, Wallace (ed.) 1997. *Understanding Canada: Building on the New Canadian Political Economy.* This selection of papers applies a political economy perspective to understanding a variety of important questions having to do with the structure of power and class in Canada. Chapters include analyses of changes in the nature of Canadian capitalism in recent years, the position of labour in the changing economy, the state in the era of globalization, and the decline of state-funded welfare in Canada in recent years.

Evans, Bryan, and John Shields 1998. *Reinventing the State: Public Administration Reform in Canada.* Halifax: Fernwood. This book looks at the trend toward a shrinking role for government in Canadian society in the 1990s and links this trend to such contemporary developments as globalization and the state economic crisis. The authors suggest alternatives to this reduced role of government in the lives of Canadians.

Forcese, Dennis 1997. *The Canadian Class Structure* (4th ed.). Toronto: McGraw-Hill Ryerson. This text focuses on class-based inequalities in Canada, but also touches on other topics in social inequality, including gender, age, ethnicity, and race.

Global Transformations Retrieved January 6, 2003 (http://www.polity.co.uk/global/research.htm). A site with good background for researching issues related to globalization. Readers should know that the Global Transformations site is hosted by a publisher (Polity Press) in England. However, it is a useful and comprehensive resource.

Laxer, Gordon 1989. *Open for Business.* Toronto: Oxford University Press. In this monograph, Laxer employs a comparative perspective to examine the historical pattern of foreign ownership in the Canadian economy.

Ornstein, Michael, and Michael Stevenson 1999. *Politics and Ideology in Canada.* Montréal and Kingston: McGill-Queen's University Press. This book examines the question of ideological power in Canada. The analysis compares the perspectives of Canada's elite leadership with those of the general public on a range of important issues, such as state power and support for government welfare programs.

SOCIO-ECONOMIC BASES OF SOCIAL INEQUALITY

A. INCOME, WEALTH, AND POVERTY
B. OCCUPATION
C. EDUCATION

In the previous section we saw that the private ownership of productive economic property contributes to a fundamental social division in Canadian society. For a very small number of Canadians, variously defined as an elite or as a ruling, upper, or capitalist class, ownership provides power and privilege. However, beyond ownership there are many other dimensions of social inequality, three of which are explored in this section. These include inequalities that are tied to *income, wealth, and poverty; occupation;* and *education.*

These three bases of inequality are closely interrelated. A causal connection runs from education through occupation to income, in that schooling typically affects job prospects, and a person's job largely determines income. Furthermore, income has consequences beyond an individual's own lifetime, influencing, for example, the educational opportunities of one's

children, and thus their jobs and incomes too. Several issues involved in this complex interrelationship should be emphasized.

First, in the study of these forms of inequality, it is necessary to clarify whether the focus is on individuals or families. When seeking to explain the occupations or incomes of people, sociologists normally study individuals. However, when looking at intergenerational job mobility or the inheritance of wealth, the focus is mainly on families. Thus, the unit of observation (individuals or families) should be made clear.

Second, discussions about inequality often involve the idea of transmission across generations. To what degree is social inequality *reproduced* over time? Research of this type investigates how family origin or family background influences the attainment of education, occupation, or income levels. Questions of the openness or rigidity of opportunities in society are central here, as is the awareness that inequalities endure across generations.

Third, the relations among the three dimensions—income or wealth, occupation, and education—are not fixed and, although they are intertwined, the associations among them are not perfect. That is, even though these forms of inequality are closely tied in Canada, some people with little education do earn large incomes, for example. Such individuals are relatively rare, however, as are people who live in poverty or lack jobs despite having high levels of education. In other words, the connections linking these three types of inequality are not deterministic, but *probabilistic* (although often quite strong).

Fourth, while social inequality is a feature of all societies, the *degree of inequality is variable*. At different times and in different societies the amount of inequality varies. Sociologists studying inequality in Canada, therefore, have been concerned with how inequality here compares with that in other countries, and also with how levels of inequality may be changing over time.

Explanations for the levels of social inequality in Canada often vary. While this section of the book stresses facts about inequality, issues of interpretation are equally important. Contrary to popular wisdom, facts do not speak for themselves. For example, how are we to understand or explain the consistent finding that women on average earn less money than men? As the selections in Section 3 indicate (see, e.g., Chapter 17 by Creese and Beagan) there are several competing and even conflicting reasons that sociologists have put forward to explain gender inequality.

Throughout this book, you will encounter certain ideas that are consistent touchstones for interpreting social

inequality. Two of these basic perspectives are raised here, so that you will recognize, compare, and assess them when you think about the reasons behind social inequality in Canada.

One way people try to explain inequality is by pointing to its positive consequences for societal well-being. This line of reasoning holds that people will only be motivated to acquire useful skills and to work at responsible jobs if they receive high rewards for doing so. In this way, people with drive, talent, and ability will be encouraged to use these attributes for the benefit of both themselves and the society in general. From this perspective, tangible incentives, including high incomes, prestige, and influence, must go to those occupying key positions in society. The *achievement* principle is central to this explanation for differences in income, prestige, or rank (see Davis and Moore 1945 for more detail).

A very different argument is taken by those who emphasize that certain groups in society benefit more than others from the way in which social structures are organized. Tensions and disputes over aspects of inequality are seen to stem from the opposing interests of different groups, as one group attempts to control profit or privilege at the expense of another group. For some researchers, these interest groups are class-based, while for others they are defined by nonclass factors such as gender or ethnicity. In all of these instances, however, the interpretation is that conflict or struggle is the key to understanding social inequality. The struggle for control over economic resources, power, and privilege is understood as the key motor of social change (see, e.g., Wright 1985 for a class-based account of this perspective).

The tension between these two perspectives underlies much of the writing on inequality, although there are several variants of each approach. In general, though, those who stress achievement tend to focus on equality of opportunity. They also emphasize the freedom of individuals to pursue their own goals, interests, and destiny. However, an emphasis on equality of condition or outcome, for all people, usually comes from those who argue that the control and accumulation of power and profit by one group gives them (and their children) an unfair advantage in society. These competing ideas continue to inform much of the discussion about the causes of social inequality in the present day.

INCOME, WEALTH, AND POVERTY

We begin this section by exploring the distribution of money. At the extremes of the income distribution are affluence and poverty, the rich and the poor. The readings in this section examine how economic rewards are distributed in Canadian society, how that distribution has changed over time, what governments have and have not done in attempting to influence the distribution, and what arguments are made for and against income redistribution.

The first reading, by Peter Urmetzer and Neil Guppy, explains that while the economic pie has grown bigger in the post–World War II era, the sizes of the slices apportioned to various income groups have remained remarkably stable. What makes this surprising is that these decades since World War II have often been described in terms of a growing welfare state. Whatever else the state may have done during this period, it is not true that the government played Robin Hood, taking from the rich and giving to the poor. The state looked after everyone's welfare equally, such that very little, if any, redistribution of income occurred. More

recently—that is, in the 1980s and 1990s—the size of the economic pie has not grown, for wages and salaries have been stubbornly stable. For many people this has meant working harder and longer just to keep pace with inflation. One consequence is the resistance of Canadians to any tax increases.

Many believe that the government uses the tax system to collect from the rich to give to the poor. As Urmetzer and Guppy describe, the poor do receive some transfer income, but so too do the rich. The result is that little income redistribution occurs. To understand this, it is important to realize that we pay tax in many forms—sales tax, income tax, gasoline tax, excise tax, and so forth. Some of these are progressive taxes, where the size of the tax bite increases with your income, while others are regressive, in that the tax bite is bigger for those with less income. People with large incomes are also able to use tax shelters (and to hire well-paid tax accountants to find such shelters). The net result is that the overall rate of tax paid by all Canadians varies surprisingly little over the entire income scale.

Income, however, is only one part of the material resources Canadians possess. For some—the super-rich—income is far less important than are assets. Wealth is accumulated and stored in land, buildings, stock, precious metals, art, and so on. As James Davies demonstrates in his paper on the distribution of wealth in Canada, there are some extremely rich families in this country. In fact, comparisons with the United States show that there are more rich families per capita in Canada. Furthermore, the distribution of wealth is far more unequal than is the distribution of income, with inheritance of wealth being the major cause of this pattern.

At the other extreme of the distribution of economic resources is poverty. The

National Council of Welfare monitors poverty in Canada and publishes many informative papers on issues faced by the poor in this country. The paper we reproduce here begins with a description of how Statistics Canada calculated their "low-income lines" (a phrasing that avoids the word poverty!). Details are also provided on how poverty lines compare to the expectations of Canadians about how much money is absolutely necessary to support a family. Poverty lines are also contrasted with average incomes, showing just how far the poverty line falls below the typical earnings of Canadians.

OCCUPATION

People's occupations are of fundamental importance, because working is what many of us do with most of our waking lives. Our jobs or careers are often at the core of our personal identities, frequently defining who we are in our own minds and in the eyes of others. And, of course, our occupations generate the incomes on which most of us make a living. Occupations also provide at least an approximate measure of where we stand on a wide variety of other inequality dimensions. These include income, education, skill level, degree of responsibility in the workplace, amount of authority over other workers, prestige ranking, and so on.

Perhaps for these reasons, occupation has been viewed by some researchers as the best overall indicator of a person's general social-class location or socio-economic rank. The relevance of occupation to the field of social inequality is revealed in the range of problems involving work or occupation that researchers in this field have addressed. These include, for example, the changing composition of the labour force, the extent to which occupational status depends on the attainment of educational credentials, the degree to which the occupational backgrounds of parents influence the occupational attainments of their children, and the problems posed by the changing nature of work in technologically advanced societies.

Such issues form the focus of the three papers chosen for our section on occupational inequality. In the first article, Douglas Baer looks at the increasingly important role that higher education plays in determining occupational attainment in Canada. This paper shows, in particular, that having a post-secondary education, though not a guarantee of occupational success, has recently become even more important as a necessary pre-condition for getting the "good" jobs in management and professional-technical fields. Those who lack advanced education, on the other hand, are more likely to be relegated to the "bad" or routine jobs in the clerical, blue-collar, and lower-level service sectors. These latter types of job are typically lower paying, less secure, and less likely to lead to a higher career position in the future than jobs that require post-secondary education.

In the second chapter, Richard Wanner assesses the question of occupational mobility and occupational status attainment in Canada. He considers the extent to which occupational advantages or disadvantages of parents are inherited by their children when the latter eventually enter the labour force as adults. He also looks at whether the amount of occupational mobility and overall patterns of status attainment have changed over time. These analyses address some of the key debates about the evolving nature of inequality in this country.

In the final chapter on occupation, Graham Lowe provides a detailed analysis of Canada's occupational structure, with special concern for the nature of present-day labour markets and the future of work. Among the major issues considered are the movement to a service-based economy in recent decades, the trend toward more "non-standard" work, including temporary and part-time employment, and the prospects for a growing gap between "good" and "bad" jobs. This selection also addresses the question of gender segregation and gender inequality in the Canadian labour force, including the gap in earnings between male and female workers. Throughout the chapter, the author considers the possible implications of several of these issues for policy-makers in business and government.

EDUCATION

How much education a person attains is arguably the most important of the three inequality dimensions under discussion in this section on income, occupation, and education. The argument would be that education is the most important because educational credentials are among the best predictors of attainment of the other two rewards. Studies of social mobility show this to be the case (Wanner 1999). Education is very often the sole avenue to the best jobs and the highest salaries.

It is little wonder, then, that academic researchers, educational practitioners, and politicians have devoted substantial attention to the question of providing equality in the opportunity to acquire education. The first selection, by Elaine Fournier, George Butlin, and Philip Giles, asks how a child's educational attainment is affected by how much education his or her mother and father possess. If there were complete equality of educational opportunity in Canada, this effect would be minimal, so that schooling attainment would depend upon your own effort and ability and not be strongly influenced by your parents'

education. Conversely, if the level of education of your parents affects your own educational attainment, this suggests that equality of educational opportunity is not strong in Canada. Fournier, Butlin, and Giles find that people's chances of proceeding to higher levels of schooling are linked to their parents' level of education. Furthermore, there is evidence that this link between parental schooling and children's schooling is the most powerful predictor of educational attainment (e.g., Guppy and Davies 1998).

Scott Davies picks up the theme of explaining how these inequalities in educational attainment come about. Why, he asks, does family socio-economic status have such an important impact on schooling destinies? He examines a host of explanations, from purely economic to cultural. If money, for example, were the key, then we would expect to see the link between parents' education and their offspring's education greatly reduced, if not eliminated, in countries where post-secondary schooling is free. There is no evidence to support this, which suggests that money is not the key factor. Another explanation could depend on the expectations of working- versus middle-class parents. Perhaps, Davies suggests, it is the social organization of family life that is the major explanatory factor. Working-class families have more rigid working lives, buffeted by shift work, tiring commuting schedules, moonlighting, and so forth, all of which make it harder for them to contribute to school-related activities than for middle-class parents. As Davies concludes, explaining the link between family origin and educational destination has proven to be a very difficult issue. His paper makes a significant contribution to such explanations, however, by showing us some promising lines of argument.

In the final selection, by Harvey Krahn, we can see that family socio-economic status and the educational attainments of a person's parents have strong predictive effects on both a person's educational and occupational goals and his/her chances of goal attainment. Using a research design that has allowed him to follow people from school into the workforce, he shows how powerful a factor family background is in affecting people's occupational outcomes.

REFERENCES

Davis, Kingsley, and Wilbert E. Moore 1945. "Some Principles of Stratification." *American Sociological Review* 10:242–249.

Guppy, Neil, and Scott Davies 1998. *The Schooled Society: Changes and Challenges in Canadian Education.* Ottawa: Statistics Canada and Nelson Publishing.

Wanner, R. 1999. "Expansion and ascription: Trends in educational opportunity in Canada, 1920–1994" (electronic version). *Canadian Review of Sociology,* August.

Wright, Erik Olin 1985. *Classes.* London: Verso Books.

C h a p t e r

5

CHANGING INCOME INEQUALITY IN CANADA

Peter Urmetzer and Neil Guppy

(Revised from the previous edition of this volume.)

INTRODUCTION

Misconceptions about income inequality are widespread. Frequently, information is tainted by personal impressions and media accounts. Thus, while the homeless have become a common and very visible feature of the urban landscape, they comprise only a small portion of Canada's population. The same is true of sports stars and executives earning the seven-figure salaries reported in the media: Only a small number of Canadians fall into this million-dollar club. These impressions, although powerful in influencing our perceptions about inequality, are unrepresentative. The fact is that most Canadians fall outside the extremes of excessive poverty and wealth. The majority of people in this country have such typical incomes that they remain inconspicuous to both the average observer and the sensationalist eye of the media.

Nevertheless, inequality does exist. Canada's economy has historically followed a cycle of bust and boom, and not all Canadians are affected equally by these cycles (see Chapter 6 on poverty). For example, an economic downturn creates a slowdown in new housing construction, causing layoffs in the building industry, while universities and colleges may benefit from the same downturn as more people upgrade their skills, translating into more jobs for teachers. Examples such as these illustrate that we need a more comprehensive way of looking at inequality, an approach that does more than focus narrowly on the rich and the poor. We need to move beyond personal and journalistic accounts, which gravitate toward the unusual.

INCOME

Some people may question the relevance of asking questions about income inequality, especially in a wealthy country such as Canada. From a social science perspective, patterns of economic inequality are important because they reveal the consequences of various social processes and political decisions. Although seldom acknowledged, many political debates directly address issues of economic distribution since economic policies have consequences benefiting some while disadvantaging others. We need some way of assessing these outcomes. We need ways of evaluating claims about the superiority of market forces over government intervention. Evidence of how these policies affect income distribution becomes an indispensable evaluation tool. Invariably, a cut in social programs or a change in tax structure or monetary policy makes some people richer and some people poorer.

The abolition of minimum wage legislation, resulting in higher profits for employers and lower pay for workers, does not affect everyone equally. The increased cost of borrowing suggests that a policy of high interest rates also has diverse consequences, as the borrower's larger interest payments end up as increased profits for investors. One person's loss is another person's gain. This holds true for the majority of economic policy decisions Canadians have grappled with over the past decade—the struggle over the welfare state, free trade, the deficit, and "globalization." Rarely are the consequences of these decisions neutral.

Statistics on income distribution serve to illuminate, at least indirectly, the outcome of these policies. Careful examination of trends in income distribution reveals patterns about the organization of Canadian society. It is this question, then, that provides the primary focus of this chapter: How has income inequality changed in Canada in recent decades? We begin by tracing changes in income.

Subsequent to the poverty and hardship of the Depression years in the 1930s, Canadians have experienced relative affluence. From the 1950s right through to the late 1970s, Canadians, whether as individuals or in families, enjoyed rising incomes and general economic prosperity. This is true even after inflation is taken into consideration.[1] Figure 5-1 charts the average real income of Canadian families from 1951 through to 2001, showing two distinct periods: (i) rising real incomes year upon year from 1951 to 1979, and (ii) income stagnation from 1980 through to 1996, with only a modest rise in the late 1990s. Notice too that this is the average income of families, not individuals.

The growth of real family incomes from the 1950s through the 1970s reflects a period of sustained and unprecedented expansion in the Canadian economy. Throughout this period, levels of productivity rose, largely based on technological advances and a more highly skilled labour force. Organized labour succeeded in tying wages to productivity and, consequently, earnings grew. However, beginning in the early 1980s, family earnings began to stagnate. This occurred despite the increasing number of married women entering the workforce (from 50% in 1980 to about 80% in 2002). Earnings of married women have done much to keep family poverty rates down. Figure 5-1 shows that although average earnings fluctuated somewhat, family purchasing power remained essentially flat from 1980 to 1996. In the late 1990s and the early 2000s family incomes rose more quickly, but even then not as fast as in the decade just after Word War II.

Averages, however, suffer from a major shortcoming: They only measure what statisticians call "central tendency"

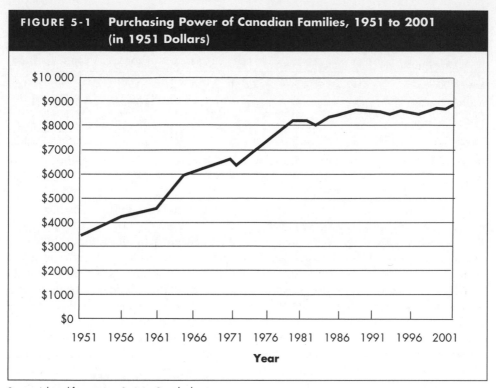

FIGURE 5-1   Purchasing Power of Canadian Families, 1951 to 2001 (in 1951 Dollars)

Source: Adapted from various Statistics Canada documents.

and are silent about dispersion or variation around that central point.[2] In order to gain a better understanding of these variations, we need an easy method of examining the *distribution* of earned income.

Distribution of Income: Quintiles

A common way to measure income distribution is to divide the population into a small number of equal-size groups, usually fifths, and then examine each group's relative share of the total income. An intuitively appealing way of doing this is to imagine a queue that contains all the families in Canada. At the head of this line is the family that earns the highest income; at the tail, the family that earns the least. This line is then divided into five equal-

size groups called fifths or quintiles. Next, the sum of the income of each of the five groups is calculated. The resulting sum for each group is then presented as a portion of the total income of all five quintiles (or the total income of all families in Canada).

As Table 5-1 shows, for the top quintile this turns out to be 45.3% in 1999. So, of all the money earned in Canada in 1999, 45.3% of it was earned by the wealthiest 20% of families. Such disproportion means that only 54.7% was left for the remaining 80%. The lowest income earners, the 20% of people at the end of the line, shared a meagre 4.4% of all income.

If income were distributed perfectly equally in Canada, every group would be allotted an identical share of income (i.e., 20%). As the table shows, the highest quintile is successful in acquiring more

TABLE 5-1	Percentage of Total Before-Tax Income Going to Families and Unattached Individuals by Quintile, 1951–1999						
Income Quintile	**1951**	**1961**	**1971**	**1981**	**1991**	**1995**	**1999**
Lowest Quintile	4.4	4.2	3.6	4.6	4.7	4.7	4.4
Second Quintile	11.2	11.9	10.6	10.9	10.3	10.2	10.0
Middle Quintile	18.3	18.3	17.6	17.6	16.6	16.4	16.1
Fourth Quintile	23.3	24.3	24.9	25.1	24.7	24.5	24.3
Highest Quintile	42.8	41.4	43.3	41.7	43.8	44.1	45.3

Source: Adapted from the Statistics Canada publications *Income in Canada*, Catalogue 75-202, 1999, and *Income Distributions by Size in Canada*, Catalogue 13-207, 1997.

than double its 20% share, while the lowest quintile receives less than a quarter of its fifth.

Table 5-1 also tracks how income shares have changed between the years 1951 and 1999. At first glance, there appears to have been little change in the proportion of income that each quintile receives. Closer examination, however, reveals a gradual shift of approximately 3% from the second and middle quintiles to the two highest quintiles. Surprisingly, perhaps, it is not the lowest of the quintiles, the point of focus of most poverty studies, where the majority of losses have occurred, but in the second and middle quintiles. The top quintile, which arguably needs it the least, has experienced the biggest increase since 1951, an increase of 2.5%. Between 1981 and 1999 this increase is especially evident, amounting to 3.6 percentage points.

As a matter of fact, between 1981 and 1999, the top quintile is the only one that can claim an increase in its share of the national income, with all of the three middle quintiles losing ground. Meanwhile, the share for the bottom quintile has remained essentially constant. This confirms what many middle-income Canadians are feeling—that it is increasingly difficult to make a living. A 3.6 per-

centage point gain for the top quintile may appear to be a trivial amount, but given that the total income generated in Canada surpasses half a trillion dollars a year, this increase translates into more than $15 billion—enough to eliminate poverty in Canada (Osberg 1992:42).

Transfers and Taxes

The figures in Table 5-1 reflect all forms of income. For example, for those families in the top quintile, earnings from stock market dividends, real estate holdings, pension plans, and professional salaries would be included. By comparison, earnings in the bottom quintile primarily consist of income from employment insurance, pension plans, wages, and government assistance (often informally referred to as "welfare"). The crucial difference to note here is between market income and government transfers. That is, income is either market based (wages, return on investment, etc.) or collected in the form of transfers (payments designed to help people who are out of work or retired, including social assistance, employment insurance payments, and government pensions). Once we acknowledge this important distinction, the distribution of income changes dramatically. As shown in Table

TABLE 5-2	Percentage of Different Income Concepts Going to Families and Unattached Individuals by Quintile, 1999		
Income Quintile	**Income Before Transfers**	**Total Money Income**	**Income After Taxes**
Lowest Quintile	2.0	4.4	5.1
Second Quintile	7.7	10.0	11.1
Middle Quintile	15.2	16.1	16.8
Fourth Quintile	25.4	24.3	24.4
Highest Quintile	49.6	45.3	42.6

Source: Adapted from the Statistics Canada publication *Income in Canada*, Catalogue 75-202, 1999.

5-2, when only market income is considered, the lowest quintile receives only 2% of all income, while the highest quintile earns nearly half (49.6%).

The second column of Table 5-2 shows that after transfer payments are taken into account, the lowest quintile sees an income increase from 2% of all market income to 4.4% of total income.[3] The highest quintile has a smaller share of the total income (45.3) than of market income (49.6).

Beyond the transfer system, the tax system can also be used to aid redistribution. Income tax, at least in theory, is a progressive tax in that high-income earners are taxed at a higher rate than low-income earners.[4] The government then takes these revenues and redistributes them in favour of poorer families. In other words, what high-income earners pay in the form of proportionally higher taxes goes into the pockets of poorer families as proportionally higher transfers. The end result is a more equitable distribution of income.

For 1999, the most recent data available, the redistributing effect of income taxation is apparent, albeit only minimally (see the right-hand column in Table 5-2). Only the highest quintile experienced a decrease in its share (from 45.3 to 42.6), with all other quintiles either staying virtually the same (the fourth) or gaining (the first, second, and third). Comparing the two columns, Income Before Transfers and Income After Taxes, shows the effect income tax has on national income, and the redistribution characteristic of the welfare state becomes obvious. Here is good evidence of the state acting as the legendary Robin Hood, taking from the rich and giving to the poor.

But this is not the full picture. At this point, we have only examined income taxes, and the bulk of government revenues comes from consumption (e.g., sales taxes, excise taxes) and property taxes. In theory, consumption taxes are flat since everyone pays exactly the same rate, regardless of income (e.g., the 7% Goods and Services Tax). However, many economists and sociologists have argued that in practice consumption taxes are effectively regressive; that is, low-income earners end up paying a higher proportion of their income in consumption taxes than do high-income earners. This conclusion is based on two related arguments.

One line of argument points out that sales taxes constitute a higher proportion of the income of a poor family than a rich one. This is best illustrated by an example. Compare two families, the Browns and the Greens, similar in many respects, with the exception of income. After income tax, the Greens earn half ($30 000) of what the Browns do ($60 000). Now both families purchase a car costing $10 000. The sales tax on this purchase, including the GST and Provincial Sales Tax (PST), would amount to around $1500 in most of Canada's provinces. In effect the Greens pay one-twentieth of their income in sales taxes (1500/30 000) while the Browns pay only one-fortieth (1500/60 000).

The argument can be made, though, that the wealthier family is likely to spend more on a car, say $20 000, and thus end up paying the equivalent proportion of sales tax. And this is a major shortcoming of this argument: It rests on hypothetical examples that can easily be countered using other hypothetical examples. The argument that consumption taxes are regressive, however, gathers steam once spending patterns are taken into consideration. This second criticism focuses less on hypothetical examples and more on outcomes.

Families in lower-income brackets are forced, out of necessity, to spend most of their income and therefore contribute a higher proportion of it to taxes. For example, a family earning $30 000 a year is likely to spend all of its income on food, shelter, clothing, and other basics. By contrast, a family earning $300 000 a year can afford to save or invest a considerable portion of its income in mutual funds or real estate holdings. Money saved is not subject to consumption taxes.

Moreover, not all products and services are taxed equally. For example, the purchase of a home is not subject to PST, and post-secondary tuition fees are taxed by neither the provincial nor federal government. We know that high-income earners are more likely to be homeowners and send their kids to university, thus benefiting from these exemptions. Low-income earners, on the other hand, have less opportunity to take advantage of these tax breaks and therefore end up paying proportionally more of their income in taxes. Thus, with consumption taxes the proportion of tax paid increases as earnings decrease, the direct opposite to the relationship found with income tax. As we saw above, income tax is structured in such a way that high-income earners pay a higher proportion of tax than do low-income earners, a structure that is considered progressive. Applying similar reasoning reveals consumption tax to be regressive.

Once both income and consumption taxes are taken into consideration, the overall redistributing effect of the Canadian taxation system becomes less apparent. As Hunter (1993:104) explains, "what taxes on income give,... taxes on spending take away." In other words, income taxes help to redistribute money, but consumption taxes erode much of this redistributive effect. The final outcome is that after different taxes (and tax breaks) are considered, very little of the Robin Hood effect remains in the welfare state.

Income Distribution in Other Countries

How fair is the distribution of income in Canada? In the abstract, this is a difficult question, and a response depends on all kinds of philosophical assumptions about merit, human rights, and inheritance. On a more practical level, though, we can answer this question by comparing Canada's income distribution to that found in other countries. Table 5-3 shows that Canada shares its income more equally than the United States, Australia, or the United Kingdom, countries that share cultural ties and economic philosophies that date back to the colonial days of the British Empire (with the exception of

Québec, of course). Canada also has the wealthiest middle quintiles of all the countries in the table. Canada, however, does less well when it comes to the lower quintiles. This is true in comparison to Western European countries in general and Scandinavian countries in particular. Not surprisingly, Sweden, often heralded as the exemplar of the welfare state, also has the most equitable distribution of income found in the West. What is surprising is that Japan, a country that cannot even boast a welfare state (but has very low unemployment), has the most generous distribution toward the lowest quintile.

Table 5-3 demonstrates that income can be distributed in a variety of ways and follows no overall or consistent pattern. Income is least equally distributed in South Africa, Mexico, and Brazil. In these countries, a wealthy top quintile occurs at the expense of an impoverished bottom quintile.

In comparison to countries in South America or Asia, Canada's distribution is more equitable. But this could change, especially as the assault on government social programs continues. The elimination or reduction of social programs would dramatically alter the distribution of income in this country, no doubt most directly affecting those in the lower quintiles. The contagion of cuts that has swept Canada in recent decades has raised concerns about the "Brazilianization" of our economy, a term that is meant to reflect the stark inequities that plague Brazil, a country completely lacking a welfare state (Therborn 1986). The fear is that by investing too much faith in markets, some

TABLE 5-3	Income Distribution According to Quintiles in Various Countries (Various Years)				
	Lowest Quintile	Second Quintile	Middle Quintile	Fourth Quintile	Highest Quintile
Sweden	9.6	14.5	18.1	23.2	34.5
Japan	10.6	14.2	17.6	22.0	35.7
Germany	8.2	13.2	17.5	22.7	38.5
Canada*	7.5	12.9	17.2	23.0	39.3
Korea (Rep)	7.5	12.9	17.4	22.9	39.3
Australia	5.9	12.0	17.2	23.6	41.3
UK	6.1	11.6	16.4	22.7	44.2
USA	5.2	10.5	15.6	22.4	46.4
Russian Federation	4.4	8.6	13.3	20.1	53.7
Malaysia	4.4	8.1	12.9	20.3	54.3
Hong Kong	4.4	8.0	12.2	18.3	57.1
Mexico	3.5	7.3	12.1	19.7	57.4
Brazil	2.2	5.4	10.1	18.3	64.1
South Africa	2.9	5.5	9.2	17.7	64.8

*Figures for Canada vary significantly from those in Tables 5-1 and 5-2 because of different working definitions necessitated by cross-national comparisons.

Source: World Bank, *World Development Indicators, 2002.*

governments, including ours from time to time, have turned their backs on social programs and ignored the poor. But the stability of income shares in this country suggests that this view may be overly pessimistic.

Given the dramatic changes that Canadian society has undergone since the Second World War, it is remarkable how obdurately stable the distribution of income has remained. In addition to an increase in the participation of women in the labour force and a decline in industrial jobs, these changes include a marked increase in government expenditures on social programs. The fact that income distribution has remained more or less constant alongside the increase in government involvement has led some commentators to question the efficacy of the welfare state as a mechanism for the redistribution of income (e.g., Teeple 1995). An often-quoted study by Hewitt (1977) argues that the redistributive effect of the welfare state is minimal at best. Hewitt's study also shows that the Canadian welfare state lags behind in its redistributive effectiveness, particularly when compared with Western European countries. Given the monumental and pervasive presence of the welfare state in Canadian society—in the form of employment insurance, pensions, education, health services, and other services too numerous to mention—most Canadians would, no doubt, find such a conclusion surprising.

On the face of it, it seems almost inconceivable that Canadian society would be identical in the absence of the welfare state. Yet the quintile approach shows precisely that: between the early 1950s and the late 1990s, a period that saw an explosion of welfare state services, income shares changed very little. Does this mean that the seemingly interminable political wrangling over social programs in Canada is essentially about nothing? The answer to this is a resounding no. Those who claim that the welfare state is ineffective must take note that the quintile approach itself does not reveal important changes in Canada's income composition. As we saw, the most common way to present quintiles is by total income; i.e., market and transfer income combined. This approach ignores how the composition of income has changed over the years, specifically the ratio of market income to government transfers. Were it not for these transfers, the poorest quintile would receive very little income (see column 1, Table 5-2).

Another change that quintiles ignore is that Canada's most costly social programs, such as health and education, are not included in income statistics because they are received in kind (i.e., as a service) rather than as monies. Nonetheless, this has an effect on income distribution, in that not having to pay for health care or education translates into a decrease in expenditure. This saving rises proportionally as income declines. For example, $1000 for an operation represents a bigger portion of income saved for someone in the bottom quintile (average income for individuals and families, $11 293 for 1999) than the top quintile ($116 364, same categories, same year) and therefore can be considered as contributing toward equality.

These observations are not consistent with views that perceive little utility in the welfare state. The reason income shares have stayed so consistent over the years is precisely because of social programs (transfers) that have steadily kept pace with a decline in market income. In short, income distribution has remained relatively uniform because of the welfare state, not despite it.

CONCLUSION

Because this chapter is an introduction to the subject, we have just scratched the surface of the various ways one can study income inequality. We have examined only how income varies among the different quintile groups and neglected the effects on income attainment of important sociological variables such as sex, ethnicity, and region. Another intriguing question asks, who occupies the different quintiles? Individuals may occupy the lowest quintile, but do so only on a temporary basis (e.g., retired individuals drawing a small pension [counted as income], but relying on extensive savings accumulated over a lifetime [not counted as income]). Many people occupy the lowest quintile at some point in their lives—as students, when learning a trade, when retired or unemployed—without suffering from the consequences normally associated with poverty, such as inadequate diet or shelter. This dynamism is not reflected in the figures. Conversely, some individuals are permanent occupants of the lower quintiles. This includes the homeless, who have increased their presence in most Canadian cities yet are not included in this type of study, primarily because they are notoriously difficult to track in income surveys.

This chapter is more descriptive than theoretical, and we do not dwell on why income inequality has changed (e.g., in market versus transfer aspects). Even a cursory inventory shows that theories abound: the advent of neoconservatism, changes in the labour market, a change in income tax structure, globalization, and so on. Whatever the issue, it is worthwhile to adopt a critical stance and ask who is likely to benefit or lose.

And who benefits is not beyond empirical verification. In this chapter we have learned that although income has risen substantially since the early fifties, income distribution has stayed relatively stable. Closer inspection, however, showed that, as no doubt many middle-class Canadians can attest, the second and third quintiles have been less successful at holding onto their share. Much of this income has escaped upward to the fourth and the highest quintile.

We also saw that the primary statistic used to compare incomes, income quintiles, is not without its problems. Its primary shortcoming is that it obscures how the composition of income has changed over the past few decades (market income versus transfer income). One reason for the stability of incomes is that social programs have done a remarkable job of subsidizing the incomes of those in the lower quintiles, thus preventing their fall into absolute poverty.

Canada has a fairly typical distribution of income for an industrial economy. As study after study shows, Canada is a wealthy country, and how to divide that wealth continues to stimulate much political debate. In the end, definitive answers about what is fair continue to elude us, and we are no closer to an answer today than when Marx, Smith, and Ricardo debated this issue over a century and a half ago. The lack of a conclusive answer, however, should not deter us from asking this question. Once we fail to do so, someone else's version of "what's fair" is sure to win out.

NOTES

1. Inflation refers to rising prices. To remove the effect of inflation we use "real" or "constant" dollars, a common procedure applied to historical comparisons of this sort. This method better reflects the purchasing power of money; that is, what a dollar can buy. A bottle of Coke that cost ten cents in the 1950s costs a dollar or

more now. The purchasing power of our money has decreased. What once cost a dime now costs a loonie. But then our incomes have increased, so the question becomes, "Is a Coke more affordable now than in the fifties?" In Canada we use the consumer price index (CPI) as a method of evaluating price changes (and inflation). By purchasing a similar basket of goods and services (e.g., milk, haircuts) month after month, we can calculate how much prices are increasing because of inflation. Incomes can then be adjusted so that we subtract or remove the effect of inflation, and examine real purchasing power, as shown in Figure 5-1.

2. When Statistics Canada presents its findings on income, it provides both average (total earnings divided by the number of cases) and median incomes (the amount earned by the family, located midway between the highest and lowest income). Statistics Canada tracks both types of income because averages can be unduly inflated by even a small number of very high incomes. For example, the average of a bank president earning $1 million a year and 100 bank clerks earning $12 000 a year would be close to $22 000, vastly overstating the salary of the average bank employee. For that reason, some argue, median income is a better indicator of what the "typical" family or individual earns (which, by the way, would be $12 000 for the bank employees in our example).

3. Between 1990 and 1999 (in constant 1999 dollars), market income for low-income families dropped from $5276 to $4590, while transfers remained almost constant at $6732 and $6703 respectively (Statistics Canada 2000). For evidence of the growing proportion of market income flowing to the highest quintile see any of the recent issues of *Income in Canada*, Statistics Canada Catalogue 75-202-XIE.

4. The precise amount of income tax people pay depends upon a complex array of factors, including the amount of money earned and the methods by which the money was earned (e.g., wages, interest, capital gains). The following information includes federal tax only. Each province also collects its share of income tax. At present, all Canadians pay no federal income tax on the first $7412 they receive. After that, any additional earnings below $30 754 are taxed at a rate of 16%. Between $30 754 and below $61 509, income is taxed at 22%. Between $61 509 and below $100 000, income is taxed at 26%. Earnings starting at $100 000 are taxed at 29%. In effect, as your income rises, you pay higher rates of income tax. This is progressive taxation.

REFERENCES

Hewitt, Christopher 1977. "The effect of political democracy and social democracy on equality in industrial societies: A cross-national comparison." *American Sociological Review* 42:450–464.

Hunter, Alfred 1993. "The changing distribution of income." In Curtis, Grabb, and Guppy (eds.), *Social Inequality in Canada* (3rd ed.). Scarborough: Prentice Hall.

Osberg, Lars 1992. "Canada's economic performance: Inequality, poverty and growth." In Allen and Rosenbluth (eds.), *False Promises, the Failure of Conservative Economics*, pp. 39–52. Vancouver: New Star Books.

Statistics Canada 2000. *Income in Canada*. Catalogue 75-202-XIE. Ottawa.

Statistics Canada Various years. *Income Distributions by Size in Canada*. Catalogue 13-207-XPB. Ottawa.

Teeple, Gary 1995. *Globalization and the Decline of Social Reform*. Toronto: Garamond Press.

Therborn, Göran 1986. *Why Some People Are More Unemployed Than Others*. London: Verso Books.

World Bank 2002. *The World Development Report*. Washington.

6

THE DISTRIBUTION OF WEALTH AND ECONOMIC INEQUALITY

James B. Davies

(Revised from the previous edition of this volume.)

INTRODUCTION

This paper addresses a series of questions about the distribution of wealth and economic inequality in Canada. First, what is wealth and how is it distributed among families in Canada? Second, what determines how wealth is distributed? Third, why should we care? Finally, how does wealth mobility affect our views about wealth inequality?

WHAT IS WEALTH?

A person's wealth equals the value of all their assets minus debts at a moment in time. This concept is also referred to as "net worth." The assets that must be included cover a wide range. They include, for example, cash, bank deposits, owner-occupied housing, guaranteed investment

certificates (GICs), registered savings plans (RSPs), stocks, bonds, mutual funds, consumer durables, real estate, and machines and equipment used in unincorporated businesses. There is also a wide variety of debts—mortgages, credit card balances, personal loans, small business loans, and so forth.

Table 6-1 indicates the relative importance of the different forms of wealth at the end of 2001. Note, first, that 35.0 % of the total value of assets is made up of real estate, the most important form of which is residential housing. Financial assets have been increasing in relative importance in recent years and now, at 56.6% of the total, are more important than nonfinancial. Among financial assets, stocks and bonds (excluding Canada Savings Bonds, or "CSBs") make up only 17.5 % of total assets. More widely distributed

TABLE 6-1   **Year-End National Balance Sheets—Persons and Unincorporated Business, Canada, 2001**

	Assets (in millions)	% of Assets
I. Nonfinancial Assets		
Residential Structures	$816 493	19.9%
Nonresidential Structures	26 465	0.6
Land	593 249	14.5
Consumer Durables	306 288	7.5
Machinery, Equipment, & Inventories	33 223	0.8
Total	1 775 718	43.4
II. Financial Assets		
Cash and Deposits	588 378	14.4
Canada Savings Bonds	23 819	0.6
Other Canadian Bonds	58 067	1.4
Life Insurance and Pensions	937 136	22.9
Stocks	658 614	16.1
Miscellaneous	52 418	1.3
Total	2 318 432	56.6
TOTAL ASSETS	4 094 150	100.0
III. Debt		
Mortgages	465 910	11.4
Other Debt	277 642	6.8
Total	743 552	18.2
NET WORTH	3 350 598	81.8

Source: These data originate from the Statistics Canada CANSIM Database, Series D16000-D160069 and Series D18639. CANSIM is an official Mark of Statistics Canada.

assets like cash, bank accounts, life insurance, and pensions make up the bulk of the total.

Some urge the use of a broader definition of wealth—one that would include, for example, the value of pension rights, both private and public. Although such wealth is illiquid, people with pension rights are better off than others. The amounts involved are also substantial. This is reflected to some extent in Table 6-1, in the pensions and insurance line. However, the value of rights to old age pension benefits (both Old Age Security and Guaranteed Income Supplement) and Canada Pension Plan/Québec Pension Plan (CPP/QPP) benefits should also be included. Estimates of such "social security wealth" in the United States vary from about 40% to 200% of conventional net worth.[1]

Finally, it is often argued that the present value of future labour earnings—that is, "human wealth"—should be included. As for social security wealth, data availability is a barrier. Estimating human wealth requires projecting future earnings. A wide range of estimates of aggregate human wealth is available. (See the appendix to Davies and Whalley 1991.) A best-guess estimate is that the total value of human wealth equals about three times that of non-human, or "physical" wealth.

HOW IS WEALTH DISTRIBUTED IN CANADA?

The best answer to the question "How is wealth distributed in Canada?" may be "We don't know." In Canada the major sources of information on the distributions of income and wealth among families are from Statistics Canada's household surveys. The most recent wealth survey, the Survey of Financial Security (SFS), was conducted in the early summer of 1999. Earlier data were provided by the Survey of Consumer Finance (SCF) for 1970, 1977, and 1984. All surveys are subject to sampling and nonsampling error. These sources of error are especially important in wealth surveys.

Sampling error is the difference between the sample value of a statistic, e.g., average wealth, and its true *population* value. The larger the sample, the smaller this error is likely to be. For characteristics like national means, it is generally small, since the sample sizes used by Statistics Canada are very large. (The SFS sampled approximately 23 000 homes.) Estimating the shape of the overall *distribution* of a highly skewed variable like wealth, however, can involve significant sampling error.[2] Most samples will select too few rich households, although a few samples will have too many rich households. This problem can be addressed by oversampling in the upper tail. This approach was not generally followed by the SCF, but the 1999 SFS uses a special high-income sample of 2000 households.

Nonsampling error is an especially serious problem in wealth surveys. It takes two forms. First, some people refuse to be interviewed. Studies indicate that the likelihood of this nonresponse varies with age, region, and income. These problems can be corrected through weighting families according to their likelihood of being in the sample. Differential response across age groups, for example, can be almost entirely corrected. However, it is only when differential response according to wealth is highly correlated with differential responses according to observable characteristics (age, region, size of urban area, etc.) that this type of error can be adequately corrected by weighting. Since the correlation is far from perfect, differential response remains a problem.

Another form of nonsampling error—misreporting—occurs because people sometimes refuse to report certain items, or make mistakes. In cases where people report that they own an asset but do not report its value, an imputed value can be assigned. However, no correction is possible if the interviewers do not know that the family owns an asset. Studies in the United States indicate that, on average, assets like bank accounts are underreported by 40% to 50%. Other assets are more accurately reported. The value of owner-occupied houses, for example, is, on average, reported with surprising accuracy. (See Davies 1979b.)

Some of the results of these combined errors are well known for the *income* distribution. While wages and salaries are, on average, reported fairly accurately, SCF estimates of average transfer payments were about 20% less than the true figures, and the shortfall was about 50% for investment income. The situation is worse for wealth surveys. The Spring 1984 SCF estimates of stock ownership, for example, were only about 14% of the year-end 1983 national balance sheet totals. Estimates for other assets are not as bad, and some, such as housing, are fairly accurately represented.

Keeping all of these reservations in mind, let us look at Table 6-2, which shows estimates of the income and wealth distributions in Canada. Note, first, that there is more dispersion in the distribution of wealth than of income. The share of the top 10% of families according to wealth is 53%. The corresponding income share, when the families are sorted by income, is 26.5%. Much the same contrast is observed in other countries.

Table 6-2 indicates that mean wealth was $199 664 in 1999, more than three times the level of mean income. This figure does not give us a good idea of the wealth of a typical family, however. The situation of an average family is better

represented by median wealth, which stood at $81 000 in 1999.[3] It is only in the top three deciles of the distribution that wealth is above the $200 000 mark. Median wealth in the top 10% of the population was $703 500. Thus, most of the top 10% of families are not millionaires. True riches are confined to quite a small fraction of the population.

It is interesting to know as much as possible about the highest wealth-holders. So far, information on the top 5% or top 1% of families is not available from the 1999 SFS. The most recent information on these select groups, in fact, is from the 1984 SCF. In that survey, there were approximately 100 000 families in this category, and their average wealth was $1 434 000. In 1999 there would have been about 120 000 families in the top 1%, and if their wealth had increased by

TABLE 6-2	Distributions of Income and Wealth, Families and Unattached Individuals, Canada, 1995 and 1999	
	Income (1995)	Wealth (1999)
Decile Shares	%	%
1	1.5	–
2	3.6	–
3	5.0	1
4	6.4	2
5	7.9	3
6	9.4	5
7	10.9	8
8	13.1	11
9	15.9	17
10	26.5	53
Mean	$54 583	$199 664
Median	46 951	81 000

Source: Adapted from the Statistics Canada publications *Family Income: 25 Years of Stability and Change*, Catalogue 75-001, Spring 1999, Vol. 11, No.1, *Canada Year Book*, Catalogue 11-402, 2001, Table 6.14, p. 216 and from *The Assets and Debts of Canadians: An Overview of the Results of the Survey of Financial Security*, Catalogue 13-595, March 2001, Table 3.1, p. 9 and Table 3.10a, p. 22.

the average amount since 1984, their mean wealth would have been $3 354 000.[4] This amount is still not what most people would consider a great fortune. Thus, the "top 1%" and the "super rich" are not the same thing. The latter are a small minority of the top 1%.

For the reasons discussed above, the figures shown in Table 6-2 are affected by important sources of error. When attempting to get an accurate picture of a highly skewed distribution, it is inevitable that less accuracy will be achieved in the "tails" of the distribution. Survey-based wealth distribution estimates invariably miss much of the upper tail. The richest family in the 1984 SCF, for example, had a net worth of only about $6 million, whereas it is well known that Canada had several billionaire families at that time.

The limitations of sample surveys mean that we should turn to alternative sources. Davies (1993) examined a number of these. They include both journalistic accounts and studies by private firms.

Various magazines and newspapers publish lists of the seriously wealthy—for example, the world's billionaires. In 1989, *Fortune* magazine included eight billionaire families with at least partial Canadian residence on such a list. In 1997, *Forbes* magazine listed four such Canadian billionaires. There is evidence that the number of Canadian billionaires increased greatly in the late 1990s and early 2000s. In May 2002, the *National Post* listed twenty-seven Canadians whose net worth was estimated to exceed $1 billion (*National Post* 2002). The top three of these individuals were Ken Thomson, a media and online database tycoon, at $27.7 billion; Galen Weston, in groceries, retail, and real estate, at $10.2 billion; and the Bombardier/ Beaudoin family, in transportation, with $4.6 billion.

There is also journalistic evidence on the sub-billionaires. The *National Post* listed twenty-three families with between $500 million and $1 billion. In an earlier era, there was even more complete information. Newman (1975) attempted to provide a complete list of all Canadian families with wealth over $20 million, or about $60 million in today's dollars. There were 160 families on his list. The list of the corporate wealthy provided by Francis (1986) indicated thirty-two families with wealth over $100 million. Using this evidence, Davies (1993) "guesstimated" that the share of the top 1% in the Canadian wealth distribution in the 1970s and 1980s was probably around 25%. This proportion implies significantly more concentration than suggested by the SCF wealth distribution, which placed the share at around 18%.

It is interesting to try to put the Canadian wealth distribution in international perspective. Sweden, the United Kingdom, and the United States have "estate-multiplier" evidence on the distribution of wealth among *individuals*, and the United States, in addition, has considerable survey evidence for families.[5] The estate-multiplier evidence indicates falling wealth inequality in Sweden, the U.K., and the U.S. from the 1920s up to the mid-1970s. Since then, there has been stability, more or less, in the U.K., a shallow rising trend in Sweden, and a sharp increase in wealth inequality in the U.S. (See Davies and Shorrocks 2000, Figure 1, p. 639.) As of 1990, the share of the top 1% was about 20% in Sweden and the U.K., and around 35% in the U.S.

Sample surveys of wealth-holding in the U.S. over the last two or three decades have consistently shown a high level of inequality, and support the conclusion that inequality has been increasing. For example, the excellent 1963 Survey of Financial

Characteristics of Consumers (SFCC) conducted for the Federal Reserve Board found a share of the top 1% of families of 31.8%. After all adjustments, including the imputation of an upper tail for wealth-holders with more than $60 million, the 1983 Survey of Consumer Finance (SCF) indicated a share of the top 1% of about 37% (Avery et al., 1988, pp. 356–361). Wolff (1994) reports that, between 1983 and 1989, the share of the top one-half percent increased by 5%, suggesting that the share of the top 1% around 1990 may have been in excess of 40% in the U.S.

The contrast between estimates of wealth inequality in Canada and the United States is interesting. While an in-depth study has not been done for Canada recently, the evidence from the 1980s indicated a share of the top 1%, at about 25%, that was considerably below comparable shares in the U.S. The fact that survey estimates indicate more wealth concentration in the U.S. than in Canada likely reflects a real difference between these countries, rather than a statistical error. There are probably many contributing reasons for this difference, including the more equal distribution of *income* in Canada. However, it is worth noting that part of the difference is also simply due to where the world's corporate wealth is held. The U.S. is clearly still the most important international centre of corporate wealth. It has "more than its share" of millionaires. In contrast, about 35% of Canadian business is foreign-owned. Thus, Canada has a large number of "missing millionaires." This pattern shows up in less concentration of wealth-holding among Canadians than among Americans.

WHAT DETERMINES HOW WEALTH IS DISTRIBUTED?

Wealth is the result of past accumulation, and comes from two main sources: labour income ("earnings"), or gifts and inheritances. Both provide resources that can be either saved or consumed. Resources that are saved can accumulate at different rates. Wise or lucky investors earn high rates of return; others, lower rates. Finally, given the lifetime path of earnings, savings, etc., up until retirement, the older the consumer, the greater tends to be his or her wealth. Thus, current wealth depends on past earnings, inheritances (including gifts), savings rates out of earnings and inheritances, rates of return, and age.

It is sometimes suggested that a large part of wealth differences might simply be explained by age. To illustrate this possibility, examples of societies that are egalitarian but that also display considerable wealth concentration are sometimes devised. For instance, consider a society with zero population growth and a zero rate of interest, in which everyone works for forty years and then retires for ten years. Assume that, while earning a constant amount during their working years, people save at a constant rate, and then "*dissave*" at a constant rate during retirement, ending life with zero wealth. The wealthiest people would be those who were at stages just before and just after retirement age. In this world, the share of the top 10% of wealth-holders would be about 19%.

At first glance, the fact that a 19% share for the top 10% could be generated from age differences alone might seem impressive. However, this does not mean that a large part of wealth concentration is explained by age in the real world, for at least two reasons. First, if we look at the top 1% in the example, we find that their wealth share is just 2%. By altering the details of the example, one could get this share to 3% or 4 %, but this would still be far short of the estimated real-world shares. Second, the assumed variation of wealth with age is not realistic. In the real world there is a less extreme pattern. On average, people save for the first few years after retirement and only dissave slowly beyond that point. (See Burbidge and Robb 1985.)

In Davies (1979a), I developed a micro-simulation model which can be used to *decompose* wealth inequality. (See Davies 1982 for a summary.) That is, it is possible to see how wealth inequality would be reduced if we eliminated differences in earnings, inheritances, savings rates, rates of return, and age. The most important factor was inheritance, followed by differences in savings rates. Differences in earnings, rates of return, and age were of lesser importance and similar to each other in impact. (See Davies 1982, Table I, p. 489.[6])

There is other evidence on the importance of inheritance. First, Wedgwood (1929) investigated the sources of wealth held by rich British decedents in a twelve-month period during 1924–1925. Of ninety-nine persons dying with at least 200 000 pounds, which was a fortune at the time, about 60% had a predecessor, usually a parent, who had died leaving at least 50 000 pounds, and about 70% had predecessors who left at least 10 000 pounds (Wedgwood 1929, pp. 138–139). This work was updated by Harbury and Hitchens (1979), who found similar results for the 1950s, 1960s, and 1970s. As reported by Brittain (1978, Chapter 1), studies by *Fortune* magazine in the U.S. on top American wealth-holders concluded that about half were "self-made." However, sample surveys of the entire population indicate that a larger fraction—

as many as 60%—of those in top wealth groups had received some inheritance (Brittain 1978, p. 18). The implication of these studies is that in both the U.K. and the U.S. at least half of the genuinely wealthy have benefited to some extent from inheritance.

While the distribution of wealth is more unequal than that of income, the distribution of inherited wealth is much more unequal than that of wealth in general. Sample surveys indicate that the majority of people have never received an inheritance (see, e.g., Brittain, 1978, p. 18), and a majority will likely never receive significant amounts in gifts or bequests. On the other hand, a small minority receive truly spectacular amounts. It is this extreme concentration, rather than the total amount being passed on, that makes inheritance an important determinant of wealth inequality.

What makes inherited wealth so concentrated? Ironically, part of the answer lies in the great importance of human wealth. The majority of families find that investing in their children's human capital, via upbringing and education, is more effective than providing gifts and bequests. But some families are in a position to provide more. First, some provide for their heirs by passing along family businesses, including farms. Second, some exhaust the attractive opportunities for investing in their children's education and upbringing before their benevolence has been used up. Third, the lure of bequests may be used to elicit attention from children in a form of exchange. (See Sussman et al. 1970 and Cox 1987.) The genuinely wealthy would almost all be in one of these three categories, and we therefore expect to see them making a considerable use of bequests.

The extent of concentration in inheritance depends on practices of estate division, fertility, and choice of marital partner. (See Atkinson 1983, pp. 183–189.) At one extreme, in some societies *primogeniture* is practised. Under this arrangement, the entire estate passes to the eldest son (or daughter in the absence of a son). This keeps large estates intact, and preserves wealth inequality over time. At the opposite extreme, many families practise equal division of estates. Especially where families are large, which was true in North America in the nineteenth and early twentieth centuries, this contributes to the rapid breakdown of wealth concentration. It appears that, in North America today, equal division of estates is the norm, although departures from this norm are observed.

Differences in fertility according to wealth can also have a sizeable effect. If the wealthy had smaller families than others, their wealth would be broken up relatively slowly by division among heirs, and wealth concentration would tend to be preserved. While this factor may have been important in some societies at some times, in Canada today, fertility differences across income and wealth groups are not large, so that it likely has a relatively small effect.

Finally, the extent of assortative mating is important. If wealthy sons marry wealthy daughters, inherited wealth can remain confined to a small minority of families. While there is positive sorting of mates according to wealth and income, the correlation in mates' backgrounds is far from perfect. Thus, there is a tendency for inequality to be broken down through wealthy children marrying nonwealthy spouses, as well as through division of estates.

WHY SHOULD WE CARE HOW WEALTH IS DISTRIBUTED?

One reason some people are concerned about the distribution of wealth is that they believe it has much to do with the distribution of power in society. This concern has several facets, since power can take political, social, or economic forms. As an economist, I am not especially qualified to comment on the first two forms of power, but it is important not to exclude them entirely from the discussion.

Some believe that the wealthy exert vastly greater political influence than others. This could be achieved through funding political campaigns, by bribing politicians and civil servants, by control of media, and through funding researchers who obtain congenial findings. Similarly disproportionate *social* power may accrue to the wealthy, e.g., through the impact of advertising and media content on values and attitudes.

While not all would agree about the extent of political and social power conferred by wealth in Canada today, there is little doubt that the wealthy can exert considerable influence by the channels mentioned. But what of the economic power created by the concentration of wealth? At first blush it might appear that the concentration of corporate wealth observed in our society must imply great concentration of economic power. However, to the extent that we maintain internationally open and competitive markets, the power of even large corporations is limited by the rigours of the marketplace.

In competitive markets, business initiatives are governed by the logic of profit and loss. In order to survive, firms have to strive to make as much profit as possible. If they do not take advantage of opportunities, someone else will. Factors like technology, consumer preferences, supplies of productive inputs, the regulatory environment, and taxes and subsidies really determine what happens. The preferences of individuals who control even large corporations may ultimately be unimportant.

One should not be complacent about the limitations that competitive and open markets place on individuals' economic power. The wealthy do not like such limitations and, like other groups, such as trade unions and professional associations, they can be expected to use their political power to try to achieve protection from competition. It is important for the electorate to be critical of weak competition policy, subsidies to private firms, special tax breaks, and other preferential treatment for private firms and wealthy individuals. In the long run, such vigilance may be more effective in preventing unhealthy concentration of power in society, and indeed in preventing undue concentration of wealth itself, than a strategy that attacks wealth concentration directly.

I turn now to a discussion of the second reason why wealth inequality may matter—that is, due to its implications for differences in economic well-being.

What determines the distribution of economic well-being at a moment in time? Often we attempt to summarize this distribution by looking at households' incomes over the calendar year. This is informative, but has its limitations. If two families have equal incomes, but one has $1 million in non-human capital and the other just $100 000, their well-being is likely to be quite different. This realization has prompted many observers to argue that we should look at wealth as well as income.

Wealth differs from income in that it is a store of purchasing power for the future. While most income is consumed in the year it is received, consumption of wealth usually takes place gradually over the lifetime of the consumer or, possibly, by his or her heirs. Thus, when we turn to wealth, we must change our focus to the long run.

The long-run differences in well-being of a cohort of Canadians of similar age are determined largely by the sum of their human and non-human resources—that is, by "total wealth." We might try to estimate the distribution of this total wealth among people aged 20–24, 25–29, 30–34, and so on up through the age spectrum. Knowing net worth, including the net value of pension rights and social security wealth, would be an important component of this exercise, but so also would be knowledge of the distribution of human wealth.

Since human wealth, on average, is considerably larger than non-human wealth, we might ask whether there is much point in studying the distribution of non-human wealth by itself. The answer is that, while looking at the distribution of wealth alone is a limited exercise, it is an important one. Although there is not a perfect correlation, people with high labour income also tend to have high wealth, so that, overall, wealth differences tend to reinforce differences in earnings. Also, the extremes reached by wealth in the upper tail are not matched by the distribution of human wealth. Thus, at the highest reaches, one can almost say that the distribution of non-human wealth *is* the distribution of total wealth. Looking at the top of the wealth distribution gives us unique and valuable information about the upper extremes of individual economic resources in our society.

Finally, we may ask a deeper question about whether the observed differences in wealth are really important. To what extent are these differences inequitable? In other words, do they represent true *inequality*? There is a wide range of possible answers to this question. Perspectives range from those of libertarians, on the right, to socialists, on the left.

Libertarians believe that, as long as wealth has been accumulated honestly, differences in wealth-holding are fair. Nobody has any superior right to that of the individual to enjoy the fruits of his or her past accumulation. Since there is no injustice, there is no "inequality." This is a highly individualistic approach.

Socialists have a very different viewpoint. The component of wealth that can be traced to inheritance, first of all, is considered undeserved, and certainly indicative of inequality. Second, some of the differences in past earnings and rates of return, which led to current differences in wealth, are regarded as unfair. In other words, aside from differences that are due purely to age, savings rates, or to "reasonable" differences in rates of return and labour earnings, all wealth differences would be regarded as unjustifiable by a true socialist.

Between the libertarian and socialist positions there is a large gap. What would a representative or "typical" Canadian think about wealth differences? It would be interesting to answer this question by means of a sample survey. In the absence of such evidence, one can only conjecture. My guess is that the typical Canadian probably believes that differences in inheritance are less justified than those in labour earnings. However, I would also guess that he or she does not believe that differences in inheritance have *no* justification. Parents' rights to pass on to their children the fruits of their labour are considered important by many. Public concern about tax loopholes is also widespread, so it is likely that the typical Canadian is also not entirely happy with differences in self-accumulated wealth. Thus, the average Canadian probably thinks that there is some true inequality involved in wealth differences.

HOW DOES WEALTH MOBILITY AFFECT OUR PERCEPTIONS OF INEQUALITY?

Wealth mobility exists if people change their relative position in the wealth distribution over time. Such mobility can take place both within lifetimes and from generation to generation. Within a lifetime, it is important to look at a person's wealth relative to others of about the same age. If this changes over time, and the change is not offset by changes in human wealth, then there is meaningful wealth mobility.

In fact, there is considerable wealth mobility both within lifetimes and across generations. (See, e.g., Menchik 1979.) While the majority of the rich have benefited from inheritance, there are many well-known, true-life "rags to riches" stories. Conversely, there are many wealthy heirs who have squandered their fortunes. And, over successive generations, there is even more mobility. It is sometimes claimed that "shirtsleeves to shirtsleeves in three generations" is typical. While this claim is exaggerated, the work by Wedgwood, Harbury and Hitchens, Menchik, and others does show that there is substantial intergenerational wealth mobility.

It is sometimes asserted that, given any level of wealth concentration, there will be less concern about inequality when there is a great degree of wealth mobility. But this is not obvious. It may depend very much on what kind of mobility we are talking about. For example, although there is wide respect for those who build up their wealth by working hard, and by saving and investing wisely, there can be great resentment of those who get rich via exploitative, questionable, or illegal activity. And, while the public probably doesn't have much sympathy with the downward mobility of spendthrift heirs, people may feel concern for those who have been forced out of business by unexpected technological change, recession, or international trade shocks.

It seems likely that people regard wealth mobility as desirable only when it occurs for good reasons. This comes back to the earlier discussion. Upward mobility that occurs through moderate inheritance, working hard, saving carefully, and perhaps also bearing risk and having good luck in investments may be considered healthy and acceptable, just as the wealth differences created by these factors may not be resented. However, people may disapprove of mobility that stems from what are regarded as excessive inheritances or earnings differences, unequal tax treatment, and so on, just as they disapprove of wealth differences that are caused by these factors.

Summing up, a reasonable degree of wealth mobility may be necessary, if the mechanisms that determine wealth differences in a society are to be regarded as fair. However, it is not *sufficient*. Hence, the fact that there is considerable wealth mobility in Canada and other Western countries shows that these societies are not caste-ridden, but it does not imply that the people of these nations should not be concerned about wealth inequality.

CONCLUSION

This chapter has tried to make clear the concept of wealth, has summarized the available evidence on how it is distributed in Canada, has discussed the determinants of wealth differences, and has asked whether these matter. The analysis has emphasized that, ideally, a comprehensive concept of wealth needs to be used—one that includes pension rights and social security wealth in addition to more narrowly defined net worth. The chapter has also stressed that even this broad concept of wealth leaves out the bulk of people's

economic resources, which take the form of expected future labour earnings or human wealth.

We have seen that wealth differences are much greater than differences in income, although the precise shape of the wealth distribution is unknown both in Canada and in countries like the United Kingdom and the United States, with much more research being done in the American case. Concentration in wealth-holding is the result of differences in inheritances, savings rates, labour earnings, rates of return, taxes paid, and age. Inheritance and the high rates of return earned by some entrepreneurs and investors together provide most of the explanation for the extreme length of the upper tail of the wealth distribution. The great stock market boom of the 1990s has drawn particular attention to the role of investment returns. It created a whole new group of billionaires in Canada and greatly lengthened the upper tail. Therefore, there may be a tendency at the moment to think of investment activity as the main source of great riches in our society. However, stock market booms come and go. Already, by the summer of 2002, there had been a "meltdown" in high-tech stocks, and the North American stock market overall lost all the capital gains it had created since 1997. With this downturn, temporary as it may turn out to be, the role of high investment returns in creating great wealth receded. In such circumstances, it may be easier to appreciate the role of other more stable factors, most notably inheritance, in creating the long upper tail of wealth-holding.

The chapter concluded by discussing why wealth differences matter. There are at least three key answers. The first is that great wealth may spell disproportionate power in our society. Although public vigilance and participation in democratic political institutions can reduce this power difference, these activities are unlikely to eliminate it completely. A second reason is that, particularly in the upper tail, differences in non-human wealth have an important influence on the distribution of economic well-being. Finally, while some wealth differences reflect factors that are widely regarded as justifiable inequalities—such as age, accepted differences in labour income, and voluntary differences in savings rates—other wealth differences, such as inheritance, unequal treatment by the tax system, and extreme differences in labour income may not win such uniform approval.

NOTES

1. Feldstein (1976) estimated aggregate social security wealth in the U.S. in 1962 at $382 billion. This was 54% of conventional net worth ($711 billion) in his study. Wolff (1987) obtains a range of figures for 1969, when conventional net worth had risen to $2904 billion. The estimates for social security wealth vary from $1194 billion (41% of net worth) to $5649 billion (195% of net worth), depending on assumptions about future growth in earnings, and social security contributions and benefits. (See Wolff 1987, Table 9.1, p. 219.)

2. A variable is skewed if its frequency histogram has one "tail" longer than the other. Distributions of income and wealth are highly positively skewed, meaning that they have very long upper tails. (A negatively skewed distribution has a long lower tail.)

3. The median is the level of wealth such that one half of the families have less and one half more. In sampling from a heavily skewed distribution such as that of wealth, the median is likely to be much more reliable than the average. Also, it is a better indicator of the wealth of the "typical" family. A family with wealth equal to the average would be at about the seventieth percentile. That is, it would be at an "upper middle" wealth level rather than in the "middle."

4. The definition of wealth used in the 1999 SFS differs somewhat from that used in the 1984 SCF. This accounts for about 10% of the apparent rise in wealth that is seen when comparing the 1984 and 1999 results. See Statistics Canada 2001.

5. Sweden, the U.K., and the U.S. have long time series of estate-multiplier estimates. Some other countries have isolated estimates. Survey evidence is available in many countries, but by far the most survey research has been done in the U.S. See Davies and Shorrocks (2000), Section 3, for a summary of the broader international evidence.

6. At about the same time that I was developing my simulation model, Michael Wolfson built another model, which he used to address similar questions. The Davies and Wolfson models differ in many respects, but they agree in ascribing the most important role in explaining the concentration of wealth in the extreme upper tail to differences in inheritance. See Wolfson (1977 and 1979). Interestingly, the conclusions from the Davies and Wolfson studies are consistent with the assessment of the famous University of Chicago economist Frank Knight, who devoted considerable thought to the determinants of personal wealth. As Knight wrote in 1923, "the ownership of personal or material productive capacity is based upon a complex mixture of inheritance, luck, and effort, probably in that order of relative importance" (Brittain 1978, p. 1).

REFERENCES

Atkinson, A.B. 1983. *The Economics of Inequality* (2nd ed.). Oxford: Clarendon Press.

Avery, Robert B., Gregory E. Elliehausen, and Arthur B. Kennickell 1988. "Measuring wealth with survey data: An evaluation of the 1983 Survey of Consumer Finances." *Review of Income and Wealth* 34 (December): 339–370.

Brittain, John A. 1978. *Inheritance and the Inequality of Material Wealth.* Washington: The Brookings Institution.

Burbidge, J.B., and A.L. Robb 1985. "Evidence on wealth-age profiles in Canadian cross-section data." *Canadian Journal of Economics* XVIII (November):854–875.

Clement, Wallace 1975. The Canadian Corporate Elite. Carleton Library No. 89. Toronto: McClelland and Stewart.

Cox, Donald 1987. "Motives for private income transfers." *Journal of Political Economy* 95:508–546.

Davies, James B. 1979a. *Life-Cycle Saving, Inheritance, and the Personal Distribution of Income and Wealth in Canada.* Ph.D. thesis, London School of Economics.

Davies, James B. 1979b. "On the size distribution of wealth in Canada." *Review of Income and Wealth* 25 (September):237–259.

Davies, James B. 1982. "The relative impact of inheritance and other factors on economic inequality." *Quarterly Journal of Economics* 47:471–498.

Davies, James B. 1993. "The distribution of wealth in Canada." In Daniel J. Slottje and Edward N. Wolff (eds.), *Research on Economic Inequality,* Vol. 4. Greenwich, Connecticut: JAI Press.

Davies, James B., and A.F. Shorrocks 1989. "Optimal grouping of income and wealth data." *Journal of Econometrics* 42:97–108.

Davies, James B., and A.F. Shorrocks 2000. "The distribution of wealth." In A.B. Atkinson and F. Bourguignon (eds.), *Handbook of Income Distribution,* pp. 605–675. Amsterdam: North-Holland/Elsevier.

Davies, James B., and John Whalley 1991. "Taxes and capital formation: How important is human capital?" In D. Bernheim and J. Shoven (eds.), *National Saving and Economic Performance.* Chicago: University of Chicago Press.

Feldstein, M. 1976. "Social security and the distribution of wealth." *Journal of the American Statistical Association* 71:800–807.

Francis, Diane 1986. *Controlling Interest: Who Owns Canada?* Toronto: Macmillan.

Harbury, C.D., and D.M.W.N. Hitchens 1979. *Inheritance and Wealth Inequality in Britain.* London: George Allen and Unwin.

Menchik, Paul L. 1979. "Inter-generational transmission of inequality: An empirical study of wealth mobility." *Economica* 46:349–362.

National Post 2002. May 25:WR4–WR6.

Newman, Peter C. 1975. *The Canadian Establishment,* Vol. 1. Toronto: McClelland and Stewart.

Oja, Gail 1986. "The wealth of Canadians: A comparison of survey of consumer finances with national balance sheet estimates." Statistics Canada, Labour and Household Surveys Analysis Division Staff Reports.

Shorrocks, A.F. 1987. "U.K. wealth distribution: Current evidence and future prospects." In Edward N. Wolff (ed.), *International Comparisons of the Distribution of Household Wealth.* Oxford: Clarendon Press.

Statistics Canada 1986. *The Distribution of Wealth in Canada, 1984.* Publication No. 13-580.

Statistics Canada 1995. *National Balance Sheet Accounts, Annual Estimates 1984–1993.* Publication No. 13-214.

Statistics Canada 1996. *Income Distributions by Size in Canada, 1995.* Publication No. 13-207.

Statistics Canada 2001. *The Assets and Debts of Canadians, An Overview of the Survey of Financial Security.* March, Publication No. 13-595-XIE.

Sussman, Marvin B., Judith N. Cates, and David T. Smith 1970. *The Family and Inheritance.* New York: Russell Sage Foundation.

Wedgwood, Josiah 1929. *The Economics of Inheritance.* London: George Routledge & Sons.

Wolff, Edward N. 1987. "The effect of pensions and social security on the distribution of wealth in the U.S." In Edward N. Wolff (ed.), *International Comparisons of the Distribution of Household Wealth.* Oxford: Clarendon Press.

Wolff, Edward N. 1994. "Trends in household wealth in the United States, 1962–1983 and 1983–1989." *Review of Income and Wealth* 40:143–174.

Wolfson, Michael 1977. *The Causes of Inequality in the Distribution of Wealth: A Simulation Analysis.* Ph.D. thesis, Cambridge University.

Wolfson, Michael 1979. "The bequest process and the causes of inequality in the distribution of wealth." In J.D. Smith (ed.), *Modeling the Intergenerational Transmission of Wealth.* New York: NBER.

POVERTY IN CANADA

National Council of Welfare

(Adapted from *The Poverty Profile 1999*, National
Council of Welfare. Reproduced with permission of the
Minister of Public Works and Government Services
Canada, 2002. Retrieved 2002,
http://www.ncwcnbes.net/htmdocument/
reportpovertypro99/Introduction.html)

INTRODUCTION

The National Council of Welfare is
encouraged that, for most Canadian individuals and families, poverty rates continued the downward trend from 1998
through into 1999. But despite eight consecutive years of economic growth and a
very impressive growth rate of nearly 5%
in 1999, it is clear that the wave of economic prosperity continued to fail the
poor. We are convinced that Canadian governments could have done more to prevent
many individuals and families from falling
into poverty. And they must do much more

for those who experience a long duration
of poverty. It is truly alarming that
between 1993 and 1998, pre-school children were the Canadians most likely to
have lived in poverty for all six years.

We were dismayed to see a rise in the
poverty rate for senior women at the same
time that the rate for seniors in general was
at an all-time low. We were also discouraged that, despite a small improvement,
the 16% of Canadian families headed by
single parents were still raising about 42%
of Canada's poor children. This is an
untenable situation in a prosperous country like ours. For Aboriginal peoples in

Canada, the situation is also one of small improvements in the face of great and pressing need.

Since 1965, Statistics Canada has used a household survey known as the Survey of Consumer Finances (SCF) to obtain information on the distribution of income and the nature and extent of poverty in private households in Canada. In 1993, Statistics Canada introduced a new survey, the Survey of Labour and Income Dynamics (SLID), with much the same objectives but using a different approach. While SCF took a snapshot of the lives of people at a particular point in time, SLID follows people for six years to see how their circumstances change over time. Starting with the 1996 reference year, SLID replaces SCF as the source of annual income estimates.

Since the publication of *Poverty Profile 1998*, our data have gone through two separate but overlapping revisions that have somewhat affected the numbers compared with earlier editions of *Poverty Profile*, but the patterns and trends remain consistent. The first set of revisions required the re-weighting of data from several years. Statistics Canada revised its low-income data for the period 1980 through 1993 in the 1994 version of *Income Distributions by Size in Canada*. These revisions included shifting population estimates to the 1991 census base, adjusting the estimates to correct undercoverage, and including non-permanent residents physically present in Canada. The National Council of Welfare has decided to use Statistics Canada's re-weighted counts for 1980 to 1993.

The second set of revisions aimed to harmonize standards and definitions between the Survey of Consumer Finances (SCF) and the Survey of Income and Labour Dynamics (SLID). For example, our data for 1996 to 1999 use the SLID

definition of a child as "all persons under 18 years of age, regardless of marital status." We have obtained data from Statistics Canada using the definition of a child for 1980 to 1995 that is consistent with the SLID definition.

Information about poverty is obtained by comparing the survey data with the low income cut-offs or LICOs of Statistics Canada. The cut-offs represent levels of gross income where people spend disproportionate amounts of money for food, shelter, and clothing. Statistics Canada has decided over the years—somewhat arbitrarily—that 20 percentage points is a reasonable measure of the additional burden. The average Canadian family spent 34.7% of gross income on food, shelter, and clothing according to 1992 data on spending patterns, so it was assumed that low-income Canadians spent 54.7% or more on the necessities of life.

The low income cut-offs vary by the size of the family unit and the population of the area of residence. There are seven categories of family size, from one person to seven or more persons, and five community sizes ranging from rural areas to cities with 500 000 or more residents. The result is a set of thirty-five cut-offs. The cut-offs are updated annually by Statistics Canada using the consumer price index.

The National Council of Welfare, like many other social policy groups, regards the low-income cut-offs as poverty lines and use the terms "poor" and "low-income" interchangeably. Statistics Canada takes pains to avoid references to poverty. It says the cut-offs have no official status, and it does not promote their use as poverty lines.

Regardless of the terminology, the cut-offs are a useful tool for defining and analyzing the significantly large portion of the Canadian population with low incomes. They are not the only measures of poverty

TABLE 7-1	Statistics Canada's Low Income Cut-Offs (1992 Base) for 1999				
Family Size	**Population of Community of Residence**				
	500 000+	**100 000–499 999**	**30 000–99 999**	**Less than 30 000**	**Rural**
1	$17 886	$15 341	$15 235	$14 176	$12 361
2	$22 357	$19 176	$19 044	$17 720	$15 450
3	$27 805	$23 849	$23 683	$22 037	$19 216
4	$33 658	$28 869	$28 669	$26 677	$23 260
5	$37 624	$32 272	$32 047	$29 820	$26 002
6	$41 590	$35 674	$35 425	$32 962	$28 743
7+	$45 556	$39 076	$38 803	$36 105	$31 485

Note: This table uses the 1992 base. Income refers to total pre-tax, post-transfer household income.

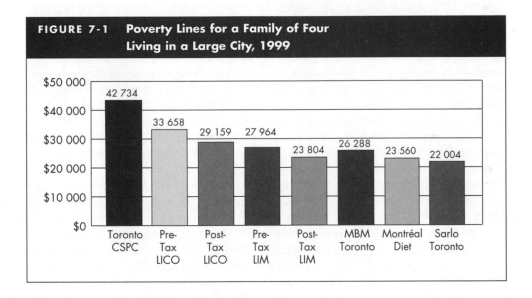

FIGURE 7-1   Poverty Lines for a Family of Four Living in a Large City, 1999

used in Canada, but they are the most widely accepted and are roughly comparable to most alternative measures.

Figure 7-1 shows eight alternative measures of poverty: two versions of the low income cut-offs of Statistics Canada (1992 base) and six other lines sometimes seen in other published reports on poverty.[1]

Toronto CSPC, the description of the first bar in Figure 7-1, refers to the budget guides of the Community Social Planning Council of Toronto, formerly the Social Planning Council of Metropolitan Toronto. The original calculation was updated to 1999 by the National Council of Welfare using the consumer price index and custom tabulations supplied by Statistics Canada.

The next two bars represent two different versions of the low income cut-offs of

Statistics Canada. The pre-tax LICO is based on total income including government transfers but before the deduction of federal, provincial, or territorial income taxes. The post-tax LICO is based on after-tax income—that is, total income including government transfers less federal, provincial, or territorial income taxes.

Pre-tax LIM and LIM post-tax refer to the low-income measures of Statistics Canada, both based on one-half of median family income. LIMs vary with family size and composition, but they are the same in all parts of the country. They do not reflect the reality of higher costs of living in large cities and lower costs of living in rural areas. The LIMs are the only lines in Figure 7-1 that do not vary from place to place in Canada.

MBM Toronto stands for the market basket measures being developed by Human Resources Development Canada for the federal, provincial, and territorial governments. The MBMs are very loosely based on the cost of buying a basket of goods and services in the local marketplace. The bar in this figure is for a family living in Toronto. The National Council of Welfare updated the figure to 1999, but the update does not reflect changes in methodology that were made after 1996.

Montreal Diet refers to the income needed for a minimum adequate standard of living for a two-earner couple with a 15-year-old son and a 10-year-old daughter in Montreal, as calculated by the Montreal Diet Dispensary and updated by the National Council of Welfare. The group also has basic needs guidelines strictly intended for short-term assistance that are somewhat lower.

Sarlo Toronto is the poverty line for Toronto calculated by Christopher A. Sarlo and updated to 1999 by the National Council of Welfare. Professor Sarlo also has "social comfort lines" that are twice as high as his poverty lines.

Poverty statistics are often broken down according to families and unattached individuals. The survey that gathered the data defined a family as a group of individuals sharing a common dwelling unit and related by blood, marriage, or adoption. The definition includes couples living in common-law relationships. Most of the data in this report is expressed in terms of families rather than the number of people in family units. Unattached individuals are defined as people living alone or in households where they are not related to other household members.

Poverty rates compare the number of poor persons, families, or unattached individuals in a particular category to all the persons, families, or unattached individuals in the same category. For example, there were an estimated 295 000 poor families with children under 18 headed by a female single parent under the age of 65 in 1999. The estimated total number of families with children under 18 headed by a female single parent under 65 was 570 000. The poverty rate was 295 000 divided by 570 000 or 51.8%.

Sometimes, the terms "incidence of poverty" or "risk of poverty" are used instead of "the poverty rate." The meaning of all three terms is the same.

Income refers to money income reported by all family members 16 years or older and includes gross wages and salaries, net income from self-employment, investment income, government transfer payments (for example, the federal Child Tax Benefit, Old Age Security, and provincial tax credits), pensions, and miscellaneous income (scholarships and child support payments, for example). The definition of income excludes gambling wins or losses, capital gains or losses, receipts from the sale of property or personal belongings, income tax refunds, loans received or repaid, lump-sum settlements of insurance policies, and income in kind.

RECENT POVERTY TRENDS

In 1999, as in 1998, most poverty rates dipped slightly. However, they remained higher than they were in the years immediately before the 1990–1991 recession. Over 4.8 million people in Canada, including 1.3 million children, lived in poverty in 1999. Poverty rates for persons under 65 years of age, especially single-parent mothers, young adults, and students aged 18 to 24 years, remained persistently high despite eight consecutive years of economic growth.

Poverty rates among seniors overall sustained a downward trend, falling from 19.7% in 1998 to 17.7% in 1999. Senior couples and unattached male seniors took the largest share of this decrease. For senior couples, the poverty rate decreased from 7% in 1998 to 4.7% in 1999; for senior unattached men, it decreased from 35.1% in 1998 to 31.9% in 1999.

One way to examine poverty is to look at the number of individuals who are living in poverty. In 1980, the poverty rate was 16.0% with just over 3.9 million people living in poverty. The number of poor people and the poverty rate rose following the recession of 1981–1982 and then declined slowly to a low in 1989 of about 3.5 million poor people and a poverty rate of 14.0%. The poverty rate and the number of poor people increased again with the recession of 1990–1991. However, unlike the 1980s, the number of poor people and the poverty rate did not decline following the 1990–1991 recession. Instead, the number of people living in poverty steadily increased to record highs while poverty rates stayed fairly constant at slightly more than 17%.

A new downward trend began in 1997 when the poverty rate was 18.2% and there were 5.1 million poor persons. A three-year decline and a poverty rate of 16.2% among poor persons in 1999 represent a sustained improvement for the first time since the mid-1980s. But this rate is still higher than it was at the beginning of the 1990s. There were about 0.7 million more poor people in 1999 at the close of the decade than in 1990.

Similar trends were evident in the child poverty statistics. In the 1980s, the number of children living in poverty and the child poverty rate rose with the recession of 1981–1982, peaking in 1984 and then declining for the rest of the 1980s. When the House of Commons unanimously passed a resolution in 1989 to work to eliminate child poverty by 2000, the number of poor children was 1 million and the child poverty rate was 15.2%. The recession of 1990–1991 drove child poverty up once again. It peaked in 1996, when more than 1.5 million children were living in poverty and the child poverty rate was 21.6%. The modest decline that began in 1997 continued through 1999 when 1.3 million children lived in poverty and the poverty rate was 18.7%. However, these figures are still substantially higher than the low of 1989.

Children are poor because their parents are poor, and a lack of good jobs is one of the main reasons for poverty among parents. The poverty rates for adults under the age of 65 tend to move up and down in line with changes in the unemployment rate. However, the link between changes in the unemployment rate and changes in the poverty rate was weaker during the 1990s than during the 1980s.

Compared with the 1980s, poverty rates in the 1990s did not fall as rapidly as unemployment rates. In the recovery from the 1990–1991 recession, the pattern changed. The unemployment rate steadily decreased, but the poverty rate was stickier. In fact, the poverty rate for adults under the age of 65 actually increased slightly. It was only between 1998 and 1999, after a downward trend in the unemployment rate over six years, that the poverty rate for working-age people decreased first to 15.5% in 1998 and then to 15.1% in 1999. The post-1991 cycle of economic growth appears to be bypassing many people at the lower end of the income scale. In 1999, the unemployment rate was 7.6% and the poverty rate was 15.2%.

While the poverty statistics for all persons give a good overview of poverty, it is often more revealing to look at poor people in terms of families and unattached individuals. Poverty rates for unattached people are normally two to three times higher than the rates for families. In 1999, the poverty rate for unattached individuals was 38.9% and the rate for families was 12.2% for a ratio of 3.2 to one.

The main reason that families have consistently lower poverty rates than unattached individuals is that they often have a second family member in the paid labour force. The percentage of younger married couples with both spouses in the work force has grown dramatically during the last generation, and two-earner couples now far outnumber one-earner couples. Many older couples are made up of spouses who both had careers outside the home and who both get pension benefits aside from the federal government's Old Age Security pension.

DEPTH OF POVERTY

An essential aspect of poverty is its severity. Poverty rates show the proportions of population groups that are poor each year; they do not show the extent of their poverty. Measures of the "depth of poverty" tell us whether people are living in abject poverty or are just a few dollars below the poverty line. In essence, depth of poverty statistics allow us to calculate the "poverty gap" to show how much additional income

would be needed to bring all Canadians out of poverty.

Figure 7-2 shows the average incomes of poor Canadians both before and after taxes as a percentage of the poverty line for the family types that were discussed previously.

With the exception of senior couples, whose post-tax sample size was too small, all family types were closer to the poverty line using post-tax measures than using pre-tax measures. However, the size of the tax effect varied. Unattached individuals under 65 were the poorest of the family types in 1999, with total pre-tax incomes that were only 51.9% of the poverty line on average for women and 53.4% on average for men. Unattached senior men and women had relatively high total income as a percentage of the pre-tax poverty line at 80.4% for men and 81.5% for women. Their income as a percentage of the post-tax poverty line was even better at 86.3% for men and 89.1% for women.

Another measure of the financial plight of poor people is how their incomes compare with average incomes. Table 7.2 presents the 1999 pre-tax and post-tax average incomes of poor Canadians and non-poor Canadians by family type. It shows that the average incomes of non-poor Canadians were, at the very least, more than twice the average incomes of poor Canadians for virtually all of the family types. For example, among couples without children, the average incomes of the poor were less than a fifth of the average incomes of the more affluent.

There is also a significant gender gap in the incomes of both poor and non-poor Canadians. Generally, families headed by men had higher average incomes than families headed by women. For example, among non-poor unattached individuals under 65 years of age, the pre-tax income

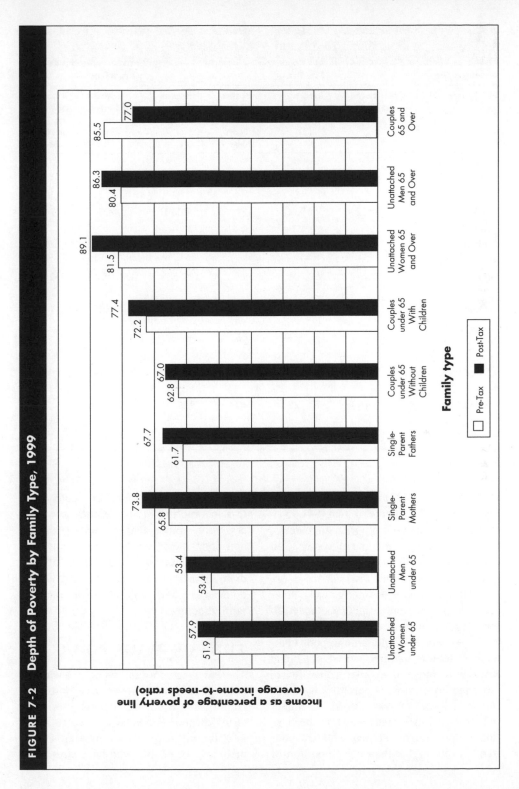

FIGURE 7-2   Depth of Poverty by Family Type, 1999

Income as a percentage of poverty line
(average income-to-needs ratio)

Family type

Pre-Tax   Post-Tax

Unattached Women under 65: 51.9 / 57.9
Unattached Men under 65: 53.4 / 53.4
Single-Parent Mothers: 65.8 / 73.8
Single-Parent Fathers: 61.7 / 67.7
Couples under 65 Without Children: 62.8 / 67.0
Couples under 65 With Children: 72.2 / 77.4
Unattached Women 65 and Over: 81.5 / 89.1
Unattached Men 65 and Over: 80.4 / 86.3
Couples 65 and Over: 85.5 / 77.0

TABLE 7-2	Average Incomes of Poor and Non-Poor Canadians, 1999					
Family Type	Pre-Tax			Post-Tax		
	Income of Poor ($)	Income of Non-Poor ($)	Income of Poor as (%) of Non-Poor	Income of Poor ($)	Income of Non-Poor ($)	Income of Poor as (%) of Non-Poor
Unattached Women Under 65	8436	38 492	22	7717	37 128	21
Unattached Men Under 65	8722	41 934	21	8068	40 477	20
Single-Parent Mothers Under 65	15 971	40 044	40	14 754	36 601	40
Single-Parent Fathers Under 65	14 466	52 706	27	12 534	51 039	25
Couples Under 65 without Children	12 232	68 012	18	10 411	66 638	16
Couples Under 65 with Children	22 892	78 564	29	20 576	76 850	28
Unattached Women 65 and Over	13 249	27 850	48	12 590	23 306	54
Unattached Men 65 and Over	13 153	32 922	40	12 390	29 437	42
Couples 65 and Over	18 185	45 724	40	*	*	*

*Sample size too small.

of women ($38 492) was, on average, less than the pre-tax income of men ($41 934). Similarly, among non-poor single parents, the average pre-tax income of women ($40 044) was only about 76% of the average pre-tax income of men ($52 706).

Among most poor family heads, however, women's average incomes tended to be slightly higher than men's average incomes. For example, among poor unattached seniors, women's pre-tax income was $96 more than men's. Likewise, among poor single parents, women's incomes were, on average, $1505 higher than men's. Differences may arise because the proportion of women who are poor tends to be higher than the proportion of

men who are poor and there tends to be less income inequality between poor and non-poor women than between poor and non-poor men. For families, there may also be differences in the number of children in male and female-headed households and child benefits could increase family income.

THE LOW-WAGE POOR

The low-wage poor or "working poor" are poor people who are normally in the labour force. Some researchers reserve the term for poor people who have full-time jobs for virtually the entire year. Others include poor people who have strong ties to the labour market regardless of the number of weeks worked or the normal hours of work each week.[2]

Overall, 25% of poor family heads under 65 worked full time in 1999, 33% worked part time, 10% were unable to work, and the remaining 32% did not work at all for wages.[3] The number of poor families was up to 828 000 in 1999, and there was a slight shift away from full-time work to part-time work or no work at all.

The patterns are slightly different for poor unattached individuals. In 1999, 16% worked full time, 38% worked part time, 28% did not work, and 18% were unable to work. In 1999, the groups that did not work and those who were employed full-time were both up by 3% while the other groups declined slightly.

Another way to define the low-wage poor is families and unattached individuals living below the poverty line who get at least half of their total income from employment. This definition puts aside the distinction between full-time and part-time work and focuses on poor people who spend a substantial part of the year in paid jobs. Fifty-nine percent of poor unattached men, 53% of poor unattached women and poor couples without children, and 55% of couples with children were working poor. However, only 24% of poor single mothers derived at least half of their income from earnings. This finding confirms earlier results: Due to parental responsibilities and not having an additional income earner, single parents are less likely to be able to support their families through employment and are more vulnerable to poverty as a result.

This report showed again that having a job, even a full-time one, is no guarantee against poverty. And the people who contribute in other meaningful ways to our society and economy, by improving their education as students or by providing care

for children and other dependants, faced the penalty of high risk of poverty. Canadians whose contributions were affected by disabilities or poor health faced a similar risk. In 1999, 40% of people with long-term illness and more than half of single-parent mothers were poor.

Poverty Profile 1999 shows that poverty rates generally continued a three-year downward trend. But Canada was still not doing as well as it was a decade earlier, despite eight years of solid economic growth. The overall improvement of 0.7% in poverty rates between 1998 and 1999 came nowhere close to matching the impressive economic growth rate of nearly 5% during that period. The Council considers this to be stagnation, at best, rather than progress. Our economic prosperity should have helped many more Canadians escape or avert poverty, including senior women living alone, whose already high poverty rate actually worsened in 1999. The National Council of Welfare also believes that Canadian governments have adequate resources at their disposal to fight poverty. That we can and must do so is far from an idle dream. The cost of poverty is one that all Canadians pay.

NOTES

1. Some of the information for Figure 7-1 comes from Chapter 2 of *The Canadian Fact Book on Poverty* (1994) by David P. Ross, E. Richard Shillington, and Clarence Lochhead, published by the Canadian Council on Social Development, and the 1996 edition of *Poverty in Canada* written by Christopher A. Sarlo and published by the Fraser Institute.

2. For a very strict definition of the term, see *The Canadian Fact Book on Poverty* (1994), p. 75. For a very loose definition, see the study commissioned by the Canadian Advisory Council on the Status of Women entitled *Women and Labour*

Market Poverty (1990) by Morley Gunderson and Leon Muszynski with Jennifer Keck, pp. 57–61.

3. "Full time" means the person worked at least forty-nine weeks during the year and the normal work week was thirty hours or more. "Part time" means the person worked less than forty-nine weeks a year or less than thirty hours a week.

THE PROS AND CONS OF REDISTRIBUTION POLICIES

Morley Gunderson

(Adapted from Morley Gunderson, *Economics of Poverty and Income Distribution*, Toronto: Butterworths, 1983, pp. 13–21. Reprinted with permission.)

INTRODUCTION

Arguments about income redistribution often evoke emotional responses because the well-being of individuals is involved and because the position of the debaters is often dependent upon where they themselves are on the income distribution scale. Whatever the motives, numerous arguments for and against income redistribution have been advanced.

ARGUMENTS FOR REDISTRIBUTION

In dealing with the arguments in favour of more equitable income distribution, it is useful to distinguish between two interrelated issues. One is the normative issue of why income redistribution should occur; the other is the positive issue of why it does occur. Income redistribution may well occur for reasons other than to satisfy a set of principles upon which society deems it should occur. The following arguments in favour of redistribution are advanced sometimes to explain why redistribution should occur, sometimes to explain why it does occur, and at other times to explain both. The first two arguments—diminishing marginal utility of income and underconsumption—are seldom advanced today; they are discussed because historically they have been advanced as arguments in favour of redistribution.

Diminishing Marginal Utility of Income

Early welfare economists advocated a move toward a more equal distribution of income on the grounds that the marginal utility of income to the rich was less than the marginal utility of income to the poor. Therefore, total utility or welfare could be increased by redistributing from the rich (who valued the income less) to the poor (who valued it more). This intuitively reasonable principle followed from the economic principles of diminishing marginal utility; that is, for a given individual the additional utility generated by an additional unit of consumption decreases as more of the commodity is consumed.

While it may be reasonable to assume that this principle eventually applies to the consumption activities of a given individual, there is no scientific basis upon which to make the comparison across individuals: Interpersonal comparisons of utility are not valid.

It may well be reasonable to assume that an extra dollar to a rich person means less than an extra dollar to a poor person, even though one could never formally prove that statement. Decisions often have to be made on the basis of beliefs that cannot be proven; for this reason, the concept of diminishing marginal utility of income may not be a bad rule of thumb.

Underconsumption View

To the extent that the poor consume a greater portion of their incomes than do the rich, redistribution from the rich to the poor could increase consumption—and hence aggregate demand—in the economy. This view has taken on particular appeal in periods of depression: Redistributing from the rich who save to the poor who consume would help the econo-

my spend its way out of the depression. The argument is in contrast to the one often advanced today that tax cuts to the rich would encourage them to invest (thereby improving the ability of the economy to produce without inflationary pressures), and this spending would eventually trickle down to the poor in the form of job opportunities and lower product prices.

While the underconsumptionist view has some intuitive appeal, there are a number of problems with the argument. First, it is not always clear that aggregate demand should be increased; in inflationary times the opposite forces may be needed. Constantly changing the income distribution so as to achieve macroeconomic objectives of having just the right amount of aggregate demand could clearly be dangerous. Second, if the objective is to change aggregate demand, then there are other well-known policy instruments, such as monetary and fiscal policies, to achieve the objective; there is no need to tinker with the income distribution. Third and most important, it is not clear what redistribution would do to aggregate consumption in the economy. Redistribution involves *changes* in income and, while the poor may well consume a larger portion of their *level* of income, it is not clear that they would consume a larger portion of small changes in that income.

It is hazardous to support redistribution on the grounds that it will have a desirable effect on aggregate demand in the economy; numerous hidden assumptions are involved for it to have such an impact. In recent years this rationale has also lost much of its effect because higher aggregate demand has not always been desirable owing to its inflationary impact. For these reasons the underconsumption view or the diminishing marginal utility of income idea tend not to be advanced today as rationales for redistribution.

Interdependent Utility

An economic efficiency rationale for redistribution can occur if potential donors (e.g., rich persons) care about the welfare of potential recipients (e.g., poor persons); that is, if the utility of the rich is a function not only of their own welfare but also of the welfare of others. Such benevolence or interdependent utility means that the donors can be made better off when the recipients are better off.

Unfortunately, such redistribution will not occur automatically through the marketplace because of the public-goods nature of redistribution. There would be insufficient incentive for an individual who cares about the poor to give to the poor, because the benefits of that redistribution would also go to other individuals who care about the poor but who do not give to the poor. In such circumstances it would make sense for the potential donors to vote for a certain amount of redistribution and to pay for that by taxes upon themselves. In that way they can share the costs of the redistribution they desire. The public-goods nature of redistribution implies that it may have to occur through the public sector under its tax system rather than through the private sector and its marketplace.

Donors may not only care about the welfare of the recipients; they may also care about the things that make up the welfare of the recipients. For example, donors may not value an increase in the leisure of the poor, but they may attach considerable weight to the poor spending on education, shelter, or food for their children. In such circumstances efficient redistribution may involve transfers-in-kind of these items rather than unconditional lump-sum transfers that the poor can use as they want.

Buy Behaviour and Avoid Conflict

Redistribution may also be seen as a device to influence the behaviour of the recipients, usually in the hope of reducing conflict between the rich and the poor. It can be used, for example, to avoid rioting, or in the extreme, revolution. Although the "War on Poverty" in the United States was conceived prior to the rioting in the 1960s, some would regard the substantial social expenditures at that time as attempts to bribe the poor to end the rioting. Marxists often regard redistribution (e.g., from land reform or from social expenditures) as a way of buying off the working classes in an attempt to thwart ultimate revolution. Such is especially the case if the redistribution is to those who pose the main threat, for example, potential leaders.

Buy Insurance

Redistribution to influence the behaviour of the poor can be thought of as insurance against consequences such as rioting or revolution, with taxes on the donors being the insurance premium. Donors may also want redistribution so as to guarantee a certain income floor in case *they themselves* should become poor. In this case they are insuring not against the behaviour of others but rather against a possible calamity that may happen to them. For this reason, donors may support, for example, certain programs like welfare, health care, or employment insurance.

Voting and the Political Process

The importance of voting and the political process has already been alluded to in the discussion of the rationales for income redistribution. Basically, the political process was seen as a device to set up taxes and transfers through the public sector, since the private marketplace would not guarantee the income distribution desired by society—the socially optimal distribution. Individuals were seen as willing to tax themselves so as to provide redistribution transfers because donors simply cared about the recipients, wanted to buy the good behaviour of the recipients, or wanted to buy insurance in case they themselves became poor.

The political process, however, may also be used in a more narrow self-interested fashion for voters to redistribute income in their favour. Downs (1957), for example, argued that individuals form political coalitions so that the state will redistribute income in their favour. Since the average income is inflated by the very high income of a few very rich people, more people will have an income that is below, rather than above, average. In seeking to maximize the probability of being reelected, politicians will try to obtain the support of the mass of voters with below-average incomes by redistributing in their favour.

This process may be offset, in part at least, by other factors. The rich, having the most to lose, will try to control the political process through mechanisms other than the "one-person, one-vote" procedure, which gives them little influence. They may use their wealth and influence to support a candidate; they may support policies to restrict the voting franchise to those with property; and they may support amending formulas requiring more than a majority vote. The rich may also try to "bribe" some of the lower-income groups out of a coalition that would involve mass redistribution. The poor themselves may not always support such coalitions because they feel they themselves will be upwardly mobile.

Marxists tend to emphasize that the rich will use the instruments of the state to maintain their position and prevent redistribution through the voting mechanism. Hence, transfers to the poor will be used selectively to co-opt revolution, and public expenditures on such items as the police and military will be used by the rich to protect their privileged position. In such circumstances the political process may be used to redistribute from the rich to the poor; however, in general, it will be used to redistribute from the poor to the rich.

Raise Income of Providers of Redistribution

Redistribution may also be supported to raise the income of those whose jobs and livelihood depend upon the redistribution *process* (as opposed to recipients who receive the transfers and donors who pay). In some cases this may be an obvious motive—for example, in the case of rich countries providing conditional aid to poor countries (on the condition that they use it to make purchases in the donor country), or providing transfers-in-kind such as farm produce or military equipment. In such circumstances the objective of the donor is probably a mixed one: to provide aid but to provide it in a form that benefits the donor country.

The motivation may be more subtle—for example, in the case of government employees whose jobs depend upon the redistribution process. (It is probably no accident that voters in Washington, D.C., tended not to support Reagan in the 1980 United States election.) Other groups, such as social workers (and even economists who do research in the area of income redistribution!), may also depend on their livelihood on the redistribution process. That is not to say that they would support income redistribution programs mainly to increase their own incomes; however, it certainly is easier to support redistribution when it is consistent with one's self-interest.

Social Contract Perspective

While theorists of social justice (e.g., Rawls, 1971) are mainly concerned with the issue of developing a set of first principles for determining how income ought to be distributed in society, and often with critically assessing the market as one instrument of income distribution, they can provide a rationale for redistribution within a market perspective. That is, income redistribution may be supported on the grounds that it is part of a social contract. We may simply prefer a society that provides a reasonable degree of equality to one that does not provide any. As Rawls (1971) suggested, if we were risk averse and had no information on where we could be in the income redistribution, we might well agree to a social contract that guaranteed a degree of equality. The fact that some individuals would not currently support such a notion simply reflects that they know where they are in the income distribution, and hence would not support redistribution from themselves to others. If they did not know whether they were going to be rich or poor, however, they might well support a social contract involving redistribution.

In this context the social contract can be thought of as a form of insurance. It is a set of principles that we agree to be bound by, presumably because the existence of the contract makes society better off than it would be without the contract—even though the contract may turn out to make some individuals worse off than they would be without the contract, once their position in society was determined or changed.

ARGUMENTS AGAINST REDISTRIBUTION

Incentive Problem

The main concern with income redistribution probably stems from its possible effect on incentives, and hence on economic growth and the size of the pie to be distributed. The concern is that if public policy taxes the rich to make transfers to the poor, then the work incentives of the rich and poor may be reduced.

The rich may have less incentive to work or invest because their earnings from these activities are being taxed. The poor may also have less incentive to work because they can afford not to, and because they often have to give up some of their transfer payments when they work.

While there may be counter-arguments as to why these effects are theoretically or quantitatively not important, or at least overemphasized, the fact remains that they can be important. In the extreme, if redistribution were to guarantee complete equality of income, what would be the incentive to work or invest? While existing redistribution schemes are not designed to achieve complete equality, the fact remains that their redistribution toward equality can have effects on the incentive to work or invest; these effects may reduce economic growth and hence the size of the economic pie available.

For this reason, those who are concerned with the adverse incentive problem tend to emphasize that it is easier to share a growing economic pie than to share one that is dwindling, because redistribution reduces incentives. Their belief is that the best way to raise the income of the poor is not through redistribution but rather through attaining growth through economic efficiency. This belief that the benefits of growth will "trickle down" to the poor is exemplified by the statement of goals in the *First Annual Review* of the Economic Council of Canada (1964:200): "The most effective 'war on poverty' will be effective achievement of potential output.... Steady economic growth would also make possible significant improvements in standards for low-income groups, and provide rising margins of income and resources over time for further advances toward more comprehensive and adequate services and facilities in the social welfare field."

Encroachment of the State

Concerns are also expressed over the fact that redistribution involves an encroachment of the state in areas where some feel that individuals or the family should be the principal decision-making unit. This can give rise to "state sovereignty" over "consumer sovereignty," and it can lead to the redistribution process being demeaning to the self-respect of recipients. It can give rise to large administrative costs that support public employees administering the redistribution. These costs may be irreversible and not necessarily responsive to the needs of the poor once a bureaucracy becomes entrenched.

Perverse Redistribution

Redistribution may end up benefiting the well-to-do more than the needy; in that sense it becomes perverse. This may occur not only because those who administer the redistribution may depend upon it for their livelihood (and they may be well-to-do professionals), but also because those who need the redistribution least may be better able than those who need it most to appropriate the benefits of redistribution. In addition, some universal programs designed to benefit everyone may in fact go disproportionately to high-income families, if, for example, they live longer to receive pensions, or if they have larger families to receive family allowances.

Some people may be poor because they lack the skills to make themselves eligible for income transfers. On the other hand, those who are skilled at making themselves eligible for transfer payments may be the least in need because they can utilize their skills elsewhere to earn a reasonable income. They are also the ones most likely to be able to obtain information on the availability of transfers and how best to become eligible, and they are probably more skilled at hiding their long-term position of wealth as opposed to their short-term low income.

As a result, there is some concern that income distribution programs beginning with the best intentions may evolve into perverse redistribution, as those least in need are best able to take advantage of the programs. This argument is not so much against the principle of redistribution but rather against what redistribution may evolve into. It becomes an argument against redistribution if such an evolution is inevitable.

REFERENCES

Downs, A. 1957. *An Economic Theory of Democracy.* New York: Harper and Row.

Economic Council of Canada 1964. *First Annual Review: Economic Goals for Canada to 1970.* Ottawa: Queen's Printer.

Rawls, J. 1971. *A Theory of Justice.* Cambridge, Massachusetts: Belknap Press.

B. OCCUPATION

EDUCATIONAL CREDENTIALS AND THE CHANGING OCCUPATIONAL STRUCTURE

Douglas Baer

THE POST-INDUSTRIAL ECONOMY

The Canadian occupational structure has undergone major changes since the early 1970s. As Clement and Myles (1994:3) note, "average wages and earnings have not grown and their distribution has become more unequal, and everywhere workers are faced with the insecurities and dislocations associated with globalization and technological change." This slowing of economic growth and widening of social inequality comes on the heels of late-twentieth-century trends, which were witnessed even during periods of sustained economic expansion prior to the 1970s. The most notable of these trends has been the shift in advanced Western economies from an economic system based primarily on the manufacture of physical goods (cars, television sets, refrigerators) to one based on

"knowledge goods" (computer software, television and movie entertainment, etc.) and on personal services (restaurant services, for example). This trend signifies what many writers refer to as a *post-industrial* economic order (Bell 1973; see also Esping-Anderson 1993; Myles et al. 1993; Clement and Myles 1994).

For people working in it, the new post-industrial economy has good and bad features compared with the previous world of work, which was dominated by industrial manufacturing. The "new" knowledge-based jobs are said to involve a less hierarchical (or "post-Fordist") structure with less routine and more room for individual initiative. For those painting an optimistic picture of this quickly emerging social future (see Bell 1973), technology has created a work world of meaningful, more pleasant jobs. At the same time, however, the new economy can also be said to promote unemployment and disruption through de-industrialization, to create a cadre of low-paid service workers whose jobs hardly partake in the advantages of the new "knowledge" economy (Myles et al. 1988), and to create a massive cultural divide between those with "good jobs" and those with "bad jobs" (Picot et al. 1990).

MORE WOMEN IN THE WORKFORCE

During the same period that the economy has moved away from an emphasis on industrial manufacturing, there has also been a rapid increase in the employment of women in the workforce. While there is a substantial literature on the continued occupational segregation of women, both between occupations and within occupations (Charles 1992; Fox and Fox 1987; Wright and Jacobs 1994; Birkelund et al. 1996; Hakim 1996), it is clear that the proportion of women in the workforce (and the proportion of the workforce that is female) has been increasing in most Western societies over the past twenty years.

Changes in the proportion of the Canadian workforce that is female can be seen in Table 9-1, which provides data from the 1971, 1981 and 1991 Canadian Censuses.[1]

The Canadian workforce steadily increased in size during this period, from 8.97 million in 1971 to 14.62 million in 1991. During the same time period, the female proportion of the workforce rose from 36.5% to 45.7%. Both changes—in the size of the workforce and in the female proportion—were slightly more pronounced in the period between 1971 and 1981 than they were in the period between 1981 and 1991.

DISCRETIONARY VERSUS ROUTINE JOBS

Which types of occupations have become relatively more or less important since 1971? To examine this question, we can employ the occupational coding scheme used by Bernard et al. (1994; see also Bernard et al. 1997). The original version of this scheme divides all jobs into twelve major categories on the basis of job skills and other related occupational attributes. For nonmanual occupations, these categories are higher managers, professionals, middle managers, semi-professionals (mostly teachers), technicians (including nurses), a single category for supervisors, forepersons, and artisans, and a category for all clerical workers. To simplify the tables somewhat, these major categories are further collapsed into (1) managers (middle and higher); (2) professionals; (3) technicians and semi-professionals; (4) forepersons, supervisors, and artisans (simply labelled "supervisors"); and (5) clerical workers. Manual workers are divided into two categories: service workers[2] and all other blue-collar workers. The division between "good jobs" and "bad jobs" does not correspond exactly to the division between manual and non-manual work.

As Rinehart (1996) notes, many white-collar jobs share with blue-collar jobs a number of negative attributes. These include low pay, a high likelihood of layoff associated with swings in the economy and with seasonal factors, routine work, an absence of job autonomy or job authority, and relatively low skill levels. In the end, only the degree of physical labour and some technical aspects of production (for example, the presence of assembly lines) differentiate blue-collar and white-collar jobs. A more important distinction, then, is probably the division between what might be called "discretionary" jobs—jobs with

TABLE 9-1	Gender Composition of Work 1971–1991			
Year	**Female**	**Male**	**Total**	**Number**
1971	36.5%	63.5%	100.0%	8 972 135
1981	42.0%	58.0%	100.0%	12 619 015
1991	45.7%	54.3%	100.0%	14 617 220

TABLE 9-2	Distribution of Discretionary vs. Routine Jobs, 1971 and 1991		
	Female	**Male**	**N**
1971	Managers	3.0%	8.3%	571 240
	Professional	0.8%	3.9%	250 000
	Semi-professional, technical	14.9%	8.3%	961 825
	Supervisors	<u>4.6%</u>	<u>15.4%</u>	<u>1 029 520</u>
	Total Discretionary	23.2%	36.0%	2 812 585
	Clerks	28.8%	6.0%	1 285 275
	Service	22.8%	11.7%	1 411 025
	Blue collar	<u>25.3%</u>	<u>46.3%</u>	<u>3 463 250</u>
	Total Routine	76.8%	64.0%	6 159 550
1991	Managers	8.5%	12.0%	1 522 415
	Professional	2.1%	5.4%	567 745
	Semi-professional, technical	17.5%	10.5%	2 003 630
	Supervisors	<u>6.3%</u>	<u>11.4%</u>	<u>1 329 310</u>
	Total Discretionary	34.5%	39.3%	5 423 100
	Clerks	29.1%	7.6%	2 543 110
	Service	18.1%	10.5%	2 039 945
	Blue collar	<u>18.4%</u>	<u>42.6%</u>	<u>4 611 065</u>
	Total Routine	65.5%	60.7%	9 194 120

skill requirements, interaction with people, and some degree of job autonomy and authority—and jobs that might be labelled "routine" jobs. This latter category would include both clerical workers and service workers.

Table 9-2 provides a picture of changes in the relative importance of the seven major job categories over the twenty-year period between 1971 and 1991. From 1971 to 1991, the number of routine jobs rose from 6.16 million to 9.19 million—an increase of 49%. At the same time, the number of discretionary jobs went from 2.81 million to 5.42 million—an increase of 92.8%. In both 1971 and 1991, there were more routine jobs than there were discretionary jobs, but the gap narrowed during the twenty-year time period.

Of the seven major occupational categories in Table 9-2, the categories with the least absolute growth (exhibiting a *decline* in relative terms) were supervisors and blue-collar workers. Many of the occupations listed under "supervisor" were forepersons and supervisors in factory settings, although white-collar supervisory jobs are also included in this category. In general, there has been a reduction in the proportion of workers involved in "lower management," signifying that jobs have tended to become less hierarchically ordered at the lower levels, or that there has been a decline in those job areas (industrial manufacturing, for example) in which multiple-level hierarchies extend down to the shop floor. Management jobs, however, are not disappearing: Of the seven occupational categories shown in Table 9-2, the category with the largest percentage increase was that of managers. The size of this group rose from 571 000 in 1971 to 1.522 million in 1991. The professional and semi-professional/technician category also saw growth rates of over 100% in the twenty-year time period. Only in the "supervisor, foreperson, and artisan" category has the expansion of discretionary jobs been relatively modest.

The percentages shown in Table 9-2 are column percentages, indicating what percentage of men and what percentage of women find themselves in a particular occupation. For example, the table shows that 3% of all women in the workforce in 1971 were employed as managers; the equivalent percentage in 1991 was 8.5%. The percentages in this table indicate that, for both males and females, the overall percentage of the workforce involved in discretionary employment has increased from 1971 to 1991. The increase has been more dramatic in the case of females; in 1971, only 23% of women in the workforce had discretionary jobs, whereas by 1991 this figure had risen to 34.5%. The comparable male percentage increased only slightly during the same time period, from 36.0% to 39.3%. For women, the major shifts were away from manual labour (down from 25% to 18%) and service work (down from 23% to 18%) and into discretionary job categories. The decline in the importance of blue-collar work was slightly less pronounced for males (dropping from 46.3% to 42.6%), but there has been an overall decline in this sort of work. The proportion of individuals in management increased in the case of males, from 8% to 12%. This increase is substantial, though not quite as dramatic as the increase observed among females. While women's likelihood of holding a management job improved in the time period from 1971 to 1991, it was still the case that, in 1991, a woman was less likely to hold a job in middle or upper management than a man (8.5% versus 12.0%).

The data presented in Table 9-2 do not show a massive expansion of jobs in the service sector—the so-called "McJobs" associated with waiting on tables and flipping hamburgers at fast-food outlets. Instead, the category of routine jobs that experienced a small amount of growth was the "clerical" category, which included receptionists, bookkeepers, secretaries, salespersons, and related occupations. Like jobs labelled "service," these jobs typically involve a moderate to high level of interaction with people, fairly low levels of formal skill requirements (for example, formal education qualifications required for the job), and relatively low earnings.

Overall, the numbers presented in Table 9-2 demonstrate the increasing importance of jobs with formal skill requirements in the newly emerging post-industrial economy. While traditional manual labour remains a significant facet of the occupational structure for males, its relative importance is declining. Many of the jobs in the expanding "discretionary" job categories have formal educational requirements in addition to specific skill requirements. All of them involve modest to high levels of generic "people skills," such as managing and coordinating the work of others, or interacting with the public.

AGE COHORTS: IS GETTING A GOOD JOB A MATTER OF BEING BORN AT THE RIGHT TIME?

The distinction between discretionary and routine jobs points to the importance of education in the process by which individuals end up with either good or bad jobs. Educational requirements are not the only factor influencing whether individuals will find themselves in one of the discretionary job categories. A body of mobility research points to the continued impor-

tance of parental social status on occupational outcomes (Erikson and Goldthorpe 1992; Westergaard 1990; Slomczysnki and Krauze 1987). For many discretionary jobs, occupational attainment may also be related to the sheer availability of positions, as members of one age cohort either block the mobility chances of successive generations by filling all available positions, or create new opportunities by retiring and leaving room for younger workers to enter vacant positions. While the demand for discretionary workers has clearly increased, it does not necessarily follow that the availability of these "good jobs" extends equally to all age groups. Some managerial jobs, for example, entail at least a nominal requirement of prior experience in the sector in question; thus, we might expect individuals who are under, say, the age of 30 or 35, to be fairly unlikely to obtain these jobs even if the demand increases. At the extreme, some professions may even be locked out to younger individuals who are better qualified than the older individuals already occupying jobs in that profession, as many graduates of teachers' college programs in the early 1990s can attest.

TABLE 9-3	Discretionary vs. Routine Jobs by Age, 1971–1991						
Year	Job Type	15–24	25–34	35–49	50–65	Over 65	Overall/Total
1971	Discretionary	16.2%	36.8%	36.8%	36.2%	39.4%	31.3%
	Routine	83.8%	63.2%	63.2%	63.8%	60.6%	68.7%
	N	2 353 215	2 026 445	2 599 910	1 699 890	292 675	8 972 135
1981	Discretionary	14.5%	39.1%	42.4%	38.5%	44.7%	33.6%
	Routine	85.5%	60.9%	57.6%	61.5%	55.3%	66.4%
	N	3 285 620	3 500 955	3 389 660	2 147 840	294 940	12 619 015
1991	Discretionary	15.6%	37.7%	45.3%	41.2%	51.3%	37.1%
	Routine	84.4%	62.3%	54.7%	58.8%	48.7%	62.9%
	N	2 720 190	4 127 365	5 102 740	2 352 530	314 395	14 617 220

Table 9-3 provides some indication of whether individuals in one particular age cohort did better than those in other age cohorts. It is clear from this table that individuals under the age of 25 were largely pegged into routine occupations in both 1971 and 1991. What changed, though, was that the proportion of individuals in this age group still in the education system went up. For employed individuals under the age of 25, the jobs they held were probably "transitional" jobs—either low-wage part-time or temporary jobs held at the same time as they went to school or between periods of schooling, or temporary jobs held just after graduation, from which they hoped to move eventually into more secure discretionary-sector jobs. It is common, when assessing the question of what happens to individuals at different levels of schooling or different levels of parental background, to focus on those who have completed their education, and to treat separately individuals under the age of university graduation (see, for example, Wanner 1996).

In Table 9-3, we follow this procedure by distinguishing those in the 15–24 age group. We also place people over the age of 65 into a separate category. The number of workers in this latter category is relatively small and also did not increase substantially from 1971 to 1991. This is because most individuals have retired at age 65. It is possible that, aside from individuals who are able to set up self-employed circumstances in their post-retirement years, these people consist mostly of high-demand workers or workers in a small number of professions in which mandatory retirement may not apply, such as medicine and law. The big increase in the proportion of people in discretionary jobs in the over-65 age group may simply reflect the increased inability of workers in routine jobs to hold on to a job or to find employment after mandatory retirement at the age of 65.

Aside from workers under the age of 25 and over the age of 65, there are slight increases in the proportions of people in the 35–49 and again in the 50–65 age group who hold discretionary jobs. In 1971, 36.8% of those in the 35–49 age group held discretionary jobs; by 1991, this percentage was 45.3%. Likewise, 41% of those in the 50–65 age group held discretionary jobs, which represents an increase from 36% in 1971. The shifts seemed to occur throughout the twenty-year period, although the improvement for the 35–49 age group was a bit higher from 1971 to 1981 (37% to 42%) than it was from 1981 to 1991 (42% to 45%). In addition to having a greater likelihood of obtaining a discretionary job, the 35–49 age group doubled in size from 1971 to 1991, a reflection of the passage through these age thresholds of the "baby boom" generation, i.e., individuals born after World War II and roughly prior to 1960. Did this generation fill up all of the "good job" spaces and leave the subsequent generation disadvantaged? From 1971 to 1991, the percentage of individuals in the 25–34 age group who were able to obtain discretionary jobs hardly changed—from 36.8% to 37.7%—while, in the entire labour force, this percentage increased from 31.3% to 37.1%. More dramatically, the proportion of individuals in the 25–34 age group who obtained discretionary jobs actually declined from 39.1% in 1981 to 37.7% in 1991; at the same time, there was an increase in the proportion of discretionary jobs across the entire workforce. These figures are at least consistent with the idea that earlier generations may have been more advantaged than those who entered the labour market between 1981 and 1991.

THE INCREASING IMPORTANCE OF EDUCATION

The importance of educational credentials in obtaining both stable, high-paying jobs and promotions into better jobs is fairly well known (see Blakely and Harvey 1988; Hou and Balakrishnan 1996; Ishida et al. 1997). All other things being equal—including the age cohort one was born into—it can be expected that better-educated individuals will do better in the job market, and will be more likely to obtain discretionary as opposed to routine jobs. The data presented below support this contention. Aside from the question of just how substantial this effect is in Canada, one can also ask about trends over the period from the 1970s. Has the general rise in educational credentials in the population, along with increasing demands on the part of prospective employers for educated individuals, eliminated the possibility that individuals without educational qualifications can still obtain a "good job"?

Table 9-4 provides an overview of the relationship between education and occupation from 1971 to 1991, using the broad categories of "discretionary" and "routine" jobs. Education is grouped into five categories: less than grade 12 (essentially, those without a high school diploma), grades 12 or 13 (usually, those with a high school diploma), some post-secondary (including community college graduates and individuals who attended but did not complete university), an undergraduate university degree, and a post-bachelor's university degree or certification (e.g., a Master's degree, a professional degree, or a Ph.D.).

It is clear from Table 9-4 that individuals with high school education are fairly unlikely to obtain non-routine or discretionary jobs, and that individuals with uni-

TABLE 9-4	Discretionary vs. Routine Jobs by Level of Education, 1971–1991					
		Grade 12	Gr. 12/13	Some Post-sec.	B.A.	Post-B.A.	Overall
1971	Discretionary	20.2%	28.3%	45.2%	78.7%	92.1%	31.3%
	Routine	79.8%	71.7%	54.8%	21.3%	7.9%	68.7%
	N	5 016 215	1 390 160	1 954 100	319 450	292 210	8 972 135
1981	Discretionary	18.9%	23.4%	40.2%	80.2%	92.0%	33.6%
	Routine	81.1%	76.6%	59.8%	19.8%	8.0%	66.4%
	N	4 763 850	2 356 020	4 177 210	857 520	464 415	12 619 015
1991	Discretionary	18.6%	25.5%	40.0%	77.6%	90.3%	37.1%
	Routine	81.4%	74.5%	60.0%	22.4%	9.7%	62.9%
	N	3 901 495	3 167 265	5 466 295	1 371 985	710 180	14 617 220

Percentages of workforce in each education category:

		Grade 12	Gr. 12/13	Some Post-sec.	B.A.	Post-B.A.	Overall
1971		55.9%	15.5%	21.8%	3.6%	3.3%	100.0%
1981		37.8%	18.7%	33.1%	6.8%	3.7%	100.0%
1991		26.7%	21.7%	37.4%	9.4%	4.9%	100.0%

versity credentials are fairly likely to obtain them. Individuals with some post-secondary education stand somewhere between these extremes. It is also clear that there has been a pronounced rise in the educational background of the Canadian workforce. In 1971, 55.9% of all individuals in the workforce did not have a high school diploma; by 1991, this proportion had dropped to 26.7%. The proportion of individuals with university education (adding the B.A. and post-B.A. columns) rose from 6.9% in 1971 to 14.3% in 1991.

At each level of education, the likelihood of obtaining discretionary work dropped from 1971 through to 1991. The competition for "good jobs" appears to have become stiffer over time, and the likelihood that a university graduate will end up with a routine job in 1991, while still fairly small, is slightly higher than it was in 1971. For individuals with one university degree (bachelor's level), the likelihood of ending up in the "routine" job sector actually went down from 1971 to 1981, from 21.3% to 19.8%, but rose to 22.4% in 1991. For individuals with post-bachelor's education, there was an increase in the likelihood of ending up with a "routine" job from 1981 to 1991, after virtually no change from 1971 to 1981. Of course, it is also the case that the size of this group of individuals increased fairly substantially from 1981 to 1991.

While the overall working population only increased from 12.6 million to 14.6 million, the number of individuals with post-bachelor's university education increased from 464 000 to 710 000 in the same period. In other words, there was much more competition for any available jobs at this level. An even more dramatic expansion took place in the group with B.A.-level education. While the overall labour force increased in size by 63% from 1971 to 1991, there was an increase

of over 300% in the bachelor's category—from 319 000 in 1971 to 1 372 000 in 1991. Despite this major increase in size, this group came very close to holding on to its relative advantage in the workforce since, as mentioned earlier, the likelihood of obtaining a "discretionary" job only dropped marginally, from 78.7% in 1971 to 77.6% in 1991.

Individuals with low levels of education do not appear to have been shut out of discretionary jobs entirely, even in 1991, since 18.6% of those with less than grade 12 education held such jobs in 1991. This may, in part, be due to older individuals, who obtained their jobs when credential requirements were not nearly so high, and continued to hold down places prior to their retirement and replacement by a new cohort with higher levels of credentials. Or it could simply be that education is not the only determining factor: It might still be possible for individuals in some sectors of the economy to hold management jobs, by establishing their own companies or by rising through the ranks of existing companies without holding educational credentials. The latter possibility is more likely to occur in the case of individuals who entered the job market decades ago, when educational credentials were less important, and can be sorted out to some degree by examining the effects of education within particular age categories.

WHAT HAPPENS TO PEOPLE WHO ARE NEW TO THE LABOUR MARKET?

Examining the occupational outcomes for individuals in a cohort in which many are still in the process of completing their education is likely to render a misleading impression of the relationship between education and occupational outcomes.

Individuals who are still in the process of completing educational credentials will typically hold part-time or summer jobs that are "routine" jobs. Such jobs hardly represent important elements in an individual's career trajectory, although small numbers of individuals, as suggested in Table 9-4, may find themselves chronically unable to obtain a good job both immediately after graduation and later in life. To obtain a sense of how succeeding generations fare in the job market, we can consider the situation of the 25–34 age group in each of the three census years. This is the youngest age category within which most individuals have completed their education. Certainly, a small number of individuals will still be in the process of completing professional university degrees after age 25, but this is the age at which the vast majority of individuals, even at the higher levels of credentialization, have entered the job market.

Table 9-5 shows that the educational credentials of those in the 25–34 age group have increased substantially over the twenty-year period from 1971 to 1991. Especially between 1971 and 1981, there was a big increase in the proportion of individuals, both male and female, with university degrees. By comparison, the proportion of individuals with university degrees remained fairly stable from 1981 to 1991, increasing slightly in the case of women (11.4% to 13.5%) and hardly at all in the case of men (from 11.9% to 12.0%).[3] By 1991, the proportion of the female workforce with university degrees in the 25–34 age group actually exceeded the proportion of men with such credentials.

The picture provided by Table 9-5 is more dramatic than that which is shown in Table 9-4, because this new table concentrates on those in the 25–34 age group, and does not include older workers who entered the workforce thirty, forty, and

TABLE 9-5	Workforce Education Level, Individuals Aged 25–34 in Workforce by Gender, 1971–1991					
		Grade 12	Gr. 12/13	Some Post-sec.	B.A.	Post-B.A.	Overall
1971	Females	309 615	125 425	225 305	35 680	21 085	717 110
	%	43.2	17.5	31.4	5.0	2.9	100.0
	Males	648 050	177 520	316 555	80 210	87 000	1 309 335
	%	49.5	13.6	24.2	6.1	6.6	100.0
1981	Females	348 805	322 090	604 670	172 885	62 010	1 510 460
	%	23.1	21.3	40.0	11.4	4.1	100.0
	Males	539 555	329 190	777 320	237 320	107 110	1 990 495
	%	27.1	16.5	39.1	11.9	5.4	100.0
1991	Females	270 070	463 030	859 880	261 895	82 790	1 937 665
	%	13.9	23.9	44.4	13.5	4.3	100.0
	Males	446 420	494 825	891 400	263 065	93 990	2 189 700
	%	20.4	22.6	40.7	12.0	4.3	100.0

even fifty years earlier. In 1971, 49.5% of the working males and 43.2% of the working females in the 25–34 age range had less than a grade 12 education. By 1991, these proportions had dropped to 20.4% in the case of males and only 13.9% in the case of females.

By 1991, individuals with less than high school education were the exception, not the norm. The most pronounced decline in the relative size of this group took place between 1971 and 1981 (from 50% down to 27% in the case of males, and from 43% down to 23% in the case of females).

Table 9-6 shows how individuals aged 25–34 with differing levels of education fared in each of the three census years. This table is also divided by gender, so that outcomes are examined separately for males and females. To simplify the table, only the percentage of individuals with discretionary jobs is displayed; in each cell, the percentage of individuals with routine jobs will simply be 100% minus the reported discretionary percentage. Thus, for exam-

ple, 91.0% of the females with less than a grade 12 education in 1971 held routine jobs (100% minus 9.0%).

In addition to showing the clear relationship between having higher education and obtaining a discretionary job, Table 9-6 contains some interesting gender patterns.

In 1971, there was a male-female difference in the likelihood of getting a discretionary job at all levels of education, but this pattern was much more pronounced in the lower education categories. By 1991, this gender difference for individuals with lower levels of education had been reduced considerably. This result occurred because the likelihood that women with low education would obtain discretionary jobs actually went up between 1971 and 1991. For men, the reverse was true: The likelihood that less-educated males would obtain discretionary jobs went down from 21% to 15% among those with less than grade 12, and from 46% to 25% of those with grade 12 or grade 13 education. It should be noted, however, that obtaining a discretionary job

TABLE 9-6	Type of Job by Education by Gender, 1971–1991, Individuals in the Workforce Aged 25–34					
		Grade 12	Gr. 12/13	Some Post.-sec.	B.A.	Post-B.A.	Overall
1971	Female % Discretionary	9.0%	17.7%	53.2%	83.0%	88.3%	30.4%
	Male % Discretionary	21.1%	46.0%	50.1%	86.3%	93.1%	40.3%
1981	Female % Discretionary	11.3%	18.0%	39.9%	77.2%	86.8%	34.8%
	Male % Discretionary	18.6%	32.9%	43.7%	83.1%	92.1%	42.4%
1991	Female % Discretionary	13.4%	21.6%	38.4%	75.4%	86.4%	37.9%
	Male % Discretionary	14.6%	24.5%	38.7%	78.3%	88.1%	37.5%

with less than some post-secondary education was still fairly unlikely for both men and women.

From 1971 to 1991, there was a drop in the proportion of discretionary jobs among individuals aged 25–34 with some post-secondary education but without a university degree. This drop occurred for both males and females. In 1991, 38% of both males and females held a discretionary job, a proportion twice as large as that for people with high school education. Even so, this 38% figure is lower than the 53% (female) and 50% (male) proportions observed in 1971.

Among those who were university educated, there was a slight erosion from 1971 to 1991 in the odds of getting a discretionary job, but this was not as severe as it was in the case of those with only some post-secondary education. For individuals with one university degree, there was a drop of roughly 8% for both males and females. For individuals with post-bachelor's credentials, the drop was roughly 2% for females and 5% for males. Here, unlike the case of individuals with some post-secondary education, the erosion was more or less continuous from 1971 through to 1991, except for males with post-bachelor's degree credentials, in which case the majority of the decline took place between 1981 and 1991.

Table 9-7 provides a detailed breakdown of occupational outcomes for the 25–34 age group, using the seven major occupational categories noted earlier, rather than the simple distinction between routine and discretionary jobs. To simplify this table, gender divisions and the intermediate 1981 year are omitted. Table 9-7 is organized so that columns add up to 100%. Each percentage represents the proportion of individuals in each education category who end up in the listed occupation. For example, 10.3% of all those individuals

aged 25–34 with less than grade 12 education ended up in a supervisory job in 1971. This figure fell to 6.5% by 1991.

Where do individuals with varying levels of education end up in the job market? Those with less than a grade 12 education are most likely to end up with blue-collar work; if anything, this likelihood is stronger in 1991 (59.3%) than it was in 1971 (54.8%). People in this education category are fairly unlikely to get jobs as managers, professionals, or semi-professionals. As mentioned in the example above, the likelihood that they will get jobs as supervisors dropped somewhat from 1971 to 1991, although this decline was balanced partially by a slight increase in the likelihood of obtaining managerial jobs, from 3.9% to 5.0%.

In 1971, individuals who had completed high school grades 12 or 13 had only a 25% probability of holding a blue-collar job; they were as likely to work in clerical occupations, which in this scheme includes retail sales jobs, and were also found working in job classifications such as semi-professionals/technicians and supervisors. By 1991, this picture had changed substantially. Individuals with only grade 12 or 13 education were much more likely to end up with blue-collar jobs (38.7%), and much less likely to obtain jobs as semi-professionals or as supervisors. There was also a slight decline in the probability that they would obtain jobs in clerical occupations.

For university-educated individuals, jobs as managers, professionals, or semi-professionals represented the norm in 1971, and the odds of working in either the service sector or in blue-collar jobs were fairly low. The likelihood that an individual would hold a managerial job increased for everyone from 1971 to 1991, but was a bit more pronounced for individuals with university education, whose chances of

TABLE 9-7	Occupational Placement of Individuals Age 25–34 by Education Level, 1971 and 1991						
	Grade 12	Gr. 12/13	Some Post-sec.	B.A.	Post-B.A.	Overall	N
Occupation							
1971							
Managers	3.9%	7.6%	6.2%	11.4%	8.4%	5.8%	116 900
Professional	0.3%	1.1%	2.2%	13.7%	43.6%	4.0%	81 110
Semi-professional, technical	2.7%	11.6%	32.9%	53.0%	36.1%	16.7%	339 005
Supervisors	10.3%	14.0%	10.1%	7.2%	4.1%	10.3%	208 415
Clerks	11.8%	24.2%	13.5%	6.2%	3.7%	13.4%	270 700
Service	16.2%	16.3%	11.2%	4.2%	1.8%	13.4%	271 800
Blue collar	54.8%	25.2%	23.9%	4.3%	2.3%	36.4%	738 515
	100.0%	100.0%	100.0%	100.0%	100.0%	100.0%	
Number:	957 665	302 945	541 860	115 890	108 085	2 026 445	
1991							
Managers	5.0%	8.8%	9.8%	15.1%	12.3%	9.5%	392 615
Professional	0.4%	0.7%	2.2%	13.8%	33.8%	4.4%	179 745
Semi-professional, technical	2.3%	5.2%	17.1%	39.5%	36.4%	15.5%	637 765
Supervisors	6.5%	8.4%	9.5%	8.4%	4.9%	8.4%	345 890
Clerks	11.5%	21.5%	18.4%	10.4%	5.7%	16.4%	675 940
Service	15.0%	16.8%	13.6%	6.7%	3.4%	13.3%	547 515
Blue collar	59.3%	38.7%	29.4%	5.9%	3.6%	32.7%	1 347 895
	100.0%	100.0%	100.0%	100.0%	100.0%	100.0%	
Number:	716 490	957 855	1 751 280	524 960	176 780	4 127 365	

obtaining such a job remained higher than those with less educational qualification. There was a drop, from 43.6% to 33.8%, in the percentage of individuals with post-bachelor's qualifications holding jobs as professionals, balanced by concomitant increases in all other job categories. The one exception is semi-professionals, which remained more or less stable at 36%. This may be a reflection of a tougher job market or an indication of an expansion between 1971 and 1991 in the number of graduates with non-professional post-graduate degrees (e.g., individuals with M.A. degrees in English and the Social Sciences) relative to graduates with professional degrees. For this group, there was an increase in the proportion of individuals ending up in blue-collar (2.3% to 3.6%), service (1.8% to 3.4%), or clerical (3.7% to 5.7%) work, but the proportions were rather small and consistently lower than those for individuals with less education.

For individuals with some post-secondary education but without a university degree, there was a slight increase in the likelihood of obtaining employment in routine jobs—the blue-collar, clerical, or service occupations. Whereas individuals with this level of education previously had a fairly high probability of obtaining jobs in the semi-professional/technician category, by 1991 they were considerably less likely to find themselves in this occupational grouping in relation to their counterparts with university degrees. These two changes suggest that this "boundary" group between routine and discretionary work encountered a dramatic shift in job prospects over the twenty-year period being studied. This is especially significant because this group was, in 1991, the category that included the largest number of individuals. With 1.75 million people, it was over twice the size of the university-educated groups (at 525 000 and 177 000). In contrast, the modal education level in 1971 was less than grade 12. In 1971, then, individuals entering the job market with some post-secondary education represented a privileged group. They were in the top quarter of the working population with respect to educational credentials, and had a fairly good chance of obtaining a discretionary job, although significant numbers still ended up with routine work (about 49%). By 1991, there was nothing special about this level of educational qualification. It represented the population average. While pockets of individuals with this level of certification obtained "good jobs"—as semi-professionals or supervisors—and were able to do so with a greater likelihood than those with less education, the times had passed many of them by, as the new economy's demand for educated workers and an increasingly competitive labour market reduced their likelihood of finding discretionary jobs to about 39%.

This is not to suggest that individuals with community college diplomas were universally disadvantaged. Had data discriminating between those with community college diplomas and those with merely some exposure to post-secondary education (dropouts from university or community college) been available from the 1971 census, a more fine-grained picture might have been produced. Undoubtedly, in some key skill areas in which industry-specific demands couple well with community college programs, graduates of these programs do very well.[4] The overall picture, however, is one in which university education has increasingly become a requirement in an ever-more competitive market for "good jobs."

CONCLUSION

A series of profound changes in the structure of the Canadian labour force seems to have originated in the period between 1971 and 1981, and continued through to 1991. These changes involved the mostly male, fairly uneducated, and largely blue-collar workforce that held down relatively secure employment being replaced by a better-educated, mixed-gender workforce that was split between those holding "good jobs" with secure employment and generous conditions and those holding less well-paying jobs with higher risks of unemployment. Education has been crucial to the changes that have been observed, both from the standpoint of analysts looking at the occupational structure as a whole and from the standpoint of individuals faced with the need to live their lives in the work world that has been created. At one level, the skill requirements of the typical job have been increased; the jobs identified here as "discretionary" require, as part of their everyday function, knowledge levels and skills that were not present in the "routine" jobs that were more predominant twenty and thirty years ago.

While there has been an expansion of jobs with skill requirements congruent with those holding university credentials, it may also be the case that there has been a degree of "credential inflation" within jobs that twenty years ago were performed quite adequately by individuals with less education. A hint of the possibility of this process lies in the evidence that some university-educated individuals find employment in areas such as clerical occupations, and that the proportion of university-educated individuals doing so has increased over twenty years, although it still remains small. The evidence would be more conclusive if it could be demonstrated that those university-educated individuals who had difficulty finding a professional, semi-professional, or managerial job were nevertheless more successful at obtaining particular clerical jobs than those individuals without university credentials. Unfortunately, this question cannot be tested with census data.

The data presented here do not necessarily point to the disappearance of work in traditional manufacturing enterprises in Canada, although it is probably in such enterprises that the replacement of human unskilled or semi-skilled workers by technology is the most pronounced. These data do suggest, though, that males having less than a university or college education can no longer expect a ready supply of jobs that require only physical strength and exertion.

The data presented here do not demonstrate that the occupational opportunity structure is closing for university graduates. Nevertheless, a small but increasing number of university graduates is also failing to secure appropriate employment and has joined the ranks of the underemployed. Post-secondary education has become an admission ticket to the job market, but not a guarantee of placement within it. Without higher education, individuals are truly disadvantaged in the workforce, but these credentials alone, with a few notable exceptions in a very small number of professions, are not sufficient for good, stable employment in a well-paying job. It is still not clear whether the retirement from the workforce of the large baby boom generation will open up enough opportunities to improve the future job picture significantly.

An equally interesting question for the future is whether the social class of one's parents has become increasingly important to a person's occupational outcome. At the very least, the increased difficulty faced by students with working-class or lower-income parents in completing university, in the face of rising tuition costs and decreased summer job opportunities, suggests that class background will be important. Without parental support, completing post-secondary education is difficult, in a way that completing high school, the "admission ticket" in a previous generation, was not.

NOTES

1. Data for these tables were taken from aggregate data tables made available by Statistics Canada and discussed in Bernard et al. (1997).

2. Are service workers correctly classified as "manual" workers? Within this group, which includes taxi drivers, babysitters, waiters, hotel clerks, and service station attendants, there can be an argument either way. Treating such jobs as a separate category renders this question unimportant for purposes of this discussion. What these jobs have in common is fairly low skill/job requirement levels, but, at the same time, a fairly high level of interaction with the public. The use of the term "service" here

is quite at odds with the use of the term by English sociologists describing a "service class of professionals, capitalists, and financiers" (see Savage 1994), but consistent with its usage by a wide variety of other researchers (see Blossfeld et al. 1993). It is important when reading the literature to determine which use of the term is applicable to the discussion at hand.

3. These results may overstate the case slightly, since people without jobs are excluded from all the tables. It should be noted, though, that to be excluded an individual had to have been without any employment over the past year. The tables include individuals who were not currently working at the time of the census but who had worked in the previous year.

4. But see Bernard et al. (1997) for an examination of 1981 and 1991 census data including a better measure of community college education (separate from those with "some" post-secondary education), which suggests findings similar to those found in Table 9-7. Bernard et al. were not, however, able to distinguish between individuals with trade school certificates and those with community college diplomas (though most of the people in this combined category were probably community college grads).

REFERENCES

Bell, D. 1973. *The Coming of Post-Industrial Society.* New York: Basic Books.

Bernard, P., D. Baer, J. Boisjoly, J. Curtis, and M. Webber 1994. *A New Typology for Work Roles for Canadian Data.* Paper presented to the Annual Meeting of the Canadian Sociology and Anthropology Association, Calgary, June 7–11.

Bernard, P., J. Boisjoly, D. Baer, J. Curtis, and M. Webber 1997. *How Canadians Work: Changes in the Makeup of the Labour Force in the 1970s and 1980s.* Ottawa: Statistics Canada.

Birkelund, G. E., et al. 1996. "The latent structure of job characteristics of men and women." *American Journal of Sociology* 102(1):80–113.

Blakely, J. and E. Harvey 1988. "Market and non-market effects on male and female occupational status attainment." *Canadian Review of Sociology and Anthropology* 25(1):23–40.

Blossfeld, H.-P., et al. 1993. "Is there a new service proletariat? The tertiary sector and inequality in Germany." In G. Esping-Anderson, *Changing Classes,* pp. 109–135. Newbury Park: Sage.

Charles, M. 1992. "Cross-national variation in occupational sex segregation." *American Sociological Review* 57(4):483–502.

Clement, W. and J. Myles 1994. *Relations of Ruling: Class and Gender in Postindustrial Societies.* Montréal: McGill-Queen's University Press.

Erikson, R., and J. Goldthorpe 1992. *The Constant Flux: A Study of Class Mobility in Industrial Societies.* Oxford: Clarendon Press.

Esping-Anderson, G. 1993. "Post industrial class structures: An analytical framework." In G. Esping-Anderson, *Changing Classes: Stratification and Mobility in Post-Industrial Societies,* pp. 7–31. Newbury Park: Sage.

Fox, B., and J. Fox 1987. "Occupational gender segregation in the Canadian labour force, 1931–1981." *Canadian Review of Sociology and Anthropology* 24(3):374–397.

Hakim, C. 1996. "The sexual division of labour and women's heterogeneity." *British Journal of Sociology* 47(1):178–188.

Hou, F., and T.R. Balakrishnan 1996. "The integration of visible minorities in contemporary society." *Canadian Journal of Sociology* 21(3):307–326.

Ishida, H., et al. 1997. "Education and promotion changes in the United States and Japan." *American Sociological Review* 62(6): 866–882.

Myles, J., et al. 1988. "Wages and jobs in the 1980s: Changing youth wages and the declining middle." Ottawa: Social and Economic Studies Division, Statistics Canada.

Myles, J., et al. 1993. "Does post-industrialism matter? The Canadian Experience." In G. Esping-Anderson, *Changing Classes,* pp. 171–194. Newbury Park: Sage.

Picot, G., et al. 1990. "Good jobs/bad jobs and the declining middle: 1967–1986." Ottawa: Business and Labour Market Analysis Group, Analytical Studies Branch, Statistics Canada.

Rinehart, J. 1996. *The Tyranny of Work.* Toronto: Harcourt Brace Canada.

Savage, M. 1994. "Social mobility and class analysis: A new agenda for social history?" *Social History* 19(1):69–79.

Slomczynski, K., and T. Krauze 1987. "Cross-national similarity in social mobility patterns: A direct test of the Featherman-Jones-Hauser hypothesis." *American Sociological Review* 52(5):598–611.

Wanner, R. 1996. *Trends in Occupational Opportunity in Canada in the Twentieth Century.* Paper presented at the Canadian Sociology and Anthropology Association Annual Meeting, St. Catharines, Ontario.

Westergaard, J. 1990. "Social mobility in Britain." In J. Clark, C. Modgil, and S. Modgil, *John Goldthorpe: Consensus and Controversy.* pp. 277–288. London: Falmer Press.

Wright, R., and J. Jacobs 1994. "Male flight from computer work: A new look at occupational resegregation and ghettoization." *American Sociological Review* 59(4): 511–536.

SOCIAL MOBILITY IN CANADA: CONCEPTS, PATTERNS, AND TRENDS

Richard A. Wanner

(A new chapter written for this volume.)

INTRODUCTION

Seymour Martin Lipset (1963) once said that Horatio Alger[1] has never been a Canadian hero. He was correct in that the myth of unlimited opportunity for ambitious young persons never became as much a part of the folk wisdom in Canada as it had in the United States. Indeed, as Lipset (1989) himself has shown, some attitude surveys find that Canadians are more likely to favour equality of result than equality of opportunity.

Nevertheless, like most industrial societies, Canada increasingly relies on educational credentials to sort persons into jobs. As recently as 1961 just 2.9% of all Canadians had earned a university degree. By 1996 this had risen to over 13%, with 40% having had at least some post-secondary education. During the same period the proportion of professionals in Canada's labour force has more than doubled, while the proportion of workers in agriculture has dropped by two-thirds to less than 3.5% of the labour force. Has this massive transformation of the labour force resulted in an increase in opportunity in Canada? Are young persons less likely to inherit the status position of their parents than they were a generation ago? Has the increased availability of higher education led to more rapid career advancement? Has a greater reliance on educational credentials in hiring created more opportunities for women and members of minority racial and ethnic groups? Sociologists have long studied issues like these under the rubric of "social mobility" or "status attainment."

CONCEPTUAL ISSUES

Social mobility has been broadly defined as the upward or downward movement of individuals or groups into different positions in a social hierarchy based on wealth, income, occupation, education, power, or any other scarce social resource. Societies with high rates of social mobility are generally regarded as more open societies, while those with lower rates are deemed to be more closed. Social mobility may be either upward, as in the daughter of a welder becoming a lawyer, or downward, as in the son of a Ph.D. dropping out of high school. This movement assumes that occupations or other status characteristics are ranked from highest to lowest in terms of status or prestige and movement is up or down the status or prestige hierarchy. Mobility may also be classified as either intergenerational, in which movement is from parents' status to one's own status, or intragenerational, in which movement takes place within a person's own career, sometimes known as career mobility.

Although social mobility is possible along all the hierarchies mentioned, most research on the phenomenon has focused on occupational mobility. This is because occupational standing is generally agreed to be closely related to both other behaviours and other indices of general social standing, such as income and education. Occupation is also relatively easy to measure in surveys, and occupational rankings have been shown to be quite consistent both over time and across societies (see Treiman 1977). Many mobility researchers (e.g., Erickson and Goldthorpe 1993) regard occupation as primarily an indicator of class position, when combined with a measure of class of worker (i.e., status as either an employer, self-employed, or an employee). Those adopting such a class-structural approach do not regard class positions as inherently ordered and are thus uninterested in movement of individuals up or down a social hierarchy (see Erickson and Goldthorpe 1993:29–35).

Until recently, most research on social mobility was restricted to men. Indeed, the large-scale mobility surveys carried out through the 1970s only rarely included interviews with women, although the 1973 Canadian Mobility Study did so. It is not that women were simply excluded from the research by predominantly male sociologists; their exclusion was justified on theoretical grounds. The argument commonly goes as follows: Stratification theory is mainly concerned with explaining inequalities that arise out of the economic and prestige structures of society, and these structures are embodied in the occupational structure; women are peripheral to the occupational structure because of their interrupted employment patterns, attachment to part-time work, and family responsibilities. Therefore, their social class or status position is determined by the occupation of the male head of household.

A major assumption underlying this argument is that it is the family and not the individual that is the relevant social unit, and that the class or status position of the unit must be determined by its (usually male) head (see Erickson and Goldthorpe 1992). As we shall see, however, since the 1970s this conventional view has been challenged, and women in their own right are increasingly incorporated into social mobility research and stratification research more generally.

Social mobility is typically studied by means of mobility tables that cross-classify a set of categories of the occupations of respondents to a survey by their fathers', or more rarely mothers', occupations. The marginal distribution of parents' occupations is termed the occupational origin, while the marginal distribution of respondents' occupations is known as the occupational destination. More recently, a technique called log linear modelling has been used to examine the underlying structure of such tables and make comparisons of tables for different groups or different countries. Later in this chapter I will describe briefly how such models have been applied in mobility research.

From data gathered for the 1973 Canadian Mobility Study (CMS) by Statistics Canada and reported in Boyd et al. (1985), we know that there has been a great deal of upward occupational mobility in Canada up to the early 1970s, but most of it has been between occupations that are very close together in terms of their relative statuses. A father who is a labourer is much more likely to have a son who becomes a machine operative than to have a son who becomes a lawyer. We have also learned that much of this upward mobility is due to the expansion of some occupations and the contraction of others over time. As we have seen, occupations at the top of the hierarchy, including professionals, for example, grew dramatically in the twentieth century, while occupations at the bottom, particularly farm occupations, declined. The result is that much social mobility has been induced by the opportunities created by this change in the occupational structure. Mobility of this kind is known as structural mobility. The mobility in a society that exceeds that permitted by shifts in its occupational structure is known as exchange mobility, or sometimes as circulation mobility or social fluidity. Most mobility research has concentrated on exchange mobility, since it is regarded as the true measure of the openness of a social system.

Although we will only deal with it briefly here, status attainment research is complementary to mobility research. Using regression models instead of log linear models, this research attempts to identify the variables intervening between parents' statuses and their offspring's statuses. Paying particular attention to educational, occupational, and income attainment, the status attainment researcher focuses on the process that results in people ending up where they do in status hierarchies.

Mobility research is not simply descriptive, serving only to measure a society's relative openness. From its beginnings (Sorokin 1927), the study of occupational mobility has been concerned with the impact of the process of industrialization on occupational structures and occupational mobility. Two contrasting theoretical positions have emerged. The first, tracing its origins to the work of Lipset and Bendix (1959), maintains that mobility rates, or at least exchange mobility rates (Featherman, Jones, and Hauser 1975), should be similar in all industrial societies because of broad similarities in their occupational structures and the status structures that underlay them. The second, with roots in Sorokin's work and partially elaborated by Treiman (1970), argues that mobility rates should increase as a result of continued industrialization, the expansion of educational opportunities, the presence of certain political ideologies, particularly socialist and democratic socialist ones, and the diminution of status differences between classes over time. This theory has been variously termed the "industrialism thesis" (Kerr et al. 1960) or the "liberal theory of industrialism" (Erickson and Goldthorpe 1993).

A second major theoretical concern in mobility research is derived from Marx's recognition that social mobility may be inimical to the process of class formation and Weber's definition of the social class structure as "composed of the plurality of class statuses between which an interchange of individuals on a personal basis or in the course of generations is readily possible and typically observable" (1947: 424). This theme of class formation and class boundaries shows up particularly in the work of European sociologists such as John Goldthorpe (1987), but is also apparent in the concern with barriers to intergenerational movement evident in the status attainment literature (Blau and Duncan 1967:58–67). Theorists such as Giddens and Parkin have both used the results of mobility studies in their attempt to understand class formation and class relationships. Giddens (1973) has explored the role of mobility processes in the institutionalization of persons in similar market positions into structurally significant social class categories and relationships.

SOURCES OF CANADIAN MOBILITY DATA

Only three large-scale sample surveys conducted in Canada have obtained the measures required for mobility and status attainment research. The 1973 Canadian Mobility Study (CMS) was a survey of nearly 45 000 men and women originally conducted to investigate rates and patterns of intergenerational occupational mobility in the Canadian population.[2] The data were collected by Statistics Canada as a supplement to their July 1973 Labour Force Survey. Though measures for some of the variables come from the Survey interviews, the bulk of the measures were included in a self-administered questionnaire left with respondents and picked up several days later by field workers (see Boyd et al. 1985).

The 1986 mobility data were collected as part of Statistics Canada's General Social Survey (GSS) program[3] and were based on telephone interviews with 16 390 respondents using random digit dialling methods. The main sample is a national sample, excluding residents of institutions and the Yukon and Northwest Territories, consisting of 9946 persons aged 15 and over. A supplementary sample of 6444 was also drawn in certain regions of New Brunswick, Québec, and Ontario with high concentrations of francophones, because of the language knowledge and use module of the survey. All social mobility questions were also asked of members of this supplementary sample. Adjustment for oversampling is included in the weights used to estimate population counts at the national level.

The 1994 (Cycle 9) General Social Survey was designed to replicate partially the education, work, and retirement items from the 1989 (Cycle 4) survey, but added new sections on the transition into retirement, social origins, and work interruptions. The sample design and interviewing methods were essentially the same as those applied in earlier GSS surveys. In 1994, the sample included approximately 11 500 respondents, including 10 000 persons in the main sample and a supplementary sample of 1500 persons aged 55 to 74.

The analysis reported in this chapter is restricted to men and women born in Canada and aged 25 to 64 at the time of the surveys. Only native-born Canadians are included because most immigrants' status origins, their education, and their parents' occupations are from another country and do not reflect Canada's opportunity structure. Both anglophone and francophone Canadian men and women are included in the analysis despite the evidence that linguistic group is often an important dimension of stratification in Canadian society. However, Boyd et al. (1981) found no substantial differences between anglophones and francophones in the patterns of effects of paternal education and occupation or respondents' education on attainment of first job, prompting them to conclude that "there is little difference between the two groups with respect to the *process* [emphasis in original] of stratification" (1981:666), although they do observe differences between linguistic groups in the average levels of the status variables. Wanner (1999a) arrived at a similar conclusion using data from the 1986 and 1994 GSS cycles in addition to data from the 1973 CMS.

In the tables that follow, I use a simple occupational classification for the Canadian labour force based on collapsing the sixteen-category classification used in the 1973 CMS (see Pineo et al. 1977) and used again in the 1986 and 1994 surveys. The eight-category classification used in the analysis preserves the conventional manual-nonmanual distinction to make these results comparable to those for other countries, as well as a distinction between higher and lower professionals. The occupational categories are rank-ordered in the sense that those at the upper end (e.g., professional or managerial occupations) have higher educational requirements, produce greater earnings, and have higher occupational prestige scores than those at the lower end (e.g., lower manual or farm occupations). Thus, the terms "upward" or "downward" mobility refer to the direction of movement on the status hierarchy on which the occupational categories are ranked.

The remainder of this chapter will be devoted to exploring patterns of intergenerational occupational mobility in Canada, as well as trends between the initial survey of 1973 and the most recent 1994 survey. First, I examine changes in Canada's occupational structure, i.e., the distribution of

workers over occupational categories both over generations and between the surveys, since the structural component of total mobility is determined by these distributions. I then use some simple methods based on percentages to explore patterns and trends in mobility tables for both men and women. I next introduce briefly the concept of a mobility model and offer some results that shed further light on the question of trends in equality of opportunity. I conclude by comparing the Canadian results to mobility patterns in other countries.

TRENDS IN THE CANADIAN OCCUPATIONAL STRUCTURE

Tables 10-1 and 10-2 present the distributions of occupational origins and destinations for both men and women for all three survey years. These represent the marginal distributions of our mobility tables, i.e., the Canadian occupational structure, and the source of structural mobility. The occupational origins of men and women, as indexed by father's occupation, are very similar. The differences are due largely to sampling fluctuation. Most striking are the massive differences in men's and women's destination distributions. Consistent with the familiar observation, women are considerably more likely than men to be found in both the upper and lower nonmanual ranks, the latter the result of large numbers of women in clerical occupations, and women are considerably less likely to be found in the upper manual, managerial, and farm categories.

As we shall see, this predisposes women to considerably more "structural" mobility than is typical of men when mobility is measured from father's occupation. It is heartening, however, that

TABLE 10-1	Percentage Distribution of Father's Occupation and Respondent's Occupation, Native-Born Men Aged 25 to 64, 1973, 1986, and 1994

	1973		1986		1994	
Occupational Category	Father's Occupation	Son's Occupation	Father's Occupation	Son's Occupation	Father's Occupation	Son's Occupation
Higher Professional	2.9	8.2	5.8	10.1	6.1	10.8
Managerial	3.4	8.4	8.8	14.0	11.6	17.8
Lower Professional	1.8	5.7	2.1	7.3	3.8	7.6
Upper White Collar	7.7	12.3	5.1	7.4	7.7	6.7
Lower White Collar	6.9	8.5	6.9	9.9	5.6	7.9
Upper Blue Collar	22.9	25.3	25.7	21.7	25.7	21.5
Lower Blue Collar	25.4	24.6	28.2	25.1	25.0	24.0
Farm	28.8	6.9	17.5	4.4	14.5	3.6
Number of Cases	10 358	10 310	3843	3825	2658	2503

women's representation in managerial occupations has grown considerably over the two decades and appears to be converging with that of men.

It is also interesting to note that the proportion of women in farming has actually grown somewhat at the same time that the proportion of men has declined dramatically. This may be the result of an increasing tendency for women to inherit the family farm or acquire a farm property in a divorce. Nevertheless, the small proportion of the overall labour force remaining in farming suggests that, in the new century, movement from farm origins will likely cease to be a significant source of structural mobility in Canada. Indeed, the overall similarity between origin and destination distributions for men is increasing so that the only way in which the absolute mobility rate can remain constant is for the association between origins

and destinations to decline, i.e., there must be more exchange mobility. At the opposite end of the socio-economic spectrum, both professional and managerial destinations are expanding among both men and women. This suggests that a large part of any upward mobility we observe will be the result of the continued expansion of these higher-ranking occupations.

In comparing the distributions of mothers' and daughters' occupations for 1986 and 1994, it is not apparent that the daughters' distributions are converging on their mothers' distributions, as was the case for sons and their fathers.[4] If anything, the daughters' distributions are becoming less like those of their mothers, as women's representation in professional and managerial occupations increases and their representation in manual occupations, particularly lower manual jobs, declines.

TABLE 10-2 Percentage Distribution of Father's Occupation and Respondent's Occupation, Native-Born Women Aged 25 to 64, 1973, 1986, and 1994

Occupational Category	1973*		1986			1994		
	Father's Occupation	Daughter's Occupation	Father's Occupation	Mother's Occupation	Daughter's Occupation	Father's Occupation	Mother's Occupation	Daughter's Occupation
Higher Professional	2.9	7.9	5.1	9.3	11.0	6.0	6.6	11.2
Managerial	3.4	2.1	7.8	4.3	7.8	10.4	7.6	13.6
Lower Professional	1.6	11.9	2.4	8.6	12.3	3.0	7.9	15.4
Upper Nonmanual	8.1	27.0	5.6	17.2	20.7	7.0	18.7	17.4
Lower Nonmanual	7.4	34.2	6.9	32.8	32.6	6.2	34.0	28.3
Upper Manual	22.9	1.8	26.7	2.4	1.7	27.8	1.0	2.5
Lower Manual	26.7	14.0	28.1	20.9	12.6	26.8	20.5	9.1
Farm	27.1	1.0	17.5	4.6	1.4	13.1	3.6	2.5
Number of Cases	10 702	6079	3746	907	2787	2655	954	2032

*A measure of mother's occupation at this level of detail is not available for 1973.

BASIC PATTERNS OF MOBILITY

What we have been examining up to now are just the marginal totals of mobility tables. These tables are quite simply created by cross-classifying an origin status (e.g., father's occupation) with a destination status (e.g., daughter's occupation). If a mobility table is percentaged across the rows, the results are termed outflow percentages, representing distributions of respondents flowing from common status origins. If the mobility table is percentaged down the columns, the results are inflow percentages, representing distributions of respondents into common status destinations. Table 10-3 displays outflow percentages for father-son mobility in 1973, 1986, and 1994.

A separate panel in the table represents each year. While these provide some useful information about the intergenerational flow of labour, they do not control for other processes related to the relative supply and demand for workers, such as differential fertility or technological change. One of the advantages of the more complex statistical models often applied in mobility analysis is their ability to control for such factors.

The first place to start in examining the welter of data available in Table 10-3 is with the diagonals of the tables, which represent status inheritance[5] or immobility. That is, along the diagonals are respondents to the surveys whose occupations are in the same category as those of their parent. These are quite consistently the highest percentages in the table, indicating that movement from origin to destination is by no means a random process, but is characterized by a sizeable amount of inheritance. In the upper left-hand corner of the top panel we see that, in 1973, 31.4% of sons who came from higher

professional origins became higher professionals themselves, i.e., inherited a higher professional status. By the 1986 survey, this figure had dropped to 20.4%, suggesting that the amount of inheritance of this sort of occupational status had declined, though the figure for 1994 appears to rebound somewhat to 25%.[6] Among the men, even stronger inheritance appears among both higher and lower manual workers, implying that the manual-nonmanual distinction represents a real barrier to mobility, and one that has remained strong over the twenty-one-year period covered by these data.

Table 10-4 presents outflow percentages for father-daughter mobility in all three surveys. Here the most obvious feature is not so much concentration along the diagonal, though there is a considerable amount of that, but the extent to which daughters are likely to end up in upper or lower nonmanual occupations regardless of their origins.

Since this would constitute downward mobility from professional and managerial origins and upward mobility from manual origins, there is considerably more mobility and less immobility from father's occupation among women than among men. By 1994, however, the proportion of women ending up in upper nonmanual occupations had declined considerably, regardless of origin status. Over time, there also appears to be less concentration along the diagonal and a greater propensity to be upwardly mobile toward both upper professional and managerial occupations.

My speculation above, concerning the increasing tendency for women to be found in farming occupations, is substantiated by the cell in the lower right-hand corner of each panel, which represents the percentage of daughters of farm fathers who themselves end up in farming. This

TABLE 10-3 Outflow Percentages from Father's Occupation to Respondent's Occupation Native-Born Men Aged 25 to 64, 1973, 1986, and 1994

Father's Occupation	Son's Occupation							
	Upper Professional	Manager	Lower Professional	Upper Nonmanual	Lower Nonmanual	Upper Manual	Lower Manual	Farm
1973								
Upper Professional	31.4	20.2	12.6	12.0	7.9	10.1	5.3	0.5
Manager	19.8	21.2	10.7	13.3	9.0	13.3	11.1	1.5
Lower Professional	14.8	12.9	19.2	11.7	9.6	17.4	12.2	2.2
Upper Nonmanual	16.6	15.0	8.2	21.8	9.6	17.1	11.0	0.7
Lower Nonmanual	11.3	11.2	6.8	19.1	11.3	20.2	18.8	1.3
Upper Manual	8.0	8.8	6.2	13.4	9.3	31.5	21.5	1.2
Lower Manual	5.5	6.7	4.7	11.5	8.7	27.9	33.3	1.6
Farm	4.7	4.5	3.3	7.4	5.6	25.0	26.5	23.0
1986								
Upper Professional	20.4	20.4	15.5	8.2	9.8	13.3	8.4	3.8
Manager	13.5	21.9	8.1	17.7	13.3	10.8	13.2	1.4
Lower Professional	20.1	7.5	17.2	10.0	9.3	25.5	10.1	0.4
Upper Nonmanual	17.3	19.5	8.9	15.6	12.5	15.9	10.3	0.0
Lower Nonmanual	11.9	18.0	12.1	11.3	13.8	9.7	21.6	1.6
Upper Manual	9.6	11.0	6.2	5.6	10.1	31.1	24.9	1.5
Lower Manual	7.6	12.0	5.5	6.0	9.9	22.7	35.3	1.0
Farm	7.5	15.3	3.5	4.9	5.0	19.2	23.6	21.0
1994								
Upper Professional	25.0	24.4	10.0	6.2	6.7	11.5	16.0	0.3
Manager	11.4	31.1	11.6	10.6	8.6	16.3	9.5	1.0
Lower Professional	25.0	31.2	9.7	4.5	7.5	3.2	18.8	*
Upper Nonmanual	10.9	21.0	11.0	17.1	8.1	17.9	12.9	1.1
Lower Nonmanual	18.7	15.3	11.9	8.4	11.2	15.3	19.2	*
Upper Manual	10.2	12.9	7.3	5.2	8.2	32.6	23.2	0.4
Lower Manual	7.6	15.3	5.7	4.1	7.9	21.9	35.1	2.5
Farm	4.3	14.3	3.6	3.6	4.4	20.5	29.2	20.1

Note: Totals of all rows should equal 100 percent, but may not due to rounding error.
*No sample cases in these cells.

TABLE 10-4   Outflow Percentages from Father's Occupation to Respondent's Occupation Native-Born Women Aged 25 to 64, 1973, 1986, and 1994

Father's Occupation	Daughter's Occupation							
	Upper Professional	Manager	Lower Professional	Upper Nonmanual	Lower Nonmanual	Upper Manual	Lower Manual	Farm
1973								
Upper Professional	24.7	5.2	22.8	28.3	14.9	0.8	3.3	0.0
Manager	16.1	2.3	15.5	32.8	24.2	4.4	4.7	0.0
Lower Professional	9.8	3.8	16.6	30.9	30.6	3.3	5.1	0.0
Upper Nonmanual	11.4	3.0	14.9	32.5	28.9	2.4	6.4	0.4
Lower Nonmanual	7.4	2.2	13.4	30.5	33.9	1.4	10.6	0.5
Upper Manual	6.5	2.0	11.0	29.5	36.1	2.0	12.3	0.7
Lower Manual	4.4	1.1	9.9	25.9	38.6	1.8	18.1	0.2
Farm	10.0	2.1	12.3	20.4	32.3	1.2	17.9	3.8
1986								
Upper Professional	19.8	12.1	15.6	24.7	20.3	0.0	5.3	2.3
Manager	15.0	12.7	16.9	24.1	24.8	0.6	5.9	0.0
Lower Professional	15.2	2.0	19.1	12.8	33.2	0.0	16.0	1.7
Upper Nonmanual	16.7	13.0	11.5	25.6	28.2	0.0	5.0	0.0
Lower Nonmanual	16.9	5.9	18.0	20.9	29.5	1.0	7.5	0.3
Upper Manual	8.3	8.7	9.5	24.9	34.1	2.1	11.9	0.4
Lower Manual	8.7	6.7	12.6	15.3	38.3	1.8	16.4	0.3
Farm	10.2	5.5	10.5	19.2	30.9	2.9	14.5	6.2
1994								
Upper Professional	12.4	24.8	25.4	10.7	16.0	7.3	3.3	*
Manager	11.9	19.4	20.9	13.8	25.4	1.6	4.6	2.4
Lower Professional	16.5	10.9	24.4	15.4	24.4	0.4	8.0	*
Upper Nonmanual	9.3	25.9	21.5	13.8	21.5	*	4.9	3.1
Lower Nonmanual	19.7	5.7	13.6	15.2	36.3	2.4	4.3	2.8
Upper Manual	10.8	13.9	13.8	20.0	30.4	3.1	7.3	0.7
Lower Manual	8.7	12.3	10.7	21.6	26.7	3.9	15.8	0.3
Farm	10.7	6.3	14.3	11.4	33.4	0.9	12.1	10.9

Note: Totals of all rows should equal 100 percent, but may not due to rounding error.
*No sample cases in these cells.

percentage steadily increased, from just 3.8% in 1973 to 10.9% in 1994. Although men from farm backgrounds were still twice as likely as women to end up in farming in 1994, the inheritance of farm occupations actually declined among men over the twenty-one-year period.

SUMMARIZING MOBILITY TABLES

Some basic summary statistics comparing relative flows in the mobility tables we have just explored are presented in Table 10-5. In this table, the percent immobile is computed as the percentage of the cases lying on the diagonal of each mobility table.[7] Upward mobility is the percentage of cases below the diagonal; downward mobility is the percentage of cases above the diagonal.

Structural mobility is computed by simply summing the positive percentage differences between origin and destination statuses and may be interpreted as the percentage of cases that would have to be reallocated to make the origin and destination distributions identical. Exchange mobility is movement in the table that is not accounted for by marginal differences and equals the sum of the percentages of immobility and structural mobility subtracted from 100%.

In the case of mobility from father's occupation shown in Table 10-5, the proportions of both men and women who are immobile have remained remarkably constant between 1973 and 1994. Another way of putting it is to say that the volume of total mobility (the "upward" plus the "downward" percentages) has also remained quite constant. Nevertheless, a net increase in exchange mobility can be observed for both men and women, largely the result of a decline in structural mobility.

The most impressive change to be observed in Table 10-5 is the shift over time in the relative balance of upward and downward mobility, with the latter increasing to a considerable extent over the twenty-year period under consideration here. This can be accounted for largely by the substantial decline in farm origins over the period, which has had the effect of eliminating a major source of upward structural mobility. In particular, for men in 1973 virtually all structural

| TABLE 10-5 | Measures of the Components of Total Mobility from Father's Occupation, Native-Born Men and Women Aged 25 to 64, 1973, 1986, and 1994 |

	Men			Women		
	1973	1986	1994	1973	1986	1994
Immobile	26.8	26.8	27.6	13.3	12.1	13.5
Mobile						
Upward	56.3	50.3	47.5	71.5	69.7	66.5
Downward	16.9	22.9	24.9	15.2	18.2	20.0
Structural Mobility	21.6	20.3	16.5	56.0	55.7	50.5
Exchange Mobility	51.6	52.9	55.9	30.7	32.2	36.0

Note: These measures are based on the eight-by-eight mobility tables shown in Tables 10-3 and 10-4.

mobility was driven by movement out of farming. By 1994, only about 60% of this structural mobility was farming-related, with only about 11% of all upward mobility originating in farming occupations.

As mentioned above, for women structural mobility from their fathers' occupations is a qualitatively different phenomenon than it is for men, involving as it does a gender shift in the transition from origin to destination distributions. As a consequence, we see considerably more structural than exchange mobility among women than among men, and considerably less immobility. What is perhaps surprising is the preponderance of upward over downward mobility among women, although this is largely the result of daughters of manual fathers finding themselves in lower nonmanual occupations. If we were to use mother's occupation as our origin distribution for women, the ratio of upward to downward mobility would be similar to that of men (see Wanner 1993).

MODELS OF MOBILITY

While we have gleaned a fair amount of information about patterns and trends in occupational mobility from an examination of some simple percentaged tables, it has rapidly become apparent to researchers in the field that these results could be misleading in a number of respects. What is required is a statistical model that reflects these patterns and trends. Such a statistical model consists of one or more equations expressing the relationship between two or more variables. These equations must be capable of being fitted to observed data so that the fit between the model and the data may be evaluated. Statistical models are an expression of hypothetical statements derived from social theories and assume that the observable world works in the way

predicted by the theory. If the model can be shown to fit observed data well, it lends support to the theory. A poor fit casts doubt on the theory.

By the late 1960s, Leo Goodman (1969) had developed an approach to modelling data organized as frequencies in cross-tabulations that closely resembled regression analysis for continuous variables. In these so-called log linear models, the dependent variable is the logarithm of the frequency count of cases in the cells of such tables, while the independent variables are membership in certain rows or columns or row-column combinations in the tables. Such log linear models were immediately applied to mobility tables and developments have been rapid since (see Hout 1983; Breen and Whelan 1994).

One variety of log linear models that has become popular with mobility researchers was developed by Xie (1992). His "log-multiplicative layer effect model"[8] is particularly useful because it provides a single parameter value that indexes the overall strength of association between occupational origins and destinations across time periods or countries, assuming that the basic pattern of association between origins and destinations is the same for the time periods or countries. The larger the value of these parameters, the stronger the association between origin and destination statuses. Alternatively, a mobility table exhibits more openness if the association is weaker. The advantage of using these parameters to index association is that their value is not affected by the marginal distributions. That is, they reflect mobility rates relative to the occupational structure, not the absolute rates shown in Table 10-5.

Table 10-6 shows the parameters indexing association from two separate log-multiplicative layer effect models, one for men and one for women. In both cases,

TABLE 10-6 **Measures of the Strength of Association* Between Father's Occupation and Respondent's Occupation for Native-Born Men and Women Aged 25 to 64, 1973, 1986, and 1994**

Year	Men	Women
1973	0.720	0.715
1986	0.484	0.498
1994	0.498	0.491

*Based on Xie's (1992) log-multiplicative layer effect model applied to the observed frequencies for Tables 10-3 and 10-4.

there is evidence of a sharp decline in the association between father's occupation and respondent's occupation between the 1973 survey and the 1986 survey, suggesting an increased openness of the system between the 1970s and the 1980s. Between 1986 and 1994, however, we see no change in the magnitude of the association for either men or women, implying that the degree of openness stayed about the same between the 1980s and the 1990s.

Why was the Canadian system of occupational stratification more open in the 1980s and 1990s than it was in the 1970s? These results are quite consistent with Hout's (1988) findings for the United States, using data assembled from a series of U.S. General Social Surveys between 1972 and 1986. He suggests that the sizeable decline in the association between men's and women's occupational origins and destinations which he observed was the result of increasing proportions of university graduates in the American labour force, a group for which he finds virtually no association between origin status and destination status. The strong association between origin and destination among those with less than a university education accounts for nearly all of the overall association. Given the strong educational expansion in Canada between the 1950s

and the 1970s (see Wanner, 1999b), it is likely that a similar interpretation would apply to this country. The failure of the association to decline further between 1986 and 1994 suggests that the expansion of university education had bottomed out by then and had no further effect on the openness of the Canadian occupational class system.

CANADA IN COMPARATIVE PERSPECTIVE

How do the trends and patterns of occupational mobility we observed for Canada compare with those for other countries? As mentioned earlier, the theories underlying mobility research can only be tested by means of either longitudinal comparisons within a single society, cross-sectional comparisons of two or more societies, or both. Relatively little cross-national research has included Canada, because Statistics Canada will not release a detailed occupational code identifying unique occupational titles, which would make it possible to create occupational categories equivalent to those available in other countries. However limited, the available research indicates that Canada is by no means the "low mobility" society some commentators have claimed it to be, and the long-term trend in Canada toward relatively greater openness is shared with most post-industrial societies.

McRoberts and Selbee (1981) compared exchange mobility from father's occupation to son's occupation in Canada and the United States using 1973 data from both countries and found there was no significant difference between the two countries. Wanner (1986) examined both structural and exchange mobility from father's to son's occupation in comparing Canada with the U.S. and found that, while exchange mobility rates were similar, structural mobility into higher-ranking occupations was less pronounced in Canada than in the U.S. This implies that, while equality of opportunity is similar in the two societies, a combination of the supply and demand for labour in Canada produces fewer actual opportunities for upward mobility. In another comparison, Wanner and Hayes (1996) used data from the 1980s to compare mobility rates and patterns among men in Australia and Canada. They found that not only were structural mobility effects far stronger in Australia, but there was also a greater association between occupational origins and destinations there—i.e., Australia is a less open society than is Canada.

Just one of the major studies comparing mobility rates and patterns in many countries has included Canada. Ganzeboom et al. (1989) undertook the massive task of analyzing 126 mobility tables from thirty-two countries, including four tables from Canada. Their results suggest that the association between status origins and destinations in Canada is fairly low, indeed lower than in such countries as Sweden, the United Kingdom, France, and the Netherlands. Consistent with trends in Canada described above, Ganzeboom et al. report that "the overall trend in association between father's and son's class

position is *down* [emphasis in original] in nearly all countries we could include in our analysis" (1989:31).

Since the appearance of the work of Ganzeboom et al. (1989), a large number of studies of social mobility have confirmed the prediction of the industrialism thesis that the association between origin status and destination status will decline. This decline in class-based ascription has been documented in Australia (Marks and Jones 1991), Canada (Wanner 1999a), Hungary (Luijkx et al. 1995), the Netherlands (DeGraaf and Luijkx 1992; Hendrickx and Ganzeboom 1998), Norway (Ringdal 1994), and France (Vallet 1999).

SUMMING UP

This chapter has attempted to provide a basic introduction to contemporary research on social mobility, including some definitions of basic terms, a brief survey of theoretical and methodological issues, and an analysis of patterns and trends in intergenerational occupational mobility among Canadian men and women. The basic message I have sought to convey is that understanding a system of stratification involves examining not only the distributions of scarce resources and how those distributions change over time, but also understanding the process whereby individuals arrive at a particular location in those distributions. This is the role of mobility and status attainment research: to understand the physiology of social inequality rather than its anatomy.

Although we have seen that Canadian society has become more open and the availability of opportunities less driven by shifts in the occupational structure since the early 1970s, Canada is still a stratified society characterized by a considerable amount of inheritance of privilege.

Theoretically derived models of mobility tables provide rich detail pinpointing exactly where it is in the social structure that mobility and immobility are taking place. Mobility research is well suited to studying the problem of class formation by viewing the occupational hierarchy as discrete, with barriers to movement forming and dissolving over time. This affords insights into the processes whereby systems of inequality are historically reproduced and transformed. That being said, since the early 1990s many scholars of social inequality have shifted their efforts from the study of social mobility, by means of the intensive analysis of mobility tables using log linear models, to other issues, including gender, racial, and ethnic inequities; problems surrounding the incorporation of ethnically diverse immigrants into industrial societies; structural barriers to mobility in labour markets; and education both as a form of stratification and as a mechanism facilitating mobility. Far from abandoning the key issues raised by social mobility research, these new lines of inquiry serve to broaden our understanding of systems of inequality and movement within them.

NOTES

1. In the late nineteenth century Horatio Alger, Jr. published a series of books for young people, the "Luck and Pluck" series, that featured poor but ambitious young men who always seemed to move from rags to riches by dint of their own efforts and a series of fortuitous events. The "Horatio Alger myth" has since then been synonymous with equal opportunity for all.

2. The Canadian Mobility Study was funded by the Canada Council. Monica Boyd, Hugh A. McRoberts, and John Porter, all of Carleton University at the time, Frank Jones and Peter Pineo, both of McMaster University, and John Goyder, University of Waterloo, served as principal investigators on the original project. See Boyd et al. (1985) for a discussion of the CMS and its methodology.

3. Since 1985, the General Social Survey has been a national survey conducted by Statistics Canada on a nearly annual basis. It was designed to monitor Canadian social trends and to provide data for addressing social policy issues. See Norris and Paton (1991) for a detailed description of the GSS program and survey methodology.

4. I do not report the distribution of mother's occupation for 1973 because the CMS reported just a four-category occupational classification for mother's occupation. As well, few of the mothers of 1973 respondents had been in the labour force, leaving a small sample size for constructing a mobility table unless work in the home is included as an occupational category.

5. The term "inheritance" is used here in the very loose sense that occupational destinations are in the same category as origins. The term is not meant to imply some sort of direct bestowal of a position. Although this still happens in advanced industrial societies, as when children inherit their parents' businesses, most people are employed by others.

6. It must be pointed out that all the data used here come from samples of the Canadian population. As a result, all the figures reported, whether percentages or coefficients of mobility models, are estimates of the actual corresponding value in the Canadian population. Because the samples are large, the estimates are probably good ones, but estimates are nevertheless subject to some error. To keep our discussion as simple as possible, I do not report the inferential statistics necessary to determine how good our estimates may be.

7. These calculations actually were not made using the outflow percentages shown in Tables 10-3 and 10-4, but on the frequency counts on which those percentages are based.

8. Erickson and Goldthorpe (1993:91–93) describe a similar model that they term a "uniform difference" model.

REFERENCES

Blau, Peter M., and Otis Dudley Duncan 1967. *The American Occupational Structure.* New York: Wiley.

Boyd, Monica, John Goyder, Frank E. Jones, Hugh A. McRoberts, Peter C. Pineo, and John Porter 1985. *Ascription and Achievement: Studies in Mobility and Status Attainment in Canada.* Ottawa: Carleton University Press.

Boyd, M., J. Goyder, F.E. Jones, H.A. McRoberts, P.C. Pineo, and J. Porter 1981. "Status attainment in Canada: Findings of the Canadian Mobility Study." *Canadian Review of Sociology and Anthropology* 18:657–673.

Breen, Richard, and Christopher T. Whelan 1994. "Modelling trends in social fluidity." *European Sociological Review* 10:259–272.

DeGraaf, Paul M., and Ruud Luijkx 1992. "From 'ascription' to 'achievement'? Trends in status attainment in the Netherlands between 1930 and 1980" ("Van 'ascription' naar 'achievement'? Trends in statusverwerving in Nederland tussen 1930 en 1980"). *Mens en Maatschappij* 67:412–433.

Erickson, Robert, and John H. Goldthorpe 1992. "Individual or family? Results from two approaches to class assignment." *Acta Sociologica* 35:95–105.

Erickson, Robert, and John H. Goldthorpe 1993. *The Constant Flux: A Study of Class Mobility in Industrial Societies.* Oxford: Clarendon Press.

Featherman, David L., F. Lancaster Jones, and Robert M. Hauser 1975. "Assumptions of social mobility research in the United States: The case of occupational status." *Social Science Research* 4:329–360.

Ganzeboom, Harry B.G., Ruud Luijkx, and Donald J. Treiman 1989. "Intergenerational class mobility in comparative perspective." *Research in Social Stratification and Mobility* 8:3–84.

Giddens, Anthony 1973. *The Class Structure of the Advanced Societies.* New York: Harper and Row.

Goldthorpe, John H. 1987. *Social Mobility and Class Structure in Modern Britain* (2nd ed.). Oxford: Clarendon Press.

Goodman, Leo A. 1969. "How to ransack social mobility tables and other kinds of cross-classification tables." *American Journal of Sociology* 75:1–39.

Hendrickx, John, and Harry B.G. Ganzeboom 1998. "Occupational status attainment in the Netherlands, 1920–1990: A multinomial logistic analysis." *European Sociological Review* 14:387–403.

Hout, Michael 1983. *Mobility Tables.* Beverly Hills: Sage.

Hout, Michael 1988. "More universalism, less structural mobility: The American occupational structure in the 1980s." *American Journal of Sociology* 93:1358–1400.

Kerr, Clark, John T. Dunlop, Frederick H. Harbison, and Charles A. Myers 1960. *Industrialism and Industrial Man.* Cambridge, Massachusetts: Harvard University Press.

Lipset, Seymour Martin 1963. *The First New Nation.* Garden City, New Jersey: Anchor Books.

Lipset, Seymour Martin 1989. *Continental Divide: The Values and Institutions of Canada and the United States.* Toronto: C.D. Howe Institute.

Lipset, Seymour Martin, and Reinhard Bendix 1959. *Social Mobility in Industrial Societies.* Berkeley: University of California Press.

Luijkx, Ruud, Peter Robert, Paul M. DeGraaf, and Harry B.G. Ganzeboom 1995. "From ascription to achievement: The status attainment process in Hungary" ("A szarmazastol a teljesitmenyig: A statuszmegszerzes folyamata Magyarorszagon"). *Szociologiai Szemle* 4:3–27.

Marks, Gary N., and F.L. Jones 1991. "Change over time in father-son mobility in Australia." *Australia-New Zealand Journal of Sociology* 27:315–331.

McRoberts, Hugh A., and Kevin Selbee 1981. "Trends in occupational mobility in Canada and the United States: A Comparison." *American Sociological Review* 46: 406–421.

Norris, D.A., and D.G. Paton 1991. "Canada's General Social Survey: Five years of experience." *Survey Methodology* 17:227–240.

Pineo, Peter C., John Porter, and Hugh A. McRoberts 1977. "The 1971 census and the socioeconomic classification of occupations." *Canadian Review of Sociology and Anthropology* 14:91–102.

Ringdal, Kristen 1994. "Intergenerational class mobility in post-war Norway: A weakening of vertical barriers?" *European Sociological Review* 10:273–288.

Sorokin, Pitirim 1927. *Social Mobility.* New York: Harper & Brothers.

Treiman, Donald J. 1970. "Industrialization and social stratification." In Edward O. Laumann (ed.), *Social Stratification: Research and Theory for the 1970s,* pp. 207–234. New York: Bobbs-Merrill.

Treiman, Donald J. 1977. *Occupational Prestige in Comparative Perspective.* New York: Academic Press.

Vallet, Louis-Andre 1999. "Forty years of social mobility in France: Temporal trends in social fluidity illuminated by recent models" ("Quarante années de mobilité sociale en France: L'évolution de la fluidité sociale à la lumière de modèles recents"). *Revue Française de Sociologie* 40:5–64.

Wanner, Richard A. 1986. "Structural and exchange mobility in Canada and the United States: A comparison." Meeting of the Research Committee on Social Stratification of the International Sociological Association, Rome.

Wanner, Richard A. 1993. "Patterns and Trends in Occupational Mobility." In J. Curtis, E. Grabb, and N. Guppy (eds.), *Social Inequality in Canada: Patterns, Problems, Policies* (2nd ed.), pp. 153–178. Scarborough, Ontario: Prentice-Hall.

Wanner, Richard A. 1999a. "Twentieth-century trends in occupational attainment in Canada." Meeting of the International Sociological Association Research Committee on Social Stratification, Madison, Wisconsin.

Wanner, Richard A. 1999b. "Expansion and ascription: Trends in educational opportunity in Canada, 1920–1994." *Canadian Review of Sociology and Anthropology* 36:409–442.

Wanner, Richard A., and Bernadette C. Hayes 1996. "Intergenerational occupational mobility among men in Canada and Australia." *Canadian Journal of Sociology* 21:43–76.

Weber, Max 1947. *The Theory of Social and Economic Organization.* New York: Oxford University Press.

Xie, Yu 1992. "The log-multiplicative layer effects model for comparing mobility tables." *American Sociological Review* 57:380–395.

LABOUR MARKETS, INEQUALITY, AND THE FUTURE OF WORK

Graham S. Lowe

(Revised from the previous edition of this volume.)

INTRODUCTION

Debate and controversy surround the present and future of work. Canadians entered the twenty-first century having experienced two decades of profound changes in their working lives. Futurists have seized upon these trends, offering conflicting images of where work is headed. Just compare, for example, Jeremy Rifkin's (1995) image of a technology-dominated "workerless world," with William Bridges' (1994) entrepreneurial "dejobbed world" of flexible work, with Richard Sennett's (1998) "new capitalism" where the sense of purpose and commitment in work has eroded.

Sociologists also are concerned about the changing work world and the implications of these trends for society. However, they reject futuristic predictions in favour of a careful consideration of evidence, explanations, and public policy options. A sociological analysis of work is rooted in a firm understanding of labour markets. This chapter examines labour markets: what they are, how they operate, major Canadian labour market trends, and the implications of these trends for social inequality.[1]

A labour market can be defined as the processes and institutions through which workers are allocated to paid jobs. Because jobs provide income and other rewards—such as pensions, paid vacations, opportunities for career advancement, and personal development and fulfillment—they have a direct bearing on an individual's living standard and quality of life. Sociologists use information about a person's job or occupation to locate her or him in the class structure. Thus, labour markets are central to understanding broader issues of how inequality is structured in a society (Van den Berg and Smucker, 1997).

A POST-INDUSTRIAL SOCIETY?

We will begin by examining changes in jobs in the context of debates about an emerging post-industrial society. The post–World War II expansion of white-collar occupations and service industries, along with increasing living standards, gave rise in the 1970s to a theory of "post-industrial society." Daniel Bell (1973) argued that the industrial phase of capitalism was over, replaced by a post-industrial society that was based on knowledge production rather than goods production. While industrialization had brought increased productivity and living standards, post-industrial society would usher in reduced class conflict and less concentration of power. Bell underscored the importance of knowledge, suggesting that it was the new basis of power. Knowledge workers, such as technicians, scientists, and other professionals, would become the new elite.

An alternative, critical view is provided by neo-Marxist scholars (Braverman 1974; Rinehart 2001). Examining changes in the "labour process"—how work is actually performed—these researchers suggest that work under corporate capitalism has become more alienating and that class divisions are widening. The growing numbers of non-managerial white-collar workers in offices, shops, or the public sector form, in this view, a new working class. More sophisticated managerial control techniques and computer technology extended the degradation of working conditions from the factory into offices and other white-collar settings.

However, a close inspection of labour market trends reveals a far more complex and contradictory picture than portrayed by either the post-industrial or the labour process perspective. In the United States, Robert Reich (1991) points out that the real winners in the high-tech, global economy are the symbolic analysts—Bell's knowledge workers. However, Reich argues that their rise to power and wealth has created even greater inequality. In Canada, John Myles (1988) has found some support for both theoretical positions. Myles shows that shifts in employment patterns across industries, coupled with changing skill requirements within industries, have created jobs at the top and the bottom of the occupational ladder, and a decline in middle-level blue-collar jobs in the manufacturing sector. In sum, the shift to a service-based economy has been accompanied by growing signs of polarization in the labour market.

EXPLAINING LABOUR MARKETS

The debates about post-industrialism draw our attention to how, and why, certain individuals or groups occupy particular locations in the labour market. Who gets to be a corporate executive, a computer technician, or a parking lot attendant? Are these jobs allocated based on ability, other personal characteristics (such as age, gender, ethnicity, or social class), luck, or some combination? These are key sociological questions, given that one's job determines one's "life chances." Furthermore, an understanding of how the labour market operates is essential for designing public policies that can shape the future of work, thereby addressing concerns about a lack of good jobs.

There are two major theoretical perspectives on labour markets. Human capital theory comes from economics, while labour market segmentation theory is more sociological. Both recognize that some jobs are better than others, in terms of pay and benefits, career opportunities, personal rewards, and social status. Beyond this similarity, the two perspectives offer alternative views of how labour markets are organized and operate.

Human Capital Theory

Human capital theory draws on neo-classical economics (Becker 1975). It assumes that the labour market is one large, open arena in which everyone with similar qualifications competes on the same basis for available jobs. The market rewards those individuals who have the greatest "human capital" as measured by education, training, experience, and ability. A job's rewards are based on its economic contribution to society. By focusing on the supply of labour, in terms of workers' characteristics, this theory does not address the influence of employers' hiring practices or the organization of work on inequality. The theory simply assumes that employers make rational hiring and promotion decisions based on ability.

This view of the labour market is similar to the functionalist theories that were popular in sociology several decades ago. These theories also saw a person's socio-economic position as a product of the functional importance of their job in society. Human capital theory presents a consensus view of society; issues of class and power are ignored. However, human capital theory does accurately predict the returns of education. There is solid evidence that, on average, individuals with university degrees have higher incomes, greater lifetime earnings, a lower risk of unemployment, and a generally higher probability of being in a "good" job, in comparison with individuals who have lower levels of education. This was starkly clear in the 1990s, when the vast majority of new full-time jobs went to university graduates.

However, human capital theory can't explain why some groups get better jobs than other groups, regardless of ability or education (Blau and Ferber 1986). For example, young people from poor families often don't even get the opportunity to apply to a university and are at risk of dropping out of high school. In 2000, the chief executive officers of the sixty largest corporations listed on the Toronto Stock Exchange received an average compensation package worth over $6 million (Krahn and Lowe 2002:104). In contrast, equally able and educated individuals in socially useful occupations—say, primary school teachers or managers of community food banks—earned far less. In addition, members of recent immigrant groups often end up working in low-status jobs, for example, as taxi drivers or security guards, even though they may be highly educated and experienced.

Labour Market Segmentation Theory

Such inequalities among different jobs provide the starting point for labour market segmentation theory (Clairmont et al. 1983; Rubery 1988; Kalleberg and Berg 1987; Gordon et al. 1982). This perspective rejects human capital theory's assumption of a homogenous labour market in which all people compete on the basis of their education and other human-capital attributes. Instead, it depicts the labour market as comprising unequal segments, where movement to a better or "primary" labour market segment from a worse or "secondary" segment is often difficult. The segmentation perspective examines the barriers that many qualified individuals face in trying to enter the primary labour market.

There are different versions of this basic labour market segmentation perspective. A dual economy model highlights the uneven development of economic sectors in industrial capitalist societies (Hodson and Kaufman 1982). This model distinguishes between core and periphery industries, with the majority of better jobs found in organizations located in core sectors, which include mainly large corporations and government. The Japanese economy is organized along these lines, with corporations like Toyota providing good careers and benefits to its workers while subcontracting for parts and services to an extensive network of small firms in which wages and working conditions are poor. In Canada, General Motors and the Royal Bank are core firms; peripheral firms would include small family-run motels or restaurants.

Small firms tend to have lower profit margins, to invest less in new technologies and worker training, to require less-skilled workers, and to be more labour-intensive than large organizations. Hence, there is greater pressure to keep down wage costs, and workers are considered to be easily replaceable. Unions and professional associations also influence labour market outcomes. The majority of public-sector workers in Canada belong to unions. Unionization also is much higher in large than in small firms. The concentration of professionals in the primary labour market creates "shelters" that limit access to individuals with recognized credentials, increasing the bargaining power of professional associations (Krahn and Lowe 2002, Chapters 3, 7).

The size, profitability, and market dominance of core firms (those in primary labour markets) enable them to use stable employment conditions to gain the cooperation of workers. This employment system is known as an internal labour market (Althauser 1989) and it also applies to governments and other public-sector organizations across Canada. These organizations are pyramid-shaped bureaucracies that recruit at specified entry-level positions and then provide security, career paths, and training to workers once inside, as long as they meet management's expectations for hard work and commitment to the organization's values. Most job openings therefore are filled internally, essentially creating a sheltered organization-based labour market.

Until recently, the internal labour market has been a hallmark of core sector organizations. In the last decade, however, widespread downsizing has shaken internal labour markets. Staff cuts, a "delayering" process whereby the bureaucratic hierarchy is flattened, and a shift to contracting out and temporary workers have all reduced internal career mobility and shaken the employee commitment that these organizations once cultivated. Even in Japan, where major corporations have developed elaborate internal labour markets based on the concept of "life-long employment," a corporate career is no longer guaranteed in return for loyalty and hard work.

Nevertheless, the dualistic thinking of labour market segmentation theory, involving primary versus secondary or core versus periphery jobs, tends to oversimplify current employment realities. A growing number of large private-sector and public-sector organizations are adopting "flexible" approaches to employment, using lower-paid part-time or temporary workers in place of full-time employees. For example, in the retail sector, grocery and department stores rely on a "just-in-time" work force. In many hospitals, unionized cleaning, laundry, and food preparation jobs have been contracted out to firms that employ lower-wage, non-union labour. Another example is the fast-food industry, in which multinational chains recruit staff from secondary labour markets populated by students, middle-aged women, and recent immigrants (Reiter 1991).

WORK IN A SERVICE ECONOMY

The post-industrialists and their critics would agree that Canada is a service-based economy. From the perspective of human capital theory, the rise of a service economy poses questions about possible changes in the relationship between education and jobs, and the relative "pay-offs" of investing in education. For labour market segmentation theory, the recent restructuring of industries and labour markets raises questions about which groups have or have not benefited from these changes.

Changing Industrial Patterns of Employment

To understand these changes, we need to look at industrial patterns of employment over time. Industry classifications focus on the type of economic activity occurring within the workplace. We can distinguish three major sectors: primary (agriculture, mining, forestry, and other resource extraction industries); secondary (manufacturing and construction); and tertiary (industries that create services rather than products). The service sector includes a wide range of industries, from finance and retail trade to education, government, and health and social services.

Much of Canada's industrialization initially entailed a drop in primary-sector employment and a growth in manufactur-

ing jobs. Service industries also expanded in this period, accounting for almost half of all jobs by 1951 (Picot 1987:11). Since then, the proportion of the work force in both the primary and the secondary sectors has declined steeply, although through technological change and new production methods these sectors still contribute significantly to national economic output. As shown in the right-hand column of Table 11-1, by 2000, the service sector accounted for almost three-quarters of all employment. Agriculture accounted for only 2.5% of all employment, while manufacturing accounted for 15%. In contrast, in 1961 these two sectors had accounted for 11% and 24%, respectively, of all jobs.

Table 11-1 also reveals the extent of industrial restructuring in the Canadian economy during the 1990s. The table reports two crucial pieces of information for understanding changing industrial patterns of employment. First, we need to examine the actual numbers of jobs gained or lost in each industry during the 1990 to 2000 period. Note that, in absolute terms, the largest employment losses occurred in agriculture, largely because of global trends in commodity markets, and in public administration, because of government budget and service cuts. It is also interesting that most new jobs were created in professional, scientific, and technical services, a sector associated with the knowledge and technology-intensive "new economy." Nevertheless, at the same time, the manufacturing industries of the "old economy" also added jobs. A second important pattern concerns the rates of employment growth or decline. Public discussions of employment trends often mistakenly focus only on these percentage changes, and this can be misleading if the actual number of jobs involved is not taken into account. For example, trade (retail and wholesale) jobs increased by a

TABLE 11-1   Changes in the Distribution of Employment Between 1990 and 2000, Canada

	Actual	Net	% Change	2000
Total of All Sectors	14 909.7	1825.7	14.0%	
Goods-Producing Sector	3867.8	103.1	2.7%	25.9%
Agriculture	372.6	−74.2	−16.6%	2.5%
Forestry, fishing, mining, oil, and gas	283.0	−22.7	−7.4%	1.9%
Construction	815.6	−1.6	−0.2%	5.5%
Manufacturing	2280.2	227.7	11.1%	15.3%
Utilities	116.4	−26.1	−18.3%	0.8%
Services-Producing Sector	11 041.9	1722.7	18.5%	74.1%
Upper Tier:				
Transportation and Warehousing	779.8	132.6	20.5%	5.2%
Information, culture, and recreation	665.5	151.0	29.3%	4.5%
Finance, insurance, real estate and leasing	867.0	18.9	2.2%	5.8%
Professional, scientific, and technical services	945.9	372.2	64.9%	6.3%
Management, administrative, and other support services	546.2	235.4	75.7%	3.7%
Educational services	974.8	128.7	15.2%	6.5%
Health care and social assistance	1526.4	241.7	18.8%	10.2%
Public administration	761.7	−71.2	−8.5%	5.1%
Lower Tier:				
Trade	2318.1	241.3	11.6%	15.5%
Accommodation and food services	960.6	187.9	24.3%	6.4%
Other consumer services	695.8	84.1	13.7%	4.7%

Source: Adapted from the Statistics Canada publication *Labour Force Historical Review,* Catalogue 71F004, 2001.

relatively modest 11.6% in the decade, but because this is such a large sector, the actual number of jobs generated in the trade sector was quite high.

Given the size and diversity of the service sector, it is useful to divide it into an upper tier, which tends to include the service occupations with the highest pay and educational qualifications, and a lower tier, which includes jobs that generally involve lower incomes and education-al requirements (Krahn and Lowe 2002, Chapter 2; also see Economic Council of Canada 1991). Currently, 47% of the employed are located in the upper-tier services and approximately 27% have jobs in lower-tier service industries, while 26% of employed Canadians work in the goods-producing sector. The distinction between upper-tier and lower-tier service industries is especially relevant to our later discussion of "good" and "bad" jobs.

Occupational Changes

We can also examine employment by looking at occupations, or the kind of work that individuals perform in their jobs. Most workers in primary and secondary industries would be classified as blue-collar (or manual) workers, while the growth of service industries is directly related to the expansion of white-collar occupations. Historically, white-collar occupations tended to be viewed as having higher status. However, as service industries grew and diversified, the white-collar occupational category came to include well over half of Canada's workers, some of whom performed less desirable jobs. Because many of the new white-collar positions—especially clerical, sales, and personal service jobs—have been filled by women, the term "pink-collar" has often been applied to these occupations.

Another related change in the labour force is the rising educational level of workers. Canadians are becoming increasingly well educated. The proportion of the work force with a university degree increased from 7% to 20% between 1975 and 2000, and over half of all workers have now completed some form of post-secondary education (Statistics Canada 2001). As Table 11-1 documents, many new jobs have been created recently in upper-tier service industries that would require some form of post-secondary education. However, the rising educational level raises the question of under-employment: Are well-educated workers, especially recent graduates, able to find jobs that adequately reward their investment in education? (See Livingstone 1999.)

NON-STANDARD WORK

Despite public concerns about declining job security, the majority of employed Canadians still have a full-time, year-round, permanent job. Public insecurity on this issue is fuelled by the recent waves of downsizing, but perhaps more so by the spread of alternatives to the standard type of employment (Lowe 2000). Non-standard work takes four main forms: part-time employment, multiple job-holding, own-account self-employment, and temporary work. These four types of non-standard work accounted for 28% of all employed Canadians (aged 15 to 64 years) in 1989, and one-third of all employed Canadians by 1998 (Krahn and Lowe 2002:86–91).

The non-standard work trend is double-edged. It has advantages, to the extent that it provides some individuals with greater choice and flexibility in how they organize their work life. For example, parents (especially mothers) with young children, university students, older workers wanting to ease out of a full-time career, or highly skilled professionals seeking the continual challenge of new projects may seek out part-time or contract work. Given women's generally greater family responsibilities compared with men's, it is perhaps not surprising that 40% of female workers in 1994 were in non-standard jobs, compared with 27% of men. Often, though, this choice involves trade-offs. The main disadvantage of non-standard work is that it tends to offer lower wages and fewer benefits than full-time work, because employers use non-standard employment as a "flexible" strategy for reducing labour costs.

Part-time work is defined as working less than thirty hours per week in one's main job. It is the most common type of non-standard employment, accounting for 18% of all employment in 2000 (Krahn and Lowe 2002:90). This is a modest increase from 1977, when part-time employment was 13% of the total. About three-quarters of part-timers are women, and youth of both genders are also concentrated in these jobs. However, what has increased more rapidly in the past two decades is involuntary part-time employment, whereby people have to accept part-time jobs because suitable full-time jobs are not available. In 2000, 25% of all part-time workers were "involuntary," up from 11% in 1975. This increase reflects the fact that the economy is not generating a sufficient number of full-time jobs to meet the needs of workers.

HOURS OF WORK

We can gain a more complete picture of how labour market restructuring affects employment opportunities by examining trends in work hours. Canada established a standard forty-hour work week in the late 1950s. Despite expectations of more leisure time due to the productivity gains of computers and other new technologies, by 2000 the average length of the work week was still just under thirty-seven hours. However, a substantial polarization in work hours has occurred, as part-time jobs increased at the same time as did jobs with long hours.

By 2000, only 59% of paid workers put in thirty-five to forty hours weekly (Krahn and Lowe 2002:83–85). Young workers (aged 15 to 24) experienced the largest drop in work hours, resulting in a sharp decline in real earnings (i.e., earnings adjusted for inflation) since the 1980s (Betcherman and Leckie 1997). Over the same period, many adult workers, especially males, have put in longer hours. This has been mainly due to organizational downsizing, which tends to increase the workloads (usually without more pay) for remaining employees, and also has occurred because of a rise in multiple job-holding. Thus, by 2000, 16% of the labour force worked more than forty hours weekly, and, in some management and professional occupations, a fifty-hour work week has become common (Canadian Policy Research Networks 2002).

The fact that some people don't have enough work while others have too much is a reflection of a more polarized labour market (Duffy et al. 1997). In this context, it is not surprising that a growing number of policy analysts and interest groups are calling for a reduced work week. Shortening the work week to thirty-five or thirty hours is seen as a way of redistributing work. This policy would redistribute income, because those with no job or with too few hours would see increased incomes, while groups of full-time workers would have small cuts in both income and hours (Human Resources Development Canada 1994). Work redistribution has attracted interest because of persistently high unemployment and the absence of effective job creation policies. During 2000, more than one million Canadians were unemployed (that is, out of a job but actively seeking one). Since the end of World War II, the long-term trend in unemployment rates has been upward, from an average of 4% in the 1950s to between 7% and 8% in the early twenty-first century.

Some public policy analysts urge governments to adopt more active job creation measures (Betcherman and Lowe 1997; MacLean and Osberg 1996; *Policy Options* July-August 1996). However, creating new jobs poses a more difficult challenge than does redistributing existing work time. Even Jeremy Rifkin (1995), who argues in *The End of Work* that there will be less work to go around in the future, advocates reducing the work week as a partial solution to unemployment. Several European nations are moving in this direction. Unionized German auto workers have negotiated shorter work hours in order to create more jobs, and in France, there is widespread popular support for a legislated thirty-five-hour work week to help reduce high unemployment.

GOOD JOBS AND BAD JOBS

There is considerable debate about whether the service economy has created more good jobs than bad ones, and how public policy can encourage the creation of better-quality jobs in the future (Banting and Beach 1995; Osberg et al. 1995; Duffy et al. 1997). The language of "good" and "bad" jobs refers to widening disparities on a range of job characteristics: wages, benefits, skill requirements, security, working conditions, and intrinsic rewards, such as the experience of challenging and satisfying work. The "good jobs"–"bad jobs" dichotomy seems to capture the basic difference between standard and non-standard jobs. In the 1980s, 44% of all employment growth was in non-standard jobs (Economic Council of Canada 1991:81), a trend that continued in the 1990s. However, not all of these non-standard jobs are what critics call "McJobs." Some of these positions earn high incomes and require high levels of skill and education; business consultants and project engineers are two good examples.

Income is an obvious criterion for identifying jobs that may be more or less desirable. If we look at the incomes of paid employees (i.e., excluding the self-employed), individuals in the service sector earn about 20% less than people in the goods-producing industries. However, there is wide variation in income within the service sector, with workers in the upper-tier industries earning much more than those in the lower-tier industries. For example, paid employees in engineering, architectural, and computer-related services earned an average of about $800 per week in the mid-1990s, almost four times as much as those in food and beverage services (Grenon 1996).

There are also substantial occupational differences in earnings. In 1995, managers reported average annual earnings of $41 352 (Statistics Canada 1997). In contrast, clerical workers earned an average of $21 825, and the combined category of waitresses, hairdressers, security guards, and other service jobs paid an average of $17 160. Some of these differences in earnings are due to a higher percentage of part-time and part-year workers in service occupations, especially in the lower-tier service industries. In some cases, the higher earnings in goods-producing industries, upper-tier services, and managerial and professional occupations are partly due to the influence of unions and professional associations. Typically, the higher earnings of managers and professionals also reflect their higher educational attainment.

Employment benefits are another measure of job quality. Benefits such as employment insurance, the Canada/Québec Pension Plan, and workers' compensation are part of the "social safety net." Although they are mandatory, such government-funded benefits only provide a minimum level of support. In addition, however, some jobs come with employer-provided benefits, which therefore give some workers much better security and living standards than others, and which again reinforce the distinction between good and bad jobs. Figure 11-1 reports access to four basic types of job benefits—a pension, supplementary health insurance, paid sick leave, and paid maternity or parental leave—by labour market status. The majority of jobs that are full-time and that are permanent jobs (often these two features go hand in hand) receive these benefits. In contrast, we see

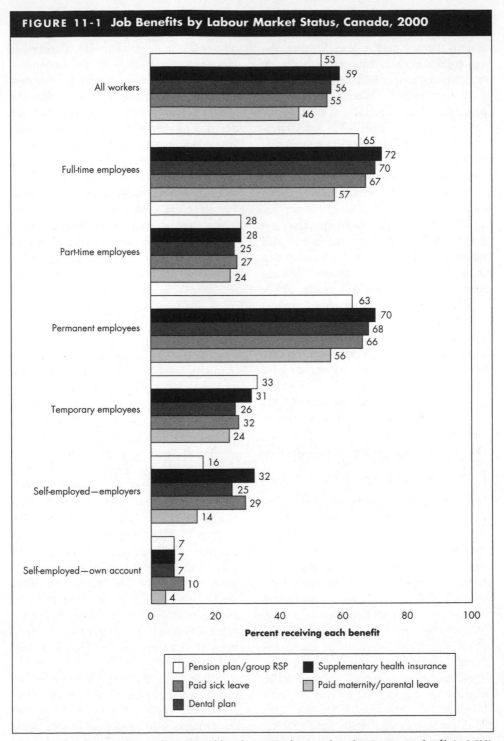

FIGURE 11-1 Job Benefits by Labour Market Status, Canada, 2000

All workers: 53, 59, 56, 55, 46

Full-time employees: 65, 72, 70, 67, 57

Part-time employees: 28, 28, 25, 27, 24

Permanent employees: 63, 70, 68, 66, 56

Temporary employees: 33, 31, 26, 32, 24

Self-employed—employers: 16, 32, 25, 29, 14

Self-employed—own account: 7, 7, 7, 10, 4

Percent receiving each benefit

☐ Pension plan/group RSP   ■ Supplementary health insurance
■ Paid sick leave   ■ Paid maternity/parental leave
■ Dental plan

Source: Canada Policy Research Networks Inc., CPRN/Ekos Changing Employment Relationships Survey, microdata file (n=2,500).

much lower levels of benefits coverage, in the range of 24 to 33%, among part-time and temporary employees. However, the group least likely to have any benefits are the own-account self-employed—the contract workers and freelancers that feature prominently in some discussions of the future of work. In terms of industrial sectors, workers in the lower-tier services typically receive few benefits. Benefits are more common in large organizations and in unionized workplaces, which also tend to be larger.

Training can also be an important job benefit; however, only about one in five workers receive work-related training that is paid for by the employer (Human Resources Development Canada 1997). Increasingly, training is viewed by workers as a personal "safety net" that increases their employability in a volatile labour market. Furthermore, workers who receive employer-sponsored training already have labour market advantages, to the extent that they are better educated, work in large firms, and often have full-time positions.

LABOUR MARKET GENDER INEQUALITIES

One of the most profound changes in Canadian society over the last three decades has been the sharp rise in female employment. In 1970, 38% of all adult women in Canada worked outside the home for pay; in 2000, this figure had reached 59.5%. Deeply rooted barriers to female employment have been eroding. Many factors underlie this change, particularly feminism's critique of traditional female stereotypes, women's rising educational levels, and economic pressures for women to support themselves or their families.

Most wives in the 1950s and 1960s left the labour force to raise families. By the 1980s, however, a growing proportion of mothers with young children were also employed, greatly increasing the female labour force participation rate (Logan and Belliveau 1995). Dual-earner families now account for three out of five families. As well, 15% of all mothers in the work force are single parents. Sociologists use terms like the double day, or the second shift, to denote the tendency for most married women to spend their days in paying jobs, yet still assume most of the responsibilities of child care and domestic chores when they get home (Hochschild 1989). Most workplaces have not adapted to this social change by becoming more flexible and family-friendly.

Gender-Segregated Employment

The concept of occupational gender segregation describes the concentration of men and women in different occupations. Gender-role socialization and education reinforce this pattern. Consequently, many women end up in occupations that are predominantly female, such as clerical work or nursing. The concept of a female "job ghetto" emphasizes the unequal rewards and opportunities built into the labour market on the basis of a worker's gender. Women in job ghettos lack easy access to the more challenging and lucrative occupations that traditionally have been dominated by men. These male segments of the labour market (e.g., senior management and some professions such as engineering) often set up success criteria that are male-biased (Kanter 1977; McIlwee and Robinson 1992).

Figures 11-2 and 11-3 describe two major trends associated with occupational gender segregation. Figure 11-2 identifies the percentage of employees in each occupation who are women. Women now compose 46% of the total labour force. Clerical and administrative jobs, along with nursing and health-related occupations, have the highest concentrations of women (75% and 86%, respectively). Teaching, social sciences, and sales and service occupations (e.g., jobs in restaurants, bars, hotels, tourism, hairdressing, child-care facilities, and domestic and building cleaning) are between 57% and 62% female. All these could be labelled job ghettos in the sense that the majority of employees are women, although pay

and other working conditions in some positions (particularly nursing and teaching) are relatively good. By contrast, 20% of workers in natural sciences, engineering, and mathematics occupations are women, and just 6% of jobs in trades, transportation, and construction occupations are held by women.

Figure 11-3 shows the distribution of the female labour force across all occupations. Clerical and administrative occupations employed almost one-quarter of all female workers in 1999, although this

FIGURE 11-2 Women's Employment by Occupational Group, Canada, 1999

Occupational Group	Women as a percentage of total employment in occupation
All occupations	45.9
Managerial	35.1
Business/finance	49.4
Natural science/engineering/mathematics	19.6
Social sciences	58.2
Teaching	62.1
Doctors/dentists/other health-related	47.1
Nursing/therapy/other health-related	86.5
Artistic/recreational	54.8
Clerical/administrative	75.3
Sales/service	58.7
Primary occupations	21.6
Processing/manufacturing/utilities	29.8
Trades/transport/construction	6.2

Source: Adapted from the Statistics Canada publication *Women in Canada 2000. A Gender-based Statistical Report*, Catalogue 89-503, September 14.

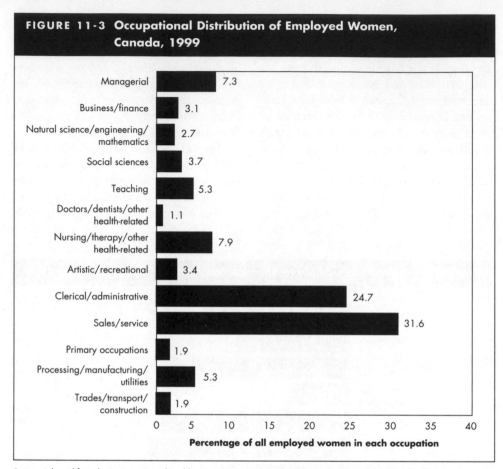

FIGURE 11-3 Occupational Distribution of Employed Women, Canada, 1999

Occupation	Percentage
Managerial	7.3
Business/finance	3.1
Natural science/engineering/mathematics	2.7
Social sciences	3.7
Teaching	5.3
Doctors/dentists/other health-related	1.1
Nursing/therapy/other health-related	7.9
Artistic/recreational	3.4
Clerical/administrative	24.7
Sales/service	31.6
Primary occupations	1.9
Processing/manufacturing/utilities	5.3
Trades/transport/construction	1.9

Percentage of all employed women in each occupation

Source: Adapted from the Statistics Canada publication *Women in Canada 2000. A Gender-based Statistical Report,* Catalogue 89-503, September 14.

proportion is down from one-third in 1991. Over half of the female labour force is in service, sales, and clerical jobs. These numbers demonstrate women's continued overrepresentation in lower-status occupations, or what we have referred to as job ghettos. Only about 10% of female workers are in traditional male areas of work, such as primary, manufacturing, and other manual occupations.

Despite these patterns, however, occupational gender segregation is slowly being reduced as women move into a broader range of occupations. Over the past twenty years, more women have entered nontraditional jobs in which men historically predominated, especially in management and some professions (Hughes 1995). Note in Figure 11-3, however, that only 7% of employed women are managers, even though this is a growing area of female employment. It appears that many women still encounter a "glass ceiling." This concept refers to the often-invisible barriers to women's advancement that persist despite formal policies—such as employment equity—that are designed to eradicate these obstacles.

The Gender Wage Gap

Male-female wage differences reveal how gender is a major source of labour market inequality. For example, female managers reported average annual earnings in 1995 of $32 306, two-thirds of the earnings of their male counterparts ($48 753) (Statistics Canada 1997). Similar differences are observed in all major occupations. The average 1995 earnings of all employed women in Canada ($20 219) represented only 65% of the average earnings of all employed men ($31 053). Examining only full-time, full-year workers, which is perhaps a more appropriate comparison, given women's higher level of part-time employment, we see that male average earnings increase to $40 610, compared with $29 700 for females. Expressed as a female-to-male earnings ratio, or gender wage gap, in 1995 full-time working women received an average of 73% of the wages of their male counterparts, up from 60% in 1970.

Women's rising incomes can be partly explained by their rising educational attainment and access to better-paying jobs. Another factor, however, is that, since 1975, real earnings for men have fallen slightly (Krahn and Lowe 2002, Chapter 3). During this period, women were moving into intermediate-level professions and junior- and middle-level management positions. At the same time, males were losing ground in well-paying (often unionized) manual jobs and in some professional and managerial occupations due to downsizing and industrial restructuring. While different factors affected male and female employment, the overall result was rising wages for some women and falling wages for some men.

Women can face two key forms of labour-market discrimination. Employers could pay women less than men for performing the same jobs, a form of wage discrimination that is rare in Canada today. More common, however, is an indirect type of discrimination, which results from the gender-segregated structure of the labour market, and from the gender-based stratification within organizations that gives men greater access to jobs with the highest rewards. Thus, when statistical models are applied that take into account male-female differences in various characteristics—in education, training, and work experience, in occupation and industry of employment, and in geographic location—the wage gap shrinks. Applying this type of analysis to men and women employed in the same jobs within a single establishment, the earnings ratio narrows even further, to between 90% and 95% (Gunderson 1994; Coverman 1988).

Given that more women than ever before are graduating from university, how has this improved their labour market success? Overall, a university education is a good predictor of higher occupational attainment for both women and men However, the National Graduate Survey found a wage gap of 92% at the bachelor level when it followed up 1990 graduates in 1992 (Wannell and Caron 1994). Even so, gender and other individual characteristics have far less impact on graduates' earnings than does program of study (Davies et al. 1996). In other words, gendered enrollment patterns in post-secondary institutions—for example, women choosing nursing and men choosing engineering—are directly linked to occupational gender segregation. Overall, there are positive signs suggesting that women will have increased employment opportunities in the future, although the path toward gender equality has clearly been far from easy.

Another important point in this regard is that most of the reduction in occupational gender segregation has resulted from women moving into male-dominated jobs, and not from men moving into female-dominated jobs. Public policy has been a catalyst for these changes. Since the mid-1980s, the federal and some provincial governments, as well as a number of large employers, have implemented employment-equity and pay-equity policies. The goal of employment equity policies is the elimination of barriers to the recruitment or advancement of four social groups that historically have been disadvantaged in the Canadian labour market: women, visible minorities, Aboriginal peoples, and persons with disabilities. Pay equity promotes the principle of equal pay for work of equal value. This policy uses job evaluation systems to compare predominantly female jobs with predominantly male jobs within the same organization, in an attempt to redress any undervaluing of women's work. Both approaches are good examples of how public policy can positively influence employer practices by promoting gender equality in the labour market. Of course, employment-equity policies address more than just gender-based inequities in the labour market. While our focus in this chapter has been on gender, it is important to apply the same kind of labour market analysis to other groups. Such analyses are discussed in other chapters of this volume.

CONCLUSION

Many of the concerns Canadians have about the future of work are, in fact, concerns about present labour market trends (Lowe 2000). Widespread feelings of economic insecurity among Canadians are a reaction to high unemployment and under-employment, the spread of non-standard work, declining real incomes, and a more polarized labour market that has clear winners and losers. A paradox in today's labour market is that some workers—the under-employed and involuntary part-timers—don't have enough work, while a growing number of full-time workers are putting in longer hours than they consider ideal. These developments have a direct impact on society, as more of the risks associated with economic change are transferred to individuals, families, and communities, and as the divide widens between the haves and have-nots. The study of labour markets can inform public policies to address these problems.

This chapter has focused on paid work in the formal economy. Such an emphasis makes sense if we consider that, directly or indirectly, the vast majority of Canadians rely for their daily living on earned income from employment. Still, it is important to recognize that a fully comprehensive discussion of work would have to include unpaid work performed in households and in volunteer-based community organizations, as well as paid work in the "informal" or "underground" economy that operates outside government regulation (e.g., the backyard mechanic who fixes your car for cash). Hence, while the paid labour market is a crucial element in the world of work, it does not account for all of the important labour that is performed by Canadians. Looking into the future, it is interesting to speculate about changes in how Canadians value and participate in all forms of work.

NOTES

1. This chapter relies extensively on data and analysis from Statistics Canada. Useful sources in this regard are two quarterly publications, *Perspectives on Labour and Income* and *Canadian Social Trends; The Labour Force* (monthly); and the *Labour Force Historical Review* CD-ROM.

Students are encouraged to visit Statistics Canada's website (http://www.statscan.ca) for regular updates and extensive background information on labour market, demographic, economic, and social trends.

REFERENCES

Akyeampong, Ernest B. 1997. "Work arrangements: 1995 overview." *Perspectives on Labour and Income* (Spring):48–52.

Althauser, Robert P. 1989. "Internal labor markets." *Annual Review of Sociology* 15:143–61.

Banting, Keith G., and Charles M. Beach (eds.) 1995. *Labour Market Polarization and Social Policy Reform.* Kingston, Ontario: School of Policy Studies, Queen's University.

Becker, Gary S. 1975. *Human Capital: A Theoretical and Empirical Analysis with Special Reference to Education* (2nd ed.). Chicago: University of Chicago Press.

Bell, Daniel 1973. *The Coming of Post-Industrial Society.* New York: Basic Books.

Betcherman, Gordon, and Graham Low 1997. *The Future of Work in Canada: A Synthesis Report.* Ottawa: Canadian Policy Research Networks Inc.

Betcherman, Gordon, and Norm Leckie 1997. *Youth Employment and Education Trends in the 1980s and 1990s.* Ottawa: Canadian Policy Research Networks Inc., Working Paper No. W03.

Blau, Francine D., and Marianne A. Ferber 1986. *The Economics of Women, Men and Work.* Englewood Cliffs, New Jersey: Prentice-Hall.

Braverman, Harry 1974. *Labor and Monopoly Capital: The Degradation of Work in the Twentieth Century.* New York: Monthly Review Press.

Bridges, William 1994. *Job Shift: How to Prosper in a Workplace Without Jobs.* Don Mills, Ontario: Addison-Wesley.

Canadian Policy Research Networks 2002. Job quality website, work hours section (http://www.jobquality.ca).

Clairmont, Donald, R. Apostle, and R. Kreckel 1983. "The segmentation perspective as a middle-range conceptualization in sociology." *Canadian Journal of Sociology* 8:245–271.

Coverman, Shelley 1988. "Sociological explanations of the male-female wage gap: Individual and structuralist theories." In Ann Helton Stromberg and Shirley Harkess (eds.), *Women Working: Theories and Facts in Perspective* (2nd ed.). Mountain View, California: Mayfield.

Davies, Scott, Clayton Mosher, and Bill O'Grady 1996. "Educating women: Gender inequalities among Canadian university graduates." *Canadian Review of Sociology and Anthropology* 33:125–142.

Duffy, Ann, Daniel Glenday, and Norene Pupo (eds.) 1997. *Good Jobs, Bad Jobs, No Jobs: The Transformation of Work in the Twenty-first Century.* Toronto: Harcourt Brace Canada.

Economic Council of Canada 1991. *Employment in the Service Economy.* Ottawa: Supply and Services Canada.

Gordon, David. M., R. Edwards, and M. Reich 1982. *Segmented Work, Divided Workers: The Historical Transformation of Labor in the United States.* New York: Cambridge University Press.

Grenon, Lee 1996. "Are service jobs low-paying?" *Perspectives on Labour and Income* (Spring):29–34.

Gunderson, Morley 1994. *Comparable Worth and Gender Discrimination: An International Perspective.* Geneva: Organization for Economic Cooperation and Development.

Hochschild, Arlie 1989. *The Second Shift: Working Parents and the Revolution at Home.* New York: Viking Penguin.

Hodson, Randy, and Robert L. Kaufman 1982. "Economic dualism: A critical review." *American Sociological Review* 47:727–739.

Hughes, Karen D. 1995. "Women in non-traditional occupations." *Perspectives on Labour and Income* (Autumn):14–19.

Human Resources Development Canada 1994. *Report of the Advisory Committee on Working*

Time and the Distribution of Work. Ottawa: Supply and Services Canada.

Human Resources Development Canada (and Statistics Canada) 1997. *Adult Education and Training in Canada: Report of the 1994 Adult Education and Training Survey.* Ottawa: Supply and Services Canada.

Kalleberg, Arne, and Ivar Berg 1987. *Work and Industry: Structures, Markets, and Processes.* New York: Plenum.

Kanter, Rosabeth M. 1977. *Men and Women of the Corporation.* New York: Basic Books.

Krahn, Harvey, and Graham S. Lowe 2002. *Work, Industry & Canadian Society* (4th ed.). Toronto: Thomson Nelson.

Livingstone, D.W. 1999. *The Education–Jobs Gap: Underemployment or Economic Democracy.* Toronto: Garamond Press.

Logan, Ron, and Jo-Anne Belliveau 1995. "Working mothers." *Canadian Social Trends* (Spring):24–28.

Lowe, Graham S. 2000. *The Quality of Work: A People Centred Agenda.* Toronto: Oxford University Press.

MacLean, Brian K., and Lars Osberg (eds.) 1996. *The Unemployment Crisis: All for Nought?* Toronto: University of Toronto Press.

McIlwee, Judith S., and J. Gregg Robinson 1992. *Women in Engineering: Gender, Power, and Workplace Culture.* Albany, New York: State University of New York Press.

Myles, John 1988. "The expanding middle: Some Canadian evidence on the deskilling debate." *Canadian Review of Sociology and Anthropology* 25:335–364.

Osberg, Lars, Fred Wien, and Jan Grude 1995. *Vanishing Jobs: Canada's Changing Workplace.* Toronto: Lorimer.

Picot, W. Garnett 1987. "The changing industrial mix of employment, 1951–1985." *Canadian Social Trends* (Spring):8–11.

Policy Options 1996. Special Issue on Unemployment 17(6).

Reich, Robert B. 1991. *The Work of Nations: Preparing Ourselves for Twenty-first-Century Capitalism.* New York: Alfred A. Knopf.

Reiter, Ester 1991. *Making Fast Food: From the Frying Pan into the Fryer.* Montréal and Kingston: McGill-Queen's University Press.

Rifkin, Jeremy 1995. *The End of Work: The Decline of the Global Labor Force and the Dawn of the Post-Market Era.* New York: Putnum.

Rinehart, James 2001. *The Tyranny of Work: Alienation and the Labour Process.* (4th ed.). Toronto: Harcourt Canada.

Rubery, Jill 1988. "Employers and the labour market." In Duncan Gallie (ed.), *Employment in Britain.* Oxford: Basil Blackwell.

Sennett, Richard 1998. *The Corrosion of Character: The Personal Consequences of Work in the New Capitalism.* New York: W.W. Norton & Company.

Sheridan, Mike, Deborah Sunter, and Brent Diverty 1996. "The changing work week: Trends in weekly hours of work in Canada, 1976–1995." *The Labour Force Survey* (June). Ottawa: Statistics Canada. Catalogue No. 71-001.

Statistics Canada 2001. *Labour Force Historical Review 2000.* Catalogue No. 71-F004-XCB.

Statistics Canada 1997. *Earnings of Men and Women 1995.* Catalogue No. 13-217.

Statistics Canada Various years. *The Labour Force.* Catalogue No. 71-001 monthly.

Statistics Canada Various years. *Perspectives on Labour and Income.* Catalogue No. 75-001.

Statistics Canada Various years. *Canadian Social Trends.* Library of Congress No. HN103.C355.

Van den Berg, Axel, and Joseph Smucker (eds.) 1997. *The Sociology of Labour Markets: Efficiency, Equity, Security.* Scarborough: Prentice Hall Allyn and Bacon Canada.

Wannell, Ted, and Nathalie Caron 1994. *The Gender Earnings Gap Among Recent Postsecondary Graduates, 1984–92.* Ottawa: Statistics Canada, Analytic Studies Branch, Research Paper Series, No. 64.

C h a p t e r

INTERGENERATIONAL CHANGE IN THE EDUCATION OF CANADIANS

Élaine Fournier, George Butlin, and Philip Giles

(Adapted from Statistics Canada, "Intergenerational change in the education of Canadians," *Education Quarterly Review,* Catalogue 81-003, 1995, 2, 2, pp. 22–23. Reprinted with permission.)

INTRODUCTION

How does a person's socio-economic status compare with his or her parents' status? Using data collected in January 1993 as part of the Survey of Labour and Income Dynamics (SLID's) preliminary interview, this article examines the relationship between a person's educational attainment and that of his or her parents by comparing the academic achievements and mobility of different generations.

Educational attainment is a strong predictor of occupational success and income level. For example, in 1993, average income for persons with a university degree was $40 247, compared with $23 644 for those with a high school diploma (Statistics Canada 1994).

THE NATURE OF EDUCATIONAL ATTAINMENT

As Grabb (1992) has noted, some sociologists have argued that academic success or failure is based mainly on individual talent and motivation rather than on factors related to social background (for example, sex, ethnicity, religion, and family social class). Put in terms of social mobility, a society may be characterized either by a weak linkage between social origin (in this article, parents' education) and personal position (educational attainment), allowing considerable intergenerational movement, or by a strong connection entailing less movement.

Readers should be mindful of structural mobility—that is, mobility arising from changes in the population as a whole. With the expansion in the Canadian educational system that started in the 1950s, there has been a general upgrading of educational levels between generations. Persons born during or after the 1950s are likely to be better educated than their parents' generation, particularly at the post-secondary levels (Pomfret 1992).

Against the backdrop of structural mobility, this article looks at circulation mobility (Creese, Guppy and Meissner 1991), which is movement attributable to factors such as an individual's talent and motivation.

Measuring Level of Education

Our educational level variable has five categories: university degree; college or university (with or without a certificate or diploma); high school diploma; some secondary schooling; and some elementary schooling or completion.

The following groups have been excluded from the analysis: respondents who did not have a university degree and are still attending school; those who did not report a level of education; and those whose parents' level of education was not reported. People who are still studying but have already reached the highest level of education (that is, university degree) have been included in the analysis; those who have not achieved a university degree and are still studying have been excluded because they may eventually reach a higher level. Respondents without a reported parents' educational level are more likely to be older. Their exclusion from the analysis will slightly bias the measures of mobility upwards since, in general, older respondents have less upward mobility.

TABLE 12-1	Educational Attainment of Canadians and Their Parents, by Sex, 1993			
	Daughters*	Sons*	Mothers*	Fathers*
Education				
Total**	100.0	100.0	100.0	100.0
University degree	12.3	15.4	3.2	7.1
College or university (with or without a certificate or diploma)	39.4	39.0	8.6	7.0
High school diploma	18.9	15.7	18.3	14.9
Some secondary schooling	15.1	15.9	20.1	18.8
Some elementary schooling or completion	14.3	14.0	49.9	52.1

* "Sons" and "daughters" correspond to the Canadian population, so these columns could also be labelled "males" and "females." On the other hand, "mothers" and "fathers" refer to the parents of those aged 15 and over in the Canadian population; some of these people are also part of the Canadian population, some were members of the Canadian population but have since died or moved out of the country, and some were never part of the Canadian population.

** Total may not sum to 100% due to rounding.

Source: Survey of Labour and Income Dynamics preliminary interview (January 1993).

CANADIANS' EDUCATIONAL ATTAINMENT HAS RISEN

Canadians have traditionally attained a higher educational level than the previous generation. In 1993, just over half the population had attended a post-secondary institution, compared with a little over 10% of their parents (Table 12-1). Moreover, while 70% of the parents had not graduated from high school, only 30% of their children had failed to do so.

Educational attainment varies considerably by age. Two out of three baby boomers (aged 25 to 44) had some post-secondary education, compared with two out of five persons born before the baby boom (aged 45 and over). Compared with baby boomers, proportionately fewer young (aged 15 to 24) people (one in two) had some post-secondary education, but since one-quarter of them did not have a high school diploma, they may have left school temporarily (dropping out is wide-

TABLE 12-2 Mother's and Daughter's Educational Attainment, 1993
Daughter's Education

Daughter's Education: Mother's Education:	University Degree	College or University (with or without a certificate or diploma)	High School Diploma	Some Secondary Schooling	Some Elementary Schooling Completion	Total %
Total*	100.0	12.2	39.3	19.0	15.2	14.3
University degree	3.1	1.5	1.1	–	–	–
College or university (with or without a certificate or diploma)	8.7	2.4	4.5	1.2	0.5	–
High school diploma	18.0	3.4	9.1	3.6	1.5	0.3**
Some secondary schooling	19.8	2.2	8.8	5.2	3.0	0.6
Some elementary schooling or completion	50.3	2.6	15.9	8.5	10.0	13.2

* Totals may not equal sum of parts due to rounding.

** High sampling variance (coefficient of variation between 16.5% and 25 %); use with caution.

Note: The shaded diagonal from top left to bottom right refers to cases with no mobility (that is, the educational level of daughter and mother are the same.)

Source: Survey of Labour and Income Dynamics preliminary interview (January 1993).

spread). Age, therefore, has a significant effect on educational level.

MOBILITY TABLES[1]

The analysis of intergenerational mobility starts with a cross-classification of a respondent's educational level with that of one parent (see below "Measuring Mobility"); for example, a daughter's educational level and her mother's (Table 12-2). The cells above the diagonal describe *downward mobility* (for example, a mother with a university degree and a daughter with a high school diploma). Each segment to the right of the shaded diagonal represents one step of *downward mobility*. Similarly, the cells below the diagonal contain cases of *upward mobility*, and each segment to the left represents one step upward. For example, four steps of upward mobility are captured by daughters with a university degree whose mothers had elementary schooling.

The cell values in a mobility table can be aggregated to show the degree of mobility. Table 12-3 contains these distributions for the four possible parent/child combinations.

Measuring Mobility

The measure of mobility depends largely on the number of categories used. The higher the number, the higher the likelihood that a person will move. (In the extreme case, with only one category, there would be no mobility.) In defining the categories, SLID has ranked the educational levels and, by doing so, has made a value judgment.

In this article, a person with a university degree is judged to have attained a higher educational level than someone with college or university (but no degree), even though this is not always the case. For example, a person can be certified as an electrician after taking courses and working several years, while another person can

---

TABLE 12-3   Steps of Intergenerational Educational Mobility, 1993

Mobility Steps	Mother/Daughter	Mother/Son	Father/Daughter	Father/Son
%				
Total	**100.0**	**100.0**	**100.0**	**100.0**
Upward Mobility				
4 steps up	2.6	3.6	2.6	3.8
3 steps up	18.1	20.1	19.3	20.3
2 steps up	20.8	19.6	20.4	18.3
1 step up	26.7	24.3	23.6	23.5
No Mobility	**26.0**	**25.3**	**26.6**	**25.9**
Downward Mobility				
1 step down	4.5	5.3	5.7	6.1
2 steps down	1.2	1.2	1.3	1.4
3 and 4 steps down	0.2**	0.5	0.5	0.5

* Totals may not sum to 100% due to rounding.

** High sampling variance (coefficient of variation between 16.5% and 25%); use with caution.

Source: Survey of Labour and Income Dynamics preliminary interview (January 1993).

obtain a university degree after only three years of university. Moreover, SLID does not take into account "equivalences" in education. For example, a person now requires a university degree to teach at all levels of education, which was not the case previously.

Two Out of Three Canadians Exceeded Their Parents' Educational Level...

Individuals who exceeded their parents' academic achievement very often gained up to three steps. In most cases, the parent had attended elementary school and the child had college or university (no degree). Of those who moved up two steps, slightly less than half had college or university education, while their parents had not graduated from high school. An equivalent proportion received a high school diploma, whereas their parents had only an elementary school education.

... and Fewer Than One in Ten Achieved a Lower Level

Only about 7% of Canadians acquired less education than their parents and most of them were just one level lower. Individuals who achieved a lower level in comparison with their fathers most often had attended but not completed college or university, while their fathers had obtained a university degree. In contrast, those with less schooling than their mothers had some high school education, while their mothers had graduated from high school.

Since the fathers are often slightly more educated than the mothers, the proportion of children with lower academic achievement than their fathers is a little higher. Logically, children of parents with the highest educational attainment cannot move up but have to settle for achieving

the same level or moving down one or more steps.

Sex of Child or Parent Does Not Affect Mobility

Traditionally, research into social mobility has focused on the impact of the father's occupation on the son's. If the mother was not in the labour market, she was excluded from the analysis. Yet this study has shown that the mother's education is no less important an influence than the father's on the educational attainment of the child. Intergenerational mobility is similar regardless of the sex of the parent or child (Figure 12-1).

As gender is not a significant variable in the analysis of educational mobility, a person's educational attainment was compared with the highest level reached by either the mother or father, rather than looking at each separately. This simplifies the analysis because only one comparison is made. However, it has the effect of lowering the apparent achievement of each individual because only the parent with the higher level is considered.

Overall Upgrading Does Not Account for All Educational Achievement

For the seven out of ten Canadians whose education differed from their parents', SLID has sought to determine what proportion of the change was attributable to overall upgrading of educational levels (structural mobility), and what proportion was due to individual abilities and merit (circulation mobility). For example, in an environment in which the distribution of educational levels was identical from one generation to the next, circulation mobility would explain any changes in the child's educational attainment compared with the

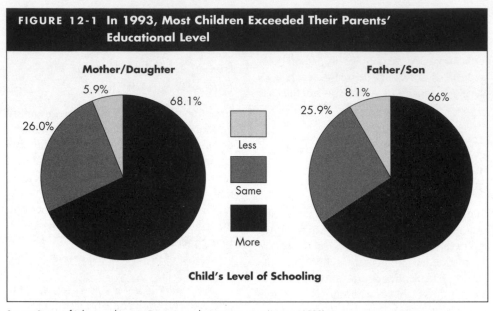

FIGURE 12-1 In 1993, Most Children Exceeded Their Parents' Educational Level

Mother/Daughter

5.9%
68.1%
26.0%

Father/Son

8.1%
66%
25.9%

Less

Same

More

Child's Level of Schooling

Source: Survey of Labour and Income Dynamics preliminary interview (January 1993).

parents'. Cases of upward mobility and downward mobility would balance each other.

The General Social Survey (GSS) also measured the changes attributable to overall upgrading and to individual abilities and merit, using their 1986 data (see below, "Structural Mobility and Circulation Mobility"). By comparing an individual's educational attainment with that of the parent who reached the higher level, SLID found that structural mobility was 33% and circulation mobility was 37%; 30% of the population remained at the level of the previous generation. If persons who did not move were excluded, structural mobility accounted for just under half the increase in educational attainment, and circulation mobility accounted for the remainder. These results suggest that the improved educational attainment of persons from disadvantaged backgrounds need not be linked solely to the general increase in educational attainment.

A calculation of mobility for each parent/child combination in this study yielded results comparable to the GSS. For the mother/son combination, however, the results were different, with much greater structural mobility observed by SLID than by the GSS. The latter calculated mobility using six educational levels, while SLID used only five. This likely affects the results, because the higher the number of categories, the greater the chances of movement.

Parents' Post-Secondary Education Makes a Difference

The figures for post-secondary attainment range from just over 40% for children whose parents did not complete secondary school, to 65% for children of high school graduates, to almost 80% for those whose parents had a post-secondary education (Figure 12-2).

Structural Mobility and Circulation Mobility

Structural mobility refers to changes linked to the general increase in the educational level of the population, whereas circulation mobility results from individual effort. To calculate these two types of mobility, the Survey of Labour and Income Dynamics (SLID) used the same definitions as the 1986 General Social Survey (GSS). To measure the effect of structural mobility, an index of dissimilarity was calculated. This index, expressed as a percentage, reflects the difference between two distributions; in this case, the educational level of daughters and their mothers (Table 12-2). Structural mobility is one-half of the absolute difference between the percentages in the two univariate distributions for each educational level (Creese, Guppy and Meissner 1991). An index of 0% would mean that the two univariate distributions are identical, whereas an index of 100% would mean

that they are extremely different. In this case, structural mobility is 41%. If the proportion of cases with no mobility (the sum of the shaded cells in Table 12-2, i.e., 26%) and the proportion of structural mobility (expressed by the index) are subtracted from 100%, a proportion of 33% for circulation mobility is obtained. This figure corresponds to all other movements in the table.

Individuals under the Age of 40 Achieved a Lower Level Than Other Canadians

It was relatively easy for most Canadians to attain if not exceed their parents' educational level, since 62% of all parents did not graduate from high school. However, for individuals under the age of 40, it was more difficult to surpass their parents' level, which was higher than that of parents of individuals aged 65 or over. In fact, the proportion of parents with

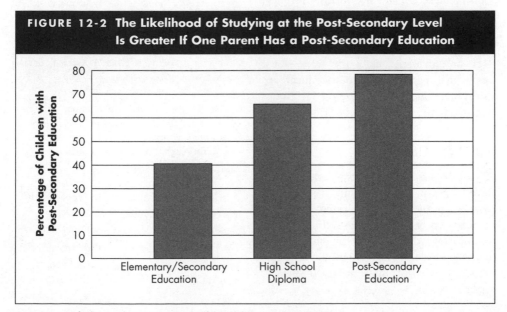

FIGURE 12-2 The Likelihood of Studying at the Post-Secondary Level Is Greater If One Parent Has a Post-Secondary Education

Source: Survey of Labour and Income Dynamics preliminary interview (January 1993).

TABLE 12-4	Educational Attainment of Canadians in Comparison with Their Parents, by Age, 1993			
	Total	Higher	Same	Lower
Age				
15–39	100.0	60.1	26.2	13.7
40–64	100.0	63.9	27.3	8.8
65 and over	100.0	46.1	44.1	9.8

Source: Survey of Labour and Income Dynamics preliminary interview (January 1993).

post-secondary education ranges from 11% for parents of individuals aged 65 and over, to more than 25% for parents of individuals under 40.

Moreover, almost 70% of the parents of Canadians aged 65 and over had only an elementary education, so it was difficult for their children to achieve a lower level by comparison. Thus, 44% of individuals aged 65 and over attained the same educational level as their parents (elementary in 80% of cases). Still, 46% achieved a higher level than their parents. A large proportion of these persons are in the "secondary" category, one step above their parents' elementary level, and an almost equally large proportion are in the "college or university" category, three steps above their parents' elementary education. Most individuals in the 40-to-64 age group are also in the latter category (Table 12-4).

CONCLUSION

The increase in Canadians' educational level is not merely the result of structural changes in the education system, but also depends on each individual's abilities and merit. However, there is a link between the parents' educational level and that of their children. Children have a much greater chance of studying at the post-secondary level if one parent has a post-secondary education. While some may believe that the father's educational level has a greater impact on the children's education, this study reveals that the mother's educational attainment is probably equally important.

NOTE

1. This section applies methods drawn from Creese, Guppy, and Meissner 1991.

REFERENCES

Creese, G., N. Guppy, and M. Meissner 1991. *Ups and Downs on the Ladder of Success: Social Mobility in Canada.* General Social Survey Analysis Series, Catalogue 11–612E, No. 5. Ottawa: Statistics Canada.

Grabb, E. 1992. "Social stratification." In James J. Teevan (ed.), *Introduction to Sociology: A Canadian Focus* (4th ed.), pp. 195–235. Scarborough: Prentice-Hall Canada.

Pomfret, A. 1992. "Education." In James J. Teevan (ed.), *Introduction to Sociology: A Canadian Focus* (4th ed.), pp. 369–402. Scarborough: Prentice-Hall Canada.

Statistics Canada 1994. *Income Distributions by Size in Canada*, 1993. Catalogue 13–207. Ottawa.

STUBBORN DISPARITIES: EXPLAINING CLASS INEQUALITIES IN SCHOOLING

Scott Davies

INTRODUCTION

Canada has been transformed over this century from a predominantly rural, agricultural society to an urban, post-industrial nation. Whereas one hundred years ago most people were self-employed in family-owned farms and small businesses, today the vast majority earn their livelihood by competing in the labour market. Coinciding with these changes, the school system has expanded enormously, greatly increasing the educational attainments of Canadians. Most Canadians, regardless of social origin, earn more school credentials than did their ancestors. Indeed, Canada has more citizens attending school at its various levels—elementary, secondary, and post-secondary—than almost any other country (see Guppy and Davies, forthcoming).

Schooling has become an increasingly important determinant of one's chances of securing a good job and a stable income, and by extension, education has become a prime arena for social competition. Schools sift and sort people into highly stratified career paths.

This raises a key question: Have all Canadians benefited equally from the expansion of the school system? Recent studies have examined trends in educational outcomes by race, gender, and social class.[1] As for race, most visible minorities, whether immigrant or Canadian-born, fare better in school than Whites, except for Aboriginal Canadians (Geschwender and Guppy 1995; Davies and Guppy 1998). Non-Aboriginal minorities, taken as a group, are less likely to drop out of high school, and are more likely to attend university. With the exception of Aboriginals, race or ethnic heritage is not a strong predictor of Canadians' educational attainment.

In terms of gender, Canadian educational trends resemble those of most other nations: an overall movement toward male-female parity (Bradley and Ramirez, 1996). Whereas males still earn more advanced degrees (masters, doctorates) and continue to dominate lucrative fields of study such as computer science and engineering, females are catching up in these and other areas. Females now attend and graduate from university at higher rates than males, and are less likely to drop out of high school. Despite some lingering female disadvantages, the main trend in Canadian education, as elsewhere, is toward gender equality.

However, a very different story emerges for social class. Whether measured by high school dropout rates, standardized test scores, or university attendance rates, youth from working-class and underclass backgrounds do not fare as well as their middle- and upper-class peers. Students' class origin markedly influences their school success regardless of their race, gender, or ethnicity. Certainly, the relation between class and educational outcomes is not a perfect fit. Within every socio-economic status (SES) category a wide range of outcomes exists, and some working-class students are very successful in school. Nevertheless, SES is the strongest and most enduring social determinant of educational attainment. Indeed, in Canada, as in most nations, socio-economic disparities in educational attainment have persisted despite decades of educational expansion and reform (see Shavit and Blossfeld 1993; Deng and Treiman 1997).

This chapter presents and evaluates sociological explanations for the persistence of these SES inequalities. While acknowledging the variation in education achievements within any SES category, I dwell on explanations of the unequal average attainments of working-class versus middle-class youth. I focus on Canada, though drawing heavily on American and British research, since socio-economic patterns of educational inequality in Canada and the United States are remarkably similar, and because much British research on the topic has influenced Canadian sociologists.[2]

HOW INEQUALITIES EMERGE: SELECTION AND CUMULATIVE DISADVANTAGE

Educational inequality is best understood as a series of dissimilar transition and survival rates between groups (see Mare 1993 for an elaboration). Schooling is laddered, with student pools becoming smaller and smaller with successive transitions. For instance, most students now finish elementary schooling and enter high school. But since approximately 20% of Canadians who enter high school fail to graduate by age 24 (Frank 1996), the pool of high school graduates is selective relative to the entering high school cohort. Since SES is an important predictor of dropping out (Gilbert et al. 1993), high school graduates have a smaller proportion of working-class students than high school entrants. In turn, another selection takes place when only some high school graduates pursue post-secondary schooling. The "survivors" of this transition are again relatively select, as the proportion of students from lower SES origins again shrinks (for Canada, see Guppy and Davies, forthcoming; for other countries, see Shavit and Blossfeld 1993). And there is still more. In the U.S., lower SES students are less likely to attend prestigious universities, even controlling for academic ability (Davies and Guppy 1997). What causes these class disparities in educational attainment?

ECONOMIC ARGUMENTS: MONEY MATTERS

Perhaps the most elemental explanation for working-class underachievement in school focuses on how working-class families face economic constraints that impede their educational progress. Although publicly funded, school attendance and performance requires money to pay for optional field trips, learning materials, and private tutors (e.g., piano, reading). Research shows that class background affects students' decisions about attending university, even controlling for their academic ability. This is usually interpreted as an effect of the increasingly prohibitive costs of tuition (Porter et al. 1979, Gambetta 1996, Steelman and Powell 1991). Private schools, which send the vast majority of their graduates to universities, are largely unaffordable to lower-income families. Wealthier parents are more likely to pay for additional private tutoring outside school hours (though lower-income parents would hire tutors "if they had the time and/or money" [Environics 1997]). Another economic factor is the quality of public schooling. Public schools in more affluent neighbourhoods enjoy superior resources and attract better teachers.[3] Though resource level itself does not directly produce better educational outcomes, better-funded schools produce an environment that is more conducive to educational success.

Nevertheless, economic resources—whether used for tuition, transportation, private tutors, or to avoid the need for part-time work—are not the sole factor that affects school outcomes. Countries that largely eliminated university tuition fees, such as Great Britain, France, and Australia, have class inequalities in university attendance similar to those in Canada and the U.S. This suggests that pure economic factors, while palpable, are not all-determining. There is an explanatory gap, something unexplained by economic factors. To complement economic explanations, sociologists have turned to the realm of culture.

CLASS AND FRAMES OF REFERENCE

People's economic conditions affect their sense of life options. SES origins influence their perceptions of the kinds of jobs they are likely to obtain, and the lives they are likely to lead. Judgments about school are thus influenced by these surrounding economic conditions. In particular, this context shapes the various "push" factors providing disincentives for remaining in school, and the "pull" factors providing incentives to leave school. Working-class students confront two obvious push factors: economic constraints (as elaborated above), and their underachievement relative to middle-class children (as elaborated below). Other factors give push and pull forces extra strength and efficacy.

When explaining socio-economic disparities in education, the key factor is the gap between people's abstract values and their concrete aspirations and expectations (see Mickelson 1990). Everyone "values" education in an abstract sense. Whether through surveys, interviews, or policy statements, virtually all Canadians stress the importance they place on education. Our consumer-driven, success-striving society encourages people to pursue the "North American dream" of a prestigious, well-paying job. As a result, the number of young people wanting professional careers greatly exceeds the number of such positions that exist. Hopes for professional jobs are unrealistically high (Jacobs, Karen, and McClelland 1991).

Expressing an appreciation for education is one thing, but converting desires into reality is another. Part of this gap between expressed values and reality can be traced to factors beyond the economic realm.

"Frames of reference" refer to people's sense of desirable yet possible life options, their mental horizons that influence what they expect they can realistically attain. Immediate family and friends influence these frames greatly. We develop expectations by comparing ourselves to similar people, aligning our aspirations and efforts accordingly. These frames of reference shape our ideas of what kinds of jobs and lifestyle we want, and the role school plays in our desires.

Social class strongly influences people's frames of reference. Middle-class students have higher expectations for jobs and education than do working-class students, even controlling for differences in measured academic ability. Their higher aspirations can be attributed largely to the influence of their family and friends (Sewell and Hauser 1980; McClelland 1990).[4] These differences in frames of reference explain part of the socio-economic gap in educational success (Sewell and Hauser 1980; Jacobs, Karen, and McClelland 1991).

How does class shape these frames? In some instances, people's past experience and current social position cause them to "come to terms" with their circumstances and adjust their expectations to what is "realistic." When asked what they would like to be when they grow up, very young children often reply "police officer," "nanny," or "teacher." As they grow older,

learning about the jobs of their parents' friends, these choices change. The choices change again as young people hear others encouraging or remaining mute about their occupational dreams. When confronting barriers, economic or otherwise, they often lower their original goals. Additionally, "pull factors" disproportionately entice working-class youth out of school. Especially for youth not faring well in school, domestic and employment roles act as school-leaving incentives. Relatively secure blue-collar jobs requiring few educational credentials appear as viable alternatives to schooling (Brown, 1987), as do marriage plans. Even among the previously ambitious, and among the talented, early marriage reduces aspirations (Jacobs, Karen, and McClelland 1991).

PUSH FACTORS: THE STRUCTURE OF SCHOOLING

Working-class students in most countries, including Canada, are more likely than their middle-class counterparts to be streamed into less challenging, terminal programs in high school (Davies 1992; Curtis, Livingstone, and Smaller 1992). The very existence of these streaming systems, critics contend, disadvantages working-class students. These youth would fare better in a non-streamed high school environment that offered them the same curricula and expectations as other students. Being stuck in lower tracks offers these students less challenging work, and lowers their expectations and aspirations for the future. Once in different tracks, fatalistic frames of reference are reinforced, as opportunities to rise in school and learn are limited. The incentives of available jobs and/or impending domestic roles, when combined with streaming, lead these youth to perceive school as irrelevant to their future. School becomes a pointless dress rehearsal that is irrelevant to their upcoming roles.

American Catholic schools place far fewer students in lower streams, and as a result greater proportions of working-class students in these schools score well on standardized tests, graduate from high school, and attend post-secondary institutions (Lee, Bryk, and Smith 1993). Such research findings encourage the "de-streaming" movement, which seeks to abolish differential grouping and to mix students of all abilities. In the early 1990s, Ontario removed streams in grade 9, and planned eventually to phase out all streaming. However, for a variety of reasons—but largely due to teacher complaints about the practical difficulties imposed by heterogeneous ability groups—the government ended the experiment. Nevertheless, American research suggests that de-streaming could be a valid tool for easing class disparities in schooling if practical problems associated with student heterogeneity can be overcome.

Another factor shaping frames of reference, and their relation to class, is knowledge about education. Even when students from humble origins have lofty aspirations, and are academically gifted, other factors mitigate against their success. The daunting variety of choices available in modern post-secondary education, such as the distinctions between community colleges and universities, different types of degrees, the informal ranking of institutions, and the wide variety of programs available within any institution, creates an elaborate system of selection with many ports of entry. To make wise choices and maximize one's benefit, one must understand how the system operates; for example, what are the efficacious strategies for success or the informal rank-

ings of programs and institutions? Such navigational savvy is held disproportionately by students from middle-class origins. These youth have superior information about the academic marketplace, and they are more likely to know which fields offer lucrative rewards and how to find competitive advantages. As a result, students from disadvantaged origins have a lower probability of survival in advanced stages of the education system (Davies and Guppy 1997).

MORE PUSH FACTORS: THE CULTURE OF SCHOOLING

A notable characteristic of class inequality in education is that disparities in skills, such as the ability to read, write, and reason, can be detected from the earliest days in school (Alexander, Entwisle, and Horsey 1997). Why does this occur? As has been well documented, some parents can pass on to their children non-material resources that facilitate school success. Because parental education attainment better predicts student success than parental income or class position, many sociologists have looked to the role of non-material resources in facilitating class differences in educational attainment.

More educated parents pass on to their children "human capital"—basic reading, writing, and vocabulary skills, disciplined work habits—giving their children a distinct advantage in school. More highly educated parents spend more time helping their children with school-related activities (Environics 1997), a finding that is likely a consequence of their more flexible work schedules and greater familiarity with academic matters (Lareau 1989).

Another cultural approach places less emphasis on particular skills and focuses instead on cultural tastes and aesthetics. "Cultural capital," the signature concept of

French sociologist Pierre Bourdieu (Bourdieu and Passeron 1990) refers to the advantage enjoyed by students who possess sophisticated (as opposed to merely competent) conversational abilities and who have acquired a taste for literature and the arts.

In addition to the culture of the home, the culture of the classroom is also important. Many sociologists focus less on working-class culture and more on possible school cultures in order to understand class disparities. For instance, Bourdieu contends that since schools reward children who possess a certain type of cultural sophistication that is less likely to be found among the working class, schools in essence are rewarding middle-class culture. The way school is conducted—expected styles of speech, dress, and the content of the curriculum—are deemed to be largely foreign to working-class youth.

For instance, Basil Bernstein's (1973) research in East London (England) led him to postulate that middle-class children and working-class children come to school speaking different "codes"—that is, different styles of language with different grammatical rules and themes that lead to different ways of communicating. Schooling, Bernstein argued, is conducted in the more elaborate code of the middle class, putting working-class students at a distinct linguistic disadvantage. Other cultural idioms used in schools also may be class-biased. For instance, critics of standardized testing have long contended that such tests are more tests of "culture" than of cognitive ability, in that success in these tests is dependent upon having a certain cultural exposure (Contenta 1993).

Another longstanding charge of systematic bias in North American schools is that teachers, themselves middle class, hold higher expectations for middle-class students than for working-class students (see Wineburg 1987). Teachers are said to generalize, perhaps unconsciously, from the physical and social attributes of students (e.g., dress, demeanour, and speech style) to their abilities. According to this argument, teachers subtly expect well-dressed, presentable, and articulate children to be good students, and expect those with the opposite traits to be poorer students. This typecasting is also said to create a self-fulfilling prophecy. Whether via body language or the attention they give to students, teachers are said to express their expectations by treating students differently, and students are said to internalize these subtle messages. Thus, students for whom teachers have low expectations are said to eventually develop poor self-images, which in turn lead to poor academic performance.

Creating bold theories of working-class underachievement is one thing; providing convincing empirical evidence to support such theories is another. How have these theories fared over decades of sociological research?

Results are mixed, offering only qualified support. Beginning with cultural capital theory, sociologists have tested whether school outcomes are statistically correlated with various indicators of cultural capital, such as whether students have attended art galleries or museums, or whether their household provides reading material such as newspapers, magazines, and books. Findings suggest that students who regularly visit art galleries and museums achieve superior test scores (DiMaggio 1982). High school students exposed to household reading material are more likely to complete high school, attend selective universities, and enter lucrative post-secondary programs (Davies and Guppy 1997; Tanner, Davies, and O'Grady 1997). However, the link between cultural capital and class background is not exactly as Bourdieu imagines. Class background affects school success independently of cultural capital, and conversely, students with cultural capital enjoy advantages in school, independently of SES (Aschaffenburg and Maas 1997). Not all middle-class youth participate in high-status culture—far from it—and not all lower SES children are excluded from this culture.

Bernstein's theory of language codes is less successful. His theory, while popular in the 1970s, lacks any large-scale empirical confirmation, and many researchers are highly skeptical as to whether it is applicable beyond the setting of East London in the 1960s and 1970s. Similarly, sweeping claims that working-class students are culturally alienated in schools appear to be based more on assertion than argument and detailed evidence. Examples of successful "working-class schools," where such students thrive in a culturally proletarian environment, would aid the case for these theories, but, to my knowledge, no such schools exist. In fact, research suggests that working-class student performance is raised in schools that have a more middle-class composition.

As with studies of cultural capital, research on teacher biases offers mixed findings. Proof for the famous "self-fulfilling prophecy" thesis was originally said to be provided by the famous "Pygmalion in the classroom" experiment (Rosenthal and Jacobson 1968). Rosenthal and Jacobson tested whether labelling a group of elementary students as "gifted" (when in reality they were chosen at random) would cause those children to markedly improve not only their grades but their IQ scores as well. Any improvement, the researchers reasoned, would be strong evidence of the self-fulfilling prophecy. One year later, the researchers claimed they had evidence of a strong labelling effect. The study quickly became famous and remains one of the best known in the history of educational research.

Other studies quickly followed that argued that teacher typecasting was a root cause of working-class and minority underachievement in schools.

But is there clear evidence to support this claim? Few observers at the time noticed that the actual Pygmalion results were weak and uneven, and that the conclusions drawn from the data far overshot the content of the actual study, which did not directly test whether teachers negatively stereotyped working-class students. Subsequent attempts at replication have produced mixed results. Teacher expectations do not appear to consistently influence student ability.

Other types of research on teacher expectations find nuanced effects. While some conclude that teacher expectations are largely the consequence of the academic actions of students, and not vice versa (see Wineburg 1987; Farkas et al. 1990; Hurn 1993:170–176), some suggest working-class students do endure biased treatment. Teachers from high-status origins appear to have lower expectations and give lower grades to low SES students (Alexander, Entwisle, and Thompson 1987). These students, even controlling for academic ability, are less likely to be assigned to upper tracks (Hurn 1993: 165–170). Thus, while sweeping claims that schools are culturally biased and directly "push out" able working-class students may be overstated, evidence suggests that those youth encounter some unequal treatment in schools.

SOCIAL CAPITAL AND ACTIVE CAPITAL

What might account for the complex and somewhat inconsistent effects found in research on resources and school biases? Research frequently underplays agency. The concept of cultural capital points to a potential. Parental endowments in human capital and cultural capital aid educational success, but their influence is contingent upon whether those resources are acted upon in those families. Families with impressive resources "on paper" may not spend time helping their children. Exposure to music, art galleries, and world travel may offer advantages, but only if this potential is actualized through strategic action.

Family advantages can be reinforced in different ways. Having a sizable income, for instance, can boost one's cultural capital in the form of tutoring services, attending cultural events, or travelling to exotic locales. Money allows one to take advantage of one's knowledge of the school system. Knowledge that a high LSAT score is crucial to one's chances of acceptance into law school, for example, is especially helpful if one can afford the books and study courses that can improve such scores. Conversely, families that lack advantages in some areas can compensate by excelling in other areas. For instance, many Asian immigrant parents possess little of the dominant cultural capital, few English skills, and have relatively little direct contact with teachers, yet compensate by enrolling their children in private tutoring and monitoring their children's homework at higher-than-average rates (Schneider and Coleman 1993).

"Active capital" (Looker 1994) refers to the conversion of potential resources—economic or cultural—into real educational advantage. Research shows that academic advantages are enjoyed by children whose parents more actively monitor their children's homework, spend more time with their children, and intervene positively if their children run into difficulties at school (Schneider and Coleman 1993; Lareau 1989).

What activates capital? At one level, motivation is an individual, idiosyncratic

matter. Yet, sociologists know that individual effort does not occur in a social vacuum, but is embedded in broader social contexts. Relationships among students, parents, neighbouring communities, and educators can influence and channel an individual's actions. In conceptualizing these broader social effects, Coleman has referred to "social capital" as the set of collective expectations within a community that affects the goal-seeking behaviour of its members (see Coleman 1988). Communities create social capital by forging reciprocal norms of obligation among parents, youth, and schools. Such norms breed strong bonds of trust, cooperation, and mutual respect, and can channel motivation and effort. Conversely, communities with weak obligations and expectations may be less committed to their educational goals.

Differences in social capital can reinforce socio-economic disparities. Studies show that parents from lower SES categories are less active in their children's schooling (Schneider and Coleman 1993). Working-class parents are disadvantaged vis-à-vis middle-class parents by their relatively inflexible work schedules, less detailed knowledge of the school system, lesser familiarity with the social culture of teaching, and by schools that do not actively encourage parental participation (Lareau 1989; Epstein 1995).

However, these effects can be counteracted. Working-class students appear better motivated in more academically oriented schools. Researchers have found that schools with strong expectations of success raise the attainment of all children, particularly lower SES students (Willms 1986; Shouse 1996). Schools of mixed socio-economic composition benefit working-class children by exposing them to an enriched academic environment, high-status role models, and peers with high aspirations (see Hurn 1993:168).

THEORIES OF DEEP CULTURAL DIVISIONS: DEPRIVATION AND RESISTANCE

Notions of frames of reference and forms of capital, described above, portray middle-class versus working-class families as having different outlooks and unequal resources regarding school. These cultural differences are not seen to be "deep," in the sense of reflecting profoundly dissimilar values or norms, but rather stem from their adjustments to their respective socio-economic conditions. Yet, some sociologists see much deeper cultural differences. A controversial idea that has haunted sociologists for over forty years is that working-class children are outperformed by their middle-class counterparts because of a fundamental mismatch between the cultural orientations required for school success and the culture of lower socio-economic groups. There are two versions of this thesis.

The first version, called "cultural deprivation" or "cultural deficit" theory, was popular in the 1950s and 1960s (see Hyman 1953). In this view, modern schools, as part of the societal contest for economic status and social climbing, require of the populace a set of "middle class" orientations aimed at achievement, competition, and aspiration for upward social mobility. Families from lower socio-economic strata, these theorists reasoned, desire the same material goals of income and wealth as their middle-class counterparts, but fail to embrace the attitudes or orientations needed to reach those goals. Working-class families were seen to be behind the times, mired in a pre-modern value set.

Cultural deficit theory met a barrage of criticism in the late 1960s and early 1970s. Much of this criticism consisted of moralistic charges of elitism and "blaming the victim," but there were substantive sociological criticisms as well. Perhaps the most powerful was a challenge to the claim of deep cultural divisions rooted in class. Writers such as William Ryan (1971), drawing on notions of frames of reference, passionately argued that virtually everyone in North America shares common aspirations for material wealth, but the working class adjust their expectations in response to their lower objective chances of realizing their aspirations.

The idea of deep cultural division did not vanish, however, but resurfaced in a new guise. Many sociologists in the 1970s and 1980s, influenced by Marxism, offered a novel account of deep cultural differences to explain why working-class students underperformed. In what became known as *Resistance theory* (see Davies 1995 for a review), Marxists such as Paul Willis (1977) argued that class disparities in school stem less from a working-class inability to compete, but more from their *unwillingness* to compete. This unwillingness, they argued, is rooted in a profound culture clash. Rather than sharing an orientation of status striving, Willis and his followers argued, the working class has its own defiant mores, which it forged through historic struggles with its capitalist employers. These values are said to include a preference for solidarity over competitiveness, pride in manual labour, and an antagonism to institutional authority.

Resistance theorists make two crucial inferential leaps. First, they argue that many, if not most, working-class youth are generally indifferent to school, exert little effort in classes, and participate in school deviance. Second, they argue that these anti-school subcultures have a proletarian character that, in essence, is a youthful version of factory culture. The solidarity of the shop floor is said to be mimicked by close peer relationships among teens. The pride in heavy, manual labour is said to be expressed by their disparaging of the "pencil-pushing" that pervades school work, and a resentment toward the second-class status that is accorded to manual labour in schools. The antagonism to authority, as visibly expressed in workers' conflicts with factory supervisors and bosses, is transferred to student-teacher relations.

These subcultural values, in this account, lead these youth to reject school and eagerly anticipate the "real world" of employment. Simply put, working-class kids get working-class jobs by developing rebellious subcultures, thereby condemning themselves to educational failure. While acknowledging that not all working-class students engage in deviance, resistance theorists view working-class resistance to school as a prime cause of their educational underachievement.

Resistance theory has had a huge impact in sociology, but has sparked much criticism. Willis and his followers stand accused of greatly exaggerating the extent to which working-class students actually oppose school, and of offering overly romantic interpretations of school deviance. Indeed, most concrete instances of "resistance"—often amounting to little more than expressions of boredom—are simply unconvincing as evidence of a deep and ideologically charged cultural division.

CONCLUSION: CHANGING SOCIETY, PERSISTING INEQUALITIES?

Class disparities in education stem from a variety of factors—unequal economic constraints, different frames of reference and endowments in various forms of capital, and some forms of bias in school. Each of these interacting factors have multiple levels of influence, from the individual, to the family, to the surrounding community, to the school. Documenting class inequalities is relatively easy, but the complexity of how class affects schooling makes convincing explanations backed by solid evidence much harder to find. Part of this difficulty stems from the fact that society and its educational institutions are constantly changing.

Schools have changed. One possible reason why recent research on school bias finds such uneven effects is that teachers and their methods have been continually altered over recent decades. While the notion of the self-fulfilling prophecy perhaps had a stronger reality thirty years ago, educators today are generally far more sensitive and alert to issues of equity and bias. Teacher colleges focus much of their training on issues of "diversity." Curricula and tests have been modified constantly in an effort to better suit a diverse student body.

Cultural configurations are shifting as well. Sociologists, more than before, doubt that social class is a primary source of cultural division in our society. Before the mid-1980s, many commonly referred to a "working-class culture" as a recognizable and coherent entity. These ideas led Resistance theorists, like the Functionalists before them, to depict a deep culture clash between working-class youth and schools. But this notion of such a distinct culture, in semi-opposition to the middle class, seems less and less plausible in North America. Most sociologists now stress instead race, ethnicity, religion, or region as more potent sources of social attachments, self-conceptions, group loyalties, and cultural conflict. Class may continue to shape frames of reference and senses of people's life options, but it is not a source of deep cultural attachment. An essential irony is that while working-class culture may have faded, class remains the key objective barrier to school success.

These culture shifts can be linked to changing economic conditions. De-industrialization is transforming the job structure that helped forge class-differentiated frames of reference. Until the mid-1980s, blue-collar jobs in resources and manufacturing that required few educational credentials attracted many working-class youth, particularly males, out of school. But the stock of such jobs is now smaller. More school leavers now encounter service-sector jobs (often requiring educational credentials, even if not high levels of skill) or the spectre of unemployment. Further, on average, women are marrying and bearing children at later ages and, perhaps as a result, female educational attainments among all classes have shot upwards. Thus, two viable alternatives that previously attracted many working-class students out of school have been recently undercut.

What impact will this change have on frames of reference and aspirations? One might expect that the weakening of these pull factors will strengthen most youth's attachments to schooling. As our society transforms itself into a "knowledge economy," lifetime learning is being hailed as the next source of educational expansion. People of all descriptions, so the argument goes, will return to school numerous times over their employment lifetimes to upgrade their skills. Will this alter the frames of reference of those who would not otherwise consider post-secondary schooling? It might, but we need to remember that educational inequality is a relational concept, not an absolute measure of attainment. Often overlooked is the fact that over the past four decades, working-class families have substantially boosted their attainments, but inequalities have remained largely stable because the middle class has boosted equally its attainments. An understanding of inequality requires not only recognition of the barriers faced by working-class youth, but the advantages and strategies of middle-class youth. Even if working-class frames of reference change and school biases are removed—which would render working-class students more competitive—middle-class families will likely develop new strategies to keep ahead. The sharp increases in recent years in the number of families seeking private schooling and private tutoring is a likely indication of a new middle-class strategy aimed at maintaining a competitive edge in education.

NOTES

1. Although the terms "class" and "socio-economic status" (SES) have different theoretical and empirical meanings in sociology, I use them interchangeably to refer to one's relative economic standing. Canadian trends are taken from data cited in Guppy and Davies (1998).

2. Two very important and related topics—group differences in "equity"—that is, the power to shape and influence the content and form of education, and the question of how class interacts with region, race, ethnicity, or gender—cannot be pursued here for reasons of space.

3. This tends to be a much starker phenomenon in the U.S. than in Canada. In fact, schools in neighbourhoods populated by racial minorities in urban areas like Toronto and Vancouver receive greater funds than the average.

4. The relation between frames of reference and class, like the relation between educational outcomes and class, is far from a perfect fit. Research needs to be further developed to understand why there is wide range within any class. One possibility is that low-income communities that are less tight-knit and bonded allow their members to develop expectations that are atypical of those communities (see Portes and Sensenbrenner 1993). Some low-income

communities may have resources that can compensate for their class position (see Kao, Tienda, and Schneider 1996).

REFERENCES

Alexander, Karl L., Doris R. Entwisle, and Maxine S. Thompson 1987. "School performance, status relations, and the structure of sentiment: Bringing the teacher back in." *American Sociological Review* 52(5): 665–682.

Alexander, Karl L, Doris R. Entwisle, and Carrie S. Horsey 1997. "From first grade forward: Early foundations of high school dropout." *Sociology of Education* 70(2): 87–107.

Aschaffenburg, Karen, and Ineke Maas 1997. "Cultural and educational careers: The dynamics of social reproduction." *American Sociological Review* 62(4):573–587.

Bernstein, Basil (ed.) 1973. *Class, Codes and Control, Vol. 2: Theoretical Studies Towards a Sociology of Language.* London/Boston: Routledge & Kegan Paul.

Blossfeld, Hans-Peter, and Yossi Shavit 1993. "Persisting barriers: Changes in educational opportunities in thirteen countries." In Shavit, Yossi, and Hans-Peter Blossfeld (eds.), *Persistent Inequality: Changing Educational Attainment in Thirteen Countries*, pp. 1–24. Boulder, Colorado: Westview Press.

Bourdieu, Pierre, and Jean-Claude Passeron 1990. *Reproduction in Education, Society and Culture* (2nd ed.). London: Sage.

Bradley, Karen, and Francisco O. Ramirez 1996. "World polity and gender parity: Women's share of higher education, 1965–1985." *Research in Sociology of Education and Socialization* 11:63–92.

Brown, P. 1987. *Schooling Ordinary Kids: Inequality, Unemployment, and the New Vocationalism.* London: Tavistock.

Coleman, James S. 1988. "Social capital in the creation of human capital." *American Journal of Sociology* 94:s95–s120.

Contenta, Sandro 1993. *Rituals of Failure: What Schools Really Teach.* Toronto: Between the Lines.

Curtis, Bruce, David W. Livingstone, and Harry Smaller 1992. *Stacking the Deck: The Streaming of Working Class Kids in Ontario Schools.* Toronto: Our Schools/Our Selves.

Davies, Scott 1992. "In search of the culture clash: Evaluating a sociological theory of social class inequalities in education." Doctoral dissertation, Department of Sociology, University of Toronto.

Davies, Scott 1995. "Reproduction and resistance in Canadian high schools. An empirical examination of the Willis thesis." *British Journal of Sociology* 46(4):662–687.

Davies, Scott, and Neil Guppy 1997. "Fields of study, college selectivity, and student inequalities in higher education." *Social Forces* 75(4):1417–1138.

Davies, Scott, and Neil Guppy 1998. "Race and Canadian education." In Vic Satzewich (ed.), *The Racist Imagination: The Sociology of Racism in Canada.* Toronto: Thompson Educational Publishing.

Deng, Zhong, and Donald J. Treiman 1997. "The impact of the cultural revolution on trends in educational attainment in the People's Republic of China." *American Journal of Sociology* 103(2):391–428.

DiMaggio, Paul 1982. "Cultural capital and school success: The impact of status culture participation on the grades of U.S. high school students." *American Sociological Review* 47(2):189–201.

Environics 1997. *Focus Canada Report 1997–2.* Toronto: Environics.

Epstein, Joyce L. 1995. "School/family/community partnerships." *Phi Delta Kappan* 72(5): 701–712.

Farkas, George, P. Grobe, D. Sheehan, and Y. Shuan 1990. "Cultural resources and school success: Gender, ethnicity and poverty groups within an urban school district." *American Sociological Review* 55(1): 127–142.

Frank, Jeffrey 1996. *After High School: The First Report of the School Leavers Following-up Survey, 1995.* Ottawa: Minister of Public Works and Government Services Canada.

Gambetta, Diego 1996. *Were They Pushed or Did They Jump? Individual Decision Mechanisms* *in Education.* Boulder, Colorado: Westview Press.

Geschwender, Jim, and Neil Guppy 1995. "Ethnicity, educational attainment, and earned income among Canadian-born men and women." *Canadian Ethnic Studies* XXVII (1):67–84.

Gilbert, Sid, Lynn Barr, Warren Clark, Matthew Blue, and Deborah Sunter 1993. *Leaving School: Results from a National Survey Comparing School Leavers and High School Graduates 18 to 20 Years of Age.* Ottawa: Statistics Canada.

Guppy, Neil, and Scott Davies 1998. *Education in Canada: Recent Trends and Future Challenges.* Ottawa: Statistics Canada and Nelson Canada.

Hurn, Christopher J. 1993. *The Limits and Possibilities of Schooling* (3rd ed.). Boston: Allyn and Bacon.

Hyman, Herbert H. 1953. "The value systems of different classes: A social psychological contribution to the analysis of stratification." In Reinhard Bendix and Seymour Martin Lipset (eds.), *Class, Status and Power: A Reader in Social Stratification*, pp. 426–442. Glencoe, Illinois: Free Press.

Jacobs, Jerry A., David Karen, and Katherine McClelland 1991. "The dynamics of young men's career aspirations." *Sociological Forum* 6(4):609–639.

Kao, Grace, Marta Tienda, and Barbara Schneider 1996. "Racial and ethnic variation in academic performance." *Research in Sociology of Education and Socialization* 11:263–297.

Lareau, Annette 1989. *Home Advantage: Social Class and Parental Intervention in Elementary Education.* London: Falmer.

Lee, Valerie E., Anthony S. Bryk, and J.B. Smith 1993. "The organization of effective secondary schools." *Review of Research in Education* 19:171–268.

Looker, E. Dianne 1994. "Active capital: The impact of parents on youths' educational performance and plans." *Sociology of Education in Canada: Critical Perspectives on Theory, Research and Practice.* Toronto: Copp Clark Longman.

Mare, Robert D. 1993. "Educational stratification on observed and unobserved components of family background." In Y. Shavit and H.P. Blossfeld (eds.), *Persistent Inequality: Changing Educational Attainment in Thirteen Countries,* pp. 351–376. Boulder, Colorado: Westview Press.

McClelland, Katherine 1990. "Cumulative disadvantage among the highly ambitious." *Sociology of Education* 63(2):102–121.

Mickelson, Rosalyn A. 1990. "The attitude-achievement paradox among black adolescents." *Sociology of Education* 63:44–61.

Porter, Marion, John Porter, and Bernard Blishen 1979. *Does Money Matter?* Downsview, Ontario: Institute for Behavioural Research.

Portes, Alejandro, and Julia Sensenbrenner 1993. "Embeddedness and immigration: Notes on the social determinants of economic action." *American Journal of Sociology* 98(6):1320–1350.

Rosenthal, R., and L. Jacobson 1968. *Pygmalion in the Classroom.* New York: Rinehart and Winston.

Ryan, William 1971. *Blaming the Victim.* New York: Vintage.

Schneider, Barbara, and James S. Coleman 1993. *Parents, Their Children, and Schools.* Boulder, Colorado: Westview Press.

Sewell, William, and Robert Hauser 1980. "The Wisconsin longitudinal study of social and psychological factors in aspirations and achievements." *Research in Sociology of Education and Socialization* 1:59–99.

Shavit, Yossi, and Hans-Peter Blossfeld (eds.) 1993. *Persistent Inequality: Changing Educational Attainment in Thirteen Countries.* Boulder, Colorado: Westview Press.

Shouse, Roger C. 1996. "Academic press and sense of community: Conflict and congruence in American high schools." *Research in Sociology of Education and Socialization* 11:173–202.

Steelman, Lala Carr, and Brian Powell 1991. "Sponsoring the next generation: parental willingness to pay for higher education." *American Journal of Sociology* 96(6): 1505–1529.

Tanner, Julian, Scott Davies, and Bill O'Grady 1997. "Whatever happened to yesterday's rebels? Longitudinal effects of teenage delinquency on educational and occupational attainment." Unpublished manuscript, University of Toronto.

Teachman, Jay D. 1987. "Family background, educational resources, and educational attainment." *American Sociological Review* 52: 548–557.

Willis, P. 1977. *Learning to Labour.* Farnborough: Saxon House, Teakfield.

Willms, J. Douglas 1986. "Social class segregation and its relationship to pupils' examination results in Scotland." *American Sociological Review* 51(2):224–241.

Wineburg, Samuel S. 1987 "The self-fulfilment of the self-fulfilling prophecy: A critical appraisal." *Educational Researcher* 16(9): 28–37.

CHOOSE YOUR PARENTS CAREFULLY: SOCIAL CLASS, POST-SECONDARY EDUCATION, AND OCCUPATIONAL OUTCOMES

Harvey Krahn

(A new chapter written for this volume.)

INTRODUCTION

Rapid advances in the science of genetics over the past decade have made it possible for parents to pre-select the sex of their children with little chance of error (Boseley 2002). And, with cloning specialists shifting their attention from the animal world to the human species, it may be only a matter of time before someone chooses to bring a perfect copy of her- or himself into existence (Radford 2002). While the ethical implications of such actions need to be seriously debated, science has brought us to the point where parents literally can choose their children.

What if the laws of time and physics could be reversed, and we could choose our parents? Given the opportunity, whom would you choose? Famous parents? Gorgeously beautiful parents? A loving, caring mother and father? Someone who would get off your back? This chapter concludes that, if you are concerned about your own educational and career future, and if you really could select your parents, you would clearly benefit from making them better educated and more affluent.

SOCIAL CLASS AND LIFE CHANCES

Throughout much of the twentieth century, sociologists from different theoretical camps have debated the extent to which *social class*—one's position in an economic hierarchy defined by occupation, education, or income—affects people's life chances (Grabb 2002). There has generally been agreement that, compared with their working-class counterparts, middle-class North Americans enjoy a more comfortable and worry-free existence, tend to live longer and healthier lives, and are more likely to pass such advantages on to their children (Forcese 1997; Allahar and Côté 1998; Corak 1998). Even so, since at least the Second World War, counter-arguments about the decline in importance of social class have also frequently been heard.

For example, it has been argued that the affluence generated by the post-war economic expansion in western democracies has essentially eliminated the large pockets of perpetual poverty and the huge income disparities that had seemed so inevitable in earlier eras (Lenski 1973). Related to this, the rapid expansion of post-secondary institutions in Canada and the United States during the 1960s and 1970s (Clark 2000) allowed many more talented young people, even those born into poorer families, to acquire post-secondary credentials and, thus, move into better-paying professional careers. Daniel Bell (1973) proposed that, in post-industrial society, rigid social inequalities based on accidents of birth (e.g., were you born into a wealthy or a poor family?) were replaced by more fluid and less severe income differences based on educational attainment.

More recently, several European social theorists (Giddens 1991; Beck 1992) have suggested that the rapid social and economic change characteristic of globalized, post-modern society have provided young people with more opportunities to shape their own destinies, even though post-modern society has also generated more risks. In short, the argument goes, social class is no longer as relevant an explanation of social inequality as it once was; it is "an increasingly outmoded concept" (Clark and Lipset 1991:397).

However, researchers examining the connections between individuals' educational accomplishments and career outcomes and their family of origin continue to see persistent intergenerational patterns. Young people from more advantaged backgrounds are more likely to succeed in school and, subsequently, in the labour market (Looker 1997; Davies and Guppy 1997; de Broucker and Lavallée 1998; Davies 1999; Butlin 1999; Knighton and Mirza 2002). The most obvious explanations for such social class effects is that wealthier parents can pay for better and more secondary and post-secondary education.

In addition, children from more advantaged backgrounds are less likely to participate in non-academic (vocational) secondary school programs that typically leave graduates without the high school credits required for university entrance (Wotherspoon 1995; Andres and Krahn 1999). This "streaming" may be a function of teachers and advisors providing more encouragement and advice to middle-class youth compared with their less advantaged peers. It may also reflect the educational choices of working-class youth who typically report lower educational and occupational aspirations (Andres et al. 1999) than their middle-class peers. The latter are more likely challenged by their parents and teachers to "aim higher."

Related to these patterns is the differential distribution of *cultural capital* (Bourdieu 1986). Children from more affluent backgrounds are more likely to have been exposed to the experiences (e.g., pre-school education, a "book" culture in the home, exposure to the fine arts) and beliefs (e.g., "You have to get a university degree to be successful in life") that are valued in the formal education system and, so, are more likely to enjoy and do well in school (Andres 1994; Looker 1994; Davies 1999). In contrast, working-class youth without such advantages are more likely to do poorly and may, sometimes, even reject the values of an educationally focused society (Willis 1977).

Thus, despite the observations of social theorists who describe the declining relevance of social class, research findings clearly demonstrate that social class continues to matter. The most convincing evidence comes from longitudinal studies that track individuals as they move into, through, and out of the formal educational system into their adult occupational careers. The research results discussed below are taken from such an over-time study that monitored the educational and occupational ambitions and experiences of a large sample of Canadian youth over a fourteen-year period.

RESEARCH DESIGN AND METHODS

The *Edmonton School-Work Transition Study* began in 1985 as part of a larger longitudinal study of high school and university graduates in three Canadian cities (Edmonton, Toronto, and Sudbury).[1] Since this paper focuses only on the experiences of the Edmonton high school "class of 1985," the following discussion of research methods will be restricted to this educational cohort.

The original 1985 sample included 983 high school seniors from six different Edmonton high schools representing both middle- and working-class sections of the city. Survey participants completed questionnaires in class in May and early June of that year. Follow-up surveys were conducted by mail in 1986, 1987, 1989, and 1992. In each follow-up survey, attempts were made to contact only those individuals who had participated in the previous wave of data collection (e.g., in 1987, no attempt was made to contact those who had not completed the 1986 survey). By 1992, cumulative sample attrition had reduced the sample to 404 of the original

members of the class of 1985 (41% of the baseline 1985 sample).[2]

The 1999 follow-up survey was conducted by telephone since many of the postal addresses recorded in 1992 were out of date. In addition, the 1999 survey attempted to contact as many of the original 1985 respondents as possible, whether or not they had participated in all four intervening waves of data collection. Ultimately, after many telephone calls to locate and interview the study participants, 509 interviews were completed with original members of the Edmonton high school class of 1985 (about 5% completed questionnaires that they had asked to be mailed to them). This represented 52% of the original 983 respondents, and 57% of the 894 who had provided follow-up information in 1985. Almost all of the original sample members who did not participate in the study in 1999 could not be located or, if located, could not be reached by telephone, despite repeated call-backs. Very few (only 6% of the potential respondents) refused to participate in the 1999 survey.[3]

1985 Sample Characteristics

Fifty-one percent (n = 261) of the 509 respondents were female, and 49% (n = 248) were male. Two-thirds (65%) were born in 1967, making them either 17 or 18 at the time they were first interviewed in 1985. One in four (26%) were one or more years older (born pre-1967) while 9% were younger (born in 1968). All but three of the 509 respondents (99%) were single when first interviewed in 1985.

Eighty-five percent of the sample members were born in Canada, while 15% were immigrants, a proportion very similar to the proportion of immigrants in the city of Edmonton in the mid-1980s. Twelve percent of those who answered the survey question about race indicated that their mother was either Aboriginal or a member of another visible minority group. The same response pattern was observed for a second question about the racial origin of respondents' fathers.[4] On average, sample members had lived in Alberta for 14.8 years and in Edmonton for 13.7 years.

Two-thirds (65%) of the respondents' mothers were employed (either full time or part time) when the baseline survey was conducted in 1985, as were 86% of the fathers of sample members. Six percent of the fathers were unemployed at the time, as were 2% of the mothers. A considerably higher proportion (15% of fathers and 11% of mothers) had been unemployed at some time in the previous year. In total, 22% of the 509 sample members indicated that one or both of their parents had been unemployed at some point in the previous twelve months.

When surveyed in 1985, 38% (of those who answered the question) indicated that their mother had acquired at least some post-secondary education, with 18% saying their mother had a university degree. A full 50% (of the respondents who answered the question) noted that their father had participated in the post-secondary system following high school, with 28% indicating that their father had a university degree.[5] In total, 29% of the sample members reported that at least one of their parents had completed a university degree. In the following analyses, this simple binary variable—whether or not at least one parent had completed a university degree—is used to measure family socio-economic status (SES), a proxy for the concept of social class.

It is important to remember that all of the respondents in this study had managed to get to grade 12. Thus, high school dropouts are absent from the sample. Since the probability of dropping out of high school is inversely correlated with

family socio-economic status (Gilbert et al. 1993; Tanner et al. 1995), it is likely that the very poorest sector of Edmonton's population (in 1985) was underrepresented in the study. Even so, there is still considerable variation in socio-economic status within the sample.

SOCIO-ECONOMIC STATUS (SES) AND HIGH SCHOOL EXPERIENCES/ PERFORMANCE

In total, two-thirds (64%) of the 1985 survey participants were enrolled in academic high school programs that should, if successfully completed, provide graduates with the course credits needed for university entrance. The remainder were enrolled in a range of non-academic programs. Using parents' university education as our basic measure of socio-economic status (SES), it is apparent that there is a strong relationship between family social status and the type of high school program in which youth participate (Table 14-1). Five out of six (84%) students from higher SES families were enrolled in academic high school programs, compared with only a small majority (55%) of students from families in which neither parent had completed university. While this study cannot explain the process whereby "streaming" into different high school programs occurs, it can tell us whether it makes a difference for educational and occupational attainment.

Table 14-1 also demonstrates a strong relationship between family SES and students' performance in high school. One-half (51%) of the survey respondents from families where at least one parent had acquired a university degree reported average grades of 70% or higher in their senior year in high school, compared with only 35% of the young people from less advan-

TABLE 14-1 High School Program and Grades by Parents' University Education, Edmonton High School Seniors, 1985

Parent(s)' Education	No Degree	Degree	Total
High school program			
Academic	55	84	64
Non-academic	45*	16	36
Grades in past year			
< 60%	16	12	15
60–69%	49	37	45
70–79%	28	34	30
80%+	7*	17	10
Total %	100	100	100
(N)	(360)	(149)	(509)

* Differences in percentages are statistically significant ($p < 0.05$; chi-square test).

taged family backgrounds. Again, this study cannot clearly identify the determinants of these grade differentials. However, other research suggests that the greater "cultural capital" available to middle-class youth is part of the explanation. In addition, as Table 14-2 below suggests, young people from university-influenced households probably learn to place more value on higher education and, hence, may put more effort into doing well in high school. As university students know, higher high school grades improve one's chances of being accepted into university and, furthermore, into programs that lead to higher-paying careers and into "better" (higher-status) universities.

SOCIO-ECONOMIC STATUS (SES) AND EDUCATION VALUES

When first surveyed in 1985, the Edmonton high school seniors in the study were asked to indicate how much they agreed or disagreed with a wide array of statements about different aspects of education and work. Table 14.2 displays aver-

age responses to four of the education-related statements, broken down by our measure of SES (parents' university education). Only a minority of these young people agreed that "most of the classes at school are a complete waste of time" (mean score = 2.29 on a 1–5 scale) while a majority agreed that "overall, I have enjoyed my time in high school" (mean = 3.79). Differences by socio-economic status were inconsequential. These findings reinforce those reported by other researchers (Tanner et al. 1995; Davies 1999) who have concluded that there is very little evidence of "resistance" to formal education among high school students in Canada or of greater "resistance" among young people from less advantaged backgrounds.

However, we observe a somewhat different pattern of responses to the remaining two statements featured in Table 14-2. A very large majority of high school seniors agreed that "continuing my education will help me get a good job" (mean = 4.16), while a very small minority agreed that "for the sort of job I'm likely to get, you don't really need much education"

TABLE 14-2 **Education Values by Parents' University Education, Edmonton High School Seniors, 1985**

	Mean Scores*		
Parent(s)' Education	No Degree	Degree	Total
"Most of the classes at school are a complete waste of time."	2.26	2.36	2.29
"Overall, I have enjoyed my time in high school."	3.78	3.83	3.79
"Continuing my education will help me get a good job."	4.12	4.25	4.16
"For the sort of job I'm likely to get, you don't really need much education."	1.83†	1.61	1.76
(N)	(360)	(149)	(509)

* Respondents were asked to agree or disagree with each statement on a five-point scale, with "1" representing "strongly disagree" and "5" representing "strongly agree."

† Differences in means are statistically significant ($p < 0.05$; F-test).

(mean = 1.76). Sample members from higher SES families were somewhat more likely to agree with the first statement and significantly more likely to disagree with the second. Thus, while we find no evidence of outright "resistance" to the idea of formal education among less advantaged Canadian youth, we do see that, to some extent, they are less convinced of the ability of post-secondary education to improve their future labour market position. Nevertheless, even among 12th graders from families where neither parent had completed university, a solid majority acknowledged the career value of investments in post-secondary education.

SOCIO-ECONOMIC STATUS (SES) AND EDUCATIONAL/ OCCUPATIONAL ASPIRATIONS

The hints in Table 14-2 that middle-class youth are somewhat more confident of their ability to translate formal education into career success suggests that we might want to examine the post-secondary education plans and future occupational aspirations of these high school seniors. When asked in 1985, virtually all of the sample members indicated that they intended to acquire some post-secondary education—only 7% of the total sample said they intended to finish high school and nothing more (Table 14-3). One-half (51%) planned a college (or technical school) education,[6] while four out of ten (42%) expected to acquire a university degree, including 17% who intended to complete a second degree. Knowing that, by 2000, only about 60% of all Canadian labour force participants had at least some post-secondary education (Krahn and Lowe 2002:46), it would appear that not all of these 1985 study participants would, eventually, reach their educational goals.

These 1985 survey participants were also asked, "What kind of job or career do you want eventually?" and answered with responses like "teacher," "mechanic," "rock star," "engineer," "hairdresser," and "lawyer." Recognizing that many high school seniors may not have firm career plans, their answers to a question like this still signal general preferences for employment in the future. To simplify the analysis, the many different specific

TABLE 14-3   **Post-Secondary Education Plans and Occupational Aspirations by Parents' University Education, Edmonton High School Seniors, 1985**

Parent(s)' Education	No Degree	Degree	Total
Post-secondary education plans			
Finish high school	9	1	7
1–2 years college	58	34	51
3–4 years university	22	34	25
5+ years university	11*	31	17
Occupational aspirations			
Managerial/professional	55	69	59
Other	45*	31	41
Total %	100	100	100
(N)	(360)	(149)	(509)

* Differences in percentages are statistically significant (p < 0.05; chi-square test).

occupational aspirations recorded by sample members in 1985 have been collapsed into two basic categories, "managers/professionals" (managers of all kinds and professionals such as nurses, lawyers, teachers, engineers, and artists) and "other occupational aspirations" (included here are all other lower-status occupations as well as the "don't know" responses provided by a small minority of respondents). Table 14-3 demonstrates that well over half (59%) of the total sample hoped to someday be in a managerial or professional occupation, the type of job that typically pays better, provides more fringe benefits, and is generally more rewarding (Krahn and Lowe 2002). Since, by 2002, only 34% of all employed Canadians were in managerial or professional occupations (Krahn and Lowe 2002:67), it is again apparent that not all of these high career aspirations would have been attained.

Along with the high educational and occupational aspirations of the total sample, what stands out in Table 14-3 are the statistically significant SES differences.

Specifically, two-thirds (65%) of the survey respondents from university-educated families expected to acquire one or more university degrees, compared with only one-third (33%) of those from families where neither parent had completed a university degree. The SES differences in occupational aspirations are not quite as large, but are still pronounced: Sixty-nine percent of the 12th graders from more advantaged backgrounds hoped to become a manager or professional someday, compared with only 55% of the high school seniors from lower SES backgrounds. Thus, class background does matter for education and career plans.[7] Does it also matter for post-secondary education and career outcomes?

SCHOOL-WORK TRANSITIONS BY 1992

Only 404 of the original 1985 sample members participated in the 1992 follow-up survey. By this time, seven years after high school graduation, most of the study participants had effectively completed their transition from school to work, although a minority were still involved (mainly full time) in the post-secondary system and a small proportion were continuing with (part-time) training relevant to their current jobs. Figure 14.1 shows that 6% of the total sample (n = 404) had completed an apprenticeship by 1992, while 37% had acquired a college or technical school diploma. Within this category, two-thirds had received their diploma from a technical school and one-third had obtained a college diploma. Almost one-third of the study participants (32%) had obtained a university degree, and a small proportion (3%) had acquired a second degree. In total, 69% of the sample had acquired at least one post-secondary credential by 1992 (some had obtained several credentials—for example, a first and second degree, or a degree and a diploma).

With the exception of apprenticeships, an area where female respondents were conspicuously absent (2%, compared with 11% of males), Figure 14-1 reveals only small gender differences. Male sample members were somewhat more likely to have obtained a college or technical school diploma, while female study participants were a bit more likely to have received a university degree by 1992. Obviously, a more detailed analysis of the type of diploma or degree would have highlighted more distinct patterns of gender segregation (e.g., females with education degrees and males with engineering degrees). Overall, 67% of the young women in this study had acquired some kind of post-secondary credential by 1992, compared with 71% of the men who participated in the 1992 follow-up survey.

SCHOOL-WORK TRANSITIONS BY 1999

By 1999, the Edmonton 12th graders who had first participated in the study fourteen

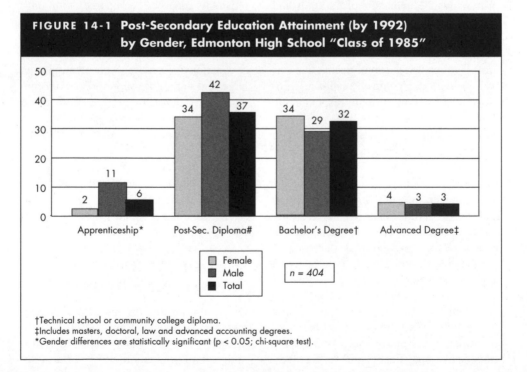

FIGURE 14-1 Post-Secondary Education Attainment (by 1992) by Gender, Edmonton High School "Class of 1985"

n = 404

Female
Male
Total

†Technical school or community college diploma.
‡Includes masters, doctoral, law and advanced accounting degrees.
*Gender differences are statistically significant (p < 0.05; chi-square test).

years earlier were now 32 years of age, on average. Two-thirds (66%) were married or in a long-term relationship, one-half (52%) were raising children, and six out of ten (61%) had purchased a home. One in six (18%) were still participating in some kind of formal education, but most of this activity was part time and much of it was career training relevant to current occupations. Figure 14-2 reveals that, by 1999, sample members had acquired some additional post-secondary credentials.

Twelve percent had completed an apprenticeship by 1999 (8% of the women and 17% of the men in the sample). Forty-three percent now had a college or technical school diploma. While the proportion with university degrees had not increased since 1992, by 1999, 5% of the total sample reported a second degree. Thus, it is apparent that the bulk of the school-work transition (and virtually all of the undergraduate university education) of these Edmonton youth had been completed

within the first seven years following high school. In the next seven-year period, some study participants acquired additional non-university credentials and a few more went on to post-secondary training. In addition, gender differences in the acquisition of post-secondary credentials declined.

SOCIO-ECONOMIC STATUS (SES) AND SCHOOL-WORK TRANSITIONS

In total, 71% of the sample members reported at least one post-secondary credential by 1999. Fourteen years earlier, 93% had planned to obtain such credentials (Table 14-3). The central question addressed in the following analyses is whether family SES or, in other words, class background had an impact on post-secondary educational attainment. Figure 14.3 demonstrates, very clearly, that the answer is "yes."

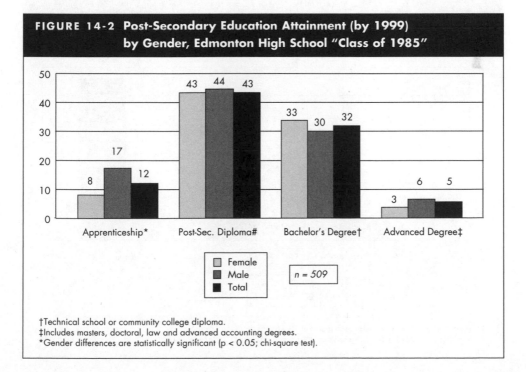

FIGURE 14-2 Post-Secondary Education Attainment (by 1999) by Gender, Edmonton High School "Class of 1985"

Female
Male
Total

$n = 509$

†Technical school or community college diploma.
‡Includes masters, doctoral, law and advanced accounting degrees.
*Gender differences are statistically significant (p < 0.05; chi-square test).

By 1999, 14% of the sample members from lower SES families had completed an apprenticeship, compared with 9% of the respondents from more advantaged backgrounds. Similarly, we see a small SES difference in the acquisition of post-secondary diplomas (46% versus 37%). However, we see a much larger difference in the opposite direction with respect to university education.[8] Figure 14-3 shows that, if at least one parent had completed university, the odds of children in this family completing university are almost three times as high as they are for children from families without a university tradition (56% compared with only 21%).

These findings document the huge impact of class background but cannot directly explain the differences. However, it is very likely that education values and ambitions, as well as familiarity with academic issues and discourse, differed significantly in the two types of families. Furthermore, as we have already noted in Table 14-1, children from more advantaged backgrounds were much more likely to complete an "academic" high school program that provided all of the necessary prerequisites for university education. Thus, Figure 14-4 reveals that only 4% of the 1985 sample members whose parents had not completed university and who had been enrolled in "non-academic" high school programs had completed a university degree by 1999. In sharp contrast, 62% of the higher SES graduates of "academic" high school programs had a degree by 1999 (a ratio of 15 to 1). These differences in "cultural capital" were no doubt augmented by differences in parents' financial

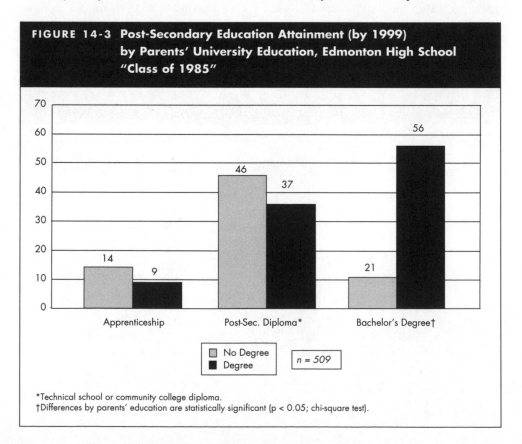

FIGURE 14-3 Post-Secondary Education Attainment (by 1999) by Parents' University Education, Edmonton High School "Class of 1985"

Legend:
- No Degree
- Degree

n = 509

*Technical school or community college diploma.
†Differences by parents' education are statistically significant (p < 0.05; chi-square test).

resources, the result being that middle-class youth were much more likely to have obtained university credentials by 1999.

SOCIO-ECONOMIC STATUS (SES) AND OCCUPATIONAL OUTCOMES

How well had the class of 1985 turned its post-secondary credentials into satisfactory employment? By 1999, 87% of the sample members (n = 442) were employed. Only 4% (n = 19) were unemployed, while the remaining 9% (n = 48) were out of the labour force, frequently for family-related reasons. Almost half (48%) of the employed study participants were in managerial or professional jobs, including 15% in managerial positions, 11% in science or engineering professional positions, and 10% in professional positions in the health care sector. Seven percent of the employed sample members were teachers, while the remaining 5% were in a range of other professional occupations. Just over one-third (36%) were in lower-status clerical, sales or service occupations, while 16% reported a variety of skilled and semi-skilled blue-collar occupations.

Female respondents were overrepresented in teaching (11% versus 4% of males), health-related occupations (16% versus 4%), and clerical jobs (30% versus 6%). In turn, male respondents were significantly overrepresented in science and engineering occupations (17% versus 4% of females) and blue-collar jobs (26% versus 4%). However, when all the different higher-status occupations are combined into a single category, gender differences in managerial/professional employment were non-significant.

Figure 14-5 documents the extent to which family background (SES) and

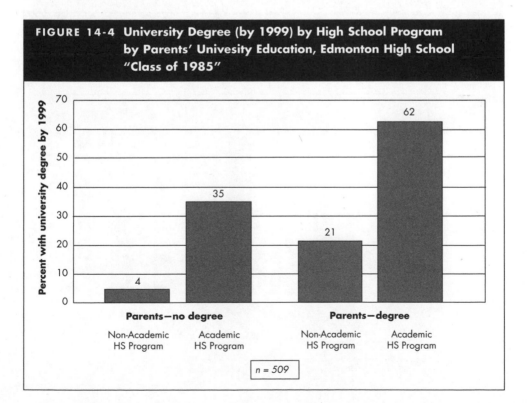

FIGURE 14-4 University Degree (by 1999) by High School Program by Parents' Univesity Education, Edmonton High School "Class of 1985"

Percent with university degree by 1999

- Parents—no degree
  - Non-Academic HS Program: 4
  - Academic HS Program: 35
- Parents—degree
  - Non-Academic HS Program: 21
  - Academic HS Program: 62

n = 509

respondents' own educational attainment had influenced their career outcomes. While 48% of all employed sample members were in managerial/professional occupations, the odds of having acquired a higher-status occupation were considerably higher (66%) for young people from families where at least one parent had completed university. Within this subgroup, 89% of those who had themselves acquired a university degree were in a managerial or professional position when surveyed in 1999, compared with only 38% of sample members without a degree.

While a much lower proportion of sample members from non-university families had themselves completed university (see Figure 14-3 above), those who had acquired a degree despite their disad-

vantaged background were still highly likely (78%) to be in a higher-status occupation by 1999. In contrast, only 30% of lower SES sample members without a degree were in managerial or professional positions. Looking at Figure 14-5 in another way, when we focus on only those sample members with a degree, or on only those without a degree, in each case we see a class advantage. For example, among university graduates, 89% from a higher SES background were in managerial/professional occupations in 1999, compared with 78% from lower-status families. Thus, taking educational attainment into account, individuals from higher SES families still do somewhat better than their less advantaged counterparts.

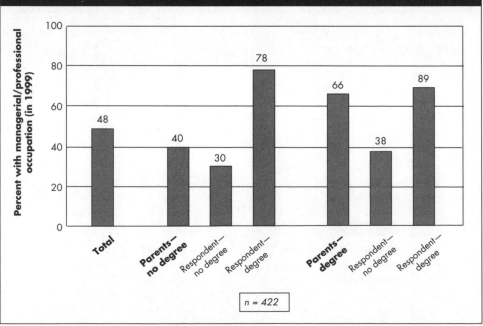

FIGURE 14-5 Managerial/Professional Occupation (in 1999) by Respondents' University Education by Parents' University Education, Edmonton High School, "Class of 1985"

SOCIO-ECONOMIC STATUS (SES) AND THE FIT BETWEEN ASPIRATIONS AND OUTCOMES

In Table 14-3 we observed that 59% of these young people had aspired to managerial or professional occupations when completing high school in 1985. The 1999 follow-up study revealed that very few (only 12%) were in exactly the same job they had mentioned fourteen years earlier (e.g., nurse, automobile mechanic). Less than one-third (30%) were in the same general type of occupation (e.g., health-related occupations, science and engineering). Using an even broader category, we find that only 36% had both aspired to a managerial/professional occupation and then, eventually, moved into such a career. Having observed that SES strongly influences both educational attainment and occupational outcomes, we now turn to a final research question: Does SES also influence one's chances of finding the type of employment that one had hoped to obtain?

Figure 14-6 provides a clear answer. A total of 268 respondents (59% of the total longitudinal sample) had aspired to managerial or professional occupations back in 1985 (see Table 14-3). Sixty percent of these "high goal" individuals had attained these goals by 1999 (Figure 14-6). However, by the age of 32, only 53% of "high goal" sample members from less advantaged families were employed in a managerial or professional occupation, compared with 73% of "high goal" study participants from higher SES families. This big difference is largely explained by the previous findings that the children of university-educated parents were almost three times as likely as their less advantaged peers to themselves obtain a university degree (Figure 14-3), and that a

university degree significantly enhances one's chances of employment in a professional or managerial occupation (Figure 14-5). Because of the latter, within both the lower and higher SES groups the acquisition of a university degree doubled the odds of obtaining the higher-status employment to which one had aspired when leaving high school (Figure 14-6). However, as we saw earlier (Figure 14-3), lower SES sample members were much less likely to obtain a university degree.

SUMMARY AND POLICY IMPLICATIONS

Summarizing the findings from this longitudinal study of school-work transitions, we have seen that middle-class youth (1) typically do better in high school and are more likely to complete academic high school programs that will improve their chances of gaining entry to university; (2) are somewhat more likely to recognize the labour market value of post-secondary education; and (3) have higher educational and occupational aspirations. In the fourteen years following high school completion, (4) members of this cohort acquired an impressive array of post-secondary credentials. (5) They were somewhat more likely to obtain college and technical school diplomas compared with university degrees. The over-time survey data clearly show that (6) children of university-educated parents were much more likely to obtain a university degree themselves; and, as a result, (7) were much more likely to move into managerial or professional employment and (8) to find the type of higher-status employment to which they had originally aspired when leaving high school. In short, these data analyses clearly demonstrate that social class, as measured by SES or parents' university education, continues to matter. In

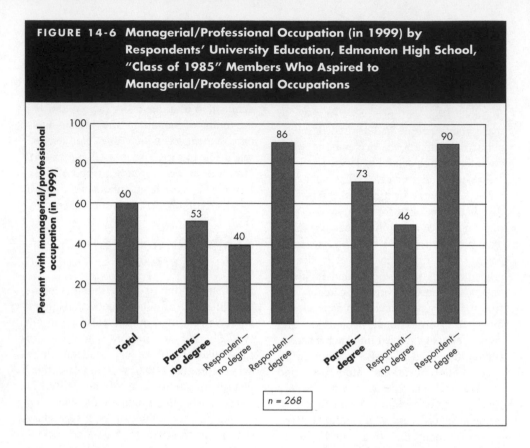

FIGURE 14-6 Managerial/Professional Occupation (in 1999) by Respondents' University Education, Edmonton High School, "Class of 1985" Members Who Aspired to Managerial/Professional Occupations

fact, it matters a great deal. So choose your parents carefully!

Class matters as a result of "streaming" into academic and non-academic programs in high school. It matters because of the different education values, and the different education and occupational aspirations, of teenagers from lower and higher SES families. It matters because more affluent parents can provide more financial support for their children's post-secondary education. Ultimately, class matters the most because of the different post-secondary educational "choices" made by young people from more and less advantaged backgrounds since, in our credential-focused society, a university degree continues to be the prerequisite required to compete for most of the

better-paying, higher-status, and often more satisfying types of employment.

If social class matters this much, should we, as members of society, do something to reduce these SES-based differences in education and career opportunity? If you begin with the premise that public policy interventions are always inappropriate, then the answer is "no." Alternatively, you might argue that unequal education and employment opportunities as a result of family background are unfair. You might also propose that an economy in which some potentially very talented people do not have equal opportunity to compete for the best jobs is an economy that is less productive than it could be. In that case, your answer would be "yes." Either argument invites suggestions for public policy responses.

Having observed the impact of "streaming" in the high school system—and specifically the much higher probability of obtaining a university degree if one completes an "academic" high school program—we should look carefully at how high school programs are organized and how young students are channeled into them. On one hand, it is difficult to reject the argument that some young people may not have the ability or aptitude to complete highly challenging high school courses that lead to university entrance. High school programs that lead into non-university careers are a useful and important alternative. On the other hand, it is possible that some young people who could complete "academic" high school programs are not encouraged to try, or are even actively discouraged, perhaps because of cultural capital deficits.

High school counsellors and others involved in advising young people about educational and career choices nccd to be acutely conscious of the significant impacts they can have on students' futures. In addition, high school programs, both "academic" and non-academic, need to be designed in such a way that young people in them can continue to make choices. For example, several Canadian provinces have designed youth apprenticeship programs that allow high school students to apprentice for trades while still obtaining the high school credits needed for university entrance, should they decide to go this way in the future (Lehmann 2000).

The longitudinal survey data examined in this paper highlight a substantial class effect on occupational outcomes, via post-secondary educational attainment. In other words, children of university-educated parents are much more likely to complete university themselves and, as a result, are more likely to obtain higher-status and more rewarding occupations. Greater access to cultural capital among middle-class youth is part of the explanation, but material capital—money—also plays an important role. Most of the Edmonton youth in this study had completed university by the late 1980s or early 1990s. As we might expect, many had taken out student loans, and many were still paying back these loans in 1999 when they were last surveyed. And, no doubt, many had relied heavily on parents to help finance their post-secondary education.

However, the cost to students of a university education in the late 1980s was relatively low compared with the situation today. In 1980, Canadian universities received only 13% of their total revenue from students' tuition fees. By 1995, this had risen to 24% (Little 1997:2), and tuition fees have continued to rise steadily in almost all provinces since then. In a number of larger universities, professional faculties have more than doubled their tuition fees in the past several years. As tuition costs continue to increase across the country, universities and provincial governments are promising to put in place funding programs to assist the less advantaged to attend university and other post-secondary institutions. It remains to be seen whether these new sources of financial assistance will be sufficient and, furthermore, whether they will really be directed toward the most needy. If not, we can expect to see an even more pronounced impact of social class on educational and occupational attainment in the future. As we have observed, class already matters a great deal with respect to post-secondary education. Without appropriate policy interventions of the type discussed above, it may matter even more in the future.

NOTES

1. The author of this chapter and Dr. Graham S. Lowe have been co-principal investigators in this study since 1985. The Population Research Laboratory, Department of Sociology, University of Alberta, has been responsible for data collection and processing. The largest funding source for this study has been the Social Sciences and Humanities Research Council of Canada (SSHRC). Alberta Learning has also provided significant amounts of funding.

2. Only 894 of the original 983 respondents provided their name and address for follow-up purposes. Hence, the 1992 sample of 404 represented 45% of the original respondents who might have participated.

3. Additional analysis of attrition bias in this longitudinal study (not reported here) indicates that female respondents were somewhat more likely to remain in the study from start to finish, as were 1985 respondents with higher educational aspirations.

4. Fourteen percent of the sample members did not answer these questions (or respond to the 1986 follow-up survey when the question was first included).

5. Ten percent of the 509 sample members did not answer these questions, presumably because they were unsure about how much education their parent(s) had acquired.

6. Included in this category are about 5% of the total sample who stated that they expected to complete one or two years of university.

7. Additional analyses (not reported here) checked for gender differences in high school experiences/performance, education values, and education and career plans. No statistically significant gender differences were observed.

8. Since only 5% of the total sample had completed a second degree by 1999, these results are not examined in this and subsequent analyses.

REFERENCES

Allahar, Anton, and James Côté 1998. *Richer and Poorer: The Structure of Inequality in Canada.* Toronto: James Lorimer.

Andres, L. 1994. "Capital, habitus, field, and practice: An introduction to the work of Pierre Bourdieu." In L. Erwin and D. MacLennan (eds.), *Sociology of Education in Canada*, pp. 120–135. Toronto: Copp Clark Pitman.

Andres, Lesley, Paul Anisef, Harvey Krahn, Dianne Looker, and Victor Thiessen 1999. "The persistence of social structure: Cohort, class, and gender effects on the occupational aspirations and expectations of Canadian youth." *Journal of Youth Studies* 2(3):261–282.

Andres, L., and H. Krahn 1999. "Youth pathways in articulated post-secondary systems: Enrolment and completion patterns of urban young women and men." *Canadian Journal of Higher Education* 19(1):47–82.

Beck, Ulrich 1992. *Risk Society: Towards a New Modernity.* London: Sage Publications.

Bell, Daniel 1973. *The Coming of Post-Industrial Society.* New York: Basic Books.

Boseley, Sarah 2002. "Call for ban on sex choice clinics." Special Report: The Ethics of Genetics. Retrieved December 13, 2002 (http://www. guardian.co.uk/guardian/).

Bourdieu, Pierre (R. Nice, Trans.) 1986. "The forms of capital." In J.C. Richardson (ed.), *Handbook of Theory and Research for the Sociology of Education*, pp. 241–158. New York: Greenwood Press.

Butlin, George 1999. "Determinants of post-secondary participation." *Educational Quarterly Review* 5(3):9–35.

Clark, Terry Nichols, and Seymour Martin Lipset 1991. "Are social classes dying?" *International Sociology* 6:397–410.

Clark, Warren 2000. "100 years of education." *Canadian Social Trends* (Winter):3–7.

Corak, Miles (ed.) 1998. *Labour Markets, Social Institutions, and the Future of Canada's Children.* Ottawa: Statistics Canada and Human Resources Development Canada.

Davies, Scott 1999. "Stubborn disparities: Explaining class inequalities in schooling." In James Curtis, Edward Grabb, and Neil Guppy (eds.), *Social Inequality in Canada: Patterns, Problems, and Policies* (3rd ed.), pp. 138–150. Toronto: Prentice Hall.

Davies, Scott, and Neil Guppy 1997. "Fields of study, college selectivity, and student inequalities in higher education." *Social Forces* 75(4):1417–1438.

de Broucker, Patrice, and Laval Lavallée 1998. "Getting ahead in life: Does your parents' education count?" *Canadian Social Trends* (Summer):29–41.

Forcese, Dennis 1997. *The Canadian Class Structure* (4th ed.). Toronto: McGraw-Hill Ryerson.

Giddens, Anthony 1991. *Modernity and Self-Identity: Self and Society in the Late Modern Age.* Oxford: Polity Press.

Gilbert, Sid, L. Barr, W. Clark, M. Blue, and D. Sunter 1993. *Leaving School: Results from a Longitudinal Survey Comparing School Leavers and High School Graduates 18 to 20 Years of Age.* Ottawa: Minister of Supply and Services.

Grabb, Edward G. 2002. *Theories of Social Inequality: Classical and Contemporary Perspectives.* 4th ed. Toronto: Harcourt Canada.

Knighton, Tamara, and Sheba Mirza 2002. "Postsecondary participation: The effect of parents' education and household income." *Educational Quarterly Review* 8(3):25–32.

Krahn, Harvey, and Graham S. Lowe 2002. *Work, Industry and Canadian Society* (4th ed.). Scarborough, Ontario: Thomson Nelson.

Lehmann, Wolfgang 2000. "Is Germany's dual system still a model for Canadian youth apprenticeship initiatives?" *Canadian Public Policy* 26(2):225–240.

Lenski, Gerhard 1973. *Power and Privilege: A Theory of Social Stratification.* New York: McGraw-Hill.

Little, Don 1997. "Financing universities: Why are students paying more?" *Education Quarterly Review* 4(2):10–26.

Looker, E. Dianne 1994. "Active capital: The impact of parents on youths' educational performance and plans." In Lorna Erwin and David MacLennan (eds.), *Sociology of Education in Canada: Critical Perspectives on Theory, Research and Practice*, pp. 164–187. Toronto: Copp Clark Longman.

Looker, E. Dianne 1997. "In search of credentials: Factors affecting young adults' participation in post-secondary education." *The Canadian Journal of Higher Education* 27(2):1–36.

Radford, Tim 2002. "Italian promises cloned human baby in January." Special Report: The Ethics of Genetics. Retrieved November 28, 2002 (http://www.guardian.co.uk/guardian/).

Tanner, Julian, H. Krahn, and T.F. Hartnagel 1995. *Fractured Transitions from School to Work: Revisiting the Dropout Problem.* Don Mills, Ontario: Oxford University Press.

Willis, Paul 1977. *Learning to Labor: How Working Class Kids Get Working Class Jobs.* New York: Columbia University Press.

Wotherspoon, Terry 1995. *The Sociology of Education in Canada: Critical Perspectives.* Toronto: Oxford.

FURTHER REFERENCES— SECTION 2: SOCIO-ECONOMIC BASES OF SOCIAL INEQUALITY

Income, Wealth, and Poverty

Ambert, Anne Marie 1998. *The Web of Poverty: Psychosocial Perspectives.* Binghamton, New York: The Haworth Press. An interesting attempt to link social structure and individual circumstance in the debate about poverty. Focuses upon both Canada and the United States.

Blais, Francois, and Jennifer Hutchinson 2002. *Ending Poverty: A Basic Income for all Canadians.* Toronto: James Lorimer & Company. They explore the idea of a universal basic income for all Canadians.

Halli, Shiva S., and A. Kazemipur 2000. *The New Poverty in Canada: Ethnic Groups and Ghetto Neighbourhoods.* The authors present a picture of urban poverty in Canada.

Hurtig, Mel 1999. *Pay the Rent or Feed the Kids: The Tragedy and Disgrace of Poverty in Canada.* Toronto: McClelland and Stewart. Hurtig documents the indicators of poverty and the growing disparity among Canadians.

National Council of Welfare (http://www.ncwcnbes.net/). The Council has produced publications such as the *Poverty Profile* and, most recently, the *Child Poverty Profile.*

Poverty Reduction (http://www.acdi-cida.gc.ca/poverty). Information about Canada's efforts at national and international poverty reduction.

Statistics Canada *Quarterly Perspectives on Labour and Income.* Ottawa: Statistics Canada. Published four times a year, this is an excellent source of up-to-date information on various topics related to the study of inequality.

Statistics Canada 2000. *Income in Canada.* (75-202-XIE) Ottawa. This annual publication presents highlights and summary statistics on income and low income of families. The income concepts covered are market income, government transfers, total income, income tax, income after tax, and low income.

Statistics Canada (http://www.statcan.ca). For example, see the research paper *The Evolution of Wealth Inequality in Canada, 1984–1999.*

The Vanier Institute of the Family (http://www.vifamily.ca/). Publications about important issues and trends critical to Canadian families.

Occupation

Betcherman, Gordon, and Graham Lowe 1997. *The Future of Work in Canada. A Synthesis Report.* Ottawa: Canadian Policy Research Networks Inc.

Canadian Labour Congress (http://www.clc-ctc.ca). This site provides information on work from the unionized worker's perspective.

Duffy, Ann, Daniel Glenday, and Norene Pupo (eds.) 1997. *Good Jobs, Bad Jobs, No Jobs: The Transformation of Work in the 21st Century.* Toronto: Harcourt Brace Canada. In this collection of papers, the editors provide a range of analyses dealing with the apparent polarization of occupations into "good" and "bad" categories in recent years, and also of the problems of unemployment and underemployment for many workers.

Industry Canada (http://www.ic.gc.ca). This site provides information on the Canadian economy, trade, and jobs.

Krahn, Harvey, and Graham Lowe 2002. *Work, Industry, and Canadian Society* (4th ed.). Scarborough: Thomson Nelson. This text provides a comprehensive review of employment, the labour market, and workplace trends in Canada, and helps students to interpret these trends using different theoretical perspectives.

Lowe, Graham 2000. *The Quality of Work: A People-Centred Agenda.* Toronto: Oxford University Press. This monograph considers a number of important issues in the analysis of work in the contemporary era, including the future direction of occupational growth and the crises and problems posed for young people, the less educated, the unskilled, and others in their attempts to integrate themselves into the changing "new economy."

Rinehart, James 2001. *The Tyranny of Work* (4th ed.). Toronto: Harcourt Canada. This monograph explores the nature of work in Canada from a critical perspective, with a particular emphasis on the labour process and the alienating nature of work under capitalism.

Statistics Canada *Perspectives on Labour and Income* and *Canadian Social Trends.* These two quarterly publications are invaluable sources of information on Canadian labour market and employment trends and issues.

Van den Berg, Axel, and Joseph Smucker (eds.) 1997. *The Sociology of Labour Markets: Efficiency, Equity, Security.* Scarborough, Ontario: Prentice Hall Allyn and Bacon Canada. This collection of essays covers the major theoretical perspectives on labour markets and presents research findings from various studies of how labour markets operate.

Education

Castellano, Marlene Brant, Lynn Davis, and Louise Lahache (eds.) 2000. *Aboriginal Education: Fulfilling the Promise.* Vancouver: UBC Press. The authors document the significant gains made in Aboriginal education in recent years.

Council of Ministers of Education, Canada (http://www.cmec.ca/). CMEC is the national voice for education in Canada. For example, see *The Transition from Initial Education to Working Life: A Canadian Report for the OECD Thematic Review.*

Guppy, Neil, and Scott Davies 1998. *The Schooled Society: Changes and Challenges in Canadian Education.* Ottawa: Statistics Canada and Nelson Publishing. An assessment of Canadian education, from Confederation to the present, using materials from the Canadian Census. Recent decades are stressed.

Krahn, Harvey, and Jeffery W. Bowlby 2000. *Education-Job Skills Match: An Analysis of the 1990 and 1995 National Graduate Surveys.* Hull: Human Resources Development Canada.

Pocklington, Tom, and Allan Tupper 2002. *No Place to Learn: Why Universities Aren't Working.* Vancouver: UBC Press. The authors cast a critical eye on how Canadian universities work—or fail to work.

Programme for International Student Assessment (PISA) 2000. (http://www.cmec.ca/pisa/2000/indexe.stm) *Measuring Up: The Performance of Canada's Youth in Reading, Mathematics, and Science. First Results for Canadians Aged 15.* The Programme for International Student Assessment, conducted in 2000 by the Organization for Economic Cooperation and Development (OECD), tested over 250 000 students from thirty-two countries.

Robertson, Heather-Jane 1998. *No More Teachers, No More Books: The Commercialization of Canada's Schools.* Toronto: McClelland and Stewart. The author reports on the increasing commercialization of education in Canada.

The Society for the Advancement of Excellence in Education (http://www.saee.bc.ca/). Provides nonpartisan education research and information to policy-makers, education partners, and the public.

Statistics Canada 2001. *Education in Canada 2000.* Ottawa: Minister of Industry. An annual review of statistics on Canadian education.

ASCRIPTION AND SOCIAL INEQUALITY

A. GENDER
B. ETHNICITY, RACE, AND ANCESTRY
C. AGE
D. REGION

A historic moment was signalled by the signing in 1948 of the Universal Declaration of Human Rights (a United Nations initiative) proclaiming the rights of all citizens. In the next decade, inspired principally by Martin Luther King, the U.S. civil rights movement riveted attention on the plight of Blacks in North America. Throughout this era, the promotion of equality in human rights spread to include other ethnic, linguistic, and religious groups. Based also on equal rights for groups defined by sex, nationality, region, and physical ability, powerful social movements arose in the aftermath of the Second World War, transforming politics, economics, and culture the world over.

Many grievances of these disadvantaged groups were long-standing, with, for example, the struggles of women and Aboriginal peoples having had a tortuously long history. But in the late 1940s and early 1950s, following a world war in which millions had died battling Hitler's racism, a new surge of human energy focused on promoting and advancing the opportunities of oppressed people. The racial bigotry of fascism had been crushed at immense cost, and a world sensitized to the brutality of human hatred was more accommodating to the idea of equal opportunity.

Perceiving a maturing of industrial capitalism in the post-war era, some social thinkers came to believe that the political fault lines of society, in the past often based on territory, religion, race, and ethnicity, would dissolve as democratic freedoms and economic opportunities flourished. With economic prosperity would come political modernization. An era of equal opportunity would follow, in which merit and effort would determine the distribution of social resources. Traditional social cleavages would pale in the face of a growing meritocracy, in which competence, achievement, and motivation would determine individual life chances.

In sharp contrast to this modernization view, other social thinkers foresaw growing conflict along class lines. Rather than a maturing of competitive capitalism, these theorists saw a period of monopoly capitalism, in which a class of wealthy owners prospered at the expense of others. The gap between the rich and the poor would widen, they believed. As consciousness of class interests grew, the eclipse of traditional cleavages would result, and class antagonism would obliterate old hostilities. The significant fault line of modern society now would be based on class interests grounded in the differential ownership of private property. Traditional conflicts among religious, racial, or regional groupings would be forgotten.

Neither of these two perspectives has served us particularly well in understanding the most recent social movements dominating the Canadian political scene. Neither view fits closely with the facts. The women's movement, the quest for native self-government, the rise of Québec nationalism—these are all phenomena whose emergence, and magnitude, theorists of class antagonism or political modernization did not anticipate. People from a diversity of class backgrounds expressed group rights with vigour and dedication in a variety of "modern" countries.

At the core of any of these particular movements is a collective membership based on birthright. The women's movement or the Black civil rights movement focuses upon social groups defined by birth. Sex, for example, is not attained or achieved; it is determined at conception, and individuals have no say in the matter. However, as an ascribed attribute, sex is important sociologically only to the extent that people use it as a significant marker. Others react to us, make judgments about us, and generally orient themselves to us based on a variety of ascribed features, including our sex, race, age, ethnicity, and region.

Although distinctions involving sexes, races, or age groups are based on birthright, notice that it is the socially constructed distinctions around these birth-

rights that are significant for sociologists. The concept of "race" perhaps best illustrates this point. In apartheid South Africa "race" was established by committee (under the *Population Registration Act*). This occurred because no group was "pure-blooded," no genetic differentiation could separate "white," "mixed," and "black" South Africans—such was the history of sexual mixing.

This is true more widely, in that all human groups are genetically mixed populations. The distinctions we make are based on those observable physical characteristics that we collectively choose to use as group markers. Race is not a biological construct, but a socially created system of classification. No "pure" racial groups exist.

Not only a process of social differentiation is at work here, but also invariably a hierarchical structuring, a stratification of dominant and subordinate groupings, occurs. Races were not only separated (differentiated) in South Africa; they were also ranked (stratified). The degree and the strength of this hierarchy vary across societies, but inequality based on ascription is a common feature of all societies. Ascriptive attributes are correlated with different scarce rewards: income, power, prestige. This is the context—the "vertical mosaic," as John Porter (1965) labelled the phenomenon of ascriptive inequality in Canada—within which various social groups have rallied to press for increased human rights.

In Canada these social movements have found expression in an array of formal agencies and organizations, including the Assembly of First Nations, the National Action Committee on the Status of Women, the Canadian Human Rights Commission, and the National Advisory Council on Aging. Government policy initiatives in such areas as multiculturalism, bilingualism and biculturalism, nontraditional job training for women, and regional development have reinforced these movements.

GENDER

Social scientists distinguish between sex and gender. Sex is a biological concept referring to physiological differences between women and men (e.g., reproductive functions, hormonal variation). Gender is a social concept referring to socially constructed differences between women and men (e.g., femininity and masculinity).

In modern Canada, masculine traits entail being adventurous, forceful, and stern, whereas more feminine attributes include being gentle, sensitive, and warm. What it means to act or to think in a feminine, as opposed to a masculine, way depends on social expectations that vary both in time and space (see, e.g., Mackie 1991:1–7). As you will know from your own experience, although gender roles are social creations that we learn, there are powerful social expectations that allow relatively little deviation (which is why we treat gender here as ascribed).

The importance of this distinction for us is to underscore the idea that many differences between women and men are more the result of gender roles than of biological destiny. In modern Canada, women occupy a disadvantaged position on a variety of inequality dimensions, but this ought not to be regarded as some immutable, unchangeable fact of human nature. Although women who work full time, full year, earn only about 73% of what men do and typically find themselves in jobs with relatively little power and responsibility, this does not mean that such inequalities are unalterable. Instead, as we noted in our preface, it means that the economic, political, and ideological control of privileged groups play a formidable role in structuring and maintaining inequality.

Sociology has played an important role in addressing gender inequality. In the first chapter of this section, Janet Siltanen uses the discipline of sociology as a focus to show how women's experiences and gender inequalities have been addressed by different scholars. From a period in which women were largely invisible in scholarly research, two more recent stages have occurred. Beyond stage one, where women's experience was made visible, stage two was a period in which analysts and researchers sought to understand and explain that experience. In a third and more recent stage, the concept of gender, along with the related question of sexual identity, has become more contested.

In their chapter on who does the housework in Canadian households, Kevin McQuillan and Marilyn Belle look at recent Canadian evidence that confirms the well-established tendency for women to do consistently more housework than men. They show also that domestic labour still tends to be divided along conventional gender lines, with women performing most of the traditional "female-typed" tasks, such as cooking, inside cleaning, and laundry work, and men doing more of the traditional "male-typed" jobs, such as yard work and household maintenance. There is some tendency for men to do more domestic labour today than in the past. However, the gender differences remain evident, even after considering which member of the couple has greater economic power (e.g., which person generates a higher income) or which member of the couple has more free time available. The authors offer a number of suggestions as to why women continue to do more of the domestic labour than men, including the possibility that, because of continuing gender differences in socialization, women still give the idea of a "clean house" greater symbolic value than do men, as well as the likelihood that the division of household labour is really an everyday reflection and reproduction of the patriarchal nature of contemporary Canadian society.

Gillian Creese and Brenda Beagan, in the final chapter in the Gender subsection, review trends in women's employment opportunities between 1930 and 2002, pointing to specific policy changes of particular significance to women. Their empirical evidence considers employment rates, earnings ratios, and occupational segregation, and they especially highlight policies dealing with both pay and employment equity.

ETHNICITY, RACE, AND ANCESTRY

As much as any country in the world, Canada has developed as a nation of immigrants. In the first paper in the Ethnicity, Race, and Ancestry section, Monica Boyd and Michael Vickers provide us with detailed evidence on the changing nature of immigration in Canada over the past 100 years. Among the many important patterns they identify is the movement away from European immigration and toward larger proportions of non-White or visible minority immigrants in recent decades, as well as the shift away from individual male immigration and toward more female and family-based immigrants in the latter decades of the 1900s. The authors also note the considerable ebb and flow in the number of immigrants that came to Canada in different stages or time periods. Interestingly, the amount of immigration at the end of the 1900s was very nearly back to the highest level experienced at any time within the twentieth century—that is, to the level that occurred at the beginning of the 1900s.

Boyd and Vickers spell out the various factors that have made for the ebb and flow, most of them rooted in politics and public policy. This chapter provides one of several illustrations in the book of how social status distributions and public policy are closely related.

What are the implications for inequality of the ways in which ethnicity, race, and ancestry are socially constructed? The next selection, by Feng Hou and T.R. Balakrishnan, starts to address this question. The analyses of recent census data in this article demonstrate that educational attainment and income vary considerably across ethnic groups. The data show particularly that some "visible minorities" have lower levels of income than other ethnic groups, and have lower incomes than would be expected from their education levels. Further, some "non-visible minorities"— e.g., certain European-origin groups—have attained income parity with the majority "charter groups," the British and French. This has occurred despite the fact that these European-origin groups have somewhat lower educational attainment levels than the average for the total population. Most visible minorities have higher educational attainment but lower incomes than the average for the population.

Hou and Balakrishnan go on to speculate about the causes of these patterns. They hypothesize that some groups may do better than their educational credentials suggest they should because of "economic mobilization within the ethnic community." The ethnic community provides social support by providing employment and business opportunities for ethnic group members. Further, the authors believe that the earnings disadvantages of some visible minorities are likely related, at least in part, to employment discrimination. Programs intended to compensate for discriminatory practices against ethnic and racial group members have helped to lessen income inequality, but the effects of discrimination have not been completely erased (cf., e.g., Agocs and Boyd 1993).

Frances Henry's work appears next in the Ethnicity, Race, and Ancestry section. Her research, including the results from earlier studies she conducted with Effie Ginzberg, shows that there were explicit and undeniable processes of discrimination in hiring practices among samples of job interviewers. The results held across two samples of interviewers studied a few years apart. Using an experimental design in which job applications were made in person, these researchers measured the extent of preferential hiring of Whites relative to Blacks. Not content with this single procedure, they altered the research design to incorporate job searches by telephone as well, and examined the success rates of different "audible" minorities. Based on these two types of evidence, Henry arrived at a "discrimination ratio" of 3:1, showing that racial minorities suffered substantial obstacles compared with the dominant White majority group in their ability to find employment.

Henry was also involved in a follow-up study a few years later, which showed the same pattern of results as the original study, once a variation in the procedure from the first to the second study was taken into account. In this second study, conducted in a time of expansive hiring, when the Black applicants approached employers first, they were as likely to get jobs as the White applicants applying later. If the White applicants applied first, they were more likely to get a job offer than the Black applicants applying after them.

Henry's work dramatically demonstrates one of the very direct forms that discrimination still takes in Canadian society. Other, more subtle forms of discrimination also occur in the labour market. Word-of-mouth hiring procedures, the use of irrelevant job qualifications, biased screening techniques, and systematic misinformation are all examples of more disguised forms of preferential treatment in employment. Such discrimination practices are likely implicated in some differences in earnings between visible minorities and other groups shown in the earlier selection by Hou and Balakrishnan.

We should mention, too, that Reitz (1988) has built upon the work of Henry, by making Canada-British comparisons. Reitz noted that a study very similar to that of Henry had been undertaken in Britain as well. Comparisons across the Canadian and British studies do *not* suggest that there is less employment discrimination by race in Canada, as popular understanding might hold. (People tend to think that Canadians are comparatively high in tolerance and acceptance of racial and ethnic minorities.) Reitz argues that there are, however, *other* important Canadian-British differences around race and ethnicity. He makes the case that there is less *racial conflict*, rather than less racial discrimination, in Canada. He attributes the national difference to various factors that differ across the countries, including (1) the better average socio-economic status of visible minorities in Canada than in Britain (because of immigration policies concerning who is accepted for admission to the country); (2) the greater stability of immigration policy in Canada, with less debate over the appropriateness of immigration to the country; and (3) Canada's policies of multiculturalism and bilingualism, which give legitimation to minority ethnic and racial communities, and which have no counterparts in Britain.

Historical evidence reveals, of course, a litany of discriminatory acts around ethnicity and race in Canada. We need think only of Black slavery, Chinese head taxes, and Japanese internment to know that there have been many serious instances of discrimination in Canada. Another example is the treatment of Aboriginal peoples by the majority groups over the centuries. As Judge Rosalie Abella (1984:33) reported in her Royal Commission on inequality of opportunity in Canada, "it is not new that their [Aboriginal peoples'] economic conditions are poor. Study after study has documented the facts." What is less often realized, Abella continues, is that their economic plight has taken its inevitable toll on social conditions. Native people are angry over the disproportionate numbers of native people who drop out of school, who are in prison, who suffer ill health, who die young, who commit suicide. They are saddened by the personal, communal, and cultural dislocation of their people.

In the next selection, Charles Menzies examines the relations of Aboriginal peoples with the rest of Canadians, showing that none of this is outdated. Ancestry matters, and it matters as much now for First Nations people as it did at the time of first European contact. He enumerates forms of disadvantage in socio-economic attainment and important life chances experienced by Aboriginal peoples in Canada. He traces some of the history of dislocation that has beset the Aboriginal peoples of Canada, pointing out that this dislocation has its origins in the imperialist encroachment of European nations in pursuit of riches from North America's resources. For several centuries Aboriginal peoples have been placed in an increasingly dependent position, with their protests over land claim settlements or their calls for greater self-determination going unheeded. More recently, while these old demands remained unresolved, a new Canadian constitution was signed that contains no statements on the Aboriginal rights of the indigenous population. These rights, including self-government, have remained a basic demand of the

Aboriginal peoples. Menzies describes how some progress toward self-determination has been made in recent years. However, he cautions us that this process will be particularly helpful for Aboriginals only if it is built on a sound economic base.

AGE

Gender and ethnicity/race/ancestry are but two ascribed attributes that have served to unite people around social issues. Age is a third. Consider this: Is it reasonable to have a minimum wage policy specifying that people under a certain age—often 16, 17, or 18—should be paid a lower wage rate than people a few weeks or months older? Should people be forced out of the labour force once they reach the age of 65, even if they are willing and able to continue working? Especially in the last decade, age discrimination has become a rallying point for social protest. One particularly dramatic incident occurred in 1985, when Canadian pensioners successfully organized to oppose legislation proposed by the federal government to reduce pension benefits for seniors. Using the concepts of age grading and dependency, Guppy, Curtis, and Grabb show how age relates to a variety of dimensions of social inequality.

The relation between age and inequality has also been explored in the context of the welfare state and the aging population. Put succinctly, can we afford the old-age-security system now in place in Canada, once a greater percentage of our population is over the age of 65? If the answer to this question is no, then given the link between poverty and old age (especially among older women), the consequences could be catastrophic. John Myles takes on this debate in the next selection, investigating in particular various ways of understanding the "crisis" in old-age security. He contrasts a demographic perspective, focusing on the number of elderly people, with a social conflict perspective, featuring the class interests of capital versus labour, as explanations for the crisis in old-age security.

REGION

The last subsection on ascription shifts our attention from individual attributes to the community and regional contexts in which Canadians live. On first consideration, it might seem odd to include region as an issue under the topic of ascription. After all, people can choose to move from region to region. Thus, region of residence could be viewed as an achieved or attained status, because it can be changed by individual choice in a way that ascribed statuses like gender or race cannot.

Nevertheless, there clearly are ascribed aspects to the region variable. Region of birth, for example, is not a matter of personal choice and, moreover, is a good predictor of a person's ultimate place of residence. That is, people who are born in a particular region often stay in the same locality during their adult lives, because of the strong community allegiances, regional identities, and social ties that arise in early life and that constrain people to stay where they are, in spite of pressures or opportunities to go elsewhere. This may be especially true in a region like Québec, where the French language is another strong bond keeping a large proportion of the population in that part of the country. However, the holding power of regional ties is apparent throughout the entire country—in the Atlantic provinces, the West, and elsewhere.

Region can also have lasting effects on people's stratification position and life chances. This occurs for at least two reasons. First, some Canadians have developed stereotypes about regional cultures and personality traits. We hear some people speak of "rednecks" from the West,

"laid-back" Vancouverites, "unsophisticated" Newfoundlanders, and "anti-Canadian" Québecers, for example. Certain expectations are then formed and judgments are made on the basis of what are typically misleading perceptions or impressions. Such attitudes, in turn, can have negative effects on how we deal with and relate to each other. Second, and equally important, inequalities of reward and opportunity are also structured by the communities and regions in which Canadians live. The regional disparities of the country often reinforce many of the structural inequalities that arise within the larger population, including the differences in corporate economic power, wealth, income, occupation, education, and so on that were discussed in Sections 1 and 2 of the book.

We begin our consideration of regional differences with Fred Wien and Catherine Corrigall-Brown's analysis of regional socio-economic differences. Their chapter provides considerable information on the extent of regional inequality in Canada with regard to unemployment, income, and related social indicators such as health, life expectancy, and educational attainment. The authors also review key explanations for regional inequalities and discuss some of the policies that governments have implemented to alleviate problems of regional disparity.

The second paper, by Kenneth Stewart, examines the position of Québec in Canada's regional make-up, and the possible role of the federal government's economic policies in defining this position. Stewart makes the somewhat provocative and controversial argument that Ottawa's long-standing policy of transferring wealth from the richer provinces to poorer areas, especially to Québec and the Atlantic region, has made these areas increasingly dependent economically. At the same time, in Stewart's view, these policies have actually encouraged the cause of Québec independence.

The central concern of our section on Social Ascription is the degree to which social inequalities are related to ascriptive factors. Despite the optimistic view of those who believe that ascribed statuses are becoming less and less important in contemporary Canadian society, the evidence reviewed in this section reveals that people's life chances continue to be affected in significant ways by race, ethnicity, ancestry, gender, age, and region. We are still a long way from the elimination of ascriptive inequalities.

REFERENCES

Abella, Judge Rosalie Silberman 1984. *Equality in Employment: A Royal Commission Report.* Ottawa: Minister of Supply and Services.

Agocs, Carol, and Monica Boyd 1993. "The Canadian ethnic mosaic recast for the 1990s." In J. Curtis, E. Grabb, and N. Guppy (eds.), *Social Inequality in Canada: Patterns, Problems, Policies* (2nd ed.), pp. 331–352. Scarborough, Ontario: Prentice-Hall.

Mackie, Marlene 1991. *Gender Relations in Canada.* Toronto: Butterworths.

Porter, John 1965. *The Vertical Mosaic.* Toronto: University of Toronto Press.

Reitz, Jeffrey G. 1988. "Less racial discrimination in Canada, or simply less racial conflict? Implications of comparisons with Britain." *Canadian Public Policy* 14, 4:424–441.

Chapter

INEQUALITIES OF GENDER AND CLASS: CHARTING THE SEA CHANGE

Janet Siltanen

(A new chapter written for this volume.)

If we date the women's movement in Canada from the late 1960s, it becomes possible to speak about "before" and "after" on virtually every topic that has been raised by feminists. This does not mean that everything changed in the way that the participants and supporters of the movement intended. But there was a sea change. ...

(Hamilton 1996:42)

INTRODUCTION

Second-wave feminism was a movement for intellectual as well as political change. As the quote from Hamilton identifies, a vast range of topics was affected by its challenge to take seriously women's experience and gender inequality.[1] Sociology and, within it, the study of inequality were not exempt from this challenge. As people turned to existing traditions of stratification analysis, looking for intellectual resources and inspiration to address women's experience, they found little of either. Worse, they often found exactly the same male-oriented ideas and practices they were trying to challenge outside of academia.

In "before" forms of stratification analysis, men are the main characters of interest and, if women appear at all, it is usually in peripheral, supporting roles. The first collection of sociological research on Canadian society, published in 1961, clearly reveals this problem (Blishen et al. 1961). The five stratification chapters illustrate the different positioning of women's and men's experience in the "before" mode of analysis. In a chapter reporting on the extent to which children grow up to have occupations similar to their parents, women do not appear. Only male parents are thought to have occupational experience of relevance to their children's future. In three chapters, women are present, but only briefly and marginally as the wives, daughters, or mothers of the main research subjects. In only one chapter are women included in the central interests of the research. The study uses information on men's and women's income and education to create a socioeconomic scale. But it is telling to note that the need to create separate scales for women and men is regarded as a "technical problem" and is not approached as a source of analytical interest.

The "sea change" in sociology, and in the study of inequality specifically, has meant that women's lives, and the inequalities between women and men, are less likely to be ignored or marginalized as topics relevant to the study of inequality. In the "after" forms of stratification analysis, women's experience and issues of gender are more frequently in the foreground. It is possible to observe some of this "sea change" by comparing different editions of the book you are now reading.

Social Stratification: Canada, published in 1973, was the first collection of research wholly dedicated to the study of inequality in Canada. It was, and remains, an important landmark in Canadian sociology. At the same time, it has definite "before" characteristics: Women's experience, and the analysis of inequalities between women and men, are absent from the stratification agenda. The themes organizing the book are, the editors say, an expanded list of the dimensions of the "Canadian Social Stratification System": occupational prestige, authority, income or wealth, education, ethnicity, and religion.

In a footnote to this list, Curtis and Scott (1973:4, 7n) state that while it "includes [the] most important dimensions of stratification in industrial societies it is not necessarily complete (for example, age and sex stratification might be included in a longer list)." In the collection as a whole, only one of the twenty-one articles addresses women's experience in any extensive fashion, and it focuses on low income and poverty.

But this relegation of "sex stratification" to the end of a long list of inequality topics was to end. With the sea change, stratification analysis began to open up to the significance of women's experience, and gender, for the analysis of inequality. In a 1993 edition of the book, gender appears as a dimension of stratification significant enough to warrant its own section of articles. In the third edition, the gender section remains, and in addition the editors (Curtis et. al. 1999:v) draw attention to the fact that "we have worked very hard to ensure that various dimensions of inequality, for example, gender and ethnicity, have not been confined exclusively to isolated sections. While separate sections ... are maintained, we include several articles in other sections that deal with these dimensions as well." There is a definite "after" taste to this later presentation of gender as a form of inequality that is important—not ghettoized as a specialized interest—and incorporated into other aspects of stratification analysis.

Incorporating gender has been a significant advance in the sociological study of inequality. Over the course of the last thirty or so years, there has been a close and critical engagement with conventional theories of inequality and methods of stratification analysis over the appearance and representation of women's experience and gender inequality. Earlier engagements were often focused on the inclusion of women or the sexual division of labour as analytical considerations. The beginning of a more elaborate sociological interest in "gender" itself is usually attributed to Oakley (1972) who advocated distinguishing between the biologically given features of "sex" and the socially constructed characteristics of "gender"—a formulation that shaped the interest in gender inequality for at least two decades.[2] Thus, while earlier arguments addressed stratification by "sex," later formulations used the concept of gender.

It is important to realize that the conceptualization of gender has its own history. Early analyses of stratification regarded being male or female as an "ascriptive" characteristic—that is, a "natural" attribute beyond the influence of individuals or societies. However, the concept of gender was introduced as a challenge to the idea that feminine and masculine characteristics are natural and not subject to change. A gender perspective regards being masculine or feminine as a very social achievement that requires intense effort and scrutiny on the part of individuals and societies. Further, inequalities associated with being male and female came to be seen as socially created consequences of the way society is organized around gendered identities. For example, the gap in earnings between women and men is not a consequence of natural abilities or chromosome patterns. It is a result of how ideas of gender enter into the social organization of paid and domestic work. Later, the division between the natural and the social started to break down as the conceptual foundation for gender and questions of race, sexuality, and sexual orientation emerged to confront the tendency to define gender in universal terms. This development has had a significant impact on how we think about gender inequality.

As the theorization of gender developed, incorporating gender into theories of inequality posed tougher challenges. My purpose here is to show how challenges to stratification theory have intensified as the conceptualization of gender underwent its own development and critique.

The "after" era of stratification analysis has had many trajectories of theoretical elaboration and change, and feminist sociologists have had a go at just about all of them.[3] As an introduction to this important and lively area of scholarly work, we can identify three levels in the challenge to theories of inequality in the Canadian context. The challenges are distinguished as levels, rather than phases or stages, and the levels contain two important attributes. First, the challenge intensifies with each level. Higher levels imply more extensive challenges to revise and re-think stratification approaches. Second, each level is relevant. While we will see some chronological sequencing as we move from levels one to three in the examples discussed in this chapter, challenges at levels one and two are not historically obsolete.

In this chapter I use examples from the challenges to Marxist class analysis. I do this because it is in this area of scholarly work that some of the sharpest and most interesting debates have occurred, both within Canada and internationally. Not all forms of stratification analysis have witnessed such intense scrutiny, nor provoked such profound questioning about the foundational dynamics of society.[4] As gender itself becomes a contested concept, as has happened recently in some quarters of analysis, contesting stratification on behalf of gender becomes a more elaborate and complex task. Marxist class theory has faced the toughest challenges yet—a testament to people's attachment to it despite its explanatory vulnerability in the face of women's experience and gender inequality.

THE THREE LEVELS
OF CHALLENGE

The first level of challenge is to make women visible! The challenge of recognizing the existence of two sexes involves the basic but fundamental argument that the study of stratification in sociology cannot be about men only. The inclusion of women and women's experience in the analysis of stratification is an essential condition for the credibility and validity of theories of inequality. One response to this challenge has been to see how women would fit into already developed theoretical concepts and arguments of class analysis. While this gives women an analytical presence, sometimes "fitting women in" provides only a description of the inequality between women and men, and not an explanation of it. And sometimes gender inequality actually disappears from view. As significant as this level of challenge is, it leads somewhat inevitably to further challenges, such as *how* women's experience is to be included and *how* inequalities between women and men are to be addressed.

At the second level of challenge, inclusion of women into existing theoretical frameworks is not sufficient, and the focus shifts to the need to identify and examine gender inequality. Here arguments take issue with what counts as inequality and the ability of existing theoretical concepts to explain gender inequality. The insistence on the visibility and explanation of gender inequality forces a more substantial revision of class analysis. However, as we shall see, there has been a range of responses to this challenge, depending on how gender inequality is conceptualized.

At the third and most challenging level, the concept of gender is itself unsettled. Just as gender challenged class in terms of its claim to represent general experience, the possibility that gender has a single, unified meaning is challenged. Class and gender, it is argued, can no longer confront each other as if they each defined a homogeneous terrain of inequality. Inequalities cohering around, for example, sexuality and race specify gender as well as the relationship between gender and class. The need to particularize the meaning of gender (to say where, when, and how it is significant), as well as the configuration of class/gender relations, leads to further, deeper, questioning about the significance of class. At its strongest, this third-level challenge calls for a major re-positioning of class and a fundamentally new approach to theories of inequality.

Let us consider now some examples of how Canadian scholars have worked through the three levels of challenge.

Level One: The Challenge of Two Sexes

In the "before" studies of stratification in Canada, many research projects and reports were exclusively and explicitly about men's experiences. Canadian sociology was by no means unique in this regard, and feminist sociologists in Canada joined a chorus of voices, including those from the United States and Britain, objecting to the exclusion of women from the realm of stratification inquiry.

Marxist approaches to a class analysis of capitalism were very male-oriented. A "Y" chromosome seemed to be a prerequisite for entry into the work sites and industrial disputes of class action! For example, in *Class, State, Ideology and Change*, a "before" anthology bringing together Marxist scholarship throughout the 1970s in Canada, women's experience is discussed in one article out of twenty-two (Grayson 1980). Significantly, it is an example of "institutionalized practices of excluding women" (Smith 1980:264).

In Marxist analysis more generally, however, scholars did find some attention to women's experience—particularly in terms of their oppression within the family. The classic reference point in Marxist scholarship for the discussion of women's position within capitalist society is Engels' late-nineteenth-century classic *The Origins of the Family, Private Property and the State*. In this work, Engels argues that women are essentially excluded from the central dynamic of capitalist commodity production. They are locked away in a privatized family form, which ensures clear inheritance lines for accumulated private property. Indeed, at the time of Engels' writings, women were themselves part of the private property of fathers or husbands. Women's liberation, Engels asserted, requires release from this privatized existence, and rests with their full entry into the public world of productive relations.

Analysts in the mid-twentieth century found some much-valued company in Engels' recognition and objection to women's unequal position within the family. However, this analysis did not travel easily into contemporary arrangements. Two aspects concern us here. First, people were not content to see housework and child care as simply a private service to the husband. As Zaretsky pointed out, "Engels fails to specify the place of women, as housewives and mothers, in relation to capitalist production" (1976:94). Second, by the 1960s the double shift was well established as the main profile of women's work. Women were not only labourers in the domestic sphere; they were now proletarianized as wage labourers. They were heading for "liberation" in Engels' sense of the term, although for women it often felt like anything but! So Marxist analysis needed to consider how to include, in the analysis of contemporary capitalism, women's position as both domestic and wage labourers.

Marx's own writings are not helpful in this regard. His argument is that the dynamic of capitalism would do away with any distinctive social features of the labourers themselves. While women did work as wage labourers during Marx's time and did have some distinguishing characteristics in terms of where and how they were employed, these divisions within wage labour were in his view antithetical to the dynamic of capitalism and destined to fade away. He also paid little attention to the activities of social reproduction located within the household. Although the reproduction of the working class was an important concept that entered into calculations of the value of labour power and into the reproduction of capital, Marx was not interested in analyzing directly how this was accomplished. These matters can, he said, be "safely" left "to the workers' drives for self-preservation and propagation" (1976:718).

Despite this limited assistance from Marx and Engels in determining how women might be included in the analysis of late-twentieth-century capitalism, there was a concerted effort to incorporate women's contemporary experience into Marxist class analysis. Two areas received special attention in Canadian scholarship: the identification of women's domestic work as labour within capitalism and the positioning of women's wage labour.

Domestic Labour as Productive Labour

In order to bring domestic labour into the dynamics of capitalist production, many attempts were made to understand domestic labour in terms of the existing labour theory of value. In Marxist analysis, a distinguishing feature of capitalism is the commodification of the capacity to labour. Labour power is bought (by capitalists) and sold (by wage labourers) for use in capitalist production. As a commodity, labour has a "use value"—the usefulness of labour in the actual process of production—and an "exchange value"—what labour power is worth when bought and sold. When used in production, labour produces enough to cover the costs of its own reproduction, as well as an amount that is surplus to this and appropriated by the capitalist. The division of the working day into necessary labour time and surplus labour time is what the great struggle between labour and capital is about. Productive labour is labour that produces a surplus, and the appropriation of this surplus is the basis of exploitation in capitalism.

The "domestic labour debate" was about whether and how women's domestic labour could fit into this value scheme for understanding the basis of the exploitative relationship between the capitalist and working classes. While some argued against stretching the concept of surplus value to include contributions from labour not exchanged as a commodity, others argued that domestic labour was indeed "productive" in the Marxist sense, although indirectly. Capitalism depends on domestic labour on a daily basis (the care of the male wage labourer) and an intergenerational basis (the care of children). Productive labour is itself produced by domestic labour. Therefore, domestic labour contributes, in a central though indirect way, to the production of surplus value. While there were many more permutations within the debate, the useful observation for current purposes is that "the explicit aim of the domestic labour debate ... was to come to an understanding of the relationship of the private household to capitalist commodity production" (Fox 1986:182).[5]

Women as a Reserve Army of Labour

When it came to fitting women into theories of the distribution and dynamics of wage labour, people turned to the concept of the reserve army of labour. As mentioned above, a key aspect of the conflict between capitalists and labour is the division between necessary and surplus labour time. Workers want the division to favour the former and capitalists want the division to favour the latter. Maintaining a reserve pool of labour is identified by Marx as one way of disciplining workers to accept lower and lower definitions of what is necessary to reproduce labour power. Large numbers of unemployed people, or people employed casually and on poor terms, create competitive pressure on the employed population to accept degradations in their employment conditions and remuneration in order to keep their jobs. Maintaining a reserve army of labour is a strategy to extract higher levels of surplus value.

It was argued that capitalists used women's wage labour as a form of reserve. Women are, in Connelly's (1978) formulation, "last hired and first fired." The ideology defining men as the primary breadwinners of families make women's claim to paid work open to manipulation, and creates a vulnerability that can be used to the advantage of capitalist production. The real or threatened use of cheaper female labour can be used to exert a competitive pressure on the male labour force, helping to dampen men's demands around wages and conditions. While the experience of the Second World War is often referred to as the prime example of using women as a reserve of labour, it was argued that this practice continued subsequently as a feature of the organization of the capitalist labour force.

Limitations of the "Stretch to Fit" Strategy

At this level of challenge to conventional theory, the interest is to recover women's experience, giving it visibility and relevance. This in itself is an important strategy and achievement. Obviously, those who responded positively by attempting to fit women into existing formulations of class analysis recognized the claims of the feminist critique and saw the significance of the need to have women's experience included. As additional motivation, a theory of class that has no place for women's experience was going to lose relevance as an explanation of contemporary inequality. While there was considerable debate about whether Marxist categories could be "stretched to fit" aspects of women's experience, there was, even among those who initially saw value in the attempt, a recognition that to comprehensively address the inequality in women's and men's experience, concepts and ideas needed to be derived from the problematic of gender inequality itself. Further, many analysts were concerned that the aim of addressing the oppression of women was being subsumed by an agenda to salvage Marxist theory. Attempts to bring feminism and Marxism together were producing, in Hartmann's (1981) well-known metaphor, an "unhappy marriage" with the identity of feminism becoming obscured by the partnership.

Responding to the critique of neglect by fitting women into existing frameworks leaves unanswered the question of why women were not there in the first place. This is not an accidental absence—it's not that people just forgot to put them in! As Crompton and Mann archly comment, "It is not the case ... that gender has been simply omitted from stratification analysis by default" (1986:2). The exclusion of women's experience is a reflection of the particularity of the theoretical framework. While claiming to be a *general* theory, it was in fact a gendered theory—from the vantage point of, and primarily about, male experience.

Several commentators of the time insisted that such practices of active exclusion amounted to a form of intellectual sexism in the academic approaches to the analysis of inequality. As an early American commentator observed, "sex has rarely been analyzed as a factor in stratification processes and structures, although it is probably one of the most obvious criteria of social differentiation and one of the most obvious bases of economic, political and social inequalities" (Acker 1973:340).[6] Indeed, the "before" analysis of stratification fits many of the criteria Eichler identified as "sexist" research (1988).

Women's experience was omitted from stratification theory and research because it was thought to be irrelevant to the identification and location of the processes of inequality as defined by Marxist analysis. It is not surprising, then, that many aspects of what was identified as women's oppression and gender inequality, both within the experience of labour as well as outside of it, were just not being captured by the Marxist analysis of class. This includes, for example, issues of sexuality, the medical domination of women's reproductive health, the experiences of violence, and the silencing of women's creative and political voices. It was, in part, the discontent with how the "stretch to fit" strategy narrowed the conceptualization of what counts as gender inequality and women's oppression that prompted some to move to the second level of critique.

Before moving on to examine the next level of challenge, it is important to observe briefly that the need to be alert for this first level of challenge has not diminished. While much has changed, some theories of inequality, including neo-Marxist ones, continue to construct their vision of society aligned with the centrality of male experience. Recent examples that focused on men's experience are theories that identify working class politics, the compulsion of wage labour, and class struggle as the central dynamics in the formation of welfare states. What feminists have argued, repeatedly, is that this historical story leaves out women and "women's issues" from the development of the welfare state. Almost twenty years ago, Andrew (1984) was motivated by the absence of women from this area of work to insist that the history of welfare state development needed to be reinterpreted to bring women's experience and contributions to light. And, more recently, similar arguments have had to be made against formulations in the comparative welfare state literature that exclude much of women's experience through their "focus on male workers' decommodification" (O'Connor et al. 1999:19). As we seem fated to continually discover, the privileging of men's experience is by no means an obsolete feature of sociological accounts.

Nevertheless, having won, for the most part, the argument about the necessity of including women's experience, the manner of inclusion becomes a key area of attention. For many this raised significant questions about the conceptualization of gender, and its explanatory status vis-à-vis class.

Level Two: The Challenge of Gender Inequality

At this level of challenge, the inclusion of women's experience is a necessary but not sufficient response to the interest in inequalities between women and men. As identified by Maroney and Luxton, there is a need to move "beyond the stage of 'adding women on' to make a genuine attempt to theorize gender" (1987:9, 11). The general challenge is to include a concept of gender in the analysis of inequality, and there have been many discussions about how this might be done. In all responses to this second-level challenge, class is not abandoned as a general explanatory theory. Sociologists discuss how gendered experience is to be positioned with respect to class processes. As we shall see, there have been different interpretations of just how challenging it is to conventional frameworks to think about inequalities of gender *and* class. The conceptualization of gender can range from an empirically identified dichotomous variable, at one end of the spectrum, to a theoretical concept referring to a systematic and socially structured relationship of inequality, at the other end. There is a fairly broad consensus that some sort of revision to contemporary forms of Marxist class analysis is required—the disputed question is, how much?

Starting in the 1980s, there emerged in Canadian scholarship a debate about the appropriate positioning of gender inequality in relation to theories of class inequality. There were two related questions: (1) Is there a uniquely identifiable structure of social processes responsible for producing gender inequalities; and (2) if there is such a structure, how does it connect with the structure and dynamic of capitalism?

One position in the debate advocated using Marx's method of analysis—dialectical materialism—to revise class analysis in ways that better reflect the historical and contemporary reality that the working class has two sexes. In doing so, Armstrong and Armstrong (1986) answered "no" to the first question. They argued that both gender inequality and class inequality are a product of the capitalist system. "Patriarchy and capitalism are not autonomous, not even interconnected systems, but the same system. As integral forms, they must be examined together" (1986:226). In this view, a sexual division of labour is a definitive feature of capitalism and, therefore, class is gendered and gender classed. A key aspect of Armstrong and Armstrong's argument is that all aspects of class, at all level of analysis, are gendered.[7]

This contrasted with the positions of Connelly (1986:241) and Jensen (1992:201), who both argued that the significance of gender is specified by the level of analysis. The abstract analytical level of capitalism is gender-free, but specific formations of capitalist societies must be analyzed as forms of gendered class. Jensen argues that "a system of gendered power can be acknowledged and resisted without immediately requiring that it be articulated at the highest level of abstraction to the capitalist mode of production" (1992:215). In her formulation, gender and class would not have the same analytical status. We can accept, Jensen argued, that gender relations are not reducible to class relations without sacrificing the analytical primacy of class.

For Connelly, a similar specification of levels of analysis resolves the need to acknowledge gendered relational forms that pre-existed capitalism and went into the formulation of capitalist relations. She takes issue with Armstrong and Armstrong's notion that "the sexual or gendered division of labour is essential at the level of the capitalist mode of production" (Connelly 1986:245). It is at the level of concrete social formations that capital exists alongside and in competition with other forms. The analytical question is how "the capitalist mode of production, as it operates in specific societies, determines or refines particular social, political and ideological forms" (1986:246). It is also at the level of specific, concrete social formations that the relation of class and gender is relevant. "At this level the focus is on how the relations of production intersect, combine and conflict with the relations of gender in different classes and within different historical periods within one society, and in different societies" (1986:246).

Although there is some disagreement in these three positions as to the exact formulation of the gender and class relation, all agree that a theory of capitalism can be revised to explain gender inequalities. A different position is adopted by those analysts who identify gender inequality as having a more autonomous relation to capitalism. They answer "yes" to question (1) Is the structure of gender independent of capitalism? and go on to explore answers to question (2) How does this gender structure relate to capitalism? Class and gender are historically connected, but there are independent processes also affecting the trajectory of each. Whereas the previous arguments limited the contemporary operation of gender to within levels of capitalist class formations, this alternative approach is premised on the more limited operation of class.

For example, in *Relations of Ruling*, Clement and Myles (1994) adopt something akin to a "dual systems" approach in setting out the relationship between gender and class. Dual systems theory (Hartmann 1981) was developed in response to the observation that the categories of capitalism are "sex-blind." These categories could identify the "empty places" of capitalist social organization but they could not give an explanation of who filled those places. A theory of gendered hierarchy, or patriarchy, was needed to identify the positioning of individuals within the structure of capitalism. In setting out their orientation to the contemporary configuration of class and gender, Clement and Myles state, "The significant fact about the postindustrial division of labour, then, is not so much that the working class of industrial capitalism has come to an end. Rather, a new working class employed in services has grown up along-side it. And superimposed on this material division of labour is a social division based on gender" (1994:35).

One aim of their analysis is the gendering of class theory, and they conclude that the "class structures of the developed capitalist economies are also neo-patriarchal structures…" (1994:140). They refer, ultimately, to the "feminization of the class structure" which occurs "not despite, but because of patriarchy" (1994:243, 245).

One way to think about the turn to dual systems theory is that it involves the recognition that class categories cannot be the basis of a general theory of inequality. The argument that the dynamics of capitalism cannot account for patterns of inequality that have been thought of as central to the operation of capitalist relations of production—patterns such as who fills what positions and what people earn—is a major blow to any claim that the general structuring principle of industrial or post-industrial society is the market relations of the capitalist mode of production.

This possibility provides the framework for an investigation by Li (1992) into the extent to which race and gender "fractionalize" class categories. In one of his research questions, Li asks, "what are the consequences of race and class as bases of class fractions on earnings within each specific class?" (1992:492). The dependent variable in the analysis is earnings from employment and self-employment. The independent variables include the main three that are of interest—social class, race, and gender—plus controls for industrial sector, education, and hours of work. Li uses the neo-Marxist class scheme developed by Erik Olin Wright to define social class. This means using five class categories (employers, managers, professionals, petty bourgeoisie, and workers) distinguished on three dimen-

sions: (1) ownership of capital, (2) control of capital, and (3) control of labour.

In the analysis, Li finds that "race and gender fractionalizations operate more strongly among wage-earners than among those who own and control capital" (1992:503). He concludes that his analysis says something to the debate about the relative importance of class, gender, and race in processes of inequality. At least in the case of income inequality, his results suggest that class carries no ultimate explanatory weight. Processes producing race and gender as lived experiences of differentiation and inequality carry equal weight.

The growing recognition of the significance of race and ethnicity in identifying different experiences of inequality *among* women led analysts to realize they could not be content with a simple, dichotomous presentation of gender. Detailed investigations of women's experiences of inequality showed the importance of recognizing differences between women. Ng's (1986) investigation of a community-based employment counselling and placement agency reveals the minute acts and assumptions that come together to create "immigrant women" as a distinct category of labour. Research into patterns of employment in the garment industry (Gannagé 1987) showed a form of work organization etched by ethnic, gender, and skill distinctions creating complex networks of solidarities and feelings of division. Research on work within the domestic sphere also exposed inequalities between women. Arat-Koc (1989) examined the lives of immigrant women working as live-in domestic workers in Canada, a situation in which housework "becomes the responsibility of *some* [women] with subordinate class, racial and citizenship status, who are employed and supervised by those who are liberated from the direct physical burdens" (1989:53). She concludes that the domestic service relationship, between female employer and female employee, is one that adds class and race complexities to gender inequalities.

This research on patterns of inequality within gender categories foreshadows the shift to the third level of challenge. It is evidence that a dichotomous concept of gender, with a single fixed meaning, is too limited a formulation for the many variations and possibilities of gendered experience. The recognition of variation within gender, race, and class categories, and of different patterns of relations between these forms of experience, sets the scene for a more nuanced and complex picture of inequality.

Level Three: The Challenge of Multiple Genders

As attempts to develop an understanding of the relationship between class and gender proceeded, debates within feminism and feminist sociology were beginning to unsettle previously held ideas about gender. The notion that we could separate sex from gender started to break down, as people came to accept the impossibility of separating the "natural" and the "social." Delphy (1993) shook the foundations of the sex/gender division by inverting what had become the common formulation and suggesting that our understanding of biological sex is a consequence of gendered thinking. Analysts were on the lookout for tendencies to essentialize gender—that is, to use concepts of femininity and masculinity as if they had singular, fixed, and ahistorical social meanings.[8] More dramatically still, the fissures within women's experience—the differences and inequalities between women—were demanding their due attention. Authors argued that the naturalizing process challenged by feminists in terms of gender identities was noticeable in the case of race, even within

feminist analysis itself (Kobayashi and Peake 1994). Racialized difference and inequality had been erased in most approaches to gender and class. As Bannerji expresses it, "the type of difference encoded by 'race' adds a peculiar twist to gender. In societies such as ours in Canada not only is all labour gendered … but all forms of gendered labour are 'raced'" (1995:31). In addition, and in part inspired by post-modernist approaches, researchers are increasingly aware that the meanings of gender and class, and even their salience, can be highly varied depending on context and the particular circumstances being investigated. There is, in other words, a trend toward regarding the relevance and substance of dimensions of stratification as questions for, and not assumptions of, research.

As theoretical work around the concept of gender starts to confront the need to be more specific about the meaning and significance of gendered experience, a similar contextualizing is being suggested in terms of class. In effect, the claim that class has meaning as an abstract, general process of inequality is abandoned—and its place in explanations of inequality becomes more open to investigation. One strategy has been to focus on intersections of inequality dimensions, including class, gender, race, and sexuality, with commitments to investigate the potential relevance of all dimensions.

In Canadian scholarship, the main development that builds on the problematizing of gender challenges the practice of assuming the validity of theoretical (including class) perspectives. There is a move to a multi-dimensional approach to inequality with no presumption of the *relative importance or particular configuration* of any dimension. As Creese and Stasiulus set it out, "When we shift our theoretical lens to the intersections between and among relations of gender, race, class and sexuality, we extend the boundaries of political economy by challenging the 'categorical hegemony' attempted by many Marxists with class, many feminists with gender" (1996:8). As they note, however, care must be taken not to regard patterns of intersectionality as socially or historically pre-determined.

As analysts try to work with formulations of intersectionality, a key aspect is the multiple determination of inequality and the rejection of any notion of conceptual hierarchy. For example, in Evans and Wekerle's approach to the development of the Canadian welfare state, they reject "a position that placed gender in contestation to, or ranked in a hierarchy with class and race" (1997:9) and commit themselves to promoting a perspective that examines "variability over time and place." This position is also adopted by Seccombe and Livingstone in their proposed development of a materialist understanding of group consciousness in the context of work. They aim to "break with a 'class first' framework that treats gender, generational and race relations as subsidiary to, or somehow derived from, class relations" (1996:131).

Analysts of how inequality was organized in the past are also adopting this research approach. For example, Parr summarizes the current intellectual challenge as needing to think "beyond this history of fixed dualisms and its accompanying assertion of an ahistorical hierarchy of oppressions … to rethink the categoricalism that canonizes gender, class, race, ethnicity and nationality, and to see past the conceptual signage, which has illuminated the previously invisible but now threatens to obstruct our view of the living space beyond" (1990:8). Her very detailed historical analysis of the dramatically different patterns in the use of female and male labour in two Ontario manufacturing towns is an excellent example of how

intricacies of inequality can be highly variable within and across specific settings. Her conclusion that "neither breadwinners nor domestic workers were ever so thoroughly or continuously and completely proletarianized as existing theories of work assume" (1990:242) hints at the more limited range of class narratives. She counsels us to adopt an approach of "presuming less" about the relevance of theoretical categories and their relation to configurations of daily life in specific settings (1990:231).

Such hints and conjectures bring Canadian work on gender inequalities into conversation with more iconoclastic positions on the future of class as an analytical concept. There are exciting and dramatic arguments, inspired by the gender critique of class, that challenge the entire narrative of "capitalism" and ask us to consider whether current circumstances require a completely new framework for analysis. For example, Gibson-Graham, while continuing a commitment to Marxism, and to the analysis and struggles against exploitation, nevertheless wants to "divorce Marxism from one of its many and problematic marriages—the marriage to 'the economy' in its holistic and self-sustaining form" (1996:264). They would like to see an end to capitalism "as we knew it" for, in their view, our form of knowing has created a more unitary, total and powerful entity than exists.

Bottero (1998) is even more radical in her suggestion that the legacy of class analysis is a separation of the social and the economic that continues to distort attempts to analyze inequality. Her provocative assertion is that explanations of gender inequality have accepted the general "market nature of society—and it is this which must be rejected, if gender is to be theorized in structural terms. To do so, however, involves fundamental revision of both class and gender theory" (1998:485).

CONCLUSION

One major achievement of the analysis of inequalities between women and men is acceptance of the idea that these are socially created and amenable to change. Class analysis, too, broke with previous explanations that argued that there was something inevitable and natural about the presence of inequality in society. The analysis of Canadian society in terms of class presents a view that inequality is the result of a system of organization in which the production of profit is given priority over the needs of people. As radical as this view was, and still is, in challenging the dominant idea of Canada as a just and gentle society, class analysis produced its own set of analytical limitations and theoretical exclusions. While the theories were not entirely silent on the question of inequality between women and men, many came to accept that the categories of class analysis were indeed "sex-blind." The investigation of how class and gender inequalities relate to one another has been a huge effort among those who seek to understand inequality in order to bring it to an end.

This chapter has set out a progression of challenges to class analysis from the position of women's experience and gender inequality. The first level of challenge came from the realization that traditional forms of analysis were ideological constructions that excluded women's experience. At this basic but essential level, there is the insistence that women's lives be recognized and included in stratification analysis. As attention shifts from the fact of exclusion to the manner in which women's experience and gender inequality are to be included, the conceptualization of class comes under more intense scrutiny. Attempts to stretch existing

components of class analysis to fit gender inequality are found wanting. There is a wish to consider a full range of gender issues and experiences of inequality. At its most developed, this second level of challenge sees limits in the explanatory capacity of class categories. Class continues to be given pride of place in explaining inequality, but analysts recognize that other structures and processes, such as gender, are needed to fill in significant aspects left unexplained. As the conceptualization of gender itself becomes contested, the direction of theory and research is toward more complex understandings of how the multiple forms of gender are embedded in patterns of inequality. Researchers working at this third level of challenge abandon explanations that put class first, and try to examine both the meaning and salience of intersecting dimensions of inequality. As with all other potentially relevant forms of inequality, the significance of class in any specific investigation must be established, not presumed.

The hope of many is that there is a way to continue the immensely creative, critical, and politically progressive impulses of the legacy of Marx's theory of class, without remaining caught in conceptual snares that conceal and distort significant aspects of the history and organization of society. For some of those interested in pursuing explanations of gender inequality, this means continuing to work with the concept of class; for others, it means cutting these ties and heading further out to sea toward as yet uncharted territory.

NOTES

1. Hamilton (1996) gives a good description of first-wave and second-wave feminism in Canada. First-wave feminism is associated with struggles in the late eighteenth and early nineteenth centuries—particularly the fight for legal recognition, voting rights, and breaking down barriers in

education and employment. Second-wave feminism reached its height between the 1960s and 1980s. Primary issues were inequalities in the family, reproductive choice and control, equal pay, pornography, and domestic violence. The distinction between liberal, radical, and socialist feminists is associated with second-wave feminism.

2. Marshall (2000) and Ferree et al. (1999) are good introductions to the current state of thinking about gender.

3. See Hamilton (1996) for a quick overview of contemporary Canadian feminist interests. Vosko (2002) provides an informative account of the development of, and current interest in, feminist political economy in Canada.

4. In this paper, the terms inequality and stratification are used interchangeably. In the sociological literature, the two have been distinguished, although there are different presentations of what the two terms mean. I follow here the practice of regarding the sociology of stratification as the analysis of structured social inequality, including class analysis. Inequality is, of course, a much broader phenomenon than class as this paper discusses. See Grabb (2002) for a discussion of the two terms that contrast stratification with class analysis.

5. See Hamilton and Barrett (1986) for some retrospective thoughts from key participants on the longer-term contribution of this debate.

6. Readers interested in similar engagements with neo-Weberian approaches to class analysis can follow the work of Boyd (who draws inspiration from Acker) to challenge "the assumption that women were irrelevant in the area of stratification analysis aside from their family roles and their marital status" (1985:29).

7. For consistency, I use gender here, although Armstrong and Armstrong did not frame their argument in this way.

8. For an example of this argument in the area of gender inequalities in paid work, see Siltanen (1994) and Pratt and Hanson (1993).

REFERENCES

Acker, Joan 1973. "Women and social stratification: A case of intellectual sexism." *American Journal of Sociology* (78):936–945.

Andrew, Caroline 1984. "Women and the welfare state." *Canadian Journal of Political Science* 17:667–683.

Arat-Koc, Sedef 1989. "In the privacy of our own home: Foreign domestic workers as solution to the crisis of the domestic sphere in Canada." *Studies in Political Economy* (28):33–58.

Armstrong, Pat, and Hugh Armstrong 1986. "Beyond sexless class and classless sex: towards feminist Marxist." In Roberta Hamilton and Michel Barrett (eds.), *The Politics of Diversity*, pp. 208–37. Thetford: Thetford Press Limited.

Bannerji, Himani 1995. *Thinking Through: Essays on Feminism, Marxism, and Anti-Racism.* Toronto: Women's Press.

Blishen, Bernard R., Frank E. Jones, Kaspar D. Naegele, and John Porter (eds.) 1961. *Canadian Society: Sociological Perspectives.* New York: The Free Press of Glencoe.

Bottero, Wendy 1998. "Clinging to the wreckage? Gender and the legacy of class." *Sociology* 32(3):469–490.

Boyd, Monica 1985. "Educational and occupational attainments of native-born Canadian men and women." In M. Boyd et al. (eds.), *Ascription and Achievement: Studies in Mobility and Status Attainment in Canada,* pp. 229–295. Ottawa: Carleton University Press.

Clement, Wallace, and John Myles 1994. *Relations of Ruling: Class and Gender in Postindustrial Societies.* Montréal & Kingston: McGill-Queen's University Press.

Connelly, Patricia 1978. *Last Hired, First Fired: Women and the Canadian Work Force* Toronto: The Women's Press.

Connelly, Patricia 1986. "On Marxism and feminism." In Roberta Hamilton and Michel Barrett (eds.), *The Politics of Diversity*, pp. 241–254. Thetford: Thetford Press Limited.

Creese, Gillian, and Daivia Stasiulis 1996. "Intersections of gender, race, class and sexuality." *Studies in Political Economy* 51(Fall): 5–14.

Crompton, Rosemary, and Michael Mann (eds.) 1986. *Gender and Stratification.* Cambridge: Polity Press.

Curtis, James, Edward Grabb, and Neil Guppy (eds.) 1999. *Social Inequality in Canada: Patterns, Problems, and Policies.* Scarborough: Prentice Hall Allyn and Bacon Canada.

Curtis, James E., and William G. Scott (eds.) 1973. 3rd ed. *Social Stratification: Canada.* Scarborough: Prentice-Hall.

Delphy, C. 1993. "Rethinking sex and gender." *Women's Studies International Forum* 16:1–9.

Eichler, Margrit 1988. *Non-sexist Research Methods.* Wellington: Unwin Hyman.

Engels, F. 1972 [1884]. *Origin of the Family, Private Property and the State.* New York: International Publishers.

Evans, Patricia M., and Gerda R. Wekerle (eds.) 1997. *Women and the Canadian Welfare State: Challenges and Change.* Toronto: University of Toronto Press.

Ferree, Myra Marx, Judith Lorber, and Beth B. Hess (eds.) 1999. *Revisioning Gender.* Thousand Oaks: Sage Publications.

Fox, Bonnie 1986. "Never done: The struggle to understand domestic labour and women's oppression." In Roberta Hamilton and Michel Barrett (eds.), *The Politics of Diversity,* pp. 180–189. Thetford: Thetford Press.

Gannagé, Charlene 1987. "A world of difference: The case of women workers in a Canadian garment factory" In H. J. Maroney and M. Luxton (eds.), *Feminism and Political Economy—Women's Work, Women's Struggles.* Toronto: Methuen.

Gibson-Graham, J.K. 1996. *The End of Capitalism (As We Knew It): A Feminist Critique of Political Economy.* Cambridge: Blackwell Publishers.

Grabb, Edward G. 2002. *Theories of Social Inequality: Classical and Contemporary Perspectives* (4th ed.). Toronto: Harcourt Canada.

Grayson, J. Paul 1980. *Class, State, Ideology and Change: Marxist Perspective on Canada.* Toronto: Holt, Rinehart and Winston.

Hamilton, Roberta 1996. *Gendering the Vertical Mosaic: Feminist Perspectives on Canadian Society.* Toronto: Copp Clark.

Hamilton, Roberta, and Michele Barrett (eds.) 1986. *The Politics of Diversity.* Thetford: Thetford Press.

Hartmann, Heidi 1981. "The unhappy marriage of Marxism and feminism: Towards a more progressive union." In L. Sarpent (ed.), *Women and Revolution,* pp. 1–41. London: Pluto Press.

Jensen, Jane 1992. "Gender and reproduction, or babies and the state." In M. Patricia Connelly and Pat Armstrong (eds.), *Feminism in Action: Studies in Political Economy,* pp. 201–236. Toronto: Canadian Scholars' Press.

Kobayashi, A., and L. Peake 1994. "Unnatural discourse: Race and gender in geography." *Gender, Place and Culture* 1(2):225–243.

Li, Peter S. 1992. "Race and gender as bases of class fractions and their effects on earnings." *Canadian Review of Sociology and Anthropology* 29(4):488–523.

Maroney, Heather Jon, and Meg Luxton 1987. "From feminism and political economy to feminist political economy." In Heather Jon Maroney and Meg Luxton (eds.), *Feminism and Political Economy: Women's Work, Women's Struggles,* pp. 5–50. Toronto: Methuen.

Marshall, Barbara L. 2000. *Configuring Gender: Explorations in Theory and Politics.* Peterborough: Broadview Press.

Marx, Karl 1976. *Capital.* Middlesex: Penguin.

Ng, Roxanna 1986. "The social construction of immigrant women in Canada." In R. Hamilton and M. Barrett (eds.), *The Politics of Diversity.* London: Verso.

Oakley, Ann 1972. *Sex, Gender and Society.* New York: Harper and Row.

O'Connor, Julia S., Ann Shola Orloff, and Sheila Shaver 1999. *States, Markets, Families: Gender, Liberalism and Social Policy in Australia, Canada, Great Britain and the United States.* Cambridge: Cambridge University Press.

Parr, Joy 1990. *The Gender of Breadwinners: Women, Men, and Change in Two Industrial Towns 1880–1950*. Toronto: University of Toronto Press.

Pratt, G., and S. Hanson 1993. "Women and work across the life course." In C. Katz and J. Monk (eds.), *Full Circles—Geographies of Women over the Life Course*, pp. 27–54. London: Routledge.

Seccombe, Wally, and David Livingstone 1996. "'Down to earth people': Revising a materialist understanding of group consciousness." In David Livingstone and J. Marshall Mangan (eds.), *Recast Dreams: Class and Gender Consciousness in Steeltown*, pp. 131–194. Toronto: Garamond Press.

Siltanen, Janet 1994. *Locating Gender: Occupational Segregation, Wages and Domestic Responsibilities*. London: UCL Press.

Smith, Dorothy E. 1980. "An analysis of ideological structures and how women are excluded: Considerations for academic women." In J. Paul Grayson (ed.), *Class, State, Ideology and Change: Marxist Perspective on Canada*, pp. 252–267. Toronto: Holt, Rinehart and Winston.

Vosko, Leah F. 2002. "The pasts (and futures) of feminist political economy in Canada: Reviving the Debate." *Studies in Political Economy* 68 (Summer):55–83.

Zaretsky, Eli 1976. *Capitalism, the Family, and Personal Life*. London: Pluto Press.

WHO DOES WHAT? GENDER AND THE DIVISION OF LABOUR IN CANADIAN HOUSEHOLDS

Kevin McQuillan and Marilyn Belle

(Revised from the previous edition of this volume.)

INTRODUCTION

Although the study of housework was once seen as a marginal topic in sociology, the classic work by Friedan (1963) and Oakley (1974) forced sociologists to take the issue seriously and to explore the ways in which sociological theory can help us to understand the factors that determine the performance of household work. In recent years, the study of housework has become the focus of a growing body of sophisticated research. Work in this area has not yet produced a consensus, but certain findings do appear consistently in the literature. The most well documented finding is that women perform a greater share of the domestic chores than men (Shelton and John 1996). The relative shares performed by men and women vary according to the characteristics of the individuals and the circumstances of the households in which they live, but women almost invariably perform the larger share of the domestic duties (Shelton 1992). However, there is also evidence that the situation has been changing (Sullivan 2000). Sociologists are now struggling to understand the role of men in the household and to identify the factors that may lead some couples to a more balanced sharing of housework.

The present analysis has three goals. First, it briefly reviews the findings of recent research on housework, noting areas that have seen significant change. Second, it examines some of the most important attempts at explaining the findings in this area. And, finally, it presents some recent Canadian data on the topic, looking at how much housework is done and by whom in households in which a heterosexual couple resides.

RECENT RESEARCH ON HOUSEWORK

The tone for modern research on the problem of housework was set by Betty Friedan's (1963) classic study of American women, *The Feminine Mystique*. Discussing what she termed "the problem that has no name," Friedan explored the sense of dissatisfaction felt by many American women in the post-World War II era who felt trapped in the household, their lives entirely taken up by the care of their husband, their children, and their home. Friedan and later observers (Cowan 1983) noted that the emergence of modern technology—washing machines, vacuum cleaners, dishwashers—had not lessened the demands on women in the household. On the contrary, Friedan entitled a chapter in her book, "Housewifery expands to fill the time available," and went on to describe how the introduction of labour-saving gadgets simply led to an increase in the standards demanded of housekeepers. Higher standards of cleanliness, decoration, and childcare, which, with the growth of suburbia, included the chauffeuring of children to numerous activities, made the performance of housework a daunting task. What Friedan and others also emphasized, of course, was that meeting these rising standards of care was a woman's responsibility—husbands and children might offer occasional "help," but it was women who were ultimately responsible and who would face the condemnation of relatives and friends if the household failed to meet expectations.

Whether the situation Friedan described was a new one that emerged in the prosperity that followed World War II, or the modern incarnation of a long-standing pattern, is a subject of much dispute. There is considerable agreement among historians that women have long been almost exclusively responsible for such traditional household tasks as cooking, laundry, and the care of young children (Tilly and Scott 1978; Segalen 1980; Sabean 1990). Nevertheless, many would also argue that the growth of wage labour and the increasing separation between domestic labour and paid work performed outside the home fundamentally changed our perception of housework (Coontz 1992; Fox 1993). When men worked in closer proximity to their families—indeed, when they worked side-by-side with their wives and children on the family farm or at a trade—all forms of work were seen as contributing to the economic well-being of the family. But as men began to work in ever larger numbers in factories and offices while the majority of married women remained in the home, a more rigid division of labour emerged, and housework, which increasingly became the responsibility of wives and mothers, developed into an isolating and devalued form of labour.

In recent decades, of course, we have seen yet another transformation of the working world, one that has brought ever-greater numbers of women into the labour market. The proportion of married women employed outside the home has risen dramatically, from less than 27% in 1966 to more than 63% in 2000 (Labour Canada 1978; Statistics Canada 2001). In light of such changes, researchers have sought to determine whether a more egalitarian sharing of household tasks is beginning to emerge, or whether women continue to carry the major load when it comes to doing housework. The question is difficult to answer because good evidence on the changing distribution of household labour has not been readily available. The evocative work of Friedan (1963), Oakley (1974), and Luxton (1980) suggested a rather rigid division of family duties, but only in the 1970s did data on housework from large samples of households become available. Some of the early work using these data (Meissner et al. 1975) confirmed that women performed the lion's share of household tasks. This research also pointed to a clear division of labour by task, with women taking almost sole responsibility for chores such as cooking, cleaning, washing dishes, and doing laundry, while men's contributions were limited to outdoor work and certain elements of childcare.

More recent studies conducted in a number of developed societies suggest that women continue to perform the majority of domestic chores, even when employed in the labour force (Baxter 1997). However, these studies also suggest that some movement toward a more egalitarian division of labour has been occurring (Shelton and John 1996; Coltrane 2000). Research based on the Canadian General Social Survey (Marshall 1993), as well as analyses of specific communities (Bernier et al. 1996), has found that men are doing more housework than in the past, though still not as much as their wives. Similarly, a series of American studies found that men in dual-earner couples nearly doubled their contribution to indoor work between the early 1970s and mid-1980s. However, more recent data suggest that the increase in men's contribution may have begun to level off. Bianchi et al. (2000) found that, since 1985, men's reported hours of housework have not increased. Another recent study by Juster et al. (2002) reported no change in the hours of housework performed by American men between 1989 and 1999.

Many studies of domestic labour emphasize that it is not only the amount of time spent that differs between men and women, but also the nature of the work performed (Blair and Lichter 1991). Men's contributions tend to be limited to certain types of tasks. Males are most likely to do maintenance, repairs, and yard-work, though many men also make significant contributions to childcare, shopping, and cooking (Berk 1985; Ferree 1991; Lupri 1991). Such tasks as laundry and vacuuming still seem to be largely handled by women (Coltrane 1996; Twiggs et al. 1999). Men are also less likely to take on the "managerial" side of housekeeping. They may, for example, go grocery shopping, but will usually rely on a list of required items drawn up by their wives. These patterns lead some women to express considerable frustration with having to plan and supervise the chores that their husbands agree to do (Luxton 1983). However, Allen and Hawkins (1999) note that some women are reluctant to relinquish control over the organization of household tasks, and this may inhibit men's involvement in housework.

Overall, then, the evidence indicates that women continue to do significantly more than their partners, though the gap has closed somewhat over time. It is also true, of course, that the amount of work that men and women do varies greatly across different households. An enormous amount of research has been undertaken on this problem, and we will do no more in this paper than summarize some of the major findings. One point that does seem clear is that higher-status women—those with higher education and better-paying jobs, for example—normally do less housework than other women (Brines 1993; Marshall 1993; Shelton and John 1996; McFarlane et al. 2000). The result is a more equitable distribution between partners in such cases, even though the men in these households do not always increase the amount of work that they perform. It appears that, instead of males doing more work, the higher incomes earned in such families may allow couples to purchase services rather than do the work themselves. For example, these families may be more likely to hire a cleaning service or eat out at restaurants rather than cook for themselves at home (Cohen 1998).

It is clear that the arrival of children has a significant effect on the work patterns of family members. Not surprisingly, young children place additional demands on adults in the household. Most, though not all, studies indicate that a larger number of children in a family greatly increases the amount of housework mothers perform, while the effects for fathers are far less (Berk 1985; South and Spitze 1994; Bianchi et al. 2000). Fathers may, of course, do a significant amount of childcare, but their wives often end up using the resulting time that they themselves save to do other household tasks. Children, as they grow older, are also able to take on some of the housework burden. Nevertheless, some researchers suggest that children today are doing far less in the home, choosing to spend their time on schoolwork and extracurricular activities rather than on household chores (Goldscheider and Waite 1991; Gager et al. 1999). Moreover, when they do contribute, sons and daughters are likely to follow traditional patterns, with girls doing more around the house and boys taking on outdoor tasks like mowing the lawn (Blair 1992; Cohen 2001).

One of the more interesting lines of recent research has focused on the effects of people's attitudes on the sharing of housework. We might expect that men who hold more egalitarian ideas about gender roles are significantly more involved in doing housework. To some extent, this is true. Most studies do find a more equitable distribution among couples holding egalitarian values (Goldscheider and Waite 1991; Shelton and John 1996). Still, good intentions on the part of husbands are not always enough. Some analysts argue that a more equal distribution of housework is only likely to come about when women feel this to be important and are ready to insist on a more even division of labour (Presser 1994:94; Coltrane 1995:265).

A related line of work has focused on the differences between legally married and cohabiting couples. The suggestion here is that couples who choose to cohabit may be less inclined to hold traditional views or to follow traditional patterns concerning the division of household labour. Although the evidence in this regard is mixed, several studies have found that cohabiting couples do exhibit a slightly more egalitarian division of housework (South and Spitze 1994; Baxter 2001; Batalova and Cohen 2002). However, some of this difference is attributable to the different demographic characteristics of cohabiting couples. Moreover, as Gupta (1999) notes, both married and cohabiting men do significantly less housework than men who live alone.

The effects of many variables, such as education, income, and gender role attitudes, are also mediated by external factors. One innovative line of research has emphasized the importance of work schedules that are usually imposed by employers. Presser (1986, 1994) has noted that men, even those who do not hold especially progressive attitudes, are more likely to play an important role in housework when husbands and wives work different shifts. Whether they like it or not, men who find themselves at home with the children while their partners are off at work are pressed into performing various household chores out of sheer necessity (Brayfield 1995). Oddly, then, changing work patterns over which individuals have little control may sometimes lead to greater changes in the household than a transformation of people's ideas about what is fair.

EXPLAINING GENDER DIFFERENCES

Most of the recent attempts to account for patterns of housework have built on one of three theoretical approaches: time availability models, resource-power theories, and gender theories of domestic labour. Because excellent reviews of these approaches are already available (Berk 1985; Shelton and John 1996), this section of the chapter highlights only the literature that is most salient for the analysis undertaken in this paper.

First, time availability models, which have their roots in neo-classical economic theory (Becker 1981; Coverman 1985), emphasize competing demands on the time of household members. The amount of housework that needs to be done is a function of the characteristics of the household and its members. The number of dependent children in the household, for example, increases the absolute amount of work that must be done. How household members respond to these demands is influenced by the other commitments they have made. Most important among these other commitments is their involvement in the paid labour force. As their hours of paid labour increase, the availability of household members to fulfill their roles diminishes, and the hours of housework performed decline. It has been suggested that households may benefit from a degree of role specialization. If some members are better positioned to find paid employment, or are able to attract higher wages than are other household members, it is in the household's interest to allocate a greater share of the household work to the members who have more limited opportunities in the paid labour market. In practice, this has usually meant that women assume a greater share of household labour.

A second perspective is contained in resource-power theories. These theories adopt a more sociological view of the operations of the household, one that stresses the role of power differentials in the allocation of household tasks (Blood and Wolfe 1960; Greenstein 1996). The disproportionate share of housework performed by women reflects, not their greater availability to do domestic labour, but the lower level of resources they bring into the household. Because women are more likely to work in part-time jobs or to have lower incomes when they work full time, they typically earn less than their partners. This puts women at a relative disadvantage in bargaining over the distribution of housework (Brayfield 1992; Nakhaie 1995). In addition to income, other valued traits, such as higher education or occupational prestige, may strengthen the position of one partner in the bargaining process. The result is that, on average, women do a larger share of the housework. By the same logic, however, it can be argued that, in households in which wives hold greater resources than their partners, a more equitable distribution of household tasks should occur (Greenstein 2000).

The resource-power and time-availability approaches are, of course, more sophisticated than these brief summaries suggest. Research using these frameworks has drawn attention to important factors that influence the division of household labour. Yet, empirical research on housework in a variety of settings indicates that the variables these theories identify account for only a modest proportion of the variance in either the absolute amount or relative share of housework performed by men and women. Moreover, analyses that include such factors still show large differences between males and females. These findings suggest that the greater share of work undertaken by women does not simply reflect differences in human capital attributes between women and their partners.

A third approach builds on gender theories of social behaviour. These theories have tried to remedy the shortcomings in the first two approaches by directing explicit attention to the influence of gender on the distribution of household work. The earliest work in this tradition emphasized the different perceptions of household work that women and men may hold. Friedan (1963) underlined the sense of obligation women felt to ensure proper order in the household. Oakley's (1974) path-breaking study, based on detailed interviews with British housewives, vividly depicted the different views and expectations of men and women concerning what chores needed to be done and how they should be done. More recently, Ferree (1991) has redirected attention to differences between men and women in what might be called the symbolic significance of household labour. Performing household tasks is more likely to be viewed by women as something more than accomplishing necessary work. Doing housework and doing it well may be an expression of love and commitment. It may also indicate the successful performance of one's role and hence be a mark of social status (Robinson and Milkie 1998).

A second stream of thought, popular among current writers, emphasizes the relational element of gender (Hartmann 1981; Berk 1985; West and Zimmerman 1987). Proponents of this view accept that males and females experience socialization differently, and that this shapes their values and behaviour. However, these theorists argue that gender is not simply a characteristic of individuals or even a learned role, but takes on its full sociological significance when viewed as an ongoing relation. In this view, the daily actions of men and women are guided by our ideas about appropriate conduct for men and women. These actions, in turn, serve to reinforce differences between the sexes. Goffman (1977) illustrates this process in his discussion of the choices men and women make about appropriate partners. Women tend to choose men as boyfriends and husbands who are older, taller, and stronger. While it is true that men, on average, are taller and stronger than women, it is still quite possible to conceive of situations in which a substantial proportion of couples include women who are taller and stronger than their husbands. Similarly, in the case of age, there is no necessary reason why the vast majority of husbands should be older than their wives. Goffman contends that, in making the choices they do, men and women are guided by their sense of what is appropriate and desirable. At the same time, these choices serve to reinforce the notion that men are more powerful and "naturally" occupy a more dominant role in the marriage. Building on this theme, Berk (1985) and others argue that this image of the male as the dominant partner leads women in couple relationships both to take on a larger share of the workload and to consider such arrangements fair.

PATTERNS OF HOUSEWORK IN CANADA

In this final section of the chapter, we will examine some recent evidence on patterns of housework in Canadian households. The analysis is based on a series of time-use surveys that form part of Statistics Canada's General Social Survey Program (Statistics Canada 1990, 1993, 1998). The surveys were conducted by telephone in 1986, 1992, and 1998, with interviews spread evenly across the twelve calendar months. Basic demographic information was collected on all household members, with one member selected at random to complete the time-use survey.

Respondents maintained a time-use diary and supplied additional social and demographic information about themselves and the households in which they lived. Although the survey covered all types of households, the present analysis focuses only on those households that contained a married or cohabiting couple. The total number of households included in the analysis ranges from 4785 to 5800.

Respondents who completed the time-use diary supplied information on their activities over a twenty-four-hour period. Individuals were asked to report on their main activity in each fifteen-minute period during the day. The data were weighted to allow for estimates of the amount of time spent per week on various activities. In the results presented here, the housework measures are reported in hours per week.

The diary approach allows for great specificity in the reporting of activities. The original survey data provided detailed reports of the activities of respondents. We have reduced these activities to a smaller set of categories that match those commonly used in recent research. The major categories are cleaning, cooking, maintenance and yard work, paying bills, childcare, and shopping. As other authors have noted, a small number of respondents report spending an extremely large number of hours on a particular type of work. Following South and Spitze (1994), we set the maximum number of hours recorded for any category of activity at the ninety-fifth percentile and recoded all values above that level equal to this maximum. We then summed the recoded values to give a measure of the total amount of housework done by a respondent.

Data were also available on a wide range of demographic characteristics that allow us to assess the importance of a number of variables identified by the various theoretical perspectives. Time availability models point to the importance of the demands that household members face inside and outside the home. In the empirical analysis, we included three factors that might be expected to influence the amount of labour to be done and the ability of the respondents to carry it out. These factors are the number of dependent children, the number of hours spent at paid employment, and home ownership. The time-availability approach would lead us to expect that home ownership and a larger number of dependent children would increase the amount of housework, while longer hours of paid work would reduce the amount of housework people do.

Resource-power models stress that it is not just the number of hours worked outside the home that counts, but also the resources that flow from that work. Thus, higher income should allow an individual to limit his or her involvement in household work. Past studies have differed in the treatment of these variables. Both absolute and relative measures have been employed. Given the limitations in the way income was measured in the survey, it was not possible to use a proportional measure. In this analysis, the income variable refers to the reported income of individuals, which was grouped into categories. A second important measure of personal resources is the education level of respondents. Higher education might be seen as conferring great power on individuals, but may also expose people to more egalitarian ideas on issues of gender. To assess the influence of education, we used a simple dichotomous measure indicating whether the respondent had any post-secondary education. This approach seemed reasonable given provincial differences in education systems, but also because one might expect that post-secondary education would be the most likely level required to bring about a change in attitudes regarding appropriate roles for men and women.

Finally, age, common-law status, and gender were included in the analysis. Because previous research has often found that the amount of housework done first increases with age, but then declines among those in the older age groups, we have included both the age variable (measured in years) and the square of the respondent's age. If there is indeed a curvilinear relationship between age and amount of housework done, the sign of the coefficient for the age measure should be positive while the sign for the age squared measure should be negative.

RESULTS

We begin with some simple descriptive results on the amount of housework done by men and women in couple households. Table 16-1 presents evidence from the 1986, 1992, and 1998 surveys. These findings confirm what many previous studies have found: Women, on average, do significantly more housework whether or not children are present, although the gap is significantly larger in families with children. Men do spend more time on housework when children are present, but the increase among women is greater. In 1998,

women in families with children did about twice as much housework as men. It is important to remember, however, that both dual-earner and single-earner households are included in this section of the analysis.

While the difference between men and women is still large, it is also true that the gap has narrowed somewhat between 1986 and 1998. In families with children, and also in those without children, men have increased the number of hours they spend on domestic labour over this period, while women have marginally reduced their involvement. Thus, for example, among couples with children, men's domestic workload was only 35% of their partners' contributions in 1986, but increased to 51% in 1998.

Table 16-2 focuses only on the most recent survey and breaks down the time spent on domestic work by the specific tasks being performed. This breakdown makes it apparent that gender differences also extend to the type of work that people are doing. Women spend more time than men on all types of tasks, except for household maintenance and repairs, which are traditionally male responsibilities. The differences are greatest in the categories of cooking and cleaning, where women spend about three times as many hours as men on these activities. Aside from main-

---

TABLE 16-1   Mean Hours of Housework Performed in Couple-Households per Week, by Gender and Presence of Children, 1986, 1992, and 1998

	Males			Females		
Household Type	1986	1992	1998	1986	1992	1998
Couples without Children	11.7	14.0	14.0	25.0	23.2	23.1
Couples with Children	12.1	16.6	17.3	34.9	35.7	34.0

Source: Adapted from the Statistics Canada publications *General Social Survey, Cycle 2: Time Use, Mobility, and Language Use (1986)*. Public Use Microdata, Catalogue 12M0002, 1988, *General Social Survey, Cycle 7: Time Use (1992)*. Public Use Microdata File, Catalogue 12M0007, 1996, and *General Social Survey, Cycle 12: Time Use (1998)*. Public Use Microdata File, Catalogue 12M0012, 1999.

TABLE 16-2 **Mean Hours of Household Work in Couple-Households on Selected Tasks, by Gender and Presence of Children, 1998**

Task	Couples without Children		Couples with Children	
	Males	Females	Males	Females
Cooking	2.4	5.7	2.5	6.4
Cleaning	3.0	10.0	3.2	11.5
Childcare	–	–	4.5	7.6
Maintenance	3.3	1.9	2.5	1.4
Shopping	5.0	5.4	3.8	6.1

Source: Adapted from the Statistics Canada publication *General Social Survey, Cycle 12: Time Use (1998) – Public Use Microdata File*, Catalogue 12M0012, 1999.

tenance, men are most likely to contribute to shopping and childcare, though even here women do significantly more.

The results presented in these two tables indicate that there have been noticeable changes in the division of household work in recent years. Men have increased their contribution somewhat, though women continue to do significantly more and remain predominantly responsible for such tasks as cooking and cleaning. To understand the situation better, however, it is important to see how the characteristics of couples influence the distribution of domestic labour. This can be a difficult task given the great variability among households and the limited information contained in the survey. However, in Table 16-3, we address this problem using multiple regression analysis. This technique allows us to examine the simultaneous effects of a number of individual and household characteristics on the amount of housework performed in an average week. In this analysis, households with children and those without children are analyzed separately.

The results in Table 16-3 provide a degree of support for the predictions of time-availability models. The coefficients for the hours employed variable are negative and statistically significant, indicating

that the more hours persons devoted to a paid job, the less work they did at home. On the other hand, if their dwelling was owned by a member of the household, individuals spent significantly more time on housework. In couple-only households, for example, those who owned their homes spent about two and a half (2.425) hours per week more on housework than did those who rented their place of residence. Among couples with children, more children generally meant more work for the parents, although the effect varied by the age of the child. The younger the child, the greater the demands on the parent (Beaujot 2000:210). Each additional child aged 0–4 required an average of four and a half hours of extra work per week. This figure declined to just over two hours (2.244) for children aged 5–12, while having a teenager in the house was actually associated with fewer hours of domestic work for parents. Older children are, of course, better able to care for themselves and may also do some jobs that parents would otherwise end up doing.

Variables associated with the relative-resource theory received less support in the analysis. Neither personal income nor education was significantly associated with the amount of housework undertaken. However, as mentioned above, the analysis

TABLE 16-3 Coefficients for Regression of Hours of Housework per Week on Selected Variables, for Couples with and without Children

Independent Variables	Couples without Children	Couples with Children
Hours Worked for Pay	-0.321†	-0.398†
Owned Dwelling	2.425†	1.655*
Post-secondary Education	0.924	0.756
Annual Personal Income	-0.062	-0.470†
Couple Living Common-Law	0.150	-0.972
Age	0.230*	1.001†
Age Squared	-0.002*	-0.013†
Female	7.361†	11.105†
Child Aged 0–4		4.500†
Child Aged 5–12		2.244†
Child Aged 13–18		–0.847*
Constant	12.575	7.250
R^2	0.264	0.480
Number of Cases	2586	2919

Note: * $p < 0.05$; † $p < 0.01$

Source: Adapted from the Statistics Canada publication *General Social Survey, Cycle 12: Time Use (1998)—Public Use Microdata File*, Catalogue 12M0012, 1999.

that is possible with this survey was less than ideal. Income was grouped into rather large categories, and it was not possible to determine whether the respondent made more or less than his or her partner. In the case of education, there is more of a story to tell. When the analysis is performed separately for men and women (data not shown in the tables), post-secondary education is not associated with hours of housework among women; however, among men, those with post-secondary education performed about two hours more housework per week than did men with no post-secondary education. This lends some support to the idea that higher education may change men's ideas and behaviour regarding their housework obligations.

As expected, the effects of the age variable are positive, but those of the age-squared variable are negative, suggesting that the association between age and hours of housework is curvilinear. Therefore, it appears that, as men and women move toward middle age, they may invest more of their time in the care of their family and household. However, as they continue to age, they begin to reduce the hours they spend on domestic chores. This may occur because older people tend to have less energy and less inclination to commit a large amount of time to the upkeep of their homes.

It is striking to see that, even with these controls on the effects of a variety of other factors suggested by leading theories, there continues to be a large difference in the hours of household labour performed by women and men. Among couples without children, women did over seven (7.361) hours more per week than men, while, in families with children, women worked approximately eleven hours more. As yet, neither the changes in the labour market nor the changes in the ideas of men and women about gender roles have created a situation in which men and women share equally in the burdens of maintaining the home.

CONCLUSION

The findings of this paper reinforce the conclusions of a number of similar studies while also raising some new issues for future research. Although some change has occurred, women continue to carry the major burden of housework in couple households. Men do contribute to the work of the household, but they spend significantly less time than their partners on these activities, and their efforts are concentrated on a narrow range of tasks.

Obviously, the amount of work done by both men and women varies significantly with a number of characteristics of both individuals and households. Work outside the home leads both men and women to reduce the amount they do at home. This may result in less work being done or it may lead families to use some of the money they earn to hire others to perform necessary chores. With large numbers of women now in the paid labour force, the long-term consequence of this pattern may be a change in perceptions regarding women's duties at home. The arrival of children, a joyful event for most families, also brings about greater pressure on mothers and fathers and leads to a significant increase in housework. While this study could not really assess the significance of changing ideas about the roles of men and women in the household, it is interesting to note that men with post-secondary education did contribute more to domestic work than did those who had not achieved this level of schooling.

One of the great challenges for research in this area is to understand why gender consistently appears as the strongest predictor of hours of housework, even in the presence of a wide range of controls. Many attempts have been made to account for these enduring differences. Some have pointed to the different perceptions and evaluations of housework, or what might be called the symbolic significance of household labour (Spitze 1988; Ferree 1991). Both performing the work itself and being able to display the results of that work—a clean, well-decorated house, well-dressed children, etc.—may mean very different things to men and women. Women may be more likely to draw status and self-esteem from doing such tasks and doing them well. Women may also see the performance of these tasks as a way of communicating love and caring for other members of the household. For men, on the other hand, housework may be seen in simpler, more pragmatic ways, and may lead many men to resist increasing their contribution to the household even when their partners increase their hours of paid work. In simple terms, the additional labour may just not seem worth it to men.

It is also true, however, that couple-living is associated with larger differences in the amount of housework done by men and women, and this is particularly true once children enter the picture (Beaujot 2000). This pattern could reflect greater specialization and what economists would term "a rational division of labour." Or, as recent sociological approaches suggest, it may indicate an unconscious process whereby gender relations in the larger society, which generally give greater power to men than to women, are carried over and reproduced within the household. The result of this process is that women are more likely to be placed in a disadvantaged role at home. Evaluating the competing claims of these theories is by no means easy, since the empirical evidence can be used to support various interpretations. The sheer tenacity of gender differences underlines the sociological significance of these patterns, however, and should lead researchers to explore more fully the different ways in which men and women adapt to the many demands placed on them inside and outside the home.

REFERENCES

Allen, Sarah M., and Alan J. Hawkins 1999. "Maternal gatekeeping: Mothers' beliefs and behaviors that inhibit greater father involvement in family work." *Journal of Marriage and the Family* 61:199–212.

Batalova, Jeanne A., and Philip N. Cohen 2002. "Premarital cohabitation and housework: Couples in cross-national perspective." *Journal of Marriage and the Family* 64:743–755.

Baxter, Janeen 1997. "Gender equality and participation in housework: A cross-national perspective." *Journal of Comparative Family Studies* 28(3):220–247.

Baxter, Janeen 2001. "Marital status and the division of household labour." *Family Matters* 58:16–21.

Beaujot, Roderic P. 2000. *Earning and Caring in Canadian Families.* Peterborough, Ontario: Broadview Press.

Becker, Gary S. 1981. *A Treatise on the Family.* Chicago: University of Chicago Press.

Berk, Sarah Fenstermaker 1985. *The Gender Factory: The Apportionment of Work in American Households.* New York: Plenum.

Bernier, Christiane, Simon Laflamme, and Run-Min Zhou 1996. "Le travail domestique: tendances à la désexisation et à la complexification." *Canadian Review of Sociology and Anthropology* 33(1):1–21.

Bianchi, Suzanne M., Melissa A. Milkie, Liana C. Sayer, and John P. Robinson 2000. "Is anyone doing the housework? Trends in the gender division of household labor." *Social Forces* 79(1):191–228.

Blair, Sampson Lee, and Daniel T. Lichter 1991. "Measuring the division of household labor." *Journal of Family Issues* 12:91–113.

Blair, Sampson Lee 1992. "The sex-typing of children's household labor: parental influence on daughters' and sons' housework." *Youth and Society* 24(2):178–203.

Blood, Robert O., and Donald M. Wolfe 1960. *Husbands and Wives.* Glencoe, Illinois: Free Press.

Brayfield, April A. 1992. "Employment resources and housework in Canada." *Journal of Marriage and the Family* 54:19–30.

Brayfield, April A. 1995. Juggling jobs and kids: The impact of employment schedules on fathers' caring for children." *Journal of Marriage and the Family* 57:321–332.

Brines, Julie 1993. "The exchange value of housework." *Rationality and Society* 5:302–340.

Cohen, Philip N. 1998. "Replacing housework in the service economy: Gender, class, and race-ethnicity in service spending." *Gender & Society* 12(2):219–231.

Cohen, Rina 2001. "Children's contribution to household labour in three sociocultural contexts." *International Journal of Comparative Studies* 42(4):353–367.

Coltrane, Scott 1995. "The future of fatherhood." In William Marsiglio (ed.), *Fatherhood: Contemporary Theory, Research, and Social Policy.* Thousand Oaks, California: Sage Publications.

Coltrane, Scott 1996. *Family Man: Fatherhood, Housework, and Gender Equity.* New York: Oxford University Press.

Coltrane, Scott 2000. "Research on household labor: Modeling and measuring the social embeddedness of routine family work." *Journal of Marriage and the Family* 62:1208–1233.

Coontz, Stephanie 1992. *The Way We Never Were.* New York: Basic.

Coverman, Shelley 1985. "Explaining husbands' participation in domestic labor." *The Sociological Quarterly* 26:81–97.

Cowan, Ruth Schwartz 1983. *More Work for Mother.* New York: Basic Books.

Ferree, Myra Marx 1991. "The gender division of labor in two-earner marriages." *Journal of Family Issues* 12(2):158–180.

Fox, Bonnie J. 1993. "The rise and fall of the breadwinner-homemaker family." In Bonnie

J. Fox (ed.), *Family Patterns, Gender Relations.* Toronto: Oxford University Press.

Friedan, Betty 1963. *The Feminine Mystique.* New York: Dell Publishing.

Gager, Constance, T., Teresa M. Cooney, and Kathleen Thiede Call 1999. "The effects of family characteristics and time use on teenagers' household labor." *Journal of Marriage and the Family* 61:982–994.

Goffman, Erving 1977. "The arrangement between the sexes." *Theory and Society* 4:301–331.

Goldscheider, Frances K., and Linda J. Waite 1991. *New Families, No Families? The Transformation of the American Home.* Berkeley: University of California.

Greenstein, Theodore N. 1996. "Husbands' participation in domestic labor: Interactive effects of wives' and husbands' gender ideologies." *Journal of Marriage and the Family* 58:585–595.

Greenstein, Theodore N. 2000. "Economic dependence, gender, and the division of labor in the home: A replication and extension." *Journal of Marriage and the Family* 62:322–335.

Gupta, Sanjiv 1999. "The effects of transitions in marital status on men's performance of housework." *Journal of Marriage and the Family* 61:700–711.

Hartmann, Heidi I. 1981. "The family as the locus of gender, class, and political struggle: The example of housework." *Signs* 6: 367–394.

Juster, F. Thomas, Hiromi Ono, and Frank Stafford 2002. "Time use: Diary and direct reports." Institute for Social Research, University of Michigan.

Labour Canada 1978. *Women in the Labour Force: Facts and Figures.* Ottawa: Minister of Supply and Services.

Lupri, Eugen 1991. "Fathers in transition: The case of dual-earner families in Canada." In Jean E. Veevers (ed.), *Continuity and Change in Marriage and Family.* Toronto: Holt, Rinehart and Winston.

Luxton, Meg 1980. *More Than a Labour of Love: Three Generations of Women's Work in the Home.* Toronto: Women's Press.

Luxton, Meg 1983. "Two hands for the clock: Changing patterns in the domestic division of labour." *Studies in Political Economy* 12:27–44.

Marshall, Katherine 1993. "Employed parents and the division of labour." *Perspectives on Labour and Income* 5(3):23–30.

McFarlane, Seth, Roderic Beaujot, and Tony Haddad 2000. "Time constraints and relative resources as determinants of the sexual division of domestic work." *Canadian Journal of Sociology* 25(1):61–82.

Meissner, Martin, Elizabeth W. Humphreys, Scott M. Meiss, and William J. Scheu 1975. "No exit for wives: Sexual division of labour and the cumulation of household demands." *Canadian Review of Sociology and Anthropology* 12:424–439.

Nakhaie, M.R. 1995. "Housework in Canada: the national picture." *Journal of Comparative Family Studies* 26(3):409–425.

Oakley, Ann 1974. *The Sociology of Housework.* New York: Pantheon.

Presser, Harriet B. 1986. "Shift work among American women and child care." *Journal of Marriage and the Family* 48:551–563.

Presser, Harriet B. 1994. "Employment schedules among dual-earner spouses and the division of household labor by gender." *American Sociological Review* 59:348–64.

Robinson, John P., and Melissa A. Milkie 1998. "Back to the basics: Trends in and role determinants of women's attitudes toward housework." *Journal of Marriage and the Family* 60:205–218.

Sabean, David Warren 1990. *Property, Production, and Family in Neckarhausen, 1700–1870.* Cambridge: Cambridge University Press.

Segalen, Martine 1980. *Mari et Femme dans la Société Paysanne.* Paris: Flammarion.

Shelton, Beth Anne 1992. *Women, Men, and Time: Gender Differences in Paid Work, Housework, and Leisure.* Westport, Connecticut: Greenwood.

Shelton, Beth Anne and Daphne John 1996. "The division of household labor." *Annual Review of Sociology* 22:299–322.

South, Scott J., and Glenna Spitze 1994. "Housework in marital and nonmarital households." *American Sociological Review* 59:327–47.

Spitze, Glenna 1988. "Women's employment and family relations: A review." *Journal of Marriage and the Family* 50:595–618.

Statistics Canada 1990. *The 1986 General Social Survey, Cycle 2: Time Use, Social Mobility And Language Use.* Public Use Microdata File Documentation and User's Guide. Ottawa, Ontario.

Statistics Canada 1993. *The 1992 General Social Survey, Cycle 7: Time Use.* Public Use Microdata File Documentation and User's Guide. Ottawa, Ontario.

Statistics Canada 1998. *General Social Survey 1998, Cycle 12: Time Use.* Public Use Microdata File Documentation and User's Guide (Codebook). Ottawa, Ontario.

Statistics Canada 2001. *Labour Force Historical Review, 2000* (machine readable data file). Ottawa, Ontario. Statistics Canada 2001-10-22.

Sullivan, Oriel 2000. "The division of domestic labour: Twenty years of change?" *Sociology* 34(3):437–456.

Tilly, Louise, and Joan Scott 1978. *Women, Work and Family.* New York: Holt, Rinehart and Winston.

Twiggs, Joan E., Julie McQuillan, and Myra Marx Ferree 1999. "Meaning and measurement: Reconceptualizing measures of the division of household labor." *Journal of Marriage and the Family* 61:713–724.

West, Candace, and Don Zimmerman 1987. "Doing gender." *Gender and Society* 1: 125–151.

GENDER AT WORK: STRATEGIES FOR EQUALITY IN NEO-LIBERAL TIMES

Gillian Creese and Brenda Beagan

(Revised from the previous edition of this volume.)

INTRODUCTION

Not long ago, working women were considered unusual, if not neglectful of home and family. Today, most women, like most men, are gainfully employed. In reality, of course, paid employment is only part of the work most women do. Domestic labour is unpaid work that must be accomplished, usually on a daily basis, to sustain household members. In 1998 women with full-time jobs, and a male partner and children at home, performed 4.9 hours of domestic work each day; men performed significantly less domestic work each day, at 3.3 hours (Statistics Canada 2000:111).[1] That time difference of 1.6 hours per day amounts to women working an additional 584 unpaid hours, or 73 additional eight-hour shifts, every year. That inequitable division of unpaid domestic work has a significant impact on inequalities experienced in the labour market. As governments across Canada engage in neo-liberal reforms that downsize the public sector, cut social programs and services, and privatize "caring work" back into individual households, gendered work disparities, both paid and unpaid, will likely grow. This chapter explores the major trends in women's paid work, identifies strategies to achieve greater equality, and considers the impact of neo-liberal reforms on gender equity in the workplace.

TRENDS IN WOMEN'S LABOUR FORCE PARTICIPATION

The number of women in the labour force has increased steadily since the Second World War, when only one in four women were employed (24% in 1951) (Calzavara 1993:312). In 2000, 56% of women over the age of 15 years were employed, with women making up 46% of the workforce[2] (Statistics Canada 2001:4). Our grandmothers were most likely to be in the labour force prior to marriage and childbearing, perhaps returning once their children had grown up and left home. Today most women remain employed through their child-rearing years. Seventy percent of women with children under 16 years of age are in the labour force, including 61% of those with children under the age of 3 (Statistics Canada 2001:6). While women have increased their rates of labour force participation, the pattern for men has gone in the opposite direction, from 84% in 1951 to 68% in 2000 (Calzavara 1993:312; Statistics Canada 2001:4).[3] As a result of these twin trends, the participation rates of women and men are now more similar than different. The majority of women and men are employed (or seeking employment) throughout most of their adult lives.[4] One key difference that remains, however, is the likelihood of part-time versus full-time employment. In 2000 almost two million women, more than one quarter of the female labour force (27%), were employed part time; only 10% of men worked part time (Statistics Canada 2001:6).[5]

It is worth noting some key variations in employment trends among different groups of women (Table 17-1). Compared with immigrant women, especially more recent immigrants, Canadian-born women have higher rates of employment, lower levels of unemployment, and earn higher incomes. Full-time earnings for recent

TABLE 17-1	Employment, Unemployment, and Employment Income Differences among Women in Canada, 1996		
	Percent Employed	**Percent Unemployed**	**1995 Average Employment Earnings, Full Year, Full Time**
	Ages 25–44	**Ages 25–44**	**Ages 25–44**
Immigrant Women	74	12	28 643
Immigrant Women arriving after 1991	64	19	21 900
Canadian Born	80	9	30 704
	Ages 15–64	**Ages 15–64**	**Ages 15–64**
Visible Minority	53	15	27 508
Not Visible Minority	63	9	30 479
	Ages 15–64	**Ages 15–64**	**Ages 15–64 (1996: Income from All Sources*)**
Aboriginal	41	21	13 300
Non-Aboriginal	53	10	19 350

* Income differences vary widely for Aboriginal women on reserves ($11 100) and those living in major urban areas ($14 800). Although employment income is not specified, Statistics Canada notes that 64% of Aboriginal women's incomes derive from employment, in comparison with 70% for non-Aboriginal women.

Source: Adapted from the Statistics Canada publication *Women in Canada 2000: A Gender-Based Statistical Report*, Catalogue 89-503, September 14.

immigrants average only 71% of the earnings of Canadian-born women ($21 900 versus $30 704). Similarly, visible minority women experience lower rates of employment, higher levels of unemployment (15% versus 9%), and lower employment earnings than other women ($27 508 versus $30 479). Immigrant status and visible minority status overlap; 69% of visible minority women are immigrants (Statistics Canada 2000:220).

Recent research suggests that there is no significant income gap based on visible minority status among women who are born in Canada (Pendakur and Pendakur 1998:543). On the other hand, significant differences are evident between Aboriginal and non-Aboriginal women in Canada; Aboriginal women have double the unemployment rates (21% compared with 10%) and lower incomes than other women (see Table 17-1). Another notable division among women is tied to ability/disability status. Women with disabilities have about half the employment rate of those without disabilities (30% compared with 63%) (Canadian Council on Social Development 2002).[6] Notwithstanding this great diversity among women, however, the gender gap between women and men is even more marked and continues to form a central feature of the Canadian labour market.

OCCUPATIONAL SEGREGATION AND THE INCOME GAP

Not only are more women employed today, women are employed in a much broader range of occupations than at any time in the past. In little more than two decades women have made major inroads into such prestigious and traditionally "male" professions as medicine, dentistry, law, and corporate management. In spite of these success stories, occupational segregation

on the basis of gender remains firmly entrenched in the Canadian labour market. Compared with men, women work in a narrower range of occupations, and remain concentrated in those areas with lower pay and less social prestige.

A majority of women (56.3%) are employed in just two occupational sectors: clerical and administration (24.6%) and sales and service (31.7%) (see Table 17-2). When we add nursing (7.9%) we account for nearly two-thirds of all women in the labour force (64.2%). As Table 17-2 shows, most occupational sectors are either dominated by men or, less often, dominated by women. Men dominate the following fields: management (64.6%), especially senior management (89.1%), natural sciences, engineering and mathematics (89.9%), primary industries (89.7%), trades, transport, and construction (96.7%), and processing, manufacturing, and utilities (70.2%). Together, nearly two-thirds of men work in these six occupational sectors (62.2%). In contrast, women predominate in only three areas: teaching (63.1%), nursing (87.7%), and clerical and administrative work (75.4%). Thus, while it is true that some women have made considerable occupational gains over the last two decades, most women continue to work in the "pink collar" or feminized occupations.

When women enter into an occupation previously dominated by men, one of two processes usually happens: The occupation becomes re-gendered, or subdivisions develop within the occupation. It is rarely the case that an occupation becomes truly integrated by gender. When an occupation re-genders, it is usually in the direction of feminization; what was "men's work" becomes redefined as "women's work" (Reskin and Padavic 1994). A job may lose its appeal for men due to declines in job security, wages, or prestige (Reskin and Roos 1990); as men lose interest,

TABLE 17-2	Distribution of Employment in Canada, by Occupation and Gender, 2000		
Occupation	Women	Men	Women as a Percentage of Employment
Senior Management	0.3	0.8	20.9
Other Management	7.1	10.7	36.3
Total Managerial	7.4	11.4	35.4
Business/Finance	2.9	2.6	48.5
Natural Sciences/Engineering/Mathematics	2.8	9.6	20.1
Social Sciences/Religion	4.0	2.3	60.1
Teaching	5.1	2.6	63.1
Doctors/Dentists/Other Health	1.2	0.9	52.7
Nursing/Therapy/Other Health Related	7.9	1.0	87.7
Artistic/Literary/Recreational	3.3	2.3	54.7
Total Professional	27.4	21.3	52.3
Clerical/Administrative	24.6	6.8	75.4
Sales/Service	31.7	19.2	58.4
Primary	1.7	5.7	20.3
Trades/Transport/Construction	2.0	24.8	6.3
Processing, Manufacturing/Utilities	5.3	10.7	29.8
Total	100%	100%	46.0%

Source: Adapted from the Statistics Canada publication *Women in Canada: Work Chapter Updates*, Catalogue 89F0133, August 2001.

women are more able to enter the job, driving wages and prestige down and causing men to lose interest more rapidly (Padavic 1991). Alternatively, as women enter an occupation, horizontal segregation may occur as women and men gravitate to different specialties, different sectors, or different types of clients (Roos and Reskin 1992). For example, while about 50% of medical school graduates are female, women disproportionately enter family practice, pediatrics, and psychiatry while the most highly paid medical specialties are still almost exclusively male (Association of Canadian Medical Colleges 1998).

Gendered occupational segregation might not be so noteworthy were it not for the marked economic consequences for most women. As Table 17-3 shows, women earn less than men within each occupational sector, even those in which women predominate. Overall, women employed full time, full year in 1997 earned 72 cents for every dollar men earned ($30 915 compared with $42 626). When part-time workers are included, women's average earnings drop to 64 cents for every dollar men earned (Statistics Canada 2000:156). Even women in clerical jobs, among the most "feminine" occupations, earned $6700 less per year than men in the same occupation (Table 17-3)! As economic restructuring progressed through the 1990s, with the loss of many high-wage unionized jobs in predominantly male sectors of employment, the gendered wage gap fluctuated, though the

TABLE 17-3 Average Annual Earnings, by Occupation and Gender, Full-Time, Full-Year Workers, 1997

Occupation	Women	Men	Women's Earnings as a Percentage of Men's
Managerial/Administrative	37 092	56 640	65.5
Natural Sciences	41 221	49 962	82.5
Social Sciences/Religion	37 280	55 767	66.8
Teaching	40 888	50 305	81.3
Medicine/Health	35 407	62 354	56.8
Artistic/Recreational	29 324	41 251	71.1
Clerical	28 151	34 863	80.7
Sales	28 843	39 475	73.1
Service	21 516	33 225	64.8
Agriculture	18 366	25 126	73.1
Processing	26 886	40 655	66.1
Product Assembly/Fabrication/Repair	24 384	38 111	64.0
Transport Equipment Operation	30 253	38 396	78.8
Material Handling	22 810	35 821	63.7
Total	30 915	42 626	72.5

Source: Adapted from the Statistics Canada publication *Women in Canada 2000: A Gender-Based Statistical Report*, Catalogue 89-503, September 14, 2000.

TABLE 17-4 Women's Earnings as a Ratio of Men's Earnings, Full-Time, Full-Year Workers

Year	Women's Earnings as a Percentage of Men's
1990	67.7
1999	69.9

Source: Adapted from the Statistics Canada website at http://www.statcan.ca/english/Pgdb/labor01b.htm and from the Statistics Canada CANSIM II database at http://cansim2.statcan.ca/cgi-win/CNSMCGI.EXE, Table 202-0102.

general pattern remained stable.[7] (see Table 17-4).

As Table 17-5 illustrates, the gendered wage gap appears across all educational levels, ranging from a low of 65% of men's wages for women with some secondary schooling, to a high of 75% for those with some post-secondary training. In 1997 a woman with a university degree earned an average annual income of $42 661, con-

siderably more than most female workers, but $15 269 less than the average man with a university degree. One reason for this is that occupational segregation cuts across educational levels. Most often, women and men with similar levels of education are trained in different fields and are not employed in the same jobs. While women are a majority of university students enrolled in bachelor's degrees in

TABLE 17-5　Average Annual Earnings, by Education and Gender, Full-Time, Full-Year Workers, 1997

Educational Attainment	Women	Men	Women's Earnings as a Percentage of Men's
Less than Grade 9	21 403	30 731	69.6
Some Secondary school	22 846	35 367	64.6
Secondary School Graduate	27 525	37 705	73.0
Some Post-Secondary	28 360	37 812	75.0
Post-Secondary Certificate/Diploma	29 539	41 868	70.6
University Degree	42 661	57 930	73.6
Total	30 915	42 626	72.5

Source: Adapted from the Statistics Canada publication *Women in Canada 2000: A Gender-Based Statistical Report*, Catalogue 89-503, September 14, 2000.

health professions (70.8%), education (69.5%), fine arts (63.4%), and humanities (62.2%), women are a minority in the fields of science and mathematics (29.7%) and engineering (21.5%) (Statistics Canada 2000:95). Differences in educational fields result in different occupational opportunities.

Even within identical occupations requiring specialized educational qualifications, however, a gendered wage gap remains. For example, one study found the following inequities within the professions: Female judges earned 72.5%, doctors 65.7%, lawyers 58.1%, senior managers 54.6%, and university professors 74.6% of what their male counterparts earned (Armstrong and Armstrong 1994:46). Although women working in traditionally male-dominated professions are economically advantaged relative to other women, they remain disadvantaged relative to their male colleagues.

EVERYDAY INEQUALITIES ON THE JOB

As we have seen, women have entered formerly male occupations, but most are either in new female subspecialties or

occupations that become feminized; in either case, women typically continue to earn less than their male colleagues. Ensuring equality of access to diverse occupations is not enough to ensure equality on the job. Simply getting into an occupation or profession where women have historically been underrepresented does not ensure that women's experiences there will be the same as men's. There may still be significant barriers to full participation. When women enter a traditionally male workplace they often face highly gendered workplace cultures. Men may engage in boundary "heightening," exaggerating gender differences to exclude women by increasing sexual banter (Reskin and Padavic 1994) or resorting to sexual harassment (Cockburn 1991).

More commonly, in traditionally male-dominated jobs, women may face "subtle sexism," an everyday kind of gender inequality that has been internalized "as 'normal,' 'natural,' or 'acceptable'" (Benokraitis 1997:11). For example, women lawyers have been found to face instances of hostile humour, isolation, diminishment, devaluation, and discouragement that cumulatively exclude them, rendering them less confident and less productive (Haslett and Lipman 1997). Women in medicine struggle to dress professionally while seeking to balance femininity, authority, comfort, and practicality; yet they are still often mistaken for nurses (Beagan 2002). Operating rooms are designed to fit typical male proportions: The operating tables, the clamps, the instruments—everything is built for a man's hand and a man's height. When a small woman is in the operating room, she faces physical problems, and may become seen as *being* a problem when she places extra demands on staff to accommodate her differences (Beagan 2002).

While any single incident or event may appear to be too trivial to confront, the power of these everyday forms of gender inequality lies in the "aggregate burden" they accumulate through daily repetition. Over time these micro-level inequities may "constitute a formidable barrier to performance, productivity, and advancement" (Haslett and Lipman 1997:51). Such daily gender practices, which occur at the level of everyday interactions between individuals, may be intentional or unintentional (Frehill 1997); nonetheless they constitute the commonplace processes through which gender inequality is enacted and perpetuated at work (O'Brien 1998).

SEEKING SOLUTIONS: STRATEGIES FOR EQUALITY IN NEO-LIBERAL TIMES

There are four main strategies proposed to achieve greater gender equality in the labour market: (1) policies to hire more women in higher-paying jobs traditionally held by men (employment equity); (2) programs to raise the monetary value of work traditionally performed by women (pay equity); (3) attempts to organize a larger segment of the low-wage workforce (unionization); and (4) strategies to accommodate and, equally important, to redistribute domestic responsibilities linked to the household (domestic labour). Each of these strategies promises some improvement in the situation of women workers; each also has limitations; and each initiative is currently being undermined by neo-liberal reforms.

Employment Equity

Given the depth of gendered occupational segregation, one of the most important policy initiatives is the incorporation of employment equity programs to eliminate barriers to employment and implement positive policies and practices to correct systematic disadvantages experienced by women, Aboriginal peoples, people with disabilities, and people in visible minority groups. The federal *Employment Equity Act* was passed in 1986 and revised in 1996. It requires public sector and federally regulated private sector employers with 100 or more employees to develop plans to ensure their staff represents the qualified workforce available. For example, if women make up 40% of trained biologists, eventually 40% of biologists employed in a government department should be women. The Act applies to about 8% of the Canadian labour force (Treasury Board of Canada Secretariat 2002).

Seven provinces (British Columbia,[8] Manitoba, Saskatchewan, Québec, Nova Scotia, New Brunswick, and Prince Edward Island) developed employment equity policies that apply to the provincial public service. Ontario introduced employment equity legislation in 1994, under a New Democratic Party government. Grounded on a belief in the existence of systemic oppression requiring systemic remedies, it applied to most employers in the province. In 1995 a newly elected Progressive Conservative government made repeal of the Act one of its first actions, arguing that "special measures" are themselves discriminatory (Bakan and Kobayashi 2000).

By all reports the success of employment equity in achieving its goals has been modest. Until the early 1990s improvements were minimal; since 1996 stronger enforcement mechanisms have meant steady improvements for women, particularly Aboriginal women, though people with disabilities are still significantly underrepresented and people from other visible minority groups have seen little improvement (Bakan and Kobayashi 2000). The increasing employment of women and Aboriginal peoples in the public sector has occurred as governments shifted drastically from permanent positions to term contract and casual positions. Moreover, the target groups have been hired largely into administrative support and clerical positions (Bakan and Kobayashi 2000).

Several limitations of employment equity restrict its impact in equalizing job opportunities for women. First, it only covers a fraction of the workforce, almost entirely limited to the public service. Furthermore, recent neo-liberal policies in some provinces (for example, Ontario and British Columbia) have further reduced rather than expanded coverage. Second, at the federal level employment equity was very poorly enforced until the 1996 revisions. Even now, an employer cannot be required to take steps that would cause "undue hardship" on the employer (Treasury Board of Canada Secretariat 2002). Third, equality is defined as the proportion of women employed relative to the proportion of women available in the trained workforce. This fails to address systemic gender segregation which, as we have seen, results in very small proportions of women qualified for some occupations.

Pay Equity

While employment equity policies seek to equalize women's representation in male-dominated occupations, pay equity policies seek to address the consistent underpaying of "women's jobs" relative to comparable "men's jobs." As early as the 1950s legislation was passed in most provinces requiring equal pay for equal work, but occupational segregation meant that women and men seldom did the same work (Wilson 1996:129). Beginning in the late 1970s the federal government and several provinces[9] introduced legislation that requires "equal pay for work of equal value"—meaning jobs that are comparable in terms of skill, effort, working conditions, and responsibility—which is usually assessed through complex systems of job evaluation. This process allows very different job categories to be compared across segregated occupations (for example, comparing male janitors and female receptionists working at a university, or female nurses and male lab technicians working at a hospital).

At the federal level pay equity is addressed through the *Canadian Human Rights Act* section 11 prohibiting wage discrimination between male and female employees performing work of equal value. It is a complaints-based model, in which pay practices only come under scrutiny if a complaint is made. Cases can take years to process, at enormous cost. The burden is on the workers who make the complaint to bear the cost of systemic change; in effect, only workers represented by large unions have recourse to this measure (Iyer 2002). In 2001 the federal government set up a task force to review its own policies.

Some provinces developed more proactive pay equity legislation. Ontario's 1987 *Pay Equity Act* requires all private and public sector employers with ten or more employees to achieve and maintain pay equity by classing jobs as predominantly male or female and comparing the value of work done in each job class using a gender-neutral job comparison system (Iyer 2002). However, it is limited in that it only compares job classes, not male and female workers within job classes. Furthermore, there is little enforcement by the government.[10]

Though pay equity has led to significant pay settlements for some groups of women, at neither the federal nor provincial levels has it resulted in a significant reduction of the gendered wage gap (Iyer 2002). It is usually limited to comparisons within an individual workplace, so in predominantly female workplaces there may be no appropriate male comparators. Moreover, the majority of the workforce is not covered by pay equity legislation. Some provinces have never passed pay equity legislation, while others, such as British Columbia, have recently repealed these initiatives.[11] Iyer (2002) concludes that pay equity is of greatest benefit to women in large unionized workplaces who are employed full time in specific sectors. The most economically vulnerable women, and those most likely to experience wage discrimination, are least likely to benefit from pay equity policies.

Unionization

Another potential solution is to increase rates of unionization in low-wage sectors, sectors that are also disproportionately female. On average, unionized workers enjoy higher wages and better benefits than their non-union counterparts, and the gap is greatest for part-time workers, the vast majority of whom are women. In 1998 the average wage for unionized part-time workers was $16.71 an hour compared with $9.76 for non-union part-timers; full-time unionized workers earned

$19.01 an hour compared with $15.50 for non-union full-timers (Akyeampong 1998:42). Moreover, on average, "full-time unionized women earned 90% of their male counterparts' hourly wages" (34). Historically, unions were male preserves centred in blue-collar industries like manufacturing, construction, logging, and mining. Over the last three decades large numbers of public-sector workers also formed unions, bringing civil servants, nurses, teachers, and postal workers into the labour movement. Today, employees in the public sector are more than three times as likely as those in the private sector to be members of unions (Akyeampong 1998:34). As a result of these changes in patterns of unionization, 46% of all union members today are women (Statistics Canada 2000:106).

Men are slightly more likely than women to be union members, 33% compared with 31% in 1999 (Statistics Canada 2000:106). And while unionization does decrease the gendered wage gap for the same job, unions have not decreased gender segregation in the workplace. Moreover, unions have historically been male-dominated institutions and women still remain underrepresented in positions of leadership. Issues of gender equity are often not seen as union priorities. Women unionists have identified a number of strategies that would make unions more sensitive to gender equity. These include targeting union organizing among part-time and low-wage workers, pursuing solidarity bargaining so the gap between higher- and lower-paid workers becomes narrower,[12] and focusing on stronger bargaining for "women's issues" such as day care, pay equity, employment equity, and policies on sexual harassment (Creese 1999:209-220).

Of course most employees (nearly 70%) are not covered by collective agreements of any kind. And during the last decade government policies to reduce employment in the public sector, contract out public services to private for-profit companies, and curtail the ability to organize unions and to strike have been adopted by governments across the country, most notably in Ontario, Alberta, and British Columbia. Such policies are intended to decrease rates of unionization, lower wages in the public sector, and generally limit the influence of unions. As long as these policies dominate the political agenda, it is less likely that unionization will provide a solution for most women seeking equality at work.

Domestic Labour

One of the most important dimensions of the gendered division of labour, as we noted earlier, is the uneven distribution of domestic labour in the household. Even when women work full time in the labour force, most retain primary responsibility for childcare, elder care, housework, shopping, and food preparation. This extra domestic work (seventy-three additional eight-hour shifts every year for women with children at home) may limit women's ability to compete for jobs or promotions that demand long hours, to relocate for employment purposes, or to pursue further education to upgrade skills. The uneven division of labour in the household disadvantages women in the workplace, making it difficult to compete with male colleagues who often have a wife to shoulder the greater burden of domestic responsibilities. We need to recognize that workplaces have been structured around the experience of men who have someone else to care for home and hearth; as such, most workplaces allow little flexibility for employees to perform domestic tasks (Hessing 1992).

Unfortunately, neo-liberal policies are likely to intensify domestic work by down-loading more responsibilities back to individual households. Patients are released from hospital earlier to be cared for at home (usually by wives, mothers, or daughters). Home-care services are cut back for the elderly who must turn to relatives for support (usually daughters or daughters-in-law). Public funding for day-care is cut and subsidies reduced, forcing some parents (usually mothers) out of the labour market or into lower-paying part-time jobs. Class sizes are increased and special education teachers are reduced so more children require additional help at home (often from mothers). All of these policy decisions result in more domestic work that disproportionately falls on women's shoulders.

If we wish to level the playing field for women and men in the workplace we need to support public programs designed to meet the needs of employed women and their families. Initiatives that will improve gender equity in the workplace include government-supported low-cost daycare and better maternity and paternity leave provisions; adequate social services in areas such as health, education, and home care; and "family friendly" employee programs such as on-site daycare, flex-time, family leave, and a work culture that does not demand excessive overtime or frequent relocation to qualify for promotions. These measures would improve the situation of all parents, especially single mothers, who make up one in every five families with children (Statistics Canada 2000:33). In the long run, however, men must also begin to take on a much larger share of domestic responsibilities. Although men are doing more domestic work today than in the past, the division of labour is still far from equal.

Without significant change on the domestic front, gender segregation in low-paying jobs will likely remain the reality for most women. Women who do pursue high-powered careers, for example, in areas like law, are still more likely to be single and/or childless (Hagan and Kay 1995; Reskin and Padavic 1994). Men do not have to make a choice between children and a successful career, and women should not have to either. Redefining the domestic division of labour may also help to break down the sharp gendered distinctions and social value attached to men's work and women's work. We might just begin to "do gender" differently at work if we also do it differently, and more equitably, at home.

CONCLUSION

In the period since the Second World War, labour force participation rates of women and men have become more similar than different, but major differences remain in the gender segregation of occupations, in the wages earned by women and men, and in the uneven distribution of unpaid work in the household. Gender segregation and a significant income gap are not easy to overcome, and contemporary neo-liberal policies pose a significant barrier to achieving greater gender equity. Measures proposed to provide women with access to more and higher-paying jobs in the labour market include employment equity, pay equity, unionization, and various initiatives by governments, employers, and men in their individual households, to better support families and equalize responsibilities for domestic labour. Although none of these proposals alone provides a solution to existing forms of gender inequality, in combination these strategies could promise to substantially improve the situation of women in the workplace.

NOTES

1. In two-person households without children there was less domestic labour performed, but women still did the lion's share: Women performed 3.2 hours of domestic labour each day, while men performed 2.3 hours (Statistics Canada 2000:111).

2. Labour force participation rates vary with economic conditions across the country, ranging from the lowest levels in Newfoundland (42.9% of women and 50.2% of men) to the highest levels in Alberta (61.9% of women and 75.2% of men) (Statistics Canada 2001:10).

3. Reasons for the decline in men's labour force participation include the development of universal old age pensions, income security programs for ill and injured workers, and economic restructuring and job loss.

4. The unemployment rates for women and men have fluctuated during the last few decades but are currently almost identical. In 2000 the unemployment rate for adult women was 6.7%, and for men 6.9% (Statistics Canada 2001:8).

5. Women are also less likely to be self-employed: 12% of women and 19% of men were self-employed in 2000 (Statistics Canada 2001:16).

6. Yearly employment earnings are not available, but in 1998 women with disabilities aged 35–49 years earned a median hourly wage of $12.36 compared with $15.05 for women without disabilities (82%) (Canadian Council on Social Development 2002).

7. Two decades of job losses, mostly full-time unionized jobs, in the primary and secondary industries, and an increase of lower-wage, often part-time, jobs in the service sector, have produced a notable decline in young men's wages (Morissette 1997:8-12). Given this, we might expect some narrowing of the gendered gap simply due to the decline in men's wages without reflecting a real increase in women's wages.

8. The Liberal government in British Columbia recently eliminated the employment equity policy in the public service. The policy had been implemented by the previous New Democratic government.

9. Manitoba, Nova Scotia, New Brunswick, Ontario, Prince Edward Island, and Québec all have pay equity legislation. British Columbia, Newfoundland and Labrador, Saskatchewan, and the Yukon use human rights codes to address pay equity.

10. Failure to enforce legislation makes its value questionable. Iyer (2002) notes that among Ontario private-sector employers of fifty or fewer employees, non-compliance with the *Pay Equity Act* is as high as 90%.

11. A pay equity provision was added to the *Human Rights Code* by the NDP government in British Columbia just prior to the 2001 election, but was quickly repealed by the new Liberal government (Iyer 2002).

12. Traditionally, unions negotiate for percentage wage increases that, over time, increase the gap between higher- and lower-wage workers. Solidarity wage bargaining requires a commitment to raise the wages of workers at the bottom end of the pay scales (usually women) more than those at the top (usually men) to narrow the wage gap over time. This is a common practice in some countries, for example, in the Swedish labour movement, but uncommon in Canada.

REFERENCES

Akyeampong, Ernest 1998. "The rise of unionization among women." *Perspectives on Labour and Income* 10(4):30–43.

Armstrong, Pat, and Hugh Armstrong 1994. *The Double Ghetto: Canadian Women and Their Segregated Work* (3rd ed.). Toronto: McClelland & Stewart.

The Association of Canadian Medical Colleges 1998. *Canadian Medical Education Statistics* 20.

Bakan, Abigail, and Audrey Kobayashi 2000. *Employment Equity Policy in Canada: An Interprovincial Comparison.* Ottawa: Status of Women Canada (March).

Beagan, Brenda L. 2002. "Micro inequities and everyday inequalities: 'Race,' gender, sexuality and class in medical school." *Canadian Journal of Sociology* 26:4:583–610.

Benokraitis, Nijole V. 1997. "Sex discrimination in the twenty-first century." In Nijole V. Benokraitis (ed.), *Subtle Sexism: Current Practice and Prospects for Change*, pp. 5–33. Thousand Oaks, California: Sage.

Calzavara, Liviana 1993. "Trends and policy in employment opportunities for women." In James Curtis, Edward Grabb, and Neil Guppy (eds.), *Social Inequality in Canada* (2nd ed.), pp. 311–326. Toronto: Prentice Hall Canada.

Canadian Council on Social Development 2002. *Disability Information Sheet* Nos. 2 and 4. Retrieved May 27, 2002 (http://www.ccsd.ca/drip/research/dis4/index.htm).

Cockburn, Cynthia 1991. *In the Way of Women: Men's Resistance to Sex Equality in Organizations.* London: Macmillan.

Creese, Gillian 1999. *Contracting Masculinity: Gender, Class and Race in a White-Collar Union, 1944–1994.* Don Mills, Ontario: Oxford University Press.

Frehill, Lisa M. 1997. "Suble sexism in engineering." In Nijole V. Benokraitis (ed.), *Subtle Sexism: Current Practice and Prospects for Change,* pp. 117–135. Thousand Oaks, California: Sage.

Hagan, John, and Fiona Kay 1995. *Gender in Practice: A Study of Lawyers' Lives.* New York: Oxford University Press.

Hallock, Margaret 1991. "Unions and the gender wage gap: An Analysis of pay equity and other strategies." Labour Education Research Center, Working Paper No. 8, February. Eugene: University of Oregon.

Haslett, Beth Bonniwell, and Susan Lipman 1997. "Micro inequities: Up close and personal." In Nijole V. Benokraitis (ed.), *Subtle Sexism: Current Practice and Prospects for Change*, pp. 34–53. Thousand Oaks, California: Sage.

Hessing, Melody 1992. "Talking on the job: Office conversations and women's dual labour." In Gillian Creese and Veronica Strong-Boag (eds.), *British Columbia Reconsidered: Essays on Women*, pp. 391–415. Vancouver: Press Gang Publishers.

Iyer, Nityz 2002. *"Working Through the Wage Gap": Report of the Task Force on Pay Equity.* Victoria, British Columbia: Attorney General's Office.

Morissette, Rene 1997. "Declining earnings of young men." *Canadian Social Trends* 46(Autumn):8–12.

O'Brien, Jodi 1998. "Introduction: Difference and inequalities." In Jodi O'Brien and Judith A. Howard (eds.), *Everyday Inequalities: Critical Inquiries*, pp. 1–39. Malden, Massachusetts: Blackwell.

Padavic, Irene 1991. "Attractions of male blue-collar jobs for Black and White women: Economic need, exposure, and attitudes." *Social Science Quarterly* 72(1):33–49.

Pendakur, K., and R. Pendakur 1998. "The colour of money: Earnings differentials and ethnic groups in Canada." *Canadian Journal of Economics* 31(3):518–548.

Reskin, Barbara, and Irene Padavic 1994. *Women and Men at Work*, Thousand Oaks, California: Pine Forge Press.

Reskin, Barbara, and Patricia Roos 1990. *Job Queues, Gender Queues: Explaining Women's Inroads Into Male Occupations.* Philadelphia: Temple University Press.

Roos, Patricia, and Barbara Reskin 1992. "Occupational desegregation in the 1970s: Integration and economic equity?" *Sociological Perspectives* 34(1):62–91.

Statistics Canada 2000. *Women in Canada 2000: A Gender-Based Statistical Report.* Ottawa: Minister of Industry, September.

Statistics Canada 2001. *Women in Canada: Work Chapter Updates.* Ottawa: Minister of Industry, August.

Statistics Canada 2001. Income Statistics Division. "Average earnings by sex and work pattern." Retrieved October 25, 2001 (http://www.statscan.ca/english/Pgdb/People/Labour/labor01b.htm).

Treasury Board of Canada Secretariat 2002. "Overview of the Employment Equity Act (1996) from a Public Service Perspective." Retrieved May 8, 2002 (http://www.tbs.sct.gc.ca/Pubs_pol/TB_852/OVER1E.html).

Wilson, S.J. 1996. *Women, Families and Work* (4th ed.). Toronto: McGraw-Hill Ryerson.

THE EBB AND FLOW OF IMMIGRATION IN CANADA

Monica Boyd and Michael Vickers

(A new chapter adapted from Statistics Canada, *100 Years of Immigration in Canada*, adapted from the Statistics Canada publication *Canadian Social Trends*, Catalogue 11-008, Autumn 2000, pp. 2–11. Reprinted with permission.)

INTRODUCTION

Record numbers of immigrants came to Canada in the early 1900s. During World War I and the Depression years, numbers declined but by the close of the twentieth century, they had again approached those recorded almost 100 years earlier. Despite the superficial similarities at the beginning and the end of a century of immigration, the characteristics of immigrants are quite different. This change reflects many factors: developments and modifications in Canada's immigration polices; the displacement of peoples by wars and political upheaval; the cycle of economic "booms and busts" in Canada and other countries; Canada's membership in the Commonwealth; and the growth of communication, transportation, and economic networks linking people around the world.

These forces have operated throughout the twentieth century to alter the basic characteristics of Canada's immigrant population in five fundamental ways. First, the numbers of immigrants arriving each year have waxed and waned, meaning that the importance of immigration for Canada's population growth has fluctuated. Second, immigrants increasingly chose to live in Canada's largest cities. Third, the predominance of men among adult immigrants declined as family migration grew and women came to represent slightly over half of immigrants. Fourth, the marked transformation in the countries in which immigrants had been born enhanced the ethnic diversity of Canadian society. Fifth, alongside Canada's transition from an agricultural to a knowledge-based economy, immigrants were increasingly employed in the manufacturing and service sectors of the economy. This article provides an overview of these important changes over the last 100 years.

THE EARLY YEARS: 1900–1915

The twentieth century opened with the arrival of nearly 42 000 immigrants in 1900. Numbers quickly escalated to a record high of over 400 000 in 1913. Canada's economy was growing rapidly during these years, and immigrants were drawn by the promise of good job prospects. The building of the transcontinental railway, the settlement of the prairies, and expanding industrial production intensified demand for labour. Aggressive recruitment campaigns by the Canadian government to boost immigration and attract workers also increased arrivals: between 1900 and 1914, more than 2.9 million people entered Canada, nearly four times as many as had arrived in the previous fourteen-year period.

Such volumes of immigrants quickly enlarged Canada's population. Between 1901 and 1911, net migration (the excess of those arriving over those leaving) accounted for 44% of population growth, a level not reached again for another seventy-five years. The share of the overall population born outside Canada also increased in consequence, so that while immigrants accounted for 13% of the population in 1901, by 1911 they made up 22%.

Most of the foreign-born population lived in Ontario at the start of the century, but many later immigrants headed west. By 1911, 41% of Canada's immigrant population lived in the Prairies, up from 20% recorded in the 1901 Census. This influx had a profound effect on the populations of the western provinces. By 1911, immigrants represented 41% of people living in Manitoba, 50% in Saskatchewan, and 57% of those in Alberta and British Columbia. In contrast, they made up less than 10% of the population in the Atlantic provinces and Québec, and only 20% in Ontario.

Men greatly outnumbered women among people settling in Canada in the first two decades of the twentieth century (Urquahart and Buckley 1965). The 1911 Census recorded 158 immigrant males for every 100 females, compared with 103 Canadian-born males for 100 females. These unbalanced gender ratios are not uncommon in the history of settlement countries such as Canada, Australia, and the United States. They often reflect labour recruitment efforts targeted at men rather than women, as well as the behaviour of immigrants themselves. In migration flows, particularly those motivated by economic reasons, men frequently precede women, either because the move is viewed as temporary and there is no need to uproot family members, or because the man intends to become economically established before being joined by his family. By the time of the 1921 Census, the gender ratio for immigrants had become less skewed, standing at 125 immigrant males for every 100 immigrant females. It continued to decline throughout the century, reaching 94 per 100 in 1996.

Of course, women also immigrated for economic reasons in the early decades of the century. There was strong demand for female domestic workers, with women in

What You Should Know about This Study

This article draws on numerous data sources, with the principal sources being the 1901 to 1996 Censuses of Population, and immigration statistics collected by Citizenship and Immigration Canada. It also draws on research by historians and sociologists specializing in immigration issues. A full bibliography is available on the Canadian Social Trends website at http://www.statcan.ca/english/indepth/11-008/sthome.htm.

Immigration: the movement of people into a country for purposes of legal settlement.

Net migration: the difference between immigration and emigration (the flow of people leaving the country permanently).

Immigrants/foreign born: principally people who are, or have been, landed immigrants in Canada. A landed immigrant is a person who has been granted the right to live in Canada permanently by immigration authorities. Some are recent arrivals; others have resided in Canada for many years.

Non-permanent residents: people from another country who live in Canada and have work, student, or Minister's permits, or claim refugee status. They are not included in the immigrant population after 1986, except in growth projections.

Refugee: according to the 1951 United Nations Convention on refugees, a refugee is a person who "… owing to well founded fear of being persecuted for reasons of race, religion, nationality, membership of a particular social group or political opinion, is outside the country of his nationality and is unable, or owing to such fear, is unwilling to avail himself of the protection of that country …" As a signatory to this convention, Canada uses the UN definition of a refugee in assessing who is eligible to enter Canada as a refugee.

Visible minority population: the *Employment Equity Act* defines visible minorities as "persons, other than Aboriginal peoples, who are non-Caucasian in race or non-white in colour." The visible minority population includes the following groups: Blacks, South Asians, Chinese, Koreans, Japanese, Southeast Asians, Filipinos, Arabs and West Asians, Latin Americans and Pacific Islanders.

England, Scotland, and Wales being most often targeted for recruitment. Between 1904 and 1914, "domestic" was by far the most common occupation reported by adult women immigrants (almost 30%) arriving from overseas. Men immigrating from overseas during that period were more likely to be unskilled and semi-skilled labourers (36%) or to have a farming occupation (32%) (Urquahart and Buckley 1965). Historians observe that, contrary to the image of immigrants being farmers and homesteaders, immigrants at the turn of the century were also factory and construction workers. And although many did settle in the western provinces, many also worked building railroads or moved into the large cities, fuelling the growth of industrial centres.

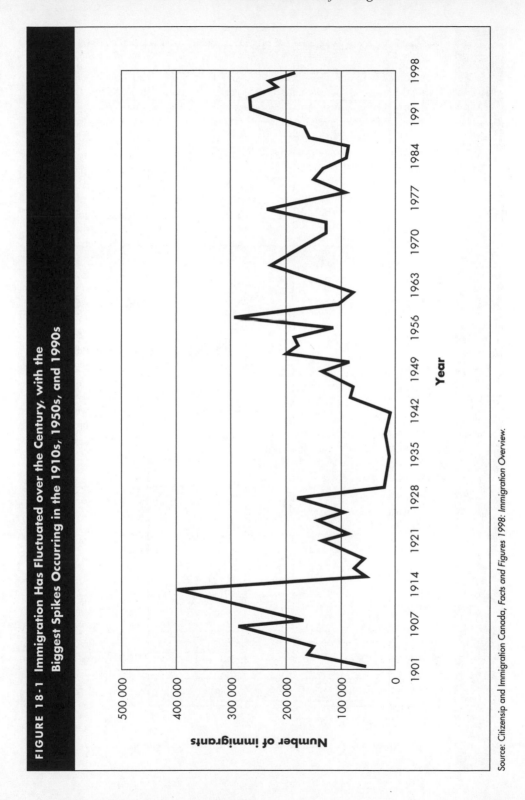

FIGURE 18-1 Immigration Has Fluctuated over the Century, with the Biggest Spikes Occurring in the 1910s, 1950s, and 1990s

Source: Citizensip and Immigration Canada, *Facts and Figures 1998: Immigration Overview.*

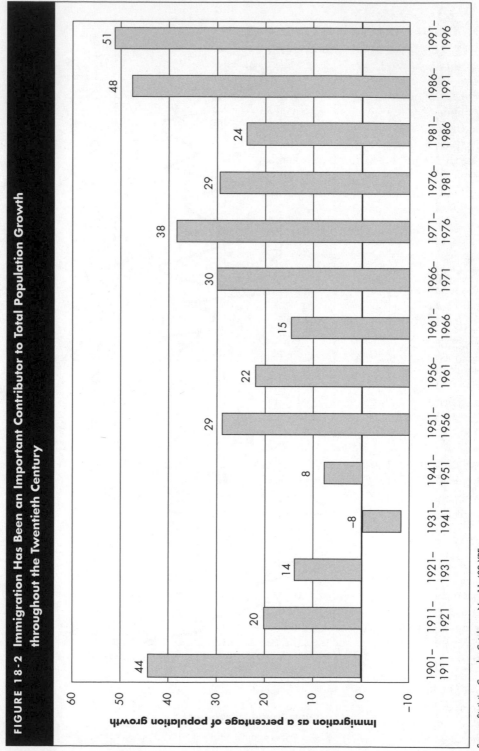

FIGURE 18-2 Immigration Has Been an Important Contributor to Total Population Growth throughout the Twentieth Century

Source: Statistics Canada, Catalogue No. 11-402-XPE.

IMMIGRATION FROM OUTSIDE BRITAIN AND THE U.S. BEGINS TO GROW IN 1910S

At the start of the century, the majority of immigrants to Canada had originated in the United States or the United Kingdom. However, during the 1910s and 1920s, the number born in other European countries began to grow, slowly at first, and then rising to its highest levels in 1961 and 1971.

This change in countries of origin had begun in the closing decades of the nineteenth century, when many new groups began to arrive in Canada—Doukhobors and Jewish refugees from Russia; Hungarians; Mormons from the U.S.; Italians; and Ukrainians. This flow continued up until World War I. It generated public debate about who should be admitted to Canada: For some writers and politicians, recruiting labour was the key issue, not the changing origins of immigrants; for others, British and American immigrants were to be preferred to those from southern or eastern European countries.

By comparison, immigration from Asia was very low at this time, in dramatic contrast to the situation at the end of the twentieth century. Government policies regulating immigration had been rudimentary during the late 1800s, but when legislation was enacted in the early 1900s, it focused primarily on preventing immigration on the grounds of poverty, mental incompetence, or on the basis of non-European origins. Even though Chinese immigrant workers had helped to build the transcontinental railroad, in 1885 the first piece of legislation regulating future Chinese immigration required every person of Chinese origin to pay a tax of $50 upon entering Canada. At the time, this was a very large sum. The "head tax" was increased to $100 in 1900, and to $500 in

1903. This fee meant that many Chinese men could not afford to bring brides or wives to Canada.[1]

The Act of 1906 prohibited the landing of persons defined as "feebleminded," having "loathsome or contagious diseases," "paupers," persons "likely to become public charges," criminals, and "those of undesirable morality." In 1908, the Act was amended to prohibit the landing of those persons who did not come to Canada directly from their country of origin. This provision effectively excluded the immigration of people from India, who had to book passage on ships sailing from countries outside India because there were no direct sailings between Calcutta and Vancouver. Also in the early 1900s, the Canadian government entered into a series of agreements with Japan that restricted Japanese migration[2] (Calliste 1993; Kelley and Trebilcock 1998; Troper 1972).

THE WARS AND THE GREAT DEPRESSION: 1915–1946

With the outbreak of the First World War, immigration quickly came to a near standstill. From a record high of over 400 000 in 1913, arrivals dropped sharply to less than 34 000 by 1915. Although numbers rebounded after the war, they never again reached the levels attained before 1914. As a result, net immigration accounted for about 20% of Canada's population growth between 1911 and 1921, less than half the contribution made in the previous decade. However, the influence of earlier foreign-born arrivals continued, reinforced by the more modest levels of wartime and post-war immigration: At the time of the 1921 Census, immigrants still comprised 22% of the population.

The number of immigrants coming to Canada rose during the 1920s, with well above 150 000 per year entering in the last three years of the decade. But the Great Depression and the Second World War severely curtailed arrivals during the 1930s and early 1940s—numbers fluctuated between 7600 and 27 500. Furthermore, there was actually a net migration loss of 92 000 as more people left Canada than entered between 1931 and 1941. The 1930s is the only decade in the twentieth century in which this occurred. By the time of the 1941 Census, the percentage of the total population that was foreign-born had fallen to just under 18%.

While more men than women had immigrated to Canada in the first three decades of the century, the situation was reversed when immigration declined in the 1930s and 1940s. During this period, women outnumbered men, accounting for 60% of all adult arrivals between 1931 and 1940, and for 66% between 1941 and 1945 (Urquahart and Buckley 1965). As a result of these changes, the overall gender ratio of the immigrant population declined slightly.

While lower numbers and the predominance of women among adult immigrants represented shifts in previous immigration patterns, other trends were more stable. The majority of immigrants continued to settle in Ontario, Manitoba, Saskatchewan, Alberta, and British Columbia. Increasingly, though, they gravitated to urban areas, foreshadowing the pattern of recent immigration concentration in large cities that became so evident in the last years of the century.

Britain was still the leading source of immigrants, but the arrival of people from other parts of the globe also continued. During the 1920s, the aftershocks of World War I and the Russian Revolution stimulated migration from Germany, Russia, Ukraine, and eastern European countries including Poland and Hungary (Kelley and Trebilcock 1998). During the Depression, the majority of immigrants came from Great Britain, Germany, Austria, and Ukraine. Fewer than 6% were of non-European origin.

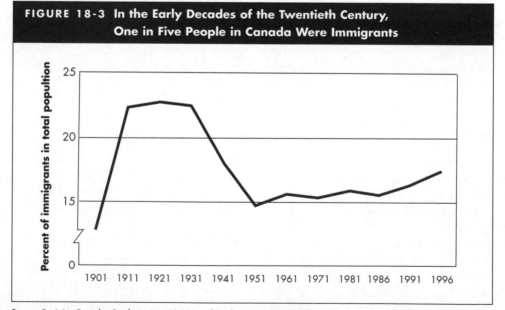

FIGURE 18-3 In the Early Decades of the Twentieth Century, One in Five People in Canada Were Immigrants

Source: Statistics Canada, Catalogue No. 99-936 and Product No. 93F0020XCB.

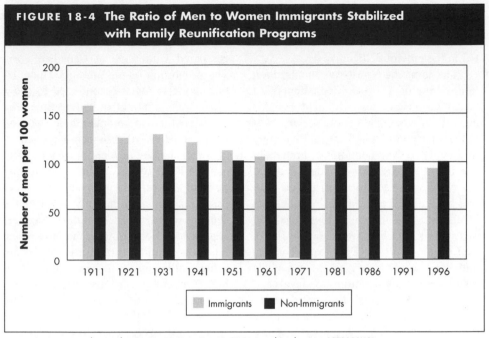

FIGURE 18-4 The Ratio of Men to Women Immigrants Stabilized with Family Reunification Programs

Source: Statistics Canada, Catalogue Nos. 99-936, 93-155, 93-316, and Product No. 93F0020XCB.

Public debate over whom to admit and the development of immigration policy to regulate admissions was far from over. Regulations passed in 1919 provided new grounds for deportation and denied entry to enemy aliens, to those who were enemy aliens during the war, and to Doukhobors, Mennonites, and Hutterites (Kalbach 1970). The 1923 *Chinese Immigration Act* restricted Chinese immigration still further (Avery 2000). Responding to labour market pressures following the Crash of 1929 and the collapse of the Prairie economy, farm workers, domestics, and several other occupational groups, as well as relatives of landed immigrants, were struck from the list of admissible classes. Asian immigration was also cut back again (Kalbach 1970).

Then, with the declaration of war on Germany on September 10, 1939, new regulations were passed which prohibited the entry or landing of nationals of coun-tries with which Canada was at war. In the absence of a refugee policy that distinguished between immigrants and refugees, the restrictions imposed in the interwar years raised barriers to those fleeing the chaos and devastation of World War II. Many of those turned away at this time were Jewish refugees attempting to leave Europe (Abella and Troper 1982). War-related measures also included the forced relocation—often to detention camps—of Japanese-Canadians living within a 100-mile area along the British Columbia coastline. It was argued that they might assist a Japanese invasion.

THE BOOM YEARS: 1946–1970

The war in Europe ended with Germany's surrender on May 6, 1945; in the Pacific, Japan surrendered on August 14. With the return of peace, both Canada's economy and immigration boomed. Between 1946 and 1950, over 430 000 immigrants arrived, exceeding the total number admitted in the previous fifteen years.

The immediate post-war immigration boom included the dependents of Canadian servicemen who had married abroad, refugees, and people seeking economic opportunities in Canada. Beginning in July 1946, and continuing throughout the late 1940s, Orders-in-Council paved the way for the admission of people who had been displaced from their homelands by the war and for whom return was not possible (Kalbach 1970; Knowles 1997). The ruination of the European economy and the unprecedented boom in Canada also favoured high immigration levels.

Numbers continued to grow throughout most of the 1950s, peaking at over 282 000 admissions in 1957. By 1958, immigration levels were beginning to fall, partly because economic conditions were improving in Europe, and partly because, with the Canadian economy slowing, the government introduced administrative policies designed to reduce the rate of immigration. By 1962, however, the economy had recovered and arrivals increased for six successive years. Although admissions never reached the record highs observed in the early part of the century, the total number of immigrants entering Canada in the 1950s and 1960s far exceeded the levels observed in the preceding three decades.

During this time, net migration was higher than it had been in almost fifty years, but it accounted for no more than 30% of total population growth between 1951 and 1971. The population effect of the large number of foreign-born arrivals was muted by the magnitude of natural growth caused by the unprecedented birth rates recorded during the baby boom from 1946 to 1965.

Many of the new immigrants settled in cities, so that by 1961, 81% of foreign-born Canadians lived in an urban area, compared with 68% of Canadian born. The proportion of the immigrant population living in Ontario continued to grow, accelerating a trend that had begun earlier in the century; in contrast, the proportion living in the Prairie provinces declined.

Such shifts in residential location went hand-in-hand with Canada's transformation from a rural agricultural and resource-based economy in the early years of the century to an urban manufacturing and service-based economy in the later years. Post-war immigrants were important sources of labour for this emerging economy, especially in the early 1950s. Compared with those arriving at the turn of the century, the post-war immigrants were more likely to be professional or skilled workers, and they accounted for over half of the growth in these occupations between 1951 and 1961.

Although the largest number of immigrants arriving after World War II were from the United Kingdom, people from other European countries were an increasingly predominant part of the mix. During the late 1940s and 1950s, substantial numbers also arrived from Germany, the Netherlands, Italy, Poland, and the U.S.S.R. Following the 1956 Soviet invasion of Hungary, Canada also admitted over 37 000 Hungarians, while the Suez Crisis of the same year saw the arrival of almost 109 000 British immigrants (Kalbach 1970; Kelley and Trebilcock 1998; Avery 2000; Hawkins 1972). During the 1960s, the trend increased. By the time of the 1971 Census, less than one-third of the foreign-born population had been born in the United Kingdom; half came from other European countries, many from Italy.

NEW POLICIES HELP DIRECT POST-WAR IMMIGRATION TRENDS

Much of the post-war immigration to Canada was stimulated by people displaced by war or political upheaval, as well as by the weakness of the European economies. However, Canada's post-war immigration policies also were an important factor. Because they were statements of who would be admitted and under what conditions, these policies influenced the numbers of arrivals, the types of immigrants, and the country of origin of new arrivals.

Within two years of the war ending, on May 1, 1947, Prime Minister MacKenzie King reaffirmed that immigration was vital for Canada's growth, but he also indicated that the numbers and country of origin of immigrants would be regulated. Five years later, the *Immigration Act* of 1952 consolidated many post-war changes

Children of Immigrants

One of the main reasons why people choose to uproot themselves and immigrate to another country is their desire to provide greater opportunities for their children. Thus, one of the main indicators used to measure the success of an immigrant's adaptation to Canadian society is the degree of success that their children achieve.

Such success is measured primarily in terms of socio-economic factors, such as increased educational attainment and level of occupational status, compared with the preceding generation. Analysis of data from the 1986 and 1994 *General Social Surveys* indicate that second-generation immigrants (Canadian-born children with at least one foreign-born parent) are generally more successful than their immigrant parents, and equally or more successful than third-generation children (both of whose parents are Canadian-born).

These findings are consistent with the "straight line" theory of the process of immigrant integration, which asserts that integration is cumulative: With each passing generation since immigration, the measurable differences between the descendants of immigrants and the Canadian-born are reduced until they are virtually indistinguishable. However, this theory's dominance has been challenged in recent years by analysts who argue that it is based primarily on the experiences of immigrants who were largely White and European, and whose children grew up during a period of unprecedented economic growth. They argue that this theory applies less well to more recent immigrants because it ignores changes in the social and economic structure of Canada in the latter half of the twentieth century. Also, it discounts the impact of barriers facing young immigrants, who are predominantly visible minorities, in their ability to integrate successfully.

Possible evidence of such barriers to the integration of the children of immigrants may be seen in an analysis of ethnic origin data for Canada's largest cities from the 1991 Census. This study found that among members of the so-called "1.5 generation"—the foreign-born children of immigrant parents—non-European ethnic origin groups were more likely to live in households that were more crowded and had lower per-capita household incomes than those with European origins.

For more information, see M. Boyd and E.M. Grieco, 1998, "Triumphant transitions: Socioeconomic achievements of the second generation in Canada," *International Migration Review*; and M. Boyd, 2000, "Ethnicity and immigrant offspring," *Race and Ethnicity: A Reader*.

to immigration regulations that had been enacted since the previous Act of 1927. Subsequent regulations that spelled out the possible grounds for limiting admissions included national origin; on this basis, admissible persons were defined to be those with birth or citizenship in the United States, the United Kingdom, Australia, New Zealand, the Union of South Africa, and selected European countries.

In 1962, however, new regulations effectively removed national origin as a criterion of admission. Further regulations enacted in 1967 confirmed this principle and instead introduced a system that assigned points based on the age, education, language skills, and economic characteristics of applicants. These policy changes made it much easier for persons born outside Europe and the United States to immigrate to Canada.

The 1967 regulations also reaffirmed the right, first extended in the 1950s, of immigrants to sponsor relatives to enter Canada. Family-based immigration had always co-existed alongside economically motivated immigration, but now it was clearly defined. As wives, mothers, aunts, and sisters, women participated in these family reunification endeavours: Women accounted for almost half of all adult immigrants entering Canada during the 1950s and 1960s. As a result of this gender parity in immigration flows, gender ratios declined over time for the foreign-born population.

GROWTH AND DIVERSITY: 1970–1996

In the 1960s, changes in immigration policy were made by altering the regulations that governed implementation of the *Immigration Act* of 1952. But in 1978, a new *Immigration Act* came into effect. This Act upheld the principles of admis-

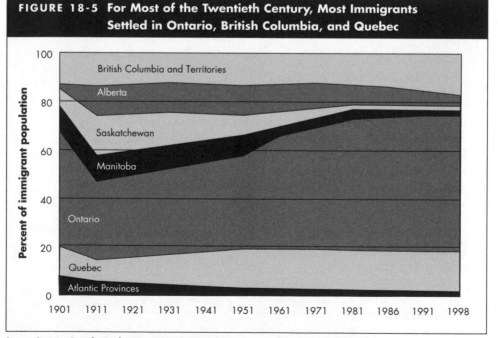

FIGURE 18-5 **For Most of the Twentieth Century, Most Immigrants Settled in Ontario, British Columbia, and Quebec**

Source: Statistics Canada, Product No. 93F0020XCB and 1901 Census of Population (Bulletin VIII).

sions laid out in the regulations of the 1960s: family reunification and economic contributions. For the first time in Canada's history, the new Act also incorporated the principle of admissions based on humanitarian grounds. Previously, refugee admissions had been handled through special procedures and regulations. The Act also required the minister responsible for the immigration portfolio to set annual immigration targets in consultation with the provinces.

From the 1970s through the 1990s, immigration numbers fluctuated. The overall impact, however, continued to be a significant contribution to Canada's total population growth that increased as the century drew to a close. During the early and mid-1970s, net migration represented nearly 38% of the total increase in the population; with consistently high levels of arrivals between 1986 and 1996, it accounted for about half of the population growth. These percentages exceeded those recorded in the 1910s and the 1920s. The cumulative effect of net migration from the 1970s onward was a gradual increase in the percentage of foreign-born Canadians. By the time of the 1996 Census, immigrants comprised just over 17% of the population, the largest proportion in more than fifty years.

Having an immigration policy based on principles of family reunification and labour market contribution also recast the composition of the immigrant population. It meant that people from all nations could be admitted if they met the criteria as described in the immigration regulations. The inclusion of humanitarian-based admissions also permitted the entry of refugees from countries outside Europe. As a result, the immigrants who entered Canada from 1966 onward came from many different countries and possessed more diverse cultural backgrounds than earlier immigrants. Each successive census recorded declining percentages of the immigrant population that had been born in European countries, the United Kingdom, and the United States.

Meanwhile, the proportion of immigrants born in Asian countries and other regions of the world began to rise, slowly at first and then more quickly through the 1980s. By 1996, 27% of the immigrant population in Canada had been born in Asia and another 21% came from places other than the United States, the United Kingdom, or Europe. The top five countries of birth for immigrants arriving between 1991 and 1996 were Hong Kong, the People's Republic of China, India, the Philippines, and Sri Lanka. Together, these five countries accounted for more than one-third of all immigrants who arrived in those five years.

IMMIGRATION THE LARGEST CONTRIBUTOR TO GROWTH OF VISIBLE MINORITY POPULATION

The visible minority population has grown dramatically in the last two decades. In 1996, 11.2 % of Canada's population—3.2 million people—identified themselves as members of a visible minority group, up from under 5% in 1981. Immigration has been a big contributor to this growth: About seven in ten visible minorities are immigrants, almost half of whom have arrived since 1981.

Most immigrants live in Canada's big cities, with the largest numbers concentrated in the census metropolitan areas (CMAs) of Toronto, Montréal, and Vancouver. This continues the trend established earlier in the century. Proportionally more immigrants than Canadian-born have preferred to settle in urban areas, attracted by economic opportunities and by the presence of other immigrants from the same countries or regions of the world. In 1996, 85% of all immigrants lived in a CMA, compared with just 57% of the Canadian-born population. As a result, the largest CMAs have a higher concentration of immigrants than the national average of just over 17%. In 1996, 42% of Toronto's population, 35% of Vancouver's and 18% of Montréal's were foreign-born.

The attraction to urban centres helps to explain the provincial distribution of immigrants. Since the 1940s, a disproportionate share has lived in Ontario and the percentage has continued to rise over time. By 1996, 55% of all immigrants lived in Ontario, compared with 18% in British Columbia and 13% in Québec.

RECENT IMMIGRANTS' ADJUSTMENT TO LABOUR FORCE CAN BE DIFFICULT

Just as immigrants have contributed to the growth in Canada's population, to its diversity, and to its cities, so too have they contributed to its economy. During the last few decades, most employment opportunities have shifted from manufacturing to service industries, and immigrants are an important source of labour for some of these industries. However, compared with non-immigrants, they are more likely to be employed in the personal services industries, manufacturing, and construction. Moreover, the likelihood of being employed in one industry rather than another often differs depending on the immigrant's sex, age at arrival, education, knowledge of English and/or French and length of time in Canada.

Living in a new society generally entails a period of adjustment, particularly when a person must look for work, learn a new language, or deal with an educational system, medical services, government agencies, and laws that may differ signifi-

cantly from those in his or her country of origin. The difficulty of transition may be seen in the labour market profile of recent immigrants: Compared with longer-established immigrants and with those born in Canada, many may experience higher unemployment rates, hold jobs that do not reflect their level of training and education, and earn lower incomes.

In 1996, immigrants aged 25 to 44 who had arrived in the previous five years had lower labour force participation rates and lower employment rates than the Canadian-born, even though they were generally better educated and more than 90% could speak at least one official language (Badets and Howatson-Leo 1999). Both male and female immigrants who were recent arrivals were more likely than the Canadian-born to be employed in sales and services occupations and in processing, manufacturing, and utilities jobs. However, the proportion of immigrant men in many professional occupations was similar to that of Canadian-born men; in contrast, recent immigrant women were considerably less likely than Canadian-born women to be employed in occupations in business, finance, administration, health, social sciences, education, and government services. Recent immigrants also earned less on average than the Canadian born (Picot and Heisz 2000).

In the past, the disparities between recent immigrants and the Canadian-born have often disappeared over time, indicating that initial labour market difficulties reflect the adjustment process. The differences in the 1990s may also result from the diminished employment opportunities available during the recession, also a period of difficulty for the Canadian-born who were new entrants to the job market. Nevertheless, the gaps in employment rates and earnings widened between recent immigrants and the Canadian-born during the 1980s and 1990s, suggesting that new-

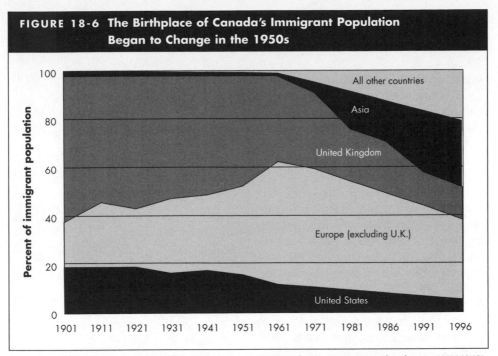

FIGURE 18-6 The Birthplace of Canada's Immigrant Population Began to Change in the 1950s

Source: Statistics Canada, Catalogue Nos. 99-517 (Vol. VII, Part 1), 92-727 (Vol. I, Part 3), 92-913, and Product No. 93F0020XCB.

comers were having an increasingly difficult time in the initial stages of labour-market adjustment.

SUMMARY

Few would quarrel with the statement that the twentieth century in Canada was an era of enormous change. Every area of life, ranging from the economy to family to law, was altered over the course of a hundred years. Immigration was not immune to these transformative forces. The size and character of immigration flows were influenced by economic booms and busts, by world wars and national immigration policies, and indirectly by expanding communication, transportation, and economic links around the world.

The ebb and flow of immigration has presented the most volatile changes over the last 100 years. The century began with the greatest number of immigrant arrivals

ever recorded. Thereafter, levels fluctuated, often with dramatic swings from one decade to the next. The lowest levels were recorded in the 1930s during the Depression. By the close of the century, though, the number of immigrants arriving annually were again sufficiently large that net migration accounted for over half of Canada's population growth.

Other changes in immigration are better described as trends, for they followed a course that was cumulative rather than reversible. The high ratio of men to women immigrants dropped steadily throughout the century. There were two main reasons for this decline. First, the number of men immigrating fell during the two wars and the Depression; and second, the number of women immigrants increased in the last half of the century as a result of family reunification after World War II and of family migration, in which women, men, and their children immigrated together.

Even in the 1900s and 1910s, the foreign-born were more likely to live in urban areas. After the initial settlement of the Prairies in the early 1900s, the trend toward urban settlement accelerated. By the 1990s, the vast majority of recent immigrants were residing in census metropolitan areas, mainly those of Toronto, Vancouver, and Montréal.

Government policies regulating who would be admitted and under what conditions also evolved. Much of the effort during the first fifty years of the century focused on restricting immigration from regions of the world other than the U.S., Britain, and Europe. This position changed in the 1960s, when national origin was removed as a criterion for entry. The policies enacted thereafter entrenched the basic principles guiding admissions, such as family reunification, economic contributions, and humanitarian concerns. With these changes, the source countries of immigrants to Canada substantially altered. By 1996, close to half of the foreign-born in Canada were from countries other than the U.K., the U.S., and Europe.

As a result of these changes, Canada at the close of the twentieth century contrasted sharply with Canada 100 years before. Immigrants had increased the population; they had diversified the ethnic and linguistic composition of the country; and they had laboured in both the agrarian economy of old, and in the new industrial and service-based economy of the future.

NOTES

1. As evidence of this fact, the 1911 Census recorded 2790 Chinese males for every 100 Chinese females, a figure far in excess of the overall ratio of 158 immigrant males for every 100 immigrant females.

2. It should be noted that although Asians were the most severely targeted by efforts to reduce immigration by non-Europeans, other ethnic groups such as Blacks from the United States and the Caribbean also were singled out.

REFERENCES

Abella, Irving, and Harold Troper 1982. *None Is Too Many: Canada and the Jews in Europe, 1933–1948.* Toronto: Lester & Orpen Dennys.

Avery, Donald 2000. "Peopling Canada." *The Beaver* 80(1):28–38.

Badets, Jane, and Linda Howatson-Leo 1999. "Recent immigrants in the workforce." *Canadian Social Trends* (Spring):16–22.

Calliste, Agnes 1993 "Race, gender and Canadian immigration policy: Blacks from the Caribbean, 1900–1932." *Journal of Canadian Studies* 28(4):131–148.

Hawkins, Freda 1972. *Canada and Immigration: Public Policy and Public Concern.* Montréal: McGill-Queen's University Press.

Kalbach, Warren 1970. *The Impact of Immigration on Canada's Population.* Ottawa: Dominion Bureau of Statistics.

Kelley, Ninette, and M. J. Trebilcock 1998. *The Making of the Mosaic: A History of Canadian Immigration Policy.* Toronto: University of Toronto Press.

Knowles, Valerie 1997. *Strangers at Our Gates: Canadian Immigration and Immigration Policy, 1540–1997.* Toronto: Dundurn Press.

Picot, Garnett, and Andrew Heisz 2000. *The Performance of the 1990s Canadian Labour Market.* Ottawa: Statistics Canada. Catalogue No. 11F0019MIE00148, No. 148.

Troper, Harold 1972. *Only Farmers Need Apply: Official Canadian Government Encouragement of Immigration from the United States, 1896–1911.* Toronto: Griffin House.

Urquhart, Malcolm, and Kenneth Buckley 1965. *Historical Statistics of Canada.* Toronto: Macmillan.

THE ECONOMIC INTEGRATION OF VISIBLE MINORITIES IN CONTEMPORARY CANADIAN SOCIETY

Feng Hou and T.R. Balakrishnan

(Abridged from the authors' "The integration of visible minorities in contemporary society," *Canadian Journal of Sociology* 21[3], 1996, pp. 307–326. Reprinted with permission.)

INTRODUCTION

Two hypotheses have been advanced to explain ethnic stratification in Canada. The first is the "ethnically blocked mobility" thesis, introduced first in Porter's *The Vertical Mosaic* (1965), which considers ethnicity to be an important factor in Canadian class structure. In this view, the socio-economic achievement of members in an ethnic group is related to their entrance status when they immigrated to Canada. An entrance status inferior to that of the charter groups may be intensified by the ethnic affiliation of the members. Ethnic affiliation may restrain the status aspirations and achievement motivations of the members of the ethnic group. As a consequence, they may have limited educational qualifications and may find themselves in a segmented labour market (Blishen 1970; Porter 1975). This view has come under attack in the past two decades following some empirical studies. On the basis of the finding that ethnic occupational dissimilarity decreased over 1931–1971, Darroch (1979) questioned the assumption that the entrance status of an immigrant group may lead to permanent stratification linked to ethnicity. Some studies also indicate that any privileged position the charter groups may have had historically in the occupational structure was being effectively challenged by other European ethnic groups (Pineo and Porter 1985; Tepperman 1975:149–152).

Furthermore, some authors have suggested that simplistic claims of ethnic identity as a hindrance to social mobility must be rejected because the causal relationship between ethnic identity and social mobility is minimal or non-existent (Isajiw, Sever, and Driedger 1993).

The second hypothesis, the discrimination thesis, attributes the inferior position of some ethnic minority groups to the socio-economic structure of the society. In this view, unequal relations arise that systematically discourage and exclude some minorities from fully participating in mainstream society. For example, visible minorities may be put into an inescapable socio-economic trap because of racial prejudice and discrimination such that access to the full range of job opportunities and other socio-economic resources of the country may be limited for them. Often they are forced to stay at the periphery of the civic, political, and economic centres of society (Driedger 1989; Wiley 1967). Although passage of human rights legislation and official promotion of multiculturalism are aimed at eliminating structural discrimination in Canadian society, it is believed that discrimination persists in institutional settings and interpersonal relations. Some institutions or individuals may limit rights or access to resources for certain ethnic groups by deliberately or otherwise imposing sets of unfair entry restrictions (Elliott and Fleras 1992). Although it can manifest itself in many ways, discrimination is often identified in income disparity among ethnic and racial groups (Li 1988; Satzewich and Li 1987; Reitz 1990).

The objective of this paper is to examine the differences in social mobility among various ethnic groups in contemporary Canadian society. In particular, we will compare the entrance status and mobility experiences of the two strata of Porter's (1965) ethnic hierarchy of socio-economic status, namely, those of Southern and Eastern European groups such as the Italians, Poles, Greeks, and Portuguese, who immigrated mostly between 1950–1970, and some visible minorities such as Blacks, Chinese, and South Asians who immigrated mostly after 1970. We hope to discover whether ethnicity and/or visibility remains an important determinant of social stratification in Canadian society. Furthermore, we investigate variations in the integration processes between and within the two strata.

THE ROLE OF EDUCATION

Virtually all ethnic groups in Canada have experienced overall improvement in education attainment over the past several decades. Hence the relative differences among ethnic groups have attenuated (Herberg 1990; Shamai 1992). As a group, Asians have experienced the greatest improvement. This fact may imply that there is a place in the vertical mosaic for the upward mobility of some ethnic groups (Shamai 1992). However, some studies attribute the apparent success of Asians to the immigration point system and an increase in the number of Asian immigrants over the last two decades (Beaujot, Basavarajappa, and Verma 1988:32–35). It has also been suggested that new immigration regulations may have been more stringently applied in the selection of non-European than traditional European immigrants, thereby increasing their entry levels of human capital (Kalbach and Richard 1988). Therefore, it is important to control for immigration status when comparing educational levels among ethnic groups. Meanwhile, the educational attainment of immigrants is a good indicator of entrance status. Hence a comparison of the educational attainments of adult immigrants and those of the Canadian-born, and those of individuals who immigrated as children, may partially reflect the extent of blocked mobility.

EXPLAINING INCOME DIFFERENCES

Influences of confounding factors on income differences are complicated. Without careful controls, ethnic differences in income may be either exaggerated or underestimated. For instance, it has been found that foreign-born visible minority members are at a disadvantage in the wage labour force, yet visible minorities who are native-born and self-employed do substantially better than the general self-employed Canadian-born population (Maxim 1992). Based on simple comparison of total income, certain visible minority groups have higher incomes than some White ethnic groups. However, this may simply be due to group differences in education and occupational structure. Therefore, multivariate analysis is essential in adjusting the effects of other influential factors, such as schooling, age, sex, nativity, language, occupation, and labour-force activity (Boyd 1992).

Education, income, and occupational status are highly related, but they also reflect different dimensions of social stratification. Education is usually achieved early in life, and in contemporary society it depends primarily on personal motivation, as well as the economic and cultural background of one's family. Occupational attainment and income come later in an individual's life cycle and are more likely to be influenced by socio-economic conditions. They are also the major factors in establishing quality of lifestyle and social prestige. Hence, to detect discrimination, it is necessary to examine the causal links between education, occupation, and income (Herberg 1990). Some minority groups may have high educational attainments, due either to the selectivity of

immigration or to high aspirations and individual efforts. However, they might have low occupational returns from this education and consequently lower income. Similarly, the same type of occupations may yield different incomes for different ethnic groups.

Using 1981 census data, Herberg (1990) analyzed the differentiation among Canadian ethno-racial groups in education and compared these patterns to those for occupation and income. He found that Chinese, East Indians, Japanese, Blacks, and Filipinos had educational or both educational and occupational attainments that were higher than the income positions they held in relation to the charter groups of British and French, or to other European groups such as the Portuguese and the Greeks. He concluded that different rates of returns from personal qualifications may reflect the effect of institutional and individual discrimination, which persist in spite of federal and provincial human rights legislation (Herberg 1990).

However, Herberg's conclusions about the degree of consonance of occupational standing with a group's educational attainment, and a group's income level relative to its educational and occupational foundations, were based only on a comparison of rankings over educational, occupational, and income statuses. Thus, it is not clear whether ethnicity and/or race was the sole factor contributing to group differences in occupation or income. Using the 1981 census data, Li (1988:117–119) controlled for the effects of education, age, gender, occupation, and industry on ethnic differences in income, and found that Chinese and Blacks were the most disadvantaged in terms of income. However, adequate attention was not given by Li to the effects of age at immigration, period of immigration, and official language proficiency.

Using 1986 census data, Balakrishnan (1988) found that minority groups who immigrated mostly since 1970 had higher educational attainment but lower incomes than the national average, even after controlling for age, year of immigration, education, and official language. However, Balakrishnan did not take occupation into account, nor did he study South Asians (Balakrishnan 1988). Similar findings of relatively lower income of recent immigrants after controlling for factors such as age, education, and language are reported by Beaujot and Rappak, although they did not do the analysis for separate ethnic groups (Beaujot and Rappak 1988). Based on 1971, 1981, and 1986 census data, Kalbach and Richard (1988) also found that groups with non-European origin were relatively high or above average with respect to levels of educational attainment, primarily due to stringent selectivity of immigration, but lower than expected in terms of economic rewards. In explaining the inconsistencies, however, they confined their analysis to the role of religious orientation on acculturation and socio-economic status achievement for post-war ethnic minority groups (Kalbach and Richard 1988).

Ethnic stratification needs to be analyzed dynamically. An increase or decline in relative socio-economic status over time indicates the extent of integration of minorities into the mainstream Canadian society. Simple comparisons over time are one way to examine the change of relative position among ethnic groups. However, the continuous flow of new immigrants makes comparisons of the socio-economic status of recent immigrant groups such as visible minorities with other European groups difficult without proper control for selectivity at entry and duration of stay. An ideal approach is to compare the trends of change between immigrant parents and their children, but this cannot be done

without specific survey data. An approximation to this approach is to compare first-generation immigrants with those whose parents were foreign-born, or with those whose grandparents were foreign-born, as was done in a study in the United States (Neidert and Farley 1985). Unfortunately, this information is not available in the Canadian census data. In this study, members of specific ethnic groups are identified by their immigration status, age, and year of immigration.

From the above theoretical considerations, we hypothesize that visibility and social distance will manifest themselves in the degree and speed of integration. Therefore, we predict that European groups such as Italians, Portuguese, Greeks, and Poles will find it easier to integrate than Blacks, Chinese, South Asians, and other visible minorities. We view equality in income as the final measure of integration. When education and occupation are controlled for, we would expect the visible minorities to have lower incomes only if visibility is a negative factor. Similarly, while incomes of visible minorities will increase with duration of stay in Canada, such an increase will still be small compared to those of European minority groups.

DATA AND METHOD

The data for this paper are from 1991 three percent individual files of Canadian Census Public Use Sample. The ethnic groups specified in this study include the two charter groups—British and French—and four European groups—Italians, Greeks, Poles, and Portuguese. For visible minorities, four groups are specified: Blacks, Chinese, South Asians, and other visible minorities (Arabs and West Asians, Filipinos, Vietnamese, Other East/Southeast Asians, Latin/Central/South Americans). Only those 30–60 years of

TABLE 19-1 Sample Size and Percentage Distribution of Educational Levels by Ethnicity and Immigration Status for Population Aged 30–60 Years, 1991

	British	French	Polish	Greek	Italian	Portuguese	Black	Chinese	South	Other Visible	Total Population
(1) Sample Size											
Total	81 401	78 096	3643	2086	10 190	3113	3783	7503	5294	8748	304 652
Canadian-born	69 803	76 975	1626	242	3076	114	495	717	412	1346	235 029
Age at immigration											
<10	2098	142	237	110	1490	244	53	126	59	75	8374
10–19	1892	189	227	532	2377	607	438	827	543	541	12 525
20–29	5145	512	595	917	2595	1222	1562	2565	2215	3068	28 276
≥30	2463	278	958	285	652	926	1234	3268	2065	3718	20 448
(2) Percentage Distribution											
Total University & +	21.4	16.7	27.0	9.5	12.8	4.3	17.7	31.8	33.4	39.3	21.3
Some post-sec.	34.9	28.9	34.7	19.3	25.0	16.0	41.3	26.1	26.0	26.1	32.9
≤Grade 13	43.7	54.3	38.3	71.2	62.2	79.7	41.0	42.1	40.6	34.6	45.8
Canadian-born											
University & +	20.8	16.4	23.2	28.9	24.9	17.5	13.9	42.5	25.5	38.9	20.2
Some post-sec.	33.7	28.9	31.9	32.6	35.0	27.2	34.3	30.3	27.7	30.6	33.0
≤Grade 13	45.5	54.7	44.9	38.4	40.1	55.3	51.7	27.2	46.8	30.5	46.8
Age at immigration											
<10											
University & +	27.4	38.0	31.6	20.0	20.5	12.3	41.5	48.4	54.2	42.7	27.2
Some post-sec.	38.5	33.1	33.3	33.6	34.2	36.1	35.8	32.5	27.1	36.0	36.9
≤Grade 13	34.1	28.9	35.0	46.4	45.3	51.6	22.6	19.0	18.6	21.3	35.9
10–19											
University & +	21.0	32.3	18.9	6.6	4.4	4.4	20.8	34.3	25.6	33.3	17.8
Some post-sec.	39.5	33.9	35.2	15.8	21.0	18.6	45.9	28.3	33.9	28.5	32.1
≤Grade 13	39.5	33.9	45.8	77.6	74.6	77.0	33.3	37.4	40.5	38.3	50.1
20–29											
University & +	26.0	41.4	26.6	5.5	3.4	3.7	19.3	34.4	39.2	41.2	25.6
Some post-sec.	44.6	35.0	39.8	17.0	15.0	13.7	45.4	25.6	27.7	27.0	34.1
≤Grade 13	29.3	23.6	33.6	77.5	81.6	83.1	35.3	40.0	33.1	31.8	40.3
≥30											
University & +	24.0	36.0	34.2	7.7	6.3	1.9	15.1	26.2	30.3	38.6	28.1
Some post-sec.	43.3	30.5	36.5	16.1	12.1	10.6	37.5	24.7	21.6	23.2	28.8
≤Grade 13	32.7	33.5	29.2	76.1	81.6	87.5	47.4	49.1	48.0	38.2	43.1

Source: The 1991 Census Public Use Sample.

Notes: (1) "Other Visible" minorities here include Arab and West Asians, Filipino, Vietnamese, other East/Southeast Asian, Latin/Central/South American. (2) Education: "university & +," with university certificate or diploma and above; "some post-secondary," non-university education or without university certificate.

age were selected, based on the consideration that most people within this age range
have completed their formal education.
The resultant sample size for the selected
ethnic groups ranges from 2086 to 81 401
(see Table 19-1).

RESULTS

Educational Attainment

Table 19-1 shows differentials in educational attainment among the selected ethnic groups. For each ethnic group, a proportional distribution of three educational
levels is calculated respectively for the
whole group, Canadian-born, and immigrants by age at immigration.

Considerable heterogeneity exists both
among the selected groups of European
origin and among visible minorities. We
will discuss each ethnic group first, and
then try to identify some common patterns.

Among the four groups of European
origin, the Polish group is distinguished
from the others, in that the Poles have the
highest educational attainment, higher
than British and total population. Clearly,
this is due to the fact that Polish immigrants at all entry ages had higher education levels. The overall education levels of
the other three European groups—Italians,
Portuguese, and Greeks—are the lowest
among all the selected groups. This can be
explained by the very low levels of education among those immigrants who came to
Canada after the age of 10. For these three
groups, the Canadian-born and immigrants who came as small children have
much higher education levels than the
older immigrants. This may suggest that in
spite of the low entrance status of immigrants, their children do achieve education
levels similar to those of the population
average.

Among visible minorities, the
Chinese, South Asians, and "other" visible

minorities have much higher education
levels than the British and the total population among both the Canadian-born and
the foreign-born segments. The average
education level of Blacks, on the other
hand, is lower than that of the British and
that of the average for the total population.
Among the Canadian-born, Blacks have
the smallest proportion with university
education. An exception are those Blacks
who immigrated before the age of 19. In
this group, there was a larger proportion
with university education. However, they
account for only a small portion of the
Blacks (about 13%).

With the exception of Blacks, the
blocked mobility thesis does not appear
applicable to visible minorities, at least
with regard to education. Education has
long been regarded as the prerequisite for
gaining access to high-paying and prestigious jobs in Canada and in other societies.
The ambition to integrate into and get
ahead in society may encourage members
of ethnic minorities to acquire necessary
educational credentials. This is clear from
the fact that the Canadian-born and those
who immigrated before the age of 10
among most minorities have education levels similar to or higher than the British and
total population. Even the low socio-
economic status of some minority groups at
entrance did not limit their children's
mobility achievements. The belief that education can eventually equalize social and
economic opportunities may be the underlying reason for the "over-achievement" in
education of children of immigrants.

Income

Equality of opportunity in a society
implies that an individual's accomplishments are basically determined by personal attributes and efforts. Earnings are the
rewards for an individual's investment in
human capital. Therefore, income differ-

TABLE 19-2   **Multiple Classification Analysis Showing Wage Income Differences Among Ethnic Groups, for Employed Workers Aged 30–60 (in Dollars, Grand Mean = $26 521), Canada, 1990**

Variable & Categories	No. of Cases	Unadjusted Deviation	(1)	(2)	(3)	(4)	(5)
				Deviation from Grand Mean			
Ethnic Group		(.09)	(.05*)	(.04*)	(.05*)	(.06*)	(.04*)
British	71 357	2297	823	816	977	1083	798
French	63 694	−1555	−61	−525	−276	284	−22
Polish	3144	−1458	−389	1462	445	−26	781
Greek	1707	−5474	−1577	−4382	−2748	−5168	−3195
Italian	8489	808	2453	534	1177	173	1203
Portuguese	2572	−3034	2829	136	1458	2	1812
Black	3340	−4150	−3526	−3607	−3687	−2226	−3039
Chinese	6399	−3551	−1153	342	635	−2340	−245
South Asian	4600	−3254	−2457	−1036	−2163	−3112	−1956
Other visible	7298	−6131	−4359	−1918	−3600	−4897	−3402
Others	88 964	520	−189	20	−204	−174	−246
Immigration		(.09)		(.06*)	(.07*)	(.08*)	(.06*)
Canadian-born	201 832	216		−135	52	234	33
Im.<1960	13 686	2818		1421	1401	1216	1268
61–70	15 476	2424		2673	2101	1718	2094
71–80,<20	2815	−2758		527	599	−72	508
71–80,≥20	14 450	−139		1829	993	222	1057
81–91	13 305	−8262		−4617	−5893	−7024	−5494
Schooling		(.25)	(.18*)		(.25*)	(.18*)	(.18*)
uni. & +	60 900	9221	6551		9316	6645	6590
some post-sec.	90 577	132	100		−97	122	76
≤grade 13	110 087	−5210	−3707		−5073	−3777	−3708
Occupation		(.31)	(.21*)	(.28*)		(.21*)	(.21*)
manager.	39 052	13 198	10 088	11420		10 129	10 046
profess.	51 025	4200	2194	5500		2220	2159
c.s.s.	94 752	−6215	−2326	−3166		−2261	−2291
other	76 735	−1834	−3719	−5559		−3839	−3720
Home Language		(.10)	(.07*)	(.07*)	(.07*)		(.06*)
English/French	237 261	678	515	484	519		417
other	24 303	−6620	−5029	−4726	−5072		−4075
Gender		(.30)	(.30*)	(.32*)	(.29*)	(.30*)	(.30*)
male	141 439	6153	6102	6469	6019	6134	6115
female	120 125	−7246	−7184	−7617	−7088	−7223	−7200
Province		(.08)	(.08*)	(.08*)	(.09*)	(.08*)	(.08*)
Ontario	107 931	2199	2100	2012	2257	2116	2102
Québec	71 339	−1882	−1890	−1709	−1661	−1958	−1870
Others	82 294	−1253	−1116	−1158	−1520	−1077	−1136
R Squared			.214	.193	.178	.215	.217

Notes: 1) Deviation—deviation from grand mean; the numbers in brackets for unadjusted means are eta values which measure the variation across the categories of each factor. The square of eta indicates the proportions of variance explained by all categories of the factor. 2) The numbers in brackets for MCA models are beta values that are equivalent to the standardized partial regression coefficient. 3) * significant at α< .01.

entials among individuals should simply reflect their differences in education, occupation, age, and other achieved social and economic characteristics. The ascribed status of individuals, such as ethnicity and race, should not enter into the equation. In this sense, any ethnic differences in income may be an important indicator of discrimination.

Table 19-2 presents the results of Multiple Classification Analysis (MCA), which is a modified form of analysis of variance. Wage income of employed workers aged 30–60 is the dependent variable. Control variables include immigration status, schooling, occupation, home language, gender, province of residence, and age. The continuous variable age is introduced in the models as a covariate. Thus, its effects are controlled statistically, which means that each group would have the same age distribution as the average of total population. The effect of each category in each factor is indicated as the deviation of the category mean income from the grand mean. The first column of the table lists the sample distribution across the categories for each variable. The second column lists the income deviation from grand mean for the categories of each variable. Model 5 controls for all the selected variables. Compared with Model 5, Models 1 to 4 identify the various effects of immigration status, schooling, occupation, and language on the income levels of various ethnic groups. Model 1 controls for all the selected variables except immigration status. In Model 2, schooling is not controlled; in Model 3, occupation is not controlled; and in Model 4 the effect of home language is not controlled. '

All the selected ethnic groups have a lower "average unadjusted income" than the British. Compared with the total population, only Italians have a higher average unadjusted income than the British. When adjusted for the effects of all the selected control variables, the income variation across ethnic groups decreases (Model 5). However, the remaining ethnic differentials are still statistically significant. All the visible minorities have average incomes lower than the grand mean and especially lower than that of the British. On the other hand, among the four selected minority groups of European origin, only the Greeks still have an average income lower than the grand mean, while the other three groups have average incomes close to or higher than the British. Assuming that similar educational and occupational attainment should yield similar incomes, there does not appear to exist systematic income inequality among European groups. Nevertheless, ethnic differentials in income still exist, and visible minorities are generally at a disadvantage in this regard. However, ethnic inequality in income is not exclusively along the colour line, since some non–visible minorities, for example, the Greeks, suffer as much as certain visible minorities.

Besides the income variations due to possible discrimination as implicitly suggested in Model 5, various factors also strongly influence the income differentials among ethnic groups. The difference between Model 1 and Model 5 reflects the effect of immigration status. Among the four European minorities, only the Polish group is in a disadvantaged position due to its composition in age at and period of immigration, as indicated by the fact that its income level increases after controlling for this variable (from −389 to +781). Meanwhile, immigration status is detrimental to the income level of all the visible minorities, with recency of immigration depressing their earnings. The effect of schooling is revealed by comparing Model 2 with Model 5. Poles, Chinese, South Asian, and other visible minorities have higher-than-expected income levels before controlling for education. This suggests that these minority groups would obtain incomes even lower than their present overall income levels if they had the same education levels as the total population. The effect of occupation is shown by the differences between Model 3 and Model 5. It seems that only the Greeks and the Chinese among the minority groups have benefited from their occupational structure, because they have higher income levels before controlling for occupation. All the selected minorities except Blacks would likely improve their incomes if they had higher proficiency in the official languages (Model 4 vs. Model 5). We assume that when the home language is neither English nor French, proficiency in these languages is likely to be low and, hence, it is detrimental in the labour market as far as earning potential is concerned. Overall, there are evident variations within non-visible minority groups and within visible minorities in terms of the effects of various factors on their income levels. Improvement in education and official language proficiency would benefit the income levels of the Greek, Italian, and Portuguese groups. Large proportions of new immigrants and difficulties with the official languages are the major problems for the Polish and Chinese groups. Immigration status, schooling, and occupational structure are all unfavourable to Blacks. Immigration status, occupational structure, and difficulties with official languages are the drawbacks to South Asians and other visible minorities.

If we treat the income differentials among ethnic groups in Model 5 as an indicator of inequality after controlling for qualifications, the discrepancy between unadjusted income deviation and the income deviation in Model 5 should show how much the observed unadjusted income deviation is due to discrimination and how much is due to group differences in qualifications. In this sense, the low level of unadjusted income for the Portuguese is totally related to their corresponding qualifications. Immigration status and language can mostly explain the low level of unadjusted income for Poles and Chinese. For Greeks, Blacks, South Asians, and other visible minorities, however, a large portion of their low unadjusted income cannot be explained by controlling for qualifications.

CONCLUSION

This study arrives at two basic conclusions. First, the integration processes for non-visible minorities and visible minorities are different and distinct. In explaining the success of Italians and Poles in the United States since 1920, Greeley (1976: 25) suggests that their social mobility has "come first in income, then in education, and finally in occupation," because most immigrant groups must acquire some kind of basic financial success before they can exploit the opportunities of educational and occupational mobility. He further suggests that income parity comes before educational and occupational parity in the case of ethnics, although education is a more general institution for facilitating upward mobility in American society. Based on the 1981 census data, and survey data in Toronto, Reitz (1990) suggests that the above pattern may still exist for the immigrants of some European groups. However, he believes that the relative success in income of those immigrants with low entrance status may not mean income parity coming before education and occupation, but rather that it has more to do with "the priority needs of immigrants from impoverished backgrounds" (Reitz 1990:189). His tentative explanation is that income mobility for ethnic minorities often depends on minority businesses based on resources within the ethnic community (Reitz 1990). Our analysis suggests that Italian and Portuguese groups obtain much higher income levels relative to their educational and occupational achievements. The relative positions of the Polish group in occupation and income are similar to those of the Italian and Portuguese. According to the mobility model suggested by Greeley, we may say that the Polish group has reached the second step in the mobility process—that is, improvement in education. Before and around the early 1980s, the Polish group had a lower educational level than the average of total population (Herberg 1990; Shamai 1992). The 1991 data show that Poles have achieved a higher educational attainment than either the British or total population due to the selectivity of immigration and the upward mobility of their Canadian-born segment in education (Table 19-1). It is possible that other European minority groups will experience a similar process. In fact, Canadian-born and young immigrants among them have achieved an educational level and occupational status close to or even higher than the British or the average of total population.

On the other hand, visible minority groups generally have higher educational attainment than the average of the total population and the charter groups. The selectivity of immigration only contributes partly to the achievement of visible minorities in education. Their Canadian-born and young immigrant segments have also attained much higher levels of education than the charter groups and the average of total population, with the exception of Blacks. On the other hand, the percentages of visible minority groups working in managerial and professional occupations are generally smaller than for the British and the French. For the Chinese, difficulties with the official languages may be the major factor influencing their occupational status. However, Blacks, South Asians, and other visible minorities have lower

occupational status than the British and French, even adjusting for educational qualifications. In spite of their remarkable accomplishments in education and occupational attainment, visible minorities are generally disadvantaged in income. In this sense, we can say that visible minorities follow a different path of integration into Canadian society.

The second conclusion, which is closely related to the first, is that ethnic differences in socio-economic status still exist in contemporary Canadian society. However, racial/ethnic minority groups are not necessarily disadvantaged in all the dimensions of socio-economic stratification. Social inequality is primarily manifested in income inequalities. Italians and Portuguese have lower levels of educational and occupational achievements than the average of total population, yet they have relatively higher incomes than other groups. The average incomes of all the visible minorities remain significantly lower than for the British and average population. Compared with their relative position in educational attainment, the income achievements of the Chinese, South Asians, and other visible minorities are lower than would be expected. The income differences would be even larger if these three visible minorities had not attained higher educational levels than the average of total population.

In Canada, income differentials exist among many ethnic groups, with some of these differentials explained by variations in educational and occupational distributions. After adjusting for these factors, some ethnic groups, such as Italians, Poles, and Portuguese, are no longer in inferior positions. In contrast, most visible minorities receive less income return from educational and occupational achievements. The important question that remains to be answered is why some European groups gain relatively high incomes while visible minority groups do not. The collective capacity for economic mobilization within an ethnic community may be able to explain the success of Italians in Toronto, as suggested by Reitz (1990). However, that may not be the reason for more recent and smaller groups like Poles and Portuguese. For the majority of ethnic minorities, average incomes will depend on the conditions in the broader labour market. Therefore, income inequality on the basis of qualifications is most probably related to discrimination. All the visible minorities experience a certain amount of income inequality. This suggests that visibility has an additional effect on income inequality in Canadian society. In a sense, the disparate integration processes of non-visible and visible minorities are not only determined by group differences in some demographic factors such as immigration status and language, and by motivations as manifested in the improvement of education, but also probably by social inequality. It has been suggested that ethnic disparities have decreased continuously first in education, then in occupation over the last several decades in Canada. The existing ethnic income disparity, as a remaining "vestige of the elitist sponsorship that once drove the Canadian society in all socioeconomic elements," is believed to be similar to those in education and occupation two or three decades ago, and may decline over time (Herberg 1990:218). However, our analyses show that while income equality has materialized in spite of educational differences for some European groups, it has not for visible minorities. Whether the increasing proportion of visible minorities and their longer stay in Canada will reduce income inequalities in the future is an important issue, and will continue to have implications for policy interventions.

REFERENCES

Balakrishnan, T.R. 1988. "Immigration and the changing ethnic mosaic of Canadian cities." *Report for The Review of Demography and Its Implications for Economic and Social Policy.* Ottawa: Health and Welfare Canada.

Beaujot, Roderic, K.G. Basavarajappa, and Ravi B.P. Verma 1988. *Income of Immigrants in Canada.* Ottawa: Minister of Supply and Services Canada.

Beaujot, R., and Peter J. Rappak 1988. "The role of immigration in changing socioeconomic structures." *Report for The Review of Demography and Its Implications for Economic and Social Policy.* Ottawa: Health and Welfare Canada.

Blishen, Bernard R. 1970. "Social class and opportunity in Canada." *Canadian Review of Sociology and Anthropology* 7:110–127.

Boyd, Monica 1992. "Gender, visible minority, and immigrant earnings inequality: Reassessing an employment equity premise." In Victor Satzewich (ed.), *Deconstructing a Nation: Immigration, Multiculturalism and Racism in '90s Canada.* Halifax: Fernwood.

Darroch, Gordon A. 1979. "Another look at ethnicity, stratification and social mobility in Canada." *Canadian Journal of Sociology* 4:1–25.

Driedger, Leo 1989. *The Ethnic Factor: Identity in Diversity.* McGraw Hill-Ryerson.

Elliott, Jean L., and Augie Fleras 1992. *Unequal Relations: An Introduction to Race and Ethnic Dynamics in Canada.* Toronto: Prentice-Hall.

Greeley, Andrew M. 1976. "The ethnic miracle." *The Public Interest* 45:20–36.

Herberg, Edward N. 1990. "The ethno–racial socioeconomic hierarchy in Canada: Theory and analysis of the new vertical mosaic." *International Journal of Comparative Sociology* 31:206–221.

Isajiw, Wsevolod W., Aysan Sever, and Leo Driedger 1993. "Ethnic identity and social mobility: A test of the 'drawback model.'" *Canadian Journal of Sociology* 18:177–196.

Kalbach, Warren E., and Madeline A. Richard 1988. "Ethnic–religious identity, acculturation, and social and economic achievement of Canada's post-war minority populations." *Report for The Review of Demography and Its Implications for Economic and Social Policy.* Toronto: University of Toronto Population Research Laboratory.

Li, Peter S. 1988. *Ethnic Inequality on a Class Society.* Toronto: Thompson.

Maxim, Paul 1992. "Immigrants, visible minorities, and self–employment." *Demography* 29:181–198.

Neidert, Lisa J., and Reynolds Farley 1985. "Assimilation in the United States: An analysis of ethnic and generation differences in status and achievement." *American Sociological Review* 50:840–850.

Pineo, Peter C., and John Porter 1985. "Ethnic origin and occupational attainment." In Monica Boyd, John Goyder, and Frank E. Jones (eds.), *Ascription and Achievement: Studies in Mobility and Status Attainment in Canada.* Ottawa: Carleton University Press.

Porter, John 1965. *The Vertical Mosaic.* Toronto: University of Toronto Press.

Porter, John 1975. "Ethnic pluralism in Canadian perspective." In Nathan Glazer and Daniel Moynihan (eds.), *Ethnicity: Theory and Experience.* Cambridge, Massachusetts: Harvard University Press.

Reitz, Jeffrey 1990. "Ethnic concentrations in labour markets and their implications for ethnic inequality." In Raymond Breton, Wsevolod Isajiw, Warren Kalbach, and Jeffrey Reitz, *Ethnic Identity and Equality.* Toronto: University of Toronto Press.

Satzewich, Victor, and Peter S. Li 1987. "Immigrant labour in Canada: The cost and benefit of ethnic origin in the job market." *Canadian Journal of Sociology* 12:229–241.

Shamai, Shmuel 1992. "Ethnicity and educational achievement in Canada 1941–1981." *Canadian Ethnic Studies* 24:43–51.

Tepperman, Lorne 1975. *Social Mobility in Canada.* Toronto: University of Toronto Press.

Wiley, Norbert F. 1967. "The ethnic mobility trap and stratification theory." *Social Problems* 15:147–69.

TWO STUDIES OF RACIAL DISCRIMINATION IN EMPLOYMENT

Frances Henry

INTRODUCTION

Until the publication of our report *Who Gets the Work?* (Henry and Ginzberg 1985), efforts to demonstrate that there is racial discrimination in the Canadian employment arena had been limited to census data analysis, personal reports of victims of discrimination, and attitude studies. Each of these three types of research is limited in its capacity to prove that discrimination based on race is actually the cause of discrepancies in income and access to employment. Critics, skeptics, and racists have easily been able to doubt the presence of racial discrimination in view of weaknesses inherent in these indirect measures of discrimination. *Who Gets the Work?* sought to test directly for the presence or absence of discrimination in the Toronto labour market through the process of field testing—a quasi-experimental research technique.

For the first time in Canada, a study tested racial discrimination in employment by actually sending individuals, White and Black, to apply to advertised positions in order to find out if employers discriminate by preferring White to non-White employees. We believe we were successful in proving definitively that racial discrimination in Canada affected the employment opportunities of non-White Canadians. Whites had greater access to jobs than did equally qualified non-Whites.

Our study was guided by two questions. One, is there a difference in the number of job offers that White and Black applicants of similar experience and qualifications receive when they apply to the same jobs? And two, are there differences in the ways in which White and Black job applicants are treated when they apply for work? Both questions were tested by two procedures: in-person testing and telephone testing.

DEFINING DISCRIMINATION

Discrimination can take place at any point in the employment process. It may exist in such areas as recruitment, screening, selection, promotion, and termination. At the level of employee selection, for example, discrimination against non-Whites can take place when job applicants are called to the initial interview. To the extent that the employer's staff or the other employees themselves practise discrimination, either as a result of racial attitudes of the interviewer or because of instructions to screen out non-Whites as a matter of company policy, non-Whites will not get beyond the initial screening of job applicants. Similarly, in terms of promotion policies, non-Whites may be hired at lower levels, but their promotion to the upper ranks is effectively stopped by discriminatory barriers to mobility. For example, the employer may believe that the other employees will not accept a non-White as their supervisor.

Discrimination in employment can be intentional as well as inadvertent. Employers may not realize that their practices and policies have the effect of excluding non-Whites. The use of standard tests of personality or intelligence to select employees places certain minority groups at a disadvantage since they come from cultures other than the one for which the tests were designed. Recruiting through in-house, word-of-mouth techniques often excludes minority applicants since they do not hear about available positions. Requiring Canadian experience and education can effectively eliminate non-Whites, many of whom are immi-

grants, from job opportunities even though such experience is not necessary to successful job performance.

Thus, there are numerous types of discrimination and numerous ways in which discrimination can be carried out. Our study concentrated essentially on the entry point and/or the selection procedure. In this study, the dynamics of discrimination are studied as discriminatory practices occur; that is, when a job seeker either makes an inquiry on the phone or comes in person to be interviewed. It is at this point that the applicant can run into a prejudiced employer or "gatekeeper" who either presumes that non-Whites are not desired, or merely acts according to company policy. The telephone inquiry is particularly crucial at this stage since it is often the first approach made by the job applicant. An individual can be screened out; that is, told quickly and efficiently either that the job has already been filled or that the applicant's qualifications are not suitable. In all likelihood, the applicant will not know that he or she has been the victim of discrimination.

For the purposes of this study, we defined discrimination in employment as those practices or attitudes, willful or unintentional, that have the effect of limiting an individual's or a group's right to economic opportunities on the basis of irrelevant traits such as skin colour rather than on an evaluation of true abilities or potential.

IN-PERSON TESTING

In the in-person testing, two job applicants, matched with respect to age, sex, education, experience, physical appearance (dress), and personality, were sent to apply for the same advertised job. The only major difference between our applicants was their race—one was White and the other Black. We created four such teams: one junior male, one junior female, one senior male, and one senior female. The youngest teams applied for semi-skilled and unskilled jobs such as gas station attendant, bus boy, waitress, and clerk and sales help in youth-oriented stores. The senior teams applied for positions in retail management, sales positions in prestigious stores, and waiting and hosting positions in expensive restaurants. The senior team members were, in fact, professional actors. Applying for middle-class type jobs meant that they would be required not only to present a sophisticated image but also to participate in a fairly demanding job interview. Professional actors, we believed, would be more convincing in playing the many roles required for this project. The résumés of the team members were carefully constructed to be as alike as possible. In order to further control possible biases, the staff of testers was changed several times so that no individual personality could account for the results.

The younger teams were composed of high school and university students who would normally be applying for the same types of jobs that they applied for in the testing situation. Since we were not testing for sex discrimination and did not want this type of discrimination to account for any of our results, the male teams were sent to traditionally male jobs and the women went to jobs traditionally associated with women's work. In some types of jobs, for example waiter/waitress, both men and women were acceptable. Men and women were sent to such jobs but never to the same job. Each tester had a different résumé for the various types of positions that he or she was applying for, so each member of the senior female team, for example, carried several résumés, one for a secretary, another for a retail sales assistant, a third for a dental technician, etc. Each résumé contained the names of references supplied by business people and friends who had agreed to support our

research. Our applicants could thus be checked out by a potential employer who could obtain a reference for the applicant. In actuality, only two employers ever called for references.

Each evening, a listing of jobs would be selected for the next day from among the classified advertisements. Some types of jobs were excluded such as those involving driving, for which licences could be checked. Jobs that required highly technical skills were also excluded.

The testers were instructed either to go to a certain address or to phone for an appointment. They used standard Canadian accents when phoning since we did not want them to be screened out over the phone. The testers arrived within approximately one half-hour of each other so that there would be little chance that a job had been legitimately filled. In most cases the Black applicant went first. After their interviews the testers completed a summary data sheet especially designed for this project in which they wrote down the details of their treatment and the kinds of information they had been given. Their résumés listed telephone numbers, which were in actuality lines connected to the research office. Call-backs for second interviews or with offers of employment were received and recorded by the researchers. On-the-spot offers to the field testers were accepted by them. In the case of call-backs and on-the-spot offers, employers were phoned back, usually within an hour, and informed that another position had been accepted, in order to make sure that the employer could fill the vacancy as soon as possible.

Research Results: The In-Person Test

In three-and-one-half months of field testing, the testers were able to apply for 201 jobs for a total of 402 individual applications.

For our purposes, racial discrimination in employment was tested in two ways. First, was an offer of employment made to one of the applicants, both applicants, or neither applicant? Second, during the interview, were there any differences in the treatment of the two applicants? The following tables present the numerical results.

Blacks received fewer job offers than Whites. Of a total of thirty-seven valid job offers, twenty-seven went to Whites, nine to Blacks, and in one case both were offered the job. There were an additional ten cases in which both were offered jobs, but these were for commission sales which involved no cost to the employer. Our overall results therefore show that *offers to Whites outnumber offers to Blacks by a ratio of 3 to 1.*

We had thought that the nature of the job might influence whether Blacks or Whites would be hired. Only Whites received offers for managerial positions or jobs as waiters or waitresses or hosts and hostesses in the restaurant trade. A Black was offered a job in the kitchen when he had applied for a waiter's job.

As noted above, the second measure of discrimination was whether differential treatment had occurred during the interview. Table 20-2 presents the results.

Blacks and Whites were treated differently thirty-six times, and in all cases but one, the White applicant was preferred to the Black. The ways in which differential treatment took place provided a great deal of insight into the nature of discrimination and its subtleties.

Differences in treatment were sometimes very blatant, as the following examples show.

1. Mary, the young Black tester, applied for a sales position in a retail clothing store and was told that the job had already been taken. Sylvia, our White tester, arrived a half-hour later and was given an application form to fill in and told that she would be contacted if they were interested in her.

2. In a coffee shop, Mary was told that the job of cashier was taken. Sylvia walked in five minutes later and was offered the job on the spot. This pattern occurred five times. Another form of

---

TABLE 20-1   Offer of a Job versus No Offer

	Number	%
Both offered job	10	5.0
White offered job; Black not	27	13.4
Black offered job; White not	9	4.5
No offer to either	155	77.1
Total	201	100.0

TABLE 20-2   Treatment of Applicants

	Number of Cases
Treated the same	165
Treated differently	36

differential treatment was as follows: The Black was treated rudely or with hostility, whereas the White was treated politely. This occurred fifteen times.

3. Paul, our White tester, applied for a job as a waiter. He was given an application form to fill out and an interview. He was told that he might be contacted in a week or so. Larry, the Black tester, was also given an application form and an interview. But as the Manager looked over Larry's résumé, he asked Larry if he "wouldn't rather work in the kitchen."

4. Applying for a gas station job, the White tester was told that there were no jobs at present, but that he could leave a résumé. The Black tester was told that there were no jobs, but when he asked if he could leave a résumé, he was sworn at: "Shit, I said no, didn't I?"

Another form of differential treatment occurred when the wage offers to Blacks and Whites were different. There were two occasions in which the Black tester was offered less money than the White tester for the same job. On a few occasions, derogatory comments were made about Blacks in the presence of our White testers. The Blacks being referred to were our testers.

These results indicate that Black job seekers face not only discrimination in the sense of receiving fewer job offers than Whites, but also a considerable amount of negative and abusive treatment while job hunting. The psychological effects of such experiences became evident in the feelings expressed by the research staff. The Black staff felt rejected, and some doubted their own ability: "I was beginning to wonder what was wrong with me and why Jean [the White tester] was so much better than me."

In sum, the findings of the in-person test reveal that in forty-eight job contacts, or 23.8% of the cases, some form of dis-

crimination against Blacks took place. These findings indicate that Blacks and Whites do not have the same access to employment. *Racial discrimination in employment, either in the form of clearly favouring a White over a Black, even though their résumés were equivalent, or in the form of treating a White applicant better than a Black, took place in almost one-quarter of all job contacts tested in this study.* When we examine the results of telephone testing, we see that this pattern of discrimination occurs again and, if anything, more clearly and strongly.

TELEPHONE TESTING

We have all had the experience of calling for a job and being told that the job has been filled. We experienced a twinge of disappointment, but we rarely felt the need to ask ourselves seriously if we had been told the truth. Members of minority groups have good reason to question whether they have indeed been told the truth. Our study tested this by having callers' phone numbers listed in the classified employment section of the newspaper to present themselves as job applicants.

In total, 237 job numbers were phoned. Each job was called four times, once by someone with no discernible accent (apparently a White-majority Canadian), once by someone who had a Slavic or Italian accent, once by a Jamaican-accented caller, and finally by a person with a Pakistani accent. Many different jobs were called, ranging from unskilled labour, secretarial, and service, to skilled trade, to managerial. To exclude sex discrimination, callers did not cross traditional sex-role categories. Men were of the same age, education, number of years of job experience, and so on for each type of job. Callers were "older" for jobs requiring more experience and maturity. A profile was provided for each of the callers for each type of job so that they had a secretarial profile, a managerial one, one for waitressing, and so on. Jobs to be called were selected from among those that had not appeared in the newspaper the previous day; they were all new jobs. Callers within each sex were given identical lists of jobs to call on the next day and were instructed to begin their calls from the top of the list and proceed in order down the list. All callers were to begin the calling at the same time so that the time span between callers would be minimized. All callers were instructed to use standard English, full sentences, and correct grammar so that the lack of language would not be a discriminating factor against them.

In the telephone testing, discrimination was said to occur when one caller was told that the job had been filled while another caller was told that the job was still available. Discrimination was also said to take place when one caller-applicant with a certain set of qualifications was screened out and told that he or she did not qualify, although other callers with the same qualifications were told that they did qualify and were invited to apply. Another form of discrimination was identified as occurring when callers were treated differently from one another in that some and not others were screened to see if they had the experience the employer sought. It has been argued that screening some applicants and not others is not necessarily discriminatory. However, if there is no systematic discrimination present, then we would expect all racial or immigrant groups to be subject to the same proportion of screening.

Research Results: The Telephone Test

Results of this procedure were that in 52% of all jobs called there was some form of discrimination present. Either one of our testers was told that the job was filled when another tester was told that the job was open, or one of our testers was treated differently in that he or she was screened while another was not.

There were nine instances in which our accented callers were told that they did not qualify for the job even though they presented the same experience and qualifications as the White-majority callers. Needless to say, the White callers were told by these same nine employers that they qualified and were invited to apply. In addition, the employers did not perceive the need to screen all of the four minority-accented callers to the same degree. Employers who treated callers differently—that is, the 123 employers who discriminated in some way—never screened non-accented callers. Italian- or Slavic-accented callers were screened 5% of the time and the two non-White minority callers received three times as much screening as the Whites, on between 15% and 20% of all their calls.

Minority-accented callers did not receive the same information about the status of the job as did Whites. Forty-eight percent of the jobs were closed to Blacks and 62% were closed to Pakistanis in that the employers told them that the job was filled when the non-accented caller was told that the job was available. Statistical analysis revealed that there were significant differences in the treatment and the type of information that Whites and non-Whites received about work. The Toronto employers discriminated against immigrants in general, but to a significantly greater degree against non-White immigrants.

The results of our telephone testing demonstrate that to secure ten potential job interviews a White Canadian had to make about eleven to twelve calls. White immigrants had to make about thirteen calls. Racial minorities had to work harder and longer since they had to make eighteen calls to get ten potential job interviews. Clearly there were differences in what Whites and non-Whites were being told over the phone about the availability of work. And, as noted in the in-person testing, discrimination did not end when a job interview was obtained.

A RATIO OF DISCRIMINATION

An Index of Discrimination was developed by combining the results of the in-person test and the telephone testing to demonstrate the degree of discrimination experienced by equally qualified persons prior to actual employment. On the phone, Blacks were told that the job was closed to them 20% of the time, whereas the job was closed to Whites only 5.5% of the time. In the in-person test, Blacks experienced discrimination in some form in 18.3% of their job contacts. If these figures are translated into the actual chances of having success in the job search, they become even more revealing. Blacks have a 64% chance of getting through a telephone screening, which means that they can secure thirteen interviews out of twenty calls. But their chances of actually getting a job *after* an interview are only about one in twenty. White applicants, on the other hand, are able to pass through screening very successfully, 87% of the time. They can achieve an interview in seventeen out of twenty calls. Out of these seventeen interviews they manage to receive three offers of employment. *The overall Index of Discrimination is therefore 3 to 1.* Whites have three job prospects to every one that Blacks have.

AFTERMATH OF THE STUDY

Who Gets the Work? was one of those relatively rare social science studies that actually had a significant impact on public policy initiatives. It also generated considerable controversy while at the same time providing communities of colour and other disadvantaged groups with the empirical data needed to validate their grievances. Over the dozen or so years since its publication, it has remained one of the most often-cited studies in the literature on racism, ethnicity, multiculturalism, and pluralism in Canadian society. Its citations have not, however, been limited to academic materials, since it has also been frequently referred to by politicians in the federal as well as several provincial parliaments. In its first few years, it was cited at least half a dozen times in the federal parliament alone, and I have since lost count of its continuing usefulness in these political arenas.

Why did this one study generate so much interest, and why does it still continue to resonate? The answer lies in the fact that it was the first, and is still among only a small handful of studies, that actually documents empirically what many people of colour, community organizations, anti-racist groups, human rights advocates, and individual grievers to human rights commissions and others have complained about for years—racial discrimination in employment. Access to employment is a fundamental right in democratic societies, but one that is at times constrained or influenced by irrelevant social factors such as racism, sexism, and the many other factors that severely limit the life chances of people in complex societies. While complaints of racial discrimination by individuals and ethno-racial groups could easily be dismissed because they provide merely "anecdotal" evidence, *Who*

Gets the Work?, using a quasi-experimental methodology, was able to provide the all-important "numbers," which, for the first time, could be used to validate the day-to-day experiences of people of colour.

Moreover, it provided useful information not only for individual grievers but also for community groups and especially for lobby groups, such as the many employment equity organizations and committees that were created in the public and private sectors throughout the eighties and early nineties in all parts of Canada.

Perhaps its most important contribution to policy, however, lies in its impact on legislation. It was published shortly after Abella's (1984) federally commissioned report on employment equity was released. One of that report's key recommendations was employment equity legislation, and a committee of the federal parliament was in the process of preparing that legislation when the results of *Who Gets the Work?* were published. The disadvantaged groups covered by the employment equity legislation were to be women, Aboriginals, and people with disabilities. While the Abella report had also included people of colour as a target group, most politicians at the time believed that their relatively small numbers did not warrant inclusion in the legislation. It was when *Who Gets the Work?* hit the news media and was very widely disseminated throughout the country that the decision to include "visible minorities" in the federal employment equity legislation was made.[1]

A RESTUDY

Further evidence of the importance of *Who Gets the Work?* in the policy arena is provided by the fact that a restudy was commissioned. In the late eighties, the federal government asked the Economic Council of Canada to prepare a report on the benefits and disadvantages of its immigrant

policies.[2] Specifically, it wanted to find out if the numerical levels from the initial study needed adjustment; it was particularly interested in the question of the social integration of immigrants, and especially immigrants of colour. Data on these issues were, and still are, hard to come by in Canada. Accordingly, the Council contracted me to conduct a restudy (see Economic Council of Canada 1991:30ff).

The restudy followed the same research procedure as in the earlier study, except that the employers contacted were, of course, different. The same kinds of jobs were used in the study. A different set of students and actors was employed as job seekers, but they were subjected to exactly the same training and preparation as those who participated in the original study.

Allegedly distinctive about the restudy were the results of the in-person test; twenty Blacks were offered jobs compared with eighteen Whites. The telephone survey results were almost exactly similar to those of the earlier study.

The Economic Council reported on the results of the restudy as follows: "a dramatic change in that no discrimination was discernible in the in-person job offers—an outcome that cannot be accounted for by the tight labour market conditions in 1989 since the employers had the option of hiring Whites." (Economic Council of Canada 1991:30). While acknowledging that racism had not vanished from the job market, the report further stated that "our results do point to a decreasing level of prejudice in Toronto as the visible minority population grows. This reinforces the Council's broad finding that the tolerance of Canadians for immigration generally and for visible minorities in particular is, in fact, increasing" (Economic Council of Canada 1991:31).

I took great exception to the Council's interpretation of the restudy's results since the original report submitted to them provided evidence that the labour market in the late eighties had markedly tightened, and that employers seeking qualified employees were more likely to overlook the factor of race when presented with a competent applicant. Although the Council wanted to publish the report as a research monograph, I refused permission since I felt that they had misinterpreted the results in their monograph.[3]

Subsequently, Reitz and Breton (1994:84) conducted a further analysis of the results in order to counter the Council's interpretation. The research procedure clearly specified that the Black job seekers were to apply for all the jobs before the White applicants. In half the cases in which the Black was given an offer, it was made "on the spot"—that is, before the White even had a chance to apply. When Reitz and Breton removed those cases from the total sample "the results show that more job offers were made to Whites than to Blacks" (1994:84). They conclude that the research procedure may have given the Black applicant an advantage in a tight labour market, thereby offsetting employer bias. Thus, the results of the restudy are basically the same as those of the earlier study, and cannot be taken as evidence of a decrease in racial prejudice or an increase in the tolerance for ethno-racial minorities.

INTERNATIONAL COMPARISONS

My colleagues and I did not invent this quasi-experimental technique of testing for racial discrimination in employment. It had already been successfully used in a study in England conducted in the late seventies that had produced results similar to those obtained in Canada (Smith 1977; see also Reitz 1988). As well, studies were conducted in the U.S. using the same methodology in the early nineties to counteract the mythical belief that the U.S. is "well on the

way to becoming a color-blind society" (Reitz and Breton 1994:85). In the studies conducted by Turner, Fox, and Struyk (1991) in both Washington and Chicago in the 1990s, it was found that Whites also received three times as many job offers as Blacks and they were also three times as likely to be invited for a job interview.

CONCLUSION

The results of our studies clearly indicate that there is very substantial racial discrimination affecting the ability of members of racial minorities to find employment, even when they are well qualified and eager to find work. The studies examined discrimination only at the very early stages, or entry level, of the employment process. Once an applicant is employed, discrimination can still affect opportunities for advancement, job retention, and level of earnings, to say nothing of the quality of work and relationships with co-workers.

The findings also support the results of other types of studies done in Canada. We know that indirect measures of discrimination, such as those that reveal income disparities between Whites and others, all come to similar conclusions: People of colour in this country are discriminated against.

Our studies suggest that discrimination is more widespread than has been thought. Employment discrimination appears not to be the result of a few bigoted employers; there seems to be systematic bias against hiring people of colour. The systemic nature of the discrimination implies that attempting to change the behaviour or the attitudes of individual discriminators will not address the problem. What is required is redress at the system level in order to remove the barriers to the employment of people of colour so that all Canadians, regardless of colour, can achieve to their full potential.

The methodology used in our studies is very useful in providing the quantitative data on racial discrimination that appear to be required for policy decision-making. Thus, studies like *Who Gets the Work?* should be systematically replicated every few years both in the employment area and other areas (such as housing) where discrimination may occur. This would allow us to monitor changing public attitudes toward people of colour.

NOTES

1. "Visible minorities" were also subsequently included in the employment equity legislation enacted in the province of Ontario and since rescinded by the present government.

2. The Economic Council of Canada has since been disbanded.

3. The complete restudy has therefore never been published.

REFERENCES

Abella, Judge Rosalie Silberman 1984. *Equity in Employment: A Royal Commission Report.* Ottawa: Minister of Supply and Services.

Economic Council of Canada 1991. *New Faces in the Crowd: Economic and Social Impacts of Immigration.* Ottawa: Ministry of Supply and Services.

Henry, Frances, and Effie Ginzberg 1985. *Who Gets the Work? A Test of Racial Discrimination in Employment.* Toronto: Urban Alliance on Race Relations and the Social Planning Council of Toronto.

Reitz, Jeffrey G. 1988. "Less racial discrimination in Canada, or simply less racial conflict? Implications of comparisons with Britain." *Canadian Public Policy* 14(4):424–441.

Reitz, Jeffrey G., and Raymond Breton 1994. *The Illusion of Difference: Realities of Ethnicity in Canada and the United States.* Toronto: C.D. Howe Institute.

Smith, David J. 1977. *Racial Discrimination in Britain: The PEP Report.* Hammondsworth: Penguin Books.

Turner, Margery Austin, Michael Fox, and Raymond J. Struyk 1991. *Opportunities Denied, Opportunities Diminished: Discrimination in Hiring.* Washington: Urban Renewal Project.

FIRST NATIONS, INEQUALITY, AND THE LEGACY OF COLONIALISM

Charles R. Menzies

(Revised from the previous edition of this volume.)

INTRODUCTION

... it would not be accurate to assume that even pre-contact existence in the territory was in the least bit idyllic. The plaintiffs' ancestors had no written language, no horses or wheeled vehicles, slavery and starvation was not uncommon, wars with neighbouring peoples were common, and there is no doubt, to quote Hobbes, that Aboriginal life in the territory was, at best, "nasty, brutish and short."

B.C. Supreme Court Chief Justice, Allan McEachern, *Delgamuukw: Reasons for Judgment*, 1991.

Racism is racism, and racism stings. All the good intentions in the world do not take away the sting and do not take away the pain.

Patricia Monture-Angus, *Thunder in My Soul*, 1995.

The First Nations' response to Justice Allan McEachern's decision (quoted above) was angry and tearful. For the First Nations people living in the Gitksan and Wet'suwet'en Territories, the four-year-long court case was about the right to live as they and their ancestors had for millennium upon millennium. From the point of view of the governments of British Columbia and Canada, a large tract of land full of crucial economic resources was at stake and had to be defended. By opening their box of stories and experience to a court, the Gitksan and Wet'suwet'en people, elders, and chiefs had placed their trust in an institution they saw as foreign. In return, they felt that they had been repaid with insult and disdain. While McEachern's decision stands out from recent court rulings and was to a certain extent overturned in appeal,[1] his basic interpretations of First Nations people as having existed without "real" social organization or culture until the arrival of Europeans in the Americas is itself a product of the colonial encounter.

Canada is built upon a colonial system in which Aboriginal lands have been expropriated, Aboriginal institutions banned, and Aboriginal peoples relegated to marginal sectors of the mainstream economy. Put simply:

> Colonialism involves a relationship which leaves one side dependent on the other to define the world. At the individual level, colonialism involves a situation in which one individual is forced to relate to another on terms unilaterally defined by the other. (McCaskill 1983:289)

Five hundred years of European settlement in the Americas is painfully and tragically represented in standard indices of social pathologies such as high rates of suicide, un- and under-employment, and substance abuse. This is not to deny impressive and important examples of successful First Nations people. Rather, it is important to underline the fact that the structure of social inequality experienced by First Nations people is directly linked to the processes of colonialism and government policies directed at undermining Aboriginal institutions and social organization. In this chapter I describe the contemporary structure of inequality, outline the general process of colonialization and expropriation of First Peoples in Canada, and suggest strategies for improving the current situation.

STORIES TO CRY OVER

Social inequality cannot simply be captured in a set of cold, apparently objective numbers (although you will see some numbers below). Think of the everyday stories we tell among friends, in school, or at work. These stories form the basis of our regular communication. They are important sources of knowledge and cultural codes. For the social scientist, these stories are also important places to search out experiences and expressions of inequality. Who is telling the story? Where is it being told? Who is excluded from the audience? We recognize that some stories are not public, that they are in some sense restricted to special places or social settings.

An important part of my writing details the semi-private stories of Euro-Canadian men and the role their storytelling plays in the maintenance of colonial structures.[2] These are emotionally wrenching stories. While one may wish to deny or ignore them, it is more important to listen to these stories. How does it feel to be the target, the butt of the joke, the object of ridicule? A cousin told me, some years after I had given her a copy of *Stories from Home* (Menzies 1994), that the stories of hate I recounted made her cry.

"I know these men, or men just like them. My husband has worked alongside of them. We raised our children in the same community as them. To hear how they talk about us [First Nations people] in your paper still makes me cry," she said. The telling of these stories is important to my cousin, even though they are painful to hear. They reveal, more than any graph, the everyday experience of racism and inequality. Here is a version of a story I first heard while sitting on the deck of a fishing boat one summer afternoon in a northern British Columbia port.

A small gathering of men were relaxing in the quiet time between the end of work and heading up town or home for the night. Ed, a crewmember from an adjacent boat, joined our circle and began to talk about his exploits of the previous evening. He had spent most of his time participating in a 20th-year high school reunion— by all accounts it had been a smashing success.

Ed is a respected member of the local fishing community,[3] an accomplished storyteller, and an effective public speaker (the public here being a group of predominantly Euro-Canadian fishermen). I began to tune out—I'd heard this story before, at least versions of it—drink, party, and drink.... I had almost decided to leave when Ed's story took an unexpected turn.

"Jim had all this paint up at his place, so we loaded it into my car and drove back downtown. Parked off Third, took a look for the cops and then went to it."

"Doing what?" I asked.

"Hey? What do you think we were doing?"

"Painting the town red," somebody said to a chorus of laughs.

"No," said Ed, "we were painting the town white. Yeah, we painted a bloody white cross-walk from the Belmont [Hotel] right into the Empress. Help all those drunken Indians make it across the street."

"I wonder'd who did that when I came down to the boat this morning," I said. "But why is it so jagged? It's crooked."

"That's the beauty of it," said Ed. "It's designed just right. Your Indian stumbles out of the bar, into the street. 'Hey, look, he says, 'a cross-walk.' And he's right over into the other bar. First class."

The irony of Ed's own drunkenness seemed to have escaped him. He plays up a popular explanation of the so-called "Indian problem": the drunken Indian. Yet his story is only one example in a multitude of narratives of colonialism in which the disparate threads of racial superiority and intolerance are wound. Ed's story is part of the day-to-day experience of social inequality felt by people of Aboriginal descent.

THE CONTEMPORARY STRUCTURE OF INEQUALITY

Social scientists typically measure inequality using social indicators such as income level, rate of participation in employment and education, and quality of life measures such as health and housing. To demonstrate inequality objectively, it is necessary to show that significant differences between groups of people do in fact exist. In this section, statistics concerning income, health, and justice are presented. You will notice that although there are some very successful First Nations' individuals (in business, entertainment, politics), many are relatively impoverished when compared with mainstream Canadian society.

Income

Data reported by Indian and Northern Affairs (2000) show significant discrepancies between income levels of First Nations people and those of other Canadians. In 1995, the average individual income for Registered Indians (on- or off-reserve) was 60% of that for other Canadians. In terms of median family income, First Nations families earned about 61% of the national average ($25 602 versus $41 898). Maxim et al. (2001:469–471) report similar results for 1995, using data from the 1996 Census of Canada Public Use Microdata File. Based on the wage and salary incomes of people who had some income, and who were between 18 and 64 years old, these researchers found that, on average, all major categories of Aboriginal Canadians made significantly lower incomes than did non-Aboriginals. The biggest gap was for Registered Indians, who made 62% of the non-Aboriginal average. Inuit earnings were at 65%, Métis at 72%, and non-Registered Indians at 77% of the non-Aboriginal average. Another way to look at income is to examine the data for Low Income Cut-Offs. Almost half of Registered Indian families live at or below the LICOs, compared with about 17% for all Canadian families.

In examining income data one must consider more than just how much people earn. The source of income also provides important information about the structure of inequality. For the majority of Canadians over the age of 15 (Aboriginal and non-Aboriginal), earned income is a major source of income. However, Aboriginal people (especially those on-reserve) receive a higher portion of their income in the form of government transfers. About 77% of all Canadians derive their income from employment. However, only 24% of all Canadians receive the bulk of their income in the form of government transfers, compared with 42% of Aboriginal people. For on-reserve populations, the figures show 55% of the income coming from employment and 45% from government transfers.

Health

Although the basic health of First Nations people has improved over the last several decades, significant differences remain between the health of Aboriginal people and members of mainstream Canadian society (Statistics Canada 1995). Illnesses resulting from poverty, overcrowding, and poor housing have led to chronic and acute respiratory diseases, which take a heavy toll among Aboriginal people. According to the Department of Indian and Northern Affairs (2002), the average age of death for Aboriginals in 2000 had improved considerably but was still 6.3 years below that of the average for non-Aboriginal Canadians. The rate of infant mortality is almost twice the Canadian average (11.6 per 1000 versus 6.1 per 1000). More than 33% of all Aboriginal deaths are related to violence, compared with 8% in Canada generally. These statistics highlight a significant discrepancy between non-Aboriginal and Aboriginal Canadians.

The Law

The interaction between First Nations people and Canadian law occurs at a collective and individual level. Collectively, particular social institutions have been banned or restricted (such as the feast or potlatch system on the Northwest Coast). The right to vote in federal elections was denied to all status Indians until 1960. Between 1927 and 1951 activity related to land claims (e.g., protesting) was illegal (Tennant 1990; Cole and Chaikin 1990). And many Aboriginal children were forcibly removed from their home communities and placed in residential schools (Haig-Brown 1988). The impact of these assimilationist policies on First Nations individuals is clearly seen in the overrepresentation of First Nations people incarcerated in the criminal justice system.

As of 2001, Aboriginal people accounted for slightly less than 3% of the total Canadian population. However, they accounted for 18% of federal and 14% of provincial admissions to prison. In western Canada, the percentage of the in-prison population who are Aboriginal ranged between 20% and 76%, depending on the province (Correctional Services Canada 2001). The ratio of Aboriginal people incarcerated in Canadian jails has been steadily increasing over the course of the twentieth century. In Saskatchewan, for example, the percentage of the prison population of Aboriginal descent has gone from 5% in the 1920s to 76% in 2001 (Correctional Services Canada 2001). In Manitoba, 59% of prisoners are of Aboriginal descent.

Patricia Monture-Angus highlights an important difficulty with this statistical picture: "The overrepresentation of Aboriginal people in the system of Canadian criminal justice is all too often seen as an Aboriginal problem (that is, a problem with Aboriginal people)" (1996:335). In a careful examination of all aspects of the Canadian criminal justice system, Ponting and Kiely conclude that "each stage of the judicial process is punctuated with a disproportionate number of Aboriginal people. [Their data] suggest that Aboriginal people are victims of a discriminatory criminal justice system" (1997:155).

EXPLAINING INEQUALITIES: COLONIALISM'S LEGACY

The socio-economic context of First Nations people is one that is clearly disadvantaged in comparison with mainstream society. Popular explanations of this imbalance of power and resources typically blame the victim. Such explanations fail to take into account the rich, vibrant way of life that pre-existed European arrival in the Americas, or the many examples of individual and community success (more on this below). By focusing on individuals, popular explanations deny the overpowering dominance of European traditions and economic processes that were forced upon Aboriginal peoples. An important and powerful set of explanations roots social inequality in the historical and cultural phenomena of colonialism, the expropriation of First Nations land and resources, and government policies designed to undermine Aboriginal social institutions.

COLONIAL HISTORY: A NORTHWEST COAST ILLUSTRATION

On the northwest coast of British Columbia, people of European and First Nations descent have come together and separated over the years as the result of the historical movement of capital. Initial contact revolved around the exchange of commodities such as fur, iron, beads, or other trade goods.

In British Columbia, a maritime-based fur trade structured the early contacts between Europeans and First Nations (1774–1858). In this period a European-based mercantile capitalism interacted with an indigenous kin-ordered mode of production,[4] in which the control over labour power and the production of trade goods remained under the control of the native American traders who were for the most part "chiefs." They "mobilized their followers and personal contacts to deliver... otter skins, and [their] power grew concomitantly with the development of the trade" (Wolf 1997 [1982]:185). The merging of these two modes of production—one based on the family and one based on European capitalism—produced new wealth and intense inflation for both First Nations and Europeans (Fisher 1977: 8–20, Codere 1961:443–467, Wolf 1997 [1982]:184–192). However, as Europeans prospered from this fur trade and developed industrial enterprises, First Nations people lost control over trade and were displaced by a settler-based industrial capitalism.

As European settlement extended into First Nations territories, marriages between Euro-Canadian businessmen and First Nations women became increasingly common. According to several commentators, these early marriages followed customary First Nations practices and were ostensibly designed to facilitate trade and cooperation between groups (Fisher 1977).

Vancouver Island, and British Columbia more generally, began the change from colonies in which Europeans exploited indigenous labour power to colonies of settlement in the 1850s following the discovery of gold in the interior of the province. With the exception of the fishing industry, First Nations' labour power "was only of marginal significance in the economic concerns of the Europeans" (Fisher 1977:96, 109). Mining, forestry, and fishing supplanted the fur trade and became the backbone of British Columbia's economy.

The extension of industrial capitalism into this region fundamentally altered the basis for alliance. No longer valued as trading partners, First Nations were slotted into the developing resource economy as a subordinate part of the growing industrial labour force in which workers were segregated by race and gender. Union organizers and social activists have attempted, with little success, to overcome these structural divisions.

By the mid-1880s indigenous control of commercially valuable land and resources was almost completely destroyed through a variety of legal (and extra-legal) measures introduced by Canada and the provinces (McDonald 1994). One of the most insidious changes was the creation of the legal category of "food fishing" in the 1880s, which prohibited Aboriginal fishers from catching fish without a permit from the federal government (Newell 1993). At the same time, First Nations people were integrated "into virtually every major resource industry in [British Columbia] as workers and owner-operators" (Knight 1996:10).

Alliances between First Nations and non-Aboriginal resource workers have played a major role in shaping British Columbia's union movement, especially in the fishing industry. Although union organizers have attempted to include them in pan-racial organizations, First Nations workers ultimately found themselves in conflict with many of their Euro-Canadian co-workers. The major point of contention between non-Aboriginal and First Nations resource workers has been the issue of land claims. Despite their common confrontation with capital as workers, non-Aboriginal workers' associations have not been able to develop a united policy on redressing the expropriation of First Nations territories or Euro-centric attacks against First Nations social institutions. While unions have been successful in addressing some aspects of First Nations experiences as workers, they seemed incapable of effectively confronting and overcoming the racism and segregation of twentieth-century industrial society.

ASSIMILATION AND GOVERNMENT POLICIES

Colonialism is not simply an economic process. It also involves social policy and regulation. In Canada, the underlying premise of most twentieth-century social policies directed at Aboriginal people has been assimilation, and the central instrument of assimilationist policy was the residential school. "By taking children away from the old ways and 'civilizing' them into European ways, so the argument ran, 'the Indian problem' would be solved" (Barman 1996:273). However, residential schools did not fulfill their stated goals. Instead, they "served as vehicles for marginalizing generations of young men and women from the Canadian mainstream and from home environments" (Barman 1996:273).

In the early 1900s, attempts were also made to assimilate mobile Aboriginal people by settling them into agricultural communities. From the government point of view, forcing nomadic First Nations people into settlements would allow other instruments of assimilation, such as local government, church, and school, to be more easily brought into effect. Settlement also freed up large tracts of land which could then be developed by non-Aboriginal people.

SUCCESS STORIES

The story of First Nations is not all social pathology and economic disadvantage. First Nations people have maintained a strong sense of their social identity and their place within their traditional territories. On the northwest coast of Canada, for example, First Nations cultural institutions have been maintained despite concerted attacks from missionaries, government offices, and economic interests to dislodge them. The Nisga'a, Tsimshian, Gitksan, and Haida in north-coastal British Columbia have persisted in asserting their Aboriginal rights and title from the moment Europeans first arrived to occupy their land.

Examples of political organization are not restricted to British Columbia. The James Bay Cree, for example, won an important battle against the government of Québec, which guaranteed them their homeland. The Native Women's Association of Canada fought for a redress of sexual discrimination under the *Indian Act* and played an important role in the passage of Bill C-31, which reinstated status to First Nations women (and their children) who had married non-Aboriginals (Frideres 1998).

The Calder case, named after Frank Calder (an important Nisga'a leader and former member of the B.C. legislature for the New Democratic Party), began the legal process in British Columbia that led the way to the important 1995 Agreement in Principle between the Nisga'a, Canada,

and British Columbia. Throughout the 1980s, the Gitksan and Wet'suwet'en people waged a strategic struggle for the recognition of their Aboriginal rights, a struggle that included tactical blockades, legal actions, and economic restraints. Taken together, the concerted political action of First Nations people has forced Canada and non-Aboriginal Canadians to take notice (as witnessed, for example, by the apology to First Peoples in January 1998 by the federal government of Canada).

STRATEGIES FOR THE FUTURE

In *What Is the Indian Problem?*, Noel Dyck cogently argues that "the only way to rectify the ravages that Indian bands have suffered is to stop looking for 'experts' and 'masterplans' and to refuse to accept the presumption that Indians do not know what is in their best interests" (1991:162). Mainstream Canadian society has to accept its collective responsibility for the legacy of colonialism. An important first step is to accelerate the process of treaty negotiations and finally to dismantle the colonial apparatus of the Canadian state.

Self-determination is not a panacea for all the past wrongs. It is, however, an important place to start. But, for self-determination to have any meaningful remedial effect on the experience of First Nations' social inequality, it must be built upon a solid economic and resource base. The 1997 Supreme Court of Canada ruling on the Delgamuukw case (see opening quote) lays the basis for a fundamental change in Canadian law that could vastly improve the economic situation of First Nations. The court found that Aboriginal people have a right to fair compensation for lands expropriated by the Canadian state, that they have a right to use their traditional lands as they see fit, and that their oral traditions should be accorded the same evidentiary weight as written sources in cases concerning Aboriginal rights and title. This decision may well usher in a new era of economic and political cooperation between First Nations and the non-Aboriginal peoples of Canada. At the very least, it can be read as the beginning of a process of national reconciliation in which mainstream Canada finally accepts its complicity in the process of colonialism.

NOTES

1. In 1997, the Supreme Court of Canada decided that Aboriginal rights have not been extinguished and that McEachern's decision was flawed because he did not accept the Gitksan and Wet'suwet'en adaawk (oral history).

2. See, for example, Menzies 1994, 1997.

3. The physical location of this fishing community is not specifically relevant to the main issue of this chapter. Nor does this one man's storytelling necessarily reflect widespread opinion within the larger community.

4. The kin-ordered mode of production is one in which access to and control of labour power is mediated by relations of kinship. For an elaboration of this concept see Wolf (1997 [1982]:88–96).

REFERENCES

Barman, Jean 1996. "Aboriginal education at the crossroads: The legacy of residential schools and the way ahead." In David Alan Long and Olive Patricia Dickason (eds.), *Visions of the Heart: Canadian Aboriginal Issues,* pp. 271–303. Toronto: Harcourt Brace and Company.

Codere, Helen 1961. *Fighting with Property: A Study of Kwakuitl Potlatching and Warfare 1729–1930.* American Ethnological Society Monograph No. 18. New York: J.J. Augustin.

Cole, Douglas, and Ira Chaikin 1990. *An Iron Hand Upon the People.* Vancouver: Douglas & McIntyre.

Correctional Services Canada 2001. Aboriginal Offender Statistics. Retrieved September 3, 2002 (http://www.csc-scc.gc.ca/text/prgrm/correctional/abissues/know/4_e.shtml).

Dyck, Noel 1991. *What Is the Indian Problem? Tutelage and Resistance in Canadian Indian Administration.* St. John's, Newfoundland: ISER, Memorial University of Newfoundland.

Fisher, Robin 1977. *Contact and Conflict: Indian-European Relations in British Columbia, 1774–1890.* Vancouver: University of British Columbia Press.

Frideres, James S. 1998. *Aboriginal Peoples in Canada: Contemporary Conflicts* (5th ed.). Scarborough, Ontario: Prentice Hall Allyn and Bacon Canada.

Haig-Brown, Celia 1988. *Resistance and Renewal: First Nations People's Experiences of the Residential School.* Vancouver: University of British Columbia Press.

Indian and Northern Affairs 2000. *Comparison of Social Conditions, 1991 and 1996.* Catalogue No. R32-163/2000. Retrieved September 3, 2001 (http://www.ainc-inac.gc.ca/pr/sts/hac/socl_e.pdf).

Indian and Northern Affairs Canada 2002. Basic Departmental Data 2001. Catalogue No. R12-712001E. Retrieved September 3, 2001 (http://www.ainc-inac.gc.ca/pr/sts/bdd01/bdd01_e.pdf).

Knight, Rolf 1996. *Indians at Work* (2nd ed.). Vancouver: New Star Books.

Maxim, Paul S., Jerry P. White, Dan Beavon, and Paul C. Whitehead 2001. "Dispersion and polarization of income among Aboriginal and non-Aboriginal Canadians." *Canadian Review of Sociology and Anthropology* 38(4):465–476.

McCaskill, D. 1983. "The urbanization of Indians in Winnipeg, Toronto, Edmonton, and Vancouver: A comparative analysis." *Culture* 1:82–89.

McDonald, James A. 1994. "Social change and the creation of underdevelopment: A northwest coast case." *American Ethnologist* 21(1):152–175.

McEachern, Justice Allen 1991. *Delgamuukw: Reasons for Judgment.* B.C. Supreme Court.

Menzies, Charles R. 1994. "Stories from home: First Nations, land claims, and Euro-Canadians." *American Ethnologist* 21(4): 776–791.

Menzies, Charles R. 1997. "Indian or White? Racial identities in the British Columbian fishing industry." In Anthony Marcus (ed.), *Anthropology for a Small Planet: Culture and Community in a Global Environment*, pp. 110–123. St. James, New York: Brandywine Press.

Monture-Angus, Patricia 1995. *Thunder in My Soul: A Mohawk Woman Speaks*. Halifax: Fernwood Publishing.

Monture-Angus, Patricia 1996. "Lessons in decolonization: Aboriginal overrepresentation in Canadian criminal justice." In David Alan Long and Olive Patricia Dickason (eds.), *Visions of the Heart: Canadian Aboriginal Issues,* pp. 335–354. Toronto: Harcourt Brace and Company.

Newell, Diane 1993. *Tangled Webs of History: Indians and the Law in Canada's Pacific Coast Fisheries*. Toronto: University of Toronto Press

Ponting, J. Rick, and Jerilynn Kiely 1997. "Disempowerment: 'Justice,' racism, and public opinion." In J. Rick Ponting (ed.), *First Nations in Canada: Perspectives on Opportunity, Empowerment, and Self-Determination*, pp. 152–192. Toronto: McGraw-Hill Ryerson.

Statistics Canada 1995. *Profile of Canada's Aboriginal Populations*. Ottawa: Statistics Canada.

Tennant, Paul 1990. *Aboriginal Peoples and Politics: The Indian Land Question in British Columbia, 1849–1989*. Vancouver: University of British Columbia Press.

Wolf, Eric R. 1997 [1982]. *Europe and the People Without History* (2nd ed.). Berkeley: University of California Press.

C h a p t e r

AGE-BASED INEQUALITIES IN CANADIAN SOCIETY

Neil Guppy, James Curtis, and Edward Grabb

(Revised from the previous edition of this volume. Our thanks to Robin Hawkshaw for her research assistance on this paper.)

INTRODUCTION

Age defines many of our rights and privileges. For instance, obtaining a driver's licence before the age of 16 is impossible, and most car rental firms will not lease a vehicle to anyone under 21. As another example, children cannot begin formal public schooling before the age of 5, but once enrolled in school, attendance is mandatory until 16.

Age also shapes certain aspects of our working lives. Provincial wage laws often contain clauses allowing employers to pay lower minimum wages to young workers than to adults. At the age of 65, many employees are required to retire. Both minimum wage provisions and mandatory retirement may seem unfair because one

or two years of age makes little difference to how effectively most people can perform at work. However, just as with the right to drive or go to school, age is used as an automatic trigger affecting both wages and retirement.

In these examples age is used as an inflexible criterion for making decisions about what we can or cannot do. This process, often called "age-grading," can seem very unfair. Determining access to rights and privileges solely based on age, despite individual merit or ability, runs strongly against the premise of equal opportunity and merit-based decision-making. Using chronological age to fix a date in our lives at which point we can (or cannot) be counted on to act reliably or responsibly makes a huge assumption. This presumption applies to a host of formal rights, ranging from voting or running for public office, through to serving in the armed forces or drinking alcoholic beverages.

Sometimes age can be a barrier to rights and privileges, not so much by law but through social convention. In the workplace, for example, mere seniority often takes precedence over performance or merit in determining pay, layoffs, or promotions. Less formally, such activities as leaving home, having children, or investing in retirement savings plans may be constrained by age. This constraint occurs because people come to believe that these and other behaviours typically *should* take place at certain stages in the life course, but not at others.

Whether resulting from legal regulations or social norms, such age-based delineations of human behaviour are primarily social creations. In other words, while aging can be partly understood as a physiological process, it is also a social process. Age, in this latter sense, is used as a socially constructed criterion for classifying and ranking people, a process with significant implications for generating and sustaining patterns of inequality.

AGE, PUBLIC POLICY, AND HUMAN RIGHTS

The *Canadian Charter of Rights and Freedoms* was designed to ensure that all Canadians enjoy equal access to fundamental opportunities and rewards. Equal rights for people of all ages is a key Charter principle:

> Every individual is equal before and under the law and has the right to the equal protection and equal benefit of the law without discrimination and, in particular, without discrimination based on race, national or ethnic origin, colour, religion, sex, age or mental or physical disability. (Section 15.1)

The wording of Section 15.1 suggests that using age to decide the rights and privileges of individual Canadians is discriminatory. How, then, can age be used as an automatic trigger effectively barring someone from obtaining a driving licence at the age of 14 or voting in provincial elections at 15? Similarly, if someone was not hired for a job simply because she/he was too young or too old, this would clearly seem to contravene the Charter, as would forcing someone to quit a job at 65. However, this latter policy of mandatory retirement at the age of 65 is still widely applied because it is believed that under certain conditions age restrictions are justifiable.

Typically, when age-grading determines rights and privileges, the argument is that these practices place *reasonable limits* on people's activity. In obtaining a driver's licence or renting a car, for example, age-grading is justified as a reasonable criterion to invoke by citing the higher accident rates of younger drivers. Age restrictions on buying alcohol are similarly justified. Alcohol consumption impairs judgment, and so restricting access to alcohol for young people is viewed as reasonable.

Unequal access is thought to be justified in these circumstances because the infringement of individual rights and privileges is beneficial for the whole of society. In special circumstances, the rights of the individual are given lower priority than the rights of the community, and this too is reflected in the Canadian Charter, which

> guarantees the rights and freedoms set out [herein] subject only to such *reasonable limits* prescribed by law as can be *demonstrably justified* in a free and democratic society. (Section 1— emphasis added)

For example, although mandatory retirement contravenes the individual wishes of some older workers wanting to work beyond the age of 65, in 1991 the

Supreme Court of Canada ruled that mandatory retirement at 65 is reasonable since it can be justified by the jobs it opens for young workers (see also Guppy 1989; Lowe 1991). With the Canadian population aging, we can expect more challenges to age-related legislation such as mandatory retirement laws (for more information see the Canadian Bar Association Newsletter: Gillan and Klassen 2002).

Notice that of all the categories listed in Section 15.1 of the Charter (e.g., sex, race), age is fundamentally different. Age is the only universal attribute. Aging happens to everyone and, therefore, any age restrictions eventually apply to us all. Unless succumbing to a premature death, all Canadians experience every age category, whereas in our lifetime normally we occupy only one category of sex, race, and so on.

Despite this difference between age and the other attributes listed in Section 15.1 of the Charter, age is, like most of the others, an *ascribed* characteristic. Ascribed characteristics are determined at birth, rather than being chosen or achieved (as is religion or education, for example). Our age is something we cannot change. To the extent that other people use ascribed attributes to make judgments about us, our opportunities and rewards may be diminished (e.g., we are too old or too young to be doing something) or enhanced (e.g., our age is taken to signal maturity or good judgment).

AGE AND DEPENDENCY

Age-grading is also related to dependency (Turner 1988). The judgments others hold of us, or the entitlements others grant to us, depend upon whether we are believed to be responsible citizens, capable of making rational decisions about the welfare of ourselves and others. Ariès (1962 [1960])

has argued that childhood, as a recognizable feature of the life course, only began to emerge in European societies through the late 1600s. Children came to be seen as a group with special needs, especially susceptible to poverty, vagrancy, and social and moral corruption. Various child protection laws were thus enacted to safeguard children.

In contemporary Canada, the debate continues over children's rights. In the Canadian justice system, for example, policy-makers have attempted to grant special rights to young offenders (aged 12 to 17), while also requiring young persons to be accountable for their actions (see the Department of Justice website [www.canada.justice.gc.ca/en/news/nr/2002/doc_29883.html] for a discussion of the new *Youth Criminal Justice Act*).

The elderly, as a group, are also frequently defined as dependent. Partially, this is a consequence of degenerative diseases, such as Alzheimer's, that erode an individual's ability to function independently (see Burke et al. 1997). However, the social arrangements of work and family are also consequential for relations of dependency or independence. As discussed below, retirement and pension arrangements make it difficult for many Canadians, especially women, to support themselves economically in their later years. Many elderly people also find that their traditional support systems (e.g., children, other relatives) no longer live in close enough proximity to provide substantial care.

DIMENSIONS OF ECONOMIC INEQUALITY OVER THE LIFE COURSE

Dependency is common at both ends of the age spectrum. As we mature we gradually acquire more and more individual autonomy until, in our later years, dependency increases again. This ebb and flow in dependency is illustrated by examining how aging relates to various dimensions of inequality.

Figure 22-1 shows the average individual incomes, from all sources, that women and men receive at different periods in their lives. Average incomes increase for men to a peak at the age of 45, declining throughout later life. Women's average incomes are always lower, rising only moderately to about the age of 40, declining to a low plateau between 60 and 65, before rising moderately through their senior years (an increase attributable, in part, to the inheritance of their spouses' assets). The contrasting nature of the two curves for women and men reflects the greater continuity of occupational careers for men and the greater variability of

women's attachment to the labour force (Jones, Marsden, and Tepperman 1990).

Evidence shows that the wages of young workers have declined substantially since the late 1970s. An increased polarization in wage income between high and low earners has been, in part, a consequence of a 15% reduction between 1975 and 1993 in average earnings (adjusted for inflation) of young full-time, full-year workers (Picot and Myles 1996).[1] Furthermore, Betcherman and Morrissette (1994) show that the earnings of young workers have declined across all occupational and industrial sectors and for individuals within all levels of schooling. In particular, this has affected young men (Heisz, Jackson, and Picot 2002). As a consequence of this wage depression for young workers, there has been a greater dependence among young people on the

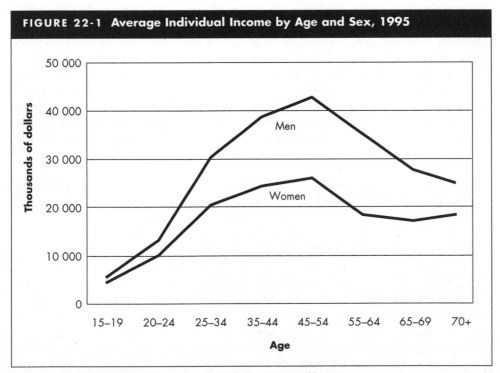

FIGURE 22-1 Average Individual Income by Age and Sex, 1995

Source: Calculated from 1996 Canadian census, total individual income reported by 1995.

welfare state (e.g., on transfer income from welfare and child tax credits).

Annual income is a good indicator of cash flow, but it says little about an individual's net worth or asset holdings. Home ownership is a good measure of the latter since this is the principal source of wealth for most Canadians (Priest 1993). In their early 20s, women and men are still leaving the family home, a pattern reflected by the decreasing percentage of people reporting living in a home that they or their immediate relatives own (see also Boyd and Norris 1995). Women leave home earlier than men, however. This pattern is caused by young women facing tighter family restrictions than young men, restrictions women seek to avoid by leaving home earlier in search of freedom and independence (Mitchell 1992). Starting at about the age of 25, more and more people report living in a family-owned home. Between the ages of 45 and 55, approximately 80% of women and men live in a family-owned home.

For women, the likelihood of remaining in a family-owned home starts to decline at around the age of 55, and drops to below 60% for elderly women. In contrast, both the timing and the decline in living in a family-owned home differ for men. About 80% of men continue living in a family-owned home past the age of 65,

and even as this rate declines among elderly men, the percentage remains substantially higher than for women.

As a consequence of these different arrangements, women are much more likely than men to live their final years in relative isolation from family members, a pattern likely to intensify in the future (Priest 1993). This means that "when men get older and frailer, most of them have built-in housekeepers and nurses—their wives. Women are not so fortunate" (National Council of Welfare 1990).

However, one area in which government social programs have been especially effective is with respect to poverty among the elderly. Many elderly people are still poor. In fact in 1999, 646 000 Canadians over 65 lived in poverty. Nevertheless, that was fewer people than in 1980 (see Table 22-1). Indeed, whereas just over one-third of all seniors lived in poverty in 1980, that percentage dropped to 17.1%, or less than one-fifth, in 1999.

Elderly women are still at much more risk than elderly men. In 1999, 48.5% of all unattached women 65 or older lived below the poverty line (see Table 22-1). Because women live longer than men on average, the older groups contain many unattached women, and unattached people having only one income to rely on have

---

TABLE 22-1   Seniors and Children Living in Poverty, 1980 and 1999

	1980		1999	
	Number	**%**	**Number**	**%**
Seniors (over 65)	742 000	34.0	646 000	17.1
Senior Couples	97 000	17.5	44 000	4.7
Senior Unattached Females	354 000	70.1	417 000	48.5
Senior Unattached Males	109 000	56.7	101 000	31.9
Children (under 18)	1 061 000	15.8	1 313 000	18.7

Source: *The Poverty Profile 1999*, National Council of Welfare. Reproduced with permission of the Minister of Public Works and Government Services, Canada 2002.

higher poverty rates than couples. Not only do many elderly women live alone or in an institution, but they also do so in poverty.

For elderly unattached men, the picture is still bleak, although proportionately not quite so desperate. Almost a third (31.9%) of these men live below the poverty line. Note too that as fewer seniors over time were living in poverty, children became the largest group among the poor. In 1999, 18.7 % or 1 313 000 children were poor, while the poverty rate for seniors fell to 17.7% or 646 000. Especially to the extent that children from poorer families have more difficulty being successful in school, this poverty creates an intergenerational cycle of disadvantage.

INCOME AND THE OLD AGE SECURITY SYSTEM

Why has the poverty rate declined for seniors? After accounting for the effect of inflation, the average income of seniors has risen substantially (22%) from 1981 to 1998 (Health Canada 2002). A variety of government programs for seniors have been of major benefit in raising the incomes of some elderly people.

The basic retirement income system for elderly Canadians works as follows (see also National Council of Welfare 1999; Oderkirk 1996). Virtually all Canadians 65 and over receive taxable Old Age Security (OAS) payments (the maximum annual benefit was $5312 per person in 2002). As well, just under four out of every ten elderly Canadians receive the Guaranteed Income Supplement (GIS), an income-tested[2] benefit designed to help the elderly poor (in January of 2002 the maximum monthly benefit for a single pensioner was $526.08 per month). As well, most provinces provide additional income supplements and special tax breaks for the elderly. However, despite these support

programs, the monies provided are not enough to keep many elderly Canadians out of poverty (see Table 22-1).

In addition to these age-related pension packages, there are two important employment-related components of the elderly income security system. One employment-related component is the Canada Pension Plan/Québec Pension Plan (CPP/QPP), while the other is the private occupational pension plans to which some Canadians subscribe. Since 1966 all Canadians who have been members of the paid labour force, either as employees or self-employed, have been required by law to contribute to the CPP/QPP. Upon retirement a pension equal to 25% of a person's average "pensionable earnings" is paid,[3] to a maximum ceiling of about $9465 annually (Human Resources Development Canada 2001). (By 1997, 76% of women 65 to 69 were receiving CPP/QPP benefits, up from 66% only five years earlier, and 25% had some income from a private pension. Still, the percentage of women receiving pensions was lower than that of men. Ninety-one percent of men were receiving CPP/QPP income, and 51% had private pensions [Statistics Canada 2000]).

CPP/QPP pension income is low for everyone. It is, however, especially low for people who only held labour force jobs intermittently (many women) and for people who earned low incomes even when they did work (again many women, as well as many members of Canada's First Nations community and the disabled population). And, of course, CPP/QPP income is zero for those who never held a labour force job.

Private occupation-based pension plans are also available and some Canadians, especially those in secure management jobs or union members, benefit from these funds as well. However, most employed Canadians are not enrolled in occupational pension plans, and the

TABLE 22-2 Seniors' Income from Private Pensions and Annuities, 1996		
	Women	**Men**
Average Amount	$2696	$7950
% Total Income	17.4	31.3
% Receiving	34.2	57.4
Average/Recipient	$7876	$13 868

Source: Canadian Labour Congress, 1999, *Incomes of Older Canadians.*

percentage enrolled declined for men but increased for women through to 1993. Since 1993, when the number of seniors covered by private pension plans peaked, workplace pension plan coverage has been declining for both men and women. Economic downturns often reduce the benefits, including pensions, that employers offer. Use of short-term contract employees and part-time workers also decreases the contributions to employer-supported pension plans. Table 22-2 shows a comprehensive breakdown of not only the percentage of people receiving income from private pensions but also the dollar amounts. The decline in pension recipients has been marked, and in 1997 only 25% of women and 51% of men received any income from private pension plans.

Although many elderly Canadians continue to live in poverty, there has been recent improvement in the overall picture. This improvement is due in large part to a strengthening of the income security system in the past two decades. Pensions now cover more Canadians (see Figure 22-2) and, since 1971, age-related pension increments have generally kept pace with or bettered inflation. The significance of this trend is that government transfer income now represents a crucial portion of the income that the elderly receive. In fact, in 1997, 65.9% of the income for unattached elderly women, 51.1% of the income for unattached elderly men, and 46.5% of the income for elderly families came as government transfer pay-

ments (National Council of Welfare 1999). The Canadian Council on Social Development tells us that, without transfers from the income security system, in 1998 only 20% of senior households had incomes of over $29 000 per year.

However, as the proportion of Canadians over the age of 65 continues to grow, there is now concern that the income security system for the elderly probably cannot withstand this growth. The Head of Statistics Canada has asked, "can we afford an aging society?" (Fellegi 1988) and has answered affirmatively. Nevertheless, opinions are divided, especially because some projections show that, among industrialized countries, Canada will have one of the highest dependency ratios by the year 2030 (Chawla 1991; Gee and Gutman 2000).

If these projections about the size of the dependent population in Canada are correct, severe pressure will be brought to bear on social benefits. Some argue that "Canadians will most likely have to choose between increasing tax rates and social security contributions or lower levels of social benefits" (Burke 1991:8). However, this too is contested hotly. Myles (1989) argues that the root of the crisis in Old Age Security lies not in the numbers of elderly (what he calls the "demographic imperative"), but in the political alignments between capital and labour in the welfare state. Myles outlines this argument in our next chapter.

FIGURE 22-2 Sources of Income of Seniors, 1998

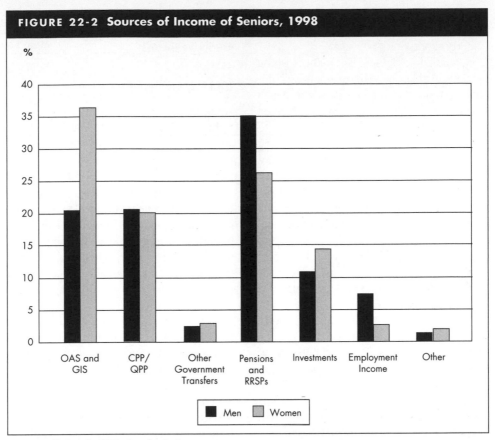

Source: Health Canada, 2001, *Canada's Seniors.*

AGE-BASED CONFLICT AND STRAIN

Age is correlated with the *distribution* of inequality and especially income derived from social programs. Seniors are vulnerable to moving into poverty because of this dependence on government transfers and the fact that many are very close to the poverty line. In addition, though, the privileges and rewards of different age groups are also *relational* in nature. Age-group relations entail issues of intergenerational equity or justice (McDaniel 2001). Mandatory retirement illustrates this relational tension between generations. The 1991 Supreme Court decision ruled that forced retirement was justifiable because

of the opportunities it creates for a younger generation, even though the decision infringes on the rights of some older workers. Tension between generations occurs when the rights and privileges favouring one age group impinge on the opportunities or fortunes of another age group.

Generational disputes can have lasting consequences. The 1960s is one historic period when intergenerational conflict led to significant social change, from policies on the Vietnam War to procedures for student involvement on many college and university committees. More recently, with the growth in the number of elderly Canadians, concern has been focused on another intergenerational trade-off. Can we continue to provide adequate funding for childhood education in the face of escalating medical costs for the care of the elderly (Foot 1996)?

Population aging also induces strain within institutions. For example, institutional strain due to aging occurs in health care. The medical system is oriented more toward treating acute illness (e.g., kidney transplants) than toward coping with chronic ailments. However, medical patients increasingly are elderly Canadians who are much more likely to suffer from chronic ailments (e.g., arthritis) that the system is least able to handle (Myles and Boyd 1988:195–196). Social strain due to age composition also occurs in the workplace when organizations must reduce their size. Tindale (1987) has documented the age-based conflicts among younger and older teachers in Ontario that resulted from the government's decision to reduce the number of teachers in the school system. Seniority, not ability, was used as the criterion to dismiss individuals, and this led to intense struggles across age groups as teachers fought to save their jobs.

However, the extent of age-based conflict must not be exaggerated. Conflict between generations has never been as prominent as have tensions between religious or ethnic groups, for example (see Davis and van den Oever 1981). While there is no denying the existence of intergenerational conflicts within families, allegiances to kin temper these disputes, thereby dampening antagonism, as do rules of inheritance and support.[4] Also, the universal nature of age mentioned earlier means that one cannot maintain a life-long identification with a specific age group. Being a member of an "adolescent gang" all of one's life is impossible. Furthermore, even though teenage "rebellion" frequently occurs, such rebellion only rarely leads to a long-term disintegration of family solidarity. Age-based conflict of a relational nature is thus not as

significant a force in Canadian society as are other conflicts based on different ascriptive factors.

CONCLUSION

Age-grading practices affect our access to rights and opportunities. Age is often an automatic trigger overriding merit or ability in determining the citizenship rights a person can, or cannot, enjoy. Several dimensions of inequality, especially income and home ownership, vary significantly across the age spectrum. The distribution of inequality, we have argued, is related to dependency. This dependency is illustrated most graphically by the number of elderly Canadians who live in, or on the edge of, poverty.

Although the income security system in Canada has improved the economic circumstances of elderly Canadians, substantial numbers of people over the age of 65 still live in poverty. The risk of living in poverty is especially acute for elderly women. Exacerbating the economic misfortunes of many women is the likelihood that they will live alone or in an institution during their final years of life. Even when living in poverty, older men are much more likely to have at least the comfort of a spouse to share the burden of later life.

The ability of taxpayers to support the swelling ranks of the aged has also been noted. Especially if immigration levels are kept low, the proportion of Canadians over the age of 65 will rise substantially in the next few decades. This trend will in turn add pressure to the old-age pension system. The ability of the welfare state to manage this pressure will depend, in part, upon accommodations reached between labour and business (Myles 1989; Denton and Spencer 1999).

We have also briefly noted other issues of intergenerational tension and have reviewed how changes in the age composition of the population can cause strains for the social system. John Myles discusses these latter themes in the next reading when he examines the dynamics of citizenship rights and income security. He explores, in particular, the crisis in Old Age Security.

NOTES

1. Average inflation-adjusted earnings of higher-paid workers have been relatively stable between 1975 and 1993.

2. Whether or not a person receives GIS income depends upon the total amount of income an individual receives. As total income rises, GIS income declines. The GIS was instituted to help the elderly poor. It is significant that 39% of all seniors receive the GIS, and that there is a significant problem of undersubscription (Canada's Association for the Fifty-Plus [CARP] 2001)

3. Numerous technical details influence exact CPP/QPP payments (see National Council of Welfare 1999 for a useful primer). CPP/QPP income is indexed to average lifetime earnings, which means that low-wage earners in the labour force also will be low-pension recipients in retirement.

4. Families can be violent, but frequently such violence is not age-related.

REFERENCES

Ariès, P. 1962 [1960]. *Centuries of Childhood: A Social History of Family Life.* R. Baldick, trans. New York: Alfred A. Knopf.

Baldwin, B., and P. Laliberte 1999. "Incomes of older Canadians: Amounts and sources 1973–1996." Canadian Labour Congress. Retrieved June 30, 2002 (http://www.clc-ctc.ca/policy/pensions/income.pdf).

Betcherman, Gordon, and Rene Morrissette 1994. "Recent youth labour market experiences in Canada." Ottawa: Statistics Canada, Analytic Studies Branch, Research Paper No. 63.

Boyd, Monica, and Doug Norris 1995. "Leaving the nest? *The impact of family structure.*" *Canadian Social Trends* 38 (Autumn):14–17.

Burke, Mary Anne 1991. "Implications of an aging society." *Canadian Social Trends* (Spring):6–8.

Burke, Mary Anne, Joan Lindsay, Ian McDowell, and Gerry Hill 1997. "Dementia among seniors." *Canadian Social Trends* 45 (Summer):24–27.

Canada's Association for the Fifty-Plus (CARP) 2001. "CARP's brief on the 2002 federal budget." October 31. Retrieved July 26, 2002 (http://www.50plus.com/carp/files/budget2k.doc).

Canadian Council on Social Development 1998. "Seniors rely on income security programs." *Insight* 7 (March). Retrieved June 26, 2002 (http://www.ccsd.ca/perception/insite7.htm).

Chawla, Raj 1991. "Dependency ratios." *Canadian Social Trends* (Spring):3–5.

Davis, Kingsley, and P. van den Oever 1981. "Age relations and public policy in advanced industrial societies." *Population and Development Review* 7(1):1–18.

Denton, Frank T., and Byron G. Spencer 1999. "Population Aging and Its Economic Costs: A Survey of the Issues and Evidence." SEDAP Research Paper No. 1. Retrieved July 25, 2000 (http://www.socsci.mcmaster.ca/~sedap/p/sedap1.PDFs).

Department of Justice 2002. "New youth justice law receives royal assent." News release. February 19. Retrieved May 7, 2002 (http://www.canada.justice.gc.ca/en/news/nr/2002/doc_29883.html).

Fellegi, Ivan 1988. "Can we afford an aging society?" *Canadian Economic Observer* (October):4.1–4.34.

Foot, David 1996. *Boom, Bust, and Echo.* Toronto: Macfarlane, Walter, and Ross.

Gee, Ellen M., and Gloria M. Gutman (eds.) 2000. *The Overselling of Population Aging: Apocalyptic Demography, Intergenerational Challenges, and Social Policy.* Toronto: Oxford University Press.

Gillin, C.T., and Thomas R. Klassen 2002. "Rethinking mandatory retirement." CBA

National Constitutional and Human Rights Law Section, April. Retrieved June 24, 2002 (http://www.cba.org/cba/newsletters/const%2D2002/co5.asp).

Guppy, Neil 1989. "The magic of 65: issues and evidence in the mandatory retirement debate." *Canadian Journal on Aging* 8(2): 173–186.

Health Canada 2001. "Canada's seniors." Retrieved June 25, 2002 (http://www.hc-sc.gc.ca/seniors-aines/pubs/factoids_2001/no20_e.htm).

Health Canada 2002. "Canada's aging population." Retrieved June 25, 2002 (http://dsp-psd.communication.gc.ca/Collection/H39-608-2002E.pdf).

Heisz, A., A. Jackson, and G. Picot 2002. "Winners and losers in the labour market of the 1990s." Retrieved June 24, 2002 (http://www.statcan.ca/english/research/11F0019MIE/11F0019MIE2002184.pdf).

Human Resources Development Canada. 2001. "Canada pension plan and old age security benefit rates effective January 2002." News release. Retrieved July 24, 2002 (http://www.hrdc.gc.ca/common/news/isp/011228.shtml).

Jones, Charles, Lorna Marsden, and Lorne Tepperman 1990. *Lives of Their Own: The Individualization of Women's Lives.* Toronto: Oxford University Press.

Lowe, Graham 1991. "Retirement attitudes, plans and behaviour." *Perspectives on Labour and Income* 3(3):8–17.

McDaniel, Susan 2001. "Born at the right time? Gendered generations and webs of entitlement and responsibility." *Canadian Journal of Sociology* 26(2):193–214.

Mitchell, Barbara 1992. "The role of family structure and social capital on the timing and reasons for home-leaving among young adults." Unpublished paper, Anthropology and Sociology. Vancouver: University of British Columbia.

Myles, John 1989. *Old Age in the Welfare State: The Political Economy of Public Pensions.* Lawrence: University Press of Kansas.

Myles, John, and Monica Boyd 1988. "Population aging and the elderly." In D. Forcese and S. Richer (eds.), *Social Issues: Sociological Views of Canada,* pp. 186–204. Toronto: Prentice-Hall.

National Council of Welfare 1990. *Women and Poverty Revisited.* Ottawa: Minister of Supply and Services.

National Council of Welfare 1999. "Pension Primer." Retrieved June 24, 2002 (http://ncwcnbes.net/htmdocument/reportpension-primer/pensionprimer.htm#_chap1).

National Council of Welfare 2002. *The Poverty Profile 1999.* Ottawa: Minister of Public Works and Government Services.

Oderkirk, Jillian 1996. "Government sponsored income security programs for seniors: Old age security." *Canadian Social Trends* 40 (Spring)3–7.

Picot, Garnett, and John Myles 1996. "Children in low-income families." *Canadian Social Trends* 42 (Autumn):15–19.

Priest, Gordon 1993. "Seniors 75+: Living arrangements." *Canadian Social Trends* 30 (Autumn):24–25.

Statistics Canada 2000. "Incomes of younger retired women: The past 30 years." *Perspectives on Labour and Income* 12(4) (Winter). Retrieved June 28, 2002 (http://www.myfinancialsite.com/retirement/news/view_news.php?article_id=1335).

Tindale, Joseph 1987. "Age, seniority and class patterns of job strain." In V. Marshall (ed.), *Aging in Canada: Social Perspectives*, pp. 176–192. Toronto: Fitzhenry and Whiteside.

Turner, Bryan 1988. "Ageing, status politics and sociological theory." *British Journal of Sociology* 40(4):588–606.

DEMOGRAPHY OR DEMOCRACY? THE "CRISIS" OF OLD AGE SECURITY

John Myles

(From *Old Age in the Welfare State: The Political Economy of Public Pensions*, by John Myles, 1989, University Press of Kansas. Reprinted with permission.)

INTRODUCTION

During the decades following World War II, the rapid growth in Old Age Security entitlements in all capitalist democracies was widely hailed as a necessary, indeed inevitable, consequence of industrialization and economic growth. Industrialization, it was thought, had simultaneously rendered the labour of older workers redundant and provided the wealth to make their labour unnecessary. A retirement wage sufficient to permit or induce withdrawal from the labour force in advance of physiological decline could, and should, be made available to all.

In the mid-seventies, however, a contrary view began to take form. According to this revised view, a combination of ris-ing entitlements and an increase in the number of retirees was creating a long-term process bound to self-destruct. In the long run, the Old Age Security systems that were the pride of the post-war state were doomed to collapse under the weight of changing demographic and fiscal realities. The "crisis" of Old Age Security had been discovered (see Myles 1981).

The roots of this crisis are usually attributed to demography: The system of Old Age Security entitlements currently in place in the capitalist democracies simply cannot withstand the projected rise in the number of old people. Wilensky (1975) argued that changing demographic realities gave rise to the modern welfare state; it is now claimed that demography will bring about its demise.

But what is the nature of this demographic imperative? In the pages that follow, I propose that the usual formulation of the demographic argument is, at best, highly misleading. This is not to say that demography is irrelevant to our understanding of the current situation. The size and composition of populations represent real constraints on any national political effort, whether for warfare or for welfare. What is required, however, is identification of the forms of social organization and institutional arrangements that make a particular demographic formation into a "problem." I suggest that to understand the current situation we must situate it within the broader context of the post-war welfare state and the political and economic foundations upon which it was constructed. The current conflict over the future of Old Age Security is a symptom of a larger conflict over the proper role of the democratic state in a market economy. This post-war Keynesian consensus upon which the welfare state was constructed has broken down, with the result that the various social institutions it spawned (including retirement wages for the elderly) have now become the focus of renewed debate and political confrontation. The implication is that the long-term future of Old Age Security—and hence of old age as we now know it—depends less on innovative fiscal management practices than on the eventual political realignments of a post-Keynesian political economy.

POPULATION AGING AND THE CRISIS IN OLD AGE SECURITY

The conventional explanation of the crisis in Old Age Security is a rather straightforward exercise in demographic accounting: The current generation of adults is simply not producing enough children to support it in its old age (Keyfitz 1980). Because of declining fertility, the size of the elderly population will grow to a point where the economic burden on the young will become intolerable. Eventually the demographic bubble will burst, Old Age Security programs will go broke, and an intergenerational "class struggle" will ensue (Davis and van den Oever 1981). To avoid this eventuality, it is argued, people must begin to show restraint now (Clark and Barker 1981). Promises that future generations will be unwilling or unable to keep should not be made to the current generation of workers (Laffer and Ranson 1977). In this scenario, we have a social responsibility to dismantle the welfare state for the sake of our children and grandchildren, who must support us in the future.

Several core assumptions underlie this argument. In this view, old-age pensions are not the product of a wage-setting process mediated by the state, but the product of an implicit social contract made between sequential age cohorts (Friedman 1978). Each cohort agrees to support the preceding cohort, under the assumption that it will receive similar treatment from the cohort that follows. But since age cohorts vary in size, the contract is inherently unstable. Although it is relatively easy to provide generous benefits to a small retired population, providing the same benefits to a very large cohort of retirees may become an intolerable burden (Keyfitz 1980). The result is a conflict between cohorts, leading to dissolution of the contract. It is argued that North Americans can expect such a dissolution when the baby-boom generation retires.

The notion of a social contract between age cohorts is a metaphor intended to enable us to understand and to predict changes in popular support for old-age entitlement programs. The question to be answered is whether the empirical evidence gives any indication that the metaphor is appropriate. Where the conditions specified by the model have been met, it would seem reasonable to expect some evidence of the intergenerational conflict and the resistance to public spending on the elderly that it predicts.

Several Western nations are already quite "old" by demographic standards. The elderly constitute more than 16% of the populations of West Germany, Austria, and Sweden—a figure that is not far from the 18% at which the North American population is expected to peak in the next century. As Heinz and Chiles (1981:iii) observe:

> Western European social security systems have already experienced the impact of population aging for some time now. The Federal Republic of Germany, for example, currently has a ratio of social security contributors to beneficiaries of less than 2:1, which is the level not projected to be reached in the United States until the year 2030, when the postwar baby boom generation reaches old age.

Moreover, the tax burden necessary to finance Old Age Security in these countries has already reached levels that exceed those projected for North America in the next century. Prior to the amendments of 1983 that reduced the projected costs of the program, the tax rate for U.S. Social Security was projected to peak at 20.1% in the year 2035 (Leimer 1979). But by 1978, the effective tax rate to support Old Age Security was already 18% in Germany, 20% in Sweden, 23% in Italy, and 25% in the Netherlands (Torrey and Thompson 1980:43). The experience of these nations, however, provides little evidence of the growing backlash and intergenerational hostility anticipated by the proponents of the conventional view.

Although several countries experienced a "welfare backlash" in the late seventies, Wilensky (1981) has shown that this pattern was unrelated either to the size of the elderly population or to levels of public spending and taxation. Indeed, according to Wilensky's estimates, the very "oldest" of the capitalist democracies (Germany, Austria, Sweden) were among the countries that experienced the least amount of popular resistance to rising welfare expenditures. And informed observers (Ross 1979; Tomasson 1982) generally agree that, despite *official* concern over rising costs, *public support* of Old Age Security systems remains high in these countries.

Moreover, where there has been popular reaction against the growth of public spending, support for the elderly appears to occupy a special place. In 1981, only 11% of Americans under the age of 65 agreed that Social Security benefits should be reduced in the future. And the majority of those under the age of 65 were prepared to accept further tax increases to keep Social Security viable (Employee Benefit Research Institute 1981). Coughlin's (1979) comparative review of public opinion poll data indicates that support for Old Age Security programs is uniformly high and shows little variation from country to country, despite wide differences in the size of elderly populations and in the quality of pension entitlements.

There are some obvious reasons for such widespread support for Old Age Security, even in the face of rising costs. First, familial bonds provide a strong basis for solidarity between generations. In the absence of suitable public provision for the elderly, adults of working age would be required to provide for their aging parents directly. For these individuals, a generous Old Age Security system is not a burden but relief from a burden. Second, those of working age are generally capable of recognizing that they will require similar support in the future. In the long run, they will suffer if the terms of the "contract" are not met.

Less obvious but perhaps more important is the fact that the key claim of the demographic model—that population aging increases the burden of dependency on the working force population—is incorrect. As Table 23-1 demonstrates, population aging has generally been associated with a decline in both total and age-based dependency, because of a decline in the size of the very young population and an increase in female labour-force participation. Canadian and U.S. projections indicate a similar trend for the future. Although the size of the elderly population will continue to grow, total age-dependency ratios will first decline and then slowly rise again to current levels (see Table 23-2). At no point are they projected to reach the levels achieved during the early sixties, the peak of the baby-boom period.

The issue for the future, then, is not the *size* of the dependent population but rather its changing *composition*—fewer children and more retirees. The usual strategy in evaluating this change is to compare *public* expenditures on the old with public expenditures on the young. Since public expenditures on the old amount to approximately three times public expenditures on the young, it is clear that total public expenditures on the non-working population must increase as the population ages. But to assess the true economic impact on the working population, we must evaluate total expenditures on the young and on the old, not just that portion passing through

TABLE 23-1	Age Dependency and Total Economic Dependency, 1959–1979							
	Youth Dependency[a] (ages 0–14)		Old-Age Dependency[a] (ages 65+)		Total Age Dependency[a]		Total Economic Dependency[b]	
	1959	1979	1959	1979	1959	1979	1959	1979
Australia	30.1	25.7	8.5	9.4	38.6	35.1	n.a.	55.0
Austria	21.8	21.1	12.1	15.5	33.9	36.6	51.8	58.5
Belgium	23.3	20.5	11.9	14.3	35.2	34.8	60.2	58.0
Canada	30.3	23.5	7.8	9.3	38.1	32.8	63.6	52.3
Denmark	25.7	21.3	10.4	14.2	36.1	35.5	54.3	47.9
Finland	30.7	20.6	7.1	11.8	37.8	32.4	52.1	51.6
France	26.1	22.6	11.6	14.0	37.7	36.6	56.3	56.9
Germany	21.0	18.9	10.7	15.5	31.7	34.4	52.0	56.9
The Netherlands	30.0	22.9	8.9	11.4	38.9	34.3	63.2	64.8
Norway	26.1	22.6	10.7	14.6	36.8	37.2	59.2	53.1
Sweden	22.8	20.0	11.6	16.1	34.4	36.1	51.4	48.5
Switzerland	24.0	20.1	10.1	13.7	34.1	33.8	54.0	54.9
United Kingdom	23.2	21.5	11.6	14.7	34.8	36.2	52.5	54.9
United States	30.8	22.8	9.1	11.2	39.9	34.0	60.1	52.4

[a] Defined as a percentage of the total population.
[b] Total non-working population as a percentage of the total population.

Source: Organization for Economic Cooperation and Development, *Labour Force Statistics, 1959–70* (Paris: OECD 1972); *Labour Force Statistics, 1968–79* (Paris: OECD 1981).

TABLE 23-2   Projected Age-Dependency Ratios for Canada and the United States

| | Dependency ratios[a] | | |
	Ages 0–17	Age 65+	Total
Canada			
1976	53.5	14.6	68.1
1986	41.9	16.1	58.0
2001	36.7	18.5	55.2
2031	33.3	33.7	67.0
United States			
1976	51.3	18.0	69.3
1985	43.5	19.0	62.5
2000	43.2	19.9	63.1
2025	42.0	29.5	71.5

[a] Dependency is defined as a proportion of the working-age population (population aged 18-64).

Sources: *Canada:* Health and Welfare Canada, *Retirement Age* (Ottawa: Ministry of National Health and Welfare, 1978), p. 17. Reproduced by permission of the Ministry of Supply and Services Canada. *U.S.:* U.S. Bureau of Census, *Current Population Reports*, "Projections of the Population of the United States: 1977–2050" (Washington, D.C.: U.S. Government Printing Office), Series P-25, No. 704.

the public purse. Information on this subject is at best incomplete. Based on the analyses of French demographer Alfred Sauvy (1948), Clark and Spengler (1980:38) conclude that total expenditures on the old exceed those on the young. In contrast, if we accept Wander's (1978) finding that the total cost of raising a child to the age of 20 is one-fourth to one-third *higher* than the total cost of supporting an elderly person from the age of 60 to death, we can expect that total intergenerational transfers (public plus private) will decline as the population ages.

The empirical foundations for the conventional view, then, appear to be rather shaky. Whatever its consequences, population aging does not seem to be a source of rising economic dependency, intergenerational conflict, or popular backlash against welfare-state spending. This does not

mean that the so-called crisis of Old Age Security is all sound and fury—only that we must look elsewhere to understand its nature and origins.

At the most general level, the current controversy over the future of Old Age Security is rooted in the broader economic crisis that has beset the capitalist democracies since the early 1970s. A protracted economic slump (characterized by declining output, rising unemployment, and inflation) brought about a radical reassessment of the post-war welfare state. Rather than a means of reinvigorating capitalism, the welfare state (including the welfare state for the elderly) is now broadly seen by both the left and the right as a fetter on capital accumulation (Gough 1979; Geiger and Geiger 1978). The crisis in Old Age Security is a symptom of this larger crisis of the welfare state.

THE ANATOMY
OF THE CRISIS

As Geiger and Geiger (1978:16) observe, the critical issue raised by the growth of the welfare state is whether or not the market retains enough of its own output to satisfy its requirements. From the viewpoint of the marketplace, the portion of the national product that is administered by the state is "out of control"; that amount is no longer directly available to provide incentives to labour (in the form of wages) or to capital (in the form of profits), nor is it directly available in the form of savings to be used for reinvestment. Access to these resources is mediated by the state. As a result, their distribution is subject to the logic of the political process rather than the logic of the market. The expansion of the public economy increasingly politicizes economic affairs and, by so doing, reverses the great achievement of the bourgeois revolutions of the seventeenth and eighteenth centuries—the removal of the state from the realm of economic decision-making (Piven and Cloward 1982:42).

Under current arrangements for the distribution of income, population aging exacerbates this process. Because increased public expenditures on the elderly are not offset by a corresponding reduction in public expenditures on the young, population aging increases the size of the public economy and reduces the share of national income directly subject to market forces. Thus, although population aging is unlikely to "break the national bank," it *will* alter the bank's structure of ownership and control. McDonald and Carty (1979), for example, estimate that public intergenerational transfers to the old and young in Canada will rise from 12.8% of GNP in 1976 to 17.8% of GNP in the year 2031.

But for whom does the expansion of public control over the distribution of income pose a problem? Any major social transformation is likely to generate conflict between those who stand to lose and those who stand to gain from such change. The trick is to identify the probable winners and losers. It is instructive to ask, then, who stands to benefit and who stands to lose as the result of yet further expansion of the public economy in general, and of the Old Age Security budget in particular. If this question can be answered correctly, we will be in a good position to predict the direction of any conflict that might ensue. More importantly, we will be better able to appreciate the logic of the current controversies and struggles over the future of Old Age Security.

In the past there have been three quite different answers to the question of who benefits from public control over income distribution. Neo-Marxists have argued that the benefits of the welfare state have gone primarily to the owners and managers of capital; "conservatives" (that is, the proponents of classical liberalism) have argued that the welfare state undermines the power of capital; and the post-war liberals have generally claimed that the welfare state benefits both labour and capital. As Piven and Cloward (1982:31) point out, however, there is a growing recognition among analysts of all political persuasions that the conservatives were right—the major consequence of the expansion of the public economy has been to alter the structure of power between capital and labour in favour of the latter. Evidence of this shift is found in the market for labour and in the market for capital.

In the labour market, the citizen's wage enhances the bargaining power of labour both individually and collectively. The effects at the individual level have been recognized for some time in the life-cycle model of earnings and labour supply. According to this model, individual workers make employment and wage decisions (whether to work and at what wage) according to the anticipated impact of such decisions on total lifetime earnings. Universal income entitlements, such as those typically contained in Old Age Security provisions, mean that some portion of each individual's total lifetime earnings is fixed by law. Thus, current decisions to work and at what wage can be made in light of the fact that some amount of future income is assured. This assurance reduces dependency on the labour market and enhances the worker's bargaining position with respect to would-be employers. When good jobs at good wages are not available, individuals may simply choose to withdraw, partially or completely, from the labour force. The "work disincentives" that result from the availability of unemployment, sickness, and old-age entitlements reduce the labour supply and drive up wage levels.

To understand the effects of the citizen's wage at the collective level, we must consider the relationship between unemployment and the bargaining power of labour (Piven and Cloward 1982:19). Under normal conditions, a rise in unemployment leads to a reduction in wages by increasing the supply of unemployed workers and the subsequent competition for available jobs. The citizen's wage increasingly insulates the working class from the reserve army of the unemployed. By absorbing the unemployed, the welfare state also absorbs much of the downward pressure on market wages that an increase in unemployment would otherwise create. Thus, wage levels tend to be higher and profit levels lower than they would otherwise be (see Block 1981:15–17). Old Age Security provisions are very much part of this process. Among the first to be absorbed in periods of rising unemployment are older workers, who join the ranks of the elderly by moving into early retirement (Clark and Barker 1981).

From the point of view of employers, this problem is compounded by the fact that the social-wage bill and the market-wage bill are interactive. Unemployment lowers the market-wage bill but simultaneously triggers an increase in the social-wage bill for unemployment, welfare, and retirement benefits. Regardless of how they are financed, public benefits must ultimately be paid for by current production. Thus, both market wages and social wages must be construed as a cost of doing business. The problem for employers, then, is that the wage bill as a whole (market wages plus social wages) becomes increasingly rigid and insensitive to market forces.

The problems of employers go beyond the obstacles in the labour market. The effects of the public economy also loom large in the capital market. When the owners and managers of capital attempt to borrow finds to invest in new facilities and equipment or to meet temporary cash-flow problems, they find themselves faced with a very powerful competitor for the supply of available savings—namely, the state. Moreover, state borrowing to finance the public economy tends to increase when individual firms can least afford the resulting rise in interest rates. Downturns in the economy produce rising unemployment, a declining tax base, and an increased level of social spending, thereby increasing government deficits and the need for state borrowing. Increased state borrowing, in turn, produces the rising interest rates that many firms in recent years have found prohibitive. In the competition for the available pool of capital, governments hold a decided advantage: The state can afford to pay the higher interest rates because of its powers of taxation, which are unavailable to private firms.

The public economy also affects the amount of capital available for investment purposes. Most national pension schemes are funded on a pay-as-you-go basis—that is, current expenditures (benefits) are paid for out of current revenues (contributions). Such a system is a form of pseudo-savings: wage earners make contributions, but no pool of capital is created. Since these contributions generate income entitlements that can be claimed on retirement, the need for other forms of saving (such as a private pension plan) is reduced. But a shift in pension financing from a pay-as-you-go to a funded basis (as practised in Sweden and Canada) simply compounds the problems of the business community.

As has long been recognized, financing a public pension system on a funded basis results in a significant shift of economic power from the private sector to the state, because the capital pool created from contributions is in the hands of government. In Canada, the funds of the Canada Pension Plan have become the major source of provincial debt financing. The funds of the parallel Québec Pension Plan have also been used to finance a state-directed program of private-sector investment. In the latter part of the seventies, recognition of this situation among the Canadian business class resulted in what came to be called the "great pension debate."

Faced with the obvious inadequacies of Canada's Old Age Security system, Canadian labour proposed, in 1975, to rectify the situation by significantly expanding the Canada Pension Plan. Objections to this proposal had little to do with the need for improvement; and the superiority of the public system over its private-sector counterparts was never seriously questioned. Rather, the principal objection was

that such a change would bring about an increase in government control over capital formation. The editors of the Toronto *Globe and Mail* (October 12, 1977) argued: "Government is already too deep into pension plans—and the savings they represent—for the good of Canada's economic future. We need more savings... but the savings should be in a variety of hands and not subject to the political vagaries of government." As Murphy (1982) has shown, the reasons for this concern are not difficult to identify. During the decade following the Canada Pension Plan legislation of 1965, corporate savings as a means of amassing new investment capital were in decline, and corporations had to turn increasingly to external sources of financing. During the same period, private pension funds grew to become the single largest source of private equity capital in Canada and the major source of corporate borrowing. Expanding the public system further would transfer a significant portion of these savings to the state and, in the words of the *Globe and Mail*, would subject them to the "political vagaries of government." In this way, democratization of the savings and investment process serves to further undermine the power of private capital. Canadian business has made abundantly clear (Business Committee on Pension Policy 1982) its view that the defence of this power must take precedence over the income requirements of the elderly.

CONCLUSION

The real crisis in Old Age Security, then, is an outcome of the adverse effects of the citizen's wage on the power of capital. State intervention to meet social needs created by or not satisfied by the market tends to transform the market itself. When workers, in their capacity as citizens, can claim a social wage that is independent of the sale of their labour power, capitalist social relations are changed. The "mixed economy" that emerges from this transformation is not a happy marriage between complementary principles of social organization but a unity of opposites, a system of tolerated contradictions. Democratic control over wage and capital formation is the antithesis of capitalist control over wage and capital formation; when the one expands, the other must contract. The principal losers are the owners and managers of capital. The result is not an intergenerational class struggle but simply an expression of the traditional struggle between labour and capital. The problem is not one of state control per se but, rather, one of *democratic* control of the state. State policies that assign resources on the basis of need and social equality undermine a system of assignment based on property entitlements and market value. The future of Old Age Security, then, is a problem of democracy, not of demography.

REFERENCES

Block, Fred 1981. "The fiscal crisis of the capitalist state." In R. Turner and J. Short (eds.), pp. 1–27. *Annual Review of Sociology* 7. Palo Alto, California: Annual Reviews.

Business Committee on Pension Policy 1982. *Pension Policy—Issues and Positions: Consensus of the Business Committee on Pension Policy.* Ottawa: Business Committee on Pension Policy.

Clark, Robert, and David Barker 1981. *Reversing the Trend Toward Early Retirement.* Washington, D.C.: American Enterprise Institute.

Clark, Robert, and Joseph Spengler 1980. *The Economics of Individual and Population Aging.* Cambridge: Cambridge University Press.

Coughlin, Richard 1979. "Social policy and ideology: Public opinion in eight rich nations." *Comparative Social Research* 2:1–40.

Davis, Kingsley, and Pietronella van den Oever 1981. "Age relations and public policy in advanced industrial societies." *Population and Development Review* 7 (March):1–18.

Employee Benefit Research Institute 1981. *Louis Harris Survey on the Aged.* Washington, D.C.: Employee Benefit Research Institute.

Friedman, Milton 1978. "Payroll taxes no; general revenues yes." In Colin Campbell (ed.), *Financing Social Security*, pp. 25–30. San Francisco: Institute for Contemporary Studies.

Geiger, Theodore, and Frances M. Geiger 1978. *Welfare and Efficiency. Their Interactions in Western Europe and Implications for International Economic Relations.* London: Macmillan.

Gough, Ian 1979. *The Political Economy of Welfare State.* London: Macmillan.

Heinz, John, and Lawton Chiles (eds.) 1981. "Preface in United States Senate Committee on Aging." *Social Security in Europe: The Impact of an Aging Population*, pp. iii–iv. Washington, D.C.: U.S. Government Printing Office.

Keyfitz, Nathan 1980. "Why social security is in trouble." *The Public Interest* 58:102–119.

Laffer, Arthur, and David Ranson 1977. "A proposal for reforming social security." In G.S. Tolley and Richard V. Burkhauser (eds.), *Income Support for the Aged*, pp. 133–150. Cambridge, Massachusetts: Ballinger.

Leimer, Dean 1979. "Projected rates of return to future social security retirees under alternative benefit structures." In *Social Security Administration Policy Analysis with Social Security Files*, Research Report No. 52, pp. 235–257. Washington, D.C.: U.S. Government Printing Office.

McDonald, Linda, and E. Bower Carty 1979. "Effect of projected population change on expenditures of government." Appendix 16 in *Canadian Government Task Force on Retirement Policy.* Hull, Québec: Canadian Government Publishing Centre.

Murphy, Barbara 1982. *Corporate Capital and the Welfare State: Canadian Business and Public Pension Policy in Canada Since World War II.* M.A. thesis, Carleton University, Ottawa.

Myles, John F. 1981. "The trillion dollar misunderstanding: Social security's real crisis." *Working Papers Magazine* 8(4):22–31.

Piven, Frances F., and Richard A. Cloward 1982. *The New Class War.* New York: Pantheon Books.

Ross, Standford G. 1979. "Social security: A world-wide issue." *Social Security Bulletin* 4-2(8):3–1.

Sauvy, Alfred 1948. "Social and economic consequences of the aging of Western European populations." *Population Studies* 2(1): 115–124.

Tomasson, Richard F. 1982. "Government old age pensions under affluence and austerity: West Germany, Sweden, the Netherlands, and the United States." Paper presented at the meetings of the Tenth World Congress of the International Sociological Association, August, 1982, Mexico City.

Torrey, Barbara, and Carole Thompson 1980. *An International Comparison of Pension Systems.* Washington, D.C.: President's Commission on Pension Policy.

Wander, Hilde 1978. "ZPG now: The lesson from Europe." In Thomas Espenshade and William Serow (eds.), *The Economic Consequences of Slowing Population Growth*, pp. 41–69. New York: Academic Press.

Wilensky, Harold 1975. *The Welfare State and Equality.* Berkeley: University of California Press.

Wilensky, Harold 1981. "Leftism, Catholicism and democratic corporation: The role of political parties in recent welfare state development." In Peter Flora and Arnold Heidenheimer (eds.), *The Development of Welfare States in Europe and America*, pp. 345–382. New Brunswick, New Jersey: Transaction Books.

REGIONAL INEQUALITY: EXPLANATIONS AND POLICY ISSUES

Fred Wien and Catherine Corrigall-Brown

(Revised and abridged from Fred Wien, "Canada's Regions,"
in James Curtis and Lorne Tepperman (eds.), *Understanding
Canadian Society*. Toronto: McGraw-Hill Ryerson, 1988.)

INTRODUCTION

A distinctive feature of being Canadian and living so close to the elephant next door is the continuing puzzle of what makes Canada different from the United States. An important difference between Canada and the United States is the level of overall inequality in the two countries. One measure of inequality is the Gini index, which measures inequality over the entire distribution of income or consumption, with a score of 0 representing perfect equality. Recent data show that the Gini index is 40.8 in the United States, but only 31.5 in Canada (United Nations 2001). However, while inequality in general is more pronounced in the United States, it is also important to understand the nature of inequality within these two countries. One

way in which Canada and the United States differ in their social stratification is in the significance and severity of regional inequalities within each of the countries. A leading student of regional development planning in North America, Benjamin Higgins, says that "there is probably no advanced country where regional disparities play so great a role, economically, socially, and politically, as they do in Canada." He adds that "regional disparities are a pressing problem in Canada; the proportion of the populations of lagging regions living in genuine poverty is higher and the regions designated as retarded much larger than those of the United States" (Higgins 1986:132,160; also see Higgins 1998).

This statement is perhaps not surprising. Canada is vast; there are significant natural and social barriers separating one region from another, and considerable differences in population, resources, and industrial structure as one goes from east to west and north to south. In addition, the overwhelming importance of our links to the United States through trade and investment ties has different implications for different regions.

While regional disparities are important, they do not always occupy a central place in Canada's political concerns. In times of economic expansion, when all regions are registering economic growth, we are likely to hear less about the problem, and this is also the case when important national issues dominate the political agenda. Since the 1960s, governments have sought to alleviate the hardship faced by the unemployed and the poor, and to create conditions of *socio-economic development* on a regionally equitable basis. Optimists hoped that these long-standing problems could be resolved by government intervention.

The current climate is considerably more subdued. After extensive efforts to reduce regional disparities in Canada, the stubborn problem is still not easily amenable to policy solution. Much has been learned, especially about what not to do and how ineffective many policy options have been. Those interested in regional development are undertaking a sober assessment of what has been accomplished and are searching for new solutions. New issues, such as free trade with the United States and Mexico, the rapid movement to a technology-based, post-industrial society, and the changing patterns of the ownership and investment of capital in the world economy, pose new challenges whose implications for regional inequalities are not yet clear. Perhaps the most optimistic thing that can be said is that the discovery and extraction of oil and gas off the east coast, and of diamonds

and other minerals in the Northwest Territories and Nunavut, are providing natural resource jobs and revenues in regions that have not had a lot of good prospects for a long time.

In this chapter, we review the debate on regional inequality in Canada, with appropriate comparisons to the United States. In particular, we examine: What is the extent of regional inequality in Canada? How do social science theorists explain it? What have governments, especially national ones, tried to do about the problem? How successful have these measures been? And what lessons can be drawn from this experience as we look ahead to new issues in this perplexing field?

THE DIMENSIONS OF REGIONAL INEQUALITY

While there is agreement on the importance of regionalism and regional inequality in Canada (e.g., Brodie 1997; Matthews 1980; Skogstad 2000), the definitions of region and regional inequality remain an important problem for assessing changes in inequality over time, and for implementing policy. Successive governments have, in the last few decades, taken quite different interpretations of what constitutes a disadvantaged region for purposes of targeting various policy initiatives; they make their decisions as much on political grounds as on the basis of a rational analysis of pertinent social and economic characteristics.

The issue is as follows. The larger the area encompassed by the term "region," the more likely it is that it will include significant internal variations or disparities. For example, the Western region (Manitoba, Saskatchewan, Alberta, and British Columbia) has some characteristics in common, but also enormous diversities. Similarly, the Atlantic provinces are often lumped together, but the provinces differ considerably in their potential for the development of agriculture, forestry, manufacturing, or energy, for example. On the other hand, if a small, localized area is targeted (for example, a census district or a disadvantaged area within a province), policy solutions may be hindered because the underlying conditions contributing to the problem may require consideration of a broader geographic area. Can the problems of Cape Breton be resolved in isolation from the mainland of Nova Scotia? Can the stagnation of Eastern Ontario be considered outside of the context of the developments centred around Toronto, Ottawa, or Montréal?

In practice, the province is most often used as the unit defining a region, because data are most readily available at the provincial level and less so for municipalities and other units. This is also occasioned by Canada's federal nature and the political and legal/constitutional significance of provincial governments. This is not a perfect definition, however, because of significant inequalities within each province. In Nova Scotia, for example, there are substantial differences in unemployment rates between the metro area of Halifax and the rural areas of the province.

What are some indicators of regional inequality in Canada, using provincial-level data? Typically, economic measures are used and, among these, per-capita income and unemployment rates are most prevalent. Other economic measures often cited reveal the productive capacity of the province (e.g., provincial gross domestic product per person, which measures the value of goods and services produced) and rates of poverty. Other social indicators describe the educational level of the labour force, the health of the population (e.g., infant mortality rates), or living standards (e.g., a crowding index with respect to housing). Some contemporary data measuring regional inequality are found in Table 24-1.

The figures from Table 24-1 show substantial inequalities on all the measures. For example, per-capita income in Newfoundland is only 61% of what it is in Ontario. The unemployment rate and the likelihood of having families or unattached individuals in poverty also vary sharply among the provinces. From these figures, it is obvious that social and economic outcomes of individual and family well-being differ significantly by region. Just as it makes a difference into what family one is born, so too it makes a difference in which region the family resides.

EXPLANATIONS OF REGIONAL INEQUALITY

There are some reasonably clear theoretical interpretations of regional inequality that have been prominent in the last several decades, and we examine three below. Each explains why inequalities exist and each suggests what policies might remedy the situation. The difficulty is that competing explanations suggest strategies that are incompatible with one another, and there is no agreement on which framework is the most appropriate. Many analysts feel none gives a complete explanation, and they pragmatically suggest that some wisdom is found in most, if not all, the alternatives. They may also argue that some explanations are better at explaining the origin of disparities in previous decades, while others are better under contemporary conditions.

Perspectives Emphasizing Regional Deficiencies

Students studying the *underdevelopment* of Third World countries in the 1950s and 1960s became acquainted with the modernization, or development, model. It

TABLE 24-1   Measures of Regional Inequality in Canada, by Province, Recent Years

Province	Personal Income per Capita 1999	Unemployment Rate 2001	Poverty Rate 1998
Newfoundland	18 313	17.0	19.8
Prince Edward Island	19 751	12.4	11.4
Nova Scotia	21 779	10.0	17.9
New Brunswick	21 915	11.4	14.9
Québec	23 749	9.7	22.0
Ontario	30 103	6.9	13.5
Manitoba	24 704	4.7	18.8
Saskatchewan	23 588	6.2	15.7
Alberta	27 264	5.1	14.8
British Columbia	30 480	9.7	14.6
Canada	27 058	8.0	16.4
Disparity Ratio (highest/lowest)	1.66	3.61	1.93

Source: Data adapted in part from the Statistics Canada publications *Income in Canada*, Catalogue 75-202, 1999; and from *Labour Force Information*, Catalogue 71-001, 2001.

suggested important characteristics of the traditional sector in a given country needed to be overcome if development were to proceed. The source of change, as well as the model for development, was the modern, urban, industrial sector of the country. Characterized by technologies based on machine production in large factories, the modernization approach suggested that the relationships, culture, political institutions, and social structures appropriate to modern industrial society would spread from the (modern) centre to the (traditional) periphery. This spread was to be effected primarily by the competition mechanism of the free market, which would destroy or transform the backward enterprises and the traditional characteristics of the groups working in them. Increased mobility of individuals between country and city, mass communications and transportation, formal education, and the

development of a modern state would all serve to disseminate rational, income-maximizing behaviours that would eventually be common to all members of the society.

The development perspective was also applied to explain regional underdevelopment in advanced industrial societies. It was not transferred without modification, however. While it is difficult to speak of development in Latin American countries without dealing with the overwhelming significance of the agriculture sector and the need for land reform, such is not the case in Canada. The debate in Canada also does not dwell particularly on differences in progressive or traditional attitudes, values, and social structures between one part of the country and another.

It is argued, however, that some regions of Canada are underdeveloped because their deficiencies stand in the way of improving their situation in employment and income terms relative to other regions. Several factors have been identified: location in relation to markets and therefore the burden of transportation costs; lower rates of capital investment; shortcomings in infrastructure, such as roads, railways, harbours, sewers, schools, and hospitals; lower levels of investment in education and training of the work force (human capital); inferior managerial quality; and lower levels of investment in new productive technology. Most of these factors contribute to the productivity of industry and thus to income and employment levels in the region.

Analysts proceeding from different theoretical perspectives identify other deficiencies. Keynesian economists, for example, suggest the demand for goods and services in a region may be too low and should be stimulated by government policy. Regional scientists look at the distribution of people in areas. They argue, for example, that growth in income and employment has occurred more rapidly in urban areas than in small towns or rural areas; hence, some regions may be too sparsely populated. Growth centres or development poles need to be encouraged so industries can be located next to each other in an industrial complex and take advantage of complementarities and of large urban markets for goods and services.

Running through much of the mainstream, orthodox approach to regional disparities is a faith in the operation of the free market, characteristic of neo-classical economic perspectives. Here, the deficiencies highlighted are the rigidities and other forms of interference with the market that maintain and exacerbate regional inequalities. As Courchene puts it, regional disparities are to some extent a problem of economic adjustment, a problem of interference with the natural adjustment mechanisms of the economy (Courchene 1986, 1994).

If one were focusing on interregional differences in incomes, the neo-classical approach would assume that, under free market conditions, workers would move from a low-income to a high-income area of the country as they seek to improve their economic situation. Again, however, artificial impediments prevent this "natural" equalization from occurring. If in the poorer region minimum wage rates are high, or if employment insurance payments are generous in the amount paid and the duration, then the incentive to leave the region is correspondingly reduced. The same result occurs if the actions of unions, governments, or corporations keep wages high. As these examples illustrate, the deficiency identified by neo-classical economists is not limited to the disadvantaged area, but is also built into the policies and practices of national governments, unions, or corporations in interaction with the poorer region. Courchene concludes that because the natural adjustment mechanisms of the market are not free to work as they should, provincial governments increasingly depend on federal transfers to sustain themselves, which exacerbates the problem. He suggests the various problems interact—if wages are prevented from moving downward in a poor province, then unemployment remains high. This triggers an influx of federal funds (e.g., for employment insurance). But the more money that flows in, the less incentive there is for the province or region to worry about the adequacy of wage adjustment and factor (labour, capital) mobility. "This is a vicious circle, and it is imperative that it is broken" (Courchene 1986:35; also see Courchene 1994).

The Staples Approach

Staples are "raw or semi-processed materials extracted or grown primarily for export markets and dominating the regional or national economies" (Marchak 1985:674). In view of Canada's historical reliance on staple production and export, it is not surprising that Canadian social scientists would emphasize this factor when explaining regional inequality and national development. The roots of the staples approach trace back to the writings of Mackintosh (1923), Innis (1930; 1940; 1956), and others who examined successive staples, such as furs, cod, square timbers, and wheat, in order to understand their social, political, and economic impacts, and the factors that shaped their development. More contemporary interpretations that attempt to specify the theory more clearly and to delimit its applicability are found in Watkins (1977a, 1977b) and Scott (1978). Watkins, in particular, suggests that staple theory, as elaborated in the earlier writings, only has explanatory value if applied to "new" countries such as Australia, New Zealand, or Canada. These countries historically have had few people in relation to their land and other resources, and few inhibiting traditions.

In this context, it is argued, a region's prosperity depends on the availability and marketability of its natural resources, and the region's success in using the production or extraction of the staple (and the proceeds derived from this) in developing the rest of its economy. In other words, a region will prosper if it has a valued resource that can be profitably marketed abroad, and if it can extend appropriate linkages to other economic sectors (manufacturing, services, etc.) so that they receive a stimulus from the export sector.

There are many conditions under which a given staple can become the engine of economic growth. Simply discovering a valued resource may be the key; or a change in technology or transportation may make it economical to produce a staple that has already been discovered but not exploited. Alternatively, the demand (and price) for a resource may increase, depending on levels of need in importing countries and its availability from other suppliers. In any case, if the conditions are favourable, capital and labour would likely flow into the region to develop and export the staple.

As noted above, whether the exploitation of the staple will benefit the economy of the region as a whole depends on the linkages established. For example, if a lot of equipment is required to extract or produce the staple, and if that equipment can be locally manufactured, then the manufacturing sector will be stimulated. If the natural resource can be processed locally rather than being exported in a raw state, then the regional economy will gain jobs and income. If labour is attracted to the export sector and receives high wages, then a local demand for consumer goods will be created. The region's long-term economic development, therefore, depends on the extent to which the stimulus provided by the exploitation of the staple can be generalized to diversify the economy.

Unfortunately, it is in the nature of staple production that the demand for a given staple, and therefore its price, may eventually decline. Consumer preferences may change, new synthetic alternatives may be found, the resources may be exhausted, production costs may increase, or other regions or countries may take over an established market. If the region has diversified its economy, the decline in the staple exporting sector is less of a problem. Labour and capital freed up in the declining sector can be redeployed to other productive uses. Some migration outside the region can also be expected, depending on factors such as government policy and opportunities elsewhere. It is more likely, however, that dependence on the staple product will continue and there will be a reluctance to adjust to the situation. Attempts may be made to subsidize and protect the declining industry, rather than encourage a search for alternative sources of economic growth. Governments may also seek to retain their population base, rather than encourage migration from the region. Unless a new staple can be found and developed, the region may stagnate and decline.

There are perhaps two additional, important features of staple theory as it has been developed by Canadian political economists. First, the importance of staple production for a region or country is not restricted to its narrowly economic implications. Each staple, including the way its production is organized, leaves its imprint politically, socially, and culturally on the region. For example, the transition in Alberta, from an economy dominated by farming to one dominated by energy production and export, sped up the urbanization trend in the province, encouraged the development of a large managerial/entrepreneurial class, and replaced a populist-agrarian political regime with one responsive to the new urban elite (Mansell 1986). Second, writers such as Innis (1956), Watkins (1977a, 1977b), and Drache (1976) have emphasized the negative implications of a staple economy— notably, the dependence on a foreign industrial centre through market and trade relations that are exploitative and constraining, the periodic crisis and boom/bust periods, and the distortions induced in the economy and society of an area that lacks a diversified, self-reliant, and self-regulated economic base. We will return to this theme when we discuss *dependency* theory in the next section.

Critics of a staples approach often suggest that this perspective provided important insights historically, when regional economies centred on the fur trade, the cod fishery, or wheat growing. They suggest, however, that staple production has receded in importance over time; Buckley (1958) in fact dates the decline of the utility of the approach to as early as 1820. The Economic Council of Canada concludes that "the maturing Canadian economy has reached the point where resources and transportation are no longer, as in the past, the only important determinants of regional variations in the well-being of Canadians, and we now have productive processes that are more complex and utilize natural resources somewhat differently" (1977:8).

Others disagree and continue to use the staples approach when analyzing the impact that staple development has on economies such as those of Alberta (Mansell 1986), British Columbia (Marchak 1983), Newfoundland (Royal Commission 1986) or Canada's North (Berger 1977).

Perspectives Emphasizing Exploitation and Dependence

Dependency theory first appeared in the late 1960s, and generated considerable intellectual excitement because it directly challenged the main tenets of modernization theory (Frank 1972). Articulated primarily by Latin American intellectuals, the approach contains two main arguments. First, dependency theory suggests that underdevelopment is the result of exploitation by capitalist metropolitan centres. Far from being models of modernity to be emulated, the "developed" areas prosper at the expense of the "traditional" societies.

Further, the exploitative relationship between, for example, the United States and Latin America is reproduced within both developed and underdeveloped countries, thus accounting for regional inequality. One early application of the dependency perspective to Canada by A.K. Davis (1971) divided the country into metropolitan areas (e.g., the urban industrial core) and satellite areas (e.g., the North, the West, and Atlantic Canada). Davis argued that the metropolis continuously dominates and exploits the hinterland, but the hinterland groups and interests tend to fight back against their metropolitan exploiters.

The second argument is that underdevelopment occurs when resources are drained from peripheral to central areas. The latter control the terms of trade for products. Thus, raw materials are exported from satellite regions at prices below their true value, and manufactured goods from the central area are sold at exorbitant prices. Banks headquartered in core areas drain the regions of their savings and invest them outside these areas, while labour is attracted to the core when needed, but sent back to the periphery when not needed. Often, the multinational corporation is regarded as the chief agent of exploitation, and the relationship between core and periphery is seen as uniformly negative. In other versions, multinationals located in a peripheral area and producing goods for a local market can be acknowledged as a source of growth and dynamism, since they need to create some internal prosperity in order to sell their consumer goods. However, while some local wealth is generated, substantial losses of capital resources from the area occur through profit remittances, interest payments, and royalties. If the result is not uniform underdevelopment in the peripheral region, it is at best uneven development or dependent development (Cardoso 1972).

Numerous Canadian studies in the dependency tradition emphasize this theme—for example, examinations of the de-industrialization of the Maritimes from 1890 to 1920 and its continuing underdevelopment in the interim (Archibald 1971; Acheson 1977; Forbes 1977; Matthews 1977; House 1981; Bickerton 1990). A similar perspective has been used in studies of agriculture and oil development on the prairies (Fowke 1957, 1968; Pratt 1976; Knuttila and McCrorie 1980) and in examinations of Native-White interactions in the context of resource development in the Canadian North (Watkins 1977b; Kellough 1980; Elias 1975).

If development is externally controlled and exploitative, economic and social distortions will arise in the dependent area. In economic terms, development usually focuses on extracting raw materials according to a timetable dictated by the external interests. The development of an integrated, balanced economy in which local resources are harnessed by local entrepreneurs to meet local needs is hampered by external decision-making and the co-optation of social resources. Here, the dependency theory argument is similar to the more pessimistic version of the staples theory, which suggests that the backward, forward, and final demand linkages that would stimulate the development of a balanced economy do not, in fact, materialize.

In social terms, dependency theory focuses on the class structure of the metropolitan and satellite areas. While different analysts of particular regions or countries will identify various kinds of social class constellations, all analyses identify dominant elites and subordinate labourers in both centre and periphery. Parts of the dominant periphery elite are linked to the centre elite and serve as its agent in the satellite area (Matthews 1980; Dos Santos 1971; Stavenhagen 1974). In the Canadian context, for example, Clement argues that a portion of the economic elite of Canada's peripheral regions has been bought out by Central Canadian and American business interests, and serves those interests in the region (Clement 1983).

Dependency theory as an explanation for regional inequality in Canada has numerous critics. Some question the applicability to the Canadian context of a model articulated initially to explain underdevelopment in the Third World. In contrast to Third World countries, Canada is not generally characterized by low returns for labour (i.e., low wages), low returns for exported resource products, or a large traditional population sector (Marchak 1985). Others have questioned whether the theory has much to add to what has already been articulated, perhaps more appropriately for Canada, by staples theorists such as Innis and Watkins. In many ways, the debate has moved to larger questions and broader perspectives due to dissatisfaction with the rather simplistic dyadic relationships of dependency theory (Friedman and Wayne 1977). Indeed, in the 1970s and 1980s, a good deal of attention was devoted to encapsulating dependency theory (and also staples theory) within the broader Marxist paradigm. (See Veltmeyer 1979; Naylor 1975; Clement 1975, 1977; Niosi 1978, 1981; Brym and Sacouman 1979.)

PUBLIC POLICY MEASURES

While regional issues are of ongoing importance in Canada, perhaps the earliest policies explicitly directed to alleviating regional disparities were the measures undertaken to counter the drought and Depression experienced by Canada's regions in the 1930s. World War II intervened and shifted attention to the need for mobilization in support of the war effort, and to national reconstruction when the war ended. Economic prosperity lasting until the mid-1950s kept regional inequalities off the national agenda.

In more recent decades, however, regional disparities have been a more important consideration in government policy. In part, this has been due to less favourable economic circumstances during certain periods, and, in part, it has been due to a more interventionist approach by governments in resolving social and economic problems. Perceptions of the issue also changed with the growing recognition that the relative gap between regions was the important consideration, and not their absolute level of poverty or well-being, or their current rates of economic growth or stagnation.

In examining the policies pursued, one is struck by the variety of measures implemented and by the frequent changes in approach. There are myriad policies designed to promote regional development or reduce disparities, and all three levels of government are active in the field. And while some policies are clearly and explicitly directed at the problem, others have only indirect implications, while still others are not directed at the problem at all, and end up frustrating the intent and effect of the more explicit approaches.

There is considerable and frequent change in policies, in part because regional development policies are important for voter support. Thus, each successive government wants to put its stamp on regional development efforts. The approaches change, as well, because conditions change—policies appropriate during a period of economic growth may be inappropriate in a period of decline.

What is the source of regional development policy? One source is the theoretical perspectives outlined in the previous section, each suggesting certain policies consistent with the analysis presented. Political concerns also influence regional policy. A good example is the 1970s shift in resources and attention designed to counteract separatist sentiment in Québec.

Following are the major kinds of initiatives that have been undertaken by the federal government—sometimes in cooperation with the provinces and sometimes unilaterally:

1. Investments in infrastructure such as roads, harbours, schools, hospitals, wharves, and railroads.

2. Human capital investments and personal adjustment. Here the emphasis is on providing education, training, and mobility grants for those unemployed people who wish to change careers or move to an area that offers better opportunities.

3. Policies of industrial assistance. These have included tax exemptions, tax credits, loan guarantees, or cash grants to individual firms to encourage them to locate in a depressed area. The same measures have been used to help new firms get started or to help existing firms expand, diversify, or export more of their products. Much debate has taken place about the effectiveness of industrial assistance policies. They have been criticized for supporting capital-intensive (rather than employment-intensive) establishments, and for attracting "footloose" industries to a region—that is, firms with few backward and forward linkages and with little commitment to staying in their new location.

4. Policies directed to resource and sectoral development. The federal government, under its Department of Regional Economic Expansion in the 1970s, and more recently under other auspices, has signed general development agreements with the provinces. The agreements have provided federal financial support for the development of forestry, agriculture, or tourism. In the early 1980s, attention was given to stimulating the economy through investments in energy-sector mega-projects such as the extraction of coal in British Columbia and oil in Alberta. In the late 1990s, major new oil and natural gas developments off the east coast also attracted government support.

5. Compensatory and transfer policies. By far the greatest amount of federal money in support of the provinces and their residents is spent not for explicit development policies, but as cash transfers to the provinces and to individual citizens or families. Equalization grants, funds for hospitals, medicare, and post-secondary education, as well as payments for employment insurance and family allowances, make up the bulk of these transfers. They greatly overshadow the budgets of the explicit regional development programs mentioned above (Lithwick 1986). The grants to the provinces have made the provincial governments of the poorer regions very dependent on federal transfers for their total spending budget. The dependence of individuals on personal transfer income is also substantial in the poorer provinces and is growing over time.

Because of the importance of federal transfer payments for understanding regional development in Canada, we should consider some of the ways in which these programs have changed over time. Before 1977–1978, the federal and provincial governments participated in a principle of 50:50 sharing of the costs of health care, post-secondary education, employment insurance, and other programs. Subsequently, however, the federal government became concerned with the escalating costs of the programs that were administered by the provinces. For this reason, from 1972 to 1977, there was a transition to what is referred to as block funding, a program in which funding assistance comes in one lump sum and is not designated for specific uses.

From 1977 to 1995, the federal government transferred money to the provinces through Established Program Financing (EPF) with block funding. Faced with cutbacks and, therefore, the need for flexibility, the provinces and territories agreed in 1977 to have health care and post-secondary education funding assistance come in block funds as opposed to funding intended for particular programs. The period after 1997 saw the EPF system replaced with Canadian Health and Social Assistance Transfers (CHST). This new CHST system encompassed both the old EPF as well as Canada Assistance Plan (CAP) transfers. CAP transfers were used to provide income assistance to Canadians in need. During this period, the CHST to the provinces dropped significantly. For example, in 1994–1995, federal transfers to the provinces for EPF and CAP totalled $18.7 billion. This number fell to $12.5 billion in CHST transfers in 1998–1999 (Finance Canada Official Estimates, Statistics Canada 1999). The 1999 and 2000 federal budgets saw a partial restoration of the CHST and the institution of one-time transfers. This, however, has not restored transfer payments to their original levels.

There has been an evolution in the policies designed to stimulate regional development. These policies have been pursued within several organizational frameworks. In the late 1950s and for much of the 1960s, discrete policies, such as the Federal Fund for Rural Economic Development, were administered by a variety of departments. The Trudeau administration, beginning in 1969, tried to consolidate all relevant programs under the newly created Department of Regional Economic Expansion (DREE). DREE was disbanded in 1982, however, in favour of an approach that provides for a federal co-ordinator's office in each region and the consideration of regional implications by Cabinet for all economic policies, not just those explicitly directed to regional development.

The current structure of regional development policy dates from 1987, when the federal Progressive Conservative government created four new joint federal-provincial agencies to deal with issues of regional inequality. First, the Atlantic Canada Opportunities Agency (ACOA) was made responsible for co-ordinating economic development in Atlantic Canada; acting as an advocate of the region in the development of national economic policy; aiding in the establishment, expansion, and modernization of small- and medium-sized enterprises; funding programs to provide employment replacements for the declining fishery; and promoting government cooperation with private-sector institutions. The second agency was the Federal Office of Regional Development–Québec (FORD–Q), which defined the overall direction of regional policy in Québec, and negotiated intergovernmental agreements designed to assist the long-term economic development of Québec regions with low incomes, slow economic growth, or high unemployment. Third, the Federal Economic Development Initiative in Northern Ontario (Fed Nor) funded research and development, business creation, expansion, and modernization in Northern Ontario. Finally, Western Economic Diversification Canada (WD) sought to move the Western economy away from traditional natural resource-based activities, gave repayable contributions to business and specific sectors or activities that were risky or innovative, and created partnerships with business to help Western Canadian businesses obtain federal contracts (Skogstad 2000). Beginning in 1993, the Liberal government in Ottawa championed greater decentralization and a larger role for the provinces in determining regional development programs as ways to improve federal-provincial relations and to avoid duplication.

As noted above, however, regional development policy is only one aspect of federal policy. Other policies, whether intended or not, also have regional consequences. In fact, one theoretical approach to the explanation of regional inequalities focuses on broader areas such as those governing tariffs, trade, transportation costs, and fiscal and monetary policy. Building on the work of Fowke (1952), writers in this tradition advance the argument that a given set of national policies is successful for only a limited period of time. Then international conditions change, internal political pressures build up, and the search is on for a new set of national policies, one that will set the economy on a new path of development (Brodie 1997).

In this view, the political economy of Canada has been characterized by three sets of national policies: the first lasting from 1867 to the 1940s, the second from World War II to the 1970s, and the third in the past three decades. While the intent of such policies is to find a new formula for promoting national economic growth, in fact they have had uneven impacts on the regions. In the present era, for example, when the emphasis is on free trade agreements, market-driven development, and a reduced role for the state, there is less room to sustain regional development and equalization policies of the kind described above. Success in the new economy is likely to be linked to how well different regions can integrate into the continental and global market. Some regions, such as British Columbia with its access to

the Pacific Rim, are likely to be more successful in this venture than others, as long as the Asian economies remain healthy (Brodie 1997).

THE PERSISTENCE OF REGIONAL DISPARITIES

There is widespread agreement among experts in regional development on the main conclusions to be drawn about trends in the extent of regional disparities in Canada. First, in per-capita income—one of the main measures usually employed to measure regional inequality—the gap between the richest and the poorest provinces has decreased over time. Table 24-2 shows that the poorest provinces improved their relative per-capita incomes from 1961 to 1999. For example, Newfoundland and Prince Edward Island went from under 60% of the national average in 1961 to 68% and 73% respectively in 1999. However, the data show some decline between 1996 and 1999. The richer provinces, Ontario, Alberta, and British Columbia, have experienced a slight decrease or remained stable in relation to the national average. In most provinces, there has been considerable improvement in relative per-capita incomes over the period.

Second, Table 24-3 shows that much of the improvement can be attributed to transfer payments, such as employment insurance, family allowances, old age security, payments under the Canada Assistance Plan, and so forth. When these kinds of compensatory transfers to individuals and families are excluded from per-capita income, as they are in Table 24-3, the improvement in relative per-capita incomes is usually rather small. Put another way, the attack on regional inequality has resulted in greater equity in the country as a result of transfers from the richer provinces to the poorer ones (via the

TABLE 24-2	Personal Income per Capita, by Province, 1961–1999 (Relative to the National Average, Canada = 100)					
Province	**1961**	**1971**	**1980**	**1990**	**1996**	**1999**
Newfoundland	58.2	63.6	64.0	71.4	79.2	67.7
Prince Edward Island	58.8	63.7	71.0	73.6	82.5	73.0
Nova Scotia	77.5	77.4	79.1	81.8	84.2	80.5
New Brunswick	67.8	72.2	71.1	76.9	82.9	81.0
Québec	90.1	88.8	94.5	92.7	94.8	87.8
Ontario	118.3	117.0	107.0	113.4	105.4	111.3
Manitoba	94.3	94.0	89.5	86.8	94.4	91.3
Saskatchewan	70.8	80.3	91.0	80.2	92.1	87.2
Alberta	100.0	98.9	111.6	99.0	103.7	100.8
British Columbia	114.9	109.0	111.3	101.0	105.2	112.6
Canada	100.0	100.0	100.0	100.0	100.0	100.0
Disparity Ratio (highest/lowest)	2.03	1.84	1.74	1.59	1.34	1.66

Sources: Adapted from Polese (1987) with data adapted in part from the Statistics Canada publications *National Income and Expenditure Accounts, Annual Estimates,* Catalogue 13-201, 1991; *Provincial Economic Accounts, Annual Estimates,* Catalogue 13-213, 1996; and from *Income in Canada,* Catalogue 75-202, 1999.

TABLE 24-3	Earned Income per Capita, by Province, 1966–1999 (Relative to the National Average, Canada = 100)						
Province	**1966**	**1971**	**1976**	**1981**	**1986**	**1990**	**1999**
Newfoundland	52.6	54.8	56.1	53.4	57.2	58.9	54.0
Prince Edward Island	53.6	57.0	60.2	59.0	66.1	65.4	63.6
Nova Scotia	71.5	74.2	74.2	73.4	79.3	77.5	74.2
New Brunswick	65.1	68.1	69.0	64.9	70.1	70.5	72.4
Québec	89.2	87.8	90.4	89.9	90.4	90.2	84.5
Ontario	118.3	119.2	112.5	110.6	114.3	117.2	113.7
Manitoba	91.0	93.7	93.9	92.9	89.6	84.5	86.5
Saskatchewan	92.3	78.7	99.5	98.9	86.5	76.6	82.0
Alberta	99.0	98.6	105.0	114.4	106.3	100.9	104.8
British Columbia	111.0	109.5	109.5	109.7	99.4	101.5	116.9
Canada	100.0	100.0	100.0	100.0	100.0	100.0	100.0
Disparity Ratio (highest/lowest)	2.25	2.17	2.00	2.14	2.00	1.98	2.16

Sources: Adapted from the Statistics Canada publications *Provincial Economic Accounts, Annual Estimates,* Catalogue 13-213, and from *Income in Canada,* Catalogue 75-202, 1999.

TABLE 24-4	**Provincial Unemployment Rate, by Province, 1966–2001** **(Relative to the National Average, Canada = 100)**							
Province	1966	1971	1976	1981	1986	1991	1996	2001
Newfoundland	171	135	189	186	208	178	201	213
Prince Edward Island	–	–	135	150	140	163	152	155
Nova Scotia	138	113	134	134	140	116	130	125
New Brunswick	156	98	155	154	150	123	121	143
Québec	121	118	123	137	115	115	122	121
Ontario	76	87	87	87	73	93	93	86
Manitoba	82	92	66	79	80	85	77	59
Saskatchewan	44	56	55	61	80	71	68	78
Alberta	74	92	56	50	102	79	73	64
British Columbia	135	116	121	88	131	96	92	121
Canada	100.0	100.0	100.0	100.0	100.0	100.0	100.0	100.0
Disparity Ratio (highest/lowest)	3.88	2.41	3.43	3.72	2.85	2.50	2.96	3.61

Source: Adapted from the Statistics Canada publication *The Labour Force*, Catalogue 71-001, 1966–1996, 2001.

federal treasury), but it has not significantly improved the productive capacity of the poorer regions, which would enable them to generate higher earned incomes relative to the national average on the basis of their own productive resources.

Similarly discouraging data are provided in Table 24-4, which gives the results for unemployment rates, another common measure of regional disparity. We see increased disparity between 1971 and 1981, reduced disparity in the subsequent decade, and then again increased inequality between 1991 and 2001 as the extremes moved further apart.

Although it is important to examine the economic indicators of regional inequality, it is also important to study its social indicators. Because inequality can manifest itself in many ways external to the economy, such as in the social and political spheres of life, an examination of these domains will provide additional insight into the patterns of regional inequality in Canada. One social indicator

of regional inequality is education level. By examining average provincial education levels, it can be seen that those provinces considered "have-not" provinces display not only economic disadvantages, but also lower general levels of education. Compared with the more prosperous provinces, we find that larger proportions of the population in these provinces have attained less than high school graduation and lower proportions of the population have completed postsecondary education (see Table 24-5).

An examination of the health indicators of inequality, particularly life expectancy, reveals that those provinces that are the most disadvantaged economically also have the populations that tend to have the shortest life expectancies. This is the case even though, in theory, health care is universally accessible in all provinces. Infant mortality rates, however, are an interesting anomaly. Although we might expect these rates to be highest in the Atlantic provinces, for example, we find

TABLE 24-5	Social Indicators of Regional Inequality, by Province, Recent Years					
	Education, 1997			Health, 1997		
Province	Less Than High School	High School Graduate	Completed Post-Secondary	Infant Mortality (per 1000)	Life Expectancy (Male)	(Female)
Newfoundland	59.2	19.4	21.4	5.2	74.5	80.0
Prince Edward Island	44.4	26.7	28.9	4.4	n.a.	n.a.
Nova Scotia	45.1	19.3	35.6	4.4	75.0	80.6
New Brunswick	48.4	25.2	26.4	5.7	75.2	81.2
Québec	50.4	19.4	30.1	5.6	74.9	81.2
Ontario	37.7	30.7	31.5	5.5	76.3	81.5
Manitoba	45.8	24.6	29.6	7.5	75.5	80.6
Saskatchewan	46.8	28.1	25.2	8.9	75.7	81.5
Alberta	28.1	36.0	35.9	4.8	76.4	81.5
British Columbia	31.7	33.8	34.5	4.7	76.5	82.1
Canada	44.3	26.3	29.4	5.5	75.8	81.4
Disparity Ratio (highest/lowest)	2.11	1.87	1.68	2.02	1.03	1.03

Source: Adapted in part from the Statistics Canada publication *Report on the Demographic Situation in Canada*, Catalogue 91-209, 2000.

that the Atlantic provinces, particularly Prince Edward Island and Nova Scotia, have relatively low infant mortality rates, even lower than the rates for the economically advantaged provinces, such as Ontario, Alberta, and British Columbia. This evidence suggests that, while it is clear that certain regions are disadvantaged in many economic and social domains, this is not an all-encompassing trend and there can be interesting and important deviations from this overall tendency.

We began this chapter by suggesting that regional inequality was a substantial and persisting problem in Canada, which made it unusual among advanced industrial (or post-industrial) societies. We are, perhaps, in a somewhat better position now to assess the similarities and differences between the experiences of Canada and the United States in order to gain a comparative perspective on the issue of regional inequality.

Geography's influence is important. While Canada has significant natural resources, the United States has the added advantage of a wide dispersion of good agricultural land, mineral resources, and forests. The American population is also more evenly distributed and its urban centres are more balanced in size and location at various points along the coast and in the interior. By contrast, much of the Canadian population is concentrated in the Toronto to Montréal corridor, as is the preponderance of Canada's manufacturing capacity and financial institutions. The greater concentration in Canada is explained not only by the advantages of a central location to serve the more peripheral areas of the country, but also because most foreign (especially American) investment is located in southern Ontario, close to the major American markets and American head offices. Thus, the overwhelming importance of the United States in trade and investment exerts its influence on the regional distribution of productive resources and population in Canada (Semple 1987). The United States has no similar relationship to a foreign power. Many different centres relate to a number of international contexts: Boston/New York, which is on the Atlantic and related to Europe; Miami, which is in the south and is oriented to Latin America; Los Angeles and San Francisco, which are on the Pacific coast and oriented to Asia; and so forth. In addition, regional centres in the interior provide urban focal points for their surrounding areas: St. Louis, Minneapolis-St. Paul, and Chicago, to name a few. Canada is also much more dependent on resource exports and is therefore more subject than the United States to the distortions, uncertainties, and pitfalls that this kind of economic development brings, as the staples and dependency theorists have described.

Another significant difference between Canada and the United States is the cultural make-up and distribution of the two populations. In Canada, the large concentration of the French-speaking population in Québec and adjacent areas overlaps with regional disparities. In the United States, the significant ethnic and racial minorities are not concentrated in one area. Higgins (1986) argues that the United States has had an extraordinary mobility of labour and capital, and that this has helped to even out regional disparities. The attachment of Canadians to their cultural communities is said to have reduced mobility.

As a result of these factors, regional disparities are less significant in the United States, and less entrenched. Significant reductions in regional disparities have taken place over the long term, and in the short run some regions decline (as New England did in the 1970s), while others grow rapidly (as did the so-called Sunbelt in the same period). The intractable problems of localized underdevelopment seem more associated with the problems of decay, neglect, and exploitation of core areas within large urban centres than with large geographic regions. In the urban context, however, racial and ethnic divisions often overlap with areas of underdevelopment.

It is also important to note that regional inequality in both Canada and the United States is not solely represented by examining inter-provincial differences. We must also consider the inequalities within provinces that arise from urban-rural differences. As noted earlier, Davis (1971) describes the Canadian experience as a tension between metropolis and hinterland, which can be seen to characterize the relationships both between and within provinces. Social policies have tended to reinforce metropolis-hinterland power imbalances and inequalities, so much so that some authors refer to areas of northern and rural Canada as a domestic Third World (see Graham et. al. 2000).

One measure of inequality within regions is average family income. The general trend is that, with increased community size, there is an increase in average family income within each region. For example, in Canada as a whole, families living in rural areas earned only 87% of the total average income for Canadian families, whereas families in urban areas with over 100 000 people earned 107% of the national average. This relationship can be generally seen in all regions of Canada (Statistics Canada, Catalogue No. 13-207, April 1999). Similarly, average levels of education tend to be highest in the largest cities (Juteau 2000).

There are many reasons why urban-rural inequalities arise. First, corporate and economic power resides primarily within large cities, where head offices are situated. Firms, especially in the expanding service sector, are more likely to locate in urban areas close to large markets and adjacent to other firms. Political power is also concentrated in large urban centres, especially in provincial and federal capital cities. Finally, ideological power is centred in urban areas in a number of ways. This is illustrated in the concentration of mass media organizations—the major newspapers, television and radio networks, publishing companies, etc.—and in the centres of higher learning and research, represented in major universities and institutes.

CONCLUSION

The stability of regional inequality patterns in Canada is impressive, perhaps more so than the changes caused by more than thirty years of concerted effort (e.g., Polese 1987; Brodie 1997). This is not to say that the policy measures undertaken have failed, since there is improvement on some measures and because the situation could have worsened without these measures.

Also, much has been learned in the process. For example, it is now clear that transferring funds to provincial governments and to families and individuals reduces inequalities in regional per-capita incomes, and is defensible on equity grounds. The debate continues about whether these transfers have a negative effect on the economic development of the region by interfering with the adaptive processes, as Courchene (1986, 1994) maintains.

The key issue is clearer now than it was before: how to bring about self-sustaining, indigenous economic development in the disadvantaged regions. How should or can a region overcome locational disadvantages, resource shortages, or external dependencies? A good deal of searching and experimenting is taking place. In the Atlantic region, for example, there is considerable interest in community-based economic development—setting up nonprofit community development agencies that rely on local initiatives and external support to promote economic and social development (MacLeod 1986). Consistent with this trend, there is concern that regional development policy has been too narrowly focused on economic measures and has neglected necessary and complementary community development initiatives. Provincial governments have charted plans for the economic development of their provinces, e.g., in Nova Scotia through a policy of "building competitiveness," and in Newfoundland through "building on our strengths" (Royal Commission on Employment and Unemployment 1986). And significant changes have taken place in the private sector as the trend toward the consolidation of ownership in the hands of a few local families continues in provinces such as New Brunswick.

In addition, the federal government has retreated from regional development issues—in budget terms because of restrained spending; in ideological terms as renewed faith is placed in the workings of the market; in priority terms as national issues such as health care reform, the war on terrorism, and the implications of free trade and globalization dominate the agenda; and in political terms, by conceding to provincial demands for more control over regional projects.

Thus, the future of Canada's disadvantaged regions will also be shaped by events and trends impinging on the regions from outside, as well as by internal dynamics. For example, there has been considerable debate surrounding the issue of how the North American Free Trade Agreement (NAFTA) of 1994 will affect Canada's regions and regional politics. Three main ways have been noted. First, the relative success of the regions increasingly depends on how they integrate into continental and global markets, rather than the national market. Second, there is concern about the de-industrialization of Ontario after the implementation of NAFTA's precursor, the Free Trade Agreement (FTA) of 1989. Brodie concludes that the Canadian economy has very much "lost its centre" (1997:257). Some provinces, such as those in Atlantic Canada, are increasingly rationalizing their health and education systems as well as their procurement policies on regional, as opposed to provincial, bases. Finally, NAFTA further constrains the capacity of the federal government to deal with issues of regional inequality, because the federal government must conform to international trade rules under the agreement before it can address the concerns of the Canadian regions.

The shift to an information-based economy, signalled by the continued growth of the service sector and the increased significance of knowledge-based industries, also provides both opportunities and problems. The trend is potentially positive for disadvantaged regions in that the new technology could overcome some locational and natural resource disadvantages (Macrae 1986). There are questions, however, about the speed of adoption of new technology in disadvantaged regions, and about limitations on the size of markets and urban centres, among other considerations (Lesser 1987; Osberg, Wien, and Grude 1995). The study of regional inequality is therefore at a turning point in that the perspectives and policies that have been prevalent for many years are increasingly being questioned, especially with respect to their results and usefulness in dealing with present and future issues.

REFERENCES

Acheson, T.W. 1977. "The Maritimes and 'Empire Canada.'" In D.J. Bercuson (ed.), *Canada and the Burden of Unity*. Toronto: Macmillan.

Archibald, Bruce 1971. "Atlantic regional underdevelopment and socialism." In L. LaPierre et al. (eds.), *Essays on the Left*. Toronto: McClelland and Stewart.

Berger, Justice Thomas R. 1977. *Northern Frontier, Northern Homeland: The Report of the Mackenzie Valley Pipeline Inquiry*. Ottawa: Supply and Services Canada.

Bickerton, James 1990. *Nova Scotia, Ottawa, and the Politics of Regional Development*. Toronto: University of Toronto Press.

Boudeville, J.R. 1968. *Problems of Regional Economic Planning*. Edinburgh: Edinburgh University Press.

Brodie, Janine 1997. "The new political economy of regions." In Wallace Clement (ed.), *Understanding Canada: Building on the New Canadian Political Economy*. Montréal and Kingston: McGill-Queen's University Press.

Brym, Robert, and James Sacouman (eds.) 1979. *Underdevelopment and Social Movements in Atlantic Canada*. Toronto: New Hogtown Press.

Buckley, Kenneth 1958. "The role of staple industries in Canada's economic development." *Journal of Economic History* 18 (December):439–450.

Cardoso, Fernando 1972. "Dependency and development in Latin America." *New Left Review* 74 (14) (July–August):83–95.

Clement, Wallace 1975. *The Canadian Corporate Elite*. Toronto: McClelland and Stewart.

Clement, Wallace 1977. *Continental Corporate Power: Economic Linkages Between Canada and the United States*. Toronto: McClelland and Stewart.

Clement, Wallace 1983. *Class, Power, and Poverty: Essays on Canadian Society*. Toronto: Methuen.

Courchene, Thomas 1986. "Avenues of adjustment: The transfer system and regional disparities." In Roger Savoie (ed.), *The Canadian Economy: A Regional Perspective*. Toronto: Methuen.

Courchene, Thomas 1994. *Social Canada in the Millennium: Reform Imperatives and Restructuring Principles.* Ottawa: Renouf Publishing.

Davis, A.K. 1971. "Canadian society and history as hinterland versus metropolis." In R.J. Ossenberg (ed.), *Canadian Society: Pluralism, Change and Conflict.* Scarborough, Ontario: Prentice Hall.

Department of Development 1984. *Building Competitiveness: The White Paper on Economic Development in Nova Scotia.* Halifax: Government of Nova Scotia.

Dos Santos, Theotonio 1971. "The structure of dependence." In K.T. Fann and D.C. Hodges (eds.), *Readings in U.S. Imperialism.* Boston: Porter Sargent.

Drache, Daniel 1976. "Rediscovering Canadian political economy." *Journal of Canadian Studies* 11(3) (August):3–18.

Economic Council of Canada 1977. *Living Together: A Study of Regional Disparities.* Ottawa: Supply and Services Canada.

Elias, Peter 1975. *Metropolis and Hinterland in Northern Manitoba.* Winnipeg: The Manitoba Museum of Man and Nature.

Forbes, Ernest 1977. "Misguided symmetry: The destruction of regional transportation policy for the Maritimes." In D.J. Bercusson (ed.), *Canada and the Burden of Unity.* Toronto: Macmillan.

Fowke, Vernon 1952. "The national policy—old and new." *Canadian Journal of Economics and Political Science* 18(3) (August): 271–286.

Fowke, Vernon 1957. *The National Policy and the Wheat Economy.* Toronto: University of Toronto Press.

Fowke, Vernon 1968. "Political economy and the Canadian wheat grower." In Norman Ward and Duff Spafford (eds.), *Politics in Saskatchewan.* Toronto: Longmans Canada.

Frank, Andre Gunder 1972. "Sociology of development and underdevelopment of sociology." In James Cockcroft et al. (eds.), *Dependence and Underdevelopment: Latin America's Political Economy.* New York: Doubleday.

Friedman, Harriet, and Jack Wayne 1977. "Dependency theory: A critique." *Canadian Journal of Sociology* 2(4) (Winter):399–416.

Graham, John R., Karen J. Swift, and Roger Delaney 2000. *Canadian Social Policy: An Introduction.* Scarborough, Ontario: Prentice Hall Allyn and Bacon.

Higgins, Benjamin 1959. *Economic Development: Principles, Problems, and Policies.* New York: W.W. Norton.

Higgins, Benjamin 1986. "Regional development planning: The state of the art in North America." In Donald Savoie (ed.), *The Canadian Economy: A Regional Perspective.* Toronto: Methuen.

Higgins, Benjamin 1998. *Employment Without Inflation.* New Brunswick, New Jersey: Transaction Publishers.

House, Douglas 1981. "Big oil and small communities in Coastal Labrador: The local dynamics of dependency." *Canadian Review of Sociology and Anthropology* 18(4) (November):433–452.

Innis, Harold 1930. *The Fur Trade in Canada.* Toronto: University of Toronto Press.

Innis, Harold 1940. *The Cod Fisheries.* Toronto: University of Toronto Press.

Innis, Harold 1956. *Essays in Canadian Economic History.* Mary Q. Innis (ed.). Toronto: University of Toronto Press.

Isard, Walter 1975. *Introduction to Regional Science.* Englewood Cliffs, New Jersey: Prentice Hall.

Juteau, Danielle 2000. "Patterns of social differentiation in Canada: Understanding their dynamics and bridging the gaps." *Canadian Public Policy/Analyse de Politiques* XXXVI Supplement (2):S95–S107.

Kellough, Gail 1980. "From colonialism to economic imperialism." In J. Harp and J. Hofley (eds.), *Structured Inequality in Canada.* Scarborough, Ontario: Prentice Hall.

Knuttila, K.M., and J.N. McCrorie 1980. "National policy and prairie agrarian development: A reassessment." *Canadian Review of Sociology and Anthropology* 17(3) (August):263–272.

Lesser, Barry 1987. "Regional development: Some thoughts arising from a review of research sponsored by the Institute for Research on Public Policy." In William Coffey and Mario Polese (eds.), *Still Living Together: Recent Trends and Future Directions in Canadian Regional Development.* Montréal: The Institute for Research on Public Policy.

Lithwick, Harvey (ed.) 1978. *Regional Economic Policy: The Canadian Experience.* Toronto: McGraw-Hill Ryerson.

Lithwick, Harvey 1986. "Regional policy: The embodiment of contradictions." In Donald Savoie (ed.), *The Canadian Economy: A Regional Perspective.* Toronto: Methuen.

Mackintosh, W.A. 1923. "Economic factors in Canadian history." *Canadian Historical Review* IV(1) (March):12–25.

MacLeod, Greg 1986. *New Age Business: Community Corporations That Work.* Ottawa: The Canadian Council on Social Development.

Macrae, Norman 1986. "A forecast of what the knowledge-based society will bring." Presentation to the Symposium on the Revolution in Knowledge: Atlantic Canada's Future in the Information Economy. Halifax: Dalhousie University.

Mansell, Robert 1986. "Energy policy, prices and rents: Implications for regional growth and development." In William Coffey and Mario Polese (eds.), *Still Living Together: Recent Trends and Future Directions in Canadian Regional Development.* Montréal: The Institute for Research on Public Policy.

Marchak, Patricia 1983. *Green Gold: The Forest Industry in British Columbia.* Vancouver: The University of British Columbia Press.

Marchak, Patricia 1985. "Canadian political economy." *Canadian Review of Sociology and Anthropology* 22(5) (December): 673–709.

Matthews, Ralph 1977. "Canadian regional development strategy: A dependency theory perspective." *Plan Canada* 17(2):131–43.

Matthews, Ralph 1980. "The significance and explanation of regional differences in Canada: Towards a Canadian sociology." *Journal of Canadian Studies* 15(2):43–61.

Meire, Gerald M. 1984. *Leading Issues in Economic Development* (4th ed.). New York: Oxford University Press.

National Council of Welfare Reports 1998. *Poverty Profile 1998.* Ottawa: Minister of Public Works and Government Services.

Naylor, Tom 1975. *The History of Canadian Business* (Vols. 1 and 2). Toronto: Lorimer.

Niosi, Jorge 1978. *The Economy of Canada.* Montréal: Black Rose Books.

Niosi, Jorge 1981. *Canadian Capitalism.* Robert Chodos (trans.). Toronto: Lorimer.

Osberg, L., F. Wien, and J. Grude 1995. *Vanishing Jobs: Canada's Changing Workplaces.* Toronto: Lorimer.

Pinchin, Hugh 1986. "A framework for assessing the impact of free trade in North America." In W. Shipman (ed.), *Trade and Investment Across the Northeast Boundary: Québec, the Atlantic Provinces, and New England.* Montréal: Institute for Research on Public Policy.

Polese, Mario 1987. "Patterns of regional economic development in Canada: Long term trends and issues." In William Coffey and Mario Polese (eds.), *Still Living Together: Recent Trends and Future Directions in Canadian Regional Development.* Montréal: The Institute for Research on Public Policy.

Poschmann, Finn 1998. "Where the money goes: The distribution of taxes and benefits in Canada." C. D. Howe Institute *Commentary* 105 (April).

Pratt, Larry 1976. *The Tar Sands.* Edmonton: Hurtig Publishers.

Ross, David, Katherine J. Scott, and Peter J. Smith 2000. *The Canadian Fact Book on Poverty.* Ottawa: Canadian Council on Social Development.

Ross, David, and Peter Usher 1986. *From the Roots Up: Economic Development as if Community Mattered.* Croton-on-Hudson, New York: Bootstrap Press.

Royal Commission on Employment and Unemployment 1986. *Building on Our Strengths.* St. John's, Newfoundland: Queen's Printer.

Savoie, Donald 1986a. "Introduction: Regional development in Canada." In *The Canadian*

Economy: A Regional Perspective. Toronto: Methuen.

Savoie, Donald 1986b. "Defining regional disparities." In *The Canadian Economy: A Regional Perspective.* Toronto: Methuen.

Savoie, Donald 1986c. *Regional Economic Development: Canada's Search for Solutions.* Toronto: University of Toronto Press.

Scott, A.D. 1978. "Policy for declining regions: A theoretical approach." In H. Lithwick (ed.), *Regional Economic Policy: The Canadian Experience.* Toronto: McGraw-Hill Ryerson.

Semple, R. Keith 1987. "Regional analysis of corporate decision making within the Canadian economy." In William Coffey and Mario Polese (eds.), *Still Living Together: Recent Trends and Future Directions in Canadian Regional Development.* Montréal: The Institute for Research on Public Policy.

Skogstad, Grace 2000. "Regional development policy." In Dietmar Braun (ed.), *Public Policy and Federalism.* Burlington, Vermont: Ashgate.

Stavenhagen, Rodolfo 1974. "The future of Latin America: Between underdevelopment and revolution." *Latin American Perspectives* 9(1) (Spring):124–148.

United Nations 2001. "Human development report." United Nations Development Program. Retrieved May 2002 (http://www.undp.org/ hdr2001/indicator/index.html).

Veltmeyer, Henry 1979. "The capitalist underdevelopment of Atlantic Canada." In R.J. Brym and R.J. Sacouman (eds.), *Underdevelopment and Social Movements in Atlantic Canada.* Toronto: New Hogtown Press.

Watkins, Mel 1963. "A staple theory of economic growth." *Canadian Journal of Economics and Political Science* 29(May):141–158.

Watkins, Mel 1977a. "The staple theory revisited." *Journal of Canadian Studies* 12 (Winter):83–95.

Watkins, Mel 1977b. *Dene Nation—The Colony Within.* Toronto: University of Toronto Press.

Watson, William 1987. "The regional consequences of free(r) trade with the United States." In William Coffey and Mario Polese (eds.), *Still Living Together: Recent Trends and Future Directions in Canadian Regional Development.* Montréal: The Institute for Research on Public Policy.

FISCAL FEDERALISM AND QUÉBEC SEPARATISM

Kenneth G. Stewart

(Revised from Kenneth G. Stewart, "Fiscal federalism
and Québec separatism." *Policy Options* June 1997,
pp. 30–33. Reprinted with permission.)

INTRODUCTION

To the English Canadian mind Québec is
an enigma, the reasons for Québec's dissatisfaction with the country a bewildering
puzzle. Is it not the case that existing constitutional and legislative arrangements
provide the province with virtually complete autonomy in the areas of language
and culture, and with great independence
in many other areas as well, including
immigration? Should it be necessary to
effectively bribe the province to remain
within Confederation, the bribes taking the
form of federal largesse in a multiplicity of
programs ranging from dairy quotas to
equalization payments? In their longstanding rejection of any option involving outright separation of the province, do not
Québecers themselves recognize the historical symbiotic unity of the nation and
the essential role that Québec plays in creating a uniquely Canadian culture? How
does one reconcile this with widespread
support for political leaders committed to
separation, to a point that includes the election of openly separatist governments in
1976, 1981, and 1994, the election to fifty-
three of seventy-five federal seats members advocating separation in some form,
and a 49.6% vote in the last referendum in
favour of pursuing a separatist agenda?

FISCAL FEDERALISM

The thesis of this essay is that the emergence of separatism in the last three decades is related to Canada's system of fiscal federalism. Prior to 1957 the fiscal responsibilities of Canada and the provinces were divided along lines such that, to a very large extent, those who were taxed were in turn the beneficiaries of that taxation. In 1957 the government of Louis St. Laurent introduced a system of equalization payments from well-off provinces to poorer provinces, having the laudable objective of equalizing the public services available to all Canadians. This was followed, in the 1960s and early 1970s, by the establishment and expansion of a variety of cost-shared and other social programs. These fall into essentially two categories: federal transfers to individuals, and transfers from the federal government to the provincial governments. The most important examples of the former are employment insurance and pensions; the latter consist primarily of transfers associated with the financing of health, education, and welfare.

These programs were created in a historically unique spirit of generosity and social progress of which Canadians have rightly been proud. At the same time they have had two noteworthy consequences that were not anticipated. The first is that the financing of these programs has given rise to one of the highest debt levels in the industrialized west, second only to Italy among the G-7 countries, and a comparatively high tax burden.

The second noteworthy consequence is that this system of fiscal federalism has led to vast cross-subsidies between individuals and regions that have served to undermine the economic and political foundations of the country in a way that is only now coming to be fully appreciated.

The erosion of the economic foundations of the country, particularly in the areas of government expenditure and finance, is now well documented. As just one example, Employment Insurance (EI) (formerly Unemployment Insurance, or UI), generates cross-subsidies not only between individuals and regions but also across industries. Because seasonal industries are subsidized at the expense of non-seasonal ones, workers have been attracted to low-skill seasonal employment. In addition to resulting in a self-propagating expansion of EI payments, there has been an artificial inducement for excessive numbers of workers to enter low-skill industries, which cannot, ultimately, support them. When the natural resource base upon which the industry depends is exhausted, as has happened in the east coast fishery and may be close to occurring in the west, large numbers of low-skill workers are left to demand compensation. By this process, the coastal communities of Atlantic Canada have been reduced in a generation from proud self-reliance to embittering and pitiable dependence on handouts from the rest of the country.

The many problems with EI specifically, and with Canada's patchwork quilt of income security programs generally, have been well known for many years. The 1986 report of the Newfoundland Royal Commission on Employment and Unemployment noted that "[t]he income security system as a whole, in Canada and in Newfoundland as a province of Canada, was never designed rationally to serve a set of well-defined goals..." and further found that the EI system "... undermines the intrinsic value of work..., undermines good working habits and discipline..., undermines the importance of education..., is a disincentive to work..., undermines personal and community initiatives..., discourages self-employment and

TABLE 25-1   Net Federal–Provincial Transfers, Fiscal Year 1991–92

Province	Total ($ millions)	Per Capita ($)
Newfoundland	881	1 536
Prince Edward Island	189	1 446
Nova Scotia	698	775
New Brunswick	907	1 249
Québec	2 984	436
Ontario	–5 015	–506
Manitoba	762	697
Saskatchewan	388	390
Alberta	–809	–321
British Columbia	–986	–306

Source: T. Courchene, 1994, *Social Canada in the Millennium*, Table 17. Toronto: C.D. Howe Institute.

small-scale enterprise..., encourages political patronage..., distorts the efforts of local development groups..., [and]... has become a bureaucratic nightmare."

These are the reasons the 1986 report of the federal Commission of Inquiry on Unemployment Insurance concluded that "... a fundamental transformation of the design of the program and of the structure of the organization was essential." Yet a decade later the essentials of the system remain much as originally conceived. Instead of being willing to use the experience of the past thirty years to recognize the weaknesses in Canada's social programs and revise them accordingly, there is a tendency to view the original 1960s conception of these programs as a sacred trust to be defended at all costs.

Less well understood is the erosion of the nation's political foundations that has taken place during this time as a result of Canada's system of cross-subsidies. Direct transfers of funds from the federal to the provincial governments are associated primarily with three program categories: Established Programs Financing of health care and post-secondary education; the Canada Assistance Plan for the financing of welfare; and the equalization payments referred to earlier. Thomas Courchene of Queen's University has computed the net transfers arising from these programs; his figures are reproduced in Table 25-1. They indicate that, as intended, these payments have the effect of transferring income from the "have" provinces of Ontario, Alberta, and British Columbia, to the remaining seven provinces. In per-capita terms, by far the greatest beneficiaries are the four Atlantic provinces; however, their populations are small—in total, no more than one-third that of either Québec or Ontario. In contrast, although its net per-capita transfers are relatively modest, due to its population, by far the single greatest beneficiary of Canada's system of fiscal federalism is Québec.

Very much the same pattern is revealed if we consider recent data on equalization payments, which account for the vast majority of the transfer funds flowing from the more prosperous to the less prosperous provinces. Estimates for 2000–2001 show that Québec received about $4.49 billion under this arrangement. The amounts distributed to the Atlantic provinces were $1.22 billion for

Nova Scotia, $1.13 billion for New Brunswick, $1.04 billion for Newfoundland, and $236 million for Prince Edward Island. Manitoba received $1.07 billion and Saskatchewan $315 million. The "have" provinces—Ontario, Alberta, and British Columbia—received no payments under this plan, but, on the contrary, were net contributors to the equalization fund (see Tress and Perry 2000: Table 8.2.)

In regions that are beneficiaries of the system, two effects are notable. The first is a natural tendency to resent the system. Dependency breeds contempt for those upon whom one is dependent. Sometimes this resentment takes the form of denial that one is a net receiver of transfers; at other times it takes the form of claiming that the subsidies are entitlements having some objective historical basis. The other side is the resentment of the system by those who pay the bills, a resentment that has developed rapidly in recent years as the inequities and perverse incentives of the system become more apparent.

Paradoxically, the second notable effect on the receiving provinces is to attempt, where possible, to negotiate an expansion of the system and an increase in the payment flows. The Atlantic provinces, Manitoba, and Saskatchewan—because their populations are relatively small—are limited in their ability to do this. There is only one province that both benefits from the system and has a large enough population to give it the political clout to negotiate in earnest for an increase in the benefits it receives: That province is Québec.

Negotiations, of course, can take a variety of forms, and often it is in one's interest to negotiate in a way that does not reveal ultimate objectives. In addition to negotiating within a given set of rules, one may seek to change the rules so as to improve one's negotiating power. In doing this, it is unwise to motivate the proposed rule changes in these terms; instead it is preferable to cite other pretexts, such as historical, cultural, or linguistic grievances, real or invented. At times good negotiation may take the form of engaging in brinkmanship and aggressive rhetoric which cites injustices of the past, of which there are always some to be found.

It is important that these observations not obscure the objectives of the current Québec leadership, which undeniably seeks separation. Why would such a leadership be elected to power by a populace that, for the most part, does not share that goal? For the same reason that I might elect firebrand Marxists to the executive of my union local even if I believe that Marxism is nonsense; I may simply believe that they will be the best negotiators.

Canada's system of equalization and transfer payments, and federal sponsorship of other social programs such as employment insurance, were originally conceived in part as a unifying influence. Instead, by creating vast cross-subsidization between regions, which decouples the benefits of expenditure from the costs of taxation, they have had exactly the opposite effect of balkanizing east and west and serving as a propellant to separatism. Just as employment insurance and welfare sometimes have an economic effect on individuals contrary to that which was originally intended, so too has fiscal federalism had unanticipated political consequences.

The parallel I have drawn between these political and economic effects extends in another disturbing direction. In the same way that Canada seems stuck in a 1960s time warp in trying to deal with the economic consequences of fiscal federalism, a similar myopia seems to pervade its political consequences. Instead of seeing the system as an incentive which incites Québec to ever higher levels of political brinkmanship, modifications to the constitutional rules governing its negotiation that favour the province are proposed as a solution. The history of the past three decades shows just what to expect of all attempts to buy off Québec in this way; in any system of cross-subsidies the political action will always come to revolve around the nature and magnitude of the subsidies, and regardless of what specifics are negotiated there will always be demands for increased subsidies.

CONCLUSION

The solution to Canada's political and economic problems requires a fundamental rethinking of fiscal federalism in a way that resurrects the principle that, at least at the margin, those who benefit from public programs should also bear their cost. This will not, of course, end separatism among some elements of Québec society: That will always be present in some form. But it would reduce the incentive of the Québec populace to elect leaders who are then in a position to advance their own separatist agenda. Canadians must ask themselves what kind of country it will ultimately be easier for Québec to leave: a financially sound Canada, or a dissipated one?

REFERENCES

Commission of Inquiry on Unemployment Insurance 1986. Ottawa: Government of Canada.

Royal Commission on Employment and Unemployment 1986. *Building on Our Strengths.* St. John's, Newfoundland: Queen's Printer.

Tress, Karen, and David B. Perry 2000. *Finances of the Nation.* Toronto: Canadian Tax Foundation.

FURTHER REFERENCES—SECTION 3: ASCRIPTION AND SOCIAL INEQUALITY

Gender

Calliste, Agnes, and George Dei (eds., with the Assistance of Margarida Aguiar) 2000. *Power, Knowledge and Anti-Racism Education: A Critical Reader*. Halifax: Fernwood. An examination of social spaces through the lens of an anti-racist feminist scholarship and practice.

Cossman, Brenda 1997. *Bad Attitudes on Trial: Pornography, Feminism, and the Butler Decision*. Toronto: University of Toronto Press. Legal battles over what is and what is not pornography are the focus of this collection. It raises key issues related to inequality and the legal system.

Policy Action Research List (PAR-L) (http://www.unb.ca/PAR-L/) An electronic network of individuals and organizations interested in women-centred policy issues in Canada. They maintain a good list of feminist resources.

Ross, Becki 1995. *The House That Jill Built: A Lesbian Nation in Formation*. Toronto: University of Toronto Press. A historical account of the rise of the lesbian movement in Canada.

Statistics Canada 2000. *Women in Canada 2000: A Gender-Based Statistical Report*. Ottawa: Statistics Canada.

Status of Women in Canada 2001. (http://www.swc-cfc.gc.ca/) For example, see the research paper by Damaris Rose, *Revisiting Feminist Research Methodologies: A Working Paper*.

Warner, Tom 2002. *Never Going Back: A History of Queer Activism in Canada*. Toronto: University of Toronto Press. Using interviews and archival material, the author presents a history of gay and lesbian liberation in a Canadian context.

Young, Lisa 2000. *Feminists and Party Politics*. Vancouver: University of British Columbia Press. This book examines the effort to bring feminism into the formal political arena through established political parties in Canada and the United States.

Ethnicity, Race, and Ancestry

Anderson, Kay J. 1991. *Vancouver's Chinatown*. Montréal and Kingston: McGill-Queen's University Press. A case study, including analyses of public documents and official records from three levels of government, on racial discourse in Vancouver's Chinese quarters, 1975–1980.

Assembly of First Nations 2002 (http://www.afn.ca/). This website promotes cooperation between First Nations peoples and the people of Canada.

Breton, Raymond, Wserolod W. Isajiw, Warren E. Kalbach, and Jeffrey G. Reitz 1990. *Ethnic Identity and Equality: Varieties of Experiences in a Canadian City*. Toronto: University of Toronto Press. Studies of ethnic inequality and the persistence of ethnic culture in Toronto. Special attention is given to the topics of ethnic identity retention, residential segregation, occupational and labour market concentrations, and political organization.

Canadian Race Relations Foundation 2002 (http://www.crr.ca/). This organization provides a national framework for fighting racism.

Driedger, Leo (ed.) 1987. *Ethnic Canada: Identities and Inequalities*. Toronto: Copp Clark Pitman. This collection of twenty-one articles presents a good overview of issues of ethnic inequality, including the social standing of ethnic and racial groupings, ethnicity and collective rights, ethnic stereotypes, discrimination, and affirmative action.

Elliott Jean Leonard, and Augie Fleras 2000. *Unequal Relations*. Toronto: Prentice Hall Canada. An introduction to patterns of racial and ethnic group inequalities and racial/ethnic group relations in Canada.

Henry, Frances, Carol Tatom, Winston Mattis, and Tim Rees 1995. *The Colour of Democracy: Racism in Canadian Society*. Toronto: Harcourt Brace. An overview of racist ideology and practice in Canada, including specific chapters related to separate institutional spheres (e.g., education, law).

Kalbach, Madeline A., and Warren E. Kalbach (eds.) 2000. *Perspectives on Ethnicity in Canada: A Reader*. Toronto: Harcourt Canada. This collection looks at a diverse set of issues in the study of ethnicity, including the definition of ethnicity and race, changes in the ethnic composition and identity of the Canadian population, and problems of inequality, prejudice, and discrimination.

Li, Peter S. (ed.) 1999. *Race and Ethnic Relations in Canada* (2nd ed.). Toronto: Oxford University Press. This informative volume contains twelve chapters on such topics as the nature of race and ethnicity, their demographic aspects, the role of the state in race and ethnicity, language policy and multicultural policy, occupational stratification, the political economy of race, and ethnicity and relevant feminist theorizing.

Pal, Leslie A. 1993. *Interests of State: The Politics of Language, Multiculturalism and Feminism in Canada.* Montréal: McGill-Queen's University Press. This book covers the history, since 1900, of various groups, mostly funded by the Department of Secretary of State, that have been active in the areas of language, multiculturalism, and gender relations. An analysis of public policy initiatives by these groups and their power struggles with various organizations is included.

Ponting, Rick (ed.) 1997. *First Nations in Canada: Perspectives on Opportunity, Empowerment, and Self-Determination.* Toronto: McGraw-Hill Ryerson. An overview of many of the First Nations' issues confronting all Canadians. Contributors bring a variety of perspectives to the issues.

Reitz, Jeffrey, and Raymond Breton 1994. *The Illusion of Difference: Realities of Ethnicity in Canada and the United States.* Toronto: C.D. Howe Institute. A comparative assessment of ethnicity as understood in both Canada and the United States.

Satzewith, Vic (ed.) 1998. *Racism and Social Inequality in Canada.* Toronto: Thompson Educational Publishing. The chapters in this reader deal with such topics as racism and immigration policy, race and educational attainment, racism in the justice system, the problems of ethnic stereotypes of First Nations peoples, and other central questions concerning racism in Canada.

Warry, Wayne 1998. *Unfinished Dreams: Community Healing and the Reality of Aboriginal Self-Government.* Toronto:

University of Toronto Press. Drawing on research among Anishnawbe communities and material from the Royal Commission on Aboriginal Peoples, this volume explores the political and social processes required for a successful move to self-government.

Age

Children and Youth (http://www.hrdc-drhc. gc.ca/menu/youth_child.shtml). Links to Human Resources Development Canada's and other government child and youth programs, services, and research.

Division of Aging and Seniors (http://www. hc-sc.gc.ca/seniors-aines). A site supported by Health Canada devoted to issues of seniors and aging.

Gee, Ellen M., and Gloria M. Gutman (eds) 2000. *The Overselling of Population Aging: Apocalyptic Demography, Intergenerational Challenges, and Social Policy.* Toronto: Oxford University Press. A collection of papers dealing with implications of population aging.

Health Canada 2002. *Canada's Aging Population.* Ottawa: Minister of Public Works and Government Services. A reflection on the impact of aging on Canada.

Heinz, Walter R. (ed.) 1999. *From Education to Work: Cross-National Perspectives.* Cambridge: Cambridge University Press. Includes Canadian material, in a comparative perspective.

Novak, Mark W., and Lori Campbell 2001. *Aging and Society: A Canadian Perspective* (4th ed.). Toronto: Nelson Canada. A recent state-of-the-art treatment of aging in Canadian society.

Social and Economic Dimensions of an Aging Population 2002 (http://socserv.socsci. mcmaster.ca/sedap/). Papers on aging from a Canadian multi-disciplinary research program.

Related Websites

Division of Aging and Seniors (http://www. hc-sc.gc.ca/seniors-aines).

Social and Economic Dimensions of an Aging Population (http://socserv.socsci.mcmaster.ca/sedap/). Papers on aging from a Canadian multi-disciplinary research program.

Children and Youth (http://www.hrdc-drhc.gc.ca/menu/youth_child.shtml). Links to Human Resources Development Canada's and other government child and youth programs, services, and research.

Region

Atlantic Canada Opportunities Agency 2002 (http://www.acoa-apeca.gc.ca/). See "Peripheral Regions in the Knowledge-Based Economy" (http://www.acoa-apeca.gc.ca/e/library/reports/peripheral.shtml).

Barry, Donald, and Ronald C. Keith (eds.) 1999. *Regionalism, Multilateralism and the Politics of Global Trade.* Vancouver: University of British Columbia Press. This book provides an examination of the relationship between regionalism and globalism. A discussion of regional issues in other countries as well as interregional relationships is offered. This text also examines the Canadian government's various responses to regionalism.

Braun, Dietmar (ed.) 2000. *Public Policy and Federalism.* Burlington, Vermont: Ashgate. The third chapter of this book, by Grace Skogstad, offers an overview of Canadian regional development policy.

Canadian Centre for Analysis of Regionalization and Health 2002 (http:// www.regionalization.org/). The regionalization of health care in Canada.

Clarke, Harold D., Allan Kornberg, and Peter Wearing 2000. *A Polity on the Edge: Canada and the Politics of Fragmentation.* Peterborough, Ontario: Broadview Press. This book provides a discussion of six critical events in Canadian politics from the 1988 federal election to the 1998 re-election of the Parti Québécois. It provides an interesting examination of regional issues in relation to Canadian politics and considers the impact of these events on regional politics in Canada.

Clement, Wallace (ed.) 1997. *Understanding Canada: Building on the New Canadian Political Economy.* Montréal and Kingston: McGill-Queen's University Press. The chapter by Brodie provides an excellent overview of the issues surrounding regionalism in Canada. She examines the bases of regionalism as well as provides an overview of the national policies that deal with issues of regionalism.

Coffey, William, and Mario Polese 1987. *Still Living Together.* Montréal: Institute for Research on Public Policy. This book considers recent trends and future directions in regional development in Canada. Regional differences in income distribution, economic development, technological change, state policy, and various other issues of relevance to regional inequality are addressed.

Courchene, Thomas J. 1994. *Social Canada in the Millennium: Reform Imperatives and Restructuring Principles.* Ottawa: Renouf Publishing. This book offers an examination of provincial economic disparities. It also provides an assessment of federal government policy as it relates to specific social programs such as employment insurance, family benefits, and pension plans. In addition, an overview of the major federal transfer and equalization programs is offered.

De Benedetti, George, and Rodolphe Lamarche (eds.). 1994. *Shock Waves: The Maritime Urban System in the New Economy.* Moncton, New Brunswick: The Canadian Institute for Research on Regional Development. This book analyzes regionalism from the perspective of the Maritime provinces. It discusses the role of the public sector and free trade in regional development.

Poschmann, Finn 1998. "Where the money goes: The distribution of taxes and benefits in Canada." C. D. Howe Institute *Commentary* 105 (April). This paper offers an analysis of federal transfers to individual and regions and a discussion of various specific types of transfers, such as education and health.

The Prairie Centre 2002 (http://www.prairiecentre.com/links.htm).

Savoie, Donald 2000. *Community Economic Development in Atlantic Canada: False Hope or Panacea?* National Library of Canada: The Canadian Institute for Research on Regional Development. This book provides a discussion of past efforts to promote community economic development in Atlantic Canada from the 1960s through the 1990s. Case studies are used to illustrate particular development policies.

Strategis 2002. For example, see (http://strategis.ic.gc.ca/SSG/ra01580e.html) No. 18, "Regional disparities in Canada: Characterization, trends and lessons for economic policy."

Young, Lisa, and Keith Archer (eds.) 2002. *Regionalism and Party Politics in Canada.* Don Mills, Ontario: Oxford University Press. This text examines overall theoretical approaches to the study of regionalism and discusses the contemporary Canadian political party system as it relates to regional issues.

SOME CONSEQUENCES OF SOCIAL INEQUALITY

The preceding three sections have described this country's main patterns of social inequality with respect to social class, income/occupation/education, and social ascription. Also, various interpretations have been offered for the patterns of inequality. Further, one of the *effects* or *consequences* of social inequality received considerable attention: the ways in which the struggles between classes and between elites have resulted in certain social trends. For example, all of the selections in Section 1, particularly those by Grabb, Brym, and Laxer, suggest how the economic structure of this country has changed as a result of both the interplay between capitalists and the state elite and the struggle between classes. The same is true of several selections in other sections; e.g., Urmetzer and Guppy's and Gunderson's chapters on income, and Creese and Beagan's pieces on gender

relations. It is difficult to describe Canada's unequal class and elite relations for very long without spelling out how aspects of history have been determined by them.

There is a second important type of consequence of social inequality, though, that was not featured in Sections 1, 2, or 3. This concerns the *consequences for the experiences of individuals* that flow from different forms of social inequality. Here the focus is on how the day-to-day living of Canadians is affected, as opposed to how the society is changing or not changing with time. In this instance, *consequences* refer to any aspects of the experiences of individuals that are influenced by differences in social inequality, including people's life chances, beliefs, and patterns of behaviour.

Our purpose in Section 4 is to portray this second type of consequence. There are a vast number of such consequences, because social inequality touches so many aspects of people's lives. Thus, in the six selections in this section we cannot pretend to give the last word on the consequences of social inequality, but we will provide some enlightening examples. To suggest how broad the range of consequences of social inequality for individuals can be, we can recall the views of Hans Gerth and C. Wright Mills, who wrote that they "include everything from the chance to stay alive during the first year after birth, to the chance to view fine arts, the chance to remain healthy and grow tall, and if sick to get well again quickly, the chance to avoid becoming a juvenile delinquent... and... the chance to complete a university or higher educational grade" (1953:313). These observations are no less true for Canadian society now than they were for the U.S. when they were written years ago.

There are many reasons behind the various consequences of social inequality for individuals in any society, but two are particularly important for our type of society. First, the existence of social inequality in the form of economic advantage means that some can "buy" more or "afford" more of the valued aspects of social life, the "life chances" of the society. Some can easily afford to take time off work when they believe their children might benefit from a doctor's examination; others cannot readily afford this. Some can afford to live in the best neighbourhoods, with the best in leisure and educational facilities for their children; others cannot. There are many such differences in life chances between "haves" and "have-nots."

Second, because differences in economic advantage involve differences in economic interest, we can expect that awareness of these interests will develop. If the pursuit of economic interests

becomes pronounced between the haves and have-nots, it can be expected to lead to differences in the areas of political beliefs, behaviour, and life chances. For the same reason, social barriers between the haves and the have-nots may develop, and these, in turn, may lead to still other differences in beliefs, behaviour, and opportunities. In other words, *subcultures of different ways of thinking and acting* can easily develop out of the differing interests that surround separate social classes and status groups.

There is no easy way of predicting the full details of these subcultures in advance, no way of saying precisely how they will differ in beliefs, behaviour, and opportunities. For an understanding of the prevalence and character of inequality-based subcultures in any society for any particular time period, a careful large-scale research effort is required. The selections in this section will suggest that this is a very large task, and will give examples of appropriate research topics and research approaches.

The selections here are limited to three categories of consequences of social inequality: (1) people's differences in *life chances*; (2) their differences in *ways of thinking* concerning social inequality; and (3) their differences in *lifestyle and orientation to social interaction*.

We shall first deal with the issue of differences in life chances. We will start with an aspect of life chances that involves the toughest of definitions: that of life expectancy. This is "toughest" in the sense that good health and continued life are among the prized possessions in Canadian society, and undoubtedly *the* most prized possession for many Canadians. This being the case, using the criterion of good health/life expectancy puts our society's patterns of inequality to a strong test. It would clearly cast doubt on the idea that ours is a society of vast equality if we found good evidence that differences in economic circumstances create differences in how healthy people are and how long they live.

Precisely this pattern has been shown to be true of other countries. One of the most complete international studies of this topic was conducted some years ago in the United States by Kitagawa and Hauser (1968). They matched 340 000 death certificates (for deaths occurring during a four-month period) with census records. Using educational attainment level as an indicator of socio-economic status, they found a strong inverse relationship between death rates and social status. For example, among White men between the ages of 25 and 64, the death rate for those with less than eight years of schooling was 48% higher than the rate for the college-educated men.

A research review by the National Council of Welfare (1990) also has dramatically shown that social inequality has a significant impact on life expectancy in Canada. This monograph indicates, for example, that when researchers studied data on income levels in Canadian cities in 1971 and 1986, they found, at both times, that there were markedly better life expectancy figures for areas with higher average income levels. Among the results was the sobering finding for 1986 that males in the highest income areas had a life expectancy fully 5.7 years greater on average than males in the lowest income areas. This discrepancy was down only slightly from a gap of 6.2 years in 1971.

The first selection in Section 4, which is excerpted from a recent Health Canada document, gives still further evidence on the relationships between socio-economic status and health and mortality in Canada. Several measures of "life chances" are used, including self-reported health, being stricken with chronic diseases or diseases that are among the major causes of death, injuries, disability and activity limitation,

life expectancy, and potential years of life lost. As the report shows, income and socio-economic status are among key factors in predicting people's success with these life choices. The higher people's incomes and socio-economic statuses, the healthier they are and the longer they live. Presumably, this pattern occurs because important factors in health and longevity—diet, lifestyle, social support networks, education, employment and working conditions, safe and clean physical environments, and coping skills—are also related to income and socio-economic status. Other social status factors—particularly gender, age, and First Nations status—are also shown to be related to health and longevity.

The next selection in this section asks us to consider another serious problem of life chances. The author, Tracy Peressini, reminds us that most people take for granted certain basic comforts of life—a roof over their heads and three meals per day—even if they are quite poor. Peressini emphasizes that a small but growing category of Canadians does not have access to these life comforts. The author reviews attempts to estimate the number of homeless people in this country, and she discusses what we know about their social background and personal characteristics and life circumstances. Also discussed are explanations of how people arrive at the dismal circumstance of homelessness. Explanations for homelessness vary from social structural reasons to individual-level factors. Each avenue of explanation accounts for some cases of homelessness, but not all cases. Whatever the appropriate explanation for particular people, the homeless almost always end up being very poor and unable to afford housing. Peressini goes on to discuss public policy, emphasizing that a major problem is that the issue of affordable housing is largely left in local municipal or provincial hands to solve; it is not a federal government responsibility. Thus, there have been few sustained, country-wide initiatives directed at the problem.

The second type of consequence of social inequality addressed in this section has to do with differences in *ways of thinking*. Here we could start by recalling Karl Marx's famous observation that it is not the consciousness of men that determines their being, but rather their social being, primarily their location in the class structure, that determines their consciousness. We can ask to what extent this view is correct for Canada today. Are the different social classes and social status groups aware of their differences? Do individuals try to safeguard or promote their class or group interests? Going further, we can ask whether the different classes and status groups develop still other differences in beliefs and behaviour over time.

Questions of this type, designed to probe the degree and extent of class and status consciousness, or common thinking by classes and strata, raise problems of obvious significance for understanding the dynamic aspect of Canada's structure of social inequality. For example, class consciousness of common interests has existed at many times and places, and has at times led to organized class actions and class struggles that changed the whole structure of societies (see, e.g., the discussions in the selections by Laxer, Conley, and Brym in Section 1). However, class consciousness does not follow automatically from objective class differences. People may have a class position that differs markedly from that of others without being particularly aware of this difference. Thinking and conduct are not determined merely by objective position in the economic or social order, but depend in part upon the way in which people perceive and interpret their social circumstances. For example, socialization through the

education system and the media probably will have some effect upon people's thinking about their class or status position and its meaning. It is likely that these influences, widespread across classes and status groups as they are, will tend to lead people of differing classes and statuses to have a *common assessment* of social inequality. Some scholars believe that much of what is taught in the education system and through the media is supportive of, or justifies, existing patterns of social inequality. Such ideas have been labelled "dominant ideology" because they generally aid in the domination of the have-nots by the haves (e.g., Parkin 1972; cf. Abercrombie et al. 1980).

Also, Canadians "carry with them" various achieved and ascribed backgrounds and related sets of experiences at any given point in their lives. A person has, simultaneously, the experiences of a class position, a level of education achieved, an occupation, a certain level of income, an ethnic status, a race, a gender, and an age group. It is, therefore, difficult to know which of these sets of experiences will most influence the person's perceptions of social inequality. We cannot assume the presence of common class or status thinking, but must investigate how Canadians evaluate and respond to their differing circumstances.

Fortunately, over the past few years there have been some well-developed national sample surveys of adult Canadians' beliefs about social inequality, which have helped us to understand this issue better. For example, Johnston and Ornstein (1982) have explored the relationship between social class, defined in the Marxist sense, and three sets of ideological beliefs: beliefs having to do with support for redistribution of income, social welfare expenditures, and the labour movement. As would be expected from the interests involved for each class, the bourgeoisie had a more right-wing position on these issues, and the working class had a more left-wing position. The bourgeoisie were less likely to favour pursuing equality through income redistribution and greater social welfare, and they were less supportive of the labour movement. The difference in beliefs between the classes, however, was far from complete. Many members of one class shared in the majority beliefs of the other class, and vice versa. Johnston and Ornstein went on to show how the attitudes of the working class were affected by education, family background, and a number of aspects of working conditions, but the working conditions were more important. Rates of pay, the distinction between manual work and nonmanual work, and whether the job was unionized or not were related to the beliefs about social inequality.

The third selection in Section 4 presents other relevant information. It reports on Canadians' beliefs about the causes of social inequality and how these beliefs are related to people's social statuses. The analyses show that there is widespread support for two sets of beliefs: (1) that it is an individual's personal characteristics (ambition, hard work, and natural ability) and educational attainment that determine how he or she gets ahead; and (2) that social background factors (social class of parents, race, gender, and region) have comparatively little to do with success or the lack of it. These beliefs are sometimes differentially distributed across social statuses, as the analyses show, but this is not the case for all dimensions of social status. Further, there is remarkably high support for each set of views among people, regardless of their achieved and ascribed statuses. Social status is not highly predictive of these beliefs. The authors argue that these beliefs are part of a "dominant ideology" that simultaneously describes and reinforces the system of social inequality in this society.

The third category of consequences of social inequality explored in this section has to do with *effects upon lifestyles and social interaction*. Archibald (1976) is among the researchers who have looked at this issue in detail. He presented a Marxian-oriented theory of how interaction between higher-class and lower-class individuals takes place. The theory presumably also applied to interaction between higher-status and lower-status people, and interaction between those with much power and those with less power. Using a sweeping review of results from many studies already conducted by others, the author arrived at the generalization that interactions between unequals will necessarily involve some interpersonal threat and exploitation by the more powerful. The interactions will involve some conflict and coercion, however subtle these may be at times. The literature contains alternative theories based on the idea that there is largely consensus, cooperation and exchange in interaction between unequals. Archibald acknowledged that these processes may occur, but insisted that they are not the most common forms of interaction between unequals; interactions based on conflict and cohesion are believed to be more common.

The selection by Jeffrey Reitz and Raymond Breton looks at one type of interaction between unequals in Canada, that between the majority group and minority ethnic and racial groups. The authors explore the results of various Canadian and American studies of discrimination and prejudice on the part of the majority toward various minority racial and ethnic groups. Reitz and Breton find that levels of discrimination and prejudice depend upon the minority outgroup involved, and the type of response to the outgroup that is in question. However, the levels of negative responses tend to be low in an absolute sense for most measures and for most outgroups, suggesting reasonably high levels of tolerance of minority groups. Returning to the consideration raised by Archibald's work—whether interaction between high- and low-status groups is characterized by coercion and conflict or by consensus and cooperation—we would have to conclude that there must be considerable consensus and cooperation in ethnic/race relations in the two countries. Of course, Henry's studies of employment discrimination and Hou and Balakrishnan's study of differences in income across ethnic groups in Section 3 of this volume are also relevant to the issues discussed by Reitz and Breton.

Reitz and Breton argue that Canada and the United States are more or less the same in levels of discrimination and prejudice. This will come as a surprise to those who think, following the popular view (in this country), that Canada is the nation of tolerance par excellence. The authors believe that there is simply an "illusion of difference" in the perceptions of Canada versus the United States among Canadians (Reitz and Breton 1994).

Two of the most important predictors of social status differences in involvement in community activities must be: (1) how much time people have available for activities outside work; and (2) what financial resources they have to apply to leisure time use. The next selection in this section, by Cara Williams, explores these issues by looking at the reported time use of high- and low-income people in large national samples of Canadians. Among the results are the perhaps surprising facts that high-income Canadians spend more time at work and less time at leisure activity and with their families. This is likely to be explained, though, by the greater opportunities to work long hours, for good pay,

among the more highly paid. Also, the work of the highly paid is likely more satisfying than the work of low-income people. The latter spend much more time on domestic work and at home than do the more highly paid. (Of course, the highly paid are typically better able to hire help with housework and childcare.) Both the high- and the low-income categories report, in large proportions, that they are greatly "rushed" and would like to spend more time with their families. As the author goes on to show, there are some commonalities and quite a few differences in the way that people in the two income levels use the leisure time that they do have available.

It will no doubt prove very informative if further research is undertaken to provide lifestyle profiles for the various social status groups. For example, we need to know more about the different leisure lifestyles of women versus men, the various ethnic and racial groups, and age groups. Further, we do not yet know much about whether the differences among various status groups result from the income and work characteristics of people in these groups. The next selection, by James Curtis, Edward Grabb, Tom Perks, and Tina Chui, shows the kind of detailed analyses that might be generated for a wide range of leisure activities. However, in this particular paper, the authors focus more narrowly on mainly political involvements and community activities.

In this final selection, the authors ask whether Canadians who are higher in regard to various social statuses—majority versus minority ethnic group members, immigrants versus non-immigrants, middle-aged versus the young and old, men versus women, those with high education versus those low in education, those with higher versus lower incomes, and so on—are also higher in involvement in political and associational behaviour. The measures of involvement ranged across several forms of "mass" activity that are generally felt to be open to all Canadians, including voting, following politics in the media, interest in politics, attending political meetings, participating in other forms of voluntary associations, public protest activities, and support for social movements. Contrary to the view that there is full openness of political participation, people's social statuses were sometimes found to be related to forms of political involvement. The "haves" were sometimes more involved than others, but this was not always the case, and the patterns often were not strong. The authors emphasize that socio-economic status and ascriptive social statuses are stronger predictors of other more intensive forms of political activity, such as running for and achieving political office. That is, while the "mass" political activities are structured in only a modest way by social status, there is evidence of a more marked degree of inequality for the achievement of higher levels of political power.

It is interesting, though, that the data showed the *public protest* activities—signing a petition, boycotting, engaging in strikes and demonstrations, and occupying facilities—were more common for higher-status individuals than for lower-status individuals. To the extent that these activities arise out of dissatisfaction with life's circumstances, one would think that lower-status people would have more reason to protest. This is likely the case for *levels of dissatisfaction*. However, lower-status people do not protest more; they generally protest less. The reason for this apparent inconsistency likely involves two issues. First, higher-status people have greater time and resources for protest than those lower in social status. Further, higher-status people have *interests* (if not high levels of dissatisfaction) to pursue through protest actions and other forms of mass political involvement.

REFERENCES

Abercrombie, Nicholas, Stephen Hill, and Bryan S. Turner 1980. *The Dominant Ideology Thesis.* London: George Allen and Unwin.

Archibald, W. Peter 1976. "Class and social interaction." *American Sociological Review* 41(5):819–837.

Gerth, Hans, and C. Wright Mills 1953. *Character and Social Structure: The Social Psychology of Social Institutions.* New York: Harcourt Brace and World.

Johnston, William, and Michael Ornstein 1982. "Class, work and politics." *Canadian Review of Sociology and Anthropology* 19(2): 196–214.

Kitawaga, Evelyn M., and Philip M. Hauser 1968. "Education differentials in mortality by cause of death: United States, 1960." *Demograph* 5:318–353.

National Council of Welfare 1990. *Health, Health Care, and Medicare.* Ottawa: National Council of Welfare.

Parkin, Frank 1972. *Class, Inequality and Political Order.* London: Paladin.

Reitz, Jeffrey, and Raymond Breton 1994. *The Illusion of Difference: Realities of Ethnicity in Canada and the United States.* Toronto: C.D. Howe Institute.

SOCIAL INEQUALITY AND HEALTH

Health Canada

(A new chapter abridged from *Toward a Healthy Future: Second Report on the Health of Canadians*, pp. 11–35, Health Canada, 1999. Reproduced with permission from the Minister of Public Works and Government Services, Canada, 2002.)

INTRODUCTION

This chapter focuses on three related questions: How healthy are Canadians? Is the health of Canadians improving? Who is healthy and who is not? The answers to these questions will help focus our efforts to improve the well-being of all Canadians. For the most part, Canadians enjoy a high level of health on virtually all measures of health. Positive health status and improvements in health, however, are not shared equally by all Canadians. This chapter shows that age and gender influence health status in a number of ways. It also shows that income and health status

are closely related on nearly all measures of health.

OVERVIEW OF PATTERNS OF HEALTH AMONG CANADIANS

Many Canadians enjoy a high level of health that continues to improve.

Self-rated health: Sixty-three percent of adult Canadians say that their health is excellent or very good and only 9% rate their health as fair or poor. These rates, which have been stable since 1985, represent one of the highest levels of self-rated

Social Inequality and Health   363

Definitions and Measures

- **Self-rated health** describes how individual Canadians experience and assess their own physical and mental health.

- **Psychological well-being** includes three measures: Sense of coherence is a perception that life is meaningful, challenges are manageable and life events are comprehensible. Self-esteem refers to an individual's sense of self-worth. Mastery describes the extent to which people believe that their life chances are under their control.

- **Selected diseases and conditions** looks at the incidence and prevalence of selected diseases and health conditions over time.

- **Disability days** measures how often health problems forced an individual to cut down on regular activities (at work, school or home) for the better part of a day in the preceding two weeks.

- **Activity limitation** measures the degree to which an individual is limited in performing their normal activities at work, home or school due to a long-term (more than six months) disability or health problem.

- **Major causes of death** reports on the principal causes of death.

- **Infant mortality** refers to the death of a live-born infant within the first year of life. **Perinatal deaths** are the combination of stillbirths and early neonatal deaths (deaths within the first seven days of life).

- **Life expectancy at birth** measures the number of years a Canadian baby born today can expect to live, based on current mortality data.

- **Potential years of life lost** describes the number of potential years lost whena death occurs prior to the age of 70.

health among citizens of developed countries.

Infant mortality: In 1996, Canada's infant mortality rate (5.6 per 1000 live births) dropped below the level of six infant deaths per 1000 live births for the first time. While this is an important achievement, it is still quite far above the infant mortality rate of Japan, which is the lowest in the world (3.8 deaths per 1000 live births).

Life expectancy: Based on current mortality patterns, a Canadian child born in 1996 can expect to live to the age of 78.6 (males 75.7, females 81.4). This life expectancy represents a new high in Canada, and is one of the highest in the industrialized world, behind only Switzerland and Japan (of the twelve OECD countries reporting this information).

Gender and age have varying effects on health status.

- Men are far more likely than women to die before the age of 70, mainly because of gender differences in deaths due to heart disease, cancer, suicide, and unintentional injuries. Rates of potential years of life lost are almost twice as high for men than women and approximately three times higher among men aged 20 to 34.

- While women live longer than men, they are more likely to suffer from long-term activity limitations and chronic conditions such as osteoporosis, arthritis, and migraine headaches.

- While older Canadians are far more likely than young Canadians to have physical illnesses and conditions, youth (aged 12 to 19) report the lowest levels of psychological well-being. Young women are particularly likely to report feeling depressed.

- Suicide rates among young men are high in Canada, compared with other countries. Suicides among Aboriginal groups (especially Inuit) have been reported to be two to seven times more frequent than in the population at large.

- While unintentional injuries among children have decreased over time, they are still the leading cause of death among children and youth. They are also a significant cause of disability in children and young people. Boys and young men tend to experience more unintentional injuries and more severe injuries than girls and young women.

Canadians with low incomes are more likely to suffer illnesses and to die early than Canadians with high incomes.

- Only 47% of Canadians at the lowest income level rate their health as excellent or very good, compared with 73% of Canadians in the highest income group.

- Low-income Canadians are more likely to die earlier and to suffer more illnesses than Canadians with high incomes. It is estimated that if the death rates of the highest income earners applied to all Canadians, more than one-fifth of all years of life lost before the age of 65 could be prevented.

Canada's Aboriginal people are at higher risk for poor health and early death than the Canadian population as a whole.

- Despite major improvements since 1979, infant mortality rates among First Nations people are still twice as high as that of the Canadian population as a whole.

- Life expectancy is significantly lower among Aboriginal people than for the overall Canadian population. High rates of suicide and fatal unintentional injuries among First Nations and Inuit young people partly account for this difference.

- The prevalence of all major chronic diseases, including diabetes, heart problems, cancer, hypertension, and arthritis/rheumatism is significantly higher in Aboriginal communities than in the general population and appears to be increasing.

SELF-RATED HEALTH

Self-rated health status has been shown to be a reliable predictor of health problems, health care utilization and longevity (Adams 1988). In the 1996–1997 National Population Health Survey (NPHS), one-quarter of Canadians aged 12 and over described their health as excellent, and more than one-third rated it as very good. Less than one in ten Canadians described their health as fair or poor. Women were slightly less likely to rate their health as excellent or very good (62%) than men (65%). Fair or poor self-rated health status increased with each successive age group, from 2% of 12- to 14-year-olds to 27% of Canadians over age 75 (Statistics Canada 1996–1997).

Figure 26-1 shows a definite gradient in self-rated health that is strongly linked to income. Among adult Canadians in the lowest income brackets, 47% rated their health as excellent or very good and 21% described their health as fair or poor.

Among Canadians with the highest income levels, 73% described their health as excellent or very good, while only 5% rated their health as fair or poor. Canadians who lived in the lowest income households were four times more likely to

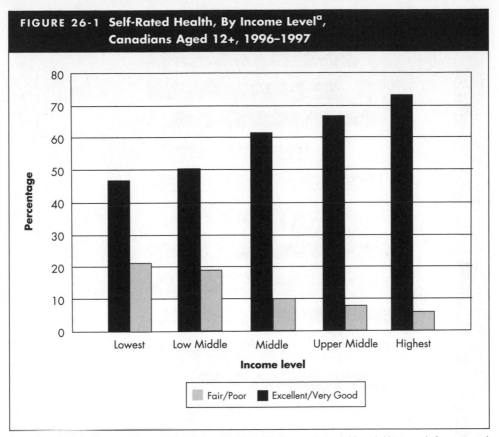

FIGURE 26-1 Self-Rated Health, By Income Level[a], Canadians Aged 12+, 1996–1997

[a] Income levels in this figure and those to follow that are based on the NPHS represent total household incomes before taxes and adjusted for family size and age-standardized.

Source: Statistics Canada, *National Population Health Survey, 1996–1997.*

report fair or poor health than those who lived in the highest-income households.

There were substantial provincial differences in self-rated health. Only 17% of Saskatchewan residents viewed their health as excellent, compared with 27% of people living in Québec. Nova Scotians were most likely to see their health as fair or poor (10%), while residents of Newfoundland (7%) and Quebec (8%) were least likely to rate their health as fair or poor.

PSYCHOLOGICAL WELL-BEING

In the 1994–1995 NPHS (Statistics Canada 1994–1995), sense of coherence, self-esteem, and mastery scores were based on a series of standardized interview questions. "High," "adequate," and "low" scores were based on peaks in the distribution of scores. This allows for intergroup comparisons, but negates the meaningfulness of statements about absolute levels of psychological well-being.

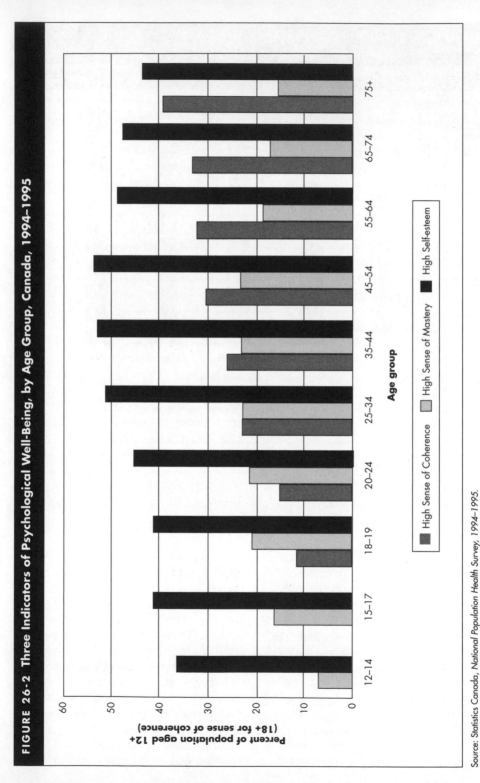

FIGURE 26-2 Three Indicators of Psychological Well-Being, by Age Group, Canada, 1994–1995

■ High Sense of Coherence   ■ High Sense of Mastery   ■ High Self-esteem

Percent of population aged 12+ (18+ for sense of coherence)

Age group

Source: Statistics Canada, National Population Health Survey, 1994–1995.

TABLE 26-1	Percentage of Canadians Reporting Low Self-Esteem, Low Sense of Mastery, and Low Sense of Coherence, by Income Level, 1994–1995		
Income Level	**Low Self-Esteem**	**Low Sense of Mastery**	**Low Sense of Coherence**
Lowest	18%	31%	47%
Middle	13%	22%	33%
Highest	10%	12%	26%

Source: Statistics Canada, *National Population Health Survey, 1994–1995.*

In 1994–1995, some 28% of Canadians had a high sense of coherence (a view of the world that life is meaningful, events are comprehensible, and challenges are manageable). Forty-nine percent had high self-esteem and 21% had a high sense of mastery (the extent to which individuals feel that their life chances are under their own control). As this was the first time these questions were asked in a national health survey, no time trends or comparisons to other countries can be provided. But within Canada, there are pronounced variations in these measures among different age groups.

In contrast to the high levels of physical health usually found among youth, psychological well-being is, on average, lowest among the youngest age groups. Sense of coherence increased with age: Seniors over the age of 75 were three times more likely than 18- and 19-year-olds to score high on sense of coherence. As Figure 26-2 shows, self-esteem and mastery improve with age to a peak in middle adulthood, followed by a modest decline in later years.

These age-related patterns are consistent with measures of poor psychological health such as depression, which declines with age (discussed later). This positive association between psychological well-being and age is a reversal from that experienced a generation ago, when seniors were more likely than younger Canadians to be depressed (Stephens 1998).

Males were slightly more likely than females to report a high sense of mastery, but the difference was small for this attribute and almost nonexistent for the other two. The lack of differences in reported self-esteem between young men and women is surprising, since many other studies have concluded that young women have lower levels of self-esteem than young men (Edwards 1993).

As Table 26-1 shows, all three measures of psychological well-being were positively linked to income level. Self-esteem and mastery were also positively related to level of education.

SELECTED DISEASES AND CONDITIONS

Chronic Diseases

A comparison of the 1994–1995 and 1996–1997 NPHS revealed that the major self-reported chronic diseases with the highest number of new cases were nonarthritic back problems and arthritis/rheumatism. Women reported higher incidence rates than men for most chronic diseases, although in some cases these differences were not statistically significant.

TABLE 26-2	First Nations/Canada Ratio of Age-Adjusted Prevalence for Selected Chronic Diseases, 1997	
Disease	**Ratio Men**	**Ratio Women**
Diabetes	3:1	5:1
Heart problems	3:1	3:1
Cancer	2:1	2:1
Hypertension	3:1	3:1
Arthritis/rheumatism	2:1	2:1

Source: Young et al., *First Nations and Inuit Regional Health Survey, 1997.*

In the 1994–1995 NPHS, 81% of all people over the age of 65 and living in private households reported that they had at least one chronic condition. Arthritis and rheumatism were the most common chronic health problems reported. Three percent of Canadians aged 12 and over reported having diabetes that had been diagnosed by a health professional. For Canadians over the age of 65, the rate was just above 10%. While there were no substantial differences in the prevalence of diabetes between the sexes or between urban and rural residents, it was significantly higher among Canadians with low incomes (James et al. 1997).

According to a recent article by Young and colleagues (1999), the prevalence of all self-reported major chronic diseases was significantly higher in Aboriginal communities than in the general population, and appears to be increasing (Table 26-2). For example, the rate of diabetes among First Nations and Inuit men was three times the rate for all Canadian men; for First Nations and Inuit women, the diabetes rate was five times the rate for all Canadian women.

In 1994–1995, chronic conditions were less common among immigrants (50%) than among the Canadian-born population (57%). Recent non-European immigrants had a particularly low prevalence of chronic conditions (37%), but as their duration of stay in Canada increased, so did the prevalence of chronic conditions. Fifty-one percent of long-term non-European immigrants reported at least one chronic condition (Chen, Wilkins, and Ng 1996).

This finding is likely due to a number of factors. First, Canada's immigration policies tend to favour immigrants who are in good health. Second, many immigrants and refugees are young when they arrive. The reasons why the prevalence of chronic conditions increases the longer they stay in Canada is less well understood. The normal aging process is clearly a factor. Also, after arrival, the adoption of unhealthy lifestyle practices such as smoking (which is more common among certain groups in Canada than in other countries) may also be a factor (Chen, Ng, and Wilkins 1996).

Depression

The 1996–1997 NPHS showed that some 6% of Canadians aged 12 and over were at possible or probable risk of depression (Statistics Canada 1994–1995, 1996–1997). Although the rates of depression reported by women (8%) were slightly higher than those reported by men (5%), the rates for both men and women were lower than in 1994–1995. Young women aged 15 to 19 were the most likely of any age-sex group to exhibit signs of depression (8% to 9%). For both males and females, depression was more likely to occur in the younger years (especially at ages 18 and 19).

For both men and women, the risk of depression was highest among those with the lowest incomes. Thirteen percent of women in the lowest income group were at risk of depression, compared with 5% of women in the highest income group. For men, the rate of depression ranged from 11% among those in the lowest income bracket to 4% among men with high incomes.

Injuries

In 1995–1996, there were 217 000 hospital admissions due to injury. By far, the highest rates of hospital admissions due to injuries were among senior Canadians over the age of 65 (235 per 10 000 population among senior women and 152 per 10 000 population among senior men). The rate of hospital admission due to injury was much lower among people under the age of 45. In this age group, males accounted for 69% of all injury admissions (Canadian Institute for Health Information 1998).

The vast majority of injuries are unintentional—nearly two out of three hospital admissions due to injury are the result of falls and motor vehicle crashes. Injuries intentionally inflicted by another person accounted for 5% of all hospital admissions due to injury, while self-inflicted injuries accounted for approximately 2% of injury admissions (Canadian Institute for Health Information 1998).

While the rate of injury due to falls is particularly high among Canadians over the age of 60, falls remained an important cause of injury among children under the age of 11, and youth aged 11 to 20. Among children, the next most important cause of

injury-related admission to hospital in 1996 was poisoning. For adolescents and adults under the age of 60, the second most important cause was motor vehicle crashes (SmartRisk Foundation 1998).

DISABILITY AND ACTIVITY LIMITATIONS

Between the 1994–1995 and 1996–1997 cycles of the NPHS, there was a decrease in the percentage of Canadian women and men who reported one or more disability days during a two-week period, and who reported a continuing health condition that limited their normal activities at home, school, or work (Statistics Canada 1994–1995, 1996–1997). Most of the improvements were among Canadians over the age of 55. Women were more likely than men to report both disability days and long-term activity limitations.

According to the NPHS, and as shown in Figure 26-3, Canadians who have activity limitations were also more likely to have low incomes. Among men in the lowest income group, 32% reported an activity limitation, compared with 12% of men in the highest income bracket. Among women, the rate of reported activity limitations ranged from 28% in the lowest income group to 16% in the highest income group. The relationship between income and disability is not yet clear. Do activity limitations and disabilities lead to low-income status or does low-income status lead to disabilities? While both factors are likely at play, this is an important area for further investigation.

Overall, immigrants to Canada were less likely than the Canadian-born population to have any long-term disability. However, the relationships between gender, socio-economic status, and disability hold true for immigrants as well. Disability was more strongly related to low household incomes and to being a

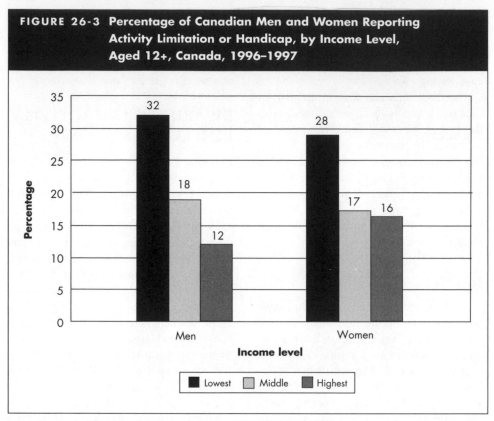

FIGURE 26-3 Percentage of Canadian Men and Women Reporting Activity Limitation or Handicap, by Income Level, Aged 12+, Canada, 1996–1997

Source: Statistics Canada, *National Population Health Survey, 1996–1997.*

woman than to immigrant status (Chen, Wilkins, and Ng 1966).

MAJOR CAUSES OF DEATH

In Canada, death rates for most of the major causes have declined since 1970, particularly in the case of coronary heart disease. The exception to this is the cancer death rate, which continued to increase until the mid-1980s and then declined steadily among men and stabilized in women.

Cardiovascular Disease

Cardiovascular disease is the major cause of death in Canada. The two major components of cardiovascular disease are ischemic heart disease, including acute myocardial infarction or heart attack, and cerebrovascular disease and stroke. In 1996, cardiovascular disease accounted for 37% of all deaths in Canada. While more men than women died of ischemic heart disease (22% versus 19%), more women died of stroke (9% versus 6%) (Statistics Canada 1996).

Deaths from cardiovascular disease have been declining in Canada since 1970 among both men and women, although more slowly in women. Canada has one of the lowest rates of cardiovascular disease mortality among all developed countries (Statistics Canada 1999).

The Atlantic provinces have had consistently higher mortality rates than the western provinces for cardiovascular disease. Provincial prevalence rates of smoking, high blood pressure, and obesity run parallel to the rates for cardiovascular disease (Heart and Stroke Foundation of Canada 1997).

Cancer

Cancer in its many forms is the second leading cause of death and the leading cause of potential years of life lost before the age of 70 (National Cancer Institute of Canada 1998). Among men, declining rates for most forms of cancer were offset by dramatic increases in the detection of (but not mortality from) prostate cancer, primarily due to the introduction of PSA testing. The incidence of new cancer diagnoses in women has remained relatively stable since the early 1980s. Cancer death rates have declined slowly for men since 1990, while they have remained relatively stable among women over the same period.

The incidence of prostate cancer was the highest among new cancers in men. The 1993 peak of new cases of prostate cancer was due to the introduction of PSA testing. At the same time, death rates from this type of cancer have remained relatively stable. Since prostate cancer is most often detected in old age and is a slow-growing cancer, many men who are diagnosed with prostate cancer die of other causes.

The number of new cases of lung cancer has declined among men since the 1980s, likely due to a decline in male smoking rates over the past thirty years. However, lung cancer death rates still far exceed death rates due to prostate cancer.

The incidence of both breast and lung cancer have been increasing among women since the 1970s. Breast cancer was estimated to be the most common newly diagnosed cancer in 1998; however, the leading cause of cancer death was still predicted to be lung cancer.

Thus, while cancer remains a serious problem, we are beginning to see signs that prevention and control strategies are working for a number of different cancer sites. These favourable results are obscured, however, by continuing increases in lung cancer incidence and mortality among women (largely as a result of increased smoking) and the recent transient surge in prostate cancer incidence (but not mortality) in males. Time will tell whether the early detection of prostate cancer affects the mortality rate.

Provincial differences in cancer incidence and deaths are rather marked. Nova Scotia has the highest male age-standardized incidence and death rates, due largely to higher lung cancer rates than the Canadian average. Among women, the highest new case incidence rate is also in Nova Scotia; the highest death rates are in Nova Scotia and Prince Edward Island.

Unintentional Injuries

Unintentional injuries are the third most important cause of death overall, accounting for 8663 deaths (29 per 100 000 population) in 1996. However, they remain the leading cause of death among Canadians aged 1 to 44, and as such are a major contributor to potential years of life lost. Although many sources persist in referring to such events as "accidents," it is estimated that 90% of deaths due to unintentional injuries are preventable. And, despite a 50% reduction in such deaths among children between 1970 and 1991, unintentional injuries remain the major cause of death among children and youth (SmartRisk Foundation 1998).

Injuries and poisonings are the number one cause of death in the First Nations population (crude rate 154 per 100 000 population). In 1993, the age-standardized injury rate for First Nations persons was 3.8 times higher than that for Canadians in general. Native children and youth have much higher death rates due to injury than do other Canadians. For Aboriginal infants, the rate of death is almost four times greater; for preschoolers, it is five times higher; and among teenagers, the injury-related death rate is three times higher (MacMillan et al. 1999).

Overall, motor vehicle crashes are the major cause of deaths due to unintentional injury. In 1994, they accounted for 38% of deaths, followed by falls (31%), poisonings (9%), drownings and suffocation (5%), and fires (4%). Motor vehicle crashes are a particularly important cause of injury and death among children and youth. However, due in part to increases in seatbelt usage and reductions in impaired driving, the number of deaths due to motor vehicle traffic crashes has declined impressively in recent years—from 5253 in 1977 to 3082 in 1996 (Transport Canada 1999). Falls remain an especially important cause of death among the elderly, accounting for nearly three out of every four deaths due to unintentional injury among Canadians over the age of 70 (SmartRisk Foundation 1998).

Suicide

Suicide is a tragic event and an important cause of potential years of life lost. In 1996, there were 3941 suicides in Canada—almost eleven per day (Statistics Canada 1997). Trends and rates associated with suicide need to be interpreted with caution, however, since official statistics tend to underreport suicide. In addition, changes over time may reflect differences in the official reporting and certification of suicide deaths.

There are dramatic sex and age differences in suicide rates. In 1996, males were four times more likely than females to commit suicide. The highest rate for male suicides was among men aged 20 to 24

(29 per 100 000 population) and 35 to 44 (30 per 100 000 population). For women, the highest rate of suicide was among those aged 45 to 54 (10 per 100 000 population) (Statistics Canada 1997).

Young men's suicide attempts are far more likely to have a fatal outcome than young women's. The reasons for this are not clear, but presumably relate to male-female differences in reaching out for help, the nature of underlying problems, learned responses to stress, and the use of lethal methods (such as firearms and hanging) by young men.

Women attempt suicide more often than men, but the ratio is a subject of debate due to wide variations in how the data are gathered. The population of attempters is large and heterogeneous and may differ in important ways from that of suicide completers. For example, most attempters will not ultimately die from suicide, though they may try repeatedly; and many people who die by suicide have not made a previous attempt (Health Canada 1994). It is likely that more suicidal acts committed by women are intended as non-fatal, compared with those by men (Canetto and Sakinofsky 1998).

Compared with other countries, Canada's rates of youth suicide are high. In 1973, Canada was the only country among twenty-one western countries in which the suicide rate for male youth aged 15 to 24 equalled or exceeded the rate for the general population of males. By 1987, only four other countries shared this pattern (Health Canada 1994). Between 1991 and 1993, the suicide rate for Canadian male youth was exceeded only in Australia and the Russian Federation (among ten industrialized countries); the female rate was higher than that of all other countries except Sweden and the Russian Federation (United Nations Children's Fund 1996).

As Figure 26-4 shows, there has been a steady and significant increase in suicide

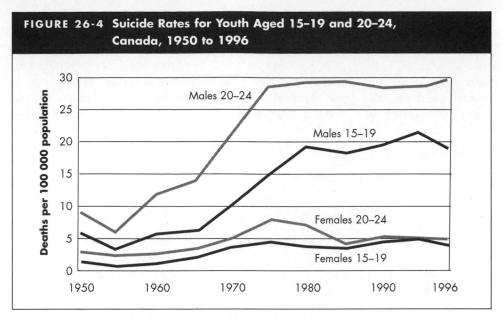

FIGURE 26-4 **Suicide Rates for Youth Aged 15–19 and 20–24, Canada, 1950 to 1996**

Source: Statistics Canada, *Health Indicators 1996,* an unpublished tabulation.

rates among young men aged 15 to 24 since 1950. The 1996 rate of 18.5 per 100 000 among 15- to 19-year-old males was almost twice as high as the 1970 rate. Suicide rates among young men aged 20 to 24 were even higher. These rates reached a peak in the early 1980s and have fluctuated around this level ever since. In 1996, the male suicide rate for this age group was 29 per 100 000. During the 1990s, there has been an average of almost thirty-nine suicides per year by children aged 10 to 14 (mostly boys), up from the average of twenty-seven per year during the 1980s (Statistics Canada 1997).

Suicide among Aboriginal groups in Canada has been reported to be two to seven times more frequent than in the population at large. In the Northwest Territories (NWT) and Nunavut combined, considerable attention has focused on an apparent increase in the occurrence of suicide in a number of communities. In 1992, the annual age-standardized suicide rate for the NWT and Nunavut combined was estimated at 23 per 100 000 population compared with 13 per 100 000 for Canada as a whole (Health Canada 1995).

In Nunavut, Inuit people represent the majority of the population. A comprehensive study conducted in 1997 on suicide in the NWT and Nunavut combined found that in a comparison of ethnic groups, the highest rate of suicide occurred among the Inuit, at 79 per 100 000, compared with 29 per 100 000 for the Dene and 15 per 100 000 for all other ethnic groups, comprised primarily of non-Aboriginal persons. A comparison of three five-year time periods between 1982 and 1996 revealed increasing rates of suicide, particularly for Nunavut. Young Inuit males were the most likely group to commit suicide. Thirty-six percent of those who committed suicide had experienced a recent family or relationship break-up and 21% were facing criminal proceedings. Understanding these and other reported circumstances on the risk of suicide requires further investigation (Isaacs et al. 1998).

Other groups at high risk of suicide include people who suffer from depression and people with substance abuse problems. Studies show that gay men, lesbians, and people who have experienced child sexual abuse may also be at higher risk (Health Canada 1995).

Homicide

There were 581 homicides reported in Canada in 1997—a decline of 9% from 1996. This continues a steady decline in the homicide rate in Canada. Following rapid increases in the late 1960s and early 1970s, the rate of homicide in Canada in 1997 reached its lowest point since 1969. Males accounted for nearly two-thirds (64%) of all homicide victims and 84% of accused persons (Fedorowycz 1998).

Canada's 1997 homicide rate of 1.92 per 100 000 was less than one-third that of the United States (6.70), but higher than that of most European countries, including England and Wales (1.00) and France (1.66).

There were 193 homicides committed with firearms in 1997, nineteen fewer than in 1996. Despite this drop, firearms continue to be used in about one out of three homicides (Kong 1998).

Infant Mortality

In 1996, infant mortality rates fell below 6 per 1000 live births for the first time (Statistics Canada 1998a). While this is an important achievement, it is still quite far above the infant mortality rate of Japan, which is the lowest in the world at 3.8 deaths per 1000 live births (Organization for Economic Co-operation and Development 1998).

Perinatal complications were the most important single cause of both infant mortality and perinatal death (Statistics Canada 1999). There are substantial dif-ferences in infant mortality rates among the various income groups in Canada. Although rates among First Nations people have fallen dramatically since 1979, the 1994 infant mortality rate was twice as high among First Nations people than in the Canadian population as a whole (Health Canada 1996). These findings are explored in more detail in Health Canada's *Toward a Healthy Future*, 1999, Chapter 3 on Healthy Child Development.

Deaths Attributable to Smoking

As a cause of early death, smoking far outweighs suicide, motor vehicle crashes, AIDS, and murder combined (Ellison et al. 1998). In Canada, smoking is estimated to be responsible for at least one-quarter of all deaths for adults between the ages of 35 and 84 (Collishaw and Leahy 1988). In 1991, more than 45 000 deaths were attributed to smoking (Ellison et al. 1995). Overall, men are still more likely than women to smoke and to smoke heavily; hence, death rates due to smoking are substantially higher among males than females. This gender difference, however, can be expected to disappear as smoking rates converge.

LIFE EXPECTANCY AT BIRTH

Based on current mortality patterns, a Canadian child born in 1996 could expect to live to the age of 78.6 (males 75.7; females 81.4). This life expectancy represents a new high in Canada, possibly due to declines in the mortality rates for several of the leading causes of death. At all ages, women have a greater life expectancy than men. The gap in life expectancy at birth has continued to narrow, however, from 7.5 years in 1978 to 5.7 in 1996 (Statistics Canada 1998b).

Immigration contributes to high life expectancy rates in Canada. Immigrants, particularly those from non-European countries, have lower mortality rates and higher life expectancies than residents who are Canadian-born. In 1991, 41% of male and 57% of female non-European immigrants could expect to live to the age of 85, compared with 23% of male and 45% of female Canadian-born residents (Chen, Ng, and Wilkins 1996).

According to a 1991 study by Robine and Ritchie, Canadian men in the highest quarter of income distribution can expect to live 6.3 years longer and 14.3 more years free of disability than those in the lowest quartile. For women, the differences are 3.0 and 7.6 years respectively (Robine and Ritchie 1991).

Another study, conducted by Michael Wolfson in 1993, shows the strong inverse relationship between career earnings and age of death for Canadian men; as earnings increased, the rate of premature mortality decreased. Wolfson's findings also suggest that this pattern is not primarily due to people being unable to work because of illness and thus unable to earn higher incomes, but rather because low economic status leads to exposure to unhealthy life conditions, and thus to poorer health and earlier death (Wolfson et al. 1993).

Consistent with these findings are the results of a study on the life expectancy of status Indians, many of whom live in low-income situations. As Figure 26-5 shows, the life expectancy of the status Indian population in 1990 was seven years less than that for the overall Canadian population in 1991 (Department of Indian Affairs and Northern Development 1993).

POTENTIAL YEARS OF LIFE LOST

Potential years of life lost (PYLL) concerns the loss of life before the age of 70 (Statistics Canada 1999). Therefore, addressing the causes of PYLL would be

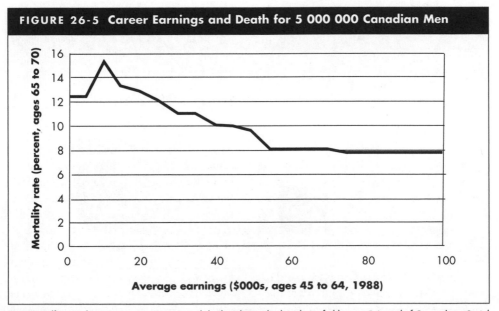

FIGURE 26-5 Career Earnings and Death for 5 000 000 Canadian Men

Mortality rate (percent, ages 65 to 70)

Average earnings ($000s, ages 45 to 64, 1988)

Source: Wolfson et al. 1993. "Career earnings and death: A longitudinal analysis of older men," *Journal of Gerontology: Social Sciences* 47(4):S167–S179.

expected to make a major difference to life expectancy and health status in general.

In 1996, there were more than one million PYLL due to all causes. The most important cause of PYLL was cancer (30% of total). Unintentional injuries (19%) and heart disease (13%) were the second and third most important causes. Cancer has been the leading cause of PYLL since 1984 and, along with suicide, is the only major cause of PYLL to have increased since 1970.

Between 1970 and 1996, there was a marked improvement in premature mortality due to unintentional injuries among young Canadians, especially for ages 10 to 19.

Potential years of life lost per 100 000 population allows us to compare the burden of premature mortality among various groups. Overall, these rates are almost twice as high among men as among women, and approximately three times higher among men aged 20 to 34. The higher rates of premature mortality among

men in general are attributed largely to the higher rates of cancer, heart disease, suicide, and unintentional injuries.

PYLL per 100 000 population varies substantially by province and territory, from a low of 3453 in Ontario to highs of 4742 in the Yukon Territory and 7695 in the Northwest Territories and Nunavut combined (Figure 26-6). The rates of PYLL in the Northwest Territories and Nunavut are more than double that for the rest of Canada. Premature deaths from unintentional injuries and suicides in the three territories account for much of the difference.

There are marked differences between socio-economic groups in terms of PYLL. A 1995 study by Wilkins found that residents of the poorest neighbourhoods had death rates from circulatory disease, lung cancer, injuries, and suicide that were significantly higher than rates for residents of the richest neighbourhoods. In other words, people who are economically disadvantaged do not suffer more from a particular

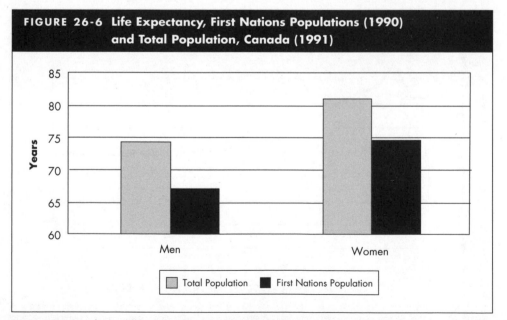

FIGURE 26-6 Life Expectancy, First Nations Populations (1990) and Total Population, Canada (1991)

Sources: Department of Indian Affairs and Northern Development; Statistics Canada, *Births and Deaths, 1993.*

TABLE 26-3   Potential Years of Life Lost per 100 000 Population, by Cause and by Province and Territory, 1996

	Total	Neoplasms	Accidents	Suicide	Respiratory	Heart Disease	Stroke	All Others
Newfoundland	3 731	1 152	759	224	77	663	110	737
Prince Edward Island	3 687	1 189	829	188	144	542	138	557
Nova Scotia	3 983	1 264	860	367	147	592	64	689
New Brunswick	3 736	1 126	758	394	77	589	82	711
Québec	4 032	1 192	735	660	108	521	98	717
Ontario	3 453	1 079	601	284	110	475	93	810
Manitoba	4 066	1 147	936	351	140	546	121	824
Saskatchewan	4 203	1 086	964	508	161	523	82	879
Alberta	3 943	1 009	963	529	129	492	86	735
British Columbia	3 986	960	828	279	102	385	75	1 357
Yukon Territory	4 742	775	1 788	457	86	559	0	1 078
Northwest Territories and Nunavut	7 695	1 479	2 309	1 480	370	481	269	1 308

Note: Small differences occur between the total and the sum of the cause columns because of rounding.

Source: Health Canada, Laboratory Centre for Disease Control. Calculated from Statistics Canada, Health Statistics Division, *Health Indicators, 1999* (Statistics Canada Cat. No. 82-221-XCB).

disease, but show an increased vulnerability to early death due to a variety of causes. Wilkins concluded that if the death rates of the highest income group for all causes of death applied to all Canadians, more than one-fifth of all years of life lost before aged 65 could be prevented (Wilkins 1995).

HOW DOES CANADA COMPARE WITH OTHER COUNTRIES?

Many health measures indicate that Canadians enjoy a standard of health that is among the best in the world. Compared with other developed countries that are members of the Organization for Economic Co-operation and Development (OECD), Canada ranks third in life expectancy, behind only Switzerland and Japan. Canadian mortality rates are among the lowest in the industrialized world, behind only those of South Korea, Japan, Iceland, and Switzerland. And among countries reporting self-rated health status, Canada ranks behind only Norway, and well ahead of such countries as Sweden, Spain, Finland, Germany, and South Korea (OECD 1998).

Yet, there is clearly room for improvement. Although Canada's infant mortality rate has decreased steadily, the rate of improvement may have been lower than that in most industrialized countries. In 1990, Canada ranked fifth among seventeen OECD countries; by 1996, it ranked twelfth. That year, Canada's rate of 5.6 deaths per 1000 live births was lower than those of only the United States, New Zealand, Greece, Australia, and the United Kingdom (Statistics Canada 1996). However, this more recent ranking may be largely due to changes in the way infant mortality is reported in various countries.

DISCUSSION

Reducing Inequities

As Canada stands poised to enter a new millennium, reducing persistent inequities in health status remains one of our greatest challenges to achieving population health. Canadians with low incomes and low levels of education (which are often related) are more likely to have poor health status, no matter which measure of health is used. They are also more likely to die earlier than other Canadians, no matter which cause of death is considered.

This chapter also shows that poor health is not just the result of economic deprivation even though health status improves for all Canadians with each step up the economic ladder. Current thinking suggests that this may be related to increased susceptibility to disease processes related to the stresses of disadvantage and the coping skills people possess, in addition to increased exposure to threats in the physical environment (Evans 1992).

This report recognizes the inherent challenges in achieving the goal of reduced inequities. Virtually all societies struggle with this problem. Achieving complete equality in health status among all Canadians is an unrealistic goal. But achieving "equitable" or fair access to the opportunities and supportive environments all people need to be healthy is both a laudable and achievable goal in a caring, civilized society. The United Nations report on human development suggests that efforts to reduce relative poverty, and to increase opportunities in education, employment, wages, and participation in political and economic spheres are the key strategies for reducing inequities and, therefore, improving the health and well-being of Canadians.

Addressing Differences in Population Groups

This report and others point to the urgent need to find effective ways to improve the health of Canada's Aboriginal people. Failure to address inequities in the health and socio-economic status of Aboriginal people will inevitably lead to continuing disparities and to an increase in illness, suffering, and early deaths for this population.

Aboriginal communities have the lead role in finding ways to enable their people to take control of and improve their health. However, to do so will require all policy-makers and practitioners (both Aboriginal and non-Aboriginal) to work with Canada's Native peoples to find culturally appropriate ways to improve their health and well-being.

Gender Has an Important Influence on Health

In the last half of [the twentieth] century, women have lived longer than men; however, the gap in life expectancy at birth between women and men has continued to narrow—from 7.5 years in 1978 to 5.7 years in 1996 (Statistics Canada 1998c). This may be due to a number of factors including increases in stress on women and decreases in the major causes of premature death among men, especially ischemic heart disease and lung cancer.

While this reduction in two of the major causes of death among men is welcome, premature mortality rates continue to be substantially higher among men than women. If male mortality rates are to be further reduced, increasing attention needs to be paid to other major causes of death among men, including fatal injuries and suicide.

While a decrease in lung cancer deaths is good news for men, cancer death rates have remained stubbornly persistent for women, mainly due to continuing increases in lung cancer mortality. At the same time, smoking rates among young women have continued to escalate. Indeed, adolescent women are now more likely to smoke than adolescent men. Unless the trend toward increased smoking among young women is quickly reversed, lung cancer will increasingly become a major killer of women.

Quality of life is as important as quantity. While women live longer than men, they also suffer more from chronic diseases and disabilities. Efforts to prevent these problems in the senior years are essential to maintaining and improving the health of both women and men, but may be particularly important to women.

This chapter also suggests a need to address the psychosocial well-being of young people. Low scores for psychological well-being, high scores for probable depression and high rates of suicide are warning signs that many of Canada's young people are greatly troubled. Increases in substance use and multiple risk behaviours are further signs of youth distress. Enhanced employment opportunities, incentives for higher education, and nurturing communities are all prerequisites for improving the well-being of Canada's young people.

Increasing Health Promotion and Disease and Injury Prevention Activities in Key Areas

Most of the causes of disease, disability, and early death explored in this chapter are preventable. In the cases of heart disease and cancer, we are beginning to see some positive results from ongoing efforts to prevent and reduce these diseases. These initiatives (and others) need to continue, with an increased focus on Canadians with low incomes and low levels of education.

Deaths and disabilities due to smoking and unintentional injuries are almost all preventable. As such, they must remain a high priority for policy-makers and practitioners. In terms of injuries, we need to pay attention to and better understand gender and age differences in risk-taking behaviour, the causes of both intentional and non-intentional injuries, and how they are best prevented. Reducing the very high rates of injury and injury-related deaths among Aboriginal young people must also be a priority for action.

REFERENCES

Adams, O. 1988. "Health status." In Health and Welfare Canada, *Canada's Health Promotion Survey 1985: Technical Report.* Catalogue No. H39-119/1988.

Canadian Institute for Health Information 1998. *National Trauma Registry Report: Hospital Injury Admissions, 1995–1996.* Ottawa: CIHI.

Canetto, S., and I. Sakinofsky 1998. "The gender paradox in suicide." *Suicide and Life-Threatening Behaviour* 28(1):1–23.

Chen, J., E. Ng, and R. Wilkins 1996. Statistics Canada. "The health of Canada's immigrants in 1994–1995." *Health Reports* 7(4):33–45. Catalogue No. 82-003-XPB. Ottawa: Statistics Canada.

Chen, J., R. Wilkins, and E. Ng 1996. "Health expectancy by immigrant status, 1986 and 1991." *Health Reports* 8(3):29–37. Ottawa: Statistics Canada.

Collishaw, N.E., K. Leahy 1988. "Mortality attributable to tobacco use in Canada." *Canadian Journal of Public Health* 79:166–169.

Department of Indian Affairs and Northern Development 1993. Statistics Canada, *Births and Deaths, 1993.*

Edwards, P. 1993. *Self-Esteem, Sport and Physical Activity.* Ottawa: Canadian Association for the Advancement of Women and Sport and Physical Activity.

Ellison, L., Y. Mao, L. Gibbons 1995. "Projected smoking-attributable mortality in Canada, 1991–2000." *Chronic Diseases in Canada* 16: 84–89.

Ellison, L., H.I. Morrison, M. de Groh et al. 1998. *Health Consequences of Smoking Among Canadian Smokers: An Update.* Ottawa: Health Canada, Laboratory Centre for Disease Control.

Evans, R. 1992. *Why Are Some People Healthy and Other People Not?* Canadian Working Paper Number 20. Toronto: Institute for Advanced Research, Program in Population Health, December.

Fedorowycz, O. 1998. "Homicide in Canada, 1997." *Juristat* 18(12). Catalogue No. 85-002-XPE. Ottawa: Statistics Canada.

Health Canada 1994. *Suicide in Canada. Update of the Report of the Task Force on Suicide in Canada.* Catalogue No. H39-107/1995E. Ottawa: Minister of Supply and Services Canada.

Health Canada 1995. *Suicide in Canada: Update of the Report of the Task Force on Suicide in Canada.* Catalogue No. H39-107/1995E. Ottawa: Health Programs and Services Branch.

Health Canada 1996. *Health Programs Analysis, First Nations and Inuit Health Programs.* Ottawa: Medical Services Branch.

Heart and Stroke Foundation of Canada 1997. *Heart Disease and Stroke in Canada.* Ottawa: Heart and Stroke Foundation of Canada.

Isaacs, S., S. Keogh, C. Menard et al. 1998. "Suicide in the Northwest Territories: A descriptive review." *Chronic Diseases in Canada* 19(4):152–156.

James, R., T. Kue Young, and A. Cameron et al. 1997. "The health of Canadians with diabetes." *Health Reports* 9(3):47–52.

Kong, R. 1998. "Canadian crime statistics, 1997." *Juristat* 18, 11. Catalogue No. 85-002-XPE. Ottawa: Statistics Canada.

MacMillan, H., C. Walsh, E. Jamieson et al. 1999. "Children's health." *First Nations and Inuit Regional Health Survey.* Ottawa: First Nations and Inuit Regional Health Survey National Steering Committee.

National Cancer Institute of Canada 1998. *Canadian Cancer Statistics, 1998.* Toronto: National Cancer Institute of Canada.

Organization for Economic Co-operation and Development 1998. *OECD Health Data 98* (CD-ROM).

Robine, J., and K. Ritchie 1991. "Healthy life expectancy: Evaluation of global indicators of change in population health." *British Medical Journal* 302:457–460.

SmartRisk Foundation 1998. *The Economic Burden of Unintentional Injury in Canada.* Toronto: SmartRisk Foundation.

Statistics Canada 1994–1995. *National Population Health Survey, 1994–1995.* Special tabulations. Ottawa: Statistics Canada.

Statistics Canada 1996. *Health Indicators 1996.* Unpublished tabulations.

Statistics Canada 1996–1997. *National Population Health Survey, 1996–1997.* Special tabulations. Ottawa: Statistics Canada.

Statistics Canada 1997. Health Statistics Division. *Health Indicators, 1997.* Catalogue No. 82-221-XDE. Ottawa: Statistics Canada.

Statistics Canada 1998a. "Births 1996." *The Daily*, July 8. Catalogue No. 11-001-XIE. Ottawa: Statistics Canada.

Statistics Canada 1998b. *Compendium of Vital Statistics 1996.* Catalogue No. 84-214-XPE (Fall). Ottawa: Statistics Canada.

Statistics Canada 1998c. "Deaths 1996." *The Daily*, April 16. Catalogue No. 11-001-XIE. Ottawa: Statistics Canada (http://www.statcan.ca).

Statistics Canada 1999. *Health Indicators, 1999.* Catalogue No. 82-221-XCB. Ottawa: Statistics Canada.

Stephens, T. 1998. *Population Mental Health in Canada.* Report prepared for the Mental Health Promotion Unit, Health Canada, May.

Transport Canada 1999. *Total Collisions and Casualties 1977–1996.* Ottawa: Transport Canada. Retrieved 1999 (http://www.tc.gc.ca/roadsafety/Stats/stats96/st96tote.htm).

United Nations Children's Fund 1996. *Progress of Nations, 1996.* New York: UNICEF.

Wilkins, R. 1995. "Mortality by neighbourhood income in Canada, 1986 to 1991." Presented at the Conference of the Canadian Society for Epidemiology and Biostatistics, St. John's, Newfoundland, August.

Wolfson, M., G. Rowe, J. Gentleman et al. 1993. "Career earnings and death: A longitudinal analysis of older men." *Journal of Gerontology: Social Sciences* 47(4): S167–179.

Young, T., J. O'Neill, B. Elias, et al. 1999. "Chronic diseases." *First Nations and Inuit Regional Health Survey, 1997.* Ottawa: First Nations and Inuit Regional Health Survey National Steering Committee.

CANADA'S HOMELESS: PATTERNS AND POLICIES

Tracy Peressini

(A new chapter written for this volume.)

INTRODUCTION

As little as two decades ago, homelessness was seldom noticed or discussed in Canada. Over the last twenty years, however, homelessness has become recognized as a significant social problem requiring attention and social action (Bogard 2001). Researchers argue that the homeless are one of the fastest growing segments of the population (e.g., Nunez and Fox 1999) and that this signals growing inequality between the rich and the very poor in society (Wright 2000). Now that we have entered the twenty-first century, the consensus among social scientists and policy analysts is that, like poverty, homelessness has become an all-too-persistent feature of society (Hoch 2000). It is, therefore, essential that we understand the nature and extent of the problem of homelessness in Canada.

This chapter discusses the size and characteristics of the homeless population and reviews the current state of knowledge on homelessness. Our primary concern is with the ways in which social advocates, researchers, and government officials have addressed the problem, and with their attempts to study and improve the lives of the homeless. Theories of homelessness are also described and evaluated. The chapter concludes with a discussion of current social policies aimed at helping the homeless.

DEFINING AND COUNTING THE HOMELESS

How many homeless people are there in Canada? Typically, this is the first question asked about the homeless. Answering the question, however, has proven to be challenging, controversial, and political. There is a lack of agreement as to who the "homeless" are, so much so that the inconsistency across definitions has been dubbed the "homeless muddle" (Ellickson 1990:45). The disagreement reflects the disparate and incompatible agendas and politics of the key players involved with the problem. On the one hand, social advocates and service providers prefer definitions that address the full spectrum of homelessness, definitions that are broad and include anyone from those who are at risk of homelessness (e.g., those who have some form of housing, but are at imminent risk of losing it) to those who are already without a permanent home. On the other hand, government officials and policy analysts prefer definitions that are restricted to those who currently do not have a permanent place to live, typically those actually living on the street and/or living in shelters for the homeless. For example, using a broad definition of homelessness, American social advocates in the 1980s estimated that the homeless population was in excess of one million people (Hombs and Snyder 1982); at the same time, the U.S. government, counting only street people and shelter users, estimated that between 250 000 and 350 000 people were homeless (U.S. Department of Housing and Urban Development 1984). The debate over appropriate definitions has been one of the driving forces behind studies of homelessness since the early 1990s.

Of course, how we define homelessness directly affects the size of the population that is counted. This, in turn, determines the degree of social response that is needed to address the problem (Fitzgerald et al. 2001:121). The estimated size and composition of the homeless population guide government officials and policy analysts in estimating the amount of funding that should be allotted for programs and services to address the social, economic, and health needs of the home-

less (Springer 2000). Definitions, therefore, not only specify who will be counted, but also determine who "counts." In other words, the act of defining who is homeless results in a political and moral statement about who is worthy of public assistance and resources and who is not (Rossi 1989).

Not surprisingly, then, the first question the Canadian federal government asked after they established the National Secretariat on Homelessness in 1999 was: How many homeless people are there in Canada? Answering the question led the Secretariat head-first into the debate over definitions, and the government is still grappling with definitions and measurement procedures.

Part of the problem is that only two concerted attempts have been made to count the homeless nationally, and these used different approaches. The most recent study was conducted by Statistics Canada during its work on the 1991 Canadian Census. In an effort to improve its count of the Canadian population, Statistics Canada supplemented the national census with a count of persons using soup kitchens in sixteen Canadian cities (Begin et al. 1999). Unfortunately, due to the limited nature of the data collected, the results of the supplemental survey were not released. The problem is that soup kitchens serve a quite diverse population, from the housed and working poor to those who are literally homeless. Studying the homeless population in this way results in an estimate that is both inaccurate (it includes both the housed poor and the homeless) and incomplete (only a fraction of the homeless eat at soup kitchens).

Another national estimate was undertaken in 1987 by the Canadian Council on Social Development (CCSD), in partnership with the Canada Mortgage and Housing Corporation. Using a national survey of temporary and emergency shelters, the CCSD estimated that roughly 7751 people slept in a shelter or hostel on any given night in 1987 (McLaughlin 1987). The researchers then combined this tally with estimated numbers obtained from key informants such as the police, service providers, and hospital administrators across the country. In this way they arrived at a national estimate of between 130 000 and 250 000 homeless Canadians, representing between 0.5% and 1.0% of the total population (McLaughlin 1987).

At best, the CCSD's estimate is a partial count, because many homeless people do not use a shelter or come into contact with the key informants on an average day. At worst, the CCSD's estimate is a very rough guess, because the numbers obtained from shelter providers are generally not based on a genuine count of their clients, but instead are an estimate of the number of people using their shelter on any given night. The final number, then, was a collection of key informants' impressions of the size of the population. The CCSD's count also was higher than it might have been because of who was defined as homeless. They asked key informants to provide them with a combined count of both the at-risk and the homeless populations, which resulted in a considerably increased estimate.

A comparison with an American count conducted by the Urban Institute in 1987 (Burt and Cohen 1989) demonstrates how the size of the population expands and contracts depending on how homelessness is defined. Comparing the Canadian estimate by CCSD with the American estimate provided by the Urban Institute, while controlling for the difference in the size of the Canadian and American populations, leads to the conclusion that there were 4.5 times as many homeless Canadians as Americans in 1987. In other words, nine in every 1000 people were homeless in Canada, compared with an

American rate of 2 in 1000 (Peressini and McDonald 2000). Are there really more homeless people per capita in Canada than in the United States? Local and regional counts of Canada's homeless suggest that the answer is no. The difference in the above rates is due to differences in who was defined as homeless and how they were counted. The Americans based their estimate on a physical count of the shelter users and street people in twenty cities with populations over 100 000 (Burt and Cohen 1989).

While there are differences of opinion about numbers and rates, we have made more headway in coming to a consensus over definitions. Most researchers and social advocates acknowledge that the United Nations' definition of homelessness is the ideal. According to the UN definition, persons are homeless if they meet one of two criteria: (1) They have no home and live either outdoors or in emergency shelters or hostels; and (2) they live in homes that do not meet the UN's standards for a minimal home (i.e., protection from the elements, access to safe water and sanitation, affordable price, secure tenure and personal safety, and accessibility to employment, education, and health care) (Springer 2000). In practice, however, many studies employ a variant of the narrower definition stipulated in the United States under the *Stuart B. McKinney Homeless Assistance Act* (U.S. Congress, House of Representatives 1987). The Act defines homeless individuals as (1) persons who lack a fixed, regular, and adequate nighttime residence; or (2) persons who have a primary nighttime residence that is either a supervised or publicly operated shelter designed to provide temporary living accommodations (including welfare hotels, congregate shelters, and transitional housing for the mentally ill), an institution that provides temporary residence for individuals intended to be institutionalized, or a public or private place not designed for, or ordinarily used as, a regular sleeping accommodation for human beings (see Hirschl 1990:444–445).

Because of the absence of a reliable national estimate of the number of homeless Canadians, many Canadian cities began to conduct regular censuses of their homeless populations. Unfortunately, no consistent procedure has been used in the counts. Therefore, the numbers cannot be combined to obtain a rough national estimate of the size of the homeless population. Also, the accuracy of the counts varies considerably across Canada's cities. The City of Toronto uses the Homeless Management Information System (HMIS), which allows them to monitor the number of people staying in their emergency and transitional shelters. Through the HMIS, the city can collect personal and demographic information from those who use the shelter system on a nightly basis, and it allows them to track usage over time. Based on data collected over the past decade, Toronto reports that the yearly number of people staying in emergency shelters increased from 22 000 to 30 000 (City of Toronto 2001). Regardless of the procedures used, and whatever the absolute numbers, several major cities have reported that the number of people staying in emergency and temporary shelters, as well as those living on the streets, has increased. The estimates of increases over the last decade range anywhere from 40% in Toronto to 121% in Calgary (Harkness 2001; City of Toronto 2001).

THE FACE OF HOMELESSNESS IN CANADA

Most experts agree that the face of homelessness has changed over the last twenty years. Today's homeless population is comparatively more diverse. The homeless now come from all classes and demographic groups, including men and women, children and youth, families, students, seniors, immigrants, Aboriginal people, and people from Canada's various ethnic communities. They have experienced problems with poverty, unemployment, family violence, child abuse, divorce, mental illness, depression, physical disabilities, substance abuse, and deviance. They are present in every city, region, and province across Canada. However, the images of bag ladies, beggars, squeegee kids, and skid-row alcoholics have prevailed and are the impressions that most often come to mind when the issue of homelessness is raised. Street people are the most visible of the homeless, but researchers have found that they make up less than 10% of the population (Dennis and Iachan 1993). In fact, most homeless persons do not actually live on the street; they live in temporary and emergency shelters, with friends and family, in their cars, indoors in public spaces, and in abandoned buildings. They also move into and out of public institutions such as group homes, psychiatric wards, shelters, and prisons. They are the invisible poor and most of them do not ever cross our paths as we move around the community. As one homeless sole-support parent in Calgary recently told a local reporter, "you can see me on the street and not know I'm homeless" (Slobodian 2002:B2).

The reality of homelessness is that, for many, it is a complex process of exits from and returns to homelessness. Researchers in the U.S. have found that the majority of the homeless population experience multiple spells of homelessness, with initial spells being of a relatively short duration (usually from seven to thirty days) and subsequent spells of progressively longer duration (Piliavin et al. 1993). For most people, homelessness is not a lasting condition, but a short-term situation that they move into and out of as they lose and regain their housing. Certainly, no one chooses to be homeless, but extreme poverty offers little economic stability and it only takes a personal crisis—such as the loss of a job, a missed child support payment, or an illness—to cause them to lose their housing. That the homeless quickly recover their housing is a testament to their resilience and resourcefulness. Sadly, though, the fact that they experience recurring episodes of homelessness is a reflection of the wide-ranging cuts in federal support of Canada's social safety net over the last two decades.

In part, it is the rapid turnover rate in the homeless population that prevents us from seeing the many different types of persons affected by homelessness. The other factor that limits the visibility of the homeless is the availability of shelters, programs, and services for some of them. For example, women, particularly women with children, tend to have access to a highly developed and well-coordinated system of short- and long-term shelters and services that is very effective in preventing them from having to stay on the streets (Bogard 2001; Passaro 1996). There generally is no adequate system of shelter and services for homeless men. The only services available to men, who are expected to find a job and support themselves, are drop-in centres and overnight homeless shelters. The shelters provide refuge on a nightly basis, but force users onto the street the very next morning. Thus, men tend to be more often associated with the street population, and more visible, because they have no place to stay during the day (Passaro 1996).

Not only are men the most visible of Canada's homeless, they also constitute the largest demographic group of homeless persons. This is one of the least recognized facts about the homeless among

policy-makers. Virtually every study of homelessness in Canada has found that men make up from 70% to 90% of the population (Layton 2000), and yet the problem of male homelessness is often addressed only through the provision of overnight shelters.

The gender bias in public and policy responses to homelessness can be seen in the greater attention paid to homelessness among women, children, and families. Homeless families, in particular, have been the focus of a great deal of attention. Even though we do not know how many homeless one- and two-parent families there are in Canada, many government researchers and social advocates single out this group and note their rapid growth in the last decade. For example, using data from the shelter user database, the City of Toronto, in their latest Report Card on Homelessness, highlighted the fact that between 1988 and 1999 the number of two-parent families looking for shelter in Toronto increased from 320 to 2070; an increase of over 600%. This increase, however, is not nearly as impressive when the number of homeless families is compared with the number of single homeless persons. Of the 30 000 people seeking shelter in Toronto in 1999, just over 1700 consisted of families, compared with more than 24 000 single persons, the majority of whom were men (City of Toronto 2001:3). The point of this example is not to diminish the plight of homeless families, but to demonstrate that there is a selective perception and assessment of the level of need among the homeless based on their demographic characteristics.

It is important to remember that the experience of homelessness is devastating and demoralizing for everyone who experiences it. As Koegel, Burnam, and Farr (1990) have noted, homelessness is characterized by a levelling process, in which personal and demographic characteristics have no observable impact on a person's ability to adapt and to survive on the streets. To be homeless is to be truly disadvantaged, regardless of age, sex, ethnic background, or any other demographic characteristic. With this in mind, a brief overview of the research findings on selected social and demographic characteristics of Canada's homeless is presented below.

Local studies from across Canada indicate that, in most cases, the age of the homeless ranges between 18 and 34 years of old (Layton 2000), although the number of homeless youth may be on the rise. For example, between 1998 and 2000, the proportion of youth (aged 15–24) using the shelter system in Toronto increased moderately, from 20% to 23% (City of Toronto 2001). The number of immigrants and refugees who are homeless appears to be on the rise as well. The City of Toronto reported a 6% increase in the number of refugees and immigrants seeking admission to their shelter system over a two-year period, with the majority of them being families (City of Toronto 2001). Findings from a study conducted in Calgary indicated that the homeless tend to have an average of ten years of education, which is slightly lower than the Canadian average, and usually have worked at sometime or other in the year previous to being interviewed (Peressini 1995). Although the evidence is mostly anecdotal, it appears that sizeable proportions of the homeless population in some of Canada's cities are Aboriginal persons, ranging as high as 75% in some cases (Begin et al. 1999; Beavis et al. 1997).

Finally, there is some limited information on other personal issues and problems—such as mental illness, drug and alcohol abuse, criminal behaviour, and physical health—among Canada's homeless. Ambrosia et al. (1992), in a study of men and women using Toronto's Street Health Clinic, found that about 17% of respondents said they used alcohol on a daily basis, 44% reported using drugs in the month prior to being surveyed, and 14% had been treated at some time or other for drug and alcohol dependency. These researchers also found that anywhere from 2% to 30% of their respondents reported some form of chronic health problem such as arthritis, allergies, asthma, diabetes, and epilepsy (Ambrosia et al. 1992). Breton and Bunston, in their study of single homeless women in Toronto, found that 44% of their sample reported using drugs and alcohol prior to the survey. Over 70% of the women reported being treated for or having some form of physical illness, while roughly 40% reported being treated for some form of emotional or mental illness (Breton and Bunston 1991). Other researchers have found that the severity and likelihood of having emotional, mental, and physical health problems increases with the duration of homelessness. For example, Peressini (1995) found that a sample of chronically homeless men in Calgary was ten times more likely to suffer from and receive treatment for emotional, psychological, or substance abuse problems than were the newly homeless in the study.

EXPLAINING HOMELESSNESS

One version of how people become homeless focuses on the individual's social, behavioural, emotional, and psychological deficits, and emphasizes the role that personal pathology and disabilities play in the process of homelessness. From this perspective, homelessness occurs because of *personal limitations*, or because there is something "wrong" with *the individual*. The causes of homelessness are identified as mental or physical illness, physical disability, social alienation, social deviance and social disaffiliation (e.g., criminal behaviour, juvenile delinquency, and drug and alcohol abuse), and human capital deficits (e.g., little education, and low or inappropriate job skills and work experience). Thus, many researchers have argued that homelessness is the result of people's inability to take care of themselves, either through incapacitation, choice, or a lack of social and personal resources (Bogard 2001; Hoch 2000).

Many studies carried out over the last decade and a half have supported these types of explanation for homelessness. For example, many studies in the United States have shown that mental illness is correlated with homelessness, but this only explains homelessness for 10% to 30% of the population (Piliavin et al. 1993; Linhorst 1992). What is the source of homelessness for the remaining 70% to 90% of the population? Only some people with health problems become homeless, some with alcohol and drug abuse problems become homeless, and some of those released from prison end up on the street.

However, there are people who become homeless who do not experience these types of personal problems. To account for these other cases, some researchers argue homelessness should be understood as a consequence of the social, political, and economic structures of society, which limit or restrict access to resources and opportunities. Homelessness in this case is viewed as a result of increased poverty and unemployment, declines in social and affordable housing, cuts to welfare and health care programs, and the shift from a manufacturing economy to a service economy (Devine and Wright 1997). According to these explanations, homelessness is created when people cannot afford housing because they are unemployed, are on welfare, or work in minimum-wage-paying jobs. Homelessness is also created when the costs of housing increase due to market demand—

e.g., when low vacancy rates are combined with little new housing being built. Roth and Bean (1986) found that almost a quarter of their sample listed unemployment as the major reason given for their homelessness. Elliott and Krivo (1991), in a study of variations in the rates of homelessness across sixty major U.S. metropolitan areas, found inconsistent effects of housing availability and affordability on the rates of homelessness. A study by Tucker (1990) showed no significant correlation between the rate of homelessness and the rates of poverty and unemployment, for the various cities in his sample.

The findings in the current research literature suggest that each version of homelessness sheds some light on the problem. For many people, homelessness results from one or more noneconomic personal troubles that need to be addressed first so that they possess the functional skills and abilities to live independently and to keep their housing. On the other hand, structural factors, such as the lack of low-cost housing, often limit the ability of Canada's extremely poor to find a place that they can afford. Each avenue of explanation suggests a different set of strategies for the individual, the community, and the state. Homelessness cannot be fully understood by focusing on one or the other of the theories. More importantly, designing effective homelessness prevention and reduction policies and programs will require an integrated approach that considers and incorporates both individual- and structural-level explanations.

SOCIAL POLICY AND HOMELESSNESS

In a country where the government does not set an official poverty line, it should come as no surprise that there is no national legislation, policy, or program that addresses the problem of homelessness

(Daly 1996:25). In 1999, however, the federal government did establish the National Homelessness Initiative (NHI). The NHI is a program that provides $753 million over three years to support community programs and services designed to reduce and alleviate homelessness across Canada (Human Resources Development Canada 2001). The cornerstone of the NHI has been the Supporting Communities Partnership Initiative, which offers limited funds to build and expand emergency and transitional shelters and services to the homeless across the country. Most of the NHI initiatives are only now being implemented, so it is too early to say what impact they will have in addressing homelessness.

Currently, programs and services for the homeless are provided in two ways. First, community and faith-based groups offer programs and services; these are almost always underfunded, and the groups compete with each other for what little funding is available at the provincial and municipal levels. Second, charitable organizations such as the United Way or the Salvation Army provide services and programs. The existing system of services and programs for the homeless is a skeletal system of emergency and stop-gap measures that rarely amounts to much more than "three hots and a cot" (Feins and Fosburg 1999:9–1). At the present time, the mainstay of the NHI funding is being spent on developing emergency and transitional housing for special-needs groups such as women, children, and families and on renovating the run-down buildings that traditionally have sheltered homeless men. While the funding provided through the NHI will definitely have a positive impact on the lives of homeless women, children, and families, and will help to strengthen the existing system of emergency programs and services for them, it is doubtful that it will help in significantly reducing rates of homelessness

for men, who constitute the majority of the homeless population.

One of the most controversial aspects of the federal government's initiative is that neither poverty reduction nor the construction of new affordable housing is part of the NHI's mandate. By focusing on the support of existing programs and services, the NHI reinforces the traditional stereotype that homelessness is a product of individual choice, incompetence, failure, or pathology, and not the result of inadequacies and inequalities in the welfare system and the availability of housing. This is a sore spot for many social advocates and service providers, who have consistently pointed to cuts and freezes in Canada's social programs—such as welfare, unemployment insurance, health care, and the building of social housing—as the prime sources of the rising rates of homelessness.

For all of the differences observed across the homeless population, the homeless have two characteristics in common: a lack of housing, and a lack of economic resources to secure and retain housing. There are two main programs of poverty reduction and income support in Canada that are designed to stabilize household incomes: welfare and employment insurance (formerly called unemployment insurance). In 1995, the federal government transformed the Canada Assistance Plan (CAP) into the Canadian Health and Social Transfer (CHST) and reduced federal contributions to post-secondary education, public health, and social assistance by $7 billion (Yalnizyan 1998). The CHST is a transfer payment from the federal government to the provinces. The provinces then apply these funds as they see fit to cover the costs of education, health care, and welfare. This change in social policy has directly affected welfare rates and shelter allowances and eligibility requirements for both, in virtually every province. For example, between 700 000 and

800 000 people in Ontario had their incomes slashed when the Ontario government cut welfare cheques by 21.6% in 1995 (Yalnizyan 1998). Prior to these cuts, the maximum amount received by a single employable person in Ontario was $663 per month. As a result of the rate cuts, maximum shelter allowances were set at $320 per month, with a living allowance of $195, reducing the maximum amount to $515 per month (Yalnizyan 1998). In addition, cuts to unemployment insurance since 1991 have doubled the number of unemployed people who do not qualify for benefits and who, therefore, have no form of income. The end result is that, in Ontario alone, over a million people lost not only their source of income, but also their ability to keep their housing.

The attack on Canada's income security programs is only half of the story of increased homelessness. Since the 1980s, the federal government has withdrawn from the social housing market and downloaded the responsibility for building new social housing to the provinces. Social housing provides the working poor, those on fixed incomes, and those on welfare with decent and affordable housing. Rents are either subsidized or geared to an individual's or a family's income. Social housing programs also provide assisted or supportive housing to mentally ill and physically disabled Canadians, and play an essential role in preventing people from losing their housing and becoming homeless. Presently, the Federation of Canadian Municipalities estimates that a minimum of 45 000 new rental units will have to be built per year for the next ten years, with at least half being affordable units, to meet current demands for new and social housing. Unfortunately, cuts in the CHST have meant that provincial governments have not only had to cut income security programs, but also have had to make up the shortfall in funding out of their own

budgets, leaving them with little funding for social housing. As a result, since the 1980s there has been a freeze on new social housing starts in most provinces.

By abdicating responsibility for reducing poverty rates, and without targeting funds for new affordable and subsidized housing, the federal government's homelessness initiative is unlikely to have much impact in reducing the number of homeless in Canada. Homelessness will only be well addressed when the criteria for public expenditures and program development are based on the needs and requirements of all Canadians, including those living and dying on Canada's streets. As Wright argues, "ending homelessness is about creating a truly democratic human society beyond the barbarism of the current stock of social inequalities and economic and political violence" (2000:27). Only when our elected officials take responsibility for providing all Canadians with decent and affordable housing, stable and well-paying jobs, and universal health care will we see the end of homelessness (Wright 2000).

REFERENCES

Ambrosio, E., D. Baker, C. Crow, and K. Hardill 1992. *The Street Health Report: A Study of the Health Status and Barriers to Health Care of Homeless Women and Men in the City of Toronto.* Toronto: Street Health.

Beavis, M., N. Klos, T. Carter, and C. Douchant 1997. *Literature Review: Aboriginal Peoples and Homelessness.* Ottawa: Canada Mortgage and Housing Corporation.

Begin, P. L. Casavant, and N.M. Chenier 1999. *Homelessness.* Ottawa: Parliamentary Research Branch, Library of Parliament (PRB 99-1E).

Bogard, C. 2001. "Advocacy and enumeration." *American Behavioral Scientist* 45(1): 105–120.

Breton, M., and T. Bunston 1991. *Single Homeless Women: A Report on Their Quality of Life.* Ottawa: Health and Welfare Canada.

Burt, M.A., and B.E. Cohen 1989. *America's Homeless: Numbers, Characteristics, and Programs That Serve Them.* Washington, D.C.: The Urban Institute Press.

City of Toronto 2001. *The Toronto Report Card on Homelessness, 2001.* Toronto: City of Toronto.

Daly, G. 1996. *Homeless: Policies, Strategies and Lives on the Street.* New York: Routledge.

Dennis, M.L., and R. Iachan 1993. "A multiple frame approach to sampling the homeless and transient population." *Journal of Official Statistics* 14(5):1–18.

Devine, J.A., and J.D. Wright 1997. "Losing the housing game: The leveling effects of substance abuse." *American Journal of Orthopsychiatry* 67(4):618–631.

Dietrich, S., S. Morton-Ninomiya, D. Vandebelt, S. Adams, G. DeSantis, and A. Klassen 1999. *Understanding Homelessness in Waterloo Region: A Backgrounder.* Kitchener-Waterloo: Social Planning Councils of Kitchener-Waterloo, Cambridge and North Dumfries, and the District Health Council, Waterloo Region.

Ellickson, R.C. 1990. "The homelessness muddle." *Public Interest* 99:45–60.

Elliott, M., and L.J. Krivo 1991. "Structural determinants of homelessness in the United States." *Social Problems* 38(1):113–131.

Feins, J.D., and L.B. Fosburg 1999. "Emergency shelter and services: Opening a front door to the continuum of care." In *Practical Lessons: The 1998 National Symposium on Homelessness Research* (9-1 to 9-36). Washington, DC: U.S. Department of Housing and Urban Development.

Fitzgerald, S.T., M.C. Shelley, and P.W. Dail 2001. "Research on homelessness." *American Behavioral Scientist* 45(1):121–148.

Harkness, P. 2001. *Homelessness Report: Survey of Major Canadian Cities.* Hamilton: Social and Public Health Services, Community Support and Research Branch.

Hirschl, T. 1990. "Homelessness: A sociological research agenda." *Sociological Spectrum* 10:443–467.

Hoch, C. 2000. "Sheltering the homeless in the U.S.: Social improvement and the continuum of care." *Housing Studies* 15(6):865–876.

Hombs, M.E., and M. Snyder 1982. *Homelessness in America: A Forced March to Nowhere.* Washington, D.C.: Community for Creative Non-Violence.

Human Resources Development Canada (HRDC) 2001. *National Homelessness Initiative.* Retrieved July 2002 (http://www21.hrdc-drhc.gc.ca/home/index_e.asp). Ottawa: Government of Canada.

Koegel, P., A. Burnam, and R.K. Farr 1990. "Subsistence adaptation among homeless adults in the inner city of Los Angeles." *Journal of Social Issues* 16(4):83–107.

Layton, J. 2000. *Homelessness: The Making and Unmaking of a Crisis.* Toronto: Penguin.

Linhorst, D.M. 1992. "A redefinition of the problem of homelessness among persons with a chronic mental illness." *Journal of Sociology and Social Work* 17(4):43–56.

McLaughlin, MaryAnn 1987. *Homelessness in Canada: The Report of the National Inquiry.* Ottawa: Canadian Council on Social Development.

Nunez, R., and C. Fox 1999. "A snapshot of family homelessness across America." *Political Science Quarterly* 114(2):289–307.

Passaro, J. 1996. *The Unequal Homeless: Men on the Streets, Women in their Place.* New York: Routledge.

Peressini, T. 1995. *Disadvantage, Drift and Despair: A Study of Homelessness in Canada.* Unpublished dissertation. Waterloo, Ontario: The University of Waterloo.

Peressini, T., and L. McDonald 2000. "Urban homelessness in Canada." In T. Bunting and P. Filion (eds.), *Canadian Cities in Transition* (2nd ed.), pp. 523–543. Don Mills, Ontario: Oxford University Press.

Piliavin, I., M. Sosin, A.H. Westerfelt, and R.L. Matsueda 1993. "The duration of homeless careers: An exploratory study." *Social Service Review* (December):576–597.

Quinn, J., and C. Dunphy 1998. "Shelters on alert as weather turns ugly." *Toronto Star*, November 11.

Rossi, P.H. 1987. "No good applied research goes unpunished." *Social Science and Modern Society* 25(1):73–80.

Rossi, P.H. 1989. *Down and Out in America: The Origins of Homelessness.* Chicago: The University of Chicago Press.

Roth, D., and G. Bean 1986. "New perspectives on homelessness: Findings from a statewide epidemiological study." *Hospital and Community Psychiatry* 37(7):712–719.

Slobodian, L. 2002. "A helter-shelter life: Hope, but no home." *Calgary Herald*, June 8.

Springer, S. 2000. "Homelessness: A proposal for a global definition and classification." *Habitat International* 24:475–484.

Tucker, W. 1990. *The Excluded Americans: Homelessness and Housing Policies.* Washington, D.C.: Regnery Gateway.

U.S. Congress, House of Representatives 1987. *Stewart B. McKinney Homeless Assistance Act.* Conference report to accompany H.R. 558, 100th Congress, 1st Session. Washington, D.C.: U.S. Government Printing Office.

U.S. Department of Housing and Urban Development (HUD), Office of Policy Development and Research 1984. *A Report to the Secretary on the Homeless and Emergency Shelters.* Washington, D.C.: Department of Housing and Urban Development.

Wright, T. 2000. "Resisting homelessness: Global, national and local solutions." *Contemporary Sociology* 29(1):26–43.

Yalnizyan, A. 1998. *The Growing Gap: A Report on Growing Inequality Between the Rich and Poor in Canada.* Toronto: Centre for Social Justice.

C h a p t e r

SOCIAL STATUS
AND BELIEFS
ABOUT WHAT'S
IMPORTANT FOR
GETTING AHEAD

James Curtis and Edward Grabb

THE CONCEPT OF DOMINANT IDEOLOGY

Most social researchers would agree that, in virtually every society, certain guiding principles and basic beliefs arise that are fundamental to how that society comes to be defined or characterized. It is common for sociologists to call this set of essential values or precepts the *dominant ideology* of the society in question.

The concept of dominant ideology has been applied in two related but distinct ways by different scholars. First, some use the term in the classical Marxian sense, to indicate the *beliefs that are cherished or promoted by the most powerful group* in society. Marx argued, in particular, that the dominant ideas in nineteenth-century capitalist countries were largely the same as the beliefs held by the ruling capitalist class in those nations. These beliefs, moreover,

tend to serve the interests of the dominant *group* itself. For example, it is usually emphasized in the belief systems of capitalist societies that all people are relatively free individuals, so that inequalities between the dominant class and the rest of the population mainly occur because members of the ruling class generally work harder or have more talent and ambition than other people (see Marx and Engels 1846:39–41, 59; 1848:84–85; also Huber and Form 1973:2; Lipset 1996:24–25).

Other sociologists, however, have used the concept of dominant ideology to indicate a second and rather different set of ideas. For these analysts, the dominant ideology or dominant value system refers mainly to the *beliefs that prevail*, not within the ruling elite, but *among the people as a whole* (see, e.g., Williams 1960:409; Mann 1970). In this case, the ideology is said to be dominant in the sense that its core values are widely believed and accepted by most of the population. Of course, there is usually an overlap between the dominant group's key beliefs and those of the general populace. One likely reason for this overlap is that dominant groups typically play a significant role within the educational, religious, media, and other ideological or "idea" organizations in society, and these organizations greatly influence what viewpoints are fostered and disseminated in the population at large. Nevertheless, as some observers have noted, dominant group values and popular values are not always identical. On the contrary, the elite's beliefs and the people's beliefs are sometimes quite different from one another. In addition, even in those cases in which the values of the dominant group also appear to be widely held by the general population, the latter's commitment to these values may be comparatively less permanent, pervasive, or deeply felt (see, e.g., Parkin 1973:81–84, 92–94; Abercrombie et al. 1980; Wright et al. 1992:44; Grabb 1994:123; Gregg 1995:20; Sniderman et al. 1996:11–13, 244–245; Perlin 1997:106–107).

A related issue that often arises when discussing dominant ideology is whether this set of core values is mainly *descriptive or normative* in nature. In other words, do the ideas and principles composing the dominant value system describe what *actually* operates in a particular society, or do they prescribe what *should* operate ideally, at least if the society is faithful to its own self-definition? This is a question that has concerned various researchers studying societal values, and there is no complete agreement on which usage is more appropriate. Whichever meaning of the term is applied, however, evidence suggests that members of ruling or privileged groups are usually more likely than the rest of the population to believe that the normative or ideal version of the dominant

value system and the values that actually shape their society are basically the same. This seems to be especially true if the values in question are tied, not to abstract statements of fact or principle, but to the concrete conditions or situations that people face. For example, some studies indicate that most people will agree that equal opportunity is prevalent in their society generally, but these same people may not agree that their own opportunities are equal to those of others (see, e.g., Rodman 1963; Mizruchi 1964; Mann 1970; Huber and Form 1973; Parkin 1973; Kluegel and Smith 1986; Feldman 1988; Bobo and Hutchings 1996). Thus, most disadvantaged individuals may embrace certain dominant values, and may even accept them as accurate depictions of their society in some vague or general sense. Even so, it is advantaged groups that seem most likely to believe that these core values are consistent with the realities of their everyday existence.

INDIVIDUAL OPPORTUNITY AND ACHIEVEMENT AS DOMINANT VALUES

It appears, then, that each society tends to sustain certain key values as part of its dominant ideology, but that not everyone in a society is equally likely to agree that such values are reflected in their own life experience. Another observation that certain researchers have made about the dominant ideology in recent years is that, at least in general terms, many modern countries may also be converging toward a broadly similar group of core values. A few analysts have gone so far as to suggest the possibility that we may eventually arrive at a future set of what Giddens has called "universal values" that are "shared by almost everyone" (Giddens 1994:

20–21). This argument stems partly from the theory that we are experiencing a trend toward more and more "globalization" in modern times, with an increase in economic connections, political affinities, and cultural ties among many of the world's nation-states (see Dogan and Pelassy 1984; Kohn 1989; Giddens 1990; 1994; Inglehart 1990; Nevitte 1996).

Some might see a single global value system as at best a distant possibility. However, the idea that there is a dominant ideology shared by various modern nations may be more plausible if we confine our discussion to the industrialized liberal democracies. Thus, the work of several researchers has led to the conclusion or speculation that there is an increasing similarity in the dominant values of countries such as Canada, the United States, Australia, New Zealand, and the nations of western Europe (e.g., Lipset 1967; Hofstede 1980; Nevitte and Gibbins 1990; for discussion, see also Grabb 1994:130–131; Baer et al. 1996:325–326; Inkeles 1997:381–382).

Of the various core values that are said to be shared in all liberal democratic countries, perhaps the most central are those that emphasize the rights and freedoms of the individual (see, e.g., Marchak 1988; Allahar 1995; Inkeles 1997). It is probably for this reason that a commitment to such ideas as personal liberty and equal rights for all citizens can be found in the formal laws or stated policies of almost every contemporary democracy. Two familiar illustrations of this pattern include Canada's Charter of Rights and Freedoms and the Constitution of the United States (see, e.g., Cairns and Williams 1985; Lipset 1996).

One crucial manifestation of the emphasis on individual rights and freedoms in liberal democracies is the apparently widespread belief in what might be termed "equal opportunity for individual achievement." According to this belief, all citizens of a democracy will not be equal in the material and other rewards they attain in society. Nevertheless, such inequalities in attainment or outcome are considered both appropriate and just, as long as everyone is allowed to succeed or fail on the basis of personal merit, effort, and ability (Pammett 1996:67). This means that people generally have a more or less equal opportunity to get ahead in life, at least in the sense that any background traits or group affiliations—race, ethnicity, gender, class origin, religion, and so on—will neither help nor hinder the individual in the competition to achieve. Under such a value system, then, *individual* attributes or abilities, as opposed to *group-related* or *structural* factors, will be the main causes for people's success or lack of success.

PREVIOUS STUDIES OF BELIEFS ABOUT OPPORTUNITY AND ACHIEVEMENT

Researchers have been interested in people's beliefs about individual equality of opportunity in a number of countries, but the topic has been of special concern to American social scientists. Although the results from these American studies are somewhat varied, three relatively consistent findings can be noted.

First, a vast majority of American respondents believe in equal opportunity as a normative or ideal circumstance. As an illustration, one recent compilation of opinion poll data reported that 98% of Americans believed "everyone should have an equal opportunity to get ahead" (Inkeles 1997:379; see also Mizruchi 1964; Kluegel and Smith 1986).

Second, a clear majority, often in the range of 75%, also appear to believe that equal (or at least considerable) opportunity really does operate in their society. In one early American survey using data from the 1960s, 78% of respondents agreed with the statement that there was "plenty of opportunity" in the United States, and that "anyone who works hard can go as far as he wants" (Huber and Form 1973:90–91). Subsequent research has shown a similarly widespread belief, both in the existence of plenty of opportunity and in the importance of individual causes for success, including hard work, self-reliance, and ability. For example, in one recent survey, 74% of Americans believed that most unemployed people "have had the opportunities" but "haven't made use of them." In the same survey, 77% of the respondents said that what happens to them personally is "my own doing," while 82% attributed any lack of personal success to "not having enough ability" (Inkeles 1997:379; see also Mizruchi 1964:82; Mann 1970:428; Kluegel and Smith 1982:520; Lipset 1996:115).

The third consistent finding in most American studies is that a person's own position in the system of social inequality is correlated with whether or not that person believes in the reality of individual equality of opportunity. In particular, members of disadvantaged groups, including racial minorities and those with lower incomes, are usually less likely than people from more advantaged groups to believe that they have a lot of opportunity, especially in comparison with the opportunities of their more privileged counterparts (e.g., Huber and Form 1973:91–96; see also Robinson and Bell 1978:125, 138; Kluegel and Bobo 1993; Bobo and Hutchings 1996; Lipset 1996:126–129). These findings suggest that the less advantaged are more likely to see structural obstacles or group affiliations as playing a significant role in their chances for success.

Although Canadian research on this topic has not been as extensive as the American research, the available evidence suggests broadly similar patterns in both countries. Certainly on the issue of whether the opportunity to get ahead rests mainly on individual or group-related factors, most Canadians appear to agree with their American neighbours that individual factors are more important.

In an early Canadian study from the 1960s, which focused exclusively on people in the 13 to 20 age group, a large majority (over 75%) said that individual factors like "hard work" and achieving "good grades in school" were very important for getting ahead in Canada (Johnstone 1969:8–11). This study also found only a small proportion (under 25%) who thought that group or structural factors—having "parents with a lot of money," being "born in Canada," and coming from the "right family" or from the "right religious group"—were very important for success.

A similar image arises from more recent opinion polls. A 1986 *Maclean's* survey found, for example, that 82% of Canadians chose individual "hard work" rather than "luck" or group "privilege" as the factor that matters most for getting ahead in Canada (quoted in Li 1988:5). A 1997 *Maclean's* survey showed that 92% of Canadians agreed with the opinion that "if you are prepared to work hard, you can still get ahead" in Canada today (*Maclean's* 1998:45). Other studies have found similarly high proportions of Canadians favouring such ideas as the value of individual hard work and self-reliance, and the importance of competition to achieve excellence in life (Sniderman et al. 1996:97–100; Perlin 1997:114–120). Research by Pammett (1996:70–73) has shown that the same Canadian belief in individual causes of success is evident in many other countries, as well, including the United States and the nations of western Europe, in particular. This strong Canadian emphasis on the role of individual factors in success is also consistent with findings from a recent study of managers and executives. For example, 96% of Canadian managers said that they preferred a job that encouraged individual initiative rather than a more collective or team-based kind of work activity. It is interesting, as well, that this proportion is virtually identical to the 97% of American managers who expressed this view in the same study (Hampden-Turner and Trompenaars 1993; see also Lipset 1996:294).

Again the evidence is less extensive, but Canadian research also seems to parallel American studies in suggesting that traditionally less privileged groups, such as French Canadians and women, for example, may not be as likely as more privileged groups to believe that equal opportunity exists, or that individual factors are more important than social background factors for achieving success. The study of young people from the 1960s found that only 47% of French respondents felt that individual hard work was very important for getting ahead, compared with 94% of English respondents. At the same time, French respondents were considerably more likely than the English to believe that group-based factors, such as having parents with a lot of money or being Canadian-born, were very important (Johnstone 1969:8). Similarly, another study from the 1960s, based on a national representative sample of adults, revealed that French Canadians were significantly less likely than English Canadians to believe that all ethnic groups have equal job opportunities or government influence (Roseborough and Breton 1968:607).

While it takes a different approach to the analysis of individual factors and suc-

cess, another study by Baer and Curtis (1988) has found, using national survey data from the 1970s and early 1980s, that French Canadians were more likely than English Canadians to have a high aspiration to personal achievement (see also Baer and Curtis 1984). On each of the following agree–disagree questions, the French were significantly more likely to give the achievement-oriented response: (1) "Life is more enjoyable when you are trying to achieve some new goal"; (2) "You should always try to improve your position in life rather than accept what you have now"; (3) "A person ought to set goals for themselves which are difficult to achieve"; (4) "Unless one learns how to reduce one's desire, life will be full of disappointment and bitterness"; (5) "Those who are always trying to get ahead in life will never be happy"; and (6) "When you come down to it, the best thing is to be content with what you have since you never know what the future will bring." Baer and Curtis interpreted the greater desire to achieve among French Canadians as a response to a more disadvantaged position in income and occupational attainment compared with English Canadians.

The results of some recent Canadian opinion surveys indicate that there may also be gender differences in people's views on the opportunity structure. A 1995 *Maclean's* poll found that, while 85% of Canadian males believed that women's job opportunities had improved in the previous decade, the comparable proportion among female respondents was only 75% (Gregg 1995:22). The results of a 1996 Conference Board of Canada survey of corporate executives, as reported in a study entitled *Closing the Gap*, reveal a similar pattern. These data showed that 75% of male executives, compared with just 56% of female executives, felt that women's job opportunities had improved in the previous five years (Williamson 1997).

SOME FURTHER CANADIAN DATA FOR THE 1990S

Some additional data for the 1990s are available that relate to the question of ideological beliefs about individual opportunity in Canada. These are provided by the Canadian component of an international study conducted in 1992–1993 by the International Social Survey Program, or ISSP (for more details on the survey see Frizzell 1996). A national sample of Canadian adults was given self-administered interviews about various aspects of social inequality. Most relevant to our present purposes was a set of questions asking about thirteen factors that may affect how people get ahead in life. We present an analysis of these data in this section. Our analysis is limited to responses from people aged 21 and over, although the survey included a small number of respondents aged 18 and over as well. Our reason for selecting only the respondents who were 21 years old or older was that they are more likely than younger people to have had first-hand experience with trying to obtain full-time work and income.

The questionnaire items that deal with possible factors in getting ahead are as follows:

> To begin, we have some questions about opportunities for getting ahead. Please tick one box for each of these to show how important you think it is for getting ahead in life. First, how important is coming from a *wealthy family*?... *having well-educated parents?*... having a *good education* yourself?... having *ambition*?... a person's *religion*?... *natural ability*?... *hard work*?... *knowing the right people*?... *having political connections*?... a person's *race*?... the *part of the country* a person comes from?... being *born a man or a woman*?... a person's *political beliefs*?

[Answer options were as follows: "essential," "very important," "fairly important," "not very important," "not important at all," and "can't choose"/"don't know."]

These items, then, focus on what people think *actually happens* in Canada, and not on what *should occur* in some ideal or normative sense. In addition, because the responses in the survey come from a cross-section of the total adult population, our results profile the views on individual opportunity that are held by Canadians generally, and not just the attitudes of any one group, such as the dominant class. As well, the data include several measures that enable us to assess whether Canadians in more advantaged groups or less advantaged groups are more likely to see particular factors as the key to getting ahead. These social status measures include the respondents' gender, age, region of residence, education level, language group, employment status, income level, and self-identification with a social class.[1]

Following previous research, we would expect most Canadians in the survey to believe that individual factors such as hard work and personal ambition are the key reasons for getting ahead in life, and to believe that social background factors, such as gender or race or having wealthy parents, are less important. We would also expect, based on earlier studies, that people from the traditionally more advantaged or privileged social groupings—men versus women, those with higher incomes versus those with lower incomes, those with more education versus those with less education, English speakers versus French speakers, etc.—will be more likely than other respondents to emphasize individual factors and less likely to stress social background causes as the reasons why Canadians do or do not get ahead in life. We move now to a description of the responses of the Canadian adult sample.

| TABLE 28-1 | Views on the Factors That Are Important in How People Get Ahead in Life: Responses from a National Sample of (N=871) Canadians Aged 21 and Older |

Factors Asked About*	"Essential" or "Very Important" %	"Fairly Important" %	"Not Very Important" %	"Not at All Important" %
Wealthy Family	14.1	29.8	34.7	21.5
Well-Educated Parents	27.4	49.7	17.6	5.9
Good Education	88.6	15.0	1.2	0.2
Ambition	83.9	13.7	2.3	0.0
Natural Ability	45.0	46.3	7.2	1.4
Hard Work	80.2	16.2	3.1	0.3
Knowing Right People	34.6	48.7	14.7	2.0
Political Connections	12.9	26.5	41.0	19.5
Race	11.1	23.6	34.3	31.1
Religion	4.8	7.0	33.8	54.4
Region	8.0	25.0	31.1	35.9
Gender	14.1	20.7	28.1	37.1
Political Beliefs	7.2	19.4	34.8	33.5

Header above data columns: **Percentage Who Responded**

* The question asked was: "To begin, we have some questions about opportunities for getting ahead. Please tick one box for each of these to show how important you think it is for getting ahead in life." The characteristics were listed in the order in the table above. Excluded are respondents who said they did not know or could not choose. These two responses did not total over 4% for any of the thirteen factors.

The Perceived Importance of the Thirteen Factors

Table 28-1 shows the responses of the sample concerning each of the thirteen possible reasons for getting ahead. Of these reasons, there are three that appear to be clearly individual in nature. These are "ambition," "hard work," and "natural ability." Another factor, "having a good education," is also an individual attribute in a sense. However, it is likely to be closely tied to social background influences, such as the wealth and education of parents, as well (see the findings to this effect in the "Education" section of this volume).

The results in Table 28-1 show that the three individual factors, along with having a good education, are the four most frequently mentioned factors people choose for what's important for getting ahead in life. Most frequently mentioned is having a good education (89%). Next are the individual factors of ambition and hard work, both of which are chosen as "essential" or "very important" by more than 80% of the respondents. The fourth most commonly mentioned factor is the individual characteristic of "natural ability"; 45% said this is at least "very important" and another 46% thought this factor is "fairly important."

If we attend to the factors that are seen as "not very important" or "not at all important," we find that it is the social background factors that are most likely to be given low degrees of importance.

TABLE 28-2   Views on the Number of Individual and Social Background Factors That Are Important ("Essential or "Very Important") in How People Get Ahead in Life

Number of Factors Mentioned	Percentage of Respondents	Who Said (N) %
Individual Factors*		
None	3.4	(30)
One	18.4	(160)
Two	45.6	(397)
Three	32.6	(284)
Social Background Factors†		
None	44.7	(389)
One	23.3	(203)
Two	13.5	(118)
Three	9.0	(78)
Four	3.9	(34)
Five	3.3	(29)
Six to Eight	2.2	(20)

* The individual factors were chosen from among ambition, natural ability, and hard work.

† The social background factors were chosen from among wealthy family, well-educated parents, knowing the right people, political connections, race, religion, region, and gender.

"Religion," in particular, was frequently thought to have little importance; over 85% said it is "not very important" or "not at all important." Further, over 60% of the respondents assigned little importance to political connections, race, region, gender, and political beliefs. In contrast, only 5% or less thought that ambition, hard work, and education were of such little importance, and less than 10% thought natural ability was this unimportant.

Table 28-2 shows the number of individual and social background factors that people labelled as very important or essential. Here we see that very few respondents (only 3.4%) felt that none of the three clearly individual factors is very important, and about one third (32.6%) felt that all three are very important. The average number mentioned, from among the three, is 2.07. If we sum the responses concerning the eight social background factors (wealthy family, well-educated parents, knowing the right people, political connections, race, religion, region, and gender) we find that only an average of 1.25 factors, out of a possible total of eight, are mentioned as very important or essential. About 45% said none of these factors is that important, and another 23% of the sample said only one of the eight factors is important. Overall, then, individual factors appear to have much greater significance for Canadians when they are asked what determines who gets ahead in their society.

TABLE 28-3	Social Statuses of the Respondents and the Average Number of Mentions of Individual and Social Background Factors as Important in Getting Ahead in Life		
Social Statuses of Respondents	**(N)***	**Average Number of Individual Factors Said to Be Very Important†**	**Average Number of Background Factors Said to Be Very Important‡**
Total Sample	(871)	2.07	1.25
Gender			
Male	(440)	2.06	1.28
Female	(410)	2.09	1.21
		n.s.	n.s.
Age			
21–30	(262)	2.03	1.26
31–40	(246)	2.02	1.21
41–50	(161)	2.11	1.06
51–64	(112)	2.09	1.33
65+	(90)	2.28	1.52
		n.s.	n.s.
Language Group			
French	(258)	1.96	1.14
English and Other	(613)	2.12	1.30
		p<.005	n.s.
Region			
Eastern Provinces	(149)	2.24	1.17
Québec	(195)	1.80	1.03
Ontario	(208)	2.21	1.41
Prairies	(158)	2.15	1.35
British Columbia	(161)	2.60	1.27
		p<.001	n.s.
Current Employment			
Full Time	(460)	2.03	1.11
Part Time	(94)	2.03	1.30
Occasional	(32)	2.00	1.13
None	(270)	2.18	1.48
		n.s.	p<.05

TABLE 28-3 Social Statuses of the Respondents and the Average Number of Mentions of Individual and Social Background Factors as Important in Getting Ahead in Life *(continued)*

Social Statuses of Respondents	(N)*	Average Number of Individual Factors Said to Be Very Important†	Average Number of Background Factors Said to Be Very Important‡
Personal Income Last Year			
< 15 Thousand (K)	(200)	2.04	1.46
15–25 K	(168)	2.08	1.35
25–35 K	(162)	2.11	1.17
35–45 K	(120)	2.06	1.20
45–55 K	(68)	2.00	1.12
55–65 K	(38)	2.22	1.13
65–75 K	(19)	2.00	0.68
75 K >	(21)	2.38	0.48
		n.s.	p<.05
Subjective Social Class			
Lower Class	(23)	1.91	1.35
Working Class	(133)	2.11	1.53
Lower Middle Class	(125)	2.06	1.34
Middle Class	(361)	2.08	1.05
Upper Middle Class	(111)	2.11	1.23
Upper Class	(5)	2.40	0.80
		p<.05	p<.05
Education Attained			
< High School Grad	(1.22)	2.02	1.82
High School Grad	(175)	2.06	1.02
Some Univ./College	(285)	2.11	1.10
Univ. Grad	(187)	2.10	1.24
Graduate School	(95)	2.03	1.42
		n.s.	p<.001

n.s. = Not a statistically significant pattern.

* The first column shows the number of respondents in the sample with the particular social status characteristic.

† The second column shows the average number of mentions of the three individual factors (from among ambition, natural ability, and hard work) as "essential" or "very important" for getting ahead.

‡ The third column shows the average number of mentions of the eight social background factors (from among wealthy family, well-educated parents, knowing the right people, political connections, race, religion, region, and gender) as "essential" or "very important" for getting ahead.

Social Status and Beliefs about Getting Ahead

In Table 28-3, the proportion of "essential" or "very important" responses on the individual and social background factors is cross-tabulated with seven different social status characteristics of the respondents. Here we find, for all categories of the social status variables, that there is considerable agreement on the great importance of individual factors, and little evidence that social background factors are seen as important. There are some instances in which the respondents' own social statuses are related to how strongly they support individual and social background factors. Specifically, the French, when compared with the combined English and "Other" language groups, are less likely to mention individual factors; British Columbians are more likely to mention these factors than those from other regions, with Québecers least likely to mention them; and people who identified themselves as being in the lower class are less likely than others (particularly compared with those calling themselves "upper class") to mention individual factors as important. These differences are all statistically significant. No significant differences in responses exist across categories of gender, age, employment, income, and education.

The responses dealing with the importance of social background factors show some statistically significant differences across the categories of current employment, income, subjective social class, and education. Those who do not work see social background factors as more important than do people who are employed full time. Those with lower incomes perceive a greater impact of social background influences on getting ahead than do people making higher levels of income. The patterns by social class identification parallel the findings for income, with the "working

class," "lower class," and "lower middle class" respondents citing more social background factors as very important or essential than do the higher classes. Finally, people with lower education (less than high school graduation) and, curiously, those with the most education (those who have gone beyond a first university or college degree) are the most likely to see background factors as important. Despite these differences in responses across social status categories, the large majority of respondents generally do not mention social background factors as important. We see in Table 28-3 that, across the numerous sub-groups of the seven social status variables, there is no category of respondent that averages more than 1.82 mentions of the social background factors, even though as many as eight such factors could have been mentioned. Those with less than high school graduation cited an average of 1.82 factors, the working-class identifiers had an average of 1.53 mentions, and older respondents (65 and older) had an average of 1.52. All other social categories had lower averages. On the other hand, although there were only three possible individual factors to choose from, across all seven social status variables the average mention of individual factors is rarely below 2.0.

Other Results

The ISSP survey included questions on three social status variables—gender, education, and region—that also happen to be listed among the thirteen possible factors for getting ahead. In Table 28-4, we assess whether people's own rankings on these three social status variables are correlated with their sense of whether these same three variables are important for getting ahead in life. Given earlier studies, we might expect that the more disadvantaged groups on these three variables (women,

TABLE 28-4   Percentage Who Said Particular Social Background Factors Were Important ("Essential" or "Very Important") for Getting Ahead by the Respondents' Own Statuses with Respect to Those Factors

Respondents' Social Statuses	Percentage Saying the Factor Was Important		
	Gender %	Education %	Region %
Gender			
Male	11.7	84.3	9.1
Female	16.9	83.0	7.1
	p<.05	n.s.	n.s.
Education Attained			
< High School Grad	20.0	74.2	15.0
High School Grad	8.5	81.7	4.8
Some Univ./College	10.1	85.9	6.7
Univ. Grad	16.4	85.0	9.1
Graduate School	24.9	91.5	7.4
	p<.001	p<.01	p<.05
Region			
Eastern Provinces	13.8	90.5	6.2
Québec	8.3	78.0	8.4
Ontario	16.8	90.0	7.2
Prairies	14.7	86.6	9.6
British Columbia	17.2	73.1	8.8
	n.s.	p<.001	n.s.

the less-educated, and Canadians from poorer regions such as the Atlantic provinces) would be more likely than other respondents to see these three factors as important.

Overall, the results in Table 28-4 provide almost no support for this expectation. As expected, respondents' gender was related to their views on the importance of being born a woman or man, with women seeing this factor as more important than did men; even here, though, only 17% of women saw gender as very important, compared with 12% of men. Gender of

respondents also had no effect on their attitudes about the importance of education and region. In addition, in the case of respondents' education, it was the more highly educated, not the less highly educated that were most likely to believe that education was very important or essential; 85% or more of those with at least some post-secondary education saw education as very important, compared with 74% of those who did not finish high school. Education's effects on the perceived importance of region are somewhat curvilinear, although the least educated are, as expected, the most likely category to mention region as important for getting ahead. Education's relation to the perceived impact of gender is clearly curvilinear, with the most highly educated and the least highly educated respondents being the most likely to mention gender as important. Finally, region of residence appears to have no connection with Canadians' views on the importance of either region or gender for getting ahead. Region does have some effect on the perceived significance of education, with people from British Columbia and Québec relatively less likely than other Canadians to believe education is important for getting ahead in life.

In other data not presented in Table 28-4, respondents' education level and region of residence were found to have statistically significant relationships with evaluations of the importance of other factors. The higher the education, the more likely wealthy parents were seen as important (p<.05) and the less likely religion was cited as important (p<.05). Region was related to perceptions of the importance of wealthy parents (p<.01), with Ontarians attaching a high importance and Québecers a comparatively low importance to this factor. Also, Québecers see a relatively low importance and Ontarians a relatively high importance for natural ability (p<.05), while both Québecers and British Columbians are relatively less convinced than other respondents that hard work matters for getting ahead (p<.001). Gender was not significantly related to any of the other factors. Compared with those with lower incomes, people with higher incomes appear more likely to cite the importance of education (p<.05), and less likely to cite knowing the right people and political connections (p<.05). Respondents with higher social class identifications were much less likely than those saying they were in the lower social

class to attach importance to political connections (p<.01). Finally, relative to English and "Other" respondents, the French were less likely to attach importance to wealthy parents (p<.01), well-educated parents (p<.01), education (p<.05), or hard work (p<.001), and more likely to cite religion as important (p<.05).

CONCLUSION

Both the results of previous studies and the additional data for the 1990s presented in this chapter indicate that Canadians generally see individual attributes or abilities as very important for achieving success. That is, most Canadians endorse the idea that it is what an individual is or does, based on hard work, ambition, and natural ability, along with the achievement of higher educational credentials, that helps a person get ahead. It is apparent, as well, that relatively few Canadians, especially in the 1990s data, mention social background variables, such as class origin, gender, race, or region, as important impediments or advantages for success. These findings indicate a remarkably high level of agreement among Canadians about these core elements of the dominant ideology.

The findings reported here suggest that these ideological beliefs are *dominant* in both senses of the term noted at the beginning of this paper. That is, not only are these views *widely held* among the population as a whole, they are also dominant in that they serve *the general interests of dominant groups or elites*. Our results imply that most Canadians would agree with the claim that the people at the top of their society got there, not because of their backgrounds, but because of their own individual efforts and abilities. Such attitudes lend ideological support to maintenance of the status quo—existing arrangements by which the dominant groups should continue to do comparatively well. These beliefs also imply that, in most people's minds, the system works largely as it should, and that there is little reason to want to change it.

As expected, our analysis has revealed that those who occupy higher social statuses tend to be very supportive of dominant ideological principles. What may be somewhat surprising, however, is that large proportions of people with less advantaged social statuses are quite supportive of these ideas as well. In some cases, disadvantaged respondents do appear to discern problems with the dominant ideology, as in the tendency (albeit a modest one) for women to see the background variable of gender as more important for affecting success than do men. In addition, if we consider French Canadians as a disadvantaged category, we have found them to be slightly less likely than the rest of the respondents to mention individual factors as important. In most instances, though, there is little or no evidence of such a pattern. Instead, as with their more advantaged counterparts, only small proportions of the disadvantaged groups either cite background factors as important or reject individual factors as unimportant.

On the other hand, these results may not be all that surprising, if we consider that they are not inconsistent with many of the findings in the American studies reviewed earlier. Recall that these studies usually showed a high degree of acceptance among disadvantaged people that individual factors were crucial for success and that opportunity was good, in general. The less advantaged groups in those studies differed from the advantaged primarily on questions specifically related to whether *they themselves had been held back* by unequal opportunity or discrimination (see, e.g., Huber and Form 1973; Rodman 1963). Because the 1990s Canadian data included no measures of respondents' attitudes about factors affect-

ing their *own personal opportunity experiences*, we cannot be sure that the same pattern would have been found here. However, it is quite possible that the lower-status respondents in our 1990s data source share a similar "dual-mindedness," with a clear belief that opportunities are good for Canadians generally but a less certain sense that they themselves have had a completely fair or equal chance at success.

Another possibility is that, like many of the disadvantaged respondents in the American studies, less successful Canadians may largely blame their relatively low position, not on social background impediments, but on their own shortcomings, including a failure to capitalize on existing opportunities, for example. This type of thinking, especially among members of the lower social classes, has been interpreted by some researchers as a so-called "value stretch" (Rodman 1963; Huber and Form 1973), or a form of "passive" or "pragmatic" acceptance (Parkin 1973; Mann 1970). A key common element in these interpretations is the idea that disadvantaged groups come to apply a set of beliefs or values when judging their own situation that is somewhat different from those they apply when assessing the workings of their society as a whole. In this way, subordinate groups may be better able to cope with the sometimes stark discrepancies between what the prevailing value system leads them to believe and what they actually experience in their daily lives. Thus, either self-blaming or pragmatic acceptance may help account for the high level of acceptance and infrequent questioning of the dominant ideology among lower status groups.

Yet another possible reason behind the absence of large differences in people's beliefs across most of the social status variables is that some of the groups that were disadvantaged in the past have greatly improved their relative economic position in recent years. The French are a good example. They once were significantly disadvantaged in Canada's stratification system, but, as a number of recent studies have shown (including Hou and Balakrishnan's paper in this volume), there now is little difference between the English and French on income and other measures of inequality. It is perhaps for this reason that French Canadians in the 1990s data are far less likely to see background factors as the causes of success than they were in earlier studies (compare Johnstone 1969; Roseborough and Breton 1968; Baer and Curtis 1984).

Another point to consider when trying to understand people's attitudes about achievement and its causes concerns the important mechanisms through which our beliefs and ideas are acquired and sustained. These mechanisms are the primary socialization, teaching, and idea-transmission apparatuses of our society, especially the media, the government, and the education system. As was mentioned at the beginning of this chapter, there is reason to assume that the values fostered by these organizations will generally be consistent with the values favoured by dominant groups. Thus, some of the tendency for Canadians to see a society of considerable individual opportunity, regardless of their own personal social status rankings, may be traced to the pervasive influence of these ideological mechanisms.

An additional issue of note is the role of everyday life in shaping people's values. In the world of work, for example, most of us have probably observed situations in which either individual achievement or social background factors helped to determine who gets ahead and who does not. While such observations can sometimes provide important insight, they are unavoidably limited and incomplete in most cases. In other words, in contrast to social researchers who have the luxury of access to numerous and usually more representative sources of evidence when studying questions such as individual opportunity and achievement, most other people must form their attitudes on the basis of anecdotal experiences and impressions. One speculation we would offer is that, in this process, individual achievement may well be *more visible* or more prominent in most people's perceptions. When a person sees, for example, that relatively few high-level managers, doctors, or judges are women and Blacks, but that *at least some are* women and Blacks, that person may be apt to conclude that gender and race are becoming less and less important factors for achievement these days. Thus, many members of the public, including those occupying lower-status positions themselves, may conclude that, because there are evident exceptions to the rule, the rule no longer applies. If this type of thinking occurs, it would help explain why the dominant ideological view of individual opportunity for achievement is so widespread in the Canadian population.

Of course, one final possibility is that most Canadians are understandably happy with the chances for achievement in their society, because their country is, indeed, a land of opportunity. After all, for several years now, Canada has consistently been named by the United Nations as the best country in the world in which to live, primarily because of our relatively high level of material affluence and quality of life. Thus, perhaps the high level of support we have seen for the dominant ideology of individual achievement is to be expected. Even so, the clear evidence of structurally based inequalities and injustices to be found in existing research on Canada (including most of the chapters appearing in this volume) means there is considerable room for skepticism on this issue. It also means there is ample room for improving the situation of the disadvantaged, in Canada as in virtually every nation of the world.

NOTES

1. The questions asked concerning these social statuses should be self-explanatory, with the exception of "social class self-identification." Here the question was: "Some people consider themselves to be a member of a specific social class. Of the following groups, would you consider yourself a member of the working class, lower middle/upper working class, middle class, upper middle class, upper class [don't know, can't choose; none of these classes]." See Table 28-3 for responses according to these categories of self-identification, and for the categories for the other measures of social status.

REFERENCES

Abercrombie, Nicholas, Stephen Hill, and Bryan S. Turner 1980. *The Dominant Ideology Thesis.* London: George Allen and Unwin.

Allahar, Anton 1995. *Sociology and the Periphery* (2nd ed.). Toronto: Garamond.

Baer, Douglas, and James Curtis 1984. "French Canadian-English Canadian value differences: National survey findings." *Canadian Journal of Sociology* 9(4):405–428.

Baer, Douglas, and James Curtis 1988. "Differences in the achievement values of French Canadians and English Canadians." In J. Curtis et al., *Social Inequality in Canada: Patterns, Problems and Policies* (1st ed.), pp. 476–484. Scarborough, Ontario: Prentice-Hall Canada.

Baer, Douglas, James Curtis, Edward Grabb, and William Johnston 1996. "What values do people prefer in children? A comparative analysis of survey evidence from fifteen countries." In Clive Seligman, James Olson, and Mark Zanna (eds.), *The Psychology of Values: The Ontario Symposium*, Vol. 8, pp. 299–328. Mahwah, New Jersey: Lawrence Erlbaum.

Bobo, Lawrence, and Vincent Hutchings 1996. "Perceptions of racial group competition: Extending Blumer's theory of group position to a multiracial social con text." *American Sociological Review* 61:951–972.

Cairns, Alan, and Cynthia Williams 1985. *Constitutionalism, Citizenship, and Society in Canada.* Toronto: University of Toronto Press.

Dogan, M., and D. Pelassy 1984. *How to Compare Nations.* Chatham, New Jersey: Chatham House Publishers.

Feldman, Stanley 1988. "Structure and consistency in public opinion: The role of core beliefs and values." *American Journal of Political Science* 82:773–778.

Frizzell, Alan 1996. "The ISSP and international research: An introduction." In Alan Frizzell and Jon Pammett (eds.), *Social Inequality in Canada,* pp. 1–7. Ottawa: Carleton University Press.

Giddens, Anthony 1990. *The Consequences of Modernity.* Stanford: Stanford University Press.

Giddens, Anthony 1994. *Beyond Left and Right* Stanford: Stanford University Press.

Grabb, Edward 1994. "Democratic values in Canada and the United States: Some observations and evidence from past and present." In Jerry Dermer (ed.), *The Canadian Profile* (2nd ed.), pp. 113–139. North York, Ontario: Captus Press.

Gregg, Allan 1995. "Now and then. A nation transformed." *Maclean's* 108(1) (January 8):20–22.

Hampden-Turner, Charles, and Alfons Trompenaars 1993. *The Seven Cultures of Capitalism.* New York: Doubleday.

Hofstede, Geert 1980. *Culture's Consequences.* Beverly Hills, California: Sage.

Huber, Joan, and William Form 1973. *Income and Ideology.* New York: The Free Press.

Inglehart, Ronald 1990. *Culture Shift in Advanced Industrial Society.* Princeton: Princeton University Press.

Inkeles, Alex 1997. *National Character. A Psycho-Social Perspective.* New Brunswick, New Jersey: Transaction Publishers.

Johnstone, John C. 1969. *Young People's Images of Canadian Society.* Studies of the Royal Commission on Bilingualism and Biculturalism, No. 2. Ottawa: Queen's Printer.

Kluegel, James, and Lawrence Bobo 1993. "Opposition to race-targeting: Self-interest, stratification ideology, or racial attitudes?" *American Sociological Review* 58:443–464.

Kluegel, James, and Eliot Smith 1982. "Whites' beliefs about blacks' opportunity." *American Sociological Review* 47:518–531.

Kluegel, James, and Eliot Smith 1986. *Beliefs About Inequality.* New York: Aldine de Gruyter.

Kohn, Melvin (ed.) 1989. *Cross-National Research in Sociology.* Newbury Park, California: Sage.

Li, Peter 1988. *Ethnic Inequality in a Class Society.* Toronto: Wall and Thompson.

Lipset, S.M. 1967. "Values, education, and entre-preneurship." In S.M. Lipset and A. Solari (eds.), *Elites in Latin America*, pp. 3–60. New York: Oxford University Press.

Lipset, S.M. 1996. *American Exceptionalism.* New York: Norton.

Maclean's 1998. "Taking the pulse of a nation." Volume 110, 52, January 5.

Mann, Michael 1970. "The social cohesion of liberal democracy." *American Sociological Review* 35:423–439.

Marchak, Patricia 1988. *Ideological Perspectives on Canada* (3rd ed.) Toronto: McGraw-Hill Ryerson.

Marx, Karl, and Friedrich Engels 1846. *The German Ideology. In Marx Engels Collected Works*, Vol. 5. New York: International Publishers, 1976.

Marx, Karl, and Friedrich Engels 1848. *The Communist Manifesto.* New York: Washington Square Press, 1970.

Mizruchi, Ephraim 1964. *Success and Opportunity.* New York: The Free Press.

Nevitte, Neil 1996. *The Decline of Deference: Canadian Value Change in Cross-National Perspective.* Peterborough, Ontario: Broad-view Press.

Nevitte, Neil, and Roger Gibbins 1990. *New Elites in Old States.* Toronto: Oxford University Press.

Pammett, Jon 1996. "Getting ahead around the world." In Alan Frizzell and Jon Pammett (eds.), *Social Inequality in Canada*, pp. 67–86. Ottawa: Carleton University Press.

Parkin, Frank 1973. *Class Inequality and Political Order.* London: Paladin.

Perlin, George 1997. "The constraints of public opinion: Diverging or converging paths?" In Keith Banting, George Hoberg, and Richard Simeon (eds.), *Degrees of Freedom: Canada and the United States in a Changing World*, pp. 71–149. Montréal and Kingston: McGill-Queen's University Press.

Robinson, Robert, and Wendell Bell 1978. "Equality, success, and social justice in England and the United States." *American Sociological Review* 43:125–143.

Rodman, Hyman 1963. "The lower-class value stretch." *Social Forces* 42:205–215.

Roseborough, Howard, and Raymond Breton 1968. "Perceptions of the relative economic and political advantages of ethnic groups in Canada." In B. Blishen, F. Jones, K. Naegele, and J. Porter (eds.), *Canadian Society: Sociological Perspectives* (3rd ed.), pp. 604–628. Toronto: Macmillan.

Sniderman, Paul, Joseph Fletcher, Peter Russell, and Philip Tetlock 1996. *The Clash of Rights: Liberty, Equality, and Legitimacy in Pluralist Democracy.* New Haven: Yale University Press.

Williams, Robin M., Jr. 1960. *American Society.* New York: Alfred Knopf.

Williamson, Linda 1997. "It's still a failure to communicate." In the *London Free Press,* Friday, December 12:A19.

Wright, Erik Olin, Andrew Levine, and Elliott Sober 1992. *Reconstructing Marxism.* London: Verso.

PREJUDICE AND DISCRIMINATION TOWARD MINORITIES IN CANADA AND THE UNITED STATES

Jeffrey G. Reitz and Raymond Breton

(Abridged from Chapter 4, "Prejudice and discrimination,"
In *The Illusion of Difference: Realities of Ethnicity in
Canada and the United States*. Toronto: C.D. Howe Institute,
1994, pp. 64–89. Reprinted with permission.)

INTRODUCTION

How do Canadians and Americans compare in terms of racial and ethnic prejudice and discrimination? In this chapter, we shall attempt to answer this question, using not only measures of overt prejudice, but also measures of the extent to which people in the two countries uphold negative stereotypes of minorities, seek to maintain "social distance" between themselves and members of other groups (in this context, our analysis will consider attitudes toward immigration, minorities as neighbours, and intermarriage), and withhold support for government action against discrimination.

Prejudice is a matter of attitudes; discrimination is a matter of behaviour. Both things are difficult to measure. Our purpose here is not to resolve the problems of measurement. Rather, it is to see whether the standard indicators of prejudice and discrimination, which are perhaps flawed, suggest in any way that there is a difference between the level of prejudice and discrimination in Canada and the level in the United States. The familiar Canadian assumption that the level in Canada is lower can, we believe, be meaningfully addressed in this way.

TRENDS WITHIN EACH COUNTRY

In both Canada and the United States, a range of indicators of racial attitudes shows certain positive trends. The National Academy of Sciences report, *A Common Destiny: Blacks and American Society* (Jaynes and Williams 1989), gleaned data from dozens of national opinion polls conducted between 1942 and 1983. These polls show growing and now virtually universal verbal commitment to the principle of racial equality. White preferences for "social distance" from Blacks in various settings have declined significantly. Although popular support for government policies and programs to assist Blacks remains low and has shown no consistent trend over time, there has been no major White "backlash."

In Canada, race is less salient, and there is less research. Without doubt the climate in Canada too has improved since the Second World War, when racially exclusionary immigration policies were still in effect. For its study, *The Economic and Social Impact of Immigration*, the Economic Council of Canada assembled data from existing surveys of intolerance (Swan et al. 1991:111–113). The council reported a "positive" trend among anglophones on an index of "tolerance." However, the study did not present specific quantitative results, and the index included items on gender as well as race.

These parallel attempts at trend analysis invite several observations. First, data on racial attitudes in Canada are so much less plentiful than data on attitudes in the United States that clear comparisons are difficult. Second, the existence of positive trends in racial attitudes in both countries may be a point of similarity between them, even if in some ways these changes prove superficial. Definitive comparison must focus on specific key areas, an approach that, as we shall show, yields interesting results. And third, the comparative data are very time-sensitive. One cannot meaningfully compare U.S. data from the 1960s with Canadian data from the 1970s and 1980s. In fact, our goal here is really to measure the trajectory of change in the two countries. One might say that what is at issue is not the extent of cross-national differences, but the approximate number of years (if any) that one country may be ahead of the other in terms of changes in racial attitudes.

OVERT RACISM AND NEGATIVE RACIAL STEREOTYPES

U.S. survey research clearly shows that overt racism, by which we mean the explicit assertion of innate White superiority, is now expressed only by a small minority. Schuman, Steeh, and Bobo (1985:125) show that, as recently as the 1940s, only 50% to 60% of Americans outside the South—and even fewer in the South—endorsed the innate equality of Blacks, agreeing that "Negroes are as intelligent as White people" and can "learn things just as well if they are given the same education and training." Since the 1950s, the proportion has been at least 90%.

A survey conducted in 1990 by Decima Research Ltd. permits a comparison of the two countries. The Canadians in the survey were, overall, slightly less overtly racist than the Americans, but only slightly: 90% of the Canadians, and 86% of the Americans agreed that "all races are created equal" (*Maclean's* 1990). This difference is insubstantial. Large majorities in both countries deny overt racism.

The denial of overt racism in both countries is also reflected in the fact that few people support organizations with explicitly racist philosophies. The 1989

National Academy of Sciences study (Jaynes and Williams 1989) found that, in the United States, support for the Ku Klux Klan had increased somewhat during the late 1960s and 1970s but was still marginal. KKK groups in Canada and indigenous organizations with racist messages, such as the Western Guard or the Heritage Front, also have few members (Barrett 1987; Sher 1983; and see Schoenfeld 1991). Actually, many supporters of groups such as the KKK deny that they are racists. One-third of the respondents in a survey conducted in and near Chattanooga, Tennessee, had favourable views of the KKK. Many of them cited the KKK as a "charitable" organization and as one that supported law and order; they may have been dissembling their knowledge of its racial views (Selzter and Lopes 1986:95). In both countries, some mainstream politicians, too, have been accused of appealing to hidden racial feelings, though as a rule they deny this intention.

How widespread are hidden racist attitudes? Is there more hidden racism in one country than the other?

U.S. attitude surveys show that some of those who deny racism in fact have racist views that are easily brought to the surface. For example, when Americans are asked to explain why so many Blacks are poor, many of them refer to innate racial inferiority. The General Social Surveys (GSS) for 1988 and 1989 asked the following question:

On the average Blacks have worse jobs, income, and housing than White people. Do you think that these differences are... (a) mainly due to discrimination, (b) because most Blacks have less in-born ability to learn, (c) because most Blacks don't have the chance for education that it takes to rise out of poverty, and (d) because most Blacks just don't have the motivation or will power to pull themselves out of poverty? (Kluegel 1990:514.)

The proportion of respondents who chose the explanation "Blacks have less in-born ability," either alone or in combination with other explanations, was 20.8% (Kluegel 1990:517). Thus, although few Whites explicitly challenge the proposition (put forward in the 1990 Decima survey, for example) that all races are created equal, a significantly larger proportion refer to inherent racial inferiority when asked to explain Black poverty. Some people explain Black disadvantage as "God's plan" (Kluegel and Smith 1986:188).

Many Americans, in shifting away from overtly racist views, have embraced what Kluegel calls "individualistic" explanations for Black-White inequality (Kluegel 1990:515). They say that Blacks lack motivation or have an inferior culture. They deny "structuralist" explanations—that Blacks lack educational and employment opportunity or experience discrimination. In the 1977 GSS, the proportion of respondents who explained Black poverty by reference to innate Black inferiority was 26% (Kluegel and Smith 1986:188; see also Sniderman and Hagen 1985:30). In 1988–1989, as we have shown, it was about 21%. Through this period, most endorsed individualist explanations, and only about 25% to 30% believed that Blacks experienced any significant discrimination. In fact, the 1977 GSS showed that the same proportion felt that Blacks were given preference—that there was discrimination against Whites (Kluegel 1985:768). "Young and old Americans alike appear to believe that discrimination in the work force *currently* does not function to limit opportunity for Black workers to any substantial degree" (Kluegel 1985:771).

What are the comparable Canadian attitudes? Canadian explanations for minority-group disadvantage are not, of course, strictly comparable with American explanations. Asking Canadians about minorities in Canada is obviously not necessarily the same as asking Americans about minorities in the United States. Nevertheless, in the 1987 Canadian Charter Study about 70% of the respondents agreed that "immigrants often bring discrimination upon themselves by their own personal attitudes and habits," 25% disagreed, and the remaining 5% gave various qualified responses or "don't know" (Sniderman et al. 1991). The proportion of those who cited an "individualistic" explanation—70%—is about the same as the proportion in the United States. Thus, Canadians, like Americans, frequently deny that the minorities in their respective countries are the victims of racial discrimination. Of course, what is in fact the case in each country is arguable. We examine data relevant to the actual comparative extent of discrimination below. For now, we simply note that Canadians and Americans seem to be alike in tending to prefer individualistic explanations of minority disadvantage to explanations that cite discrimination.

ANTI-SEMITISM

In both countries, the Jewish group is long-established and largely urban, accounts for 1% to 2% of the population, and has high average levels of educational and occupational attainment and earnings (Lieberson and Waters 1988; Li 1988; Reitz 1990). Because of this similarity, comparisons of negative attitudes and behaviour toward Jews provide a particularly good indication of relative predisposition toward ethnic tolerance. For Jews, unlike Blacks, the issue of relations with the other groups arises in a very similar way in the two countries.

Studies that measure the prevalence of negative stereotypes of Jews have produced remarkably similar aggregate results in the United States and Canada. We compared results from the Charter Study in Canada in 1987 (Sniderman et al. 1992; Sniderman 1993) with those from a U.S. survey reported by Martire and Clark (1982:17) in 1981. In three of the four comparisons, about one Canadian in five and one American in five gave a response that described the Jewish group in a negative way. Canadians were more likely than Americans, however, to agree that Jews are "pushy."

There are positive stereotypes of the Jewish group as well as negative ones. Smith (1990:9), using GSS data, found that in the United States, the general population rates Jews above "Whites" in relation to the descriptive tags "rich," "hard-working," "not violent," "intelligent," and "self-supporting."

In both countries, anti-Semitic stereotypes have their greatest currency within certain other minority groups. The frictions between Jews and these other minorities are secondary ethnic conflicts, derived from broader patterns of ethnic disadvantage. In Canada, French-Canadian attitudes toward Jews are more negative than those of any other group (Sniderman et al. 1991). However, French-Canadian attitudes toward other minorities are also more negative. At the same time, there is greater pressure toward conformity—including ethnic assimilation—in Québec than there is in the rest of the country. These are classic patterns in group conflict: suspicion of outsiders and closing of ranks among insiders.

In the United States, there is a roughly parallel tension between Jews and Blacks. This tension is at least in part the result of a reactive response among Blacks, rather than an indication that Blacks have a greater predisposition to anti-Semitism than other groups. The position of Blacks in the United States has also led to tensions between Blacks and other minorities, including Asians and Hispanics (Oliver and Johnson 1984; Johnson and Oliver 1989; Rose 1989).

One can compare anti-Semitic behaviour in the United States and Canada by using the "audit of anti-Semitic incidents" that B'nai Brith, the Jewish service organization, publishes in each country. The Anti-Defamation League of B'nai Brith in the United States reported 1879 incidents in 1991 (A'DLBB 1991:29). In Canada, the equivalent organization is the League of Human Rights of B'nai Brith, whose more positive-sounding name suggests a less conflictful or more tolerant setting. Nevertheless, the number of incidents reported in Canada in 1991 was 251 (LHRBB Canada 1991:4), more than might be expected given the roughly ten-to-one U.S.-Canadian population ratio. The totals for 1982 to 1992, however, uphold the ratio—there were 12 665 incidents in the United States and 1191 in Canada. The year-to-year figures fluctuate not quite in lock step, responding similarly to events such as the Persian Gulf war, which seemed to provoke increases in anti-Semitic incidents—and anti-Muslim incidents as well—in both countries.

Thus, attitudes and behaviour reflect very similar patterns of anti-Semitism in the two countries. This case, free from some of the methodological complexities that affect other comparisons, does not support the hypothesis that Canadians are more tolerant than Americans.

SOCIAL DISTANCE

Social distance is a measure of dominant-group tolerance for social relations with members of a given minority. For a given minority, social distance is greater when the majority is unwilling to tolerate not only close relations such as marriage and family membership but also more distant relations. Thus, the majority may be unwilling to tolerate members of the minority as neighbours, as co-workers, or even as immigrants.

U.S. data show that social distances from the dominant English-origin group are greatest for Blacks and other racial minorities, less for southern Europeans, and least for northern Europeans (Bogardus 1958, 1967). Surveys of university social science students conducted since the 1920s have shown that social distance for a variety of minority groups has declined over the years, but that the rank-order of racial groups has remained fairly stable (see Owen, Eisner, and McFaul 1981; and Sinha and Berry 1991). Table 29-1 shows how racial and ethnic groups in the United States have been ranked in various years. Sinha and Barry (1991), who have applied the concept of social distance to groups such as intravenous drug users, AIDS victims, people who have attempted suicide, and homosexuals, find that ethnic and racial groups are now less socially distant from the dominant groups than are these other groups. They suggest that race and ethnicity are becoming less important than behaviour as a basis for discrimination.

Comparable Canadian data are available for national samples as well as student populations. The national data describe the "social standing" of ethnic and racial groups, which is presumably akin to social distance or group prestige. In a national survey on ethnic social standing, English- and French-Canadian respondents placed group names in ranked categories. The results in Table 29-2 show a rank-order similar to the rank-order for U.S. minorities in Table 29-1. Racial minorities, including Blacks and Asians, are at the bottom, southern Europeans

TABLE 29-1   Mean Social Distances of Ethnic and Racial Groups in the United States, 1926–1990 (as Measured on the Bogardus Social Distance Scale)

	1926	1946	1956	1966	1977	1990
Groups Included in the Bogardus Scale						
Americans (U.S. White)	1.10	1.04	1.08	1.07	1.25	1.13
English	1.06	1.13	1.23	1.14	1.39	1.15
Canadians	1.13	1.11	1.16	1.15	1.42	1.19
Italians	1.94	2.28	1.89	1.51	1.65	1.36
French	1.32	1.31	1.47	1.36	1.58	1.37
Germans	1.46	1.59	1.61	1.54	1.87	1.39
Native Americans	2.38	2.45	2.35	2.18	1.84	1.59
Poles	2.01	1.84	2.07	1.98	2.11	1.68
Jews	2.39	2.32	2.15	1.97	2.01	1.71
Blacks	3.28	3.60	2.74	2.56	2.03	1.73
Chinese	3.36	2.50	2.68	2.34	2.29	1.76
Japanese	2.80	3.61	2.70	2.41	2.38	1.86
Russians	1.88	1.83	2.56	2.38	2.57	1.93
Koreans	3.60	3.05	2.83	2.51	2.63	1.94
Mexicans	2.69	2.89	2.79	2.56	2.40	2.00
Groups Not Included in the Bogardus Scale						
Israelis	–	–	–	–	–	2.63
Palestinians	–	–	–	–	–	2.78
Iranians	–	–	–	–	–	3.03
Spread	2.54	2.57	1.75	1.49	1.38	1.90
Change in spread		+0.03	–0.82	–0.26	–0.11	+0.52

Note: The Bogardus social distance scale ranges from a low of 1.00 to a high of 7.00. The figures are based on mean ratings of the degree of distance that respondents would prefer to maintain between themselves and members of each group. The available responses are acceptance "into my family through marriage or cohabitation" (1.00), acceptance "as close friends or room mate" (2.00), acceptance "in my dorm" (3.00), acceptance "as a co-worker or class mate" (4.00), acceptance "as speaking acquaintance only" (5.00), acceptance "as visitors only to my country" (6.00), and "would not accept into my country" (7.00).

Source: Sinha and Berry, 1991:7.

rank higher, and northern Europeans higher still (Berry, Kalin, and Taylor 1977; Pineo 1977; and Angus Reid Group Inc. 1991). Driedger and Mezoff (1981) derive similar results from data on Manitoba university students (see also Dion 1985).

Calculations of social distance index values on the basis of student samples yield similar results for the two countries. The 1977 figure for Blacks in the United States was 2.03 and a comparable figure for Blacks in Canada was 2.12; for West Indians it was 2.46 (Driedger and Mezoff 1981). For Chinese, the 1977 U.S. figure was 2.29, and the 1981 Canadian figure was 2.33. For Mexicans, the U.S. and

TABLE 29-2	Social Standing of Minority Groups in English and French Canada	

	Social Standing as Ranked by:	
Minority Group	**English Canada**	**French Canada**
Own group	83.1	77.6
English	82.4	77.6
Italians	43.1	51.3
French	60.1	72.4
Germans	48.7	40.5
Native Canadians	28.3	32.5
Poles	42.0	38.0
Jews	46.1	43.1
Blacks	25.4	23.5
Chinese	33.1	24.9
Japanese	34.7	27.8
Russians	35.8	33.2

Note: The categories are placed in order of the comparable groups in Table 29-1; some groups are not included.

Source: Pineo 1977:154.

Canadian figures were, respectively, 2.40 and 2.38; for Japanese, they were 2.38 and 2.40. There is one major discrepancy: The index value for American Indians in 1977 was 1.84, whereas the value for Native Indians in Canada, or at least in Manitoba, was substantially higher, 2.70.

No one has calculated precise index values for social distance between Whites and specific minorities in both countries on the basis of national or even general-population data, let alone data collected at comparable points in time. As Table 29-2 has shown, Jaynes and Williams (1989:122–123) summarized U.S. national survey data to demonstrate that White social distances from Blacks have declined. These and other potentially comparable data address specific components of social distance, such as acceptance of minorities as neighbours, or as family members through intermarriage, rather than social distance generally. The follow-ing subsections consider four of these specific components.

Immigration

One component of social distance is attitudes toward specific groups as immigrants. Canadians favour immigration more than Americans do, despite the fact that racial-minority immigration is currently greater in Canada. In the 1990 Decima survey, 58% of Americans wanted less immigration and only 6% wanted more (*Maclean's* 1990:52). By contrast, 39% of Canadians wanted less immigration and 18% wanted more. Whether these more positive Canadian attitudes apply to "new" racial-minority immigrants is not clear. Nevertheless, in a 1976 Gallup poll, 63% of Canadians opposed racial restrictions and only 27% favoured them. In 1981, only 10% supported cutting off all non-White immigration to Canada.

American attitudes toward immigration appear to have turned negative as immigration increased after the 1960s. In a series of comparable polls, the proportion of Americans who wanted less immigration increased from 33% in 1965 to 61% in 1993. There appears to be a nearly comparable trend in Canada. Angus Reid Group Inc. (1989:4–5) reported that the proportion of Canadians who think too many immigrants are coming to Canada increased from 30% in May 1988 to 31% in February 1989 and 43% in August 1989. An Ekos Research Associates Inc. poll showed that this proportion had risen to 53% by February 1994 (*Globe and Mail* [Toronto], March 10, 1994:A1). On the other hand, Environics polls conducted in 1986 and 1989 showed a decline in agreement with the statement that "there is too much immigration to Canada," from 66% to 57% (Angus Reid Group Ltd. 1989:5).

Canadians' somewhat more positive attitudes may reflect their country's different historical and institutional context, rather than cultural predisposition. Post-war Canadian immigration, mostly European in origin, has been a major element of economic and social development policy. Reimers and Troper (1992) argue that, in the United States, immigration has ceased to be a development policy and is now perceived as social welfare, and that public support has declined accordingly. Like Americans, and perhaps for similar reasons, Britons support racial minority immigration less than Canadians do. British immigration has been an obligation to former colonial territories in the Commonwealth, rather than a program of national development (see Reitz 1988a, 1988b).

At the same time, there are signs that growing unease with immigration among White Canadians as well as among White Americans is, in fact, related to race, not just to numbers or to immigration goals. In a 1979 survey in Toronto (Breton et al.

1990:204), 63% of "majority Canadians" agreed that "present immigration laws make it too easy for certain groups to come to Canada." In identifying these "certain groups," respondents mentioned racial minorities three times more often than they mentioned other immigrant groups. European-origin immigrants shared these concerns. In the United States, a recent *Newsweek* poll asked a comparable question in a national sample: "Should it be easier or more difficult for people from the following places to immigrate to the U.S.?" About half of the respondents said that it should be more difficult for people from China or other Asian countries to immigrate to the United States, and 61% said it should be more difficult for people from the Middle East to immigrate to the United States.

These results from the two countries seem to be roughly parallel.

Community and Neighbourhood Residence

There has long been a significant cross-national difference in responses to racial minorities as neighbours. Comparative Gallup data assembled by Michalos (1982:169, 206) indicate that in 1963 only 3% of Canadians said that they would definitely move "if coloured people came to live next door" and 91% said that they would stay put. In the United States at that time, 20% said that they would move and only 55% said that they would stay.

Things have changed since the 1960s, of course. Although racial preferences for neighbours are still significant and strong in the United States, feelings have relaxed noticeably over time. In the late 1960s, U.S. movers declined to 12% and stayers rose to 65%. In 1978, only 10% would move if a Black moved next door (Schuman, Steeh, and Bobo 1985: 106–108). As late as 1981, however, a majority of northerners preferred a mostly White neighbourhood and one in four preferred an all-White neighbourhood (Schuman, Steeh, and Bobo 1985:67). In the South, two-thirds preferred a mostly White neighbourhood and the preference for an all-White neighbourhood varied between 38% and 51%. Openness to Black neighbours varies with the numbers of Blacks mentioned in the question. Whereas only 46% of White Americans said they would not move if Blacks came into their neighbourhood in "great numbers," about 85% said they would not move if Blacks moved in "next door" or onto the "same block."

Canadian attitudes may not be markedly different, but in recent available surveys the same questions have not been asked. Replies to the most closely comparable questions do not suggest extreme cross-national differences. In the 1978–1979 Ethnic Pluralism Survey in Toronto, two-thirds of the respondents said that they were willing to have a West Indian as a next-door neighbour "if you were completely free to decide yourself" (Breton et al. 1990:200). The proportion that responded positively to having Chinese, Italian, or Portuguese neighbours was about 85%.

Acceptance into Social Clubs

A willingness to accept racial minorities into private clubs would seem to indicate an even greater tolerance than does a willingness to accept them into neighbourhoods. Yet the data for both countries show more support for open membership than for open neighbourhoods. In a 1987 Gallup poll, only 15% of Americans and 12% of Canadians thought private clubs should have the right to exclude prospective members of the basis of race. The exclusion of minorities from social clubs may be regarded as a symbol of overt

racism and may therefore be rejected even if there is a desire to exclude.

Intermarriage

Both Canadians and Americans have become more tolerant of racial intermarriage in recent decades, but Canadians continue to lead Americans in this regard. In Canada, disapproval of Black-White marriages declined from 52% in 1968 to 35% in 1973 (Michalos 1982:205), and those who disapprove are now only a small minority—16%, according to a 1988 Gallup National Omnibus Newspaper poll. In 1988, according to the same poll, 72.5% of Canadians approved of Black-White marriages. Lambert and Curtis (1984) show that English-Canadian disapproval declined from 60% in 1968 to 24% in 1983; there was less disapproval in Québec.

In the United States, disapproval of Black-White marriages declined from 72% in 1968 to 60% in 1972 (Michalos 1982:205). Yet, in 1983, only 40% of Americans approved of marriages between Whites and non-Whites (Schuman, Steeh, and Bobo 1985:74–76). The 1988 GSS showed that 25% of Americans think Black-White marriages should actually be outlawed (Niemi, Mueller, and Smith 1989:170). This figure represents a decline from earlier decades, but clearly the social climate in the United States is different from the social climate in Canada. The 1989 Decima poll confirms the difference: 32% of the American respondents, but only 13% of the Canadians, said that they would be unhappy if one of their children "married someone from a different racial background." Only 15% of the Americans, but 25% of the Canadians, said that they would be "happy" (*Maclean's* 1989).

To put the differences in the context of change, attitudes in the United States today are like those in the Canada of a decade or more ago. The Canadian data cited above show a change of about 2 percentage points per year. The U.S. data in Jaynes and Williams (1989:122) show a change of 1.5 points per year. In the matter of opposition to intermarriage, two of the data sources cited above indicate a difference between the two countries of about 20 points. Given a rate of 1.5 or 2 points per year, therefore, Canada may be ten or a dozen years ahead of the United States in the trend toward acceptance of interracial marriages.

COLLECTIVE AND GOVERNMENT ACTION AGAINST DISCRIMINATION

Americans have at times regarded race relations as one of their country's leading problems, a perception that has led to pressure for government action. A poll conducted in 1963, after a decade of growing racial unrest, showed that 52% of the U.S. population considered racial problems to be the most important facing the country; only 25% gave priority to the threat of war with the Soviet Union. Later, the prominence of the race issue receded, but it continues to be more significant in the United States than it has ever been in Canada (Michalos 1982:189–201).

In the context of race, accordingly, Americans have been more likely than Canadians to favour government action. In 1970, 25% of Americans, but only 11% of Canadians, put "reducing racial discrimination" among the top three government priorities for the future (Michalos 1982:202). And, of course, the U.S. government has indeed taken more action (Jain and Sloane 1981; Jain 1989). The Canadian federal government has avoided U.S.-style legislation to mandate equal employment, on the grounds that the problem is less serious in Canada (Reitz 1988b).

The higher priority that Americans have placed on racial discrimination is attributable in part to the higher level of racial conflict in the United States; it does not necessarily indicate a greater underlying predisposition to favour government action against discrimination. Indeed, as racial conflict has declined, Americans' willingness to invoke government action against discrimination seems to have declined somewhat as well, even though racial tolerance has increased. Even as racial attitudes and social-distance scores improved in the 1970s and 1980s, Whites became more supportive of policies to assist Blacks only in the area of housing and accommodations, and less supportive of such policies in other areas, including schools.

Kluegel (1990) uses GSS data for 1986, 1988, and 1989 to probe Americans' attitudes toward assisting Blacks to achieve equality. The GSS respondents were asked the following:

> Some people think that Blacks have been discriminated against for so long that the government has a special obligation to help improve their living standards. Others believe that the government should not be giving special treatment to Blacks.... Where would you place yourself on this scale, or haven't you made up your mind on this?

Pooling the surveys, Kluegel finds that only 13.8% agreed that the government was obligated to help Blacks; 59.3% stated that the government had no such obligation, and 26.9% took a position in between. Pooled analysis of these surveys, plus others conducted in 1977 and 1985, showed that the U.S. population was evenly split between those who thought the government was doing too much—26.8%—and those who thought it was doing too little—24.7%. Kluegel makes this point:

The only substantial change between 1977 and the late 1980s in how Whites view the Black-White socio-economic gap is a decline in the attribution of that gap to inborn ability differences. This decline parallels the trend of declining traditional prejudice.... The abatement of perhaps the most invidious explanation for the Black-White status gap has not been accompanied by any noteworthy increase in attributions that favour efforts to provide equal opportunity for Black Americans. (Kluegel 1990:523)

Smith's (1990:7) analysis of the 1990 GSS data shows that negative images of Blacks in the context of work and welfare have had a direct effect on support for affirmative action for Blacks. Thus, although the explanations that Americans give for racial disadvantages have changed, there is a persistent reluctance to identify discrimination as a major cause of these disadvantages, and hence resistance to policies intended to offset discrimination. Bobo (1988:109) offers a group-conflict interpretation of this resistance, suggesting that Whites oppose "change that might impose substantial burdens on Whites."

In Canada, no survey has asked if the government has an obligation to secure equal opportunity for Blacks. The 1987 Charter Study, however, did ask respondents if the government has an obligation to ensure equal opportunity in general. The statement "while equal opportunity to succeed is important for all Canadians, it's not really the government's job to guarantee it" elicited agreement from 63.3% of the respondents and disagreement from 33.7%. By contrast, as we noted above, only 13.8% of Americans approved of government intervention to assist Blacks. Of course, Canadian opinions might be different if racial minorities were targeted as beneficiaries. Support for government action to ensure equal opportunity might

not translate into support for government action to assist a particular group.

Sniderman and Hagen (1985) show that American rejection of government intervention is linked to "individualism," and suggest that individualist values militate against collective solutions. If this is true, then Canadians, who are less committed to individualism than Americans are, might be more willing to support government intervention. However, the causal relation between values and policy may work the other way: Opposition to government assistance to Blacks may reinforce individualism, which, in turn, may be invoked to legitimate racial inequality.

Thus, although discrimination has been a bigger political issue in the United States than it has been in Canada, and although more government intervention has occurred in the United States, Americans are not more likely than Canadians to favour collective responses to discrimination. Given their greater individualism, they may be less likely. Earlier, we showed that Canadians and Americans seem to be equally uncomfortable with the idea that discrimination is an explanation for inequality. The fact that social distances are less great in Canada may not mean that Canadians are more open to government intervention to ensure racial equality.

CONCLUSION

The findings reviewed here suggest that, despite the historical differences between race relations in Canada and race relations in the United States, Canadians and Americans are roughly similar in their attitudes and behaviour toward racial minorities. In both countries, blatant racism is marginal and the social distance between racial minorities and other groups is diminishing. The incidence of anti-Semitic attitudes and behaviour is about the same in each country. A majority of both

Canadians and Americans feel that minorities are responsible for their own inequality, that discrimination is not a major cause of inequality, and that government should not intervene to ensure equality.

Although the social distance between the majority and the racial minorities has declined in both countries, it has consistently been smaller in Canada, especially in relation to intermarriage. Depending on the dimension of social distance in question, Canadian attitudes may be either comparable to American attitudes or a decade or more ahead of them.

One likely reason why social distance between the races is greater in the United States is that economic distance is greater as well. Another likely reason is that racial minorities constitute a much larger proportion of the total population in the United States than they do in Canada. Thus, there may be a sense among White Americans that exclusion is necessary to maintain a degree of racial homogeneity that White Canadians take for granted.

REFERENCES

Angus Reid Group Inc. 1989. *Immigration to Canada: Aspects of Public Opinion.* Report prepared for Employment and Immigration Canada. Winnipeg: Angus Reid Group Inc.

Angus Reid Group Inc. 1991. *Multiculturalism and Canadians: Attitude Study 1991.* National Survey Report submitted to Multiculturalism and Citizenship Canada.

Anti-Defamation League of B'nai Brith 1991. *1991 Audit of Anti-Semitic Incidents.* New York: Anti-Defamation League of B'nai Brith.

Barrett, Stanley R. 1987. *Is God a Racist? The Right Wing in Canada.* Toronto: University of Toronto Press.

Berry, John W., R. Kalin, and D.M. Taylor 1977. *Multiculturalism and Ethnic Attitudes in Canada.* Ottawa: Supply and Services Canada.

Bobo, Lawrence 1988. "Group conflict, prejudice, and the paradox of contemporary racial attitudes." In Phyllis A. Katz and Dalmas A. Taylor (eds.), *Eliminating Racism: Means and Controversies*, pp. 85–114. New York: Plenum.

Bogardus, Emory S. 1958. "Racial distance changes in the United States during the past thirty years." *Sociology and Social Research* 43:127–135.

Bogardus, Emory S. 1967. *A Forty-Year Racial Distance Study.* Los Angeles: University of Southern California Press.

Breton, Raymond, et al. 1990. *Ethnic Identity and Inequality: Varieties of Experience in a Canadian City.* Toronto: University of Toronto Press.

Dion, Kenneth L. 1985. "Social distance norms in Canada: Effects of stimulus characteristics and dogmatism." *International Journal of Psychology* 20:743–749.

Driedger, Leo, and Richard Mezoff 1981. "Ethnic prejudice and discrimination in Winnipeg high schools." *Canadian Journal of Sociology* 6:1–17.

Jain, Harish 1989. "Racial minorities and affirmative action/employment equity legislation in Canada." *Industrial Relations* 44(3): 593–613.

Jain, Harish, and P.J. Sloane 1981. *Equal Employment Issues: Race and Sex Discrimination in the United States, Canada, and Britain.* New York: Praeger.

Jaynes, Gerald David, and Robin M. Williams, Jr. 1989. *A Common Destiny: Blacks and American Society.* Washington, D.C.: National Academy Press.

Johnson, James H., and Melvin L. Oliver 1989. "Interethnic minority conflict in urban America: The effects of economic and social dislocations." *Urban Geography* 10(5): 449–463.

Kluegel, James R. 1985. "'If there isn't a problem, you don't need a solution': The basis of contemporary affirmative action attitudes." *American Behavioral Scientist* 28:761–784.

Kluegel, James R. 1990. "Trends in Whites' explanations of the Black-White gap in socioeconomic status, 1977–1989." *American Sociological Review* 55(4):512–525.

Kluegel, James R., and Eliot R. Smith 1986. *Beliefs About Inequality: Americans' Views of What Is and What Ought to Be.* New York: Aldine de Gruyter.

Lambert, Ronald, and James Curtis 1984. "Québécois and English Canadian opposition to racial and religious intermarriage, 1968–1983." *Canadian Ethnic Studies* 16(2):30–46.

League of Human Rights of B'Nai Brith Canada 1991. *1991 Audit of Anti-Semitic Incidents.* Downsview, Ontario: The League.

Li, Peter S. 1988. *Ethnic Inequality in a Class Society.* Toronto: Wall and Thompson.

Lieberson, Stanley, and Mary Waters 1988. *From Many Strands: Ethnic and Racial Groups in Contemporary America.* New York: Russell Sage Foundation.

Maclean's 1989. "Portrait of two nations: The dreams and ideals of Canadians and Americans." July 3: 23–82.

Maclean's 1990. "Portrait of two nations: Should the two countries become one?" June 25: 37–52.

Martire, Gregory, and Ruth Clark 1982. *Anti-Semitism in the United States: A Study of Prejudice in the 1980s.* New York: Praeger.

Michalos, Alex C. 1982. "North American social report: A comparative study of the quality of life in Canada and the USA from 1964 to 1974." *Economics, Religion and Morality* Vol. 5. Dordrecht, Netherlands: D. Reidel.

Niemi, Richard G., John Mueller, and Tom W. Smith 1989. *Trends in Public Opinion: A Compendium of Survey Data.* New York: Greenwood Press.

Oliver, Melvin L., and James H. Johnson, Jr. 1984. "Inter-ethnic conflict in the urban ghetto: The case of Blacks and Latinos in Los Angeles." *Research in Social Movements, Conflict and Change* 6:57–94.

Owen, Carolyn, Howard C. Eisner, and Thomas R. McFaul 1981. "A half-century of social distance research: National replication of the Bogardus' studies." *Sociology and Social Research* 66(1):80–98.

Pineo, P. 1977 "The social standing of ethnic and racial groupings." *Canadian Review of Sociology and Anthropology* 14:147–157.

Reimers, David M., and Harold Troper 1992. "Canadian and American immigration policy since 1945." In Barry R. Chiswick (ed.), *Immigration, Language and Ethnicity: Canada and the United States*, pp. 15–54. Washington, D.C.: AEI Press.

Reitz, Jeffrey G. 1980. "Immigrants, their descendants, and the cohesion of Canada." In Raymond Breton, Jeffrey G. Reitz, and Victor Valentine (eds.), *Cultural Boundaries and the Cohesion of Canada*, pp. 329–471. Montréal: Institute for Research on Public Policy.

Reitz, Jeffrey G. 1988a. "The institutional structure of immigration as a determinant of interracial competition: A comparison of Britain and Canada." *International Migration Review* 22(1):117–146.

Reitz, Jeffrey G. 1988b. "Less racial discrimination in Canada, or simply less racial conflict? Implications of comparisons with Britain." *Canadian Public Policy* 14(4):424–441.

Reitz, Jeffrey G. 1990. "Ethnic concentrations in labour markets and their implications for ethnic inequality." In Raymond Breton, Wsevolod Isajiw, Warren E. Kalbach, and Jeffrey G. Reitz, *Ethnic Identity and Inequality: Varieties of Experience in a Canadian City.* Toronto: University of Toronto Press.

Rose, Harold M. 1989. "Blacks and Cubans in metropolitan Miami's changing economy." *Urban Geography* 10(5):464–486.

Schoenfeld, Stuart 1991. "Hate groups, hate propaganda and racial conflict." Unpublished manuscript.

Schuman, Howard, Charlotte Steeh, and Lawrence Bobo 1985. *Racial Attitudes in America: Trends and Interpretations.* Cambridge, Massachusetts: Harvard University Press.

Seltzer, Rick, and Grace M. Lopes 1986. "The Ku Klux Klan: Reasons for support or opposition among White respondents." *Journal of Black Studies* 17(1):91–109.

Sher, Julian 1983. *White Hoods: Canada's Ku Klux Klan.* Vancouver: New Star Books.

Sinha, Murli M. and Brian Berry 1991. "Ethnicity, Stigmatized groups and social distance: An expanded update of the Bogardus scale." Paper presented at the annual meetings of the American Sociological Association, Cincinnati, August 23–27.

Smith, Tom W. 1990. "Ethnic images." GSS Topical Report No. 19, National Opinion Research Center, University of Chicago.

Sniderman, Paul M. 1993. "Psychological and cultural foundations of prejudice: The case of anti-Semitism in Quebec." *Canadian Review of Sociology and Anthropology* 30(2): 242–270.

Sniderman, Paul M., and Michael G. Hagen 1985. *Race and Inequality: A Study in American Values*. Chatham, New Jersey: Chatham House.

Sniderman, Paul M. et al. 1991. "Political culture and the problem of double standards: Mass and elite attitudes toward language rights in the Canadian Charter of Rights and Freedoms." *Canadian Journal of Political Science* 22(2):259–284.

Sniderman, Paul M. et al. 1992. "Working papers on anti-Semitism in Quebec." Toronto: York University Institute for Survey Research.

Swan, Neil et al. 1991. *Economic and Social Impacts of Immigration: A Research Report Prepared for the Economic Council of Canada*. Ottawa: Supply and Services Canada.

HOW HIGH- AND LOW-INCOME CANADIANS SPEND THEIR TIME

Cara Williams

(A new chapter abridged from the author's "Time or money? How high and low-income Canadians spend their time," in *Canadian Social Trends*, Statistics Canada, Catalogue No. 11-008, Summer 2002, pp. 7–11. Reprinted with permission.)

INTRODUCTION

Our supply of time is absolute. There are twenty-four hours in a day—no more, no less. Neither technological advance nor the passage of the centuries has altered this. Yet virtually every one of us has wished for more time to spend with our families, to complete a project at work or school, to enjoy our vacations, or simply to relax. While at the beginning of the twentieth century money may have been the scarcest commodity, in the latter half, time has become the scarcest resource (Sharp 1981). Indeed, by the end of the 1990s, we had a level of prosperity that was unrivalled in history—but this was accompanied by a pace of life that, according to many, was much too hectic.

Just how hectic life gets depends on many factors, one being income. Our incomes affect, among other things, the neighbourhood and housing we live in, the holidays we choose, the activities we engage in, and the time we spend on these activities. Our incomes may also be related to the number of hours we spend on paid work and household chores, the amount of time we devote to playing with our children, and the time we have left for leisure. Is there any truth to the oft-quoted phrase, "you either have time or money, but not both"? This article uses the 1998 General Social Survey (GSS) to examine

What You Should Know about This Study

Data in this article come from the 1998 General Social Survey (GSS) on time use. The survey interviewed almost 11 000 Canadians aged 15 and over in the ten provinces and provided information on how people spent their time during one day. In addition to information about time use, the 1998 GSS also asked general questions about the perception of time.

Individuals included in this article are aged 25 to 54 years, the ones most likely to be in the labour force, to have families and significant demands on their time. For purposes of this study, people were classified as high income if their total household income was equal to or greater than $80 000 and low income if their total household income was $30 000 or less. Using these definitions, approximately 2.4 million Canadians live in high-income and 1.9 million in low-income households. While virtually all working-age adults in high-income households are employed (97%), a notably smaller proportion (72%) of those with low incomes work at a job or business.

Respondents are considered employed if they reported working at a job or business in the last week or during the past twelve months.

the activities and time use of Canadians aged 25 to 54 in high- and low-income households.

HIGH-INCOME CANADIANS SPEND MORE TIME ON PAID WORK

According to popular wisdom from the 1950s, "computers and automation were going to create abundant wealth ... and ... would free us from the drudgery of work" (O'Hara 1993:1). Many believed that by the twentieth century's end we would be working a three-day week with plenty of free time to spend at our leisure. By the time the century ended, visions of a three-day work week had vanished. In many Canadian families, both parents are now in the work force, resulting in additional stress as they struggle to juggle the often-competing time demands of family, home, and work.

Most employed Canadians aged 25 to 54 spend the largest portion of their waking day doing paid work. While this is true for individuals in both high- and low-income households, those with high income spend an average of 15% more time on their paid job[1]: forty-six hours compared with forty hours spent by those with low income.

The majority of employed Canadians in high-income households (56%) report being satisfied with the number of hours they work in their current arrangement, while 20% would prefer to work fewer hours for less pay. Only about 8% were willing to work more hours for more pay. Paid employees from low-income households felt quite differently. Nearly one-third stated that they would be willing to work more hours for more pay, while only 6% said they wanted to work less time for less pay.

TABLE 30-1	High-Income Canadians Are More Likely to Work Longer Hours and More Weeks		

		Aged 25 to 54	
		High Income	Low Income
Total (millions)		2.4	1.9
% employed during the last twelve months		97	72
Average number of hours worked in the last week		46	40
Average number of weeks worked in the last year		50	41

Source: Statistics Canada, *General Social Survey*, 1998.

TABLE 30-2	Low-Income Canadians Spend Considerably More Time on Housework		

		Aged 25 to 54	
		High Income	Low Income
Time Spent on... Average Minutes per Day			
Housework		30	50
Meal preparation		40	52
Shopping		48	51
Personal care including sleeping (hours)		9.8	10.1
Leisure		277	317
Watching television		82	132
Childcare*		68	82
Playing with child		17	18
Teaching child		4	9
Reading to or talking with child		4	5

* Refers only to individuals with children living in the household.

Source: Statistics Canada, *General Social Survey*, 1998.

LOW-INCOME CANADIANS SPEND MORE TIME ON UNPAID WORK

Unpaid work such as housework and home maintenance take up much of the time left after paid work is done. While people from high-income households spend more hours on paid work, low-income individuals expend considerably more time on unpaid chores (Table 30-1, 30-2). For example, low-income Canadians aged 25 to 54 spend fifty minutes a day on housework, while those with high income perform these tasks for just thirty minutes; similarly, meal preparation takes up fifty-two minutes of low-income people's time, but only forty minutes of a high-income individual's day.[2]

Of course, because of their better financial situation, high-income Canadians

Technological Advances and the Leisure Society

The twentieth century was a period of enormous technological advance. A great number of devices—cars, washing machines, dryers, microwave ovens, and computers, to name just a few—were invented during this time specifically to make certain tasks easier and less time consuming. But the extra time these products afford us seems to be offset by the increasing number of activities we do and things we have. For example, in his book *The Tyranny of Time*, Robert Banks observes that "food preparation and ironing take less time owing to the introduction of pre-prepared foods and non-iron fabrics. But such gains are offset by the fact that, among the middle class particularly, homes and gardens are larger, material possessions requiring maintenance and services are more numerous, and standards of personal and household presentability are higher."*

These changes have been likened to an endless spiral. As early as 1970 one social commentator observed that economic growth entails a general increase in the scarcity of time. In addition to growing requirements for the care and maintenance of our ever-increasing consumption goods,

"swelling expectations lead to a constant effort to keep up with the latest products .... With so many things to use, and the need to work harder to obtain them, our lives grow more harried and pressured." †

Indeed, technological advances have allowed us to squeeze more and more activity into our waking hours. Many of us "multi-task" our way through the day. We discuss business over the cell phone as we drive to work, eat "fast food" at our desk in the office, or conduct meetings over lunch. After work we rush home to prepare dinner, attempt to have quality time with our children, drive them to their activities and do the shopping before picking them up again. Back at home we help with homework while doing the wash, then late at night start reviewing the report we brought home from the office. We have little time to relax and often cut down on badly needed sleep to get things done.

* R. Banks, 1983, *The Tyranny of Time—When 24 Hours Is Not Enough*, pp. 82–83. Downers Grove, Illinois: InterVarsity Press.

†J.D. De Graffe, Wann and T.H. Naylor, 2001, *Affluenza: The All-Consuming Epidemic*, p. 44. San Francisco: Berrett-Koehler Publisher Inc.

---

are more likely to purchase cleaning services and eat at restaurants. Indeed, on an average day in 1998, about 25% of high-income Canadians ate at least one restaurant meal compared with about 13% of those from low-income households.

Although many people find shopping a chore, most Canadians between 25 and 54 spend a fair amount of time on this activity, regardless of income: low-income individuals, an average of about fifty-one minutes a day and high-income people about forty-eight minutes a day. Of this time, between eight and ten minutes is spent grocery shopping and approximately twelve to sixteen minutes on making other everyday purchases such as clothing and gas.[3]

MORE THAN EIGHT IN TEN HIGH-INCOME CANADIANS FEEL RUSHED

Perhaps as a result of the types of jobs they have, or because they spend a larger part of their day at paid work, Canadians with high incomes are more likely to feel pressed for time than their low-income counterparts: 84% feel rushed at least a few times a week, compared with 73% of individuals in low-income households. While weekdays tend to be more hectic, for many Canadians, juggling responsibilities is a problem that continues into the weekend. Nearly 60% of high-income and about 47% of low-income individuals feel rushed every day, including Saturday and Sunday.

Although low-income Canadians are less likely to feel pressed for time, a substantial proportion still feel this way, suggesting that the pace of society and its associated stresses affect Canadians from all walks of life. These results contradict theories that suggest low-income individuals are not caught up in the time vortex.

If given more time, both high- and low-income Canadians would spend it on similar types of activities. For example, 36% of Canadians in high-income households reported wanting to spend more time with family and friends, while 19% would relax. Among those in low-income households, 33% would spend any more time they had on family and friends and 15% on relaxing.

LITTLE TIME LEFT TO SPEND EXCLUSIVELY WITH CHILDREN

Families are often the ones most affected by the scarcity of time. Work, family, and community responsibilities frequently collide, leaving parents feeling guilty about "getting it all done and remorse that they have not done enough with their children and families" (Daly 2000:2). Unheard of thirty years ago, many homes today have a special family calendar to schedule work, school, and leisure activities.

Overall, low-income Canadians aged 25 to 54 spend more time on childcare at eighty-two minutes a day than their high-income counterparts, at about sixty-eight minutes a day.[4] But as all parents can attest, much of childcare is done while engaging in other activities such as cleaning, cooking, or watching television. Considerably less time is devoted to exclusive interaction with children. In both low- and high-income households, parents report spending under five minutes a day

reading or talking with their children and less than twenty minutes a day playing with them. However, low-income parents devote more time to teaching or helping their children, at about nine minutes a day, than do parents with high income, who do so for approximately four minutes a day.[5]

LESS LEISURE TIME FOR HIGH-INCOME CANADIANS

The concept of leisure is difficult to pin down. An activity that for some is leisure (e.g. gardening, baking, building a shed) is, for others, unpaid work. Even sociologists find defining leisure somewhat difficult. Some see it as "a quality of experience" while others regard leisure as a "portion of one's time" (Wilson 1980:21–40). While gauging the quality of a person's time use cannot be done with GSS data, it is possible to examine leisure as a portion of time. On an average day, 25- to 54-year-old Canadians from high-income households spend about forty minutes less on leisure than their low-income counterparts: 4.6 hours versus 5.3 hours.[6] Of this time, sports and hobbies take up about fifty-seven minutes of high-income and forty-nine minutes of low-income people's time, while reading books or newspapers constitutes twenty-three and eighteen minutes, respectively. Both groups spend most of their leisure time watching television (high-income people eighty-two and low-income people one hundred and thirty-two minutes a day). This, despite the fact that in addition to traditional hobbies, the computer and the Internet now also compete for scarce leisure minutes.[7]

Attending events and participating in activities may also be influenced by income. According to the GSS, high-income Canadians had been twice as likely as low-income individuals to attend a concert or participate regularly in sports in the

TABLE 30-3 **High-Income Canadians Are More Likely to Attend Concerts and Go to Museums**		
	Aged 25 to 54	
	High Income	**Low Income**
In the last twelve months, did you...	%	%
Read for leisure		
Newspapers	95	84
Magazines	87	67
Books	73	63
Go to conservation or nature parks	66	43
Attend a concert	55	22
Go to a historic site	51	25
Go to a zoo/planetarium	50	33
Engage in a sport	49	24
Improve knowledge through books, TV, computer, or talking	48	31
Go to a museum/art gallery	48	25
Attend a cultural/artistic festival	32	21
Go to the library (as leisure)	31	29
Do crafts or woodworking	29	31
Attend other stage performances	24	12
Play a musical instrument	22	15
Attend a cultural/heritage performance	18	12
Do any visual arts	12	12
Take photographs (for art)	10	8
Write prose or poetry (for leisure)	8	12
Sing	8	9
Choreograph or dance	6	4*

*Subject to high sampling variability.

Source: Statistics Canada, *General Social Survey*, 1998.

preceding twelve months (Table 30-3). People from high-income households are also more likely to attend cultural or artistic festivals, or go to museums or art galleries.[8] The availability of funds, rather than differing interests between the two groups, may be responsible for these disparities.

On the other hand, similarities also exist in how the two groups spend their leisure time. For example, individuals in both high- and low-income households are equally likely to use the library, do crafts or woodworking, sing, or participate in recreational dance.

SUMMARY

Canadians from low- and high-income households live in a complex, fast-paced world. While high-income individuals spend more time on paid work, those with low income devote more time to unpaid work activities. High-income adults feel considerably more rushed and have less time for leisure. And whether living in a high- or low-income household, parents have little time left to spend with their children. This is one reason why adults in both groups report wishing they could spend more time with family and friends.

NOTES

1. Refers to individuals who were working at a job or business in the past seven days.

2. Daily times for these activities are averaged over seven days.

3. The rest of shopping time is spent on the purchase of other goods and services such as car maintenance, finances, and personal care services.

4. This is an average and includes time spent with all children up to the age of 15. Not surprisingly, individuals with small children spend more time on childcare. For more information, see C. Silver, "Being there: The time dual-earner couples spend with their children," *Canadian Social Trends*, Summer 2000.

5. These findings support figures in the United States, which show that Americans spend about six hours a week shopping and about forty minutes each week playing with their kids. Taking a weekly average, both high- and low-income Canadians spend six hours shopping but under two hours a week playing with their children.

6. Daily times are averaged over the week and include Saturdays and Sundays.

7. Indeed, more than 30% of Internet users stated that because of being on the Internet they spend less time watching television.

8. Respondents were asked if they had participated in these activities during the past twelve months.

REFERENCES

Daly, K. 2000. *It Keeps Getting Faster: Changing Pattern of Time in Families.* The Vanier Institute of the Family, p. 2. Retrieved March 21, 2002 (http://www.vifamily.ca/cft/daly/dalye.htm).

De Graffe, J., D. Wann, and T.H. Naylor 2001. *Affluenza: The All-Consuming Epidemic.* San Francisco: Berrett-Koehler.

O'Hara, B. 1993. *Working Harder Isn't Working,* p. 1. Vancouver: New Star Books.

Sharp, C. 1981. *The Economics of Time*, p. 18. Oxford: Martin Robertson and Company.

Williams, C. 2001. "Connected to the Internet, still connected to life?" *Canadian Social Trends* (Winter).

Wilson, J. 1980. "Sociology of leisure." *Annual Review of Sociology* 6:21–40.

Chapter

31

POLITICAL INVOLVEMENT, CIVIC ENGAGEMENT, AND SOCIAL INEQUALITY

James Curtis, Edward Grabb,
Thomas Perks, and Tina Chui

(Revised from the previous edition of this volume.)

INTRODUCTION

In the popular media and public discussions, Canada is normally portrayed as a free and democratic society, where all citizens have the right to influence political decisions, and where everyone is encouraged to engage in different forms of civic participation and community or collective action. In such a society, we might expect that people are relatively similar in their levels of involvement in the formal political process, and in the "parapolitics" that occurs among local organizations and community interest groups. Presumably, then, most Canadians should participate to about the same degree in such activities as voting, discussing politics, trying to influence others, joining political parties and community groups,

making public protests, and supporting social movements.

In other words, we might think that, for these types of behaviours, members of more privileged status groups do not have an advantage over other people. In fact, we might even reason that the disadvantaged have more to protest about than other people and, therefore, are more highly represented than the advantaged in public protest activities, such as signing petitions or joining in demonstrations.

Some social scientists have questioned, however, whether there really is such a broad base to political and civic engagement in Canada and other democratic countries. In particular, these researchers have doubted that individuals who rank lower on various social status dimensions have as great an opportunity or inclination to participate in these types of activities. This question is clearly an important one for students of social inequality to consider, because political action and interest group involvement are normally seen as fundamental to our basic human rights and civil liberties.

Research in Canada and other societies, especially extensive work in the United States, has shown that there is in fact a relationship between achieved and ascribed statuses and level of involvement in both politics and community or civic activities (see, e.g., Curtis 1971; Smith 1975; Curtis and Lambert 1976; Milbrath and Goel 1977; McPherson and Lockwood 1980; Palisi and Palisi 1984; Knoke 1986; Kay et al. 1987; Curtis et al. 1989; Curtis, Grabb, and Baer 1992; Curtis, Baer, and Grabb 2001; Baer, Curtis, and Grabb 2001; Curtis and Grabb 2002). These studies have found, for example, that persons with higher occupational status, education, and income are more likely than other people to join and participate in voluntary organizations of various kinds.

Some studies also indicate that disadvantaged racial and ethnic groups, such as American Blacks, are less likely to be involved in voluntary associations than are groups higher in the ethnic stratification system. However, other research also suggests that these ethnic or racial differences may be partially the result of socio-economic inequalities, rather than racial or ethnic differences per se (e.g., Smith 1975; Grabb and Curtis 1992).

Along similar lines, research indicates that middle-aged people are more likely to participate in voluntary organizations than are older and younger people, and males are more likely to do so than are females (e.g., Curtis 1971; Smith 1975; Cutler 1976; McPherson and Lockwood 1980; Edwards et al. 1984; Palisi and Palisi 1984; Knoke 1986; Curtis, Grabb, and Baer 1992; Curtis, Baer, and Grabb 2001;

Corrigall-Brown 2002). It should be noted that, with regard to gender, one apparent exception to the general pattern concerns "new" voluntary associations, which focus on support for so-called "new social movements," including animal rights groups, women's organizations, peace groups, and environment and conservation organizations. Canadian research indicates that, in these types of voluntary associations, women are more active than men (Curtis and Grabb 2002). Otherwise, however, there is a general tendency for men to participate more often, not only in voluntary associations, but also in formal politics, such as voting, political party membership, and political interest (e.g., Curtis and Lambert 1976; Milbrath and Goel 1977; Chui, Curtis, and Grabb 1993; Curtis, Baer, and Grabb 2001; Curtis and Grabb 2002).

These differences have been explained in a number of ways. One well-known early explanation suggested that such patterns are largely accounted for by the "relative centrality" of different groups in society (see, e.g., Milbrath and Goel 1977; Chui, Curtis, and Grabb 1993). According to this perspective, some people are more centrally positioned in important social networks. Persons from the higher socioeconomic strata and from the more privileged or established racial, ethnic, gender, and age groupings are perhaps the best examples. These individuals generally have more power and resources at their disposal than others do. They also tend to have greater knowledge, information, and awareness about how various organizations operate in their community and elsewhere. For these reasons, it is argued, people of higher rank or social status are more likely to be active participants in the political processes that help to shape their society.

More recently, writers have applied a different, though related, perspective that focuses on the concept of "social capital."

Although the definitions of this concept vary somewhat (see, e.g., Coleman 1988; Putnam 1995, 2000; Lin 2000), social capital can basically be thought of as a resource, or a form of social power, which arises from and is represented by people's locations in key social networks. From this perspective, as well, it is argued that those groups and individuals who are in advantaged or dominant positions in the class, gender, ethnic, and other hierarchies of society tend to be more actively engaged in political and civic affairs, both in their local communities and in society generally.

Involvement and interest in politics and other civic activities can stem from various motivations. A belief in the value of individual participation in a free society and a wish to contribute to the welfare and progress of one's community and country are two examples. It is likely, however, that the tendency for members of more prosperous and powerful status groups to be more engaged in such activities is also due to their own private or special interests. In particular, people from advantaged groups may be more highly motivated to take part in political and community life out of a desire to maintain their superior position in the stratification system, by working in and having greater control over those organizations that help decide upon important policies in the community or the wider society (see, e.g., Olson 1965; Lin 2000; Putnam 2000).

In this paper, we examine recent information dealing with the relationship between social inequality and political or community activity in Canada. We consider the relationship between people's positions on a number of different dimensions of inequality, on the one hand, and a wide range of measures of political involvement, civic engagement, and community participation, on the other hand.

DATA SOURCES AND PROCEDURES

We have used two data sources for our analyses for this chapter: one from responses to a national survey conducted in 1991 and the other from responses to a national survey in 2000. The first data source provides us with much more detailed information, so we shall begin with a discussion of that study, its procedures, and its results. We will turn to the 2000 study following our discussion of the first study.

STUDY ONE

Data Source

A national sample of adult Canadians was interviewed as part of the larger World Values Survey in 1991–1993, an international survey of more than forty countries conducted by Ronald Inglehart and associates (for details, see Inglehart et al. 1994). The present analyses are limited to the Canadian respondents aged 21 and older. Some younger respondents, aged 18 to 21, were excluded from the analyses because many were still in school and, therefore, may not have been able to give as much time to political activities as older people.

Measures of Respondents' Political and Organization Activities

Five measures of political activities were used: discussing politics,[1] attempting to persuade people on issues,[2] interest in politics,[3] expecting to vote in the next election,[4] and political group activity.[5] Table 31-1 shows the response categories for each of these types of activity. In addition, we used a measure of public protest activity, based on responses to the following questions:

Now I would like you to look at this card. I'm going to read out some different forms of political action that people can take, and I would like you to tell me, for each one, whether you have actually done any of these things, whether you might do it, or would never, under any circumstances, do it: *signing a petition, joining a boycott, attending lawful demonstrations, joining strikes, or occupying buildings or factories.*

The responses for each of these activities were given scores as follows: "Have actually done" = 3; "Might do it" = 2; and "Would never" = 1. These scores were then summed for each respondent to give her or him a measure of *participation in public protest activity*. This measure ranged from 6 (low protest activity) to 18 (high protest activity).

The survey also yielded information on the respondent's stated *support for social movements*; whether or not they were a member of organizations working for these movements. Respondents were asked:

There are a number of groups and movements looking for public support. For each of the following movements, which I read out, can you tell me whether you approve or disapprove of this movement?: *ecology or nature protection* movement; *anti-nuclear energy* movement; *disarmament* movement; human rights movement (at home and abroad); *women's* movement; and *anti-apartheid* movement.

For present purposes, the response categories for each of the six movements were assigned scores as follows: "Approve strongly" = 4; "Approve somewhat" = 3; "Disapprove somewhat" = 2; and "Disapprove strongly" = 1. Then the respondents' support ratings for the six social movements were summed for a measure with a range of 6 (low support) to 24 (high support).

These six social movements have been referred to by others as "new social move-

ments." Although some of these movements are tied to causes or issues that are not precisely new (e.g., women's rights and equality), they are called "new" because they typically have enjoyed renewed prominence in recent years. In addition, they are also seen to operate outside of or independently from more traditional movements, such as the labour union movement and early suffrage movements (see Carroll 1992; Larana et al. 1994).

Finally, we also used a measure that gauged the *voluntary organization activity* of respondents. First, each respondent reported his or her memberships in community organizations, in answer to the following question: "Which, if any, of the following do you belong to?" A checklist of sixteen possible organization categories was supplied: charities and social welfare, churches or religious organizations, education or arts groups, trade unions, political parties or groups, community action groups, human rights organizations, conservation or environmental groups, animal welfare groups, youth work groups, sport and recreation organizations, professional associations, women's groups, peace groups, health organizations, and "others." People were also asked, "And do you currently do any unpaid voluntary work for any of them?" Each respondent was given a score of 1 for each organization in which she or he was a member only, and a score of 2 for each working membership. These scores were then summed across all types of organizations, to produce a scale of voluntary organization activity. The measure ranged from 0 (no involvement) to 32 (high involvement).

Social Status Measures

Nine different measures of inequality or social status were examined for their possible relationship to the political and community activity measures. Tables 31-4 and

31-5 later in this chapter provide details on the exact categories used for each of the social status variables. Because of the international nature of the World Values Survey, *education* had to be measured using an indirect indicator, which was the respondent's age at completion of schooling; the ten values for this measure ranged from finished school "at 12 years of age or earlier" to finished school "at 21 years of age or older." Respondent's *occupational status* was measured using a set of eleven different categories that were roughly rank-ordered from high to low status. *Age* was grouped into six categories, with values ranging from younger (aged 21–29) to older (70 or more). *Gender* was divided simply into female versus male. *Household income* had ten levels, from a low of under $5000 per year to a high of $50 000 or more. *Language group* was divided into English versus French. The available race measure produced a four-fold classification: Whites, Blacks, Chinese, and All Others. Respondents were also divided into two categories according to *nativity* or country of birth: Canadian-born versus foreign-born. *Region* was a seven-category measure, running east to west, from the Atlantic region to British Columbia.

Overall Involvement in Political and Organizational Activities

Tables 31-1, 31-2, and 31-3 show the overall involvement of the respondents in the various political and organizational activities. Starting with Table 31-1, we see that a relatively large proportion of people, close to 72%, indicated that they would vote if an election were held tomorrow. This proportion is very similar to the voter turnouts in recent Canadian elections; these ranged from 69% to 75% in the 1980–1993 period, for example (Elections Canada 1993, Table 4). In addition, almost

60% said that they were either "very" interested (20%) or "somewhat" interested (39%) in politics. Close to 20% discussed politics "often," and another 57% did so "occasionally"). However, only 14% tried regularly to persuade fellow workers, friends, or family members concerning political issues. If we consider involvement in groups that are identified by the respondent as "political parties or groups," only 8% reported such involvement, with 5% saying they were simply a member of such a group, and another 3% also doing volunteer work for the group.

If we look at the other end of the scale, non-involvement, we see that 13% of the sample said they "never" attempted to persuade others of their views; almost one-quarter (23%) of the respondents never discussed politics; about 40% reported that they were "not very" interested or "not at all" interested in politics; 28% did not intend to vote; and 92% were not involved in political groups in any way.

When we turn to participation in all types of voluntary groups in the community (Table 31-1), we find that 60% had one or more memberships and about 43% were doing work in one or more organizations. About 53% had multiple memberships, and about 23% were working in more than one organization.

Overall, then, we find little evidence of mass involvement in political activity in Canada. It is true that a sizeable majority of Canadians vote federally, express some political interest, and at least occasionally engage in political discussion. However, very few are members of political parties or politically oriented organizations, and even fewer do volunteer work for such organizations. There is stronger evidence of community participation if we look at the proportion of people who belong to at least one voluntary organization of whatever type, though even here the proportion of people who are not only members, but

TABLE 31-1	Levels of Involvement in Various Types of Political and Organizational Activities: Overall National Adult Sample		
Type of Activity and Level of Involvement	**Percentage of Sample**	**Type of Activity and Level of Involvement**	**Percentage of Sample**
Discuss Politics		**Political Group Involvement**	
Often	19.7	None	92.2
Occasionally	57.1	Member, No Work	4.6
Never	23.2	Working Member	3.3
(N=)	(1618)	(N=)	(1620)
Persuade Friends		**Voting**	
Often	13.9	No	28.5
Time to Time/Rarely	73.0	Yes	71.5
Never	13.1	(N=)	(1625)
(N=)	(1619)		
		Voluntary Organization Involvement	
Political Interest		Member of None	35.9
Very	20.2	One	20.8
Some	39.3	Two	16.4
Not Very	26.2	Three Plus	26.9
Not at All	14.3	(N=)	(1625)
(N=)	(1619)	Working for None	56.7
		One	20.1
		Two	11.4
		Three Plus	11.8
		(N=)	(1625)

are also actively involved, is less than half of the total sample.

In Table 31-2 we consider rates of involvement in the various types of public protest actions. Here we see, once more, that involvement levels are generally low, with the exception of signing petitions. Seventy-seven percent of respondents report signing a petition, while another 14% think they might do so sometime in the future, and only 8% say they would never do so. However, for joining a boycott, only about one-quarter (24%) have ever done this, and 34% say they never

would do so. For attending demonstrations the parallel figures are 22% ("Have done") and 36% ("Would never do"). The rates of involvement are even lower for "Joining a lawful strike," with only 7% doing this, and 66% saying they would never do it. Finally, only 3% have occupied facilities, and 78% would never do so. If we sum the responses across these activities, to create an Index of Public Protest Activities ranging from 8 to 15, the overall sample has an average score of only 9.1.

In Table 31-3 we see that reasonably large proportions of respondents express

TABLE 31-2 Levels of Involvement in Five Types of Public Protest Activity: Overall National Adult Sample

Level of Involvement	Types of Protest Actions				
	Sign Petition %	Join Boycott %	Attend Demonstration %	Join Strike %	Occupy Facility %
Have Done	77.3	24.1	21.6	7.3	3.0
Might Do	14.4	41.8	42.0	26.4	18.6
Would Never Do	8.3	34.1	36.4	66.3	78.4
Total	100%	100%	100%	100%	100%

(N = 1625)

TABLE 31-3 Levels of Approval for Six Social Movements: Overall National Adult Sample

Social Movement	Approval Level					
	Approve Strongly %	Somewhat %	Disapprove Somewhat %	Strongly %	(N)	Total
Ecology	53.5	41.3	3.9	1.3	(1590)	100%
Anti-nuclear	32.3	41.8	19.9	6.0	(1549)	100%
Disarmament	39.3	39.8	14.8	6.1	(1555)	100%
Human Rights	57.8	35.7	5.1	1.3	(1579)	100%
Women's	35.8	48.1	12.7	3.4	(1577)	100%
Anti-apartheid	46.5	36.8	11.5	5.2	(1439)	100%

support for each of the six new social movements. Well over one-half of the sample approve "strongly" or "somewhat" with each social movement. The "strong" support ranges from a high of 58% for the human rights movement and 54% for the ecology movement to 47% for anti-apartheid, 39% for disarmament, 36% for the women's movement, and 32% for the anti-nuclear movement. When we sum the responses across all six types of social movement, producing an Index of Social Movement Support with a range of 6 to 24, we find a high average score for the overall sample of 19.6.

Social Status and Political Activity

We now consider the key question of whether or not social status is related to level of involvement in the various political and community activities. In other words, do all categories of Canadians get involved more or less equally, or do people from more advantaged groups get involved more than others?

Table 31-4 provides data on the relationship between the five forms of political participation listed in Table 31-1 and the nine different measures of social

TABLE 31-4	Social Statuses and Average Scores for Involvement in Five Types of Political Activities				

Social Status Categories		Type of Activity				
	N	**Discuss Politics**	**Persuade Friends**	**Political Interest**	**Voting**	**Political Group Activity**
Total Sample	1625	(1.96)	(2.01)	(2.65)	(.72)	(0.11)
Years of Schooling						
<12 years	32	1.84	1.97	2.35	.66	.06
13	20	1.85	1.80	2.40	.50	.05
14	73	1.68	1.88	2.45	.62	.05
15	82	1.73	1.87	2.93	.59	.04
16	170	1.77	1.86	2.42	.66	.08
17	172	1.87	2.00	2.52	.76	.05
18	297	1.90	1.99	2.61	.72	.12
19	137	1.91	2.04	2.58	.69	.10
20	93	2.04	2.02	2.74	.78	.09
21+years	519	2.18	2.10	2.88	.76	.15
eta		(.25)	(.17)	(.18)	(.13)	(.10)
significance		‡	‡	‡	†	*
Occupational Level						
Owner>10 employees	47	2.17	2.32	3.13	.75	.38
Owner<10 employees	63	2.06	2.05	2.83	.71	.05
Professional	289	2.20	2.07	2.90	.74	.18
Middle Manager	143	2.12	2.08	2.86	.76	.12
Lower Manager	191	1.88	1.94	2.52	.70	.05
Supervisor	39	2.14	2.08	2.95	.73	.15
Skilled Lab	117	1.85	1.93	2.53	.76	.07
Semi-skilled	234	1.81	1.97	2.47	.68	.09
Unskilled	228	1.78	1.97	2.38	.68	.07
Farmers	79	2.04	2.03	2.84	.75	.19
All Others	175	1.87	1.94	2.54	.69	.07
eta		(.25)	(.15)	(.23)	(.06)	(.16)
significance		‡	‡	‡	n.s.	‡
Income Level						
<$5 000	71	1.75	1.96	2.27	.62	.03
$5 000–10 000	90	1.99	1.97	2.69	.74	.10
10 000–15 000	98	1.88	1.94	2.55	.69	.04
15 000–20 000	109	1.88	1.99	2.53	.63	.02
20 000–25 000	152	1.89	1.97	2.58	.70	.14
25 000–30 000	224	1.99	1.99	2.66	.77	.14
30 000–35 000	189	1.96	2.04	2.71	.75	.09
35 000–40 000	173	2.07	2.03	2.78	.84	.11
40 000–45 000	103	2.19	2.05	2.83	.82	.17
50 000+	178	2.19	2.16	2.92	.79	.19
eta		(.17)	(.13)	(.16)	(.15)	(.13)
significance		‡	†	‡	‡	†

TABLE 31-4   *continued*

Social Status Categories	N	Type of Activity				
		Discuss Politics	**Persuade Friends**	**Political Interest**	**Voting**	**Political Group Activity**
Age						
21–29	308	1.81	2.03	2.44	.70	.08
30–39	457	1.95	2.02	2.58	.73	.11
40–49	315	2.01	2.05	2.70	.73	.14
50–59	207	2.03	2.02	2.84	.76	.15
60–69	191	2.11	1.95	2.90	.71	.09
70 & over	147	1.93	1.88	2.67	.60	.09
eta		(.14)	(.09)	(.15)	(.09)	(.05)
significance		‡	†	‡	*	n.s.
Gender						
Male	807	1.95	2.02	2.75	.73	.14
Female	818	1.94	2.00	2.56	.70	.09
eta		(.05)	(.03)	(.10)	(.04)	(.06)
significance		n.s.	n.s.	‡	n.s.	†
Language Group						
English	1251	1.98	2.00	2.71	.74	.11
French	374	1.90	2.04	2.46	.62	.10
eta		(.05)	(.03)	(.11)	(.11)	(.02)
significance	n.s.	0	n.s.	‡	‡	n.s.
Race						
Whites	1499	1.96	2.01	2.67	.73	.11
Blacks	15	2.13	2.00	2.47	.53	.13
Chinese	48	1.83	1.98	2.51	.56	.13
All Others	63	1.90	1.95	2.33	.54	.11
eta		(.05)	(.02)	(.08)	(.11)	(.01)
significance		n.s.	n.s.	*	‡	n.s.
Nativity						
Not Born in Canada	281	2.09	2.01	2.79	.69	.12
Born in Canada	1344	1.94	2.01	2.63	.72	.11
eta		(.09)	(.01)	(.06)	(.03)	(.02)
significance		†	n.s.	†	n.s.	n.s.
Region						
AT	133	1.81	1.88	2.37	.64	.15
QU	403	1.93	2.04	2.50	.63	.11
ON	611	1.99	2.01	2.74	.75	.09
MA	59	1.90	2.03	2.50	.69	.15
SK	74	1.97	1.97	2.82	.74	.12
AB	171	2.02	2.03	2.70	.74	.20
BC	174	2.04	2.02	2.88	.74	.05
eta		(.09)	(.08)	(.16)	(.14)	(.09)
significance		†	**n.s.**	‡	‡	†

n.s. = Not a statistically significant difference.
* Significant at p<.05.

† Significant at p<.01.
‡ Significant at p<.001.

status. Based on the relative centrality and social capital perspectives, we would expect the following groups to be higher in political involvement than their less advantaged counterparts: the more highly educated, those with higher incomes, those with higher occupational status, English speakers, Whites, the native-born, males, the middle-aged, and those living in the more economically powerful regions of the country, especially Ontario.

Overall, the findings confirm many, though not all, of these expectations. As predicted, education and income have statistically significant relationships with all five measures of political participation, and in the expected direction. That is, the more highly educated respondents and those with higher incomes are more likely than other people to vote, to be involved in political groups, to show interest in politics, to discuss politics, and to attempt to influence others concerning political issues.

Age, occupation level, and region are significantly related to four of the five political activity measures. As expected, the middle-aged are more involved in voting, express greater political interest, discuss politics more, and attempt to influence the opinions of others more, at least compared with younger people and (particularly) older people. Occupational status is related in the expected way to all the political activities except voting, where there is no statistically significant pattern. As for region, residents of the powerful or more prosperous regions, especially Ontario and the Western provinces, tend to be higher on political interest, discussing politics, and voting. Respondents from the Western regions also show higher levels of political group involvement.

Moving on to the other ascribed statuses (Table 31-4), we see that language group is related to discussing politics, political interest, and voting, with English speakers higher than French speakers,

which is again consistent with the relative centrality and social capital perspectives. One caution here, though, is that voting pertains to federal elections and not provincial elections. If the voting question dealt with provincial elections, it is likely that the proportions of French speakers and Québecers voting would be more similar to those of other Canadians. Race appears to be related to only two of the five measures of political activity; for political interest and voting, Whites, as expected, are more active than other groups. Finally, in the case of nativity, we find no evidence of the expected pattern: The native-born are *less* involved than the foreign-born in political interest and political discussions, and there are no significant differences by place of birth for the other three political activity measures.

In Table 31-5, we relate the nine social status variables to three different indices of activity: *political protest, social movement support*, and *community organization involvement*. Most of the relationships in Table 31-5 are statistically significant, and in the expected direction. In general, advantaged groups tend to be more involved in the three types of activity. The exceptions are that race and nativity are not significantly related to public protest and social movement support, and income is related to public protest and organization involvement, but not to support for social movements. As we would expect, those higher in education are more involved in public protest, in community interest groups, and in supporting social movements than are their less educated counterparts. The same is true for males compared with females, the middle-aged compared with other age groups, and those with higher incomes and occupational statuses compared with others. One exception concerns the relationship between gender and support for new social movements, where we find, as other

TABLE 31-5 Social Statuses and Involvement in Public Protest, Social Movements, and Voluntary Community Organizations

Social Status Categories		Average Level of Involvement				
	N	Public Protest	N	Support Movements	N	Community Groups
Total Sample	1625	9.07	1625	19.60	1625	2.66
Years of Schooling						
<12 years	29	6.83	19	17.90	32	1.75
13	20	8.35	13	17.31	20	2.45
14	67	7.66	48	19.13	73	1.60
15	75	7.91	67	18.76	82	2.15
16	153	8.19	138	19.25	170	1.69
17	158	8.46	143	19.69	172	2.23
18	271	9.12	251	19.55	297	2.48
19	120	9.23	114	19.65	137	2.42
20	89	9.35	86	19.95	93	2.77
21+ years	479	9.96	460	19.93	519	3.56
eta		(.33)		(.12)		(.21)
significance		‡		†		‡
Occupational Level						
Ow.>10em	45	9.64	44	19.43	47	3.98
Ow.<10em	59	9.10	57	19.58	63	1.94
Professional	265	10.15	259	20.06	289	4.03
Mid. Manager	131	9.32	124	19.17	143	3.04
Low. Manager	175	8.79	151	19.66	191	2.36
Supervisor	54	8.98	48	18.44	59	2.41
Skilled Lab	107	9.42	94	19.06	117	2.09
Semi-skilled	219	8.90	193	19.83	234	2.10
Unskilled	211	8.61	198	19.38	228	3.27
Farmers	73	8.47	66	18.08	79	2.21
All Others	161	7.99	132	18.96	175	2.65
eta		(.25)		(.18)		(.23)
significance		‡		‡		‡
Income Level						
<$5000	62	7.77	53	19.57	71	1.94
$5 000–10 000	82	8.37	70	19.56	90	2.27
10 000–15 000	89	7.91	77	19.21	98	1.63
15 000–20 000	100	8.68	86	19.76	109	2.31
20 000–25 000	145	8.86	124	19.23	152	2.88
25 000–30 000	211	9.03	192	19.28	224	2.65
30 000–35 000	177	9.52	170	19.58	189	2.94
35 000–40 000	163	9.77	154	19.63	173	2.73
40 000–45 000	95	9.88	94	19.87	103	3.21
50 000+	170	10.04	161	19.91	108	3.76
eta		(.28)		(.08)		(.17)
significance		‡		n.s.		†

TABLE 31-5   *continued*

Social Status Categories	N	Public Protest	N	Support Movements	N	Community Groups
Age						
21–29	275	9.35	255	20.16	308	2.19
30–39	423	9.65	392	20.18	457	2.67
40–49	288	9.51	278	19.72	315	3.11
50–59	196	8.56	173	19.34	207	3.02
60–69	172	8.05	165	8.21	191	2.69
70 & over	136	7.32	103	18.15	147	2.34
eta		(.21)		(.24)		(.11)
significance		‡		‡		†
Gender						
Male	757	9.34	701	19.22	807	2.57
Female	733	8.78	665	19.97	878	2.79
eta		(.09)		(.13)		(.03)
significance		‡		‡		n.s.
Language Group						
English	1142	8.95	1058	18.33	1251	2.80
French	348	9.44	308	20.47	374	2.28
eta		(.12)		(.17)		(.08)
significance		‡		‡		†
Race						
Whites	1385	9.08	1261	19.59	1499	2.69
Blacks	11	8.00	14	21.00	15	2.00
Chinese	40	8.63	40	19.70	48	3.33
All Others	54	9.09	51	19.06	63	2.14
eta		(.09)		(.08)		(.06)
significance		n.s.		n.s.		n.s.
Nativity						
Not Born in Canada	254	8.96	240	19.46	281	2.83
Born in Canada	1236	9.08	1126	19.62	1344	2.65
eta		(.03)		(.02)		(.06)
significance		n.s.		n.s.		n.s.
Region						
AT	125	8.08	112	19.63	133	2.61
QC	374	9.51	332	20.48	403	2.36
ON	564	8.78	526	19.70	611	2.70
MB	50	9.16	47	19.21	39	3.45
SK	69	8.86	68	18.25	74	2.61
AB	150	9.25	127	18.68	171	2.19
BC	158	9.69	154	19.73	174	2.67
eta		(.22)		(.20)		(.09)
significance		‡		‡		*

n.s. = Not a statistically significant difference.
* Significant at p<.05.
† Significant at p<.01.
‡ Significant at p<.001.

research suggests, that women are slightly higher in support than are men. Another possible exception concerns occupation, where we find that skilled workers, despite being relatively low in occupational status, have higher involvement levels on the three activity indices than might otherwise be expected. This is perhaps because of their links to labour organizations.

In the case of language group and region, the results are not entirely consistent with either the relative centrality or social capital perspectives. We find that the French and Québec respondents are comparatively high in public protest activity and social movement support, although residents of Alberta and British Columbia rank high on both of these measures as well. The results for voluntary association activity more closely follow the predicted pattern, with the English and people from Ontario being higher on this measure.

We also conducted some multivariate analyses, using a technique called multiple classification analysis (MCA). This technique allowed us to look at the relationship between any one of the social status variables and the activity measures, while simultaneously controlling for the effects of all the other social status variables. These analyses are not reported in tables here, to conserve space. However, the results are largely the same as those shown in Tables 31-4 and 31-5. These results suggest that the patterns found in Tables 31-4 and 31-5 do not change in direction, even with the inclusion of controls, although some of the relationships are no longer statistically significant after controls. Thinking of the relationships in Table 31-4, first, we find that, with controls, one of the effects of occupational status (for political discussions) is no longer significant. The effect before controls may have been largely due to the strong joint effect of educational status on both occupation and the political discussion measure. The same change occurs for the

effects of income on both political discussion and political persuasion. These appear to have resulted mainly from the effects of educational status differences. Also, one effect of race (upon political group involvement), one effect of language group (upon voting), and one effect of nativity (upon political group involvement) are not statistically significant after controls for the effects of education, occupation, and income, suggesting that it is differences resulting from these three achieved characteristics that make for the differences in political involvement by the ascribed characteristics.

Controls produce few changes in the statistical significance of the results reported in Table 31-5 for the indices of public protest, support of social movements, and involvement in community groups. The exceptions are involvement in public protest and community organizations by language group, where the language group differences are found not to be significant after controls; however, the pattern of higher involvement by Québec residents persisted with controls.

Supplemental Analyses from a Second Study

The data for our second study are from the 2000 National Survey of Giving, Volunteering, and Participating (NSGVP). This survey was conducted by Statistics Canada through telephone interviews with a representative sample of Canadians aged 15 and over. We chose as a working subsample from the NSGVP data only respondents aged 25 and over (N = 15 912). Statistics Canada placed all respondents under the age of 24 together in the same ten-year category (aged 15–24) in the data, at least for the coding in the public-use data file. Therefore, respondents in their teens could not be separated from respondents in their early twenties. The age restriction of 25 and older for the working sample was chosen to assure that respondents in our analyses had completed their schooling.

We chose four alternative measures of *current adult community participation* for our analyses. These measures were not represented well in Study One, and we wanted to determine whether the pattern of findings in the first study extended to these other measures of community activities. The measures (with the ranges given in parentheses) were total number of organizations volunteered with over the past twelve months (coded as 0 to 20),[6] total number of voluntary association memberships held last year (coded from 0 to 7, the latter for seven or more associations),[7] the number of recent elections voted in, counting the last federal, provincial, and, municipal elections (0 to 3),[8] and an index of attention to current affairs, based on responses to three questions.[9]

The social status characteristics that we used as predictors in the analyses were largely the same as in Study One. They were as follows: current employment status (full time, part time, or not working); personal income (Statistics Canada provided five categories, which included none, up to $19 999; $20,000–$39 999; $40,000–$59 999; and $60 000 and over); level of education completed (less than high school graduation, high school graduate, some post-secondary education, and university degree); age group (coded into ten-year categories between 25 and 64 years, with a final category of 65 years and over); gender; language of interview (English or French); nativity (native-born or foreign-born); and region (the Atlantic provinces, Québec, Ontario, the Prairies, and British Columbia). We again used MCA as our main analysis procedure.

To conserve space, we do not provide tables of results for Study Two. Most of the patterns of results were similar to those already discussed for Study One, but they were not entirely the same. First, the results for the achieved social statuses were as follows. The higher the education level, the higher the amount of voting over the three elections, the higher the voluntary activity (on both measures), and the greater the attention to current affairs. Income level showed very much the same patterns of direct relationships with the activity measures, in that those with higher incomes were more involved in each case. There was no occupational status measure, but there was an employment status measure. Those who were employed were more involved than those not in the work force, although it is interesting as well that, for three of the four activity measures, people working part time were somewhat more involved than people working full time. (The one exception was the index of attention to current affairs.) These findings suggest that available free time for pursuing political and community activities is a factor affecting how involved one can become, among those who are working part time or full time.

The results for the ascribed social status predictors were as follows. Age showed the expected curvilinear pattern with activity, except that following current affairs did not tail off among those aged 55–64 and 65 or older. This particular activity does not require strong effort outside the home when compared with voluntary association activity per se, because attending community events and meetings is not necessary. Thus, it makes sense that there would be little problem for older people to continue to follow current affairs. There was very little difference between the activity levels of females and males, or between the French and English language groups. The foreign-born were less involved than the native-born in voting activity, perhaps because some of the foreign-born might not yet have been eligible to vote, but the two groups were quite similar on the other three forms of activity. Surprisingly, in a reversal of the patterns of findings from the other study, people from the Atlantic provinces and Québec were slightly more involved in voting and voluntary association activity than were people from Ontario, the Prairies, or British Columbia. The above patterns also held with controls for the effects of the other predictor variables.

The present study used a more detailed measure of voting than the first study, including all three types of elections: municipal, provincial, and federal. Only federal voting was referred to in the question used in Study One. The results by region in Study Two suggest that there may be more active "local" politics in the two higher-activity regions—the Atlantic region and Québec—and this is reflected in the results. Such patterns may not be evident when the interviewer asks only about federal voting activity. The measure of voluntary association activity was also a more detailed one than that used from the earlier study. For both these forms of activity we must be cautious about drawing firm conclusions concerning regional patterns until we have still further evidence on the matter.

The NSGVP survey used in Study Two also contained six questions on the respondents' level of community activity in youth. Each of the items asked for a "yes" or "no" response. The six questions asked whether, during their "school years," the respondents were participants in "organized team sports"; were members of "a youth group"; did "some kind of volunteer work"; went "door-to-door to raise money"; were "active in student government"; or were "active in religious organizations." Interestingly, for these six items taken separately, and for an index composed of responses to all six questions, the categories of respondents who were cur-

rently more active in the community also had higher levels of involvement in their youth. In other words, those adult individuals who currently were higher in education, higher in income, employed, and in the more middle-aged cohorts were the most likely to have been involved in community activity when they were in their school-age years. In addition, being involved in voluntary activities as young people made them more likely to be involved in the community in their adulthood, and this finding held both before and after controls for the effects of the social status predictors (Curtis and Perks 2002). These results suggest that part of the explanation for people's levels of community activity as adults lies in their acquiring contact with and experience in voluntary community activities earlier in the life course. It is possible, as well, that those who were active in their youth had parents who were also active and who consequently provided encouragement, rewards, and role modelling for being active in the community.

CONCLUSION

We have examined recent Canadian data on the question of who participates in political and community affairs in Canadian society. Drawing from previous research and theory on the subject, we began with the premise that those groups that enjoy more social power, because of their higher "relative centrality" and greater "social capital" relative to other people in our society, would have higher levels of political involvement, civic engagement, and community activity. These advantaged groups include, for example, those with higher education and socio-economic status, people who speak English rather than French, males, the Canadian-born, and the middle-aged. Our predictions receive partial support in the results. The strongest support is found for education, occupational status, income, and age. For some types of activity, there is support for the effects of gender and language group. In Study Two, we also determined that individuals who were involved with community activity in their youth were generally more likely to be involved in voluntary associations as adults.

The patterns of results for race and nativity are much less consistent with, and sometimes even contradict, our expectations based on relative centrality and social capital theory. Moreover, controlled analyses show that some of the effects of race and nativity, before controls, occur because of differences in education, occupation, and income across these two characteristics. However, this latter set of findings may not so much call into question the relative centrality and social capital arguments, as suggest an important specification of them. Namely, the results may demonstrate that power and resource differences that are rooted in achieved statuses, including socio-economic status and particularly education, are the key explanations for why ascribed statuses such as race and nativity are correlated with political activity. The findings appear to cast doubt on any *comprehensive* claims about the relationship between political involvement and civic engagement, on the one hand, and social capital or relative centrality, on the other hand. Instead, a more complex set of processes seems to be at work in accounting for why individuals are more likely than others to join and participate in various political and community activities.

The patterns for region were also more complex than suggested by our working hypothesis, and do not lend themselves to easy generalizations. Perhaps our finding of higher involvement of Ontarians and people from the Western provinces can be traced to relatively greater socio-econom-

ic advantages in these regions, in which case there may be some support here for the relative centrality and social capital perspectives. Nevertheless, Québecers were found to be somewhat more involved in political protests and in support for new social movements than other Canadians, yet Québec has traditionally been a relatively disadvantaged province judging by most economic indicators. The Québec results, however, could represent a special set of circumstances, because of the typically higher levels of political unrest in that province, which stem from issues such as Québec separatism or sovereignty and the continuing debate over Canada's constitution.

In general we have found that, apart from voting in federal elections and a few other exceptions, it is rare that a majority of Canadians becomes involved in various types of social action or political activity. Perhaps the low level of involvement in behaviours such as public protest activity is an indication that most Canadians are relatively happy about the way things are in their country and, therefore, feel no strong need to participate in political or social change. Nevertheless, to the extent that political and community activities are structured by social status, it is apparent, as well, that those who are higher in social status also tend to be the people who are most involved in such actions. Because we would assume that these individuals should be happier about the status quo than those who are lower in social status, this pattern may seem surprising. One possibility is that such actions on the part of those in advantaged situations are mainly directed toward helping and promoting the interests of others less fortunate than themselves. An alternative interpretation for the greater political and civic involvement of more privileged groups is that they have a stronger desire to protect their own interests through such activities, and also possess the material and other resources necessary for participation.

We also should consider the possibility that social capital or relative centrality may explain some kinds of political and organizational involvement better than others. To some theorists, the existence of a wide range of voluntary political and community activities, as well as broad involvement by less powerful groups, may be indicative of a democratic and "pluralist" power structure in our society (e.g., Dahl 1982). A different view, however, must also be considered: It may be that people with greater social power are simply being strategic and selective when deciding which activities they choose to pursue and which organizations they choose to join. Some writers argue that voluntary organizations serve as the representatives of competing or conflicting interest groups, some of which have a much greater capacity than others to ensure that their particular policy preferences are implemented (e.g., Hayes 1978, 1983). From this perspective, we would expect that people with higher social capital and greater relative centrality, in pursuing their own desire to have access to power, would concentrate on truly influential organizations and activities, rather than on the whole range of activities.

Evidence from other research does suggest that such a pattern may be at work. For example, individuals with higher social status are significantly more likely than other people to run for political office. Moreover, they are even more likely to be successful in being elected to parliament, and even more likely still to serve as senior ministers in government (see, e.g., Forcese and de Vries 1977; Guppy et al. 1988). Over the years, those with higher social status have also are been far more likely to occupy powerful positions in Canada's system of "elites," both in public or government organizations and in the private economic and social spheres (e.g., Porter 1965; Clement, 1975, 1977; Olsen 1980; Nakhaie 1997). Therefore, while the present study gives some indication of a relatively broad base to political and community group involvement in Canada, the findings do not mean that those with privileged social statuses are rivalled by less advantaged groups or individuals in the overall power structure.

NOTES

1. "When you get together with your friends, would you say you discuss politics frequently, occasionally, or never?"

2. "When you, yourself, hold a strong opinion, do you ever find yourself persuading relatives or fellow workers to share your views? If so, does it happen often, from time to time, or rarely?"

3. "How interested would you say you are in politics: very interested, somewhat interested, not very interested, or not at all interested?"

4. "If there were a general election tomorrow, which party would you vote for?" Responses were divided into "would vote" and named choice versus "would not vote."

5. "Please look carefully at the following list of voluntary organizations and activities and say which, if any, do you belong to—political parties or groups—and which if any are you currently doing unpaid voluntary work for."

6. The question was simply, "For how many organizations did you volunteer in the past 12 months?"

7. Total number of voluntary association memberships currently held was the number of memberships reported in response to a set of questions concerning "a service club or fraternal association; a political organization; a cultural, education, or hobby organization; a religious affiliated group; a neighbourhood, civic, or community association or school group; any other organization."

8. The voting measure was based on three questions that asked, "Did you vote in the last federal election?"; "Did you vote in the last provincial election?"; and "Did you vote in the last municipal election?" Each affirmative answer was given a score of 1, and the scores were summed.

9. Attention to current affairs was based on three questions: "How frequently do you follow news and current affairs that are local and regional?"; "How frequently do you follow news and current affairs that are national?"; and "How frequently do you follow news and current affairs that are international?" Responses to each were coded as Rarely or never = 1; Several times each month = 2; Several times each week = 3; and Daily = 4. The responses to the three questions were summed.

REFERENCES

Baer, Douglas, James Curtis, and Edward Grabb 2001. "Has voluntary activity declined? Cross-national analyses for fifteen countries." *Canadian Review of Sociology and Anthropology* 38:249–274.

Carroll, William (ed.) 1992. *Organizing Dissent: Contemporary Social Movements in Theory and Practice.* Toronto: Garamond.

Chui, Tina, James Curtis, and Edward Grabb 1993. "Who participates in community organizations and politics?" In James Curtis, Edward Grabb, and Neil Guppy (eds.), *Social Inequality in Canada: Patterns, Problems and Policies* (2nd ed.), pp. 524–538. Scarborough, Ontario: Prentice-Hall.

Clement, Wallace 1975. *The Canadian Corporate Elite.* Toronto: McClelland and Stewart.

Clement, Wallace 1977. *Continental Corporate Power.* Toronto: McClelland and Stewart.

Coleman, James S. 1988. "Social capital in the creation of human capital." *American Journal of Sociology* 94:S95–S120.

Corrigall-Brown, Catherine 2002. "What do politics have to do with me? An analysis of political alienation among young Canadians." Unpublished Master's thesis. University of Western Ontario.

Curtis, James 1971. "Voluntary association joining: A cross-national comparative note." *American Sociological Review* 36:872–880.

Curtis, James, Douglas Baer, and Edward Grabb 2001. "Nations of joiners: Explaining voluntary association membership in democratic societies." *American Sociological Review* 66:783–805.

Curtis, James, and Edward Grabb 2002. "Involvement in the organizational base of new social movements in English Canada and French Canada." In Douglas Baer (ed.), *Political Sociology: Canadian Perspectives,* pp. 164–181. Toronto: Oxford University Press.

Curtis, James, Edward Grabb, and Douglas Baer 1992. "Voluntary association membership in fifteen developed countries: A comparative analysis." *American Sociological Review* 57:139–152.

Curtis, James, and Ronald Lambert 1976. "Voting, political interest, and age: National survey findings for French and English Canadians." *Canadian Journal of Political Science* 9:293–307.

Curtis, James, Ronald Lambert, Steven Brown, and Barry Kay 1989. "Affiliating with voluntary associations: Canadian-American comparisons." *Canadian Journal of Sociology* 14:143–161.

Curtis, James, and Thomas Perks 2002. "Early experiences with voluntary community activities and adult community involvement." Unpublished paper.

Cutler, Steven T. 1976. "Age differences in voluntary association membership." *Social Forces* 55:43–58.

Dahl, Robert 1982. *Dilemmas of a Pluralist Democracy.* New York: Oxford University Press.

Edwards, Patricia K., John N. Edwards, and Alan DeWitt Watts 1984. "Women, work, and social participation." *Journal of Voluntary Action Research* 13:7–22.

Elections Canada 1993. *Official Voting Results: Thirty-Fifth General Election.* Ottawa: Elections Canada.

Forcese, Dennis, and John de Vries 1977. "Occupational and electoral success in Canada: The 1974 federal election."

Canadian Review of Sociology and Anthropology 14:331–340.

Grabb, Edward, and James Curtis 1992. "Voluntary association Activity in English Canada, French Canada and the United States: Multivariate analyses." *Canadian Journal of Sociology* 17:371–388.

Guppy, Neil, Sabrina Freeman, and Shari Buchan 1988. "Economic background and political representation." In J. Curtis, E. Grabb, N. Guppy, and S. Gilbert (eds.), *Social Inequality in Canada: Patterns, Problems, Policies* (1st ed.), pp. 394–404. Scarborough: Prentice-Hall Canada.

Hayes, M.T. 1978. "The semi-sovereign pressure groups: A critique of current theory and an alternative typology." *Journal of Politics* 40:134–161.

Hayes, M.T. 1983. "Interest groups: Pluralism or mass society?" In A.J. Cigler and B.A. Loomis (eds.), *Interest Group Politics*, pp. 110–125. Washington: CQ.

Inglehart, Ronald et al. 1994. *World Values Survey, 1991–1992: Individual and Aggregate Level Codebook.* Ann Arbor: University of Michigan, Institute for Social Research.

Kay, Barry, Ronald Lambert, Steven Brown, and James Curtis 1987. "Gender and political activity in Canada: 1965–1984." *Canadian Journal of Political Science* 20:851–863.

Knoke, David 1986. "Associations and interest groups." *Annual Review of Sociology* 12:1–21.

Larana, Enrique, Hank Johnston, and Joseph Gusfield (eds.) 1994. *New Social Movements: From Ideology to Identity.* Philadelphia: Temple University Press.

Lin, Nan 2000. "Inequality in social capital." *Contemporary Sociology* 29:785–795.

McPherson, J.M., and W.G. Lockwood 1980. "The longitudinal study of voluntary association memberships: A multivariate analysis." *Journal of Voluntary Action Research* 9: 74–84.

Milbrath, Lester, and M.L. Goel 1977. *Political Participation* (2nd ed.). Chicago: Rand McNally.

Nakhaie, M. Reza 1997. "Vertical mosaic among the elites: The new imagery revisited." *Canadian Review of Sociology and Anthropology* 34:1–24.

Olsen, Dennis 1980. *The State Elite.* Toronto: McClelland and Stewart.

Olson, Marvin E. 1965. *The Logic of Collective Action.* Cambridge, Mass.: Harvard University Press.

Palisi, Bartolomeo J., and Rosalie J. Palisi 1984. "Status and voluntary associations: A cross-cultural study of males in three metropolitan areas." *Journal of Voluntary Action Research* 13:32–43.

Porter, John 1965. *The Vertical Mosaic.* Toronto: University of Toronto Press.

Putnam, Robert 1995. "Bowling alone: America's declining social capital." *Journal of Democracy* 6:65–78.

Putnam, Robert 2000. *Bowling Alone: The Collapse and Revival of American Community.* New York: Simon and Schuster.

Smith, David Horton 1975. "Voluntary action and voluntary groups." *Annual Review of Sociology* 1:247–270.

FURTHER REFERENCES— SECTION 4: CONSEQUENCES OF SOCIAL INEQUALITY

Allahar, Anton, and James Cote 1998. *Richer and Poorer: The Structure of Inequality in Canada.* Toronto: Copp Clark. The authors use a framework that centres on the role of dominant ideology to examine social inequality in Canada, with a special focus on issues of class, gender, age, and race/ethnicity. A key claim in this analysis is that Canadians are in a state of denial about the existence of major inequalities in their society.

C.D. Howe Institute (http://www.edhowe.org). This organization is a social policy research institution. It provides analyses of such policy issues of national interest as trade, the environment, health care, and culture.

Centre for Policy Alternatives (http://www.policyalternatives.ca). This organization is currently providing critical analyses of the impact upon Canada and Canadians of developments in the Canadian public education system, free trade, and electricity privatization, among others.

Curtis, James, and Lorne Tepperman (eds.) 1994. *Haves and Have-nots: An International Reader on Social Inequality.* Englewood Cliffs, New Jersey: Prentice-Hall. This volume presents research on patterns, explanations, and consequences of social inequality from numerous countries around the world.

Dunk, Thomas W. 1991. *It's a Working Man's Town.* Montréal and Kingston: McGill-Queen's University Press. This is an interesting participant observation study of male working-class culture in Northern Ontario. The volume includes a thoughtful discussion of theories of class consciousness.

Hagan, John, and Bill McCarthy 1997. *Mean Streets: Youth Crime and Homelessness.* Cambridge: Cambridge University Press. The authors present information on (1) the lives of homeless youth on the street; (2) how the youths came to be there; and (3) how they leave the streets. The social class dimensions of these phenomena are explored, along with other factors. Theories put forward in the previous literature are critiqued, and alternative theoretical interpretations are offered. The study is based on qualitative data gathered in two Canadian cities.

Health Canada 1999. *Statistical Report on the Health of Canadians.* Ottawa. Contains detailed statistics on the state of the nation's health, with attention to the consequences of gender, age, socio-economic status, and other factors for health. See also the following websites: http://www.hc-sc.gc.ca and http://www.statcan.ca.

Johnson, Holly 1996. *Dangerous Domains: Violence Against Women in Canada.* Toronto: Nelson. This book presents results from several data sources including a Statistics Canada study of violence against women. The latter provides information on characteristics of the victim and her circumstances, and characteristics of the perpetrator of the violence. Also discussed are various individual-level and societal-level explanations of violence, and problems of measurement.

Ornstein, Michael, and Michael Stevenson 1999. *Politics and Ideology in Canada.* Montréal and Kingston: McGill-Queen's University Press. This book examines the question of ideological power in Canada. The analysis compares the perspectives of Canada's elite leadership with those of the general public on a range of important issues, including such topics as state power and support for government welfare programs.

Reitz, Jeffrey G., and Raymond Breton 1994. *The Illusion of Difference: Realities of Ethnicity in Canada and the United States.* Toronto: C.D. Howe Institute. The authors give clear and concise comparisons of information from the two countries on beliefs about levels of ethnic/racial inequality; attitudes toward retention of minority cultures; the extent of ethnic culture retention; prejudice and discrimination; and the economic incorporation of minority groups.

Statistics Canada. *Canadian Social Trends.* This journal is published four times per year. Each issue contains several brief and straightforward presentations of up-to-date information on social problems, health, income and jobs, education, and demographic processes. Frequently the pieces show how people's achieved and ascribed social statuses are related to the issue in question. See also the website at http://www.statcan.ca.

Tepperman, Lorne 1994. *Choices and Chances* (2nd ed.). Toronto: Holt, Rinehart & Winston.

This introductory-level book gives interesting discussions of what is known about patterns in people's desires around education, careers, and various aspects of lifestyles.

Index